The Making of
Human Concepts

The Making of Human Concepts

Edited by

Denis Mareschal
Birkbeck College, University of London
UK

Paul C. Quinn
University of Delaware
USA

Stephen E. G. Lea
University of Exeter
UK

OXFORD
UNIVERSITY PRESS

OXFORD
UNIVERSITY PRESS

Great Clarendon Street, Oxford OX2 6DP
Oxford University Press is a department of the University of Oxford.
It furthers the University's objective of excellence in research, scholarship,
and education by publishing worldwide in

Oxford New York

Auckland Cape Town Dar es Salaam Hong Kong Karachi
Kuala Lumpur Madrid Melbourne Mexico City Nairobi
New Delhi Shanghai Taipei Toronto

With offices in

Argentina Austria Brazil Chile Czech Republic France Greece
Guatemala Hungary Italy Japan Poland Portugal Singapore
South Korea Switzerland Thailand Turkey Ukraine Vietnam

Oxford is a registered trade mark of Oxford University Press
in the UK and in certain other countries

Published in the United States
by Oxford University Press Inc., New York
© Oxford University Press, 2010

British Library Cataloguing in Publication Data

Data available

Library of Congress Cataloging in Publication Data
The making of human concepts/edited by Denis Mareschal, Paul C. Quinn, Stephen E. G. Lea.
     p. cm.
  ISBN 978-0-19-954922-1
1. Concepts. 2. Cognition. 3. Thought and thinking. I. Mareschal,
Denis. II. Quinn, Paul C. III. Lea, S. E. G., 1946-
     BF441.M236 2010
     153.2'3—dc22

                                                              2009035756

Typeset in Minion by Glyph International, Bangalore, India
Printed in Great Britain
on acid-free paper by the
MPG Books Group, Bodmin and King's Lynn

ISBN 978–0–19–954922–1 (pbk.)

10 9 8 7 6 5 4 3 2 1

Preface

The birth of a book is always a difficult process. At first comes the germination of an idea, then a long period of incubation in which this idea takes form and is shaped by the interactions between the editors. Unfortunately, many excellent ideas somehow never quite fully evolve to the stage of a book. What is required is a catalyst that will help nurture and motivate the editors to complete the journey from idea to pages in a book.

In the case of this book, a number of factors have contributed to its development. At the heart of what is fundamentally an interdisciplinary project is the realization in very different communities that there is a gap in our understanding of concepts. Although cognitive scientists, developmental psychologists, and comparative psychologists have all explored the nature of concepts, there has been surprisingly little effort to compare notes and see what the others have discovered. A second impetus is the realization that to answer questions concerning the possible uniqueness of human concepts and their origins necessarily requires learning about concepts in nonhuman species and about the nature of concepts at different ages in humans. The final impetus for the writing of this book is the joint collaborative work that exists between the editors. Denis Mareschal and Stephen Lea were both part of a remarkable research project funded by the European Commission (grant 516542-NEST) entitled 'From association to rules in the development of human concepts'. The aims of this project were to bring together comparative and developmental researchers to ask when the apparent transition from associative to rule-governed cognition occurred. Added to this was the fact that Paul Quinn and Denis Mareschal had a long-standing history of collaboration in investigating the development of conceptual abilities and that Paul Quinn spent considerable time at Exeter University, where Stephen Lea is Professor of Psychology. The ground was therefore ripe to ensure that this project would safely make the journey from idea to book.

In putting this book together, we wanted to do more than just bring together some of the greatest thinkers on concepts. We also aspired to make a book that would be accessible and useful to students and nonspecialists. Indeed, at some level, the success of a book is determined by the span of the audience it can reach. The more the ideas discussed in the book are accessible, the more they will have a broad impact. Of course, there is a danger in trying to reach out to too broad an audience. The danger is that the subtleties of a technical world can be lost. Nevertheless, we hope to have walked that fine line between making the book original and cutting edge, while also making it accessible and useful to a broad audience. This was partly accomplished by asking authors to write relatively short chapters and to keep in mind the breadth of readership of the book. It was also accomplished by including a short preview of each chapter. These previews are meant to situate the chapters within the broader theoretical contexts (and therefore to allow less-specialized readers to see the links between the different themes discussed in each chapter). They also allow us to foreshadow the key theoretical points made by each author. Thus, the book is meant to be both scholarly and didactic – to push back the boundaries of our understanding of concepts while sharing with many people the implications and consequences of those discoveries.

This book would not have been possible without the help and support of numerous people. In particular, we thank Caspar Addyman, Nadja Althaus, and Sarah Snoxall for reading and commenting on earlier drafts of several chapters. We also thank Amy Proferes for her careful proofreading and language editing. The writing of this book was supported in part by grants from the European Commission (516542-NEST, 201932-ANALOGY), and National Institutes of Health Grants HD-42451 and HD-46526. Finally, of course, we wish to thank all the contributors to this volume. Such prominent academics are often asked to contribute chapters and simply do not have time to agree to all of the invitations. We are therefore sincerely grateful that they chose to contribute to this project and to make it the success that we certainly believe it has become.

DM, PQ, SEGL; London, Newark, Delaware, & Exeter, March 2009

To family and friends who have supported
us throughout this effort

Contents

List of contributors

F. Gregory Ashby
Department of Psychology
University of California
Santa Barbara, CA
USA

Susan Carey
Harvard University
Department of Psychology
Cambridge, MA
USA

James Close
School of Psychology
Cardiff University
Cardiff
UK

Michael C. Corballis
Department of Psychology
University of Auckland
Auckland
New Zealand

Matthew J. Crossley
Department of Psychology
University of California
Santa Barbara, CA
USA

Michèle Fabre-Thorpe
Centre de Recherche Cerveau et
Cognition (CerCo)
UMR 5549 (CNRS—Université Paul
Sabatier)
Faculté de Médecine de Rangueil
Toulouse
France

Susan A. Gelman
Department of Psychology
University of Michigan
Ann Arbor, MI
USA

Ulrike Hahn
School of Psychology
Cardiff University
Cardiff
UK

James A. Hampton
Department of Psychology
City University
London
UK

Carl J. Hodgetts
School of Psychology
Cardiff University
Cardiff
UK

Frank C. Keil
Department of Psychology
Yale University
New Haven, CT
USA

Olga F. Lazareva
Department of Psychology
Drake University
Des Moines, IA
USA

Stephen E. G. Lea
School of Psychology
University of Exeter
Washington Singer Laboratories
Exeter
UK

Bradley C. Love
Department of Psychology
University of Texas at Austin
Austin, TX
USA

Denis Mareschal
Centre for Brain and Cognitive
Development
School of Psychological
Science
Birkbeck College
University of London
UK

Tetsuro Matsuzawa
Primate Research Institute
Kyoto University
Inuyama
Japan

Gregory L. Murphy
Department of Psychology
New York University
New York, NY
USA

George E. Newman
School of Management
Yale University
New Haven, CT
USA

Emmanuel M. Pothos
Department of Psychology
University of Wales
Swansea
UK

Paul C. Quinn
Department of Psychology
University of Delaware
Newark, DE
USA

Norbert Ross
Department of Anthropology
Vanderbilt University
Nashville, TN
USA

Linda B. Smith
Cognitive Development Lab
Department of Psychology
Psychological and Brain Sciences
Indiana University
Bloomington, IN
USA

Thomas Suddendorf
School of Psychology
University of Queensland
Brisbane
Queensland
Australia

Michael Tidwell
Department of Anthropology
Vanderbilt University
Nashville, TN
USA

Marc Tomlinson
University of Texas at Austin
Department of Psychology
Austin, TX
USA

Edward A. Wasserman
Department of Psychology
Delta Center
The University of Iowa
Iowa City, IA
USA

Sandra R. Waxman
Department of Psychology
Northwestern University
Evanston, IL
USA

Barbara A. Younger
Department of Psychological Sciences
Purdue University
West Lafayette, IN
USA

Part 1

Theoretical foundations

Chapter 1

Where do concepts come from?

Denis Mareschal, Paul C. Quinn, and
Stephen E. G. Lea

I think, I may be positive . . . That the power of
abstracting is not at all in [animals]; and that the having
of general ideas is that which puts a perfect distinction
between man and animal; and is an excellency which
the faculties of animals do by no means attain to.
(*John Locke, 1690, An essay concerning human
understanding*)

I take it from this that there literally isn't such a thing as
the notion of learning a conceptual system richer than the
one that one already has; we simply have no idea of what
it would be like to get from a conceptually impoverished
to a conceptually richer system by anything like a process
of learning.
(*Jerry Fodor, 1980, Fixation of belief and concept acquisition*)

Ever since people first began to reflect on the processes of human thought, scholars have grappled with an extraordinary human ability. When we think, we do not just replay what we have seen or heard. Instead, we seem to be blessed with rich ideas that allow us to make sense of the world we live in, and that allow us to organize the world in a meaningful, consistent, and predictable fashion. More specifically, these ideas allow us to group visibly different instances as the same kinds of things. They also allow us, by combining them in ways that we have never directly experienced, to speculate about what might happen in the future and to reason about hypothetical or imagined events. In short, they allow us to conceptualize the world we live in (and indeed other possible worlds), and so we refer to them as *concepts*.

Even within Western culture, philosophers, theologians, and psychologists have explained and interpreted concepts in many different ways over the centuries. Ideas about their content, and how we have used them to organize our interactions in the world, have changed dramatically over the course of human history (Russell, 1945). Even the debates about concepts have changed. However, one debate that has always remained relevant is whether this ability to conceptualize the world is something unique to human beings. The mainstream position of Western philosophy has been that only humans have truly powerful ideas that transcend the directly perceivable world of the here and now (e.g. Locke, 1690, as cited above).

Darwin's (1871) argument that the differences between humans and other species were matters of degree and not of kind struck a serious blow to this view. If humans have evolved through a gradual process from the same primordial and ecological mass that saw the birth of every other life form on earth, if our sense of being a completely different order of being distinguished from animals by our possession of an immortal soul is illusory, if we share the same anatomical and physiological building blocks as our environmental neighbours and are descended from the same ancestors, why then would our mental abilities be different in kind? In particular, why should other animals not have the same kind of concepts as humans? Perhaps, our inability to see such similarities is just the manifestation of extreme anthropocentrism?

Darwin expressed his belief in mental as well as physical continuity between humans and other animals. Of course, his position was not immediately or widely accepted. The first response was to apply in human psychology the behaviouristic techniques that were essential in animal psychology (Boakes, 1984, Chapter 2). That approach was decisively rejected by cognitive psychologists from Bartlett (1932) onwards, leading to a re-establishment of a belief in mental discontinuity between humans and all other animals. But as researchers into animal learning began to apply models and ideas from human cognitive psychology to animal behaviour (e.g. Roitblat et al., 1984), a new way of applying Darwinian continuity to mental life emerged. The debate continues even to this day (e.g. Corballis & Lea, 1999), with many thinkers arguing for a rapprochement between human and nonhuman mental abilities (e.g. Bekoff et al., 2002; Hurley & Nudds, 2005; Smith et al., 2003) while others continue to assert the qualitatively distinct character of human cognition (e.g. Bermudez, 2003; Mithen, 1996; Premack, 2007).

Within the general debate about cognitive continuity, the nature and role of concepts in nonhuman cognition have played an important part. It seems evident that any animal must have at least some primitive or limited way of organizing events and objects in the world; indeed, Ashby and Lee (1993) have argued that any species that lacked this ability would quickly become extinct. But does such an ability deserve to be called 'conceptualization'? Geach (1957) argued that it did not, and that only if an understanding could be used in an act of judgement did it deserve the description 'conceptualization': 'Experience in training dogs to "recognize" triangles can be no guide in (let us say) teaching geometry' (p. 17). The point being made here is that, while concepts do enable us to respond in the same way to discriminable objects that all fall in the same category, to be true concepts they have to do more than that; we have to be able to act on them mentally so as to discover or understand new properties of the world. Geach thus joins many other authors, both before and since, in arguing that the possession of concepts is a uniquely human mental capacity.

However, any suggestion that human and animal concepts are inherently different does raise a number of immediate questions. If human conceptual abilities are unique, then where did they come from? How and when did the human conceptual faculty appear? Wasserman (2008) argued forcefully that, as scientists, we cannot posit capacities that do not have a phylogenetic origin. Geach (1957, p. 17) rejects, in colourful terms, any suggestion that this implies that animals have any sort of concept: 'It is scholasticism in the worst sense of the word to argue that if men are descended from brutes they *cannot* have anything that the brutes did not already possess . . . the argument is just as bad whether it is used to disprove evolution . . . or to prove that brutes, from whom man is descended, *must* have concepts in at least a "rudimentary" form'. But Wasserman must be right at least to this extent: insofar as Darwinian evolutionary theory is correct, if we cannot see at least some aspects of human concepts in other species, then we must be able to specify what nonconceptual capacities have been modified, and under what selective pressures, to form the human conceptual ability. Finding rudimentary concepts in nonhumans looks like the easier task. We can be guided in it by both phylogenetic and ecological considerations: species that are closest to us in terms of descent should have the greatest similarity in their conceptual abilities to ours, and less closely related species that have experienced similar environmental pressures may have also evolved similar conceptual abilities.

Those who take for granted the unique status of human thought and concepts have looked for clues as to the source of this uniqueness. For example, Penn et al. (2008) have argued that while many different species share some of the categorization abilities of humans, what is unique in humans is our ability to conceptualize relations between things. That is, we do not simply think of things in terms of the elementary items that we encounter, but in terms of the relations between the items that we encounter in the world. This ability to think of and mentally manipulate relations allows us to escape the limitations of direct perceptions. Thus, these authors argue that there is a qualitative discontinuity between the conceptual abilities of humans and those of other life forms, though not one that depends upon language.

The truth of this assertion of Penn et al. (2008) can only be resolved through careful experimentation and observation. However a second candidate for the uniqueness of human thought is language (Chomsky, 1980; Jackendoff, 2002; Pinker, 1994), and if human concepts are dependent on human language, it follows without further argument that they are different in kind from animal concepts (except, perhaps the concepts possessed by animals who have been taught to use a human language, if we accept that this is possible). Of course, what remains unclear is whether it is language that promotes abstract thought, or rather, the capacity for abstract thought that supports language (see the debate between Piaget and Chomsky with regards to the emergence of language and abstract thought in children; Piatelli-Palmarini, 1980).

More recently, the rich networks of human cultural and social interactions have been proposed as the essential ingredient for the uniqueness of human thought (Tomasello, 1999). These elaborate social interactions are only possible, it is argued, because we humans possess a theory of mind that allows us to collaborate with other members of our species (Tomasello & Rakoczy, 2003). Here again, there is dispute about whether the underlying capacity is unique to humans. There have been many claims that at least a few nonhuman species, chiefly great apes and dolphins, possess something that can properly be called theory of mind (e.g. Gallup, 1998; Tschudin, 2001), although the evidence has been rejected as inadequate by others (e.g. Heyes, 1998). Or, it can be argued that it is not the capacity to conceptualize other minds that is unique to humans, but the way we learn to operate mentally with our concepts: Csibra and Gergely (2006) argue that human infants come to the world prepared to seek out events from which they can learn from their conspecifics, in a way that is unlike any other species. But this too is an argument that would require careful delineation, because not only do many animals learn socially, they are frequently adapted to put themselves in situations where they have opportunities to do so (as, for example, in imprinting) and in a few cases at least it is clear that adults are adapted to do things that enable infants to learn (Thornton & Raihani, 2008).

The debate over the evolutionary origins of human concepts directly mirrors the same debate about the ontogenetic origins of adult concepts. In the modern era, it was Piaget who asked how infants and children differed from adults in acquiring or constructing their understanding of the world (Flavell, 1963; Piaget, 1954). Since then, developmental psychologists have struggled with identifying when adult-like mental competence emerges and how it develops through infancy and childhood. The same is true of concepts. One of Piaget's greatest contributions was to suggest that children were not just less knowledgeable than adults, but reasoned and conceived of the world in radically different ways relative to adults (e.g. Piaget, 1972). Of course, this is not without controversy. Over the years, several authors have argued that at some basic level, infants, children, and adults all have the same fundamental concepts (e.g. Fodor, 1998; Keil, 1989; Macnamara, 1982). Indeed, as the quote at the beginning of the chapter indicates, Fodor (1980) went so far as to suggest that it is logically impossible to acquire novel concepts, and all that happens during childhood is the selection and recombination of existing conceptual tokens.

At the other end of the spectrum is the argument that adult competence is simply one point along a lifelong trajectory of development (e.g. Karmiloff-Smith, 1992; Mareschal et al., 2007; Oyama, 1985; Thelen & Smith, 1994). According to this view, the developing organism is continually adapting and responding to both internally and externally generated pressures. The concepts that we have as adults reflect the environmental and social experiences that have shaped us as infants and children. By this account, the process of development and the individual's personal history are both essential for understanding adult concepts.

Here again, echoing the claims made regarding the evolutionary origins of concepts, Leech et al. (2008) have argued that it is equally misguided to posit cognitive abilities that have no developmental antecedents. There has to be some kind of continuity between the conceptual abilities observed in adults, and those observed in children and perhaps even in infants (Quinn, 2008). This does not mean that the same conceptual systems have to be in place from infancy, only that there must be a traceable path through which the abilities present in infancy flower into those available in adulthood.

What is this book about?

The aim of this book is to try to understand where adult human concepts come from. As discussed above, this question clearly has two dimensions. One side of the question is to ask what the evolutionary antecedents of human concepts are. The other side is to ask how adult concepts emerge during child development. These two interrelated questions are held together by the same debates in the comparative and developmental literature. Moreover, investigators often face the same or similar difficulties in trying to assess the concepts available to other species and young humans because of the research participants' lack of verbal ability.

Thus, to answer these questions one needs to consider both the comparative and developmental literature. To this end, we have collected chapters from authors with interests in comparative psychology, developmental psychology, and cognitive science more generally. The authors were asked to keep the following two key issues in mind when writing their chapters:

1. In what way might human concepts be unique?
2. What roles do development and evolution play in the emergence of the ability to form concepts?

In Part 1, we asked authors to explore the nature of adult human concepts. Here, the different definitions of concepts and how they might be embodied or implemented in the adult mind are outlined (e.g. Chapter 2 by Murphy). Also examined are the processes and mechanisms by which concepts could be acquired and used in the cognitive system (e.g. Chapter 3 by Close, Hahn, Hodgetts, and Pothos and Chapter 4 by Love and Tomlinson). This section also addresses some of the basic questions surrounding the uniqueness of concepts, such as the role of language in constraining concepts (Chapter 6 by Waxman and Gelman) and the role of culture and society in determining what are meaningful adult concepts (Chapter 7 by Ross and Tidwell). Finally, the neural systems that underlie human concepts are explored, with a particular focus on whether there is some unique component that might be related to human conceptual abilities (Chapter 5 by Ashley and Crossley).

Part 2 provides overviews of the conceptual abilities of different species and developmental populations of humans. These range from birds (Chapter 8 by Lazareva and Wasserman) to nonprimate mammals (Chapter 9 by Lea), to monkeys (Chapter 10 by Fabre-Thorpe) and chimpanzees (Chapter 11 by Matsuzawa), and finally to human infants (Chapter 12 by Younger), children (Chapter 13 by Carey), and adults (Chapter 14 by Hampton). The aim of this section is to highlight anything that is unique about each of these populations and what might be shared with human adult abilities. By comparing each group side by side, the methods that are available for testing each of the competencies become clearer, and perhaps how the limitations of the methods shape the apparent similarities and differences can be observed.

In Part 3, the book turns to considerations of what might be unique about human adult concepts and what the contributions to this uniqueness might be. Chapter 15 by Keil and Newman explores whether it is appropriate to equate ontogeny with phylogeny in the study of concepts. Chapter 17 by Corballis and Suddendorf asks whether the ability to mentally travel in time (i.e. to imagine things in the past or the future) might not be what gives human concepts their power as compared to other species. Such an ability also has a developmental component. Lastly, Chapter 16 by Smith explores whether the very notion of concept is necessary to understand the cognitive behaviours that we are ultimately interested in. Indeed, the apparent discontinuity between humans and other animals as well as infants and adults may simply be an epiphenomenon of our definition of concepts.

Each chapter is preceded by a short preview. The previews are intended to provide a generalist reader with a context within which to read and assimilate each chapter. The previews lay out how the current chapter relates to the other chapters and what the key ideas raised in each chapter are. After all, a major objective of the book as a whole is to provide an interdisciplinary dialogue in which researchers who have been asking similar questions in different domains can read and share ideas with each other. We hope that these previews will ensure that readers move beyond those chapters of direct familiarity to their current research and consider the findings from complementary fields.

References

Ashby, F. G. & Lee, W. W. (1993). Perceptual variability as a fundamental axiom of perceptual science. *Advances in Psychology*, **99**, 369–399.

Bartlett, F. C. (1932). *Remembering: A Study in Experimental and Social Psychology* Cambridge: Cambridge University Press.

Bekoff, M., Allen, C., & Burghardt, G. (2002). *The Cognitive Animal* Cambridge, MA: MIT Press.

Bermudez, J. L. (2003). *Thinking without Words* Oxford: Oxford University Press.

Boakes, R. (1984). *From Darwin to Behaviourism* Cambridge: Cambridge University Press.

Chomsky, N. (1980). *Rules and Representation* New York, NY: Columbia University Press.

Corballis, M. C. & Lea, S. E. G. (1999). *The Descent of Mind: Psychological Perspectives on Hominid Evolution* Oxford: Oxford University Press.

Csibra, G. & Gergely, G. (2006). Social learning and social cognition: The case for pedagogy. In Y. Munakata & M. H. Johnson (Eds.), *Processes of Change in Brain and Cognitive Development. Attention and Performance XXI*, pp. 249–274, Oxford: Oxford University Press.

Darwin, C. (1871). *On the Origins of the Species by Means of Natural Selection* London: John Murray.

Flavell, J. (1963). *The Developmental Psychology of Jean Piaget* Princeton, NJ: van Nostrand.

Fodor, J. A. (1980). Fixation of belief and concept acquisition. In M. Piatelli-Palmarini (Ed.), *Language and Learning: The Debate between Chomsky and Piaget*, pp. 142–162, Cambridge, MA: Harvard University Press.

Fodor, J. A. (1998). *Concepts: Where Cognitive Science Went Wrong* Oxford: Oxford University Press.

Gallup, G. G. (1998). Self-awareness and the evolution of social intelligence. *Behavioural Processes*, **42**, 239–247.

Geach, P. (1957). *Mental Acts* London: Routledge & Kegan Paul.

Heyes, C. M. (1998). Theory of mind in non-human primates. *Behavioral and Brain Sciences*, **21**, 101–148.

Hurley, S. & Nudds, M. (2005). *Rational Animals* Oxford: Oxford University Press.

Jackendoff, R. (2002). *Foundations of Language: Brain, Meaning, Grammar, Evolution* Oxford: Oxford University Press.

Karmiloff-Smith, A. (1992). *Beyond Modularity: A Developmental Perspective on Cognitive Science* Cambridge, MA: MIT Press.

Keil, F. C. (1989). *Concepts, Kinds, and Cognitive Development* New York, NY: Bradford Books.

Leech, R., Mareschal, D., & Cooper, R. (2008). Analogy as relational priming: A developmental and computational perspective on the origins of a complex cognitive skill. *Behavioral and Brain Sciences*, **31**, 357–414.

Locke, J. (1690). An essay concerning human understanding. In P. Phemister (Ed.) (2008), *An Essay Concerning Human Understanding (Oxford World Classics)* Oxford: Oxford University Press.

Macnamara, J. L. (1982). *Names for Things* Cambridge, MA: MIT Press.

Mareschal, D., Johnson, M. H., Sirois, S., Spratling, M., Thomas, M., & Westermann, G. (2007). *Neuroconstructivism, Vol. I: How the Brain Constructs Cognition* Oxford: Oxford University Press.

Mithen, S. (1996). *The Prehistory of Mind* London: Thames & Hundson.

Oyama, S. (1985). *The Ontogeny of Information: Developmental Systems and Evolution* Cambridge, MA: Cambridge University Press.

Piaget, J. (1954). *The Construction of Reality on Children* New York: Basic Books.

Piaget, J. (1972). *The Principles of Genetic Epistemology* New York: Norton Books.

Piatelli-Palmarini, M. (1980). *Language and Learning: The Debate between Chomsky and Piaget* Cambridge, MA: Harvard University Press.

Penn, D. C., Holyoak, K. J., & Povinelli, D. J. (2008). Darwin's mistake: Explaining the discontinuity between human and non-human minds. *Behavioral and Brain Sciences*, **31**, 109–178.

Pinker, S. (1994). *The Language Instinct* London: Penguin.

Premack, D. (2007). Human and animal cognition: Continuity or discontinuity. *Proceedings of the National Academy of Science USA,* **104**, 13861–13867.

Quinn, P. C. (2008). In defense of core competencies, quantitative change, and continuity. *Child Development*, **79**, 1633–1638.

Roitblat, H. L., Bever, T. G., & Terrace, H. S. (Eds.) (1984). *Animal Cognition* Hillsdale, NJ: Erlbaum.

Russell, B. (1945). *The History of Western Philosophy* New York: Simon and Schuster.

Smith, J. D., Shields, W. E., & Washburn, D. A. (2003). The comparative psychology of uncertainty monitoring and metacognition. *Behavioral and Brain Sciences,* **26**, 317–373.

Thelen, E. & Smith, L. B. (1994). *A Dynamic Systems Approach to the Development of Cognition and Action* Cambridge, MA: The MIT Press.

Tomasello, M. (1999). *The Cultural Origins of Human Cognition* Harvard, MA: Harvard University Press.

Tomasello, M. & Rakoczy, H. (2003). What makes human cognition unique? From individual to shared collective intentionality. *Mind and Language,* **18**, 121–147.

Thornton, A. & Raihani, N. J. (2008). The evolution of teaching. *Animal Behaviour*, **75**, 1823–1836.

Tschudin A. J.-P. C (2001). 'Mindreading' mammals? Attribution of belief tasks with dolphins. *Animal Welfare*, **10**, 119–27.

Wasserman, E. A. (2008). Development and evolution of cognition: One doth not fly into flying. *Behavioral and Brain Sciences,* **31**, 400–401.

Chapter 2

What are categories and concepts?

Gregory L. Murphy

Editors' Preview

Chapter 2, 'What are categories and concepts?' introduces readers to some of the major vocabulary terms that will be used by authors of the subsequent chapters. It begins by defining a category as a set of things that are treated equivalently in one or another respect. For example, items within a category might evoke the same response in the context of an investigation (e.g. the members might all be looked at for the same amount of time) or on a more everyday basis outside the laboratory (e.g. the examples are referred to with a common name). Instances from the same category are treated equivalently because they tend to share groups of attributes that make the category instances similar to one another. While categories exist in the world, their mental representations, which exist inside the head, are referred to as concepts.

Concepts are considered to be important for organizing mental life because they allow us to have summary representations of our experiences with the world (e.g. the various cats that we have encountered in life can be represented in a 'cat' concept). In addition, concepts provide us with a means to identify objects, even objects that are unfamiliar to us (e.g. our concept of 'cats' allows us to readily recognize those cats not yet experienced). Concepts moreover provide us with a basis for induction, a mental process by which we generalize properties from known to unknown instances. That is, by identifying a newly encountered cat as a cat, one may conclude that the cat is likely to have the properties that we believe cats have (such as four legs, fur, a tail, whiskers, and abilities to 'meow' and beget or give birth to kittens).

Chapter 2 also introduces the reader to some of the main themes of the book. One is the diversity of categories. For example, adult humans represent categories for objects (cats, shoes, chairs), attributes (red things), and things that follow prescribed rules or meet simple definitions (e.g. bachelor, strike in baseball). We can also represent natural categories for entities that exist in the world (e.g. birds, cars) and artificial categories where an experimenter creates a particular category structure (e.g. schematic images of animals within category A being those with angular bodies, spots, and long legs, and category B being those with rounded bodies, lack of spots, and short legs). In addition, there are ad hoc categories formed on the fly to meet the demands posed by particular situations (e.g. cash, family heirlooms, loved ones, and pets are all things of value that one would take out of the house in case of a fire). We can further entertain thematic concepts (thereby linking together car and garage) as well as script concepts for items that play the same role in a routine or event (e.g. breakfast time, birthday party). At least some categories are also believed to possess an essence or underlying causal structure that is responsible for creating the similarities observed amongst the members (e.g. cats have cat DNA).

The diversity of categories relates to a second major theme of the book, and that is how the concepts of infants and nonhuman animals are like each other and unlike the concepts possessed by human adults. The variety of categories represented by human adults allows investigators to ask whether the concepts of human infants are the forerunners of the mature concepts of human adults, and whether one can find evidence that human adult concepts are also used by nonhuman animals. Exploration of the similarities and differences of conceptual behaviour of human adults, human infants, and nonhuman animals will be a recurring topic addressed by chapter authors throughout the book.

Everyone knows what a category is: it is a set of objects of some kind. Of course, not every possible set is a category. The textbooks generally say something like 'A category is a set of objects that are equivalent for some purpose'. Yes, but equivalent how? The most obvious equivalence is when the objects are all called by the same name. Clearly, all dogs must be in the same category, or else we would not call them by the same name. All Republicans must be equivalent for *some* purpose, even if they differ greatly in their individual attributes. We cannot complain too much about the vagueness of this definition, because there are all sorts of categories (as we shall see) invented for all sorts of purposes, and a more specific definition might not fit many examples.

Nonetheless, there is something troubling about this definition, because almost every conceivable set of objects is equivalent in *some* way. The objects in my office, although extremely diverse, are equivalent in their spatial location. Are they a category? The Louvre, chile rellenos, the music of Ornette Coleman, and a nasty cat might all be things that my sister likes. Do they form a category too? Indeed, I have previously complained (Murphy, 2005) that the psychology of concepts often misuses this definition by making up arbitrary categories for people to learn in an experiment. The items form categories because subjects are told to give one set of objects one name and another set of objects another name. Therefore, each set is equivalent in having a common name (or response). But this is putting the cart before the horse: dogs have the same name because they form a coherent category – they are not an arbitrary set of objects that have been given the same name. Although it is easy for us to identify categories that have common names, that does not mean that merely assigning a common name to a set of objects makes them into a meaningful category.

The purpose of this chapter is to consider more carefully the question of just what makes a category. Presumably, we ought to have a definition of what we are studying before going off and studying it. Or should we? One of my conclusions will be that it is a mistake to try to completely define categories in advance of empirical investigation, because such definitions are inevitably wrong and then have a pernicious effect on subsequent scientific investigation. So, my attempt at describing what categories and concepts are will be based not so much on a prior definition but will reflect research into different types of categories. As we discover new and unexpected kinds of categories that people apparently have, we will have a better understanding of how categories are mentally represented and of what their role is in thought.

Having reviewed these examples, I will then turn to more controversial cases in which it has been doubted (or could be doubted) whether someone 'has' a category. In particular, this issue arises for young children and nonhuman animals. If our notion of categories derives from work with adult humans, and if subpopulations of humans and other species differ from those adult people in important respects, then there are bound to be psychological differences in their representations of (putative) categories. So, do those populations have categories or not? And does the answer make any difference to our psychology of categories?

Category and concept

It is seemingly simple to distinguish *categories* from *concepts*. Categories refer to sets of objects (or events or abstract entities) in the world. Such sets are of interest to psychologists because people think about them and use them in a variety of cognitive processes. We refer to the mental representations of these sets as *concepts*.[1] So, categories are in the world, and concepts are in the head. There is a complex interaction between categories and concepts. Concepts are good things to have because they are largely accurate summaries of the world. It is useful to have a concept of dogs because dogs generally have four legs, bark, drool, are domesticated, and so on. If dogs did not have those things in common, then it would be hard to understand why people formed such concepts. But, of course, reality and the mind do not perfectly coincide. The progress of science has led to discoveries about the world that in turn led to changes in people's concepts. Many people believed that whales were kinds of fish, but now every schoolchild knows that whales are mammals. Our concepts changed to conform more perfectly to the categories of the world. Thus, although there is an important distinction to be made between the sets of entities in the world and our thoughts about them, in speaking about one, we are often indirectly speaking about the other. For example,

---

[1] Concepts of fictional entities may not correspond to an actual category. Although these are quite interesting, I will not be able to address them here.

if we say that Lee knows that dogs have four legs, we are saying something true both about dogs per se and about Lee's concept of dogs. As a result, it often makes little practical difference whether we talk about Lee's category or Lee's concept of dogs, because what we say about one has direct implications for the other.

Psychologists are interested in the kinds of categories that people form concepts of. We do not really care about categories based on obscure properties that no one thinks about or could discover (e.g. all the things that came into existence on a Tuesday; all things that are 0.5% molybdenum). As we are doing psychology, we want to know about the kinds of categories that people actually think about and use in their everyday life. I am emphasizing this point because I think that it tends to get lost in philosophical discussions about what categories are. Although in principle many things could be grouped together for many purposes to form a category, the psychological question before us is about what kinds of groupings people actually use, and for what purposes.

Therefore, in the rest of this chapter, I will focus on categories that have important psychological functions, that is, categories that people are likely to form concepts of. In some cases, we have direct evidence that people form particular categories. But to make predictions about other, yet untested cases we need to understand what the functions of categories are, in order to be able to say what categories are learned and used in general.

Kinds of categories, and their functions

Object categories are the main sort of categories studied in the field. Prototypically, such concepts refer to concrete entities, are referred to by a noun, and have many properties associated with them. These are *taxonomic categories*, which include items that are similar to one another by virtue of the properties they tend to share. Low-level, specific categories like rainbow trout or MacBook Pro laptops are especially rich in shared features, but more abstract categories like animals or electronic devices are not as rich. Less prototypical are event concepts, which nonetheless are also labelled by a noun and have many properties in common. For example, parties generally have food and drink, invited guests, music, and so on. More abstract entities often fall into categories as well. We have categories such as computational models of working memory or non-Western musical scales. Although they are abstract, members of these categories also share features and are different from members of other categories.

In general, the categories that have been the focus of most research have been groupings of entities that are similar to one another in various respects. This similarity allows us to treat the different members of the categories in similar ways (e.g. one can cook with the most ripe tomatoes, regardless of what particular variety they are, their size, or their price). To the degree that category membership indicates shared properties, then, the category is useful. If some tomatoes were inedible and some were edible, some round and some square, some having seeds and some having pits, it would not be as useful to classify something as a tomato. The fact that tomatoes are overwhelmingly edible as well as sharing other properties makes it useful to identify something as a tomato.

Categories are useful, then, to the degree that they tell us about their members. The normal, spontaneous names people use to label objects (Rosch et al., 1976), the *basic level* of categorization, tells us much about categories. When we name things as dogs, trees, houses, or books, we are communicating much about the object. If you know only that X is a dog, you can correctly make many predictions about X's properties: what it looks like, what parts it has, how it will behave, its origin, and its eventual fate. In contrast, categories like things in my office or things that came into existence on a Tuesday do not provide this kind of information. Lacking this similarity, such categories cannot help direct our behaviour.

Another type of category is single-criterion categories like red things, things with wings, or objects bigger than a breadbox – categories defined by a single property. We often do have words to refer to such categories, but they are usually adjectives, like *red* or *winged*. Logically, there is no particular reason why red things cannot be a category, and they certainly are 'equivalent for some purpose' (their colour). Nonetheless, it does not seem to be the case that people normally use such categories in terms of identifying objects and thinking about them. When presented with objects and asked to name them, people overwhelmingly provide basic category names rather than adjectival names (e.g. Berlin, 1992; Rosch et al., 1976). Unless the light is bad, no one enters a room and thinks 'Oh, red things, large things, soft things!' Instead, one notices the chairs, lush carpeting, and stereo speakers. Use of categories such as red things is generally task specific, as when one is looking for objects to fit some specific purpose. If the customs law specified an extra tariff for red items, then I am sure that customs officials would form concepts of red things. Lacking such a context, we do not normally categorize objects that way. Redness is important as an attribute (e.g. as part of the concept of tomatoes or fire trucks), but it is not very useful as a concept itself.

The problem with single-criterion categories (Lassaline & Murphy, 1996) is that they cannot provide further information about an entity. In order to classify the object as a red thing, you need to know its colour. But since the colour exhausts the category's content, no more information can be gained from classifying it. The category cannot provide any further information about the object. In contrast, suppose you identify a flying object as a bird. Now you can infer that it lives in a nest, has two feet, has a beak, came from an egg, may migrate, and so on – properties that you did not actually observe in this object. Thus, although single-criterion categories seem to logically fulfil the definition of objects that are in some way equivalent, they do not actually subserve the other functions of categories, because they do not allow one to infer any further information about its members. Although fire trucks and cherry lollypops may both be red, they do not appear to share other interesting properties, so there is little point in classifying them together.

A similar point can be made about so-called *classical categories* – those constructed from a simple definition (see Murphy 2002, Chapter 2). For example, in classic concept-acquisition studies, subjects learned concepts such as large-or-red (Bruner et al., 1956; Shepard et al., 1961). The problem here is that the criteria for membership again exhaust the category. Once subjects identified the object as large-or-red, they knew that it was in the category, but there was no further information that the category could supply. (Indeed, a disjunctive category of this sort actually provides *less* information in some sense. In order to classify the object, you must have noticed that it was red but not large, say. But the category itself is ambiguous between these features, so it does not say which property it might have had.) There is no obvious reason to form categories of this sort, unless they also include information that is not part of their definition. But then, of course, they would no longer be classical categories. Indeed, the richness of real categories seems to have been one of Eleanor Rosch's (1977) insights that led her to criticize the traditional classical view.

In this sense, then, single-criterion categories and classical categories in general certainly 'exist' and can be taught to people, but they do not serve the functions that categories are supposed to serve, and there is little evidence that people spontaneously use them. Perhaps the most likely exception is in technical contexts where definitional categories might not be degenerate. For example, if you have more than three children and earn under a certain amount of money, perhaps you are eligible for income tax credits; if you have five cards of the same suit, then your poker hand is better than a straight. In these cases, there is further information gained by identifying the category (the tax credit, the rank of your hand), and so the concept does not consist only of its membership criteria.

Beyond traditional object categories

One of the most important projects in the psychology of concepts in terms of the question, 'what is a category?' was Lawrence Barsalou's (1983, 1985) study of ad hoc or goal-derived categories. He looked at categories such as things to carry from a burning house or ways to avoid being killed by the mob. Although some of these were in fact object categories (like the former), they were not 'normal' categories in a number of respects. They did not have simple names, they often seemed to include diverse entities, and they were not generally identified in a neutral context. No one looking at an old family Bible ever said, 'Look at that thing to carry out of a burning house'.

Nonetheless, Barsalou showed that such categories are informative and helpful. People can identify members of the categories, specify which ones are more and less typical, and they can list properties of the categories. Things to carry out of a burning house are valuable, irreplaceable, portable, and often carry emotional value. In the heat of the moment, you may gaze longingly at your new, 63-inch flat-screen plasma TV that is about to be consumed by flames, but you will probably quickly realize that you had better grab a child or pet instead – and run. Interestingly, when I have recently asked students to list things to carry out of a burning house, they mention a number of items that Barsalou's subjects (c. 1980) did not, such as their mobile phones and laptops. Nonetheless, both of these share the listed features with the previously popu-lar items, children, photo albums, family jewellery, pets, etc. If you lose your laptop, all your e-mail (and possibly the latest draft of your thesis) will be gone, and that is irreplaceable. Clearly, then, this category is not an arbitrary one that is learned in a rote manner, but is a productive category that can embrace new entities that come into existence, if they fit its intention.

Ad hoc categories are different from more prototypical object categories in that they are not generally represented in long-term memory. As their name suggests, they are constructed when they are needed. People do not spontaneously identify items as members of ad hoc categories unless the category has been previously suggested to them (Barsalou, 1983). Furthermore, members of ad hoc categories do not appear very similar to one another except in the context of the category (Barsalou, 1983; Ross & Murphy, 1999).

In later work, Barsalou (1991) suggested that a related kind of category may play more of a role in long-term thought. Many of the tasks that we do in everyday life are repeated. For example, as a college student, you might have to decide how to travel from your college dorm to home, cheaply. That summer, you might have to figure out how to get to your vacation spot, cheaply. In your junior year, you might have to plan how to get to your foreign study location, cheaply. These are not exactly the same problem, but they do have a certain similarity involving long-distance travel and severe financial constraints.

Barsalou (1991) suggested that carrying out related tasks of this sort could give rise to goal-derived categories in which common solutions to related problems form a category. For example, modes of transportation such as hitchhiking, taking a bus, or flying standby might become associated together as ways to travel long distance cheaply, because you have used them to solve this problem or at least considered them as possible solutions. Such categories *do* become encoded into long-term memory, and they are drawn on when similar situations arise again. When your college-age child asks how she is going to get to Montana for her vacation (hoping for a handout), you might immediately say, 'why not take the bus?' because you have such a solution in memory for such problems. Like ad hoc categories, these categories do not have a simple word that refers to them. But given the repetition of similar kinds of tasks across our lives, it seems likely that this kind of category is quite common. And, again, they do carry information, unlike arbitrary collections or single-criterion concepts.

Thematic and script concepts

As noted earlier, concepts are typically said to include items that are similar to one another. This similarity provides their informativeness. As dogs share properties such as their limbs, shape, behaviours, and internal organs, classifying something as a dog provides much information about it. But there is another way to make categories, based not on shared properties but on what we might call external relations. The most notable example of this is *thematic categories*, those formed by members that have a specific relation. Piaget and Vygotsky claimed to find such categories in young children's responses to classification tasks, and more recent studies using standardized methods also found that young children form thematic categories (e.g. Markman, 1989; Smiley & Brown, 1979). For example, children given a large set of objects to sort might not separate the people from the vehicles but would instead put a toy man with a car, saying 'The man drives the car'. Or a dog might be grouped with a leash, because 'The dog wears the leash when it takes a walk'.

For many years, the field viewed such categories as a developmentally immature way of grouping items that was later replaced by similarity-based taxonomic categories like tomatoes and dogs. (However, this view was a bit troubled by the finding that adults in other cultures continued to make such groupings, sometimes vociferously defending them as better than taxonomic groupings; Luria, 1976; Sharp et al., 1979.) After all, putting together a dog and a leash seems to be doing violence to the concepts of both dog and leash. The group does not breathe, is not made of leather, does not have fur, does not have a handle, etc., because the properties of one are not found in the other. Therefore, there is good reason to think that there is something wrong with such a category.

It is very surprising, then, that a more careful investigation by Emilie Lin revealed that even college-educated American adults continue to use thematic categories (Lin & Murphy, 2001). For example, in a triad task, people might be asked which item is in the same category with a bee: honey or a fly? Presumably, the fly and bee share many properties, and the bee and honey, few. Nonetheless, between 49% and 73% (depending on procedural variations) of responses by adults were of the bee-honey type, even when the instructions describe a specifically taxonomic definition of 'same category'. Furthermore, a closer look at the sorting experiments that had found that adults group items taxonomically revealed that the structure of the items in those experiments was biased towards taxonomic responses. With structures that are equally susceptible to taxonomic or thematic sorting, adults sorted thematically as much as 87% of the time (Murphy, 2001). Thus, if popularity is any guide, thematic categories must be considered as 'real' categories.

Why should seemingly normal college students group together honey and bees or turkeys and Thanksgiving as the same kind of thing? (Personally, I blame the educational system.) Lin followed up her finding by looking at whether thematic pairs of this sort carry any information. For example, if you knew something about one member of the pair (e.g. honey has some chemical in it, or it occurs in a certain location), would you attribute it to the other member (bee)? In fact, people did make such inferences, suggesting that thematic groupings are informative (e.g. in contrast to single-criterion categories). Nonetheless, I wonder whether such groupings really play much of a role in everyday thought. Such groupings indicate co-occurrence more than anything else (where there is a leash, there is likely to be a dog), and so people may in fact learn them, but they lack the many shared properties of taxonomic categories that provide a strong basis for induction. Nonetheless, thematic categories provide some useful information (Markman, 1989): when you see the dog by the door, you think about getting the leash; when you hear that bees are suffering from a mysterious disease, you realize that the price of honey is going to go up.

A related kind of category is *script-based category*. Scripts are structured representations of common events, such as birthday parties, going to the movies, eating at a restaurant, or taking an exam. Script-based categories are things that play the *same role* in the script. Thus, this kind of category is also defined externally – by the script, rather than by the properties of the objects per se. For example, animals you see at the zoo are all animals, but they are further defined by the property of being viewed on a particular kind of occasion. Cake, ice cream, fruit, and pudding are all things that might be served as dessert. So, in your script for dinner, there is a role for the dessert, and all the things that commonly occur in that role are in the same script-based category.

Script-based categories appear to have more content than thematic categories do. This is because the constraints of the script permit only certain kinds of things to play the same role in it. For dessert, one usually wants a treat, which requires sweetness rather than massive amounts of protein or complex carbohydrates, which have presumably already been eaten earlier in the meal. Thus, although it is partially arbitrary what our culture normally eats for dessert (Why do Americans eat cakes but not pancakes? Why not cereal?), it is by no means completely arbitrary. Desserts tend to be sweet and fatty, and not based on meat or potatoes. Zoo animals tend to be from exotic locations and to be photogenic. In contrast, dogs and their leashes or bees and their honey share only one relation (restrains, makes) and do not have as many properties in common.

Script categories were often believed to be something that children also grew out of, by early school age (e.g. Lucariello et al., 1992). However, more recent work has suggested that children and adults both use script categories (Nguyen & Murphy, 2003; Ross & Murphy, 1999). Indeed, in a study of food categories, Ross and Murphy discovered that people spontaneously pay attention to when the food is typically served (a script attribute) when they were grouping foods into categories. Furthermore, people formed inductions from one category member to another, again suggesting that the categories provide useful information. For example, if you found out that one kind of dessert has a certain chemical constituent, you would suspect that other kinds of dessert might have the same constituent, even if they were not in the same taxonomic category.

One important aspect of categories of this sort is that they *cross-cut* taxonomic categories. Breakfast foods include foods from many different types of taxonomic categories: meat (bacon), fish (herring, lox), bread (bagels), dairy (milk, butter, cream, and cheese), beverages, and so on. Similarly, when we have been talking about ad hoc and thematic categories, we have been referring to their members by taxonomic category names. Your laptop is both a computer and something you might carry out of a burning house; your dog is both a mammal and a member of the dog-and-leash pair. It is all too easy to fall into the habit of talking about 'what category an object is in', as if there is only one such category. As basic-level categorization is the default, it is possible to think of it as 'the' category for an object. But in real life, multiple categories can be relevant, depending on the context and task.

Knowledge-based categories

Psychologists have often invented artificial categories based on their needs for theory testing rather than being based on some claim about what real-world categories are like (see Murphy, 2005). For various reasons, such categories have typically been constructed so that they make little contact with everyday knowledge. However, in real life, most new categories enter an already densely populated conceptual forest. They are similar to known categories, they may be defined in distinction to other categories, and they generally follow the laws of nature (or some other relevant domain) that we already know. These considerations typically make new categories much easier to learn than categories that must be learned by rote (e.g. Murphy & Allopenna, 1994).

People know which properties of the category are likely to be important and which are not; sometimes the category is similar enough to another that one can think of it as known-concept plus X (e.g. zebra = horse plus stripes). Furthermore, the use of prior knowledge allows one to draw inferences that were never explicitly learned. If whales have a two-part liver, then perhaps mice also have a two-part liver, because both are mammals (see Heit & Rubinstein, 1994; Proffitt, 2000). Although mammals do not share all properties, they are likely to share basic physiological structures, and so this kind of inference is strong.

Medin and Ortony (1989) argued that people believe in an *essence* that they think underlies most natural categories. In psychology experiments with artificial categories, most subjects are sophisticated enough to realize that the category is just whatever the experimenter says it is. But in the real world, there is an assumption that categories are what they are because of an underlying causal structure that gives rise to their properties. In the case of biological categories, this structure is probably assumed to be genetic. In other natural categories, the underlying cause may be physical–chemical structure. In the case of person categories, there is reason to believe that people think that races or genders or even personalities are constructed from a shared underlying essence of some kind (e.g. Hirschfeld, 1996).

If people believe in essences for some categories and normally use their vast knowledge of the world to interpret and learn new categories, then why would anyone study the learning of categories of geometric figures or dot patterns? After all, these knowledge-rich categories are the real categories, and the artificial ones are not of interest in and of themselves. Without intending to defend the field's overreliance on artificial categories, I think it is incorrect that knowledge-rich, interesting categories like female doctors, zebras, works of art, or laptops are 'real', and categories constructed from artificial, meaningless materials are not.

Even natural categories vary greatly. Not all natural categories have essences, for example. Ad hoc and script-based categories clearly exist and have a function, yet they don't have essences or some of the other properties of the natural categories people have in mind when they raise this objection. Furthermore, at least *some* categories must be learned by the hard work of forming associations or memorizing exemplars with little help from prior knowledge, just like the categories learned by unfortunate subjects in psychology experiments. Some categories simply are not related to any prior knowledge that helps you learn them. Poultry workers learn to tell the sex of day-old chicks based on an extremely difficult perceptual discrimination that is learned slowly; experts estimate that they reach their maximum level of performance after 2–6 years of one million birds sexed per year (Biederman & Shiffrar, 1987). Bird watchers who can tell the difference between the nearly identical kinds of American sparrows cannot do so based on deep biological knowledge. Somehow they have to learn how many eye bands each bird has and how the presence or absence of a whitish spot under the wing predicts category membership. There is no theory to tell them why the Bar's pine sparrow has such a spot but the hooting gable sparrow does not.

Children learn the names for different colours very slowly, and attempts to teach them colours through paired-associate learning are often unsuccessful after hundreds of trials (Soja, 1994). Yet, they eventually do learn colour names, presumably after hearing them for a few years. I am pretty good at identifying the jazz pianist Bill Evans from his recordings (personal communication), in spite of the fact that he played on a variety of different pianos, was recorded under different conditions, and was widely imitated. I can assure you that there is no role of music theory or other conceptual knowledge involved, since I do not know music theory. Instead, it was feedback-based learning of hearing dozens of his recordings over and over as well as hearing recordings of other pianists. My category learning here was no doubt much more enjoyable than the experience of the undergraduate attempting to learn to separate geometric figures into two categories, but I cannot swear that the learning mechanism was different. In all these cases, category learning seems to work via dumb old association learning of some kind, rather than through top-down construction of a concept representation or through similarity to known categories. I am not denying that people may have rich knowledge of sparrows or Bill Evans – I am only claiming that such knowledge does not always help much in learning to identify category members.

Knowledge-based categories are an important and widespread kind of category, and the research on adult categories has neglected them relative to their importance. But to conclude that these are the only kind of categories is simply unjustified. Certainly, the question of whether racial categories are thought to be based on an underlying essence is a fascinating one with considerable relevance to society. The question of whether linearly separable or nonlinearly separable categories of geometric figures are equally easy to learn is not so fascinating on the face of it. Nonetheless, one of our human capabilities is to learn difficult discriminations that may be probabilistic, and if that is what is required to make an important distinction, then we will learn them. So, such categories are 'real' categories too. This dispute has implications for developmental approaches to concepts, as the next section discusses.

Immature concepts

When asking 'what are concepts?', developmental questions are important, because there have been claims that children do not have concepts, or at least 'real' concepts. However, such claims have often been theory bound, in that investigators had a particular idea of what concepts are (or should be), and they did not find that children met their expectations (Inhelder & Piaget, 1964, being the most notable example). If there are many kinds of adult concepts, this conclusion must be re-thought.

Children's concepts are often not the same as adults'. Indeed, several chapters in this book are devoted to exploring what is unique about children's concepts (e.g. Chapters 12, 13, 15, and 16). Mervis (1987) argued that most children's categories are in a kind of overlap relationship to adults': they include many of the same items, but children's categories both omit members of the adult category and include some items that adults do not. This difference in *categories* of children and adults raises an interesting philosophical question about whether children's *concepts* should be thought of as concepts of the same thing as adults' concepts. If children do not include insects in their concepts of animals, then they clearly do not have the same animal concept as adults. But is it a concept of animals? If concepts are identified by their members, then any difference suggests that the concepts are different. One can take this viewpoint, but then one is immediately stuck with the fact that virtually no two people's concepts are going to be identical, and therefore, one should not talk about 'the concept of animals' or 'the category of blue things', given that everyone will differ at least slightly in what they think is included in these categories. Such a viewpoint will lead to chaos rather than to greater precision in discussion. We all manage to communicate with words like *animal* or *blue* even though we may differ slightly in what we would label with these names, so little harm seems to come about if we talk about people having the same concepts or both having the concept of animals. But should the same courtesy be extended to children or other creatures whose concepts differ more significantly from those of the average adult?

To study the development of concepts, there must be a way of tracking whatever is developing. If the 2-year-old differs from the 1-year-old and the 4-year-old in their concepts of animals, say, then in order to understand the developmental progression, we have to track the development of that thing across ages. And if we define that thing as in fact different things at each age, then it cannot be developing. The historical progression from an extremely simple concept (e.g. animals are anything that move) to a more mature concept (e.g. animals move, grow, and have babies) to the final adult concept can only be traced by treating the concept as the same thing. (The same argument has appeared in the philosophy of science, as scientific revolutions have changed the way that people think about mass or the elements, creating some doubt whether the same concepts are being referred to before and after the revolution; see Khalidi, 2000.) The concept of the young child might not seem very similar to that of the college-educated adult, but we need to look forward to the child's future and project that concept changing continuously into its adult form. Unless there is a break in which most of what was believed before is rejected, it seems most useful to think of the concept as continuing to exist, but changing with development.

This dispute has taken on a more substantive tone when comparing infant concepts to those of older children and adults. In particular, Jean Mandler has argued that infants can only form perceptual-motor schemas rather than real concepts (Mandler, 2004). Mandler's objection arises from a real problem in the study of infant concepts, namely that researchers are generally limited to measuring recognition of some kind, using looking or some other measure of attention. They are also limited by infants' lack of linguistic abilities to presenting stimuli without instructions and without being able to ask questions. Therefore, the *evidence* about infants' concepts generally involves their attentive responses to perceptual stimuli. For example, if an experimenter presents children with different pictures of bunny rabbits and then shows them a bunny rabbit or dog, she might find that they prefer to look at the dog (e.g. Quinn et al., 1993). If this is evidence that they have a concept of bunny rabbits, it must be evidence for a perceptual concept, since the infants were not presented with and do not know any information about the biology, history, origins, or behaviour of bunny rabbits. Thus, Mandler argues that they are only learning perceptual schemas of some kind, and not true concepts.

I think it is rather a weak argument to say that because our experiments have been limited to testing X, infants can only form concepts of type X (whatever X may be). However, this criticism does not only reflect a concern about psychology experiments, because it is certainly correct that infants do not have deep knowledge of biology or mechanics or the functions of complex artefacts – even many of the ones they encounter every day. Under these circumstances, one might wonder whether what infants are learning really qualifies as concepts.

Referring to the earlier discussion about whether children have the 'same category' as adults, I think that similar reasoning applies to the case of infants. Even assuming that infants are learning primarily perceptual information about the everyday objects around them, it seems very likely that these concepts themselves develop into the more mature concepts, and that there is a historical connection between the two. An infant's concept of, say, cats (assuming that the child lives in a home with cats) cannot be a trivial image. The infant can recognize the sleeping cat, the cat on the couch, the cat running or jumping, the cat sitting in one of a number of positions, the eating cat, the cat from above or behind, etc. No doubt this concept, even if perceptually based, allows the infant to extract cats' skeletomuscular structure, to learn about their frequent locations and behaviours, as well as nonvisual information – all of which will be part of the eventual mature concept. I cannot conceive of conceptual development as rejecting this pre-verbal concept when a later 'real' concept, embedded in more abstract knowledge, is formed. Even the school-age child who knows something about simple biology must also recognize cats standing on the fence, cats sleeping on their backs, cats meowing at the door, and so on – the very things they learned about cats as infants. That is, I think it is not only a matter of scientific convenience to talk about infants having the same concept as older children and adults but that it is likely a psychological fact that the earliest concepts gradually turn into those later concepts, with the first, primarily perceptual information turning into the more mature, complete concepts (as proposed by Quinn & Eimas, 1997).

What about the concepts of nonhuman animals? Although they clearly exhibit conceptual behaviour that is similar in some respects to those of humans (see the chapters in Part 2 of this book), there are undoubtedly differences of various kinds. Even if lab pigeons can learn to identify cats in photographs, their knowledge of cats is much less than humans have. They have never petted or held a cat (and lived!), they do not know about its biology or evolutionary history, and they probably do not know about its behaviours or role as a domestic companion. Here, whether we want to talk about the animal having the 'same concept' as humans seems a matter of convenience rather than a matter of principle. No doubt animal concepts are similar in some respects and different in some respects from those of humans, but little rests on the question of whether we say the pigeon has the concept cat or instead cat_p. In contrast, when the concept has continuity within an individual (as in development) or commonality within a community (when speakers use the same word to refer to – mostly – the same thing), calling the concept the same concept has empirical and theoretical consequences.

Research on animals is important for identifying processes underlying conceptual behaviour, and it is useful exactly *because* other animals do some things differently from the way we do them. If they did not, it would certainly be easier to test undergraduates who can read instructions and (often) follow them. The exact pattern of similarities and differences of animals' and humans' concepts are what will (we hope)

cast light on the capacities of each, more than studying either one alone would. Getting caught up in the terminological question of whether animals have 'real' concepts is more likely to hinder this investigation than help it.

Conclusion

What may be most surprising in this discussion of what categories are is their remarkable diversity. In the history of psychology, writers' definitions of categories were rather theory laden, and they therefore have claimed (or presupposed) that there is a single type of category. Psychologists such as Hull (1920) and Inhelder and Piaget (1964) defined categories as sets of things that shared some criterial properties: everything in the category had those properties, and nothing outside the set had all those properties. Thus, a category was logically defined by the set of its defining attributes. These authors probably did not realize that their definition was theory laden, because it was only later that probabilistic and fuzzy notions of categories became well known. Nonetheless, such a definition of categories had the effect of specifying that there is only one type of category and therefore only one type of concept. If confronted with thematic categories, prototype categories, or ad hoc categories, no doubt such psychologists would have argued that these things were not categories at all. Rosch, in her remarkable critique of the classical view of categories, proposed family-resemblance prototype categories as a replacement (e.g. Rosch, 1977), but she did not seem to envision that yet other kinds of categories would be necessary to explain the full range of human thought.

I would argue, then, that psychologists need to be careful not to define the notion of categories prematurely, as this has the effect of preventing discoveries that are not consistent with our first assumptions about what categories are – assumptions that inevitably are not completely correct. Furthermore, there is a tendency in the field to think that categories *really* are like the ones we have chosen to study in our laboratories. For a while, real categories were logical terms like red-or-large, or if-green-then-square, based on the groundbreaking work of Bruner et al. (1956). For a while, categories were statistical distortions of prototypes, based on the work of Posner and Keele (1968). Then they became similarity-based classes, through the impact of prototype and exemplar theories. But even though the classical view of categories has been largely discarded, it must be admitted that there are classical-like categories in certain contexts, such as categories defined by rules of games (an out in baseball, a straight in poker), by legal definitions, or in science. Clearly, we all understand categories such as odd numbers. Add to these cases like thematic categories, script-based categories, knowledge-rich categories, or goal-derived categories, we have a very diverse set of things being called categories.

Does it make any sense to call these diverse entities by the same name? Whether it does or not depends to a large degree on scientific discovery. As we learn more about knowledge-rich categories and script-based categories, we may begin to realize that they are really very different beasts. However, it is worth trying to specify now what it is that we expect to find in the kinds of categories that people form concepts of. This will be especially useful in making connections to other areas of research such as animal cognition. It seems important to know which aspects of concepts are uniquely human achievements and which can be supported by simpler learning and memory processes that are found in much of the animal kingdom. However, in order to ask that question, we must know an animal's concept when we see it. And, of course, such a concept probably will not be identical to the modal concept of the ever-popular college sophomore. So, how will we know whether it is 'really' a concept? Identifying the main properties of the concepts of adult humans will help us to understand other concepts when we find them. And being realistic about the wide variety of human concepts will help us avoid positing differences between species that do not exist.

The concepts I have discussed in this chapter share a number of attributes, though (recapitulating Rosch's discovery about object categories) not every concept has every attribute. Concepts support categorization, that is, in identifying two distinct objects as the same kind of thing. In humans, this is clearest when the things receive a common name, though that is not necessary, as in categories that do not have a conventional label (e.g. goal-derived categories, which often receive descriptions that differ across people). Another form of categorization is when people claim that two entities are the same kind of thing (without providing a name), as in a sorting or forced-choice task. Finally, subjects can treat two distinct entities in the same way, by a set of behaviours, even if they do not have a name for them. This is an indirect measure, but it also provides a form of categorization. If you do the same things with two objects, they probably form some kind of category for you. This kind of measure seems particularly applicable for nonverbal organisms.

All category types have borderline members and typicality gradations – even the supposedly classical categories like a strike in baseball, because it is often not certain whether the category's criteria have been satisfied. Furthermore, most of them include items that are similar to one another in some way (thematic categories a seeming exception here). Most importantly (and related to the previous property), categories generally seem to form a basis for induction: a property ascribed to one member seems likely to be found in other members. Indeed, I think that this function is the main source of categories' importance, because it allows us to extend what we have learned about objects in the past to new things we encounter. This is a major basis of intelligent behaviour, and if concepts did not permit this, they would serve only as memories of things we have already encountered.

Finally, a category can serve as a nexus for reasoning and learning. If you take a biology class, you might learn about properties of all animals or of vertebrates. Having a concept of animals or vertebrates gives you a place to hang this knowledge, and then to use it in everyday reasoning. ('If all vertebrates have a central nervous system, then even squirrels must have a central nervous system, all evidence to the contrary.') Obviously, this aspect of concepts is not something that your normal infant or pigeon will take advantage of very often, but to the degree that they *do* reason, they should be able to reason about classes of entities and not just individuals, if they indeed possess concepts.

Let me use a personal example to illustrate how these properties might influence our interpretation of what categories and concepts are. Initially, I was very loath to call thematic pairs a real category. (In fact, I feel myself backsliding on this even now, but

I will try to resist.) However, when confronted with the facts that people insist on classifying thematically related items together as being 'the same kind of thing' and that thematic groups support induction, it was difficult for me to rationally reject them as categories. Indeed, one experiment (Lin & Murphy, 2001, Experiment 10) showed that presenting thematic pairs together speeded judgements of taxonomic categorization, even when the thematic relation was (apparently) irrelevant to the task. So, my guess about what categories are was wrong in this case.

Intuition can only bring us so far in any scientific endeavour. Our way of thinking about categories is partly a product of our educational system based on Western culture, in which great emphasis is laid on defining features (e.g. Sharp et al., 1979). Other kinds of categories that are more removed from such a basis seem less real to us. But as psychologists, our goal must be to attempt to account for patterns of behaviour and thought. If those patterns recur in different domains, then our explanation should focus on the commonality of the domains: if script-based categories and family-resemblance categories both support classification and induction, it would be unwise to propose two different representations and reasoning processes to account for this.

When we embark on a scientific investigation, it seems only natural to specify in advance exactly what we are investigating. But we must also be flexible in changing our assumptions in the light of experience. Rather than be committed to current intuitions about what a category is, we should be guided by discoveries about what categories people appear to have and what psychological functions they share. Category-based induction was seldom thought about in the days of Hull, Bruner, or Piaget (because of the limitations of their classical categories, discussed above), but it now takes a central role in our understanding of concepts, after important empirical discoveries (Gelman & Markman, 1986; Rips, 1975). In this way, our understanding of categories is bootstrapped by new results: an initial definition or guess about what categories are leads to later discoveries that may augment or change that understanding. Further work based on the new view leads to confirmation or more change. These changes may not only add to our knowledge but actively change our view of what categories are.

Although this can be confusing and even frustrating, it also opens up the possibility of exciting discoveries: students and young scientists can hope to find new results that not only add to what we know about categories and concepts but also change what we think categories and concepts are.

Acknowledgements

The writing of this chapter was supported by NIMH grant MH41704 and by the kind support of the Beckman Institute of the University of Illinois during my sabbatical. The editors, Brian Ross, and Eric G. Taylor provided very helpful comments on an earlier draft.

References

Barsalou, L. W. (1983). Ad hoc categories. *Memory & Cognition*, **11**, 211–227.

Barsalou, L. W. (1985). Ideals, central tendency, and frequency of instantiation as determinants of graded structure in categories. *Journal of Experimental Psychology: Learning, Memory, and Cognition*, **11**, 629–654.

Barsalou, L. W. (1991). Deriving categories to achieve goals. In G. H. Bower (Ed.), *The Psychology of Learning and Motivation*, Vol. 27, pp. 1–64, New York: Academic Press.

Berlin, B. (1992). *Ethnobiological Classification: Principles of Categorization of Plants and Animals in Traditional Societies* Princeton, NJ: Princeton University Press.

Biederman, I. & Shiffrar, M. M. (1987). Sexing day-old chicks: A case study and expert systems analysis of a difficult perceptual-learning task. *Journal of Experimental Psychology: Learning, Memory, and Cognition*, **13**, 640–645.

Bruner, J. S., Goodnow, J. J., & Austin, G. A. (1956). *A Study of Thinking* New York: Wiley.

Gelman, S. A. & Markman, E. M. (1986). Categories and induction in young children. *Cognition*, **23**, 183–209.

Heit, E. & Rubinstein, J. (1994). Similarity and property effects in inductive reasoning. *Journal of Experimental Psychology: Learning, Memory, and Cognition*, **20**, 411–422.

Hirschfeld, L. A. (1996). *Race in the Making: Cognition, Culture, and the Child's Construction of Human Kinds* Cambridge, MA: MIT Press.

Hull, C. L. (1920). Quantitative aspects of the evolution of concepts. *Psychological Monographs, XXVIII*, **1.123**, 1–86.

Inhelder, B. & Piaget, J. (1964). *The Early Growth of Logic in the Child: Classification and Seriation* London: Routledge and Kegan Paul.

Khalidi, M. A. (2000). Incommensurability. In W. H. Newton-Smith (Ed.), *A Companion to the Philosophy of Science*, pp. 172–180, Oxford: Blackwell.

Lassaline, M. E. & Murphy, G. L. (1996). Induction and category coherence. *Psychonomic Bulletin & Review*, **3**, 95–99.

Lin, E. L. & Murphy, G. L. (2001). Thematic relations in adults' concepts. *Journal of Experimental Psychology: General*, **130**, 3–28.

Lucariello, J., Kyratzis, A., & Nelson, K. (1992). Taxonomic knowledge: What kind and when? *Child Development*, **63**, 978 998.

Luria, A. R. (1976). *Cognitive Development: Its Cultural and Social Foundations* Cambridge, MA: MIT Press.

Mandler, J. M. (2004). *The Foundations of Mind* Oxford: Oxford University Press.

Markman, E. M. (1989). *Categorization and Naming in Children: Problems of Induction* Cambridge, MA: MIT Press.

Medin, D. L. & Ortony, A. (1989). Psychological essentialism. In S. Vosniadou & A. Ortony (Eds.), *Similarity and Analogical Reasoning*, pp. 179–195, Cambridge: Cambridge University Press.

Mervis, C. B. (1987). Child-basic object categories and early lexical development. In U. Neisser (Ed.), *Concepts and Conceptual Development: Ecological and Intellectual Factors in Categorization*, pp. 201–233, Cambridge: Cambridge University Press.

Murphy, G. L. (2001). Causes of taxonomic sorting by adults: A test of the thematic-to-taxonomic shift. *Psychonomic Bulletin & Review*, **8**, 834–839.

Murphy, G. L. (2002). *The Big Book of Concepts* Cambridge, MA: MIT Press.

Murphy, G. L. (2005). The study of concepts inside and outside the laboratory: Medin versus Medin. In W. Ahn, R. L. Goldstone, B. C. Love, A. B. Markman, & P. Wolff (Eds), *Categorization Inside and Outside the Laboratory: Essays in Honor of Douglas L. Medin,* pp. 179–195, Washington, DC: APA.

Murphy, G. L. & Allopenna, P. D. (1994). The locus of knowledge effects in concept learning. *Journal of Experimental Psychology: Learning, Memory, and Cognition,* 20, 904–919.

Nguyen, S. P. & Murphy, G. L. (2003). An apple is more than just a fruit: Cross-classification in children's concepts. *Child Development,* 74, 1783–1806.

Posner, M. I. & Keele, S. W. (1968). On the genesis of abstract ideas. *Journal of Experimental Psychology,* 77, 353–363.

Proffitt, J. B., Coley, J. D., & Medin, D. L. (2000). Expertise and category-based induction. *Journal of Experimental Psychology: Learning, Memory, and Cognition,* 26, 811–828.

Quinn, P. C. & Eimas, P. D. (1997). A reexamination of the perceptual-to-conceptual shift in mental representations. *Review of General Psychology,* 1, 271–287.

Quinn, P. C., Eimas, P. D., & Rosenkrantz, S. L. (1993). Evidence for representations of perceptually similar natural categories by 3-month-old and 4-month-old infants. *Perception,* 22, 463–475.

Rips, L. J. (1975). Inductive judgments about natural categories. *Journal of Verbal Learning and Verbal Behavior,* 14, 665–681.

Rosch, E. (1977). Human categorization. In N. Warren (Ed.), *Advances in Cross-Cultural Psychology,* Vol. 1, pp. 177–206, London: Academic Press.

Rosch, E., Mervis, C. B., Gray, W., Johnson, D., & Boyes-Braem, P. (1976). Basic objects in natural categories. *Cognitive Psychology,* 8, 382–439.

Ross, B. H. & Murphy, G. L. (1999). Food for thought: Cross-classification and category organization in a complex real-world domain. *Cognitive Psychology,* 38, 495–553.

Sharp, D., Cole, M., & Lave, C. (1979). Education and cognitive development: The evidence from experimental research. *Monographs of the Society for Research in Child Development,* 44(1–2), 1–112.

Shepard, R. N., Hovland, C. I., & Jenkins, H. M. (1961). Learning and memorization of classifications. *Psychological Monographs: General and Applied,* 75(13, Whole No. 517), 1–42.

Smiley, S. S. & Brown, A. L. (1979). Conceptual preferences for thematic or taxonomic relations: A nonmonotonic age trend from preschool to old age. *Journal of Experimental Child Psychology,* 28, 249–257.

Soja, N. N. (1994). Young children's concept of color and its relation to the acquisition of color words. *Child Development,* 65, 918–937.

Chapter 3

Rules and similarity in adult concept learning

James Close, Ulrike Hahn, Carl J. Hodgetts, and Emmanuel M. Pothos

Editors' Preview

Chapter 3, 'Rules and similarity in adult concept learning' continues with a theme that was introduced to readers in Chapter 2, namely, that human adults can learn different types of categories. An important distinction in Chapter 3 is made between rule-based categories and similarity-based categories. Rule-based categories are those in which one can apply a rule to sort classes of entities (e.g. objects in category A are large and bright, whereas objects in category B are small and dark), whereas similarity-based categories are those in which instances resemble one another (e.g. beagles, collies, and cocker spaniels are grouped together as dogs). The distinction between rule-based categories and similarity-based categories is important because it challenges the view that all concepts are operated on by the same kind of underlying categorization process. The distinction between rule-based categories and similarity-based categories is actually consistent with the distinction between the classical view of conceptual structure (where categories are defined by singly necessary and jointly sufficient attributes) and the family-resemblance view of conceptual structure (where categories are said to be like families in which members tend to share characteristic attributes that create resemblance, but no attributes are considered to be defining).

The distinction between rule-based and similarity-based categories has also been associated with different modes of category learning. In particular, the acquisition of rule-based categories has been associated with supervised category learning in which an individual is presented with a stimulus, classifies it, and is provided with corrective feedback. The learner can discover the rule that the experimenter used to devise the categories through the feedback. By contrast, acquisition of similarity-based categories has been associated with unsupervised category learning in which an individual learns a category on his/her own, without an experimenter or teacher telling the individual what is in the category. Similarity-based categories can be acquired without feedback because the structure within a category and the natural discontinuity between categories can be spontaneously apprehended (i.e. items within a category are perceived as being alike and being different from members of contrasting categories).

Although it is tempting to equate rule-based categories with a specific type of conceptual structure (i.e. definitional) and a particular mode of learning (i.e. supervised), and similarity-based categories with a different type of structure (i.e. family resemblance) and mode of learning (i.e. unsupervised), Chapter 3 makes it clear that this manner of parsing the domain of category acquisition and conceptual structure is likely to be overly simplistic. For example, human adults in some instances attempt to learn family-resemblance categories by using single attributes (i.e. rules) as a basis for their category partitionings. In addition, many categories once thought to have a classical structure are now considered to have a family-resemblance structure. Moreover, some studies have reported that both kinds of category learning may take place for the same stimulus class over different time courses of the category-acquisition process. Nevertheless, despite these complexities, the authors of Chapter 3 argue that the distinction between rule-based and similarity-based categories in human adults is highly relevant for this book because it leads one to ask whether a firmer understanding of the distinction can be achieved with ontogenetic and phylogenetic approaches. For example, would one find evidence that one or the other type of category learning is more readily emergent in infants or children? And would one find that one or the other type of category learning is more evolutionarily primitive, based on comparisons of learning performance across nonhuman animal species?

If we gave you a set of coloured shapes and asked you to divide up this set according to the simple rule that 'all square objects belong in Category A and all round objects in Category B', this would cause you little difficulty. Similarly, if we asked you to divide up these items based on their similarity to each other, this, again, should be relatively simple. But what would you do naturally?

This chapter reviews studies of rule-based category learning within the human adult literature, and contrasts these results with evidence for similarity-based accounts of category learning (e.g. exemplar and prototype models). Specifically, the chapter considers the contrast between rule-based versus similarity-based learning within research on unsupervised (spontaneous) categorization and supervised categorization. In the closing sections, it also presents and critically evaluates hybrid models of human adult categorization that are composed of both a rule and a similarity component.

Concepts, rules, and similarity: the terminological confusion

One of the most fundamental cognitive processes human adults engage in is categorization; that is, the assignment of objects, agents, or events to a set of instances of *the same kind*. Such an assignment takes place, implicitly or explicitly, in object recognition, in the application of linguistic labels, and in any form of reasoning that involves classes of objects. Research in this area distinguishes between *categories*, that is, classes of objects in the world that somehow *go together*, and *concepts*, as the (presumed) mental representations that underlie the assignment of objects to categories. This follows the philosophical distinction between the *extension* and *intension* in the meaning of a word first introduced by Frege (1892/1970), whereby extension captures the actual objects referred to, and intension captures the characteristics or properties associated with the word (see Chapter 2 for a more in-depth discussion of this distinction).

Discerning the nature of our conceptual system and the processes by which it is acquired is hard. Understanding mental representations and processes, in general, is inherently difficult because they can only ever be inferred. Moreover, cognitive science is replete with 'mimicry theorems'; that is, demonstrations that a particular pattern of data is amenable to explanation by contrasting accounts. It has been argued, for example, that any data indicative of serial processing might be explained by an inherently parallel model, and vice versa (Townsend & Ashby, 1983). Much the same has been argued in the debate between imagistic versus propositional representations (Anderson, 1978). Unfortunately, such equivalences also seem to obtain for rule- versus similarity-based explanations (Hahn & Chater, 1998a; Pothos, 2005). Specifically, it has been shown that few, if any, behavioural criteria are uniquely diagnostic of one or the other. Moreover, even fully specified computational models can often mimic each other through simple changes to key parameters. For example, the most renowned similarity-based model in the literature, Nosofsky's (1986) Generalized Context Model (GCM), can readily capture behaviour otherwise indicative of rule-use by narrowing its attentional focus (e.g. Nosofsky & Johansen, 2002).

However, the situation for the contrast between rules and similarity is made worse by the fact that the concept of *rule* is possibly one of the most ill-defined concepts cognitive science has produced to date, and the term means very different things to different people. For instance, the very same computational mechanisms, for example, simple connectionist networks, have variously been described as implementing similarity-based computations (Rumelhart & Todd, 1993) and as implementing *implicit rules* (Andrews et al., 1995; Dienes, 1992; see also Hahn & Chater, 1998a, 1998b, for discussion of the further confusion that arises when systems are compared across levels of description). The fundamental intuition underlying the term rule is clear enough; namely, that a rule is some sort of general statement or principle 'that specifies definitively whether an object or event is of a particular sort or not' (Shanks, 1995, p. 152). Likewise, paradigm cases are easy enough to identify: a typical example of a rule in everyday usage is a statement such as 'If it has feathers and lays eggs, it's a bird'. A typical example of a rule used in laboratory experiments is the example given at the beginning of this chapter; that is, 'If something is a square, it belongs in Category A'. Formally, these correspond to universally quantified statements whose consequent classification (*bird*, *Category A*) is meant to apply to all instances that fall under its antecedent condition. In other words, the rule's antecedent specifies *sufficient* conditions for its consequent; that is, it is enough to have feathers and lay eggs in order to be a bird, or be square in order to belong to Catgeory A. These conditions are not in themselves *necessary*, however; there might be further rules that specify other ways of qualifying as a bird or a member of Category A. There are, though, particular kinds of rules that were historically very influential in the study of concepts, namely definitions. Definitions specify conditions of category membership that are both necessary and sufficient.

Three characteristics of both simple rules and definitions can immediately be identified: first, they are statements or *representations*. This is important because of the fundamental distinction between rule-guided, or 'rule-following' behaviour, and behaviour which is merely conveniently described by a rule (e.g. Chomsky, 1980; Marcus et al., 1995). Rule-following is exemplified by legal systems and their effect. The documents that encode the law *cause* particular behaviours such as paying certain amounts of tax. By contrast, merely rule-describable, but not rule-guided behaviour is exemplified by planetary motion. Planets' orbits are well-described by physical laws, but planets do not themselves consult these laws to guide their behaviour. In this latter example, the statement of the rules of planetary motion does not function causally in the generation of the planets' behaviour, as do legal rules. This is readily apparent from the fact that planetary motion is unaffected by whether or not the appropriate physical laws are known, whereas legal rules must be known for them to produce the behaviours in question. Cognitive claims that a behaviour is rule-based have traditionally been understood to mean not just that an agent's behaviour displays a particular regularity, but rather that a particular kind of representation, a 'rule', has a causal role in producing this behaviour: that is, the behaviour has the regularity it does *because* the agent possesses the rule in question (see e.g. Hahn, 2002, for an overview).

The key characteristics of rules as particular *kinds* of mental representations are given by the second two aspects apparent in the paradigm case: first, the rule makes reference to only some of the properties of the entities to which it applies; in other words, it is *abstract*. Second, the application of a rule is typically *all or none*. Whereas early uses of the term rule in both psychology and artificial intelligence (AI) conform to this paradigm case, the term has since been used to refer to a wealth of representation formats that differ substantially both from the paradigm case and each other. Examples of the range of things to which the term 'rule' has been applied are production rules (Anderson, 1983, 1993), procedures, such as social conventions and arithmetic (Cheng & Holyoak, 1985; Young & O'Shea, 1981, respectively), fuzzy rules (e.g. Kosko, 1996), weights in connectionist networks (e.g. Bates & Elman, 1993; Davies, 1995), decision bounds (Ashby & Perrin, 1988), functions such as $y = x^2$ (Shanks, 1995), or any strategy that focuses on a small subset of object features (Pothos, 2005). Consequently, 'rule' refers, at best, to a field of related terms.

Varied attempts to systematize these and provide a coherent definition have been made (e.g. Hahn & Chater, 1998a; Pothos, 2005; Smith et al., 1992). Two things about any such attempt at conceptual clarification are clear: first, though tedious, providing a systematic definition of 'rule' is necessary, because the answers to empirical questions about rule use change with the meaning of the term itself. 'Does this agent possess a rule?' has different answers depending on what 'rule' is taken to refer to, and without clarification, the question runs the risk of becoming meaningless. Second, what should count as a 'rule' is not a question that has a single *right answer*. The meaning of fundamental theoretical terms such as 'rule' should be decided by considerations of utility. Of the many possible meanings of the term 'rule', we should prefer those that give rise to theoretically interesting generalizations. For cognitive science, that means a preference for interesting generalizations across the many different research areas represented in this book: human adult behaviour as discussed in the present chapter (and Chapters 2 and 14), as well as developmental (see Chapters 12 and 15), comparative (see Chapters 8, 9, 10, and 11), and computational work (see Chapters 4 and 5). As we shall see, the diversity of meanings associated with 'rule' poses comparatively few problems when the human adult experimental literature is considered in isolation. However, the terminological issues become acute once we seek to put these findings into a wider developmental and comparative context.

With these general considerations in hand, we first summarize past research on the roles of rules and similarity in human adult concept acquisition, before, in conclusion, relating this work to that of other areas.

Concepts, rules, and similarity: empirical findings

Concept acquisition has been pursued in two distinct contexts. The first is one of spontaneous discovery, in which a learner simply encounters an unlabelled set of objects and seeks to discover or impose classifications, or partitions, on this set. The second is one in which the learner's task is to infer predefined categories from a set of labelled instances while typically receiving continuous feedback on classification performance. In parallel to distinctions made in machine learning, we refer to these two contexts as unsupervised and supervised learning, respectively.

Unsupervised learning

Both in psychology and neighbouring disciplines such as AI and machine learning, the starting point for research on unsupervised learning has been the widespread assumption that humans' spontaneous discovery of categories should be based on similarity. This is reflected in traditional clustering algorithms (e.g. Fisher, 1996; Fisher & Langley, 1990; Krzanowski & Marriott, 1995), and a wealth of psychological models of spontaneous category formation. For example, the simplicity model of unsupervised categorization (Pothos & Chater, 2002) is a computational implementation of Rosch and Mervis's (1975) idea that *good, intuitive* categories are ones that maximize within-category similarity while minimizing between-category similarity. Equally, the unsupervised component of SUSTAIN (Gureckis & Love, 2002; Love et al., 2004) is driven primarily by a *similarity constraint*, according to which more similar items end up in the same category. In other models of unsupervised categorization (e.g. Anderson, 1991; Compton & Logan, 1999), the role of similarity is less prominent, but the predictions of even these models often lead to categorizations that reflect the overall similarity structure of the stimulus domain.

Despite the fundamental role theorists have given to similarity, research has shown that people commonly use only a single feature or dimension when asked to spontaneously categorize a set of items into a given number of categories (e.g. Ahn & Medin, 1992; Imai & Garner, 1965; Medin et al., 1987; Milton & Wills, 2004; Regehr & Brooks, 1995; Wattenmaker, 1992). Such a single-feature criterion has all the properties of a typical rule identified above. It is an abstraction; that is, it involves only a small subset of the properties of the category instances (see Hahn & Chater, 1998a), and it also gives rise to an all-or-none pattern of classification. Consequently, it meets almost any definition of 'rule'.

This preference for single-feature sorts (or unidimensional categorization) is rather robust. For example, Regehr and Brooks (1995) showed that creating complex stimuli whose separate dimensions were not readily discriminable, or using an integration of features that could be described by a single, familiar descriptor, had no significant effect on participants' preference for unidimensional categorization. However, there are ways in which this preference can be reduced. For example, Medin et al. (1987) reported that correlations between the dimensions of individual objects, and a causal theme linking these dimensions, reduced unidimensional classifications (for related evidence, see also Kaplan & Murphy, 1999; Lassaline & Murphy, 1996; Spalding & Murphy, 1996). Other investigators have suggested that simply increasing the time-pressure of the classification procedure would help reduce the bias for unidimensional sorting (e.g. Ward, 1983), although recently, Milton, Longmore, and Wills (2008) have shown evidence to the contrary. Moreover, it has become apparent that the materials used might contribute to the preference for single-feature sorts. Pothos and Close (2008) used the similarity-based simplicity model (Pothos & Chater, 2002) to examine the materials of past studies. The model showed that even a similarity-based approach to classification generates seemingly rule-based, single-feature sorts for some of these materials. With a new set of materials, for which the model predicted multidimensional, similarity-based sorting, participants matched the model's predictions and based their classifications on more than one dimension. In summary, there is some research that suggests that the previous findings of an overwhelming preference for unidimensional categorization may be an artefact of the experimental materials and procedures used.

Interestingly, research into the acquisition of pre-defined categories has, in some ways, taken a complementary trajectory to that just described for unsupervised categorization: here, an initial theoretical bias towards rules was soon confronted with a wealth of evidence for similarity-based processes.

Supervised learning

Early experimental work on concept acquisition took for granted that rules were the appropriate representational format for concepts (Bruner et al., 1956). Consequently, interest centred on questions such as the different types of rules that were used in concept attainment (e.g. conjunctive, disjunctive, and probabilistic), and the impact of rule complexity on ease of learning (e.g. Bruner et al., 1956; Shepard & Chang, 1963; Shepard et al., 1961). Considering Boolean concepts of varying degrees of complexity, for example, Shepard et al. (1961) found that learning was easiest where categorization was based on a single dimension (a so-called Type I problem), followed by categorization where two dimensions were relevant (a Type II problem), then concepts where all three dimensions were relevant to differing extents (Types III, IV, and V), and finally concepts that could only be acquired through rote memorization (Type VI) (for recent attempts to explain the findings of Shepard et al. through a compression-based approach, see Feldman, 2000; but also Chater, 2000). This *preference* for unidimensional concepts seems to match that found in unsupervised categorization tasks; however, the general relevance of these results, and the dominance of rule-focused investigation in general, was severely challenged by empirical investigation of the nature of our *everyday* categories.

Philosophers had for centuries held the view that concepts associated with natural language took the form of definitions. This notion, however, was challenged by Wittgenstein around the same time that Bruner and colleagues were conducting their work. Famously, Wittgenstein's (1953) *Philosophical Investigations* exploded the almost universally shared intuition that membership of everyday categories such as 'DOG', 'GAME', or 'RED' were based on a common, core set of properties. Instead, Wittgenstein proposed that category members are related only through criss-crossing patterns of partial featural overlap, as found with *family resemblances*. Eleanor Rosch (e.g. 1975, 1976) and her colleagues (e.g. Rosch & Mervis, 1975) provided a wealth of experimental support for this view, and the so-called definitional (or *classical*) view of conceptual structure was eventually pronounced dead (Fodor et al., 1980). Evidence amassed against definitions included the existence of fuzzy category boundaries, and typicality gradients within category membership; both of these are incompatible with definitions because, here, objects either do or do not possess the core properties required, thus giving rise to clear-cut, all-or-none category membership (Barr & Caplan, 1987; Estes, 2003; Kalish, 1995; Labov, 1973; McCloskey & Glucksberg, 1978; Rosch & Mervis, 1975).

Typicality effects, in particular, prompted the formulation of an alternative, similarity-based account of our everyday concepts in the form of *prototype theory* (Rosch & Mervis, 1975; see also Posner & Keele, 1968; Reed, 1972). Further evidence for the role of similarity within categorization came from the study of basic level categories. Rosch and colleagues (Rosch & Mervis, 1975; Rosch et al., 1976) found that participants were both more accurate and faster when categorizing objects at what they termed the basic level (e.g. *dog*, *bird*) than at the subordinate (e.g. *poodle*, *robin*) or superordinate (e.g. *animal*) levels. This level, they argued, maximizes within-category similarity while minimizing between-category similarity. Subsequent research with artificial categories, for which participants were first taught names for artificial categories at the basic, subordinate, and superordinate levels, has shown analogous effects (e.g. Murphy & Smith, 1982). Research into basic-level categorization has obvious conceptual links with unsupervised categorization in that it is concerned with the question of what makes basic level categories particularly *good* categories (see also, Corter & Gluck, 1992;

Gosselin & Schyns, 2001; Jones, 1983). The cross-fertilization between the two areas, of which Pothos and Chater's (2002) simplicity model is a prime example, should therefore come as no surprise.

A second similarity-based approach in the form of *exemplar theory* soon followed (Medin & Schaffer, 1978; Smith & Medin, 1981). This gave rise to a family of related mathematical models (the context model, Medin & Schaffer, 1978; the GCM, Nosofsky, 1986; and its connectionist implementation in ALCOVE, Kruschke, 1992; as well as extensions to include reaction times, EBRW, Nosofsky & Palmeri, 1997; and EGCM, Lamberts, 1995, 2000), that have provided some of the most detailed modelling of human behaviour that cognitive science has seen to date. This modelling has, however, focused on the laboratory acquisition of artificial concepts (but, see Smits et al., 2002).

With regards to the nature of our everyday concepts, similarity-based views ran into fundamental critiques of their own. The work that led the attack on similarity was Murphy and Medin's (1985; see also Pickering & Chater, 1995) exposition of the theory-like nature of conceptual structure, a position that has become known as the *theory theory* or *knowledge approach* (Murphy, 2002). Murphy and Medin took up the philosopher Goodman's (1972) famous attack on similarity in which he labelled similarity 'explanatorily vacuous'. Goodman argued that to say two objects are similar is vacuous, as any two objects may be considered similar; for example, you and a computer are similar in that you both weigh less than one ton, two tons, etc. The statement of similarity, he argued, only becomes constrained when a person identifies in what *respects* the two objects are similar. However, when one introduces the notion of *respects*, then it is these *respects* that are doing all of the explanatory work. Murphy and Medin also pointed out that overlap in terms of simple perceptual features seemed insufficient to explain categorization, because category assignment can diverge from surface similarity, drawing on 'deeper', nonperceptual feature properties, such as causal information, as well as relational information of the kind which is readily incorporated in theories.

Despite these criticisms, however, both similarity-based approaches (exemplar and prototype) continue to find support to this day. Several factors have contributed to this: first, some of the fundamental criticisms of similarity have been addressed (see e.g. Goldstone, 1994b; Hahn, 2002; Hahn & Chater, 1997; Medin et al., 1993), and theoretical accounts of similarity that are capable of dealing with relational information and background knowledge have been developed (e.g. Goldstone, 1994a; Hahn et al., 2003; Markman & Gentner, 1993a,b). Likewise, different ways of incorporating background knowledge into essentially similarity-based models have been explored (e.g. Heit, 2001; Heit & Bott, 2000; Rodriguez, 2001). Such research has also made clear that similarity need not be restricted to *perceptual* similarity. Second, the main focus of exemplar models has, as just mentioned, been the detailed modelling of the acquisition of artificial categories in the laboratory with materials for which the criticisms of Murphy and Medin (1985) typically carry little weight. Finally, the criticisms levelled at similarity have not yet led to the formulation of a fully explicit alternative. Fundamental questions for the theory theory such as what exactly constitutes a theory, how a theory is implemented, and how it is brought to bear in real-world concepts, are all questions that have not been fully answered, even if there have been promising suggestions (e.g. Kaplan & Murphy, 1999, 2000; Murphy & Allopenna, 1994). This means that prototype accounts of our natural language concepts (see e.g. Hampton, 2001, 2003), for example, are still the most fully articulated proposals to date.

The lack of computational explicitness of the theory theory or knowledge approach has meant that critiques of similarity-based accounts of our everyday concepts have largely remained restricted to demonstrations that similarity seemingly does not suffice. Examples of this are found in the studies of Rips (1989) and Keil (1989). Both of these attempted to provide evidence for *essences*, or at least a belief in essences, in people's concepts (see also Diesendruck & Gelman, 1999; Malt, 1990; Medin & Ortony, 1989). In Rips' study, participants were informed that because of a toxic-waste disaster, a contaminated bird now looked like an insect. Crucially, participants were further told that this insect-looking bird was still able to mate with other birds of its own kind, and that its offspring looked like normal birds. Rips found that, when presented with this information, participants still chose to classify the contaminated insect-looking bird as a bird, and not as an insect. That is, given a dissociation between perceptual similarity and essential properties, people's judgements seem to reflect the essences. These essences constitute *critical features* in classification – that is, features that are either necessary or sufficient, but not necessarily both – and hence can be viewed as support for rule-based classification (see Pothos & Hahn, 2000, for detailed discussion). However, the empirical status of essentialism is less than clear (see e.g. Braisby et al., 1996; Hampton et al., 2007; Larochelle et al., 2005; Malt, 1994).

Probably the most definitive statement that can be made from the previously presented research on unsupervised and supervised learning is that, in the laboratory at least, adults are clearly capable of using both rules and similarity as a means for categorization. Indeed, more recently, there has been a steady increase in theoretical proposals that advocate that categorization decisions might be mediated by both rules and similarity.

Rules and similarity

There are numerous variants of the idea that both rules and similarity mediate categorization decisions. First, there is evidence from detailed modelling that participants faced with novel items in a supervised classification task initially search for single-feature rules (again in line with behaviour on most unsupervised tasks), and only gradually move to a similarity-based exemplar strategy when sufficiently predictive single-feature rules cannot be found (Johansen & Palmeri, 2002; for other evidence on temporal shifts see Lewandowsky et al., 2000; Rouder & Ratcliffe, 2006). Most recently, researchers have also sought evidence from eye-tracking data and have found attentional shifts commensurate with changes in strategy over the course of a concept-learning experiment (Rehder & Hoffman, 2005). Second, researchers have developed models in which participants supplement a general rule with individual stored exceptions (e.g. Nosofsky et al., 1994). That is, the choice between a rule- or a similarity-based decision is made on a stimulus-by-stimulus basis. Third, others have suggested that the choice of rule- or exemplar-strategy is determined by *general* stimulus characteristics. Support for this idea comes from superior model fits for exemplar-models with stimuli that are perceptually distinct and relatively few in number, and better fits for decision-bound categorization models – which aim to *model* the presence of a category by computing a boundary that separates the instances of one category from the instances of other categories – with stimuli that are highly confusable (e.g. Rouder & Ratcliff, 2006). Though decision bounds might not universally be viewed as 'rules' (though they are frequently referred to as such), the general point that similarity might hold sway for some materials, while some form of rule is preferred for others, is reinforced by the studies of Pothos and Close (2008) discussed earlier.

Finally, there are a number of hybrid- or dual-systems models in the literature that give a concurrent role to rule- and similarity-based processing. These models can themselves be classified into three categories on the basis of the nature of the interaction between their rule and similarity components. The first set of models assumes two independent routes that are selected stochastically on a trial-by-trial basis according to their utility (e.g. Anderson & Betz, 2001). The second set assumes a competition or race between the two components (e.g. Palmeri, 1997), and the third set assumes a blending of outputs from the rule and similarity components into a single overall response (e.g. Erickson & Kruschke, 1998; Noelle & Cotrell, 1996, 2000; Vandierendonck, 1995).

Evidence to support the idea of a conjunction of rules and similarity has also been drawn from tasks in which participants were explicitly *given* rules for classification. Even when perfectly predictive rules were given, residual effects of exemplar similarity have been found. In the earliest study of this kind, Nosofsky, Clark, and Shin (1989) noted that this may be down to the fact that the rule itself was relatively complex and relatively unnatural. However, rule complexity does not seem to be a factor in the main thread of research conducted with explicit rules. Allen and Brooks (1991) gave participants simple heuristic rules of thumb, of the kind frequently employed in medicine, with which to classify novel *creatures*. Despite the fact that participants were both aware of the rule and the instruction to use it, and the rule was sufficient to correctly classify all items, performance on novel items was significantly affected by the test items' degree of similarity to items seen during training. Allen and Brooks hypothesized that such effects would only arise with stimuli that had certain key characteristics of everyday objects, and subsequent research has sought to explore further the exact conditions necessary for these effects (Lacroix et al., 2005; Regehr & Brooks, 1993; Thibaut & Gelaes, 2006).

Most recently, it has been demonstrated that none of the hypothesized conditions are in fact necessary, and that residual effects of exemplar similarity can be found even with the interchangeable, arbitrary materials that make up the majority of categorization research (Hahn et al., 2002). These particular studies have also shown that such effects arise even where the rule in question is not an additive rule of thumb. Additive rules, as used in all of the studies by Brooks and colleagues, as well as those by Lacroix et al. (2005) and Thibaut and Gelaes (2006), have the following format: 'if X has 3 of the 5 features {a,b,c,d,e}, then X is a category member'. In other words, the rule specifies a so-called *m-of-n concept* (see Dennis et al., 1973); thus, it is formally equivalent to a prototype n (i.e. an item with *all* relevant features present) and a threshold m

(i.e. the number of matching features required) that determines the degree of similarity to the prototype that items must have in order to be category members (Hahn & Chater, 1998a). This link with prototypes was intentional, as Allen and Brooks (1991) expected similarity effects to arise only with rules that could generate family-resemblance structures. In the case of the rule specified above, an exemplar that matches the rule in four of the rule-relevant features provides a *better* match than an exemplar that matches in only three. As a consequence, the category defined by the rule has a similarity structure that gives similarity some utility in solving the categorization task. This, however, makes the observed similarity effects in rule application rather less surprising. Given this, it is consequently important for the whole project of hybrid rule/similarity accounts that the studies by Hahn et al. found exemplar similarity effects even for simple, perfectly predictive rules that applied all-or-none, and where the similarity manipulations depended entirely on the rule-irrelevant features of the stimuli. In addition, extensive modelling of these data seem to show that the effects obtained are beyond current hybrid models in the literature (Brumby & Hahn, 2007).

The intuition that both rule- and similarity-based processes are influential in human adult categorization is now prevalent in the literature, and furthermore, this view has received considerable experimental support. However, the nature of their interaction is far from fully understood. This issue should benefit from investigation in both developmental and comparative areas of research, which could provide an understanding of the developmental time-course of rule- and similarity-based categorization in both ontogenetic and phylogenetic terms. This could provide greater insight into whether one of these categorization strategies is more cognitively complex than the other, and allow researchers to gauge the impact of the more complex strategy coming online.

What do we know now?

The preceding sections of this chapter naturally raise the question of what conclusions can be drawn from the wealth of research that in one way or the other addresses the role of rules and similarity within adult categorization. A difficulty here is that it is not always entirely straightforward to identify the general questions that have been addressed. The many strands identified in the previous sections are heterogeneous enough to suggest that, at best, it is a set of loosely interrelated issues that have been targeted. For one, it is not always clear how research into the acquisition (supervised or unsupervised) of novel, artificial categories in the lab relates to the nature of our everyday concepts. This divide is manifest even in a terminological division: 'categorization' research is the most common label for experimental research with artificial categories, and 'concepts' research is more prevalent wherever a clear link with our everyday concepts is desired.

Focusing on our everyday concepts for the moment, the main conclusion of the last 30 years is clear: the definitional view as a general account of conceptual structure is dead. Though some concepts, particularly in technical areas such as law and mathematics, might have definitions, the vast majority do not. Notably, this conclusion is a negative one. No single positive (computationally explicit) account to replace the definitional view has emerged as empirically adequate, and the literature consists of a wide variety of factors – including similarity, background knowledge, interrelations of features, and possibly even beliefs about essences – that appear to influence classification in everyday life. One possible conclusion from this state of affairs is that the problem is extremely hard, and simply awaits definitive treatment; in particular, a treatment that will benefit from computational models being developed and tested with artificial materials. Another conclusion is that the question, in a sense, has no answer, and that the view of concepts and meaning that gave rise to it is itself ill-conceived (Ramscar & Hahn, 1998). Historically, a concept was seen as a minimal unit of knowledge that speakers needed to apprehend in order to produce and comprehend words successfully. Importantly, this unit of knowledge was to be distinct from encyclopedic knowledge about the entity in question. For example, to understand the term 'dog', one had to know only a core set of properties that governed the application of this term (and hence its meaning). These core properties were intended to be distinct from the many facts that we know about dogs, such as what they like to eat, that they chase sticks, and that they make faithful companions. One reason for this distinction was that encyclopedic knowledge varies across speakers, and intuitively, successful communication might require a common core. However, all subsequent unitary views of conceptual structure, whether they proclaim that concepts are prototypes, sets of exemplars, or a 'theory', have (implicitly) abandoned this idea of a common core. This is because there is no reason to assume that your prototype, your sets of exemplars, or your theory of 'dog', will be exactly like mine. Moreover, category boundaries have been shown to vary both across speakers, and within speakers, over time (see above, and Kalish, 1995). Also, on second thought, it is unclear why successful communication would require any more than sufficient overlap to allow that your and my use of a term might, on a given occasion, both pick out the same entity in the world. Maybe, then, not only do everyday terms not have definitions, they do not have any 'concepts' – in the sense of minimal, summary representations – associated with them at all. Instead, our use of everyday terms draws liberally on everything we know.

What, then, of categorization research? What conclusions has the study of artificial categories yielded? A moment's reflection suggests that it is hard to find *general insights* that are not already available simply from looking at our everyday lives: people can deal readily with categories that are based on family-resemblance structures; people can learn rules; people are very flexible in the kinds of concepts they acquire, and are sensitive to the nature of items to be classified; people can use multiple strategies, often in parallel. All of these conclusions are readily apparent in daily life; for example, one need think only of domains such as law to know that rules are prevalent throughout society. In that same domain, the combination of similarity – in the form of precedent – and general rules is commonplace. Likewise, some terms *do* have definitions, and some are even based on single features (e.g. 'even number'); however, most do not, but we learn them readily all the same. No further evidence for any of these claims seems necessary. This suggests the goal of categorization research should not be existence proofs for what we *can* do, but maybe insight into what we do *naturally*. But can such research really tell us more than what people find 'natural' in unnatural situations? Neither the nature of the materials nor the nature of the acquisition tasks generally employed bear much resemblance to real-world contexts, and this is true of research using both supervised and unsupervised tasks. Not only are materials impoverished, and often structured in very specific (and unlikely) ways, their acquisition and use typically lacks all of the functions that categories serve in the real world such as inference about unseen members of a category or unseen properties (but see, e.g. Chin-Parker & Ross, 2004), or communication. Moreover, we are not, in the real world, pressured to exhaustively sort a set of simultaneously seen objects, as happens in many unsupervised categorization experiments; nor do children (and adults) receive anything like the kind and amount of feedback given in categorization studies when learning real words (see e.g. Landauer & Dumais, 1997).

Consequently, it should come as no surprise that the less obvious, common findings of categorization research do not seem to be general in any interesting way. For example, the overwhelming finding of unsupervised categorization has been the preference for single-feature or dimension sorts, and, as mentioned variously above, this has been supported by findings from supervised tasks as well. However, the vast majority of our everyday concepts are patently not based on a single feature or dimension, and when people are asked to list the properties of everyday categories, they spontaneously and freely list multiple features (e.g. Rosch et al., 1976). This suggests already that participants' preference for single-feature sorts is an artefact of the experimental task (cf. Pothos & Close, 2008). All that remains unclear is what, exactly, it is an artefact of: the obviously contrived nature of the experimental materials, the absence of any function or utility for classifications made in the sorting task, the appeal of a *low-effort strategy*, or the experiment as a communicative situation that might give rise to the expectation of justification of one's choices, thus favouring readily verbalizable strategies (Murphy, 2002). These are all potential influences that, in addition to the factors identified earlier, might serve to bring about this seemingly anomalous preference.

These points sound critical, but they should not be taken as a condemnation of categorization research and its attempts to experimentally tease apart different models under experimentally controlled conditions. Arguably, the strength, and (properly understood) the point of this research is not in providing general answers, but in the very detail of the modelling this research has spawned (see Chapter 4). Categorization has yielded some of the most exacting and successful modelling of human behaviour throughout the study of cognition. We are inclined to think that this constitutes a worthwhile end in and of itself. Moreover, such models can and have been exported *back* to concepts research. The work of Rosch and colleagues (e.g. Rosch et al., 1976) – discussed above – provides an example where a specific question about conceptual structure links experimental research with real-world terms, both supervised and unsupervised categorization in the lab, and associated modelling efforts (e.g. Anderson, 1990; Corter & Gluck, 1992; Estes, 1994; Fisher, 1987, 1988; Gosselin & Schyns, 2001; Pothos & Chater, 2002). Equally, detailed models have allowed the exploration of relationships and interdependencies across distinct but potentially related cognitive functions, such as the relationship between categorization and identification, categorization and recognition (e.g. Nosofsky, 1986, 1988, 1991; Nosofsky et al., 1989), or categorization and attention – both perceptual and decisional (e.g. Lamberts, 1995, 2000; Maddox & Dodd, 2003).

That said, the success of categorization research to date is dependent upon one's initial premise: if the goal is simply to provide the best, most computationally explicit account of whatever the task happens to be, the fact that laboratory tasks deviate systematically and fundamentally from real-world analogues is not of importance here. However, the deviation does matter when one seeks to address the kind of broad, comparative questions that form the overarching themes of this book, such as 'in what way is human concept learning unique?' and 'how do developmental and evolutionary processes contribute to any such abilities?'. This is because the study of nonverbal (or less-verbal) agents, such as animals, infants, or younger children, requires experimental methods. These may be straightforward adaptations of the methods used in human adult categorization research, or independently developed tools. The limitations of laboratory materials and procedures highlighted above are likely to apply to both. This, in turn, gives rise to conceptual limitations. In particular, there are things that can be taken for granted with adults that require independent, further evidence when studying animals or infants. It is readily apparent that human adults *do* naturally group together entities in the world into categories, but this cannot be said for other animals or infants. For example, there have been countless studies documenting successful performance of animals on laboratory-based category-acquisition tasks, that match in basic characteristics supervised learning in the human experimental lab (e.g. Cerella, 1979; Herrnstein & Loveland, 1964; Herrnstein et al., 1976; Lubow, 1974; Malott & Siddall, 1972; Morgan et al., 1976; Poole & Lander, 1971; Savage-Rumbaugh et al., 1980; Schrier et al., 1984; Schrier & Brady, 1987; Siegel & Honig, 1970). However, while it might seem reasonable to assume that an adult mastering this task has acquired a category, and possibly a concept to boot, the corresponding assumption for animals seems weak. The mere fact that an animal can successfully solve a discrimination task and generalize to novel items, implies, strictly speaking, no more than that the animal can successfully associate individual stimuli with a particular outcome, and can on occasion, show similarity-based generalization from such individual stimuli (see, Herrnstein, 1990; Lea, 1984). There is nothing in the behaviour in and of itself that requires the animal to have acquired a category – that is, any kind of sense that the objects all *go together* (but, see Honey & Watt, 1998, 1999) – let alone a concept – that is, a single mediating representation. To establish these, further tests are required (see also, Chater & Heyes, 1994; Close et al., 2009.).

It is also here, in the comparative literature, that the terminological difficulties involved in notions such as rule come back to bite; and this is not only because the answer to questions such as 'can animals or infants learn rules?' depend on what gets to count as a rule. Even examples of 'rules' that are conceptually straightforward can present considerable experimental challenges with nonhuman animals. As discussed previously, single-feature sorts readily meet definitions for rule use (cf. Hahn & Chater, 1998a; Pothos, 2005; Smith et al., 1992). This should not be surprising, as they match the paradigm case given earlier in crucial ways. Specifically, a single feature in this context is not just an abstraction that gives rise to all-or-none classification; in the human adult case, it also respects the important distinction between rule-governed and rule-describable behaviour: participants presumably *detect* all aspects of the object, but choose to base classification on just one of its aspect (see also, Geach, 1957).

This choice implies an *internal representation*. By contrast, a creature that simply responded to a single feature of the environment on the basis of a hardwired sensitivity would no more possess a rule than a light switch that turns on whenever pressed, as there is simply nothing there to support the idea that the system is representational in the first place (see Dretske, 1999, for a wider discussion). A critical criterion in demonstrating such rule-governed, representational categorization, therefore, is that a creature must show a level of cognitive flexibility that goes beyond this hard-wired sensitivity; that is, the creature must have the capacity to flexibly apply a rule depending upon its current environment, for example.

It is not just this hard-wired case that might seem problematic, however; a simple failure to discriminate successfully on the basis of more than one stimulus feature seems similarly deficient when considering rule use. Consequently, compelling tests of single-feature rules being used by animals would seem to require, at minimum, the further demonstration that other aspects of the stimulus could first be attended to, and second, be used for discrimination if required. Related problems are posed by the fact that rules can *express* other kinds of classifiers, or their behaviour. Examples of this include the additive rule of thumb (described previously), or decision bounds. To recap, a decision bound is simply a partition line in a multidimensional space that refers to a set of points that divide two or more regions (Ashby & Perrin, 1988). One possibility is that an agent represents this boundary, or a concise description that gives rise to this boundary explicitly (e.g. 'objects larger than 1 m are to be classified as *big*'). In this case, it seems unproblematic to refer to this representation as a rule (at least for some kinds of descriptions), as is common practice (see, e.g. Ashby et al., 1998; Rouder & Ratcliffe, 2004). However, the same decision bound can be the implicit consequence of a specification, not of the boundary, but of something that characterizes the regions (e.g. a degree of similarity to a prototype, etc.). Equally, they could arise from a classifier system that has neither a clearly rule- nor clearly similarity-based character, such as most connectionist networks. Careful distinction of what is actually represented might matter little in some adult modelling contexts (though it does seem vital for attempts to assign 'rules' and 'similarity' to particular neurological systems, e.g. Ashby et al., 1998; Smith et al., 1998, as it governs the range of processes implied, such as language or working memory), but this distinction will typically be of theoretical importance where comparative statements are concerned.

In summary, general conclusions from the last few decades of research on the role of rules and similarity in categorization are difficult to identify. Furthermore, some of the most consistent findings from both unsupervised and supervised learning tasks (e.g. participants' preference for single-feature sorts) appear patently inconsistent with the current understanding of our everyday concepts. At the same time, this research has developed considerably the standard of modelling in the study of cognition, and this must be of long-term benefit, not just for this particular field.

Clearly, much remains to be done, and one of the main lessons we might take from past categorization and concepts research might turn out to be a view on what we might productively do in the future. If we want to fully understand the nature of our everyday categories, it seems likely that we will need to combine the respective strengths of concepts and categorization research. Specifically, on the one hand, we should strive to bring to the study of real-world categories the methodological rigour of categorization research, and on the other hand, bring into the lab more of the characteristics of our everyday categories and their use. This is clearly difficult, and will only be achieved incrementally. However, it is our contention that if we are truly interested in understanding what humans do *naturally*, then merging these two fields in this way has to be a top priority.

References

Ahn, W. K. & Medin, D. L. (1992). A two-stage model of category construction. *Cognitive Science*, **16**, 81–121.

Allen, S. & Brooks, L. (1991). Specializing the operation of an explicit rule. *Journal of Experimental Psychology: General*, **120**, 3–19.

Anderson, J. R. (1978). Arguments concerning representations for mental imagery. *Psychological Review*, **85**, 249–277.

Anderson, J. R. (1983). *The Architecture of Cognition* Cambridge, MA: Harvard University Press.

Anderson, J. R. (1990). *The Adaptive Character of Thought* Hillsdale, NJ: Erlbaum.

Anderson, J. R. (1991). The adaptive nature of human categorization. *Psychological Review*, **98**, 409–429.

Anderson, J. R. (1993). *Rules of the Mind* Hillsdale, NJ: Lawrence Erlbaum Associates.

Anderson, J. R. & Betz, J. (2001). A hybrid model of categorization. *Psychonomic Bulletin & Review*, **8**, 629–647.

Andrews, R., Diederich, J., & Tickle, A. (1995). A survey and critique of techniques for extracting rules from trained artificial neural networks. *Knowledge-*Based *Systems*, **8**, 373–389.

Ashby, F. G. & Perrin, N. A. (1988). Towards a unified theory of similarity and recognition. *Psychological Review*, **95**, 124–150.

Ashby, F. G., Alfonso-Reese, L. A., Turken, A. U., & Waldron, E. M. (1998). A neuropsychological theory of multiple systems in category learning. *Psychological Review*, **105**, 442–481.

Barr, R. A. & Caplan, L. J. (1987). Category representations and their implications for category structure. *Memory and Cognition*, **15**, 397–418.

Bates, E. A. & Elman, J. L. (1993). Connectionism and the study of change. In M. J. Johnson (Ed.), *Brain Development and Cognition*, pp. 623–642, Cambridge, MA: Basil Blackwell.

Braisby, N., Franks, B., & Hampton, J. (1996). Essentialism, word use, and concepts. *Cognition*, **59**, 247–274.

Brumby, D. P. & Hahn, U. (2007). Rules and exemplars in categorization: A computational exploration. *Proceedings of the 29th Annual Meeting of the Cognitive Science Society*, pp. 131–136, Mahwah, NJ: Lawrence Erlbaum Associates.

Bruner, J., Goodnow, J., & Austin, G. (1956). *A Study of Thinking New* Brunswick, NJ: Transaction Publishers.

Cerella, J. (1979). Visual classes and natural categories in the pigeon. *Journal of Experimental Psychology: Human Perception and Performance*, **5**, 68–77.

Chater, N. (2000). The logic of human learning. *Nature*, **407**, 572–573.

Chater, N. & Heyes, C. (1994). Animal concepts: Content and discontent. *Mind and Language*, **9**, 209–246.

Cheng, P. & Holyoak, K. (1985). Pragmatic reasoning schemas. *Cognitive Psychology*, **17**, 293–328.

Chin-Parker, S. & Ross, B. H. (2004). Diagnosticity and prototypicality in category learning: A comparison of inference learning and classification learning. *Journal of Experimental Psychology: Learning, Memory, and Cognition*, **30**, 216–226.

Chomsky, N. (1980). Rules and representations. *Behavioral and Brain Sciences*, **3**, 1–61.

Close, J., Hahn, U., & Honey, R. C. (2009). Contextual modulation of stimulus generalization in rats. *Journal of Experimental Psychology: Animal Behavior Processes*, **35**, 509–515.

Compton, B. J. & Logan, G. D. (1999). Judgments of perceptual groups: Reliability and sensitivity to stimulus transformation. *Perception Psychophysics*, **61**, 1320–1335.

Corter, J. E. & Gluck, M. A. (1992). Explaining basic categories: Feature predictability and information. *Psychological Bulletin*, **111**, 291–303.

Davies, M. (1995). Two notions of implicit rule. In J. E. Tomberlin (Ed.) *Philosophical Perspectives, 9, AI, Connectionism, and Philosophical Psychology*, pp. 153–183, Atascadero, CA: Ridgeview Publishing Company.

Dennis, I., Hampton, J. A., & Lea, S. E. G. (1973). New problem in concept formation. *Nature*, **243**, 101–102.

Dienes, Z. (1992). Connectionist and memory-array models of artificial grammar learning. *Cognitive Science*, **16**, 41–79.

Diesendruck, G. & Gelman, S. A. (1999). Domain differences in absolute judgments of category membership: Evidence for an essentialist account of categorization. *Psychonomic Bulletin & Review*, **6**, 338–346.

Dretske, F. I. (1999). Machines, plants and animals: The origins of agency. *Erkenntnis*, **51**, 19–31.

Erickson, M. A. & Kruschke, J. K. (1998). Rules and exemplars in category learning. *Journal of Experimental Psychology: General*, **127**, 107–140.

Estes, W. K. (1994). *Classification and Cognition* New York: Oxford University Press.

Estes, Z. (2003). Attributive and relational processes in nominal combination. *Journal of Memory and Language*, **48**, 304–319.

Feldman, J. (2000). Minimization of Boolean complexity in human concept learning. *Nature*, **407**, 630–633.

Fisher, D. (1987). Knowledge acquisition via incremental conceptual clustering. *Machine Learning*, **2**, 139–172.

Fisher, D. (1988). A computational account of basic level and typicality effects. *Proceedings of the 7th National Conference on Artificial Intelligence*, pp. 233–238, Saint Paul, MN: Morgan Kaufmann.

Fisher, D. (1996). Iterative optimization and simplification of hierarchical clusterings. *Journal of Artificial Intelligence Research*, **4**, 147–179.

Fisher, D. & Langley, P. (1990). The structure and formation of natural categories. In G. Bower (Ed.) *The Psychology of Learning and Motivation, Vol. 26*, pp. 241–284, San Diego, CA: Academic Press.

Fodor, J. A., Garrett, M. F., Walker, F. C., & Parkes, C. H. (1980). Against definitions. *Cognition*, **8**, 263–367.

Frege, G. (1970). On sense and reference. (Translated by M. Black), In P. Geach & M. Black (Eds.), *Philosophical Writings of Gottlob Frege*, pp. 36–56, Oxford: Basil Blackwell. (Original publication, 1892).

Geach, P. T. (1957). *Mental Acts* London: Routledge & Kegan Paul.

Goldstone, R. L. (1994a). Similarity, interactive activation, and mapping. *Journal of Experimental Psychology: Learning, Memory, and Cognition*, **20**, 3–28.

Goldstone, R. L. (1994b). The role of similarity in categorization: Providing a groundwork. *Cognition*, **52**, 125–157.

Goodman, N. (1972). Seven strictures on similarity. In N. Goodman (Ed.), *Problems and Projects*, pp. 23–32, New York: Bobbs-Merrill.

Gosselin, F. & Schyns, P. G. (2001). Why do we SLIP to the basic level? Computational constraints and their implementation. *Psychological Review*, **108**, 735–758.

Gureckis, T. M. & Love, B. C. (2002). Who says models can only do what you tell them? Unsupervised category learning data, fits, and predictions. *Proceedings of the 24th Annual Conference of the Cognitive Science Society*, pp. 399–404, Hillsdale, NJ: Lawrence Erlbaum.

Hahn, U. (2002). Rule-based thought. *Encyclopedia of Cognitive Science* London: Macmillan.

Hahn, U. & Chater, N. (1997). Concepts and similarity. In K. Lamberts & D. Shanks (Eds.), *Knowledge, Concepts, and Categories*, pp. 43–92, Hove: Psychology Press.

Hahn, U. & Chater, N. (1998a). Similarity and rules: Distinct? Exhaustive? Empirically distinguishable? *Cognition*, **65**, 197–230.

Hahn, U. & Chater, N. (1998b). Understanding similarity: A joint project for psychology, case-based reasoning and law. *Artificial Intelligence Review*, **12**, 393–429.

Hahn, U., Chater, N., & Richardson, L. B. C. (2003). Similarity as transformation. *Cognition*, **87**, 1–32.

Hahn, U., Prat-Sala, M., & Pothos, E. M. (2002). How similarity affects the ease of rule application. *Proceedings of the Twenty-Fourth Annual Conference of the Cognitive Science Society*, pp. 411–416, Hillsdale, NJ: Lawrence Erlbaum Associates.

Hampton, J. A. (2001). The role of similarity in natural categorization In U. Hahn & M. Ramscar (Eds.), *Similarity and Categorization*, pp. 13–28, Oxford: Oxford University Press.

Hampton, J. A. (2003). Abstraction and context in concept representation. *Philosophical Transactions of the Royal Society of London, Theme Issue*: The abstraction paths: From experience to concept, **358**, 1251–1259.

Hampton, J. A., Estes, Z., & Simmons, S. (2007). Metamorphosis: Essence, appearance, and behavior in the categorization of natural kinds. *Memory & Cognition*, **35**, 1785–1800.

Heit, E. (2001). Background knowledge and models of categorization. In U. Hahn & M. Ramscar (Eds.), *Similarity and Categorization*, pp. 155–178, Oxford: Oxford University Press.

Heit, E. & Bott, L. (2000). Knowledge selection in category learning. In D. L. Medin (Ed.), *Psychology of Learning and Motivation*, pp. 163–199, San Diego, CA: Academic Press.

Herrnstein, R. J. (1990). Levels of stimulus control: A functional approach. *Cognition*, **37**, 133–146.

Herrnstein, R. J. & Loveland, D. H. (1964). Complex visual concept in the pigeon. *Science*, **146**, 549–551.

Herrnstein, R. J., Loveland, D. H., & Cable, C. (1976). Natural concepts in pigeons. *Journal of Experimental Psychology: Animal Behaviour Processes*, **2**, 285–311.

Honey, R. C. & Watt, A. (1998). Acquired relational equivalence: Implications for the nature of associative structures. *Journal of Experimental Psychology: Animal Behavior Processes*, **24**, 325–334.

Honey, R. C. & Watt, A. (1999). Acquired relational equivalence between contexts and features. *Journal of Experimental Psychology: Animal Behavior Processes*, **25**, 324–333.

Imai, S. & Garner, W. R. (1965). Discriminability and preference for attributes in free and constrained classification. *Journal of Experimental Psychology*, **69**, 596–608.

Johansen, M. K. & Palmeri, T. J. (2002). Are there representational shifts during category learning. *Cognitive Psychology*, **45**, 482–553.

Jones, G. V. (1983). Identifying basic categories. *Psychological Bulletin*, **94**, 423–428.

Kalish, C. W. (1995). Essentialism and graded membership in animal and artifact categories. *Memory & Cognition*, **23**, 335–353.

Kaplan, A. S. & Murphy, G. L. (1999). The acquisition of category structure in unsupervised learning. *Memory & Cognition*, **27**, 699–712.

Kaplan, A. S. & Murphy, G. L. (2000). Category learning with minimal prior knowledge. *Journal of Experimental Psychology: Learning, Memory, and Cognition*, **26**, 829–846.

Keil, F. C. (1989). *Concepts, Kinds, and Cognitive Development* Cambridge, MA: MIT Press.

Kosko, B. (1996). *Fuzzy Engineering* Upper Saddle River, NJ: Prentice Hall.

Kruschke, J. K. (1992). ALCOVE: An exemplar-based connectionist model of category learning. *Psychological Review*, **99**, 22–44.

Krzanowski, W. J. & Marriott, F. H. C. (1995). *Multivariate Analysis, Part 2: Classification, Covariance Structures and Repeated Measurements* London: Arnold.

Labov. W. A. (1973). The boundaries of words and their meanings. In C. J. Baily & R. Shuy (Eds.), *New Ways of Analyzing Variation in English*, pp. 340–373, Washington, DC: Georgetown University Press.

Lacroix, G. L., Giguere, G., & Larochelle, S. (2005). The origin of exemplar effects in rule-driven categorization. *Journal of Experimental Psychology: Learning, Memory, and Cognition*, **31**, 272–288.

Lamberts, K. (1995). Categorization under time pressure. *Journal of Experimental Psychology: General*, **124**, 161–180.

Lamberts, K. (2000). Information-accumulation theory of speeded classification. *Psychological Review*, **107**, 227–260.

Landauer, T. K. & Dumais, S. T. (1997). A solution to Plato's problem: The latent semantic analysis theory of acquisition, induction and representation of knowledge. *Psychological Review*, **104**, 211–240.

Larochelle, S., Cousineau, D., & Archambault, A. (2005). Definitions in categorization and similarity judgments. In H. Cohen & C. Lefebvre (Eds.), *Handbook of Categorization in Cognitive Science*, pp. 278–303, Amsterdam: Elsevier.

Lassaline, M. E. & Murphy, G. L. (1996). Induction and category coherence. *Psychonomic Bulletin & Review*, **3**, 95–99.

Lea, S. E. G. (1984). In what sense do pigeons learn concepts? In H. L. Roitblat, T. G. Bever, & H. S. Terrace (Eds.), *Animal Cognition*, pp. 263–276, Hillsdale, NJ: Erlbaum.

Lewandowsky, S., Kalish, M., & Griffiths, T. L. (2000). Competing strategies in categorization: Expediency and resistance to knowledge restructuring. *Journal of Experimental Psychology: Learning, Memory, and Cognition*, **26**, 1666–1684.

Love, B. C., Medin, D. L., & Gureckis, T. M. (2004). SUSTAIN: A network model of category learning. *Psychological Review*, **111**, 309–332.

Lubow, R. E. (1974). High-order concept formation in the pigeon. *Journal of the Experimental Analysis of Behavior*, **21**, 475–483.

Maddox, W. T. & Dodd, J. L. (2003). Separating perceptual and decisional attention processes in the identification and categorization of integral-dimension stimuli. *Journal of Experimental Psychology: Learning, Memory, and Cognition*, **29**, 467–480.

Malott, R. W. & Sidall, J. W. (1972). Acquisition of the people concept in pigeons. *Psychological Reports*, **31**, 3–13.

Malt, B. C. (1990). Features and beliefs in the mental representations of categories. *Journal of Memory and Language*, **29**, 289–315.

Malt, B. C. (1994). Water is not H₂O. *Cognitive Psychology*, **27**, 41–70.

Marcus, G., Brinkmann, U., Clahsen, H., Wiese, R., Woest, A., & Pinker, S. (1995). German inflections: The exception that proves the rule. *Cognitive Psychology*, **29**, 189–256.

Markman, A. B. & Gentner, D. (1993a). Splitting the differences: A structural alignment view of similarity. *Journal of Memory and Language*, **32**, 517–535.

Markman, A. B. & Gentner, D. (1993b). Structural alignment during similarity comparisons. *Cognitive Psychology*, **25**, 431–467.

McCloskey, M. E. & Glucksberg, S. (1978). Natural categories: Well defined or fuzzy sets? *Memory & Cognition*, **6**, 462–472.

Medin, D. L. & Ortony, A. (1989). Psychological essentialism. In S. Vosniadou & A. Ortony (Eds.), *Similarity and Analogical Reasoning*, pp. 179–195, Cambridge: Cambridge University Press.

Medin, D. L., Goldstone, R. L., & Gentner, D. (1993). Respects for similarity. *Psychological Review*, **100**, 254–278.

Medin, D. L. & Schaffer, M. M. (1978). Context theory of classification learning. *Psychological Review*, **85**, 207–238.

Medin, D. L., Wattenmaker, W. D., & Hampson, S. E. (1987). Family resemblance, conceptual cohesiveness and category construction. *Cognitive Psychology*, **19**, 242–279.

Milton, F., Longmore, C. A., & Wills, A. J. (2008). Processes of overall similarity sorting in free classification. *Journal of Experimental Psychology: Human Perception and Performance*, **34**, 676–692.

Milton, F. & Wills, A. J. (2004). The influence of stimulus properties on category construction. *Journal of Experimental Psychology: Learning, Memory, and Cognition*, **30**, 407–415.

Morgan, M. J., Fitch, M. D., Holman, J. G., & Lea, S. E. G. (1976). Pigeons learn the concept of an 'A'. *Perception*, **5**, 57–66.

Murphy, G. L. (2002). *The Big Book of Concepts* Cambridge, MA: MIT Press.

Murphy, G. L. & Allopenna, P. D. (1994). The locus of knowledge effects in concept learning. *Journal of Experimental Psychology: Learning, Memory, and Cognition*, **20**, 904–919.

Murphy, G. L. & Medin, D. L. (1985). The role of theories in conceptual coherence. *Psychological Review*, **92**, 289–316.

Murphy, G. L. & Smith, E. E. (1982). Basic level superiority in picture categorization. *Journal of Verbal Learning and Verbal Behavior*, **21**, 1–20.

Noelle, D. C. & Cottrell, G. W. (1996). Modeling interference effects in instructed category learning. *Proceedings of the 18th Annual Conference of the Cognitive Science Society*, pp. 475–480, Hillsdale, NJ: Lawrence Erlbaum.

Noelle, D. C. & Cottrell, G. W. (2000). Individual differences in exemplar-based interference during instructed category learning. *Proceedings of the 22nd Annual Conference of the Cognitive Science Society*, pp. 358–363, Hillsdale, NJ: Lawrence Erlbaum.

Nosofsky, R. M. (1986). Attention, similarity, and the identification–categorization relationship. *Journal of Experimental Psychology: General*, **115**, 39–57.

Nosofsky, R. M. (1988). Similarity, frequency, and category representation. *Journal of Experimental Psychology: Learning, memory and cognition*, **14**, 54–65.

Nosofsky, R. M. (1991). Typicality in logically defined categories: Exemplar-similarity versus rule instantiation. *Memory & Cognition, 19*, 131–150.

Nosofsky, R. M. & Johansen, M. E. (2000). Exemplar-based accounts of 'multiple-system' phenomena in perceptual categorization. *Psychonomic Bulletin & Review, 7*, 375–402.

Nosofsky, R. M. & Palmeri, T. J. (1997). An exemplar-based random walk model of speeded classification. *Psychological Review, 104*, 266–300.

Nosofsky, R. M., Clark, S. E., & Shin, H. J. (1989). Rules and exemplars in categorization, identification, and recognition. *Journal of Experimental Psychology: Learning, Memory, and Cognition, 15*, 282–304.

Nosofsky, R. M., Palmeri, T. J., & Mckinley, S. (1994). Rule-plus-exception model of classification learning. *Psychological Review, 101*, 53–79.

Palmeri, T. J. (1997). Exemplar similarity and the development of automaticity. *Journal of Experimental Psychology: Learning, Memory, and Cognition, 23*, 324–354.

Pickering, M. & Chater, N. (1995). Why cognitive science is not formalized folk psychology. *Minds and Machines, 5*, 309–337.

Poole, J. & Lander, D. G. (1971). The pigeon's concept of pigeon. *Psychonomic Science, 25*, 157–158.

Posner, M. I. & Keele, S. W. (1968). On the genesis of abstract ideas. *Journal of Experimental Psychology, 77*, 353–363.

Pothos, E. M. (2005). The rules versus similarity distinction. *Behavioral and Brain Sciences, 28*, 1–49.

Pothos, E. M. & Chater, N. (2002). A simplicity principle in unsupervised human categorization. *Cognitive Science, 26*, 303–343.

Pothos, E. M. & Close, J. (2008). One or two dimensions in spontaneous classification: A simplicity approach. *Cognition, 107*, 581–602.

Pothos, E. M. & Hahn, U. (2000). So concepts aren't definitions, but do they have necessary 'or' sufficient features? *British Journal of Psychology, 91*, 439–450.

Ramscar, M. & Hahn, U. (1998). What family resemblances are not: The continuing relevance of Wittgenstein to the study of concepts and categories. *Proceedings of the 20th Annual Meeting of the Cognitive Science Society*, pp. 865–870, Hillsdale, NJ: Erlbaum.

Reed, S. (1972). Pattern recognition and categorization. *Cognitive Psychology, 3*, 382–407.

Regehr, G. & Brooks, L. R. (1993). Perceptual manifestations of an analytic structure: The priority of holistic individuation. *Journal of Experimental Psychology: General, 122*, 92–114.

Regehr, G. & Brooks, L. R. (1995). Category organization in free classification: The organizing effect of an array of stimuli. *Journal of Experimental Psychology Learning, Memory, & Cognition, 21*, 347–363.

Rehder, B. & Hoffman, A. B. (2005). Eyetracking and selective attention in category learning. *Cognitive Psychology, 51*, 1–41.

Rips, L. J. (1989). Similarity, typicality, and categorization. In S. Vosniadou & A. Ortony (Eds.) *Similarity and Analogical Reasoning*, pp. 21–59, Cambridge: Cambridge University Press.

Rodriguez, A. (2001). Issues in case-based reasoning. In U. Hahn & M. Ramscar (Eds.) *Similarity and Categorization*, pp. 131–153, Oxford: Oxford University.

Rosch, E. & Mervis, C. B. (1975). Family resemblances: Studies in the internal structure of categories. *Cognitive Psychology, 7*, 573–605.

Rosch, E., Mervis, C. B., Gray, W. D., Johnson, D. M., & Boyes-Braem, P. (1976). Basic objects in natural categories. *Cognitive Psychology, 8*, 382–439.

Rouder, J. N. & Ratcliff, R. (2004). Comparing categorization models. *Journal of Experimental Psychology: General*, **133**, 63–82.

Rouder, J. N. & Ratcliff, R. (2006). Comparing exemplar- and rule-based theories of categorization. *Current Directions in Psychological Science*, **15**, 9–13.

Rumelhart, D. E. & Todd, P. M. (1993). Learning and connectionist representations. In D. E. Meyer & S. Kornblum (Eds.) *Attention and Performance XIV: Synergies in Experimental Psychology, Artificial Intelligence and Cognitive Neuroscience*, pp. 3–30, Cambridge, MA: MIT Press.

Savage-Rumbaugh, E. S., Rumbaugh, D. M., Smith, S. T., & Lawson, J. (1980). Reference – The linguistic essential. *Science*, **210**, 922–925.

Schrier, A. M., Angarella, R., & Povar, M. L. (1984). Studies of concept formation by stumptailed monkeys: Concepts humans, monkeys, and letter A. *Journal of Experimental Psychology: Animal Behavior Processes*, **10**, 564–584.

Schrier, A. M. & Brady, P. M. (1987). Categorization of natural stimuli by monkeys (*Macaca mulatta*): Effects of stimulus set size and modification of exemplars. *Journal of Experimental Psychology: Animal Behavior Processes*, **13**, 136–143.

Shanks, D. R. (1995). *The Psychology of Associative Learning* Cambridge: Cambridge University Press.

Shepard, R. N. & Chang, J. J. (1963). Stimulus generalization in the learning of classifications. *Journal of Experimental Psychology*, **65**, 94–102.

Shepard, R. N., Hovland, C. I., & Jenkins, H. M. (1961). Learning and memorization of classifications. *Psychological Monographs*, **75**, (13, Whole No. 517).

Siegel, R. K. & Honig, W. K. (1970). Pigeon concept formation: Successive and simultaneous acquisition. *Journal of the Experimental Analysis of Behavior*, **13**, 385–390.

Smith, E. E., Langston, C., & Nisbett, R. E. (1992). The case for rules in reasoning. *Cognitive Science*, **16**, 1–40.

Smith, E. E. & Medin, D. L. (1981). *Categories and Concepts* Cambridge, MA: Harvard University Press.

Smith, E. E., Patalano, A. L., & Jonides, A. L. (1998). Alternative strategies of categorization. *Cognition*, **65**, 167–196.

Smits, T., Storms, G., Rosseel, Y., & De Boeck, P. (2002). Fruits and vegetables categorized: An application of the generalized context model. *Psychonomic Bulletin & Review*, **9**, 836–844.

Spalding, T. L. & Murphy, G. L. (1996). Effects of background knowledge on category construction. *Journal of Experimental Psychology: Learning, Memory, and Cognition*, **22**, 525–538.

Thibaut, J. P. & Gelaes, S. (2006). Exemplar effects in the context of a categorization rule: Featural and holistic influences. *Journal of Experimental Psychology: Learning, Memory, and Cognition*, **6**, 1403–1415.

Townsend, J. T. & Ashby, F. G. (1983). *The Stochastic Modeling of Elementary Psychological Processes* Cambridge: Cambridge University Press.

Vandierendonck, A. (1995). A parallel rule activation and rule synthesis model for generalization in category learning. *Psychonomic Bulletin & Review*, **2**, 442–459.

Ward, T. B. (1983). Response tempo and separable-integral responding: Evidence for an integral-to-separable processing sequence in visual perception. *Journal of Experimental Psychology: Human Perception and Performance*, **9**, 103–112.

Wattenmaker, W. D. (1992). Relational properties and memory-based category construction. *Journal of Experimental Psychology: Learning, Memory, and Cognition*, **18**, 1125–1138.

Wittgenstein, L. (1953). *Philosophical Investigations* G. H. von Wright, R. Rhees & G. E. M. Anscombe (Eds.), (Translated by G. E. M. Anscombe), Oxford: Basil Blackwell.

Young, R. & O'Shea, T. (1981). Errors in children's subtraction. *Cognitive Science*, **5**, 153–177.

Chapter 4

Mechanistic models of associative and rule-based category learning

Bradley C. Love and Marc Tomlinson

Editors' Preview

Chapter 4, 'Mechanistic models of associative and rule-based category learning', reviews some of the computational models that have been used to simulate the different forms of concept learning that were introduced in Chapters 2 and 3. One class of models has been designed to capture our ability to learn rule-based categories that have defining features. Such models are well suited to learn concepts such as *triangle* in which all members have three sides, angles that add to 180°, and form a closed figure. With rule-based concepts, membership is all or none, meaning that as long as an object has the criterial features of a triangle, it is a triangle, and no triangle is any better example of a triangle than any other triangle.

A difficulty with category-learning models that can just learn rules is that many categories do not seem to be rule based. For example, one might try to define the concept of *bird* with features such as, has feathers, can fly, and lays eggs, but exceptions can be found (i.e. baby male ostriches are birds, but they do not (1) have feathers, (2) fly, or (3) lay eggs). In a more famous example, the philosopher Wittgenstein argued that a concept such as *game* has no attribute shared by virtually all of its members. Rather, members of a category bear a relationship of family resemblance where there is a cluster of attributes that characterizes the family, but no attribute would hold for all members of the family.

Categories with a family-resemblance structure are learned well by models that represent prototypes. A prototype can be thought of as the central tendency of a category or as the best representative of a family in the sense of having the greatest number of attributes in common with other members of the category and the fewest number of attributes in common with members of contrast categories. Models that represent categories as prototypes can account for typicality effects in which category membership is graded, with some members judged as more representative of the category than other members, based on their greater resemblance to the prototype (e.g. robins are rated as more typical birds than are penguins).

While prototype models perform well in terms of learning natural categories that have a regular, similarity-based structure, models that represent concepts as sets of exemplars perform better at representing more complex, irregular category structures (e.g. large and dark things, and small and light things, go into one category, and small and dark things, and large and light things, go into another category, see Figure 4.3 of Chapter 4). Exemplar models represent more information about categories than do prototype models in terms of retaining data about the frequency of the exemplars, their variability, and the correlations among them. However, at the level of intuition, exemplar models are not always viewed as cognitively efficient because they store every exemplar ever encountered (e.g. is it reasonable to think that a person walking down the street will record every similar-looking bird that is experienced and store it in memory?).

Given that each of the models (rule, prototype, and exemplar) runs into one or another difficulty, investigators have more recently been implementing hybrid models where the manner in which the model represents concepts is determined by the structure of those concepts (i.e. categories that can be organized by a regular, similarity-based structure are represented as prototypes, whereas categories that have a more complex, irregular structure are represented as exemplars). There are also models that have different category-learning systems within them such that each category-learning system functions via a distinct set of operating principles. Despite the differences in the various systems of category learning, one commonality is that they all function based on experiences with exemplars. Given that human adults, human infants, and nonhuman animals all experience exemplars, one may therefore look for evidence that the various category-learning systems are continuous across development and species.

Introduction

Judging a person as a friend or foe, a mushroom as edible or poisonous, or a sound as an *l* or *r* are examples of categorization problems. As people never encounter the same exact stimulus twice, they must develop categorization schemes that capture the useful regularities in their environment. One challenge for psychological research is to determine how humans acquire and represent categories.

The focus of this chapter is on proposed category-learning mechanisms. We focus on models that attempt to explain how people acquire categories from observed examples, as opposed to verbal instruction. Most of the models that are discussed in this chapter were developed to account for adult human performance, but many of these models have also been successfully applied to studies involving humans of all ages and to other species. Category learning is a theory- and model-rich area within cognitive psychology. Models have played a prominent role in shaping our understanding of human category learning. Accordingly, proposed mechanisms are diverse, including rule-, prototype-, and exemplar-based models, as well as hybrid models and models that contain multiple systems. One general trend is towards models with increasingly sophisticated processing mechanisms that can mimic the behaviours of existing models, as well as address behaviours outside the scope of previous models.

In the course of reviewing these various models, we emphasize what the relative merits of each model reveal about the nature of human learning. When we discuss exemplar models, we devote special attention to a model of category learning that attempts to bridge work in the analogy and category-learning literatures. The model, 'building relations through instance-driven gradient error shifting' (BRIDGES), successfully accounts for findings in the child and animal learning literatures. (Tomlinson & Love, 2006) We choose to showcase this particular model because it is well matched to the overarching goals of this book, and the focus should help the reader understand the basis for all the models reviewed, which is the primary goal of this chapter.

In the remainder of this chapter, we briefly review several models of human category learning. Presentation order is organized chronologically from oldest to most recent accounts of category learning. Although more recent models offer some advantages over their ancestors, it would be a mistake to view ancestral models as being supplanted by their descendants. Each model class addresses some key aspects of human category learning and serves an important theoretical role. In fact, many older models have taken on new life as components in recently proposed multiple systems models. One common component in these multiple systems models is a rule-based system, which is the first model class that we consider.

Rule-based models

The classical view of concepts holds that categories are defined by logical rules. This view has a long history dating back to Aristotle. In Figure 4.1, any item that is a square is a member of category *A*. This simple rule determines category membership. According to the rule view, our concept of category *A* can be represented by this simple rule. Discovering this rule would involve a rational hypothesis-testing procedure. This procedure attempts to discover a rule that is satisfied by all of the positive examples of a concept, but none of the negative examples of the concept (i.e. items that are members of other categories). In trying to come up with such a rule for category *A*, one might first try the rule *if dark, then in category A*. After rejecting this rule (because there are counterexamples), other rules would be tested (starting with simple rules and progressing towards more complex rules) until the correct rule is eventually discovered. For example, in learning about birds, one might first try the rule *if it flies, then it is a bird*. This rule works pretty well, but not perfectly (penguins do not fly and bats do). Another simple rule like *if it has feathers, then it is a bird* would not work either

Category A   Category B

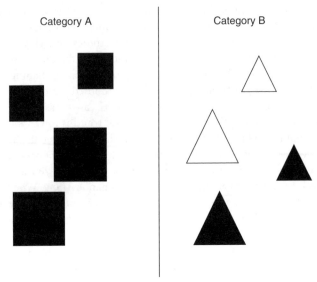

Fig. 4.1 Examples of category *A* and category *B*. A simple rule on shape discriminates between the two categories.

because a pillow filled with feathers is not a bird. Eventually, a more complex rule might be discovered like *if it has feathers and wings, then it is a bird*.

For decades, psychologists have conducted experiments to characterize the relative difficulty people have in learning various types of rules (Bruner et al., 1956; Shepard et al., 1961). These studies have provided the primary data used to develop and validate models of hypothesis testing. Some models, like RULEX, (Nosofsky et al., 1994) embody the hypothesis-testing procedure described above. RULEX starts with simple hypotheses and progresses towards more complex hypotheses until a set of rules and exceptions is discovered that properly discriminates between the categories.

As discussed in Chapter 3 in this book, the term *rule* has various, somewhat conflicting, interpretations. Here, we focus on rule-based models, like RULEX, that engage in explicit hypothesis testing. RULEX's mechanistic approach (i.e. algorithmic in the sense of Marr, 1982) contrasts with other approaches that aim to predict how difficult learning should be based on calculations of how complex the correct hypothesis is (Feldman, 2000). The latter approaches, which are not concerned with the actual process of learning, have more in common with measures of complexity and compression (Pothos & Chater, 2002). Yet other approaches, such as general recognition theory (Maddox & Ashby, 1993), aim to assess and compactly describe people's performance rather than characterize the learning process. Unlike these more abstract approaches, mechanistic models of hypothesis testing, such as RULEX, largely implement the strategic and conscious thought processes that we feel (by introspection) that we are carrying out when solving classification problems.

Although rules can in principle provide a concise representation of a concept, often more elaborate representations would serve us better. Concept representation needs to be richer than a simple rule because we use concepts for much more than simply classifying objects we encounter. For instance, we often use concepts to support inference (e.g. a child infers that members of the category 'stove' can be dangerously hot). Using categories to make inferences is a very important use of concepts (Markman & Ross, 2003). Knowing something is an example of a concept tells us a great deal about the item. For example, after classifying a politician from the USA as a Republican, one can readily infer the politician's position on a number of issues. The point is that our representations of concepts must include information beyond what is needed to classify items as examples of the concept. For example, the rule *if square, then in category A* correctly classifies all members of category *A* in Figure 4.1, but it does not capture the knowledge that all category *A* members are *dark*. One problem with rule representations of concepts is that potentially useful information is discarded. In fact, even when people explicitly use rules to classify items, performance is heavily influenced by rule-irrelevant information (Allen & Brooks, 1991; Lacroix et al., 2005; Sakamoto & Love, 2004), which is inconsistent with rules serving as the sole basis for category representations.

Perhaps the biggest problem with the rule approach to concepts is that most of our everyday categories do not seem to be describable by a tractable rule. To demonstrate this point, Wittgenstein (1953) noted that the concept 'game' lacks a defining property. Most games are fun, but Russian roulette is not fun. Most games are competitive, but ring around the roses is not competitive. While most games have characteristics in common, there is not a rule that unifies them all. Rather, we can think of the members of the category game as being organized around a family-resemblance structure (analogous to how members of your family resemble one another). Rosch and colleagues (Rosch & Mervis,1975) in their seminal work, demonstrated the psychological reality of many of Wittgenstein's intuitions. Even some paradigmatic examples of rule-based classification reveal a non-rule-based underbelly (see Love et al., 2008, for a review). Hahn and Ramscar (2001) offer one such example. Tigers are defined as having tiger DNA, which is a seemingly rule-based category definition. However, determining whether an animal has tiger DNA amounts to assessing the similarity of the animal's DNA to known examples of tiger DNA.

A related weakness of the rule account of concepts is that examples of a concept differ in their typicality (Barsalou, 1985; Posner & Keele, 1968; Reed, 1972; Rosch & Mervis, 1975). If all a concept consisted of was a rule that determined membership, then all examples should have equal status. According to the rule account, all that should matter is whether an item satisfies the rule. Our concepts do not seem to have this definitive flavour. For example, some games are better examples of the category game than others. Basketball is a very typical example of the category games. Children play basketball in a playground, it is competitive, there are two teams, each team consists of multiple players, you score points, etc. Basketball is a typical example of the category of games because it has many characteristics in common with other games. On the other hand, Russian roulette is not a very typical game – it requires a gun and one of the two players dies. Russian roulette does not have many properties in common with other games. In terms of family-resemblance structure, we can think of basketball as having a central position and Russian roulette being a distant cousin to the other family members. These findings extend to categories in which a simple classification rule exists. For example, people judge the number three to be a more typical odd number than the number forty-seven even though membership in the category odd number can be defined by a simple rule (Gleitman et al., 1996).

The fact that category membership follows a gradient as opposed to being all or none affords us flexibility in how we apply our concepts. Of course, this flexibility can lead to ambiguity. Consider the concept mother (see Lakoff, 1987, for a thorough analysis). It is a concept that we are all familiar with that seems straightforward – a mother is a woman who becomes pregnant and gives birth to a child. But what about a woman who adopts a neglected infant and raises it in a nurturing environment? Is the birth mother who neglected the infant a mother? What if a woman is implanted with an embryo from another woman? Court cases over maternity arise because the concept of motherhood is ambiguous. The concept exhibits greater flexibility and productivity than is even indicated above. For example, is it proper to refer to an architect as the mother of a building? All the above examples of the concept mother share a family-resemblance structure (i.e. they are organized around some common-alities), but the concept is not rule based. Some examples of the concept mother are better than others.

We do not want to imply that rule-based approaches do not have their place. For example, rule-based approaches might be viable for some socially defined categories. For example, determining whether currency is legal tender might largely involve applying a series of rules (Hampton, 2001). Moreover, as we will see later in this chap-ter, rule-based approaches figure prominently in multiple systems accounts. While rule-based approaches might not provide a sufficient explanation of human learning in isolation, such approaches might prove viable in certain domains or as components of multiple system models.

Prototype-based models

The prototype approach to concept learning and representation was developed by Rosch and colleagues to address some of the shortcomings of the rule approach. Prototype models represent information about all the possible properties (i.e. stimu-lus dimensions), instead of focusing on only a few properties like rule models do. The prototype of a category is a summary of all of its members (Posner & Keele, 1968; Reed, 1972; Smith & Minda, 2001). Mathematically, the prototype is the average or central tendency of all category members. Figure 4.2 displays the prototypes for two categories, simply named categories A and B. Notice that all the items differ in size and luminance (i.e. there are two stimulus dimensions) and that the prototype is located amidst all of its category members. The prototype for each category has the average value on both the stimulus dimensions of size and luminance for the members of its category.

The prototype of a category is used to represent the category. According to the pro-totype model a novel item is classified as a member of the category whose prototype

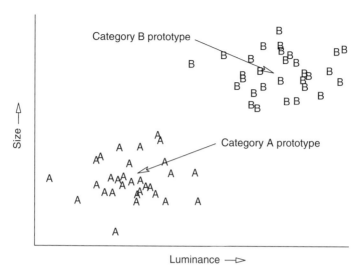

Fig. 4.2 Two categories and their prototypes.

it is most similar to. For example, a large, bright item would be classified as a member of category *B* because category *B*'s prototype is large and bright (see Figure 4.2). The position of the prototype is updated when new examples of the category are encountered. For example, if one encountered a very small and dark item that is a member of category *A*, then category *A*'s prototype would move slightly towards the bottom left corner in Figure 4.2. As an outcome of learning, the position of the prototype shifts towards the newest category member in order to take it into account. A prototype can be very useful for determining category membership in domains where there are many stimulus dimensions that each provide information useful for determining category membership, but no dimension is definitive. For example, members of a family may tend to be tall, have large noses, a medium complexion, brown eyes, and good muscle tone, but no family member possesses all of these traits. Matching on some subset of these traits would provide evidence for being a family member.

Notice the economy of the prototype approach. Each cloud of examples in Figure 4.2 can be represented by just the prototype. The prototype is intended to capture the critical structure in the environment without having to encode every detail or example. It is also fairly simple to determine which category a novel item belongs to by determining which category prototype is most similar to the item.

Unlike the rule approach, the prototype model can account for typicality effects. According to the prototype model, the more typical category members should be those members that are most similar to the prototype. In Figure 4.2, similarity can be viewed in geometric terms – the closer items are together in the plot, the more similar they are. Thus, the most typical items for categories *A* and *B* are those that are closest to the appropriate prototype. Accordingly, the prototype approach can explain why robins are more typical birds than penguins. The bird prototype represents the average bird: has wings, has feathers, can fly, can sing, lives in trees, lays eggs, etc. Robins share all of these properties with the prototype, whereas penguins differ in a number of ways (e.g. penguins cannot fly, but do swim). Extending this line of reasoning, the best example of a category should be the prototype, even if the actual prototype has never been viewed (or does not even exist). Indeed, numerous learning studies support this conjecture. After viewing a series of examples of a category, human participants are more likely to categorize the prototype as a category member (even though they never actually viewed the prototype) than they are to categorize an item they have seen before as a category member (Posner & Keele, 1968).

As the prototype approach does not represent concepts in terms of a logical rule that is either satisfied or not, it can explain how category membership has a graded structure that is not all or none. Some examples of a category are simply better examples than other examples. Moreover, categories do not need to be defined in terms of logical rules, but are rather defined in terms of family resemblance to the prototype. In other words, members of a category need not share a common defining thread, but rather can have many characteristic threads in common with one another.

The prototype approach, while preferable to the rule approach for the reasons just discussed, does fail to account for important aspects of human concept learning. The main problem with the prototype model is that it does not retain enough information about examples encountered in learning. For instance, prototypes do not store any information about the frequency of each category; yet people are sensitive to frequency information. If an item was about equally similar to the prototype of two different categories and one category was one hundred times larger than the other, people would be more likely to assign the item to the more common category (under most circumstances, see Kruschke, 1996). Of course, some of these concerns could be addressed by expanding the information that a prototype encodes.

However, other concerns seem fundamental to the prototype approach. Prototypes are not sensitive to the correlations and substructure within a category. For example, a prototype model would not be able to represent that spoons tend to be large and made of wood or small and made of steel. These two subgroups would simply be averaged together into one prototype. This averaging makes some categories unlearnable with a prototype model. One example of such a category structure is shown in Figure 4.3. Each category consists of two subgroups. Members of category A are either *small* and *dark,* or they are *large* and *light,* whereas members of category B are either *large* and *dark* or they are *small* and *light.* The prototypes for the two categories are both in the centre of the stimulus space (i.e. medium size and medium luminance). Items cannot be classified correctly by which prototype they are most similar because the prototypes provide little guidance.

In general, prototype models can only be used to learn category structures that are linearly separable. A learning problem involving two categories is linearly separable when a line or plane can be drawn that separates all the members of the two categories. The category structure shown in Figure 4.2 is linearly separable because a diagonal line can be drawn that separates the category A and B members (i.e. the category A members fall on one side of the line and the category B members fall on the other side of the line). Thus, this category structure can be learned with a prototype model. The category structure illustrated in Figure 4.3 is nonlinear – no single line can be drawn to

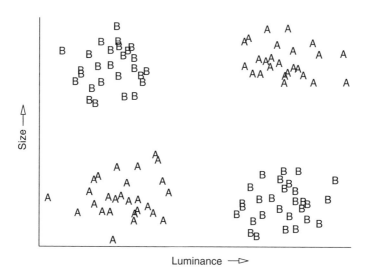

Fig. 4.3 Two categories and their prototypes.

segregate the category *A* and *B* members. Mathematically, a category structure is linearly separable when there exists a weighting of the feature dimensions that yields an additive rule that correctly indicates one category when the sum is below a chosen threshold and the other category when the sum is above the threshold.

The inability of the prototype model to learn nonlinear category structures detracts from its worth as a model of human concept learning because people are not biased against learning nonlinear category structures. While the extent to which natural categories deviate from linear structures is contended (Murphy, 2002), the general consensus is that people in the laboratory do not show a preference for linear structures in supervised learning (Medin & Schwanenflugel, 1981), though they might in unsupervised learning (Love, 2002). Some nonlinear category structures may actually be easier to acquire than linear category structures. For example, it seems quite natural that small birds sing, whereas large birds do not sing. Many categories have subtypes within them that we naturally pick out. One way for the prototype model to address this learnability problem is to include complex features that represent the presence of multiple simple features (e.g. large and blue). Unfortunately, this approach quickly becomes unwieldy as the number of stimulus dimensions increases (e.g. Gluck & Bower, 1988).

Related to the prototype model's inability to account for substructure within categories is its inadequacy as a model of item recognition. Unlike exemplar models considered in the following section (Medin & Schaffer, 1978; Nosofsky, 1986), prototypes models do not readily account for how people recognize specific items because the category prototype averages away item distinguishing information that people retain in some situations.

Exemplar-based models

Exemplar models store every training example in memory instead of just the prototype (i.e. the summary) of each category. Perhaps surprising upon first consideration, exemplar models can account for findings marshalled in support of prototype models, such as sensitivity to family-resemblance structure. At the same time, by retaining all of the information from training, exemplar models address many of the shortcomings of prototype models. Exemplar models are sensitive to the frequency, the variability, and the correlations among items. In this section, we discuss how exemplar-based models can display these behaviours.

Unlike prototype models, exemplar models can master category structures that contain substructure. For the learning problem illustrated in Figure 4.3, an exemplar model would store every training example. New items are classified by how similar they are to all items in memory (not just the prototype). For the category structure illustrated in Figure 4.3, the pairwise similarity of a novel item and every stored item would be calculated. If the novel item tended to be more similar to the category *A* members (i.e. the item was small and dark) than the category *B* members, then the novel item would be classified as a member of category *A*.

One aspect of exemplar models that seems counterintuitive is their lack of any abstraction in category representation. It seems that humans do learn something more abstract about categories than a list of examples. Surprisingly, exemplar models are capable of displaying abstraction. For instance, exemplar models can correctly predict that humans more strongly endorse the underlying prototype (even if it has not been seen) than an actual item that has been studied (a piece of evidence previously cited in favour of the prototype model). How could this be possible without the prototype actually being stored? It would be impossible if exemplar models simply functioned by retrieving the exemplar in memory that was most similar to the current item and classified the current item in the same category as the retrieved exemplar (this is essentially how processing works in a prototype model, except that a prototype is stored in memory instead of a bunch of exemplars).

Instead, exemplar models engage in more sophisticated processing and calculate the similarity between the current item (the item that is to be classified) and every item in memory. Some exemplars in memory will be very similar to the current item, whereas others will not be very similar. The current item is classified in the category in which the sum of its similarities to all the exemplars is greatest. When a previously unseen prototype is presented to an exemplar model, it can be endorsed as a category member more strongly than a previously seen item. The prototype (which is the central tendency of the category) will tend to be somewhat similar to every item in the category, whereas any given non-prototype item will tend to be very similar to some items (especially itself!) in memory, but not so similar to other items. Overall, the prototypical item can display an advantage over an item that has actually been studied. Abstraction in an exemplar model is indirect and results from processing (i.e. calculating and summing pairwise similarities), whereas abstraction in a prototype model is rather direct (i.e. prototypes are stored).

By and large, exemplar models can mimic all the behaviours of prototype models, but the opposite is not true. However, there are some subtle behaviours that the prototype model can display that versions of exemplar models cannot. For example, prototype and exemplar models predict slightly different category-endorsement gradients (i.e. probability of membership) as one moves towards the centre of a category (see Nosofsky & Zaki, 2002; and Smith, 2002, for a recent debate).

Although exemplar models are decent models of recognition, they do have some fundamental shortcomings. Exemplar models calculate recognition strength as the sum of similarity to all items stored in memory. Thus, the pairwise similarity relations among items governs recognition. However, humans often appear to build schema-like structures in memory and store items preferentially that deviate from these structures (see Sakamoto & Love, 2004, for a review). Thus, exemplar models do not correctly predict enhanced recognition for items that violate salient rules or patterns (Palmeri & Nosofsky, 1995). Exemplar models do not capture these results because exception items that violate these patterns are not exceptional in terms of their pairwise similarity relations to other items. Exception items are exceptional in terms of violating a knowledge structure stored in memory (Sakamoto & Love, 2004, 2006).

At a more philosophical level, exemplar models seem to make some questionable assumptions. For example, exemplar models store every training example, which seems excessive. Moreover, every exemplar is retrieved from memory every time an item is classified (though see Nosofsky & Palmeri, 1997, for an exception). In addition to these assumptions, one worries that the exemplar model does not make strong-enough theoretical commitments because it retains all information about training and contains a great deal of flexibility in how it processes information. In support of this conjecture, Sakamoto, Matsuka, and Love (2004) built an exemplar model that effectively built distributed knowledge structures and could account for exception recognition findings (also see Rodrigues & Murre, 2007). While their model did not explicitly build schema or exception representations, the model did learn to selectively tune exemplars (broad tunings for rule-following items and tight-tunings for exception items) and properly weight these exemplars to give rise to an exemplar model that functionally contained exception and schema-like knowledge structures. If there are no constraints on how items are processed, then in principle an exemplar model can account for any pattern of results thereby reducing the exemplar model's theoretical utility. However, in practice, exemplar models often follow previously published formalisms and serve as valuable theoretical tools.

Exemplar-based relational learning

One favourable property of exemplar models is their transparency. Their predictions are purely governed by the weighting of experienced examples. This property makes them ideally suited for computational explorations of new domains, such as relational category learning. In this subsection, we consider an exemplar model of how people learn seemingly abstract concepts by analogy to exemplars. The model, BRIDGES, provides an account of how animals (and people) learn to respond relationally (Tomlinson & Love, 2006). BRIDGES differs from other exemplar models by being sensitive to relational information.

Many of our categories are relational and therefore it is important to develop models that explain how such categories are acquired. For example, membership in the category *thief* is defined by playing the appropriate relational role in the relation *steals* rather than exhibiting some combination of concrete features (Markman & Stilwell, 2001). Differences in ability to classify relationally is often taken as a key marker of the relative mental capacities of animals, children, and adults (Thompson & Oden, 2000).

BRIDGES combines two popular approaches to cognition, exemplar-based category learning (Kruschke, 1992) and structure mapping theory (Gentner,1983). Structure mapping theory suggests that similarity is determined between two scenes by aligning the objects and relations present within one scene with the objects and relations in the other scene (Markman & Gentner, 1993). The similarity of two scenes is then a measure of how well they align. This alignment is traditionally done using an unweighted graph-matching algorithm. Figure 4.4 provides an overview of BRIDGES.

BRIDGES extends the notion of similarity used in exemplar models to an attention-weighted form of structure-mapping theory. This allows relational similarity, the degree to which mapped objects play the same role in their corresponding relations (Jones & Love, 2007), to play a variable role in the alignment process. Attention can shift between the features (e.g. *red*) and the relations (e.g. *redder*). This allows for abstraction away from the features and to the relations, but only so far as the statistics of the environment warrant. Attention is updated according to a supervised or unsupervised gradient-descent algorithm. The result is that BRIDGES is able to learn to respond differentially to the presence of relations, but its response is still affected by

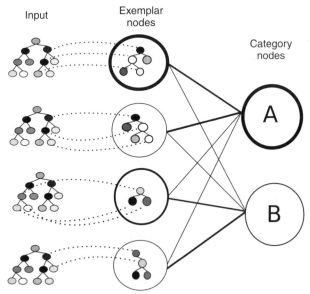

Fig. 4.4 A depiction of the BRIDGES model. The structured graphs represent the input and exemplars. These graphs encode features and their relations (e.g. man biting dog and dog biting man would have differently structured graphs). The luminance of the circles within the graphs represent attention to individual relations and features in the model. Node density reflects similarity-based activation of the nodes following the analogical match process. These activations are passed across connections weights to the category nodes.

the features of the stimuli. Figure 4.5 illustrates how attentional weighting can disambiguate between competing interpretations.

Previous simulations of same–different learning in pigeons (Young & Wasserman, 1997) and infant grammar learning (Marcus et al., 1999) have demonstrated that BRIDGES is capable of learning a variety of different relational behaviours without resorting to rules or symbol systems (Tomlinson & Love, 2006). Just like the participants in these experiments, BRIDGES generalizes to presentations of the relations with novel objects. Moreover, these relations are still clouded by the featural similarity of the individual stimuli because attention shifting is rarely complete, consistent with behavioural shifts seen in human development and acquired expertise (Chi et al., 1981; Gentner & Ratterman, 1991).

Other explanations for same–different learning centre on measures of display entropy or variability (Young et al., 2003). These explanations and BRIDGES are indistinguishable with a simple goodness-of-fit measure. However, BRIDGES makes a testable prediction different from the variability model; the responses in a same–different task should not just be based on the sameness and differentness of the array but also on the featural similarity between the test array and previous arrays the animal has been trained with, because some attention should still be on the features. Gibson and Wasserman (2004) provide just such a test and confirm BRIDGE's prediction.

In Gibson and Wasserman (2004), pigeons are trained on stimuli consisting of arrays of 16 icons drawn from one of two sets of icons, *a* and *b*. *Same* arrays always contain 16 identical *a* icons, whereas *different* arrays always contain different arrangements of the 16 unique *b* icons. When pigeons are tested with novel arrays with icons from set *c*, they behave based on the relations within the array, but when shown *different* arrays containing *a* icons, the pigeons are more likely to respond *same*, and vice versa for *same* arrays formed with *b* icons. The pigeons learn to respond to the novel relations, but their responses are still tied to the features of the exemplars used in training.

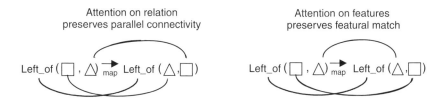

Fig. 4.5 An example comparison between two graphs is shown. There are two possible ways to map the elements in these corresponding relations. The example on the left preserves parallel connectivity by mapping elements that play the same role in each relation to one another. This solution is high in relational match, but low in featural match because the corresponding elements differ in shape features. The situation is reversed in the mapping shown in the right example. Attention weighting of mismatches determines which of these two possible mappings will be preferred by BRIDGES. BRIDGES chooses the mapping that minimizes attention-weighted mismatch.

These simulations provide insight into the differences among animals, infants, children, and adults. For the simulations just described, the exemplars were only represented with simple features and a type–token relationship. The type–token relationship assumes that the individual is able to recognize objects present in the input as members of the same type. In other words, when pigeons are presented with an array of shapes, they realize that all of the squares are members of an abstract type, square. This assumption is sufficient for an array of simple relational learning tasks. However, when modelling more complex behaviour, in children or adults, a more complex representation is often required. BRIDGES provides a tool to talk about these and other differences in a quantitative way.

Animals might not be able to succeed at complex relational reasoning tasks, but they can compare current examples to previous examples in a structured way, and from this respond in a manner consistent with an understanding of abstract relations. BRIDGES is a computational model of how this relation-like behaviour can be learned. By comparing concrete examples of the relations in a structured manner, one can learn to respond in a manner consistent with the relations, without true abstract knowledge. BRIDGES extends this core idea of exemplar models that all abstraction occurs as a result of online processing to relational categorization. BRIDGES's account serves to highlight the transparency and clarity of exemplar-based explanations.

Hybrid models

Prototype and exemplar models can be seen as opposite ends of a continuum of category representation. At one extreme, prototype models store every category member together in memory. At the other extreme, exemplar models store every category member separately in memory. Between these two extremes lie a wealth of possibilities. Categories in the real world contain multiple subtypes and exceptions. For example, the category mammals contains subcategories like cats, dogs, horses, and bats. Ideally, our mental representations would reflect this structure. Both prototype and exemplar models are inflexible in that they treat the structure of each category as predetermined. These models do not let the distribution of category members influence the form category representations take. For example, prototype models assume that categories are always represented by one node (i.e. the prototype) in memory, whereas exemplar models assume that categories are always represented by one node in memory for every category example encountered.

One reasonable intuition is that similar items should cluster together in memory (Anderson, 1991; Love et al., 2004; Vanpaemel & Storms, 2008). For example, a person walking down Congress Avenue in Austin in the fall will encounter thousands of seemingly identical grackles. The rationale for storing each of these birds separately in memory is unclear. At the same time, someone walking down the street probably would mentally note unusual or otherwise surprising birds.

Hybrid models embody these intuitions about memory. For example, Anderson's (1991) rational model computes the probability that an item belongs to an existing cluster (a prototype can be thought of as a cluster that encodes all category members). If this probability is sufficiently high, the cluster is updated to reflect its new member.

However, if the item is more likely from a new cluster, then a new cluster is created. The overarching goal of Anderson's model is to create clusters that are maximally predictive.

Love et al.'s SUSTAIN model operates along similar lines in that it incrementally adds clusters as it learns, but its recruitment process is somewhat different from that of the the rational model. SUSTAIN recruits new clusters in response to surprising events. What counts as a surprising event depends on the learner's current goals. When the learner's goals are somewhat diffuse as in unsupervised learning, SUSTAIN's operation is very similar to that of the rational model. In such cases, items that are dissimilar from existing clusters result in a new cluster being recruited to encode the item. However, in supervised learning situations, such as in classification learning (the learner's goal is to properly name the stimulus's category), items are recruited when a surprising error results. For example, upon encountering a bat for the first time and being asked to name it, a child surprised to learn that a bat is not a bird would recruit a new cluster to capture this example. If the child activates this cluster in the future to successfully classify other bats, then the cluster would come to resemble a bat prototype.

Both the rational model and SUSTAIN can be viewed as multiple prototype models in which the number of prototypes is determined by the complexity of the category structure. When categories are very regular, these models will function like prototype models. When categories are very irregular (i.e. there is no discernable pattern linking members to one another), these models will tend to function like exemplar models. SUSTAIN's sensitivity to a learner's goal allows it to capture performance differences across different induction tasks. For example, people learning through inference (e.g. *This is a mammal. Does it have fur?*) tend to focus on the internal structure of categories, whereas people learning through classification (e.g. *This has fur. Is it a mammal?*) tend to focus on information that discriminates between categories (see Markman & Ross, 2003, for a review).

Hybrid models, like exemplar and prototype models, can be coupled with selective-attention mechanisms that can learn to emphasize critical-stimulus properties. For example, in learning to classify car makes, SUSTAIN would learn to weight shape more than colour because shape reliably indicates model-type whereas colour varies idiosyncratically. The motivation for selective attention comes from the observation that people can only process a limited number of stimulus properties simultaneously. Selective-attention mechanisms have been developed through consideration of human and animal learning data (see Kruscke, 2003, for a review). In tasks that require people to actively sample stimulus dimensions, selective-attention mechanisms predict which dimensions are fixated (Rehder & Hoffman, 2005).

Importantly, selective-attention mechanisms allow non-rule models to display rule-like behaviours (see Chapter 3 in this book). When a prototype, exemplar, or hybrid model places all of its attention on one stimulus dimension, a model's operation is indistinguishable from the application of a simple rule. In terms of accounting for human data, SUSTAIN outperforms RULEX in some respects on learning problems that require acquiring a simple rule and storing exceptions to these rules (Sakamoto & Love, 2004). SUSTAIN creates a small set of clusters that encode items that follow the rules and stores exception in their own clusters. Attention is heavily biased to the rule-relevant dimensions. This allows SUSTAIN to show enhanced recognition for exceptions and rule-like behaviour for rule-following items, while maintaining some sensitivity to non-rule relevant dimensions like human subjects do. In our review of exemplar models, we discussed how selective-attention mechanisms allow BRIDGES to achieve similar ends in terms of balancing the importance of featural and relational match.

The incorporation of selective-attention mechanisms into non-rule models invites a number of theoretical questions. It is not entirely clear whether these selective-attention mechanisms should be viewed as an integral part of non-rule models or as rule mechanisms grafted onto non-rule models. One possibility is that people are relying on rule and non-rule systems, thus necessitating the need for selective-attention mechanisms in non-rule models.

Multiple systems models

Determining the best psychological model can be difficult as one model may perform well in one situation but be bested by a competing model in a different situation. One possibility is that there is not a single *true* model. In category learning, this line of reasoning has led to the development of models containing multiple learning systems. These more complex models hold that category learning behaviour reflects the contributions of different systems organized around discrepant principles that utilize qualitatively distinct representations. The idea that multiple learning systems support category learning behaviour enjoys widespread support in the cognitive neuroscience of category learning (see Ashby and O'Brien, 2005, for a review and Nosofsky and Zaki, 1998, for a dissenting opinion).

Multiple system models of category learning detail the relative contributions of the component learning systems. Some multiple system models combine the outputs of the individual systems together (Ashby et al., 1998). Over time, one system might prove more useful and dominate responding. Alternatively, the modeller can predetermine the timing of the shift from one system to another. This is sensible in cases where there is good evidence for predictable shifts, such as the shift from rule-based to exemplar-based responding in classification learning (Johansen & Palmeri, 2002).

Both of these multiple system approaches are somewhat inadequate in that they do not allow the current situation to dictate which system is operable. For example, when trying to learn how to operate a new piece of machinery, a person might use a hypothesis (i.e. rule) system, but when riding a bicycle, a more procedural system might govern responding and be updated. In some models, like ATRIUM (Erickson & Kruschke, 1998), the relative contributions of divergent systems can depend on the circumstances (cf. Yang & Lewandowsky, 2004). ATRIUM contains a rule and exemplar learning system. Which system is operable is determined by a gating system, allowing different classification procedures to be applied to different parts of the stimulus space. For example, familiar items could be classified by the exemplar system whereas rules could be applied to unfamiliar items. The power to apply qualitatively different procedures to different stimuli is the hallmark of multiple systems models.

Somewhat muddying the waters, ostensibly single-system models have been developed that also manifest this ability. In CLUSTER (Love & Jones, 2006), clusters can tune themselves (i.e. attend) to different stimulus properties and encode concepts at various levels of granularity. This allows CLUSTER to apply different procedures to different parts of the stimulus space, like ATRIUM does. For example, clusters would heavily weight colour in the domain of clothing and processor type in the domain of laptops. This tuning is accomplished by minimizing an error term that reflects the model's predictive accuracy, a technique commonly used in connectionist modelling. Tunable parameters that encode each cluster's specificity and attentional weighting of different properties are shaped by experience.

Models like CLUSTER are very rich. Consideration of such models leads to the question of what constitutes or defines a system. As previously discussed, one could even construe the selective-attention mechanism of various models as being a separate system. Fortunately, models are mathematically well specified and allow researchers to make predictions and state their theories clearly without having to be overly concerned with the semantics of what constitutes a system. The mathematical specification of models can free researchers from some potentially thorny debates.

The notion of a system perhaps takes on greater significance when considered in the context of the brain (see Chapter 5 in this book). Within cognitive neuroscience, it is generally accepted that there is a hypothesis testing system that relies on frontal circuity (Ashby et al., 1998), a dopamine-mediated procedural learning system that involves the striatum (Ashby et al., 1998), a repetition priming system that involves early visual areas (Reber et al., 2003), and a hippocampal learning system that maps onto exemplar- or cluster-based learning (Love & Gureckis, 2007). For each system, there are behavioural manipulations that tend to emphasize the system over the other systems. Lesion, patient, and imaging studies provide compelling evidence for the multiple systems view.

General discussion

In this chapter, we reviewed the relative merits of a variety of category learning models, including rule-, prototype-, and exemplar-based models, as well as hybrid models and multiple system models that combine two or more of the aforementioned model types. We also considered how inclusion of selective-attention mechanisms can increase the capabilities of these models by endowing them with the ability to manifest rule-following behaviour.

To review briefly each model family's merits, rule-based models conform to our intuition that we effortfully search for patterns that we can verbally communicate to others. In contrast to rule models, prototype models successfully reflect the graded nature of category membership. Exemplar models address deficiencies in the prototype model and can account for the learning of categories that have a nonlinear structure, such as those containing subcategories. Exemplar models also capture aspects of recognition memory performance. Hybrid models successfully transition between prototype- and exemplar-like representations depending on the complexity of the category structure. Finally, multiple system models align with emerging findings from cognitive neuroscience and intuitions that there are multiple paths or mechanisms available to categorize stimuli.

All of these models have played a critical role in driving advances in theory and in the design of key experiments. The development of new models is informed by the failings of preceding models. The history of model development is marked by the arrival of models with increasingly sophisticated processing mechanisms that can manifest the behaviours of previous models as well as additional human behaviours beyond the reach of existing models. Of course, the value in models lie more in predicting unanticipated behaviours than in simply accounting for observed behaviours. Thus, it is important for models to be somewhat constrained to have theoretical value.

We would like to end by encouraging researchers to consider conducting model-directed research. All experimenters are driven by theoretical considerations and models are ideally suited to bring these issues into focus and unite seemingly discrepant findings. In the exemplar-based model section, we described how a relatively simple model brought together powerful ideas from the analogy and category learning literatures to address learning across species and development. These kinds of advances and connections can be facilitated through model-driven explorations.

To return to one of the main themes of this book, the work reviewed in this chapter largely supports the notion that cognition is continuous across development and species. The basic mechanisms discussed in this chapter appear to apply equally well across species and development. For example, the SUSTAIN model of category learning has been successfully applied to infants and older adults (Love & Gureckis, 2007). In fact, for certain tasks, data collected from 10-month-old infants and young adults are successfully fit with the same parameter values (Gureckis & Love, 2004). Likewise, in situations where one looks at performance across species, one will likely find evidence for common representations and processes. In our discussion of BRIDGES, the same exemplar-based relational learning mechanism captures performance data from pigeons, human infants, and adults.

Does this mean there are no differences in learning across development and species? In our opinion, the answer to this question is clearly no. The convergence we observe is likely a function of the task domain. The tasks considered here can all be modelled as a process of activating past experiences in memory (represented as exemplars or clusters). It may well be that differences in such tasks are minimal across development and species. Even for this family of tasks, differences can be observed across species, particularly for cases in which task factors emphasize strategic or attentional processes, which likely rely on prefrontal regions of the brain that are most prominent in adult humans (Smith et al., 2004). In such cases, models like SUSTAIN and BRIDGES can still prove useful in quantifying differences between populations in terms of best-fitting attentional parameters. Finally, it may very well be that we underestimate the extent to which our behaviours are governed by memory-based processes. As the work reviewed in this chapter indicates, such processes can support a variety of behaviours, especially when the learning and retrieval processes are sensitive to relational match (Tomlinson & Love, 2008).

References

Allen, S. W. & Brooks, L. R. (1991). Specializing the operation of an explicit rule. *Journal of Experimental Psychology: General*, **120**, 3–19.

Anderson, J. (1991). The adaptive nature of human categorization. *Psychological Review*, **98**, 409–429.

Ashby, F. & O'Brien, J. B. (2005). Category learning and multiple memory systems. *Trends in Cognitive Sciences*, **9**, 83–89.

Ashby, F., Alfonso-Reese, L., Turken, A., & Waldron, E. (1998). A neuropsychological theory of multiple-systems in category learning. *Psychological Review*, **105**, 442–481.

Barsalou, L. W. (1985). Ideals, central tendency, and frequency of instantiation as determinants of graded structure of categories. *Journal of Experimental Psychology: Learning, Memory, & Cognition*, **11**, 629–654.

Bruner, J. S., Goodnow, J. J., & Austin, G. A. (1956). *A Study of Thinking* New York: Wiley.

Chi, M., Feltovich, P., & Glaser, R. (1981). Categorization and representation of physics problems by experts and novices. *Cognitive Science*, **5**, 121–152.

Erickson, M. A. & Kruschke, J. K. (1998). Rules and exemplars in category learning. *Journal of Experimental Psychology: General*, **127**, 107–140.

Feldman, J. (2000). Minimization of Boolean complexity in human concept learning. *Nature*, **407**, 630–633.

Gentner, D. (1983). Structure-mapping: A theoretical framework for analogy. *Cognitive Science*, **7**, 155–170.

Gentner, D. & Ratterman, M. J. (1991). Language and the career of similarity. In S. A. Gelman & J. P. Byrnes (Eds.), *Perspectives on Thought and Language: Interrelations in Development*, pp. 225–277, London: Cambridge University Press.

Gibson, B. M. & Wasserman, E. A. (2004). Time-course of control by specific stimulus features and relational cues during same-different discrimination training. *Learning and Behavior*, **32**, 183–189.

Gleitman, L. R., Gleitman, H., Miller, C., & Ostrin, R. (1996). Similar, and similar concepts. *Cognition*, **58**, 321–376.

Gluck, M. A. & Bower, G. H. (1988). From conditioning to category learning: An adaptive network model. *Journal of Experimental Psychology: General*, **117**, 225–244.

Gureckis, T. & Love, B. C. (2004). Common mechanisms in infant and adult category learning. *Infancy*, **5**, 173–198.

Hahn, U. & Ramscar, M. (2001). Conclusion: Mere similarity? In U. Hahn & M. Ramscar (Eds.), *Similarity and Categorization*, pp. 257–272, New York: Oxford University Press.

Hampton, J. A. (2001). The role of similarity in natural categorization. In U. Hahn & M. Ramscar (Eds), *Similarity and Categorization*, pp. 13–28, New York: Oxford University Press.

Johansen, M. K. & Palmeri, T. J. (2002). Are there representational shifts during category learning? *Cognitive Psychology*, **45**, 482–553.

Jones, M. & Love, B. C. (2007). Beyond common features: The role of roles in determining similarity. *Cognitive Psychology*, **55**, 196–231.

Kruschke, J. K. (1992). ALCOVE: An exemplar-based connectionist model of category learning. *Psychological Review*, **99**, 22–44.

Kruschke, J. K. (1996). Base rates in category learning. *Journal of Experimental Psychology: Learning, Memory, & Cognition*, 22, 3–26.

Kruschke, J. K. (2003). Attention in learning. *Current Directions in Psychological Science*, 12, 171–175.

Lacroix, G. L., Giguere, G., & Larochelle, S. (2005). The orgin of exemplar effects in rule-driven categorization. *Journal of Experimental Psychology: Learning, Memory, & Cognition*, 31, 272–288.

Lakoff, G. (1987). *Women, Fire, and Dangerous Things: What Categories Reveal about the Mind* Chicago, IL: University of Chicago Press.

Love, B. C. (2002). Comparing supervised and unsupervised category learning. *Psychonomic Bulletin & Review*, 9, 829–835.

Love, B. C. & Gureckis, T. M. (2007). Models in search of a brain. *Cognitive, Affective, & Behavioral Neuroscience*, 7, 90–108.

Love, B. C. & Jones, M. (2006). The emergence of multiple learning systems. *Proceedings of the 28th Cognitive Science Society*, pp. 507–512, Mahwah, NJ: Erlbaum.

Love, B. C., Medin, D. L., & Gureckis, T. (2004). SUSTAIN: A network model of human category learning. *Psychological Review*, 111, 309–332.

Love, B. C., Tomlinson, M., & Gureckis, T. (2008). The concrete substrates of abstract rule use. *The Psychology of Learning and Motivation: Advances in Research and Theory*, 49, 167–207.

Maddox, W. T. & Ashby, F. G. (1993). Comparing decision bound and exemplar models of categorization. *Perception & Psychophysics*, 53, 49–70.

Marcus, G. F., Vijayan, S., Bandi Rao, S., & Vishton, V. (1999). Rule learning by seven-month-old infants. *Science*, 283(5298), 77–80.

Markman, A. B. & Gentner, D. (1993). Structural alignment during similarity comparisons. *Cognitive Psychology*, 23, 431–467.

Markman, A. B. & Ross, B. H. (2003). Category use and category learning. *Psychological Bulletin*, 129, 592–613.

Markman, A. B. & Stilwell, C. H. (2001). Role-governed categories. *Journal of Experimental and Theoretical Artificial Intelligence*, 13, 329–358.

Marr, D. (1982). *Vision* San Francisco, CA: W. H. Freeman.

Medin, D. L. & Schaffer, M. M. (1978). Context theory of classification learning. *Psychological Review*, 85, 207–238.

Medin, D. L. & Schwanenflugel, P. J. (1981). Linear separability in classification learning. *Journal of Experimental Psychology: Human Learning & Memory*, 7, 355–368.

Murphy, G. L. (2002). *The Big Book of Concepts* Cambridge, MA: MIT Press.

Nosofsky, R. M. (1986). Attention, similarity, and the identification–categorization relationship. *Journal of Experimental Psychology: General*, 115, 39–57.

Nosofsky, R. M. & Palmeri, T. J. (1997). An exemplar-based random walk model of speeded classification. *Psychological Review*, 104, 266–300.

Nosofsky, R. M. & Zaki, S. F. (1998). Dissociations between categorization and recognition in amnesic and normal individuals. *Psychological Science*, 9, 247–255.

Nosofsky, R. M. & Zaki, S. F. (2002). Exemplar and prototype models revisited: Response strategies, selective attention, and stimulus generalization. *Journal of Experimental Psychology: Learning, Memory, & Cognition*, 28, 924–940.

Nosofsky, R. M., Palmeri, T. J., & McKinley, S. C. (1994). Rule-plus-exception model of classification learning. *Psychological Review*, 101(1), 53–79.

Palmeri, T. J. & Nosofsky, R. M. (1995). Recognition memory for exceptions to the category rule. *Journal of Experimental Psychology: Learning, Memory, & Cognition*, 21, 548–568.

Posner, M. I. & Keele, S. W. (1968). On the genesis of abstract ideas. *Journal of Experimental Psychology*, 77, 241–248.

Pothos, E. M. & Chater, N. (2002). A simplicity principle in unsupervised human categorization. *Cognitive Science*, 26, 303–343.

Reber, P. J., Gitelman, D. R., Parrish, T. B., & Mesulam, M. M. (2003). Dissociating explicit and implicit category knowledge with fMRI. *Journal of Cognitive Neuroscience*, 15(4), 574–583.

Reed, S. (1972). Pattern recognition and categorization. *Cognitive Psychology*, 3, 382–407.

Rehder, B. & Hoffman, A. B. (2005). Eyetracking and selective attention in category learning. *Cognitive Psychology*, 51, 1–41.

Rodrigues, P. M. & Murre, J. M. J. (2007). Rules-plus-exception tasks: A problem for exemplar models? *Psychonomic Bulletin & Review*, 14, 640–646.

Rosch, E. & Mervis, C. B. (1975). Family resemblences: Studies in the internal structure of categories. *Cognitive Psychology*, 7, 573–605.

Sakamoto, Y. & Love, B. C. (2004). Schematic influences on category learning and recognition memory. *Journal of Experimental Psychology: General*, 33, 534–553.

Sakamoto, Y. & Love, B. C. (2006). Vancouver, Toronto, Montreal, Austin: Enhanced oddball memory through differentiation, not isolation. *Psychonomic Bulletin & Review*, 13, 474–479.

Sakamoto, Y., Matuska, T., & Love, B.C. (2004). Proceedings of the international conference of cognitive modeling. In M. Lovett, C. Schunn, C. Lebiere, & P. Munro (Eds.), *Dimensionwide vs. Exemplar-Specific Attention in Category Learning and Recognition* Vol. 27, pp. 261–266, Mahwah, NJ: Lawrence Erlbaum.

Shepard, R. N., Hovland, C. L., & Jenkins, H. M. (1961). Learning and memorization of classifications. *Psychological Monographs*, 75 (13, Whole No. 517).

Smith, J. (2002). Exemplar theory's predicted typicality gradient can be tested and disconfirmed. *Psychological Science*, 13, 437–442.

Smith, J. D. & Minda, J. P. (2001). Journey to the center of the category: The dissociation in amnesia between categorization and recognition. *Journal of Experimental Psychology: Learning, Memory, & Cognition*, 27, 984–1002.

Smith, J. D., Minda, J. P., & Washburn, D. A. (2004). Category learning in rhesus monkeys: A study of the Shepard, Hovland, and Jenkins tasks. *Journal of Experimental Psychology: General*, 133, 398–414.

Thompson, R. K. R. & Oden, D. L. (2000). Categorical perception and conceptual judgements by nonhuman primates: The paleological monkey and the analogical ape. *Cognitive Science*, 24(3), 363–396.

Tomlinson, M. & Love, B. C. (2006). From pigeons to humans: Grounding relational learning in concrete examples. In Y. Gil & R. J. Mooney (Eds.), *Proceedings of the 21st National Conference on Artificial Intelligence* (AAAI-2006), pp. 199–204, AAAI Press.

Tomlinson, M. & Love, B. C. (2008). Monkey see, monkey do: Learning relations through concrete examples. *Behavioral and Brain Sciences*, 31, 150–151.

Vanpaemel, W. & Storms, G. (2008). In search of abstraction: The varying abstraction model of categorization. *Psychonomic Bulletin & Review*, 10, 29–43.

Wittgenstein, L. (1953). *Philosophical Investigations* Oxford: Blackwell. (G. E. M. Anscombe, trans.)

Yang, L. X. & Lewandowsky, S. (2004). Context-gated knowledge partitioning in categorization. *Journal of Experimental Psychology: Learning, Memory, & Cognition*, **30**, 1045–1064.

Young, M. E., Ellefson, M. R., & Wasserman, E. A. (2003). Toward a theory of variability discrimination: Finding differences. *Behavioral Processes*, **62**, 145–155.

Young, M. E. & Wasserman, E. A. (1997). Entropy detection by pigeons: Response to mixed visual displays after same-different discrimination training. *Journal of Experimental Psychology: Animal Behavior Processes*, **23**, 157–170.

Chapter 5

The neurobiology of categorization

F. Gregory Ashby and Matthew J. Crossley

Editors' Preview

Chapter 5, 'The neurobiology of categorization', provides a review of what is known about the neural bases for categorization. A major theme of the chapter is that categories characterized by different kinds of structures may enlist different types of learning and memory processes that in turn rely on different brain circuitry. For example, as noted in Chapters 2, 3, and 4, human adults possess the ability to rapidly learn rule-based categories in which the rule splitting the categories is explicit, verbalizable, accessible to conscious awareness (e.g. red things go into group *A*, green things go into group *B*), and believed to be stored in a declarative form of memory that enables recall of facts and events.

Human adults also learn categories that require an integration of information that is not readily verbalizable, may be slowly acquired, and may be stored in a nondeclarative procedural memory system. Figure 5.1 provides an example of categories that can be learned through an integration of information about the orientation and thickness of the bars within the circular discs on each side of the boundary. Examples of real-world categories learned through processes of information integration include determining whether X-rays provide evidence of cancerous tumours and (as was referenced in Chapter 2) determining whether day-old chicks are male or female.

Various lines of evidence acquired with different investigative techniques within cognitive neuroscience suggest that categories acquired through explicit rule learning versus information integration may be processed through two distinct brain pathways. The evidence includes studies of single-unit recording in animals (an electrode is used to register the activity of an individual neuron as an animal is performing a categorization task), brain stimulation (a brain region is directly stimulated with electric current as an animal learns a categorization task), lesion studies (a brain region of an animal is damaged to determine what effect that has on categorization performance), functional magnetic resonance imaging or fMRI (allowing one to determine which parts of the brain are active during a categorization task by tracking which brain regions are using the most oxygen), and individuals who have suffered brain damage (either through stroke, injury, or disease processes, to determine what effect the damage has on categorization abilities).

Evidence suggests that highly practised category judgements are mediated by a third brain pathway that is qualitatively distinct from both the rule-based and information-integration brain pathways that dominate early category learning. This notion is consistent with the idea that over time and with practice, categories that are initially slowly acquired can become more rapidly accessed in an automatic way. More plainly, the idea is that one can distinguish at both cognitive and neural levels between processes of category formation on the one hand, and category possession on the other hand.

The suggested scheme for the neurobiology of categorization has both phylogenetic and ontogenetic implications that are relevant to the major themes of the book. As is observed by the authors of this chapter, comparatively, one can examine particular differences in brain structures for humans and nonhuman animals that are believed to mediate categorization performance to make specific behavioural predictions for how performance should vary across species. In addition, developmentally, one can examine how early in infancy or childhood the two systems become functional and whether one system might emerge subsequently to the other.

Categorization is the act of responding differently to objects or events in separate classes or categories. It is a vitally important skill that allows us to approach friends and escape foes, to find food, and avoid toxins. The scientific study of categorization has a long history. For most of this time, the focus was on the cognitive processes that mediate categorization. Within the past decade, however, considerable attention has shifted to the study of the neural basis of categorization. This chapter reviews that work.

There is recent evidence that highly practised categorization judgements are mediated by neural pathways different from those that mediate initial category learning; so our review discusses category learning and automatic categorization judgements separately. We begin in the next section with a brief overview of the basal ganglia, which are a collection of subcortical nuclei that are especially important in categorization. Next, we focus on initial category learning. We then consider the neural basis of automatic categorization judgements. Finally, we close with some general comments and conclusions.

The basal ganglia

Many brain areas are thought to participate in category learning, including the pre-frontal cortex (PFC), the hippocampus and other medial temporal lobe structures, the anterior cingulate, and the basal ganglia. The basal ganglia seem especially important. For example, they are one of the few areas that have been identified in virtually every cognitive or behavioural neuroscience study of category learning (for a review, see Ashby & Ennis, 2006). As they play such a prominent role in the cognitive neuroscience literature on categorization, this section briefly reviews basal ganglia neuroanatomy and some key evidence implicating the striatum in category learning.

The basal ganglia are a collection of subcortical brain regions that can be divided into input structures, output structures, and collections of cells that produce the neurotransmitter dopamine. The input structures include the caudate nucleus and putamen (and other regions), which together are often referred to as the dorsal stria-tum or just the striatum. The striatum receives inputs from almost all of the cortex, and these cortical–striatal projections are characterized by massive convergence (Kincaid et al., 1998). Roughly speaking, the putamen receives input from parietal and motor areas, and the caudate receives input from visual and auditory association areas and from frontal cortex (e.g. Heimer, 1995). The anterior region of the caudate, often called the head of the caudate, is reciprocally connected to the PFC and so is often implicated in executive function tasks. The posterior (or caudal) caudate, often called the tail of the caudate, receives input from the visual association cortex (the body of the caudate is the region between the head and tail). Thus, the striatum is in a unique position in the mammalian brain since it receives direct, but highly com-pressed input from virtually the entire cortex.

Compared to cortex, the structure of the striatum is extremely simple. It contains a single layer composed predominantly of medium spiny cells. The dendrites of these cells receive input from the axons of around 15 000 cortical pyramidal cells and the medium spiny cell axons project out of the striatum to basal ganglia output structures, such as the globus pallidus. The medium spiny cells are GABAergic, and hence inhib-itory, with a low spontaneous firing rate. The cells in the globus pallidus, which are also GABAergic, project to the thalamus, which in turn, sends excitatory projections to cortex. Spontaneous activity in the globus pallidus is high (e.g. Wilson, 1995), so the globus pallidus tonically inhibits the thalamus. Cortical activation of the striatum however, causes the medium spiny cells to inhibit the pallidal cells, thereby releasing the thalamus from its tonic inhibition. Due to this functional architecture, the basal ganglia are frequently described as applying a brake on cortex because they tonically prevent the thalamus from stimulating cortex. Cortex can release the brake by stimu-lating the striatum.

Another feature of the striatum that likely contributes to the important role that it plays in category learning is that cortical–striatal synapses display an unusual form of synaptic plasticity that is ideally suited to feedback-dependent learning. In fact, the conditions required to change the efficacy of cortical–striatal synapses (i.e. to induce long-term potentiation and long-term depression) closely match the conditions for reinforcement learning (Sutton & Barto, 1998). Specifically, the best available evidence suggests that cortical–striatal synapses that were active on rewarded trials are strengthened and synapses that were active on trials that do not produce reward are weakened. The key is the neurotransmitter dopamine, which is released into the striatum from the substantia nigra pars compacta. Many studies have shown that dopamine release increases above baseline following unexpected reward, and it falls below baseline following unexpected absence of reward (e.g. Schultz et al., 1997). Many researchers have proposed that dopamine serves as the reinforcement signal in striatal-based reinforcement learning (e.g. Ashby et al., 2007; Houk et al., 1995; Wickens, 1993).

The earliest proposals that the striatum may be an important locus of category learning (Ashby et al., 1998) were motivated by a long series of lesion studies in rats and monkeys supporting the hypothesis that the striatum is both necessary *and* sufficient for visual discrimination learning. Technically, a discrimination task is a special case of categorization in which each category contains only one exemplar.

Many studies have shown that lesions of the striatum impair the ability of animals to learn visual discriminations that require one response to one stimulus and a different response to some other stimulus (e.g. McDonald & White, 1993; Packard & McGaugh, 1992). For example, in one study, rats with striatal lesions could not learn to discriminate between safe and unsafe platforms in the Morris water maze when the safe platform was marked with horizontal lines and the unsafe platform was marked with vertical lines (Packard & McGaugh, 1992). The same animals learned normally, however, when the cues signalling which platform was safe were spatial. Since the visual cortex is intact in these animals, it is unlikely that their difficulty is in perceiving the stimuli. Rather, it appears that their difficulty is in learning to associate an appropriate response with each stimulus alternative, and in fact, many researchers have hypothesized that this is the primary role of the striatum (e.g. Ashby et al., 2007; Wickens, 1993).

More recent single-unit recording studies confirm the striatal contribution to categorization. In a series of studies, monkeys were taught to classify a tactile stimulus (i.e. a rod dragged across the monkey's finger) as either 'low speed' or 'high speed' (e.g. Merchant et al., 1997). A large number of cells in the putamen showed learning-related changes in their firing properties. For example, after training, many cells fired to any movement in the low-speed category, but not to movements in the high-speed category (or vice versa). These same neurons were not active during passive experience with the stimuli or during a control motor task. Furthermore, the activity of these neurons predicted the behaviour of the monkeys.

There are several prominent basal ganglia diseases that have played an important role in attempts to understand the role of the basal ganglia in categorization. The most theoretically important of these are Parkinson's disease and Huntington's disease. In Parkinson's disease, the dopamine cells die and this depletes the striatum of the key neurotransmitter that mediates cortical–striatal plasticity. In Huntington's disease, the medium spiny cells in the striatum die.

The neurobiology of category learning

There is now overwhelming evidence that humans have multiple category-learning systems. By definition, learning requires some change in the brain that persists beyond the training event. If this change is defined as a memory trace, then it seems plausible that all major memory systems should be capable of some form of category learning (Ashby & O'Brien, 2005). Different memory systems have different properties, and each is ideally suited to a certain type of learning. In fact, we review considerable evidence that the different systems are ideally suited to learning about different types of category structures. There is evidence that changing the category structure can induce a switch from one system to another, and as a result, can cause the resulting data to differ in a qualitative manner. When reviewing the category-learning literature, it is therefore critical that we pay particular attention to which memory system is best suited to learning the type of category structures used in the research.

Declarative memory systems

Declarative memories are those accessible to conscious awareness (Eichenbaum, 1997). This includes working memory and episodic/semantic memory. Working memory is the ability to maintain and manipulate limited amounts of information during brief periods of cognitive activity (Baddeley, 1986). It is heavily used in explicit reasoning and problem-solving tasks, and more generally in any task said to depend on executive function. A huge literature is devoted to the neural basis of working memory (see, e.g. Fuster, 1989). Suffice it to say that there is overwhelming evidence linking working memory to the PFC. However, there is also evidence that the head of the caudate nucleus is critical in working-memory tasks (Hikosaka et al., 1989; Schultz & Romo, 1992), and a variety of models have been proposed that assume working memory is mediated, at least in part, by cortical–striatal loops (e.g. Ashby et al., 2005; Frank et al., 2001; Monchi et al., 2000).

Episodic and semantic memories are known to depend on the hippocampus and other medial temporal lobe structures (e.g. Squire & Schacter, 2002; Tulving, 2002). For example, medial temporal lobe damage often causes anterograde amnesia – that is, deficits on tests that depend on recent declarative memories.

As working memory is effective only for short time periods, it cannot store long-term category knowledge, but it could be the primary learning system in tasks where the categories are learned quickly. However, even in this case, episodic and semantic memory systems would presumably be required to consolidate this learning, so one would likely expect the different declarative systems to work together during category learning.

Declarative memory systems might mediate learning in any categorization task in which subjects are consciously aware of their categorization strategy. Obvious possibilities include tasks in which subjects formulate and test explicit hypotheses about category membership or explicitly memorize the category labels associated with each stimulus.

Tasks that encourage explicit hypothesis testing

In *rule-based category-learning tasks,* the categories can be learned via an explicit hypothesis-testing procedure (although, of course, they could also be learned in other ways). In most cases the rule that maximizes accuracy is easy to describe verbally (Ashby et al., 1998). In the simplest examples, only one stimulus dimension is relevant, and the subject's task is to discover this dimension and then to map the different dimensional values to the relevant categories. More difficult rule-based tasks require attention to two or more dimensions. For example, the correct rule might be a conjunction of the type: 'the stimulus is in category A if it is large and bright'. The key requirement is that the correct categorization rule in rule-based tasks is one that can be discovered by an explicit hypothesis-testing procedure. Virtually all category-learning tasks used in neuropsychological assessment are rule based, including the widely known Wisconsin card sorting test (WCST) (Heaton, 1981). Stimuli in this task are cards containing geometric patterns that vary in colour, shape, and symbol number, and in all cases the correct categorization rule is one dimensional and easy to describe verbally.

Many researchers have proposed that people generate and test explicit hypotheses about category membership in rule-based tasks (e.g. Ashby et al., 1998; Erickson & Kruschke, 1998; Nosofsky et al., 1994), and Ashby and O'Brien (2005) argued that rule-based learning is mediated primarily by declarative memory systems. The idea is that working memory is used to store hypotheses about category membership during their testing, and episodic/semantic memory systems are used for the long-term storage and consolidation of these rules. A wide variety of evidence supports this hypothesis. For example, several studies have reported that a dual task requiring working memory and executive attention has massive detrimental effects on rule-based category learning, but little or no effect on the ability of subjects to learn other types of category structures (i.e. information-integration categories; DeCaro et al., 2008; Waldron & Ashby, 2001; Zeithamova & Maddox, 2006).

The only neurobiologically detailed model of category learning, called COVIS (COmpetition between Verbal and Implicit Systems), assumes that humans have separate hypothesis-testing and procedural-learning systems (Ashby et al., 1998; Ashby & Valentin, 2005; Ashby & Waldron, 1999). COVIS assumes that learning in rule-based tasks is dominated by an explicit, hypothesis-testing system that uses working memory and executive attention and is mediated primarily by the anterior cingulate, the PFC, the hippocampus, and the head of the caudate nucleus. There are two main subnetworks in this model: one that generates or selects new candidate hypotheses, and one that maintains candidate rules in working memory during the testing process and mediates the switch from one rule to another. The COVIS hypothesis-testing system is similar to the neural network models of the WCST that were proposed by Monchi et al. (2001) and Amos (2000).

COVIS and the cognitive neuroscience literature on working memory predict that the PFC and the head of the caudate nucleus should be active in rule-based tasks. A wide variety of evidence supports this prediction. First, impaired performance on the WCST is among the most classic of all signs of PFC damage (e.g. Kimberg et al., 1997). Second, many animal-lesion studies have confirmed the important role played by the PFC in rule learning and use (for a review, see Roberts & Wallis, 2000). For example, Joel et al. (1997) reported that lesions to the medial PFC in rats impaired the animals on a simplified version of the WCST. Third, a number of neuroimaging studies have used the WCST or a rule-based task similar to the WCST, and all of these have reported task-related activation in the PFC (e.g. Konishi et al., 1999; Monchi et al., 2001; Rogers et al., 2000).

There is also strong evidence that the striatum is critical to rule-based category learning. First, there are many reports that Parkinson's disease patients are impaired in rule-based tasks (e.g. Ashby et al., 2003a; Brown & Marsden, 1988; Cools et al., 1984). Although later in the disease Parkinson's patients have frontal damage (primarily the result of cell death in the ventral tegmental area), the disease mainly targets the basal ganglia. The caudate region most affected appears to be the head of the caudate nucleus (van Domburg & ten Donkelaar, 1991), which is reciprocally connected to the PFC. Second, a number of functional neuroimaging studies of the WCST have reported task-related activation in the head of the caudate nucleus (e.g. Monchi et al., 2001; Rogers et al., 2000).

Explicit hypothesis testing requires working memory, but it also requires a number of other executive processes, including executive attention, rule selection, rule representation, and rule switching. Many studies have focused on the neural basis of one or more these processes.

There is a large literature on executive attention, which we do not review here. However, one relevant proposal is that executive attention is mediated in part by the PFC and anterior cingulate (Posner & Petersen, 1990). The (dorsal) anterior cingulate was also identified as a site of hypothesis generation in rule-based category learning (Elliott et al., 1999).

Important evidence about the neural representation of rules was obtained in a series of single-unit recording studies in which monkeys were taught to classify objects by applying either one rule (e.g. spatial) or another (e.g. associative). Each trial began with a cue signalling the animal about which rule to use with the ensuing stimulus. Several studies using this paradigm reported many PFC cells that showed rule-specific activity – that is, they fired during application of one of the rules (but not during the other), regardless of which stimulus was shown (Asaad et al., 2000; Hoshi et al., 1998; White & Wise, 1999).

A separate line of research implicates the head of the caudate nucleus in rule switching. First, stimulation of the striatum increases switching from one motor activity to another when such switching behaviours are rewarded (Jaspers et al., 1990). Second, lesioning the dopamine projection into the PFC *improves* the performance of monkeys in an analogue of the WCST, even though it impairs their spatial working memory (Roberts et al., 1994). This result at first seems perplexing, but it turns out that such lesions increase dopamine levels in the basal ganglia (Roberts et al., 1994). Therefore, if the basal ganglia are responsible for switching, and if switching is enhanced by dopamine, then lesioning dopamine fibres into the PFC should improve switching, which is exactly what Roberts et al. (1994) found. Third, van Golf Racht-Delatour and El Massioui (1999) reported that rats with lesions to the striatum had no deficits in learning which arm of a radial arm maze was initially baited, but they did have deficits when the position of the baited arm was successively switched according to a simple rule. Fourth, human fMRI studies have reported striatal activation during rule switching (e.g. Crone et al., 2005).

In summary, there is strong evidence that the PFC and head of the caudate nucleus are critical in rule-based tasks, and there is also evidence that the anterior cingulate may participate via its role in executive attention and hypothesis generation. On the other hand, several studies have reported that medial temporal lobe amnesiacs are normal in rule-based category learning (Janowsky et al. 1989; Leng & Parkin, 1988). An obvious possibility is that many rule-based tasks are simple enough (e.g. the WCST) and that working memory is sufficient for subjects to keep track of which alternative rules they have tested and rejected. If so, then a natural prediction is that medial-temporal-lobe amnesiacs should be impaired in complex rule-based tasks (e.g. when the optimal rule is disjunctive). To our knowledge, this prediction has not been tested.

Tasks that encourage explicit memorization

In *unstructured category-learning tasks*, the exemplars of each category lack any coherent structure that could be discovered via hypothesis testing. Typically, unstructured categories are created by randomly assigning a set of perceptually distinct stimuli to the contrasting categories. For example, a category such as 'my personal numbers' (e.g. phone numbers, zip code, social security number) is unstructured because there is no logical rule or similarity relationship binding these numbers together. Introspection seems to suggest that such categories can only be learned via explicit memorization. Unstructured categories are closely related to ad hoc categories in the cognitive literature (Barsalou, 1983; see also Chapter 1 in this book) and pseudocategories in the animal literature (Lea, 1984).

Historically, tasks using unstructured categories have received relatively little attention. Most efforts have been simply to show that unstructured categories are among the most difficult of all types of category structures to learn (Nosofsky et al., 1994; Shepard et al., 1961; Smith et al., 2004).

In the only known neuroimaging study using unstructured categories, successful categorization was associated with activation in the body and tail of the caudate nucleus and the putamen, but not in the medial temporal lobes (Seger & Cincotta, 2005). On the neuropsychological front, Bayley et al. (2005) reported that two patients with dense amnesia, both as a result of bilateral medial temporal lobe lesions, were nonetheless able to learn difficult unstructured categories over the course of several weeks of training, despite not being able to describe the task, the instructions, or the stimuli at the start of each session.

Introspection seems to suggest that the only way arbitrary categories of this type could be learned is via explicit memorization. Based largely on this intuition, Ashby and O'Brien (2005) speculated that the medial temporal lobes would be critical for learning unstructured categories. The Seger and Cincotta (2005) results and the Bayley et al. (2005) results, however, cast serious doubt on this hypothesis. An alternative seems to be that the medial temporal lobes might mediate our conscious recollection of specific stimuli, but that the striatum is required to associate a category response with each stimulus because of the trial-by-trial reward-mediated learning that is required. Clearly, much more work is needed on the neural basis of unstructured category learning.

What role for the hippocampus?

The failure to find a more significant role for the hippocampus in rule-based and unstructured category-learning tasks is surprising for several reasons. First, the hippocampus and other medial temporal lobe structures play a prominent role in the more traditional memory literature. Therefore, if category learning is a process of encoding and consolidating memories about categories, then it is natural to expect that the hippocampus might play a similar prominent role in category learning. Second, as described in other chapters in this book (e.g. Chapter 4), exemplar theory has been the most prominent cognitive theory of categorization for 30 years. Although there currently is no detailed neurobiological interpretation of exemplar theory, initial attempts to ground exemplar models of categorization in neurobiology have all assigned a key role to the hippocampus (e.g. Pickering, 1997; Sakamoto & Love, 2004). Thus, the success of exemplar theory also directs attention to the hippocampus.

To begin, it is important to note that the mapping of exemplar theory to the hippocampus is problematic. This is partly because the memory system postulated by exemplar theory appears qualitatively different from all of the memory systems that have been identified by memory researchers. According to exemplar theory, the memory representations that must be accessed prior to each categorization response are of each previously seen exemplar. These memory representations are detailed replicas of each exemplar (filtered by attentional processes), but they do not typically include contextual information (e.g. details about the experimental room). Thus, the closest match in the memory literature is probably semantic memory.

One problem with assuming that exemplar memory is a form of semantic memory is that semantic memory is declarative. In contrast, exemplar theorists are careful to assume that people do *not* have conscious awareness of exemplar memories. Thus, exemplar theory appears to postulate a unique memory system that has not yet been discovered by memory researchers.

It is important to note, however, that other instance-based theories postulate more traditional memory systems. For example, RULEX (Nosofsky et al., 1994) assumes people use explicit rules during categorization but they memorize exceptions. Presumably, people are aware of these exceptions, so this form of memory seems identical to semantic memory.

An obvious prediction of instance- or exemplar-based categorization theories, therefore, seems to be that patients with damage to medial temporal lobe structures should be impaired in category learning. We know of two studies that have reported category-learning deficits in amnesiacs (Kolodny, 1994; Zaki et al., 2003), and two others that reported normal performance on the first 50 trials, but impaired performance later on (Hopkins et al., 2004; Knowlton et al., 1994). On the other hand, many more studies have reported normal category-learning performance in patients with amnesia. First, many studies have shown that amnesiacs are normal in rule-based tasks such as the WCST (e.g. Janowsky et al., 1989; Leng & Parkin, 1988). Second, Filoteo et al. (2001b) reported normal performance by amnesiacs in a difficult information-integration task with nonlinearly separable categories that required hundreds of training trials. In fact, in the Filoteo et al. (2001b) study, one (medial temporal lobe) amnesiac and one control subject completed a second day of testing. Despite lacking an explicit memory of the previous session, the patient with amnesia performed slightly better than the control on the first block of day 2. This result suggests that amnesiacs do not necessarily rely on working memory to perform normally in category-learning tasks (because working memory cannot be used to retain category knowledge across days). Third, several studies have also reported that patients with amnesia have normal performance in the (A, not A) prototype-distortion task that we describe in a later section (Knowlton & Squire, 1993; Kolodny, 1994; Squire & Knowlton, 1995; Zaki et al., 2003).

In summary, there currently is no neurobiological interpretation of exemplar theory. It seems likely that such an interpretation would have to assign a key role to medial temporal lobe structures. Some evidence suggests that medial temporal lobe damage can cause category-learning deficits under certain special conditions, but many studies have reported normal category learning in patients with amnesia. The role of the medial temporal lobes in categorization is likely to be a topic of intense research in future years.

The procedural memory system

Procedural memories are nondeclarative memories of skills that are learned through practice (Willingham, 1998). Traditionally, these have been motor skills, such as those used when playing the piano. Procedural learning is qualitatively different from learning that is mediated by declarative memory systems. First, there typically is little conscious recollection or even awareness of the details of procedural learning. Second, procedural learning is slow and incremental, and third it requires immediate and consistent feedback (Willingham, 1998).

Much evidence suggests that procedural learning is mediated largely within the striatum (Willingham, 1998; Mishkin et al., 1984; Saint-Cyr et al., 1988). Neuroanatomical studies suggest that the most important striatal regions might be the body and tail of the caudate nucleus and the putamen because these regions of the striatum receive direct projections from sensory association areas of cortex (Ashby et al., 2007).

As procedural learning requires many repetitions, it is not likely to influence performance when the categories have a simple structure that can be discovered quickly via hypothesis testing. But categories that cannot be learned via hypothesis testing are common in everyday life. For example, deciding whether an animal is a wolf or a German shepherd requires integrating information from a variety of perceptual dimensions in a way that is difficult to describe verbally. The laboratory analogue of this experience is the information-integration category-learning task, in which accuracy is maximized only if information from two or more stimulus dimensions is integrated at some pre-decisional stage. Typically, the optimal strategy is difficult or impossible to describe verbally (Ashby et al., 1998). An example is shown in Figure 5.1. In this case, each stimulus is a circular sine-wave grating that varies across trials in the width and orientation of the dark and light bars. The category boundary is denoted by the diagonal line. In this case, because of the incommensurable nature of the two stimulus dimensions, this bound is difficult (or impossible) to describe verbally. Even so, healthy young adults can reliably learn such categories (for a review, see Ashby & Maddox, 2005).

COVIS assumes that information-integration categories are primarily learned via striatal-mediated procedural learning (Ashby et al., 1998; Ashby & Waldron, 1999). In fact, there is strong evidence that information-integration tasks frequently recruit the

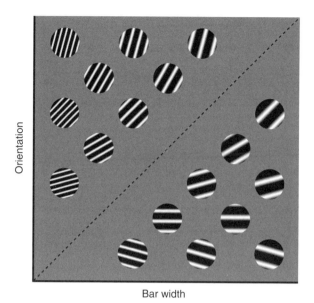

Fig. 5.1 Example of stimuli that might be used in an information-integration category-learning task. The diagonal line denotes the category boundary. Note that no simple verbal rule separates the discs into the two categories.

procedural learning system. The most popular paradigm for studying procedural learning is the serial-reaction-time (SRT) task (Nissen & Bullemer, 1987), in which subjects press keys as quickly as possible in response to stimuli that appear in various locations on the screen. A large response-time improvement occurs when the stimulus sequence is repeated, even when subjects are unaware that a sequence exists. In addition, changing the location of the response keys interferes with SRT learning, but changing the fingers that push the keys does not (Willingham et al., 2000). Thus, if procedural learning is used in information-integration tasks, then switching the locations of the response keys should interfere with learning, but switching the fingers that depress the keys should not. In fact, Ashby et al. (2003b) reported evidence that directly supported this prediction. They also reported that neither manipulation had any effect on rule-based category learning. Subsequent studies have confirmed that information-integration learning requires a consistent association between a category and a response feature (e.g. the spatial location of the response) whereas rule-based learning does not require that this mapping is consistent (Maddox et al., 2004; Spiering & Ashby, 2008).

There is also evidence that as in traditional procedural-learning tasks, information-integration category learning is most effective when the feedback signal is delivered immediately after the categorization response. For example, delaying the feedback by as little as 2.5 s after the response significantly interferes with information-integration category learning, but delays as long as 10 s have no effect on rule-based learning (Maddox et al., 2003; see also Ashby et al., 1999,2002).

If information-integration tasks recruit striatal-dependent procedural learning, then information-integration learning should also depend on the striatum. In fact, there is good evidence that the striatum plays an important role in information-integration category learning. First, several studies have reported that Huntington's disease and Parkinson's disease patients are both impaired in difficult information-integration tasks (Filoteo et al., 2001a, 2004; Maddox & Filoteo, 2001), although other studies have reported that Parkinson's disease patients learn normally if the information-integration task is simpler (Ashby et al., 2003a; Filoteo et al., 2004). Second, both known neuroimaging studies of information-integration category learning have reported significant task-related activation in the striatum (Nomura et al., 2007; Seger & Cincotta, 2002).

The perceptual representation memory system

The perceptual representation memory system (PRS) is a nondeclarative memory system that facilitates perceptual processing of a stimulus as a consequence of having seen that stimulus before (Schacter, 1990). Behavioural effects of the PRS can be observed after only a single stimulus repetition, yet are long lasting (e.g. Wiggs & Martin, 1998). Furthermore, PRS effects can be induced when two stimuli are different, but perceptually similar (e.g. Biederman & Cooper, 1992; Cooper et al., 1992).

The neural basis of the PRS is still unclear. The repetition priming thought to be mediated by the PRS is widely associated with the phenomenon of repetition suppression, in which repeated presentations of a stimulus elicit a smaller and smaller neural response in fMRI experiments. As a result, there have been specific proposals that repetition suppression is the neural signature of PRS activation (e.g. Schacter & Buckner, 1998; Wiggs & Martin, 1998). Despite this proposal, several open questions have prevented the development of a neural theory of the PRS. First, if the PRS is a purely perceptual memory system then we might expect to see its effects limited to sensory areas of cortex. Repetition suppression is not only often seen in the visual cortex, but it has also been reported in other nonsensory brain areas, including the PFC (e.g. Demb et al., 1995; Raichle et al., 1994). Second, the neural mechanisms that mediate repetition suppression are also unclear. For example, it is unclear whether repetition suppression is due to a sharpening of tuning curves (Wiggs & Martin, 1998) or because of rapid response learning (Dobbins et al., 2004).

This brief summary suggests that the PRS should be operating in any categorization experiment in which specific exemplars are shown repeatedly, or in which a category contains multiple exemplars that have high perceptual similarity. Of course, just because the PRS is activated does not mean that it aids the categorization process. To aid categorization, the PRS must give a different response when exemplars from contrasting categories are displayed. In its original description, Schacter (1990) argued that the PRS did not 'represent elaborative information that links an event to pre-existing knowledge' (p. 553). Instead, he proposed that the PRS could provide 'a basis for a feeling of familiarity' (p. 553). Thus, the PRS could assist in categorization only if exemplars from contrasting categories are associated with different levels of familiarity.

In most categorization experiments, PRS activation should be roughly equal for all categories. There is a popular exception though. In *prototype-distortion category-learning tasks*, a category is created by first defining a category prototype and then by randomly distorting the prototype to create the other category members. In the most popular version, the prototype is a constellation of dots and the category exemplars are created by randomly perturbing the location of each dot in the prototype pattern (Posner & Keele, 1968). In the (A, not A) prototype-distortion task, there is a single prototype that is used to create category A. Stimuli not belonging to the A category are random patterns. The participant's task is to respond 'Yes' or 'No' depending on whether the presented stimulus was or was not a member of category A. In this task, the category A members have a coherent structure since they are created from a single prototype, but typically every pair of 'not A' category members are visually distinct. Thus, one might expect more PRS activation on A trials than on not A trials. In practice, this effect is often accentuated because it is common to include an initial training period when only category A members are displayed.

In contrast, in (A, B) prototype-distortion tasks, two prototypes are created and the A and B categories are constructed by randomly distorting these two patterns, respectively. An important feature of (A, B) tasks is that the stimuli associated with both responses each have a coherent structure. Thus, within-category similarity is equally high in both categories, so it is natural to predict approximately equal amounts of PRS activation on A and B trials. Historically, prototype-distortion tasks have been run both in (A, B) and (A, not A) forms, although (A, not A) tasks are most common.

There have been several proposals that the PRS mediates much of the learning that occurs in the (A, not A) prototype-distortion task (Ashby & O'Brien, 2005; Casale & Ashby, 2008; Reber & Squire, 1999), and behavioural support for this hypothesis was provided by Casale and Ashby (2008). Neuropsychological support comes from studies showing that a variety of patient groups with known deficits in rule-based and information-integration category learning are apparently normal in (A, not A) proto-type-distortion learning. This includes patients with Parkinson's disease (Reber & Squire, 1999), schizophrenia (Kéri et al., 2001), or Alzheimer's disease (Sinha, 1999). Normal (A, not A) performance has also been shown in patients with amnesia (Knowlton & Squire, 1993; Kolodny, 1994; Squire & Knowlton, 1995). At least two studies have compared (A, not A) and (A, B) prototype-distortion learning on the same patients – and both studies report the same striking dissociation. Specifically, Sinha (1999) reported normal (A, not A) performance in Alzheimer's disease patients, but impaired (A, B) performance, and Zaki et al. (2003) reported this same pattern of results with amnesiacs. Sinha (1999) also reported deficits in (A, B) prototype-distortion learning in patients with amnesia.

A handful of neuroimaging studies have used prototype-distortion tasks. All of these using an (A, not A) task have reported learning-related changes in occipital cortex (Aizenstein et al., 2000; Reber et al., 1998) – in general, reduced occipital activation was found in response to category A exemplars, although Aizenstein et al. (2000) found this reduction only under implicit learning conditions. When subjects were given explicit instructions to learn the A category, increased occipital activation was observed. Studies that used (A, B) tasks have reported quite different results. Seger et al. (2000) did report categorization-related activation in occipital cortex, but they also found significant learning-related changes in prefrontal and parietal cortices. Vogels et al. (2002)

reported results from a hybrid task in which subjects were to respond *A*, *B*, or *neither*. Thus, stimuli were created either from distortions of an *A* prototype, a *B* prototype, or were just random patterns. Like Seger et al. (2000), Vogels et al. (2002) found prefrontal and parietal activation (although in different foci). However, they also reported task-related activation in orbitofrontal cortex and the striatum, and they failed to find any task-related activation in occipital cortex.

Automatic categorization

The previous section focused on category learning. However, there are many reasons to believe that the neural mechanisms and pathways that mediate category learning are different from the neural structures that mediate automatic responses to highly learned categories. For example, many neuropsychological groups that are impaired in category learning (e.g. frontal patients and Parkinson's disease patients) do not lose old, familiar categories (e.g. fruits and tools). Similarly, there is no evidence that people who lose a familiar category (i.e. who develop a category-specific agnosia) develop any general category-learning deficits (although we know of no studies that directly address this issue). As another example, there is strong evidence, much of which we reviewed in the previous section, that certain types of category learning (e.g. information-integration) are heavily dependent on dopamine. Some recent results however, indicate that instrumental behaviours that are dopamine dependent during early learning become dopamine independent after extensive training (i.e. weeks).

Neuroscience data

Compared to the amount of research that has been done on category learning, relatively few studies have examined the neural basis of automatic categorization responses. In one of the few single-unit recording studies to examine this issue, Muhammad et al. (2006) recorded from single neurons in the PFC, head of the caudate, and premotor cortex while monkeys were making rule-based categorization responses. As predicted by COVIS, they found many cells in the PFC and caudate nucleus that fired selectively to a particular rule. However, after training the animals for a year, they also found many premotor cells that were rule selective, and even more importantly, these cells responded on average about 100 ms *before* the PFC rule-selective cells. Thus, after categorization had become automatic, the PFC, although still active, was not mediating response selection.

A similar result was reported by Carelli et al. (1997). In this study, rats were trained to lever press to a tone. Thus, Carelli et al. (1997) studied an instrumental behaviour, but not categorization. The animals learned to lever press to the tone within just a few sessions, but they received many extra days of overtraining. Throughout this extended training period, Carelli et al. (1997) recorded from single units in the striatum. As expected, just after learning, many units were found that fired a burst just before the animal lever pressed. However, a few sessions later, the same striatal units still fired bursts, but now these bursts came *after* the response had been made, and therefore they played no role in response selection. In later sessions, presumably after automaticity was well established, the striatum quit responding altogether – that is, neither the tone nor the response elicited any activity from the same striatal units that apparently controlled the response earlier in training.

Choi et al. (2005) reported the results of an experiment that used a task similar to the lever-pressing task of Carelli et al. (1997). However, rather than recording from single units, each animal was injected either with a saline control or with a selective dopamine D1 antagonist at some point during training. As expected, immediately after initial learning was complete, the D1 antagonist significantly interfered with the expression of the learned behaviour in a dose-dependent manner. In contrast, after a period of significant overtraining, the D1 antagonist had no effect on the performance of the learned behaviour.

Other results indicate that during initial acquisition of a more traditional procedural learning task (i.e. the SRT task), task-related activation in the striatum is mostly in the caudate nucleus, whereas after extended training, the task-related activation shifts to the putamen (e.g. Lehéricy et al., 2005; Miyachi et al., 2002). As with the Carelli et al. (1997) and Choi et al. (2005) data, these results are problematic for any model that assumes instrumental learning is controlled by a single basal ganglia-dependent system.

We know of no neuroimaging studies that have specifically investigated automatic categorization. However, several neuroimaging studies have examined changes in neural activations during the course of more traditional procedural-learning tasks in which participants were required to execute a fixed sequence of finger movements. In general, automaticity was associated with reduced neural activation. For example, after automaticity was achieved, decreased activation (relative to initial learning) was reported in cingulate, premotor, parietal, and prefrontal cortices, as well as in the caudate nucleus (Lehéricy et al., 2005; Poldrack et al., 2005; Wu et al., 2004).

There are many reports of neuropsychological patients who seem to lose a highly specific and very familiar category (Warrington & Shallice, 1984), a condition known as category-specific agnosia. For example, a variety of patients have been identified who have near-normal categorization performance with inanimate objects, but are highly impaired in their ability to categorize living things (e.g. Satori & Job, 1988). The most widely known of such conditions is prosopagnosia, which is a category-specific agnosia that is limited to faces. Category-specific agnosias, including prosopagnosia, often occur following a lesion to visual cortex. Single-unit recording and neuroimaging studies have identified inferotemporal cortex (and especially the fusiform gyrus) as a region especially critical to the object-perception process (e.g. McCarthy et al., 1997).

A separate literature shows how experience with a category affects the representation of its members in visual cortex (e.g. Humphreys & Forde, 2001). For example, in several studies categorization training enhanced the sensitivity of cells in the inferotemporal cortex to diagnostic features compared to features that were irrelevant to the categorization judgement (e.g. Sigala & Logothetis, 2002). Note that such changes are consistent with the widely held view that category learning is often associated with changes in the allocation of perceptual attention (Nosofsky, 1986).

Despite these many results indicating a significant role for visual cortex in the categorization process, there is good reason to believe that category learning is not mediated within visual cortex. For example, when the motor responses associated with category membership are switched (i.e. from 'approach' to 'avoid' and vice versa), the firing properties of cells in the inferotemporal cortex that are sensitive to those stimuli do not change (Rolls et al., 1977). More recent studies have found similar null results in traditional categorization tasks (e.g. Freedman et al., 2003; Op de Beeck et al., 2001). In each case, single-cell recordings showed that the firing properties of cells in the inferotemporal cortex did not change as monkeys learned to classify visual objects into one of two categories. The cells showed sensitivity to specific visual images, but category training did not make them more likely to respond to other stimuli in the same category, or less likely to respond to stimuli belonging to the contrasting category. For these reasons, the best evidence seems to suggest that inferotemporal cortex does not mediate the learning of new categories. Even so, this visual-association area is crucial to the categorization process, because it appears to encode a high-level representation of the visual stimulus.

Theories of automatic categorization

In response to these differences between category learning and automatic categorization, Ashby et al. (2007) proposed a biologically detailed computational model of how categorization judgements become automatic in tasks that depend on procedural learning. The model assumes that there are two neural pathways from the relevant sensory-association area to the premotor area that mediates response selection. The longer and slower path, which is identical to the procedural learning system of COVIS, projects from the sensory-association cortex to the premotor cortex via the striatum, globus pallidus, and thalamus. A faster, purely cortical path projects directly from the sensory-association area to the premotor area. The model assumes that the subcortical path, although slower, has greater neural plasticity because it receives a dopamine-mediated learning signal from the substantia nigra. In contrast, the faster cortical–cortical path learns more slowly via (dopamine-independent) classical two-factor Hebbian learning. Due to its greater plasticity, early learning is dominated by the subcortical path, but the development of automaticity is characterized by a transfer of control to the faster cortical–cortical projection.

Although we know of no other neural theories of categorization automaticity, there are proposals that as training progresses, control of procedural-learning tasks passes from the caudate to the putamen (e.g. Costa, 2007). A theory that the development of categorization automaticity is mediated by such a shift accounts for much of the data reviewed in this section. Even so, it is not clear how such a theory could account for the normal automatic categorization behaviour of Parkinson's patients, since the effects of Parkinson's disease are particularly insidious in the putamen. In addition, because the putamen is a prominent target of the nigrostriatal dopamine system, it is not clear how this theory could account for results (e.g. Choi et al., 2005) showing that overlearned behaviours are largely dopamine independent.

Conclusions

Ten years ago, virtually nothing was known about the neurobiology of category learning and the dominant view was that humans had a single category-learning system.

During the past decade, overwhelming evidence has been collected supporting the multiple-systems viewpoint and much has been learned about the brain regions and neural pathways that mediate learning in these putative systems. During the coming years, it is likely that this trend will continue. We can expect more details to emerge about the neural mechanisms that subserve each system, and about how the various systems interact during the learning process.

One surprising result of this new cognitive-neuroscience focus on category learning is that virtually every such study has implicated the striatum. We believe there are several reasons for this. One is that the striatum plays a key role in both working memory (i.e. the head of the caudate nucleus) and procedural memory (i.e. body and tail of caudate and putamen), and the evidence reviewed above suggests that one of these two memory systems is active in virtually every category-learning situation. A second related reason is that the striatum may be the only brain region capable of reinforcement learning (Ashby et al., 2007) – that is, learning in which synapses active on trials when correct feedback is given are strengthened and synapses active on trials when error feedback is given are weakened. Whereas it might not be surprising that reinforcement learning is critical in information-integration tasks, the striatal activation observed by Seger and Cincotta (2005) in a task with unstructured categories suggests that reinforcement learning, and hence the striatum, may play an important role in a wide variety of category-learning paradigms.

The cognitive neuroscience efforts also have led directly to the discovery of a variety of important new empirical phenomena. Here we mention only one (for more examples, see Ashby & Maddox, 2005). Neuroscience evidence suggests that the trace (i.e. Ca^{2+}) of an active synapse persists for only a few seconds after a striatal medium spiny neuron fires. For this reason, COVIS (Ashby et al., 1998) predicts that information-integration learning should therefore be impaired if the feedback signal is delayed by several seconds, and also that such delays should not affect rule-based learning. These predictions were both supported by Maddox et al. (2003). It is difficult to imagine a scenario in which a researcher working within the cognitive tradition would ever think of running this experiment. Certainly, none of the current or past cognitive models of categorization offer any hint that feedback delay is an interesting independent variable to study.

Cognitive neuroscience research on categorization also offers the hope of unifying the historically separate human and animal literatures. Although the cognitive-neuroscience work has focused on human adults, all mammals have a cortex and basal ganglia, and thus, they are likely to have the same memory systems as humans. But the greatest differences between the neuroanatomy of humans and other mammals are in frontal cortex, and more specifically in the size and complexity of the PFC. Thus, although the system that humans rely on in rule-based tasks may exist in some rudimentary form in all mammals, one might expect that this system is considerably more primitive in species further down the phylogenetic scale. Healthy, young human adults learn rule-based tasks approximately ten times faster than they do an information-integration task with equally coherent and separated categories. We predict this difference is greatest in humans, and should gradually reduce across species as the size and complexity of the PFC decreases.

Finally, one of the unexpected benefits of this new focus on the cognitive neuro-science of categorization is that it has tied the categorization process more closely to other cognitive tasks. For example, because the striatum was implicated in information-integration category learning, previously unknown relationships were discovered between information-integration categorization and more traditional procedural-learning tasks (e.g. the SRT task).

Acknowledgements

Preparation of this chapter was supported in part by Public Health Service Grant MH3760-2 and by support from the US Army Research Office through the Institute for Collaborative Biotechnologies under grant W911NF-07-1-0072.

References

Aizenstein, H. J., MacDonald, A. W., Stenger, V. A., et al. (2000). Complementary category learning systems identified using event-related functional MRI. *Journal of Cognitive Neuroscience*, **12**, 977–987.

Amos, A. (2000). A computational model of information processing in the frontal cortex and basal ganglia. *Journal of Cognitive Neuroscience*, **12**, 505–519.

Asaad, W. F., Rainer, G., & Miller, E. K. (2000). Task-specific neural activity in the primate prefrontal cortex. *Journal of Neurophysiology*, **84**, 451–459.

Ashby, F. G. & Ennis, J. M. (2006). The role of the basal ganglia in category learning. *The Psychology of Learning and Motivation*, **46**, 1–36.

Ashby, F. G. & Maddox, W. T. (2005). Human category learning. *Annual Review of Psychology*, **56**, 149–178.

Ashby, F. G. & O'Brien, J. B. (2005). Category learning and multiple memory systems. *Trends in Cognitive Science*, **2**, 83–89.

Ashby, F. G. & Valentin, V. V. (2005). Multiple systems of perceptual category learning: Theory and cognitive tests. In H. Cohen & C. Lefebvre (Eds.), *Categorization in Cognitive Science*, pp. 543–578, New York: Elsevier.

Ashby, F. G., Ell, S. W., Valentin, V. V., & Casale, M. B. (2005). FROST: A distributed neurocomputational model of working memory maintenance. *Journal of Cognitive Neuroscience*, **17**, 1728–1743.

Ashby, F. G. & Waldron, E. M. (1999). On the nature of implicit categorization. *Psychonomic Bulletin and Review*, **6**, 363–378.

Ashby, F. G., Alfonso-Reese, L. A., Turken, A. U., & Waldron, E. M. (1998). A neuropsychological theory of multiple systems in category learning. *Psychological Review*, **105**, 442–481.

Ashby, F. G., Queller, S., & Berretty, P. M. (1999). On the dominance of unidimensional rules in unsupervised categorization. *Perception and Psychophysics*, **61**, 1178–1199.

Ashby, F. G., Maddox, W. T., & Bohil, C. J. (2002). Observational versus feedback training in rule-based and information-integration category learning. *Memory and Cognition*, **30**, 665–676.

Ashby, F. G., Noble, S., Filoteo, J., Waldron, E. M., & Ell, S. W. (2003a). Category learning deficits in Parkinson's disease. *Neuropsychology*, **17**, 115–124.

Ashby, F. G., Ell, S. W., & Waldron, E. M. (2003b). Procedural learning in perceptual categorization. *Memory and Cognition*, **31**, 1114–1125.

Ashby, F. G., Ell, S. W., Valentin, V. V., & Casale, M. B. (2005). FROST: A distributed neurocomputational model of working memory maintenance. *Journal of Cognitive Neuroscience*, 17, 1728–1743.

Ashby, F. G., Ennis, J. M., & Spiering, B. J. (2007). A neurobiological theory of automaticity in perceptual categorization, *Psychological Review*, 114, 632–656.

Baddeley, A. D. (1986). *Working Memory* New York: Oxford University Press.

Barsalou, L. W. (1983). Ad hoc categories. *Memory and Cognition*, 11, 211–227.

Bayley, P. J., Frascino, J. C., & Squire, L. R. (2005). Robust habit learning in the absence of awareness and independent of the medial temporal lobe. *Nature*, 436, 550–553.

Biederman, I. & Cooper, E. E. (1992). Size invariance in visual object priming. *Journal of Experimental Psychology: Human Perception and Performance*, 18, 121–133.

Brown, R. G. & Marsden, C. D. (1988). Internal versus external cues and the control of attention in Parkinson's disease. *Brain*, 111, 323–345.

Carelli, R. M., Wolske, M., & West, M. O. (1997). Loss of lever press-related firing of rat striatal forelimb neurons after repeated sessions in a lever pressing task. *Journal of Neuroscience*, 17, 1804–1814.

Casale, M. B. & Ashby, F. G. (2008). A role for the perceptual representation memory system in category learning. *Perception and Psychophysics*, 70, 983–999.

Choi, W. Y., Balsam, P. D., & Horvitz, J. C. (2005). Extended habit training reduces dopamine mediation of appetitive response expression. *Journal of Neuroscience*, 25, 6729–6733.

Cools, A. R., van den Bercken, J. H. L., Horstink, M. W. I., van Spaendonck, K. P. M., & Berger, H. J. C. (1984). Cognitive and motor shifting aptitude disorder in Parkinson's disease. *Journal of Neurology, Neurosurgery, and Psychiatry*, 47, 443–453.

Cooper, L. A., Schacter, D. L., Ballesteros, S., & Moore, C. (1992). Priming and recognition of transformed three-dimensional objects: Effects of size and reflection. *Journal of Experimental Psychology: Learning, Memory, and Cognition*, 18, 43–57.

Costa, R. M. (2007). Plastic corticostriatal circuits for action learning. *Annals of the New York Academy of Science*, 1104, 172–191.

Crone, E. A., Wendelken, C., Donohue, S. E., & Bunge, S. A. (2005). Neural evidence for dissociable components of task-switching. *Cerebral Cortex*, 16, 475–486.

DeCaro, M. S., Thomas, R. D., & Beilock, S. L. (2008). Individual differences in category learning: Sometimes less working memory capacity is better than more. *Cognition*, 107, 284–294.

Demb, J. B., Desmond, J. E., Wagner, A. D., Vaidya, C. J., Glover, G. H., & Gabrieli, J. D. E. (1995). Semantic encoding and retrieval in the left inferior prefrontal cortex: A functional MRI study of task difficulty and process specificity. *Journal of Neuroscience*, 15, 5870–5878.

Dobbins, I. G., Schnyer, D. M., Verfaellie, M., & Schacter, D. L. (2004). Cortical activity reductions during repetition priming can result from rapid response learning. *Nature*, 428, 316–319.

Eichenbaum, H. (1997). Declarative memory: Insights from cognitive neurobiology. *Annual Review of Psychology*, 48, 547–572.

Elliott, R., Rees, G., & Dolan, R. J. (1999). Ventromedial prefrontal cortex mediates guessing. *Neuropsychologia*, 37, 403–411.

Erickson, M. A. & Kruschke, J. K. (1998). Rules and exemplars in category learning. *Journal of Experimental Psychology: General*, 127, 107–140.

Filoteo, J. V., Maddox, W. T., and Davis, J. D. (2001a). A possible role of the striatum in linear and nonlinear categorization rule learning: Evidence from patients with Huntington's disease. *Behavioral Neuroscience*, 115, 786–798.

Filoteo, J. V., Maddox, W. T., & Davis, J. D. (2001b). Quantitative modeling of category learning in amnesic patients. *Journal of the International Neuropsychological Society*, 7, 1–19.

Filoteo, V. J., Maddox, W. T., Salmon D. P., & Song D. D. (2007). Implicit category learning performance predicts rate of cognitive decline in nondemented patients with Parkinson's disease. *Neuropsychology*, 21, 183–192.

Frank, M. J., Loughry, B., & O'Reilly, R. C. (2001). Interactions between frontal cortex and basal ganglia in working memory: A computational model. *Cognitive, Affective, and Behavioral Neuroscience*, 1, 137–160.

Freedman, D. J., Riesenhuber, M., Poggio, T., & Miller, E. K. (2003). A comparison of primate prefrontal and inferior temporal cortices during visual categorization. *Journal of Neuroscience*, 23, 5235–5246.

Fuster, J. M. (1989). *The Prefrontal Cortex*, 2nd edn., Philadelphia, PA: Lippincott-Raven.

Heaton, R. K. (1981). *A Manual for the Wisconsin Card Sorting Test* Odessa, FL: Psychological Assessment Resources.

Heimer, L. (1995). *The Human Brain and Spinal Cord*, 2nd edn., New York: Springer-Verlag.

Hikosaka, O., Sakamoto, M., & Sadanari, U. (1989). Functional properties of monkey caudate neurons III. Activities related to expectation of target and reward. *Journal of Neurophysiology*, 61, 814–831.

Hopkins, R. O., Myers, E. C., Shohamy, D., Grossman, S., & Gluck, M. (2004). Impaired probabilistic category learning in hypoxic subjects with hippocampal damage. *Neuropsychologia*, 42, 524–535.

Hoshi, E., Shima, K., & Tanji, J. (1998). Task-dependent selectivity of movement-related neuronal activity in the primate prefrontal cortex. *Journal of Neurophysiology*, 80, 3392–3397.

Houk, J. C., Adams, J. L., & Barto, A. G. (1995). A model of how the basal ganglia generate and use neural signals that predict reinforcement. In J. C. Houk, J. L. Davis, & D. G. Beiser (Eds.), *Models of Information Processing in the Basal Ganglia*, pp. 249–270, Cambridge, MA: MIT Press.

Humphreys, G. W. & Forde, E. M. E. (2001). Hierarchies, similarity and interactivity in object recognition: 'Category-specific' neuropsychological deficits. *Behavioral and Brain Sciences*, 24, 453–509.

Janowsky, J. S., Shimamura, A. P., Kritchevsky, M., & Squire, L. R. (1989). Cognitive impairment following frontal lobe damage and its relevance to human amnesia. *Behavioral Neuroscience*, 103, 548–560.

Jaspers, R. M., De Vries, T. J., & Cools, A. R. (1990). Enhancement in switching motor patterns following local application of the glutamate agonist AMPA into the cat caudate nucleus. *Behavioral Brain Research*, 37, 237–246.

Joel, D., Weiner, I., & Feldon, J. (1997). Electrolytic lesions of the medial prefrontal cortex in rats disrupt performance on an analog of the Wisconsin Card Sorting Test, but do not disrupt latent inhibition: Implications for animal models of schizophrenia. *Behavioral Brain Research*, 85, 187–201.

Kéri, S., Kelemen, O., Benedek, G., & Janka, Z. (2001). Intact prototype learning in schizophrenia. *Schizophrenia Research*, 52, 261–264.

Kimberg, D. Y., D'Esposito, M., & Farah, M. J. (1997). Effects of bromocriptine on human subjects depends on working memory capacity. *Neuroreport*, **8**, 3581–3585.

Kincaid, A. E., Zheng, T., & Wilson, C. J. (1998). Connectivity and convergence of single corticostriatal axons. *Journal of Neuroscience*, **18**, 4722–4731.

Knowlton, B. J. & Squire, L. R. (1993). The learning of natural categories: Parallel memory systems for item memory and category-level knowledge. *Science*, **262**, 1747–1749.

Knowlton, B. J., Squire, L. R., & Gluck, M. A. (1994). Probabilistic classification learning in amnesia. *Learning and Memory*, **1**, 106–120.

Kolodny, J. A. (1994). Memory processes in classification learning: An investigation of amnesic performance in categorization of dot patterns and artistic styles. *Psychological Science*, **5**, 164–169.

Konishi, S., Karwazu, M., Uchida, I., Kikyo, H., Asakura, I., & Miyashita, Y. (1999). Contribution of working memory to transient activation in human inferior prefrontal cortex during performance of the Wisconsin Card Sorting Test. *Cerebral Cortex*, **9**, 745–753.

Lea, S. E. G. (1984). In what sense do pigeons learn concepts? In H. L. Roitblat, T. G. Bever, & H. S. Terrace (Eds.), *Animal Cognition*, pp. 263–277, Hillsdale, NJ: Erlbaum.

Lehéricy. S., Benali, H., Van de Moortele, P. F., et al. (2005). Distinct basal ganglia territories are engaged in early and advanced motor sequence learning. *Proceedings of the National Academy of Science*, **102**, 12566–12571.

Leng, N. R. & Parkin, A. J. (1988). Double dissociation of frontal dysfunction in organic amnesia. *British Journal of Clinical Psychology*, **27**, 359–362.

Maddox, W. T. & Filoteo, J. V. (2001). Striatal contribution to category learning: Quantitative modeling of simple linear and complex non-linear rule learning in patients with Parkinson's disease. *Journal of the International Neuropsychological Society*, **7**, 710–727.

Maddox, W. T., Ashby F. G., & Bohil C. J. (2003). Delayed feedback effects on rule-based and information-integration category learning. *Journal of Experimental Psychology: Learning, Memory and Cognition*, **29**, 650–662.

Maddox, W. T., Bohil, C. J., & Ing, A. D. (2004). Evidence for a procedural learning-based system in perceptual category learning. *Psychonomic Bulletin and Review*, **11**, 945–952.

McCarthy, G., Puce, A., Gore, J. C., & Allison, T. (1997). Face-specific processing in the human fusiform gyrus. *Journal of Cognitive Neuroscience*, **9**, 605–610.

McDonald, R. J. & White, N. M. (1993). A triple dissociation of memory systems: Hippocampus, amygdala, and dorsal striatum. *Behavioral Neuroscience*, **107**, 3–22.

Merchant, H., Zainos, A. Hernadez, A., Salinas, E., & Romo, R. (1997). Functional properties of primate putamen neurons during the categorization of tactile stimuli. *Journal of Neurophysiology*, **77**, 1132–1154.

Mishkin, M., Malamut, B., & Bachevalier, J. (1984). Memories and habits: Two neural systems. In G. Lynch, J. L. McGaugh, & N. M. Weinberger (Eds.), *Neurobiology of Human Learning and Memory*, pp. 65–77, New York: Guilford.

Miyachi, S., Hikosaka, O. & Lu, X. (2002). Differential activation of monkey striatal neurons in the early and late stages of procedural learning. *Experimental Brain Research*, **146**, 122–126.

Monchi, O., Taylor, J. G., & Dagher, A. (2000). A neural model of working memory processes in normal subjects, Parkinson's disease, and schizophrenia for fMRI design and predictions. *Neural Networks*, **13**, 953–973.

Monchi, O., Petrides, M., Petre, V., Worsley, K., & Dagher, A. (2001). Wisconsin Card Sorting revisited: Distinct neural circuits participating in different stages of the task identified by event-related functional magnetic resonance imaging. *Journal of Neuroscience*, 21, 7733–7741.

Muhammad, R., Wallis, J. D., & Miller, E. K. (2006). A comparison of abstract rules in the prefrontal cortex, premotor cortex, inferior temporal cortex, and striatum. *Journal of Cognitive Neuroscience*, 18, 1–16.

Nissen, M. J. & Bullemer, P. (1987). Attention requirements of learning: Evidence from performance measures. *Cognitive Psychology*, 19, 1–32.

Nomura, E. M., Maddox, W. T., Filoteo, J. V., et al. (2007). Neural correlates of rule-based and information-integration visual category learning. *Cerebral Cortex*, 17, 37–43.

Nosofsky, R. M. (1986). Attention, similarity, and the identification categorization relationship. *Journal of Experimental Psychology: General*, 115, 39–57.

Nosofsky, R. M., Gluck, M. A., Palmeri, T. J., McKinley, S. C., & Glauthier, P. (1994). Comparing models of rule-based classification learning: A replication and extension of Shepard, Hovland, and Jenkins (1961). *Memory and Cognition*, 22, 352–369.

Nosofsky, R. M., Palmeri, T. J., & McKinley, S. C. (1994). Rule-plus-exception model of classification learning. *Psychological Review*, 101, 53–79.

Op de Beeck, H., Wagemans, J., & Vogels, R. (2001). Inferotemporal neurons represent low-dimensional configurations of paramterized shapes. *Nature Neuroscience*, 4, 1244–1252.

Packard, M. G. & McGaugh, J. L. (1992). Double dissociation of fornix and caudate nucleus lesions on acquisition of two water maze tasks: Further evidence for multiple memory systems. *Behavior Neuroscience*, 106, 439–446.

Pickering, A. D. (1997). New approaches to the study of amnesic patients: What can a neurofunctional philosophy and neural network methods offer? *Memory*, 5, 255–300.

Poldrack, R. A., Sabb, F., Foerde, K., et al. (2005). The neural correlates of automaticity during motor skill learning. *Journal of Neuroscience*, 25, 5356–5364.

Posner, M. I. & Keele, S. W. (1968). On the genesis of abstract ideas. *Journal of Experimental Psychology*, 77, 353–363.

Posner, M. I. & Petersen, S. E. (1990). Attention systems in the human brain. *Annual Review of Neuroscience*, 13, 25–42.

Raichle, M. E., Fiez, J. A., Videen, T. O., et al. (1994). Practice-related changes in human brain functional anatomy during nonmotor learning. *Cerebral Cortex*, 4, 8–26.

Reber, P. J. & Squire, L. R. (1999). Intact learning of artificial grammars and intact category learning by patients with Parkinson's disease. *Behavioral Neuroscience*, 113, 235–242.

Reber, P. J., Stark, C. E. L., & Squire, L. R. (1998). Cortical areas supporting category learning identified using functional MRI. *Proceedings of the National Academy of Sciences of the United States of America*, 95, 747–750.

Roberts, A. C., De Salvia, M. A., Wilkinson, L. S., et al. (1994). 6-hydroxydopamine lesions of the prefrontal cortex in monkeys enhance performance on an analog of the Wisconsin card sort test: Possible interactions with subcortical dopamine. *Journal of Neuroscience*, 14, 2531–2544.

Roberts, A. C. & Wallis, J. D. (2000). Inhibitory control and affective processing in the prefrontal cortex: Neuropsychological studies in the common marmoset. *Cerebral Cortex*, 10, 252–262.

Rogers, R. D., Andrews, T. C., Grasby, P. M., Brooks, D. J., & Robbins, T. W. (2000). Contrasting cortical and subcortical activations produced by attentional-set shifting and reversal learning in humans. *Journal of Cognitive Neuroscience*, 12, 142–162.

Rolls, E. T., Judge, S. J., & Sanghera, M. (1977). Activity of neurons in the inferotemporal cortex of the alert monkey. *Brain Research*, **130**, 229–238.

Saint-Cyr, J. A., Taylor, A. E., & Lang, A. E. (1988). Procedural learning and neostriatal dysfunction in man. *Brain*, **111**, 941–959.

Sakamoto, Y. & Love, B. C. (2004). Schematic influences on category learning and recognition memory. *Journal of Experimental Psychology: General*, **133**, 534–553.

Satori, G. & Job, R. (1988). The oyster with four legs: A neuropsychological study on the interaction of visual and semantic information. *Cognitive Neuropsychology*, **5**, 105–132.

Schacter, D. L. (1990). Perceptual representation systems and implicit memory: Toward a resolution of the multiple memory systems debate. *Annals of the New York Academy of Sciences*, **608**, 543–571.

Schacter, D. L. & Buckner, R. L. (1998). Priming and the brain. *Neuron*, **20**, 185–195.

Schultz, W. & Romo, R. (1992). Role of primate basal ganglia and frontal cortex in the internal generation of movements. I. Preparatory activity in the anterior striatum. *Experimental Brain Research*, **91**, 363–384.

Schultz, W., Dayan, P. & Montague, P. R. (1997). A neural substrate of prediction and reward. *Science*, **275**, 1593–1599.

Seger, C. A., Poldrack, R. A., Prabhakaran. V., Zhao, M., Glover, G., & Gabrieli, J. D. E. (2000). Hemispheric asymmetries and individual differences in visual concept learning as measured by functional MRI. *Neuropsychologia,* **38**, 1316–1324.

Seger, C. A. & Cincotta, C. M. (2002). Striatal activity in concept learning. *Cognitive, Affective, and Behavioral Neuroscience*, **2**, 149–161.

Seger, C. A. & Cincotta, C. M. (2005). The roles of the caudate nucleus in human classification learning. *Journal of Neuroscience*, **25**, 2941–2951.

Shepard, R. N., Hovland, C. I., & Jenkins, H. M. (1961). Learning and memorization of classifications. *Psychological Monographs*, **75**, (13, Whole No. 517).

Sigala, N. & Logothetis, N. K. (2002). Visual categorization shape feature selectivity in the primate temporal cortex. *Nature*, **415**, 318–320.

Sinha, R. R. (1999). Neuropsychological substrates of category learning. *Dissertation Abstracts International: Section B: The Sciences and Engineering*, **60**(5-B), 2381. (UMI No. AEH9932480).

Smith, J. D., Minda, J. P., & Washburn, D. A. (2004). Category learning in Rhesus monkeys: A study of the Shepard, Hovland, and Jenkins tasks. *Journal of Experimental Psychology: General*, **133**, 398–414.

Spiering, B. J. & Ashby, F. G. (2008). Response processes in information-integration category learning. *Neurobiology of Learning and Memory*, **90**, 330–338.

Squire, L. R. & Knowlton, B. J. (1995). Learning about categories in the absence of memory. *Proceedings of the National Academy of Science USA*, **92**, 12470–12474.

Squire, L. R. & Schacter, D. L. (2002). *The Neuropsychology of Memory*, 3rd edn., New York: Guilford Press.

Sutton, R. S. & Barto, A. G. (1998). *Reinforcement Learning* Cambridge, MA: MIT Press.

Tulving, E. (2002). Episodic memory: From mind to brain. *Annual Review of Psychology*, **53**, 1–25.

van Domburg, P. H. & ten Donkelaar, H. J. (1991). *The Human Substantia Nigra and Ventral Tegmental Area* Berlin: Springer-Verlag.

Van Golf Racht-Delatour, B. & El Massioui, N. (1999). Rule-based learning impairment in rats with lesions to the dorsal striatum. *Neurobiology of Learning and Memory*, 72, 47–61.

Vogels, R., Sary, G., Dupont, P., & Orban, G. A. (2002). Human brain regions involved in visual categorization. *Neuroimage*, 16, 401–414.

Waldron, E. M. & Ashby, F. G. (2001). The effects of concurrent task interference on category learning: Evidence for multiple category learning systems. *Psychonomic Bulletin and Review*, 8, 168–176.

Warrington, E. K. & Shallice, T. (1984). Category specific semantic impairments. *Brain*, 107, 829–854.

White, I. M. & Wise, S. P. (1999). Rule-dependent neuronal activity in the prefrontal cortex. *Experimental Brain Research*, 126, 315–335.

Wickens, J. (1993). *A Theory of the Striatum* New York: Pergamon Press.

Wiggs, C. L. & Martin, A. (1998). Properties and mechanisms of perceptual priming. *Current Opinion in Neurobiology*, 8, 227–233.

Willingham, D. B. (1998). A neuropsychological theory of motor skill learning. *Psychological Review*, 105, 558–584.

Willingham, D. B., Wells, L. A., Farrell, J. M., & Stemwedel, M. E. (2000). Implicit motor sequence learning is represented in response locations. *Memory and Cognition*, 28, 366–375.

Wilson, C. J. (1995). The contribution of cortical neurons to the firing pattern of striatal spiny neurons. In J. C. Houk, J. L. Davis, & D. G. Beiser (Eds), *Models of Information Processing in the Basal Ganglia*, pp. 29–50, Cambridge, MA: Bradford.

Wu, T., Kansaku, K. & Hallett, M. (2004). How self-initiated memorized movements become automatic: A functional MRI study. *Journal of Neurophysiology*, 91, 1690–1698.

Zaki, S. R., Nosofsky, R. M., Jessup, N. M., & Unversagt, F. W. (2003). Categorization and recognition performance of a memory-impaired group: Evidence for single-system models. *Journal of the International Neuropsychological Society*, 9, 394–406.

Zeithamova, D. & Maddox, W. T. (2006). Dual-task interference in perceptual category learning. *Memory and Cognition*, 34, 387–398.

Chapter 6

Different kinds of concepts and different kinds of words: What words do for human cognition

Sandra R. Waxman and Susan A. Gelman

Editors' Preview

Chapter 6, 'Different kinds of concepts and different kinds of words: What words do for human cognition', provides a contrast to Chapter 4. Whereas Chapter 4 focused on what could be learned about concepts based entirely on observation from examples and without verbal instruction, Chapter 6 concentrates on how language may assist categorization by facilitating the ability to extract commonalities from experience. Given that nonhuman animals presumably do not have entry into the world of links between concepts and words, the close interrelationship between word learning and concept acquisition described in this chapter highlights an important respect in which the concepts of humans may differ from the concepts of nonhuman animals.

Chapter 6 reviews evidence indicating that children, by the age of 2 understand that there are different types of words (e.g. nouns, adjectives, verbs) and that this knowledge can be recruited to unravel the meanings of the concepts referred to by words (e.g. objects, properties, actions). In particular, when young concept formers and word learners view a scene with a group of objects, object properties, and actions performed by the objects, hearing the names of the objects described in a noun phrase (e.g. 'these are blickets') promotes extraction of the commonalities amongst the objects (thereby allowing the objects to be viewed as members of the same category). In contrast, hearing the scene described with an adjectival phrase (e.g. 'these are blickish') facilitates a different construal of the scene, one in which properties of the objects are more likely to serve as a basis for category formation (i.e. objects of the same colour are likely to be grouped together). Moreover, hearing the scene described with a verb phrase (e.g. 'they're blicking'), supports categorical processing of actions performed by the objects (e.g. running, waving). Notably, the precise links between specific words and particular concepts observed at 2 years of age are not the starting points for conceptual-lexical acquisition. Rather, there appears to be a developmental course that begins at least a year earlier when different word forms (e.g. nouns, adjectives) are more broadly linked with commonalities among objects.

Chapter 6 also describes how language affects cognition beyond categorization, extending to additional cognitive processes such as object individuation and induction. For example, when infants hear that two objects can be labelled with different count nouns, they are more likely to respond to those objects as distinct individuals. In addition, when children learn that different objects have the same label, they are more likely to infer that the objects will have the same non-obvious properties. That is, given two cats of different appearances, if the cats are labelled as '*cats*', then the child will be likely to generalize a property learned about the one cat to the other cat (e.g. can see in the dark).

Chapter 6 argues further that the impact of language on categorization and other cognitive processes poses challenges for an empiricist account (one based on learned associations) of the emergence of human concepts. That is, while general learning mechanisms provided with perceptual input that has correlational structure can be used to explain how concepts are acquired by nonhuman animals, it will not provide a sufficient foundation for understanding how human concepts (those intertwined with words) are acquired. For example, the idea that words are linked with concepts by virtue of pure association is contradicted by the findings that (1) words presented in isolation do not promote categorization (i.e. they need to be presented in an appropriate linguistic context such as a noun phrase) and (2) the effects of words vary depending on the kind of word presented (e.g. nouns promote the extraction of object concepts, whereas adjectives facilitate the extraction of property concepts).

Introduction

This book addresses the nature of concepts. A consideration of human concepts is incomplete without also considering language. Language is a fundamental human capacity, one that permits us to express our own concepts and to influence the concepts of others. Although humans and nonhumans alike can form categories in the absence of language, there is nonetheless a crucial role for words in human conceptual development (see Gelman & Kalish, 2006; Waxman & Lidz, 2006; Woodward & Markman, 1998, for recent reviews). We argue that throughout human development, words are intimately linked with conceptual representations and permit us to transcend categories and concepts that are supported by immediate perceptual experiences. Even before infants produce their first words, their representations of objects and events are influenced by the words that they hear. With development, the influence of words becomes increasingly powerful and precise. Thus, we argue for strong developmental continuities in the powerful and uniquely human relation between words and concepts; we also underscore that throughout human development, decisions about categorization and naming are affected by a host of considerations that do not correlate in any simple way with perceptual properties.

Concepts, words, and development

The chapter is also motivated by our concern about the treatment of the constructs *concept, word,* and *development.* The depth and subtlety underlying each of these key constructs is often overlooked in current discussions. Consider first, the construct *concept.* The human mind is remarkable for its flexibility. We can construe any particular scene, or any element within a scene, in a number of different ways, depending upon the perspective that we adopt at the moment and the task at hand. The human mind, including the minds of infants and young children, represents a rich range of concepts, ranging from distinct individuals (e.g. Fido) to categories and kinds. Our concepts include abstractions over individual objects (e.g. dog, animal), events (e.g. pushing, thinking), and properties (e.g. fluffy, mischievous). We represent concepts that can be derived from immediate perceptual experience (e.g. fluffy, cold), as well as concepts that relate to more complex internal emotional states (e.g. happy, mad) and abstract ideas (e.g. causation, animacy). Moreover, not all concepts are 'created equal': natural kind concepts that have been encoded in language (e.g. dogs, trees) are likely very different from arbitrary groupings created for a particular research task (e.g. tall red cubes, U-shaped blocks; see Gelman & Kalish, 2006; Sloutsky et al., 2007; Smith & Heise, 1992; Vygotsky, 1962; Younger, 2003; Chapter 12, this book). Although the latter are often organized around a small set of necessary and sufficient perceptual features, decades of research document that this organizational structure is not one that characterizes some of our most foundational concepts (e.g. concepts of number, kinship relations, emotions, natural kinds, and complex artefacts), for which it is difficult, if not impossible, to identify necessary and sufficient features (Armstrong et al., 1983; Murphy, 2000; Murphy & Medin, 1985).

Consider next the construct, *word.* Words are not isolated bits of sound; they are embedded within social, symbolic, and linguistic systems. It was for this reason, among others, that research agendas from the past that used acquisition patterns of isolated consonant–vowel–consonant syllables in the lab as a basis for generalizations about language acquisition fell out of favour (Smith & Medin, 1981). These tasks fell out of favour not only because they failed to represent the diversity of word forms in human language, but also because they failed to represent the diversity of word meanings. Languages include many different kinds of words (e.g. nouns, adjectives, verbs), each of which is recruited to convey a different kind of concept (e.g. categories of objects, properties, and events, respectively).

Yet even in the current literature, most of the developmental research on words and concepts has focused on only one kind of word: nouns. Although important insights have been gained, this focus is not without costs. Chief among them is that the principles underlying the acquisition of nouns and the conceptual consequences of their use differ importantly from the principles underlying the acquisition of other grammatical forms, including adjectives and verbs, and the conceptual consequences of using these forms. In short, because 'word' is not interchangeable with 'noun', any comprehensive theory of human conceptual development will have to consider the distinct developmental trajectories and the distinct conceptual entailments of different kinds of words. Furthermore, because words are elements within a complex linguistic system, any comprehensive theory will have to consider not only words on their own but also their combinatorial power.

Third, consider the construct, *development*. Words, concepts, and the links between them evolve over the course of human development. Therefore, the fundamental developmental question is not simply whether infants or young children can represent a given concept, whether they can grasp the meaning of a given word, or whether they represent words or concepts precisely as their elders do. Instead, the developmental question is what capacities are available at the time of acquisition and how these evolve over the course of development.

Plan of the chapter

With these observations in mind, we offer a description of the problem of word learning that acknowledges the diverse range of concepts and words in the human repertoire. We then turn our focus to infants and young children, reviewing evidence bearing on the early-emerging relation between words and concepts, the conceptual power afforded by this relation, and a developmental trajectory in which an early appreciation of different kinds of words and different kinds of concepts becomes increasingly precise and powerful. We consider how this evidence bears on claims, expressed explicitly or implicitly, in recent associationist accounts of word learning and concept development (Sloutsky, 2003; Smith et al. 1996). Central to these latter accounts is the assertion that the processes underlying the acquisition of words and concepts are identical to those underlying the acquisition of any other kind of knowledge (including associative learning, similarity assessment, and attentional weighting) (Rakison & Lupyan, 2008; Sloutsky & Fisher, 2005; Smith, 2000; Smith et al. 2003). We challenge this assertion, articulating four overlapping assumptions which, separately and together, underlie this associationist view: (1) that the word–concept link is one of pure association; (2) that a word is merely an attentional spotlight; (3) that a word is merely another feature of an object; and (4) that a word indexes only a perceptual representation. To foreshadow, we demonstrate that because these accounts fail to acknowledge the diversity and flexibility of the constructs 'word' and 'concept', and because they fail to consider fully the forces underlying human 'development', they fall far short.

The problem of word learning

To acquire a human language, infants and young children must solve the problem of word learning. Although languages differ in the particular words that they use (e.g. 'dog' vs. 'chien'), and in the syntactic relationships between these words (e.g. whether or not adjectives vary across contexts to reflect the gender or number of the noun that they modify), there are also aspects of human language that are universal. We presume that the phenomena we consider within this chapter are of the latter sort. Consider an infant who observes a scene in which three cats are playing in a park. The infant has the representational capacity to construe this scene and the elements comprising it in multiple ways. For example, the infant may focus on one particular cat, cats in general, a salient property (e.g. fast, furry), the activities in which they are engaged (e.g. grooming, chasing), or any of a number of other relations. Some of these construals will correspond to words in the language the infant is in the process of acquiring. For example, for an infant acquiring English, a proper noun (e.g. 'Look, it's *Tabitha*') can be applied to a specific individual; a count noun (e.g. 'Look, it's a *cat*') can be applied to a specific individual, but also applies more broadly to other members of the same object category (e.g. to other cats, but not dogs). And if we provide an adjective (e.g. 'Look, it's *fluffy*'), the meaning is again quite different. Here, we refer to a property and not the individual or category itself, and we can extend that word to other instances of that property, independent of the particular entity embodying it (e.g. to any other fluffy thing, including [some, but not all] puppies and bedroom slippers). Finally, verbs (e.g. 'Look, they're *running*') refer to a relation or an activity at that moment in time, and are extended to similar activities, perhaps involving very different actors (e.g. horses, children) at different times and places. This analysis can be extended far beyond nouns, verbs, and adjectives to words that express a broad range of abstract concepts including number (e.g. 'three'), spatial relations (e.g. 'in'), ownership (e.g. 'mine'), causal relations (e.g. 'because'), hypotheticals (e.g. 'if'), and so on.

There is now considerable evidence that young children appreciate this nuanced relation between different kinds of words and different kinds of concepts. Although their words and concepts may be less precise or less elaborated than those of adult speakers, and their mappings may be less fine tuned, children nonetheless appreciate that there are distinct kinds of words, and recruit these distinctions as they map words to meaning (Brown, 1957; see Waxman & Lidz, 2006, for a recent review). They interpret a novel count noun applied to a scene as referring to an object kind (Markman, 1989; Waxman, 1990), a novel proper noun as referring to a specific individual (Gelman & Taylor, 1984; Hall & Lavin, 2004; Macnamara, 1984), a novel adjective as referring to a property (Klibanoff & Waxman, 2000; Mintz & Gleitman, 2002; Waxman & Markow, 1998), and a novel verb as referring to an action or event (Fisher, 2002; Waxman et al., 2009). Notice that this means that in assigning meaning to a novel word, young children pay attention not only to the word itself, but also to surrounding linguistic elements. For example, the distinction between a count noun (e.g. 'This is a kitty') and a proper noun (e.g. 'This is Kitty') rests with the unstressed determiner, 'a'. The distinction between a transitive (e.g. 'Anne pushes Josh') and intransitive verb (e.g. 'Anne and Josh are pushing') rests upon the positions of the words in an utterance (Fisher & Song, 2006; Naigles, 1990). Thus, when assigning meaning to a novel word, children are exquisitely sensitive not only to the word itself, but also to its relation among other elements within the linguistic stream.

In sum, learning the meaning of a word entails more than associating a particular sound with a particular object on the basis of co-occurrence. On the contrary, a comprehensive treatment of word learning will be one that acknowledges the rather precise dance between a range of conceptual options and a variety of linguistic forms. The problem of word learning is intimately related to the problem of concept acquisition.

But how do words and concepts come together in the developing mind? To address this question, we turn to consider whether and how words influence the conceptual systems of infants and young children. As it is beyond the scope of the current chapter to provide a comprehensive review, we focus here on two recurrent themes. The first theme illustrates the powerful, and increasingly precise, relation between words and concepts from infancy through early childhood. The second illustrates the conceptual consequences of naming on fundamental cognitive processes, including object categorization, object individuation, and inductive inference.

Theme 1: even in infancy, there is a powerful, and increasingly precise, relation between words and concepts

An early link between words and concepts

In our view, there is considerable developmental continuity in the role of words in human conceptual organization. First, even before infants begin to produce words on their own, they are sensitive to a link between words and concepts. Second, as development unfolds, this initial link between words and concepts becomes increasingly precise, tuned by the infants' experience with the objects and events they encounter and the structure of the language being learned (see Gelman & Kalish, 2006; Waxman & Lidz, 2006, for recent reviews). Third, even in infancy, words exert a unique influence on conceptual representations, as compared to other auditory signals (Balaban & Waxman, 1997; Booth & Waxman, 2008; Fulkerson & Waxman, 2007; Gopnik & Nazzi, 2003; Graham et al., 1998; Keates & Graham, in press; Poulin-Dubois et al., 1995; Waxman & Booth, 2003; Waxman & Markow, 1995; Xu, 2002).

Thus by 2 years of age, children have made significant headway on the problem of word and concept learning. They have discovered that there are distinct kinds of words and have established a repertoire of distinct kinds of concepts. To be sure, many concepts can be established in the absence of words; the current book is testimony to the conceptual capacities of nonverbal nonhuman animals, and the same is true of preverbal infants (see Chapter 12 of this book). However, what is distinctive among humans is the capacity to forge links between concepts and words. And this distinctive capacity is evident remarkably early; young children recruit these links as they assign meaning to novel words. But how do infants break into this system? Which links between words and concepts, if any, are available as they begin the process of lexical acquisition?

In a series of experiments conducted over a decade ago, Waxman and Markow (1995) asked whether words influence infants' ability to conceptualize an object category (e.g. animal). This research focused on infants at 12 and 13 months of age who were just beginning to produce a few words on their own. During a *familiarization phase*, an experimenter offered the infant four different toys from a given object category (e.g. four animals), one at a time, in random order. This was immediately followed by a *test phase*, in which the experimenter simultaneously presented both (1) a new member of the now-familiar category (e.g. another animal) and (2) an object from a novel category (e.g. a fruit). To discover whether words influence infants' categorization, infants were randomly assigned to one of three conditions. In all three conditions, infants heard infant-directed speech; what differed were the comments the experimenter made during familiarization (see Figure 6.1). Notice that at test, infants in all conditions heard precisely the same phrase ('See what I have?').

The predictions were as follows: if infants noticed the commonality among the familiarization objects, then they should reveal a preference for the novel object at test. If words highlighted the relation among these objects, then infants hearing novel words should be more likely than those hearing no novel words to prefer the novel test object. Finally, if this link between words and concepts is general at the start, then infants in both the noun and adjective conditions should be more likely than those in the no-word condition to form categories.

All of the predictions were borne out. Infants in the no-word control condition showed no preference for the novel test object, suggesting that they had not detected the category-based commonalities among these familiarization objects. In contrast, infants in both the noun and adjective conditions revealed reliable novelty preferences. This constitutes clear evidence for an early, foundational link between words and object categories. It suggests, following in the spirit of Roger Brown (1958), that words serve as *invitations* to form categories. This apparently simple invitation has dramatic consequences: providing 12-month-olds with a common name (at this developmental moment, either a noun or an adjective) for a set of distinct objects highlighted the commonalities among them that went undetected in the absence of a novel word (in the no-word condition). Moreover, this invitation has considerable force: the novel words were present only during familiarization, but their influence extended beyond the named objects, directing infants' attention to the new – and as yet unnamed – test objects.

What is it about words?

What is the mechanism underlying this powerful invitation? We proposed that providing a shared name for a set of disparate individuals promotes infants' attention to the commonalities among them. However, it is also possible that a more general learning

Familiarization phase				Test phase	
Pink duck	Purple raccoon	Blue dog	Orange lion	Yellow cat	Red apple
Noun: See the *blicket*?		See the *blicket*?		See what I have?	
Adjective: See the *blickish* one?		See the *blickish* one?		See what I have?	
No Word: See here?		See here?		See what I have?	

Fig. 6.1 A representative set of stimuli.

From Waxman, S. R. & Markow, D. B. (1995). Words as invitations to form categories: Evidence from 12-month-old infants. *Cognitive Psychology*, **29**, 257–302.

mechanism is at play. After all, we know that infants devote more attention to objects that have been named than those that remain unnamed (Baldwin & Markman, 1989). Perhaps, then, it is simply the presence of a word that heightens infants' interest in the objects, and object categorization then comes along 'for free'. If this is the case, then infants should successfully form object categories, whether the familiarization objects are named with the *same* or with *different* words. To test this possibility, we compared the conceptual consequences of providing either the *same* or *different* words for a set of objects, focusing on infants at 6 and 12 months (Fulkerson et al., 2006; Waxman & Braun, 2005). When the familiarization objects (e.g. four different animals) were introduced with the *same* name, infants at both ages successfully formed object categories. This replicates Waxman and Markow (1995) and reveals a facilitative effect of naming at 6 months, in infants who are just beginning to identify distinct words within the stream of language. Importantly, however, when the same objects were introduced with *distinct* names, infants at both 6 and 12 months failed to form categories. Thus, by 6 months and perhaps earlier, infants not only are sensitive to the *presence* of a word, but also track carefully the *details* of that word and the entities to which it is applied. In this way, naming can not only support the establishment of a stable repertoire of object categories, but can also provide infants with a means of tracing the identity of individuals within these categories (see section on 'Object individuation', below).

We have also asked whether the facilitative effect of naming on infants' categorization can be attributed specifically to the presence of a consistently applied *word*, or whether it might be attributed more generally to an attention-engaging function associated with any kind of auditory stimulus. Put differently, when it comes to forming object categories, are words privileged over other, nonlinguistic auditory stimuli? Evidence from Waxman and Markow (1995) suggests that words are indeed privileged vis-à-vis object categorization. Recall that all infants in their foundational study heard infant-directed speech, yet only those hearing novel words within this context successfully formed categories. Several more recent studies have approached this question by comparing the effects of words to nonlinguistic stimuli, including tones, melodies, and mechanical noises produced by simple toys. Taken together, the results point to a privileged effect of names as early as 6 months of age. For example, Balaban and Waxman (1997) documented that words (e.g. '. . .a bird!') promote object categorization, but that tones (matched precisely to the word condition in amplitude, duration, and pause length) do not. Moreover, the evidence indicates that other, more complex nonlinguistic stimuli (e.g. repetitive, nonlinguistic mouth sounds; brief melodic phrases) also fail to promote categorization (Balaban & Waxman, 1997; Ferry et al., in press; Fulkerson & Waxman, 2007; but see Gogate et al., 2001; Sloutsky & Lo, 1999).

This is not to say that nonlinguistic stimuli cannot be presented in such a way as to facilitate the formation of object categories. On the contrary, there are circumstances in which nonlinguistic stimuli can promote object categorization. Importantly, how-ever, they do so *only* when it is made clear to the infant that these nonlinguistic stimuli are meant to have referential status and are meant to be interpreted as object names. For example, when nonlinguistic stimuli are presented within familiar naming routines or when they are produced intentionally by an experimenter who is interacting directly with the infant and a salient object, then nonlinguistic stimuli can promote object categorization (Fulkerson, 1997; Fulkerson & Haaf, 2003; Namy & Waxman, 1998, 2000, 2002; Woodward & Hoyne, 1999). In contrast, when the very same kinds of sounds are presented in the absence of social, pragmatic, or linguistic cues, infants fail to interpret them as names for things and they fail to support object categorization (Balaban & Waxman, 1997; Campbell & Namy, 2003; Fulkerson & Haaf, 2003).

Interestingly, the same is true for words. As we have pointed out, human languages are comprised of different kinds of words, each with its own conceptual, linguistic, and/ or referential function(s). As we have also pointed out, infants do not interpret novel words in a vacuum, but are instead influenced powerfully by the context in which they are presented. Recall, for example, that when assigning meaning to a novel word, infants and young children are exquisitely sensitive to the surrounding words, or the grammatical context, in which it is presented. If it is presented as a count noun (e.g. 'this is a dax'), they map the word to an object category; if it is presented as a proper noun (e.g. 'this is Dax'), they map it to a distinct individual; if it is presented as a verb (e.g. 'John is going to dax the puppy'), they map it to an event category. The observation that infants use the surrounding context to arrive at the meaning of a novel word raises a very interesting question: how do they interpret words that are presented in isolation?

While words seldom occur in isolation in naturally occurring speech (Aslin et al., 1996; Brent & Siskind, 2001), when they do, they rarely represent names for objects. Instead, isolated words tend to be commands (e.g. 'Stop!') or exclamations (e.g. 'Wow!'). Infants appear to be sensitive to this state-of-affairs. When novel words are presented in naming phrases (e.g. 'Look at the dax!'), infants as young as 6–12 months interpret them as names for objects and readily map them to the objects with which they occur. But when the very same words are presented in isolation (e.g. 'Look! Dax!'), their referential status is ambiguous, and infants fail to establish this mapping (Fennell & Waxman, in press; Fennell et al., 2007; Fulkerson & Waxman, 2007; Namy & Waxman, 2000).

This finding reveals that the conceptual status of words comes not from the sound of a word itself, but rather from its role within the linguistic and social system in which it is embedded. This finding, important in its own right, also fortifies the view that infants (like adults) take into consideration more than associations alone when establishing word meaning (see section below). After all, even in experiments in which words are presented in isolation, the presence of the novel word (e.g. 'blick') is correlated perfectly with the presence of an object. Yet, this correlation alone, however perfect, is not sufficient to support the establishment of a word–object mapping (Baldwin & Markman, 1989; Baldwin et al., 1996; Sabbagh & Baldwin, 2001). Instead, infants take into account the surrounding context and the referential status of the novel word.

In sum, infants begin the process of word learning with a broad initial link between words and commonalities among objects. Although this link initially encompasses a broad range of words (including at least nouns and adjectives), it is not so broad as to include nonlinguistic sounds. This initial link between words and concepts provides infants with a means to establish a rudimentary lexicon and sets the stage for the evolution of the more precise links between different kinds of words and different kinds of concepts. Notice that it is to the learner's advantage to begin with only the most general expectations: different languages make use of different grammatical categories, and they recruit these to convey meaning in slightly different ways. A broad initial link between words and concepts enables the learner to break into the system of word learning in the first place.

Increasingly precise links between kinds of words and kinds of concepts

When and how do infants begin to build more precise links between different kinds of words and different kinds of concepts? To the best of our knowledge, the earliest evidence comes from infants at roughly 14 months of age (Booth & Waxman, 2008; Waxman & Booth, 2003). Booth, Waxman, and their colleagues conducted a series of studies to examine how infants interpreted novel words when the objects with which they were presented offered the possibility of more than one candidate meaning. For example, infants were introduced to sets of objects (e.g. four purple animals) that shared both category-based commonalities (e.g. animal) and property-based commonalities (e.g. colour: purple things). At issue was (1) whether infants could construe this set of objects flexibly, either as members of an *object category* (e.g. animals) or as embodying an *object property* (e.g. colour: purple), and (2) whether their construals were influenced differently by different kinds of words (e.g. nouns vs. adjectives). Retaining the logic of Waxman and Markow (1995), infants at 11 and 14 months were familiarized to four distinct objects, all from the same object category (e.g. animals) and all embodying the same object property (e.g. purple). In the *test phase*, infants were required to extend the novel word they had heard during familiarization to one of two test objects: a category match (e.g. a blue horse; same category as familiarization objects, but new property) versus a property match (e.g. a purple spatula; same property as familiarization objects, but a new category). The experimenter's comments varied as a function of the infant's condition assignment. See Figure 6.2.

Infants' expectations regarding word meaning became increasingly precise from 11 to 14 months. At 11 months, infants displayed a broad link between word and concept. They were sensitive to both the category- and property-based commonalities, and were willing to map novel nouns and novel adjectives to either type of commonality. By 14 months, the link between words and concepts was more precise. Infants mapped novel *nouns* specifically to category-based commonalities, but not to property-based commonalities. But they continued to map novel *adjectives* broadly to either category- or property-based commonalities. Thus, by 14 months, infants acquiring English are sensitive to at least some of the relevant cues in the speech stream that distinguish nouns from adjectives (e.g. the presence of unstressed determiners and pronouns), and they recruit these distinctions actively when mapping words to meaning.

More recently, this paradigm has been adapted to examine infants' expectations for yet another kind of word – verbs (Waxman et al., 2009). Once again, we maintained the same logic, but this time presented infants with a series of dynamic scenes (e.g. a man waving a balloon) during familiarization. We constructed the test trials to ask (1) whether infants could construe these scenes flexibly, noticing the consistent action (e.g. waving) as well as the consistent object (e.g. the balloon) and (2) whether their construals would vary with the grammatical form of the novel word used to describe

Familiarization phase			Test phase	
			Property-match	Categ –match
Purple lion	Purple elephant	Purple dog Purple bear	Purple spatula	Blue horse
Noun: These are blickets. This one is a blicket and this one is a blicket.		These are blickets. This one is a blicket and this one is a blicket.	Look at these.	Can you give me the blicket?
Adjective: These are blickish. This one is blickish and this one is blickish.		These are blickish. This one is blickish and this one is blickish.	Look at these.	Can you give me the blickish one?
No Word: Look at these. Look at this one and look at this one.		Look at these. Look at this one and look at this one.	Look at these.	Can you give me one?

Fig. 6.2 A representative set of stimuli.

From Booth, A. E. & Waxman, S. R. (2008). Taking stock as theories take shape. *Developmental Science*, **11**, 185–194; and Waxman, S. R. & Booth, A. E. (2003). The origins and evolution of links between word learning and conceptual organization: New evidence from 11-month-olds. *Developmental Science*, **6**, 130–137.

the scene. To examine the influence of language on their construals, infants were randomly assigned to a verb, noun, or no word (control) condition. We reasoned that if infants have specific expectations for both verbs and nouns, then they should map words from these grammatical categories differently, mapping nouns specifically to object categories and verbs specifically to event categories. The results were straightforward. By 24 months, infants mapped nouns specifically to the participant objects, and not to the actions in which they were engaged at the time of naming. Perhaps more provocatively, the results revealed for the first time that infants map verbs specifically to the categories of events, and not to the participant objects that were present at the time of naming (Waxman et al., 2009).

Taken together, these results support the claim that: (1) infants begin the task of word learning equipped with a broad expectation that links novel words (independent of their grammatical form) to a broad range of commonalities; (2) this initially general expectation gives way to a more specific set of expectations, linking *particular* kinds of words (e.g. nouns, adjectives, verbs) to *particular* kinds of concepts (concepts of objects, properties, and actions); and (3) these more specific links do not all emerge concurrently. Instead, infants appear to tease apart first the grammatical form *noun* and map this form specifically to object categories. This noun-category link sets the stage for the evolution of more specific expectations linking adjectives and verbs to their respective meanings.

Thus, words influence infants' construals of the objects and events that they observe, and in the second year of life, the links between kinds of words and kinds of concepts become increasingly precise. These distinct links between kinds of words and kinds of concepts support our capacity to move flexibly and nimbly among various construals. In addition, naming permits us to consider the perceptible commonalities that we can observe first-hand, but at the same time to move beyond these to consider the deeper, perhaps hidden commonalities that characterize some of our most fundamental concepts (see Diesendruck, 2003; Diesendruck et al., 1998; Gelman & Kalish, 2006; Waxman et al., 1997). We turn to these issues next.

Theme 2: words have conceptual consequences beyond categorization; they support individuation, inductive inference, and causal reasoning

When young children acquire novel words, they acquire more than names for things. Word learning engages and supports some of the most fundamental logical and conceptual capacities of the human mind, including the processes of object individuation, inductive inference, and reasoning about causal and nonobvious properties.

Object individuation

Object individuation, or the ability to track the identity of distinct individuals over time and place, is a fundamental conceptual and logical capacity (Macnamara, 1986). It permits us to know whether, for example, the kitten we see now is the same kitten we saw previously, or whether they are two different individuals. Under certain experimental conditions, infants have difficulty tracking the identity of two distinct objects (Xu & Carey, 1996). But when each of the objects is labelled with a distinct count noun label, babies successfully track these as distinct individuals (Van de Walle et al., 2000; Wilcox & Baillargeon, 1998; Xu, 1999; Xu & Carey, 1996). Apparently, providing distinct names for distinct objects not only fails to promote categorization (Keates & Graham, 2008; Waxman & Braun, 2005), but also highlights their uniqueness (rather than their commonalities) and supports very young infants' ability to trace their identity over time.

Inductive inference

A chief function of categories is to support inductive reasoning (Murphy, 2002; Smith & Medin, 1981). Induction is the capacity to extend knowledge to novel instances, for example, inferring that a newly encountered mushroom is poisonous on the basis of past encounters with other poisonous mushrooms. All organisms use categories as a structure for forming inductive inferences. Detecting food, enemies, or prey all require responding to new and perceptibly distinct items as if they were comparable to previously viewed items, and drawing appropriate inferences accordingly. One of the most central, accessible, and predictive cues to membership in an object category is perceptual similarity. However, when they are provided with names for things, children do not rely on similarity alone to make category judgements. Below we discuss how words play an important role in the sorts of inductive inferences that children make.

The world is filled with objects for which appearances can be deceiving. These may be the result of evolutionary processes (e.g. a legless lizard resembles a snake more than it resembles a typical lizard) or the product of human ingenuity (e.g. a sponge can be painted to resemble a chunk of granite). In either case, a recurring issue facing infants, children, and adults alike is how to reason when there is a conflict between category membership (i.e. what a thing is) and perceptual similarity (i.e. what a thing is like) (Flavell et al., 1983; Malt, 1994). A clear pattern of developmental evidence has emerged from research on this topic conducted over the past 20 years. Young children, like adults, use category membership as a basis for inductive inference even when it conflicts with perceptual similarity. When faced with such conflicts, words provide critical cues to category membership.

Figure 1 from Gelman & Markman (1986, 1987) illustrates this point. The leaf-insect and the leaf are overall more similar: both are large, green, with striped markings on the back, and share overall shape. Children are highly attentive to these similarities, and when asked to sort pictures in the absence of labelling, rely heavily on perceptual features. However, if each item is given a label (e.g. 'leaf', 'bug', 'bug') and they are asked to draw novel inferences about the leaf-insect, children more often rely on category membership as conveyed by the label. Once children learn a new fact about one member of a category, they generalize the fact to other members of that category, even if the two category members look substantially different. Children are more willing to make category-based inferences when the perceptual and category information are in accord than when they conflict – thus, children do not rely on category labels *exclusively* to guide their inferences. Nonetheless, conventional labels powerfully direct children's responses. These effects are not just due to children discounting the information in drawings, as children draw inferences to dissimilar category members even when the perceptual cues are detailed and realistic, as with three-dimensional objects and photographs (Deák & Bauer, 1996; Gelman & O'Reilly, 1988). These effects are also not due to a desire to comply with experimental task demands, as children use the novel labels in conversations with others who had notbeen present during initial labelling (Jaswal et al., 2009).

The effect of labelling on induction holds for a range of concepts, including types of animals (e.g. bird, fish, rabbit), types of natural substances (e.g. gold, cotton), and types of social categories (e.g. male, female, smart, shy) (Cimpian et al., 2007; Gelman et al., 1986; Giles, 2005; Heyman & Gelman, 2000a,b; Hirschfeld, 1996; Waxman & Shumer, 2008). Hearing a novel social category given its own kind label (e.g. 'She is a carrot-eater') leads to 5- and 7-year-olds to infer that the behaviour is more stable and enduring than when the same category is described otherwise, with a nonlabel descriptive phrase (e.g. 'She eats carrots whenever she can') (Gelman & Heyman, 1999; Liu et al., 2007). Furthermore, hearing a label for a familiar social category can lead children (8–12 years) to treat an individual's ability as more innate and less susceptible to change (Heyman, 2008). Labelling effects extend beyond childhood into adults (Carnaghi et al., 2008; Reynaert & Gelman, 2007; Yamauchi, 2005), including judgements about one's own characteristics (Walton & Banaji, 2004) as well as those of others (Baron, 2007; Diesendruck & haLevi, 2006).

This appreciation that words can signal nonobvious properties seems to be in place at the very start of word learning (Gelman & Coley, 1991; Jaswal & Markman, 2007; Jaswal, 2007; Keates & Graham, 2008). For example, in a series of studies, an experimenter introduces a 13-month-old infant to a target object. For half the infants, the experimenter named the target object with a novel noun; for the remaining infants, no names were provided. All infants then witnessed the experimenter perform an action with the object. Crucially, this action revealed a property of the object that was not available by visual inspection alone (e.g. that it made a particular noise when shaken). Infants were then provided with an opportunity to explore a series of other objects. The results were striking. Infants who had heard no name generalized the hidden property narrowly, trying to elicit it only with test objects that strongly resembled the target object. But infants who heard the target labelled with a novel noun revealed a very different pattern. They now generalized the 'hidden' property more broadly to include other members of the object category, even those that did not bear a strong a perceptual resemblance to the target object (Booth & Waxman, 2002a; Gopnik & Sobel, 2000; Graham et al., 2004; Jaswal & Markman, 2007; Nazzi & Gopnik, 2001; Welder & Graham, 2001).

By 4 years of age, children display subtlety and flexibility regarding when they do and do not make category-based inductive inferences (Gelman, 2003). They do not use a simple matching strategy, in which they extend properties only when two items share identical labels. For example, items that receive a common adjective label do not show the naming effect; the shared label must be kind-referring (Gelman & Coley, 1991). Children also do not use novel labels as the basis for induction when the labels fail to capture a perceptually coherent set (Davidson & Gelman, 1990; Gelman & Waxman, 2007; Sloutsky et al., 2007). These results reveal that children assess the extent to which entities are members of the same category (often conveyed via a label or phrase, though not necessarily), and independently assess the extent to which the property in question is a relatively enduring (vs. temporary or accidental) feature (but see Sloutsky, 2003, for debate). Category-based induction results only when the entities belong to a category and the property is relatively enduring.

Importantly, labels do not exert their effects from simple association with an object, as speaker cues regarding communicative intent powerfully influence whether or not a child makes use of the label. Jaswal (2004) showed preschool children (3 and 4 years of age) anomalous category instances (e.g. a cat that looked like a dog) and asked them to make various inductive inferences (i.e. would it drink milk or eat bones?). As others have found, labelling the items greatly reduced children's reliance on perceptual similarity (i.e. without labels, children typically reported that the cat-like animal would drink milk, but when it was labelled as 'a dog' then they typically reported that it would eat bones). What is most significant for present purposes, however, is that children's use of the label was powerfully affected by whether the label appeared to be applied intentionally or not. When the experimenter prefaced the label with an additional phrase that clarified that the label was certainly intentional and not merely a slip of the tongue (e.g. 'You're not going to believe this, but this is actually a dog'), they were much more likely to make use of the label in drawing inductive inferences.

Causal and nonobvious properties

Young preschoolers extend novel words on the basis of causal powers more than outward properties (Gopnik & Sobel, 2000). For example, if a red cylinder ('a blicket') causes a machine to light up, then children report that another 'blicket' is more likely to be a blue cube that causes the machine to light up, than a red cylinder that does not cause the machine to light up (see also Legare et al., 2008). Similarly, by 7–9 years of age, children treat causal features as more central for novel word extensions. In one set of studies, children learned descriptions of novel animals, in which one feature caused two other features. When asked to determine which test item was more likely to be an example of the animal they had learned, children preferred an animal with a cause feature and an effect feature rather than an animal with two effect features (Ahn et al., 2000). These findings provide support for a 'causal status hypothesis' (Ahn, 1998; Gelman & Kalish, 1993; Rehder, 2003), according to which causal features are more central than effect features, in both labelling and conceptual reasoning.

Children also privilege internal, nonobvious properties in their word extensions. By 4 or 5 years of age, children often recognize that an animal cannot be transformed into another kind of thing (for example, the word 'skunk' cannot be applied to an object that was originally 'a raccoon', even if the animal is transformed to look just like a skunk). Instead, labels are applied stably, despite striking transformations and perceptual change (Gelman & Wellman, 1991; Keil, 1989). When children learn a new category label, they are especially likely to learn the word when told that instances with the same label share nonobvious, internal features as contrasted to superficial features (Diesendruck et al., 1998). This finding is culturally general, appearing not only among middle-class children in the US, but also in middle-class and favela-dwelling children in Brazil (Diesendruck, 2001). Functional features are also central in children's early word extensions (Booth & Waxman, 2002b; Kemler Nelson, 1999; Ware & Booth, 2007).

This finding highlights another important way in which words permit humans to transcend what is available in their perceptual world. Words permit us to retain and sustain our flexible representations, highlighting different construals or perspectives depending upon the task at hand. Other animals have concepts. None has our flexibility and ease of alternative representations. Language is essential not only in permitting these various construals, but in sustaining them. Using a word can shift the hearer's attention or perspective, or make less-salient relations more accessible.

Taken together, the research we have described converges on the view that although human and nonhuman animals share the capacity to form categories in the absence of language, there is nonetheless a crucial role for words in human conceptual development (see Gelman & Kalish, 2006; Waxman & Lidz, 2006; Woodward & Markman, 1998, for recent reviews). We have interpreted this work as evidence that throughout human development, words are more than isolated entities that are somehow attached to particular objects or events. Instead, we have suggested that words, embedded within human linguistic and social systems, are intimately linked with our conceptual representations and permit us to transcend categories and concepts that are supported by immediate perceptual experiences. This interpretation, however, is not uncontroversial.

Simple attentional mechanisms?

We now consider the implications of this evidence for a family of approaches that share a commitment to the view that word and concept acquisition can be accounted for fully on the basis of simple attentional mechanisms (Sloutsky, 2003; Smith, 2000). Following in the empiricist tradition, this family of approaches makes several assumptions: that the raw materials for word meanings and concepts are built up from sensory experiences, that these experiences are operated upon by means of general-purpose processes (including associative learning, similarity assessment, and attentional weighting), and that these processes can account fully for the acquisition of words and concepts. We have argued for a different view. Although we acknowledge the benefits of trying to account for complex mental representations with a minimum of conceptual architecture, and although we acknowledge that general learning principles, sensory experiences, and correlational structure within the environment are certainly at play in the acquisition of words and concepts, we assert that these cannot provide a complete account for the acquisition of words and concepts. In short, they are insufficient because they fail to acknowledge the contribution of abstract conceptual information in words and concepts throughout development, and because they fail to acknowledge the diversity in the kinds of words and kinds of concepts that are the hallmarks of human cognition.

Below we briefly review four interrelated assumptions found in associative and similarity approaches, and evaluate them in light of the evidence presented in the previous sections. To foreshadow, we demonstrate that each assumption, though appealing in its own way, falls short because it uses too blunt a tool when considering the notions of 'word', 'concept', and 'development'.

Assumption No 1: the word–concept link is one of pure association

One of the key debates in the field of nonhuman primate communication is whether the symbols that apes acquire are truly symbolic. The question can be rephrased as: is a sign merely *associated with* a given environmental cue, or does the sign *refer*? The debate rests on the assumption that human signs do refer (Saussure, 1966), and is concerned with whether or not this referential capacity extends to apes – with arguments on either side (e.g. Gardner, et al., 1989; Matsuzawa, 2003; Pinker & Bloom, 1990; Savage-Rumbaugh, 1993; Seidenberg & Petitto, 1979; Terrace, 1979). Ironically, the debate now is no longer only about apes, but also about human children. Within developmental research, there are strong assertions that word learning requires nothing more and nothing less than establishing an association between a word and a perceptual/sensory experience (Samuelson & Smith, 1999; Sloutsky, 2003; Smith, 2000). However, there are also strong reasons to doubt that this is the case.

Importance of social and interpersonal cues The process of word learning is steeped in subtle social and interpersonal information exchange. Hearing a word in the context of an object does not automatically or promiscuously connect that word with the object, as should be the case if word learning was based on associative processes alone. In seeking to establish the meaning of a novel word, children consider the gaze of the speaker (Baldwin, 1995), the extent to which the speaker's behaviour seems intentional versus accidental (Akhtar & Tomasello, 2000; Carpenter et al., 1998; Jaswal, 2004), the speaker's degree of certainty (Sabbagh & Baldwin, 2001), the trustworthiness of the speaker (Koenig & Echols, 2003; Koenig et al., 2004), etc. That these links require more than associative mappings can be seen in children with autism, who have difficulty gauging social implications. They correspondingly have difficulty with these mappings (Baron-Cohen et al., 1997; Tager-Flusberg, 2000), but not with establishing other kinds of associations. Similar conclusions can be drawn from the research with human infants. Words are interpreted as 'names for things' only if they are embedded within a social, linguistic, or symbolic system (Fennell et al., 2007; Namy & Waxman, 2000; Woodward & Hoyne, 1999). Strikingly, when words are presented in isolation, infants do not form associations between them and the objects with which they are introduced. It is only when they are embedded within a linguistic or social context that clarifies their referential status that infants interpret words as names for things. The same is true for nonlinguistic elements (e.g. tones, melodies, squeaks). Presented on their own, infants do not tend to establish associations to objects or to events. Yet, when they are presented within a context that clarifies that they are intended as names for things, infants can, under certain circumstances, establish this connection. These effects illustrate the limitations of a simple associative account for word and concept learning.

Words link to mental representations – not to environmental features An experiment conducted by Preissler and Carey (2004; Preissler & Bloom, 2007) illustrates quite concretely the pitfalls of associationist models of word learning. Eighteen- and 24-month-old infants saw an experimenter point to a photograph of a whisk, and learned a word for this novel entity ('whisk'). Importantly, when given a choice of extending the novel word to a new photograph of another whisk, or to an actual three-dimensional whisk, children preferred the object as referent. They understood something subtle about naming and reference: a word is mapped to a representation (i.e. a concept), and not merely to a perceptual impression (see also Ganea et al., 2008).

A very different illustration of this point comes from the example we offered in the introduction: a host of different kinds of words may be correctly applied to the very same scene (e.g. cats playing in the park). Infants construe the scene differently, depending not only upon the presence of a word, but also, importantly, upon the kind of word presented and its position among other linguistic elements. More generally, the point is this: words cannot link solely to environmental features, because human concepts include both sensory based and abstract entities that extend beyond perceptible features. This point is developed further under Assumption No 4.

Certain kinds of words, including generic nouns, cannot be learned by association alone Word *use* (in both children's speech and adults' child-directed speech) extends beyond simply supplying a label when a referent appears. Adults use labels to refer to absent things, and children readily interpret such expressions (Baldwin, 1991; Ganea et al., 2007; Saylor & Baldwin, 2004). Likewise, children and adults frequently use nouns to refer to abstract *kinds* of things – for example, 'dogs' in the sentence 'Dogs are four-legged'. These expressions, known as generic noun phrases (Carlson & Pelletier, 1995; Gelman, 2004), emerge in children's speech by about 2½ years of age in English – which is the earliest that English speakers have productive control over the morphological devices required for their expression (plurals, articles, tense) (Gelman et al., 2008). By preschool age, children understand the semantic implications of generics as kind-referring (Cimpian & Markman, 2008; Gelman & Raman, 2003), as extending beyond current context (Gelman & Bloom, 2007), and as expressing stable and important properties (Graham and Chambers, 2005; Hollander et al. 2009). When preschoolers learn a novel label and are asked to extend that label to new instances, generics draw children's attention towards the critical feature mentioned even when it competes with similarity (Hollander et al., 2009). Likewise, when children learn a novel word introduced generically rather than specifically, they are more likely to extend the word to a taxonomic match (e.g. apple to banana) than to a shape match (e.g. apple to baseball; Tare & Gelman, in press). When asked to make comparison judgements (e.g. noting either similarities or differences), presenting the items in generic form (e.g. 'Can you tell me some things that are [the same] [different] about dogs and cats'?) leads preschool children and adults to deeper, less obvious comparisons than when the items are presented in specific form (e.g. 'Can you tell me some things that are [the same] [different] about this dog and this cat?'; Gelman et al., 2009).

The associationist model might suggest that generics are acquired by learning a limited set of forms that are associated or correlated with generic meaning in the input. Such a model was proposed by Smith, Jones, & Landau (1996) to account for how count nouns versus mass nouns are learnt. If this model accounts for the acquisition of generics, we should expect a gradual process, by which children slowly learn to map generic meaning onto each of a variety of particular forms. For example, children might first acquire the most common form, and only later acquire less-common forms. However, this description does not match the developmental facts: (1) generic referents are not observable; (2) the linguistic contexts associated with generic noun phrases vary widely; and (3) generic noun phrases have no morphological marker in some languages (e.g. Mandarin, Quechua). An associative model runs into difficulty accounting for the ease with which children acquire generic noun phrases.

Associationist models are unconstrained How is it that children acquire a basic set of concepts in a fairly regular way, across wide variations in experience, without gross deviations? The general answer, on an empiricist view, is that the structure of the input is responsible, and that basic conceptual distinctions can be recovered from low-level features of input. But it is also clear that among the myriad associations that are present in the environment, only certain associations among them, or links between words and concepts, will be detected readily; others may not be extracted at all (Booth & Waxman, 2008; Keil, 1981; Quine, 1960). Of all the possible correlations available in the input, why is it that some concepts emerge early in development and reliably across input conditions, while others do not? Why is it that some concepts are difficult to acquire or resistant to evidence from the environment? The most parsimonious answer to this question is that in addition to the structure in the input, there is also structure in the mind of the learner (Chomsky, 1959; Gelman & Kalish, 2006; Gelman & Williams, 1998; Waxman & Lidz, 2006). The acquisition of some concepts is guided not only by what is available in the input but also what is available in the mind.

Assumption No 2: a word is an attentional spotlight, nothing more

Some researchers have proposed that words focus infants' and children's attention on objects, and that the facilitative effect of words on categorization and induction comes along for free, merely as a by-product of this heightened attention (see Waxman & Braun, 2005, for a fuller articulation of this assumption and its shortcomings). Here we focus on three distinct, but interrelated, pitfalls of this assumption.

Words presented in isolation do not lead to concept formation If words acted strictly as attentional spotlights, then words presented alone would promote concept formation. There is considerable evidence documenting that this is not the case (as reviewed earlier: Fennell & Waxman, 2008; Fennell et al., 2007; Namy & Waxman, 2000).

Not all input serves equally to spotlight attention If a word is an attentional spotlight, then any attention-enhancing stimulus (e.g. tone, gesture, etc.) should serve as a spotlight as well. This is not the case. For example, as reviewed earlier, both words and tones augment infants' attention to objects, but only words serve as invitations to form categories of objects (Balaban & Waxman, 1997; Fulkerson & Waxman, 2007). In addition, many other nonlinguistic elements (tone, gesture, squeak) are attention enhancing, yet they do not serve as invitations to form object categories. Instead, if such stimuli are to evoke a categorization response, they must be presented within a social or linguistic context that somehow conveys their referential status (Namy & Waxman, 2000; Woodward & Hoyne, 1999).

Not all words are equal; not all concepts are equal If words were no more than attentional spotlights, then whether the same or different words were applied to a distinct set of objects, these should promote categorization. But this is not the case. Applying the same noun to a set of objects highlights commonalities among them and promotes object categorization; applying a different noun to each object has a very different effect, highlighting distinctions among them and promoting object individuation (Waxman & Braun, 2005; Xu et al., 2005).

Moreover, the metaphor of word-as-attentional-spotlight is too diffuse because from the beginning of word learning, different words highlight different kinds of categories. As we have seen earlier, nouns spotlight categories of objects (e.g. animal) but not properties of objects (e.g. fuzzy) (Booth & Waxman, 2009; Waxman & Markow, 1998), or the actions in which they are engaged (Waxman et al., 2009). Verbs spotlight event categories and not object categories, etc. Words do not function as a general spotlight.

Assumption No 3: a word is merely another feature

Another closely related assumption is that words are simply one more perceptual feature that items can share. So, for example, if two entities are both called 'birds', they become more perceptually similar, because they share a verbal feature in addition to their visual features (Sloutsky & Fisher, 2004). This increase in perceptual (verbal plus visual) similarity leads children to treat the instances as more alike. We do not doubt that sharing a common label highlights commonalities among objects. This observation was made over 50 years ago (Rossman & Goss, 1951). What we doubt is that the common label is nothing more than another feature in an undifferentiated similarity space (Sloutsky, 2003; Smith et al., 1996). Here, we focus on three classes of evidence that reveal that words are more than 'just another feature' attached to an object: (1) words are distinctive, and influence categorization and judgements more than (and differently from) other features; (2) different kinds of words (and different uses of words) yield different kinds of effects, none of which could be predicted on the 'just another feature' account; (3) the effects of wording are graded, not absolute. We discuss each of these points below.

Words are distinctive One serious problem with the word-as-feature account is that it cannot distinguish words from any other kind of associated auditory cues (e.g. tones). On the 'words-are-just-another-feature' account, the introduction of any additional shared feature should have the same effect on categorization and inductive inference. But it does not. As noted earlier, tones do not consistently yield the same effects as words (Balaban & Waxman, 1997; Fulkerson & Waxman, 2007).

Perhaps in an attempt to circumvent this concern, Sloutsky has argued that words are, in some sense, a 'super feature': on his view, auditory features override visual features in children's processing. This is an exceedingly tricky claim, as it is not clear how one could adequately calibrate the strength of the two dimensions (auditory, visual), and without such a calibration, it is impossible to deliver on any claim that is predicated on pitting one against the other for salience. Moreover, even if such a calibration were possible, we cannot assume that the calibration derived at one time persists across contexts. To take just one example, it is reasonable to assume that when infants first hear a new word, sound, or linguistic construction, isolating and identifying this unit in fluent speech may be difficult, and may deplete attentional resources for other tasks, including inspection of the visual input. But eventually, as this auditory unit becomes more familiar, identifying it should require less attention. Put differently, attentional demands do not operate as steady states, but are instead responsive to momentary environmental contingencies.

Different kinds of words (and different uses of words) have different kinds of effects Most crucially, where the 'words-as-features' view falls short is in failing to differentiate among different kinds of words. If words were nothing more or less than simple attentional cues, then different kinds of words should nonetheless exert the same sorts of effects on infants' and young children's construals. Yet as reviewed earlier, children notice different kinds of commonalities and render different sorts of inductive inferences, depending on whether a word is introduced as a count noun, proper noun, mass noun, adjective, preposition, or verb (Bloom, 2000; Gelman & Coley, 1991; Gelman & Markman, 1986; Waxman & Lidz, 2006). Moreover, as also noted earlier, words fail to exert effects unless they are presented in a linguistic context and have referential status. In short, children's sensitivity to different word types makes clear that children are not simply treating an auditory cue as a featural similarity.

In contrast, we propose that children interpret auditory cues as the referential signals they are intended to be. In this framework, children treat different words as referring to different kinds of concepts (i.e. count nouns label taxonomic kinds; proper nouns label individuals), and these concepts mediate children's judgements.

Assumption No 4: a word indexes a perceptual representation, nothing more

A fourth assertion offered within associationist accounts is that young children's concepts, and the words they use to describe them, are grounded exclusively in perception: '[Y]oung children's naming of objects is principally a matter of mapping words to selected perceptual properties' (Smith et al., 1996, p. 144). Although we certainly agree that perceptual features are important in the concepts held by humans and nonhumans alike, we take issue with the claim that in human concepts, perceptual features are primary. Instead, many human concepts seem to possess two distinct though interrelated levels: the level of observable reality and the level of explanation and cause. It is an open question whether nonhumans represent this second level as well (e.g. Povinelli, 2000). But certainly for humans, this two-tier structure has the capacity to motivate further development, by leading children to consider and develop deeper understandings (Wellman & Gelman, 1998). The ability to consider contrasting representations is a powerful capacity that may lead children to new insights (see also Inhelder & Piaget, 1958).

Hidden features have conceptual consequences On the words-as-perceptual-cues account, if two response items are equated for perceptual similarity with the target, but in addition, one has a conceptual, hidden commonality, then naming should not lead the child to prefer one over the other, because words map to perceptual features alone. This prediction does not fare well in the face of the evidence. For example, for infants and toddlers, providing a shared label for two distinct objects leads infants and young children to expect that despite the perceptual distance between them, those objects are members of the same the category and as such, will share nonobvious features (Booth et al. 2005; Gelman & Markman, 1987; Keates & Graham, 2008; Jaswal, 2004; Waxman & Shumer, 2008).

Moreover, many human concepts are abstract and extend beyond perceptible features of the environment: both sophisticated concepts (e.g. 'justice', 'communism') and basic, early-acquired concepts ('mine', 'good', 'cause'). As reviewed earlier, a wealth of findings indicates that children treat words as indicating a deeper set of properties (Gelman & Heyman, 1999; Gelman & Markman, 1986; Gopnik & Sobel, 2000; Graham et al., 2004; Mandler, 2004; Walton & Banaji, 2004; Yamauchi, 2005).

The problem of context sensitivity A further problem with the words-map-onto-percepts-only view is that any position that relies solely on similarity-based processing will have difficulty accounting for context sensitivity. Children's concepts and word learning are notable for the context-sensitive, selective use of similarity. Preschool-aged children realize that although a person and a toy monkey look alike, they are unlikely to share internal properties; they also understand that although a worm and a person look different, they are likely to share insides (Carey, 1985; Gelman, 2003; Keil, 1989). Simple attention to correlated attributes is not sufficient to account for these expectations. For example, 3- and 4-year-olds predict that a wooden pillow will be hard rather than soft, even though all the pillows children have previously encountered have been soft (Kalish & Gelman, 1992). Likewise, 2- to 4-year-old children are more likely to use perceptual similarity cues when similarity corresponds to function (McCarrell & Callanan, 1995; Ware & Booth, 2007). For example, after looking at pictures of two creatures that differed only in eye size and leg length, children were invited to make an inference concerning sight (e.g. 'Which one sees really well in the dark?') or movement (e.g. 'Which one can jump really high?'). Children attended selectively to different perceptual features depending on the particular function (e.g. eyes, when the question concerned sight; legs, when the question concerned movement). Giles and Heyman (2004) found that preschool children judged the same behaviour differently depending on the category of the individual involved. For example if a girl (vs. boy vs. dog) spills a child's milk, the implications differ accordingly, in how this is explained. These examples of selectivity would seem more readily explained as an instance of causal reasoning than as a reflection of attentional weights.

Conclusions

In this chapter we have argued that words and concepts are intricately intertwined throughout human development, and that the link between them has important conceptual consequences, motivating us to move beyond the information immediately available to us by virtue of our perceptual experiences. We have summarized current theoretical views and empirical evidence attesting to the power and complexity of these links between words and concepts, and have argued against the view that simple attentional mechanisms can account fully for the acquisition of words and concepts. We have also pointed out that sweeping claims about words and concepts need to be tempered by careful consideration of the kind of concept and the kind of linguistic expression that is recruited to capture it. Yet, we have noted that at their core, most approaches espousing a simple attentional view tend to treat 'word', 'concept', and 'development' as unanalysed units. This is a shortcoming: concepts that the human mind deals with are more complicated, subtle, flexible, and diverse; the words that comprise the languages of the world support this conceptual complexity, subtlety, flexibility, and diversity.

One major open question concerns what if anything is unique about human concepts. Here it is interesting to consider that nonhuman primates have full access to the broad attentional mechanisms considered earlier – including the capacity to note similarity and to track statistical features of the environment – yet only humans have a full and expressive language system. On the attentional learning view, these differences might be understood in terms of evolutionarily based differences in which sorts of features human infants attend to (as distinct from the young of other species). For example, perhaps the human species has evolved a propensity for processing auditory information, and this propensity thereby encourages attention to language. Yet, this view cannot account for the acquisition of full and expressive visuogestural languages. However, the model that we have proposed here – a model in which human learning and development are linked to mechanisms *beyond* attentional learning to include social understandings, causal reasoning, and theory-based concepts – is consistent with the acquisition underlying the full range of human languages.

Acknowledgements

Preparation of this chapter was supported by NICHD grant R01HD030410 to Waxman, and NICHD grants R01HD36043 and R56HD036043 to Gelman from the Eunice Kennedy Shriver National Institute of Child Health & Human Development.

The content is solely the responsibility of the authors and does not necessarily represent the official views of the Eunice Kennedy Shriver National Institute Of Child Health & Human Development or the National Institutes of Health. We thank Erin Leddon for helpful comments on an earlier draft.

References

Ahn, W. (1998). Why are different features central for natural kinds and artifacts? *Cognition*, 69, 135–178.

Ahn, W., Gelman, S. A., Amsterlaw, J., Hohenstein, J., & Kalish, C. W. (2000). Causal status effect in children's categorization. *Cognition*, 76, B35–B43.

Akhtar, N. & Tomasello, M. (2000). The social nature of words and word learning. In R. Golinkoff & K. Hirsh-Pasek (Eds.), *Becoming a Word Learner: A Debate on Lexical Acquisition*, pp. 113–135, New York: Oxford University Press.

Armstrong, S. L., Gleitman, L. R., & Gleitman, H. G. (1983). On what some concepts might not be. *Cognition*, 13, 263–308.

Aslin, R. N., Woodward, J. Z., LaMendola N. P., & Bever, T. G. (1996). Models of word segmentation in fluent maternal speech to infants. In J. L. Morgan & K. Demuth (Eds.), *Signal to Syntax*, pp. 117–134, Mahwah, NJ: Erlbaum.

Balaban, M. T. & Waxman, S. R. (1997). Do word labels facilitate object categorization in 9-month-old infants? *Journal of Experimental Child Psychology*, 64, 3–26.

Baldwin, D. A. (1991). Infants' contribution to the achievement of joint reference. *Child Development*, 62, 875–890.

Baldwin, D. A. (1995). Understanding the link between joint attention and language. In C. Moore & P. J. Dunham (Eds.), *Joint Attention: Its Origins and Role in Development*, pp. 131–158, Hillsdale, NJ: Erlbaum.

Baldwin, D. A. & Markman, E. M. (1989). Establishing word–object relations: A first step. *Child Development*, 60, 381–398.

Baldwin, D. A., Markman, E. M., Bill, B., Desjardins, R. N., & Irwin, J. M. (1996). Infants' reliance on a social criterion for establishing word–object relations. *Child Development*, 67, 3135–3153.

Baron, A. S. (2007, October). Cognitive developmental perspectives on social categorization and the implications for intergroup bias. Paper Presented at the Cognitive Development Society Fifth Biennial Meeting, Santa Fe, NM.

Baron-Cohen, S., Baldwin, D., & Crowson, M. (1997). Do children with autism use the speaker's direction of gaze (SDG) strategy to crack the code of language? *Child Development*, 68, 48–57.

Bloom, L. (2000). The intentionality model of word learning: How to learn a word, any word. In R. M. Golinkoff, K. Hirsh-Pasek, N. Akhtar, et al. (Eds.), *Becoming a Word Learner: A Debate on Lexical Acquisition*, pp. 19–50, New York: Oxford University Press.

Booth, A. E. & Waxman, S. R. (2002a). Word learning is 'smart': Evidence that conceptual information effects preschoolers' extension of novel words. *Cognition*, 84, B11–B22.

Booth, A. E. & Waxman, S. R. (2002b). Object names and object functions serve as cues to categories for infants. *Developmental Psychology*, 38, 948–957.

Booth, A. E. & Waxman, S. R. (2008). Taking stock as theories take shape. *Developmental Science*, 11, 185–194.

Booth, A. E. & Waxman, S. R. (2009). A horse of a different color: Specifying with precision infants' mappings of novel nouns and adjectives. *Child Development*, **80**(1), 15–22.

Booth, A. E., Waxman, S. R., & Huang, Y.T. (2005). Conceptual information permeates word learning in infancy. *Developmental Psychology*, **41**, 491–505.

Brent, M. R. & Siskind, J. M. (2001). The role of exposure to isolated words in early vocabulary development. *Cognition*, **81**(2), B33–B44.

Brown, R. (1957). Linguistic determinism and the part of speech. *Journal of Abnormal and Social Psychology*, **55**, 1–5.

Brown, R. (1958). *Words and Things* New York: The Free Press.

Campbell, A. L. & Namy, L. L. (2003). The role of social referential cues in verbal and non-verbal symbol learning. *Child Development*, **74**, 549–563.

Carey, S. (1985). *Conceptual Change in Childhood* Cambridge, MA: Bradford Books.

Carlson, G. N. & Pelletier F. J. (Eds) (1995). *The Generic Book* Chicago, IL: University of Chicago Press.

Carnaghi, A., Maass, A., Gresta, S., Bianchi, M., Cadinu, M., & Arcuri, L. (2008). Nomina sunt omina: On the inductive potential of nouns and adjectives in person perception. *Journal of Personality and Social Psychology*, **94**, 839–859.

Carpenter, M., Akhtar, N., & Tomasello, M. (1998). Fourteen- through 18-month-old infants differentially imitate intentional and accidental actions. *Infant Behavior & Development*, **21**, 315–330.

Chomsky, N. (1959). A review of *Verbal Behavior*, by B. F. Skinner. *Language*, **35**(1), 26–57.

Cimpian, A., Arce, H. C., Markman, E. M., & Dweck, C. S. (2007). Subtle linguistic cues affect children's motivation. *Psychological Science*, **18**, 314–316.

Cimpian, A. & Markman, E. M. (2008). Preschool children's use of cues to generic meaning. *Cognition*, **107**, 19–53.

Davidson, N. S. & Gelman, S. A. (1990). Inductions from novel categories: The role of language and conceptual structure. *Cognitive Development*, **5**, 151–176.

Deák, G., & Bauer, P. J. (1996). The dynamics of preschoolers' categorization choices. *Child Development*, **67**, 740–767.

Diesendruck, G. (2001). Essentialism in Brazilian children's extensions of animal names. *Developmental Psychology*, **37**, 49–60.

Diesendruck, G. (2003). Categories for names or names for categories? The interplay between domain-specific conceptual structure and language. *Language and Cognitive Processes*, **18**, 759–787.

Diesendruck, G. & haLevi, H. (2006). The role of language, appearance, and culture in children's social category based induction. *Child Development*, **77**, 539–553.

Diesendruck, G., Gelman, S. A., & Lebowitz, K. (1998). Conceptual and linguistic biases in children's word learning. *Developmental Psychology*, **34**, 823–839.

Fennell, C. & Waxman, S. R. (in press). What paradox? Referential cues allow for infant use of phonetic detail in word learning. *Child Development*.

Fennell, C. T., Waxman, S. R., & Weisleder, A. (2007). With referential cues, infants successfully use phonetic detail in word learning. In H. Caunt-Nulton, S. Kulatilake, & I. Woo (Eds.), *Proceedings of the 31st Boston University Conference on Language Development*, pp. 206–217, Somerville, MA: Cascadilla Press.

Ferry, A., Hespos, S., & Waxman, S. R. (in press). Categorization in 3- and 4-month-old infants: An advantage of words over tones. *Child Development*.

Fisher, C. (2002). Structural limits on verb mapping: The role of abstract structure in 2.5-year-olds' interpretations of novel verbs. *Developmental Science*, 5, 56–65.

Fisher, C. & Song, H. (2006). Who's the subject? Sentence structures as analogs of verb meaning. In K. Hirsh-Pasek & R. M. Golinkoff (Eds.), *Action Meets Word: How Children Learn the Meanings of Verbs*, pp. 392–423, New York: Oxford University Press.

Flavell, J. H., Flavell, E. R., & Green, F. L. (1983). Development of the appearance-reality distinction. *Cognitive Psychology*, 15, 95–120.

Fulkerson, A. L. (1997). 'New Words for New Things: The Relationship between Novel Labels and Twelve-Month-Olds' Categorization of Novel Objects' (Unpublished master's thesis), University of Toledo, Toledo, OH.

Fulkerson, A. L. & Haaf, R. A. (2003). The influence of labels, non-labeling sounds, and source of auditory input on 9- and 15-month-olds' object categorization. *Infancy*, 4, 349–369.

Fulkerson, A. L. & Waxman, S. R. (2007). Words (but not tones) facilitate object categorization: Evidence from 6- and 12-month-olds. *Cognition*, 105, 218–228.

Fulkerson, A. L., Waxman, S. R., & Seymour, J. M. (2006). Linking object names and object categories: Words (but not tones) facilitate object categorization in 6- and 12-month-olds. In D. Bamman, T. Magnitskaia, & C. Zaller (Eds.), *Supplement to the Proceedings of the 30th Boston University Conference on Language Development*, pp. 32–38, Somerville, MA: Cascadilla Press.

Ganea, P. A., Shutts, K., Spelke, E., & DeLoache, J. S. (2007). Thinking of things unseen: Infants' use of language to update object representations. *Psychological Science*, 18, 734–739.

Ganea, P. A., Pickard, M. B., & DeLoache, J. S. (2008). Transfer between picture books and the real world. *Journal of Cognition and Development*, 9, 46–66.

Gardner, B. T., Gardner, R. A., & Nichols, S. G. (1989). The shapes and uses of signs in a cross-fostering laboratory, In R. A. Gardner, B. T. Gardner, & T. E. Van Cantfort (Eds.), *Teaching Sign Language to Chimpanzees*, pp. 55–180, Albany, NY: State University of New York Press.

Gelman, S. A. (2004). Learning words for kinds: Generic noun phrases in acquisition. In D. G. Hall & S. R. Waxman (Eds.), *Weaving a Lexicon*, pp. 445–484, Cambridge, MA: MIT Press.

Gelman, S. A. (2003). *The Essential Child: Origins of Essentialism in Everyday Thought* New York: Oxford University Press.

Gelman, S. A. & Bloom, P. (2007). Developmental changes in the understanding of generics. *Cognition*, 105, 166–183.

Gelman, S. A. & Waxman S. R. (2007). Looking beyond looks: Comments on Sloutsky, Kloos, and Fisher, When looks are everything: Appearance similarity versus kind information in early induction. *Psychological Science*, 18, 554–555.

Gelman, S. A. & Kalish, C. W. (2006). Conceptual development. In W. Damon & R. M. Lerner (Series Eds.), and D. Kuhn & R. S. Siegler (Eds.), *Handbook of Child Psychology: Vol. 2 Cognition, Perception, and Language* 5th edn., pp. 687–733, Hoboken, NJ: Wiley.

Gelman, S. A. & Raman, L. (2003). Preschool children use linguistic form class and pragmatic cues to interpret generics. *Child Development*, 24, 308–325.

Gelman, S. A. & Heyman, G. D. (1999). Carrot-eaters and creature-believers: The effects of lexicalization on children's inferences about social categories. *Psychological Science*, 10, 489–493.

Gelman, R. & Williams, E. (1998). Enabling constraints for cognitive development and learning: Domain specificity and epigenesis. In W. Damon & R. M. Lerner (Series Eds.), and D. Kuhn & R. Siegler (Eds.), *Cognition, Perception, and Language, Vol. 2. Handbook of Child Psychology*, 5th edn., pp. 575–630, New York: Wiley.

Gelman, S. A. & Kalish, C. W. (1993). Categories and causality. In R. Pasnak & M. L. Howe (Eds.), *Emerging Themes in Cognitive Development*, pp. 3–32, New York: Springer-Verlag.

Gelman, S. A. & Coley, J. D. (1991). Language and categorization: The acquisition of natural kind terms. In J. P. Byrnes & S. A. Gelman (Eds.), *Perspectives on Language and Thought: Interrelations in Development*, pp. 146–196, New York: Cambridge University Press.

Gelman, S. A. & Wellman, H. (1991). Insides and essences: Early understandings of the non-obvious. *Cognition*, 38, 213–244.

Gelman, S. A. & O'Reilly, A. W. (1988). Children's inductive inferences with superordinate categories: The role of language and category structure. *Child Development*, 59, 876–887.

Gelman, S. A. & Markman, E. M. (1987). Young children's inductions from natural kinds: The role of categories and appearances. *Child Development*, 58, 1532–1541.

Gelman, S. A. & Markman, E. M. (1986). Categories and induction in young children. *Cognition*, 23, 183–209.

Gelman, S. A. & Taylor, M. (1984). How 2-year-old children interpret proper and common names for unfamiliar objects. *Child Development*, 55, 1535–1540.

Gelman, S. A., Raman, L., & Gentner, D. (2009). Effects of language and similarity on comparison processing. *Language Learning and Development*, 5, 147–171.

Gelman, S. A., Collman, P., & Maccoby, E. E. (1986). Inferring properties from categories versus inferring categories from properties: The case of gender. *Child Development*, 57, 396–404.

Gelman, S.A., Goetz, P. J., Sarnecka, B. S., & Flukes, J. (2008). Generic language in parent–child conversations. *Language Learning and Development*, 4, 1–31.

Giles, J. W. (2005, October). Priming effects in children's reasoning about aggression. *Paper Presented at the Cognitive Development Society*, San Diego, CA.

Giles, J. W. & Heyman, G. D. (2004). When to cry over spilled milk: Young children's use of category information to guide inferences about ambiguous behavior. *Journal of Cognition and Development*, 5, 359–382.

Gogate, L. J., Walker-Andrews, A. S., & Bahrick, L. E. (2001). The intersensory origins of word comprehension: An ecological-dynamic systems view. *Developmental Science*, 4, 1–18.

Gopnik, A. & Nazzi, T. (2003). Words, kinds and causal powers: A theory perspective on early naming and categorization. In D. Rakison & L. Oakes (Eds.), *Early Category and Concept Development: Making Sense of the Blooming, Buzzing Confusion*, pp. 303–329, New York: Oxford University Press.

Gopnik, A. & Sobel, D. (2000). Detecting blickets: How young children use information about novel causal powers in categorization and induction. *Child Development*, 71, 1205–1222.

Graham, S. & Chambers, C. G. (2005, March). Preschoolers' attention to linguistic cues in the acquisition of generic knowledge. *Paper Presented at the Biennial Meetings of the Society for Research in Child Development*.

Graham, S. A., Baker, R. K., & Poulin-Dubois, D. (1998). Infants' expectations about object label reference. *Canadian Journal of Experimental Psychology*, 52, 103–112.

Graham, S. A., Kibreath, C. S., & Welder, A. N. (2004). 13-month-olds rely on shared labels and shape similarity for inductive inferences. *Child Development*, 75, 409–427.

Hall, D. G. & Lavin, T. (2004). The use and misuse of part-of-speech information in word learning. In D. G. Hall & S. R. Waxman (Eds.), *Weaving a Lexicon*, pp. 339–370, Cambridge, MA: MIT Press.

Heyman, G. D. (2008). Talking about success: Implications for achievement motivation. *Journal of Applied Developmental Psychology*, **29**, 361–370.

Heyman, G. D. & Gelman, S. A. (2000a). Preschool children's use of novel predicates to make inductive inferences about people. *Cognitive Development*, **15**, 263–280.

Heyman, G. D. & Gelman, S. A. (2000b). Preschool children's use of traits labels to make inductive inferences. *Journal of Experimental Child Psychology*, **77**, 1–19.

Hirschfeld, L. A. (1996). *Race in the Making: Cognition, Culture, and the Child's Construction of Human Kinds* Cambridge: MIT Press.

Hollander, M. A., Gelman, S. A., & Raman, L. (2009). Generic language and judgments about category membership: Can generics highlight properties as central? *Language and Cognitive Processes*, **24**(4), 481–505.

Inhelder, B. & Piaget, J. (1958). *The Growth of Logical Thinking from Childhood to Adolescence* New York: Basic Books.

Jaswal, V. K. (2004). Don't believe everything you hear: Preschoolers' sensitivity to speaker intent in category induction. *Child Development*, **75**, 1871–1885.

Jaswal, V. K. (2007). The effect of vocabulary size on toddlers' receptiveness to unexpected testimony about category membership. *Infancy*, **12**, 169–187.

Jaswal, V. K. & Markman, E. M. (2007). Looks aren't everything: 24-month-olds' willingness to accept unexpected labels. *Journal of Cognition and Development*, **8**, 93–111.

Jaswal, V. K., Lima, O. K., & Small, J. E. (2009). Compliance, conversion, and category induction. *Journal of Experimental Child Psychology*, **102**(2), 182–195.

Kalish, C. W. & Gelman, S. A. (1992). On wooden pillows: Multiple classification and children's category-based inductions. *Child Development*, **63**, 1536–1557.

Keates, J. & Graham, S. (2008). Category labels or attributes: Why do labels guide infants' inductive inferences? *Psychological Science*, **19**, 1287–1293.

Keil, F. C. (1981). Children's thinking: What never develops. *Cognition*, **10**, 159–166.

Keil, F. C. (1989). *Concepts, Kinds, and Cognitive Development* Cambridge, MA: MIT Press.

Kemler Nelson, D. G. (1999). Attention to functional properties in toddlers' naming and problem-solving. *Cognitive Development*, **14**, 77–100.

Klibanoff, R. S. & Waxman, S. R. (2000). Basic level object categories support the acquisition of novel adjectives: Evidence from preschool-aged children. *Child Development*, **71**, 649–659.

Koenig, M. A., Clément, F., & Harris, P. L. (2004). Trust in testimony: Children's use of true and false statements. *Psychological Science*, **15**, 694–698.

Koenig, M. A. & Echols, C. H. (2003). Infants' understanding of false labeling events: The referential role of words and the people who use them. *Cognition*, **87**, 181–210.

Legare, C., Gelman, S. A., Wellman, H. M., & Kushnir, T. (2008, July). The function of causal explanatory reasoning in children. Poster Presented at the Annual Meeting of the Cognitive Science Society. Washington, DC.

Liu, D., Gelman, S. A., & Wellman, H. M. (2007). Components of young children's trait understanding: Inferring trait labels from behaviors and predicting behaviors from trait labels. *Child Development*, **78**, 1543–1558.

Macnamara, J. (1984). *Names for Things* Cambridge, MA: MIT Press.

Macnamara, J. (1986). *A Border Dispute* Cambridge, MA: MIT Press.

Malt, B. C. (1994). Water is not H_2O. *Cognitive Psychology*, **27**, 41–70.

Mandler, J. M. (2004). *The Foundations of Mind: Origins of Conceptual Thought* New York: Oxford University Press.

Markman, E. M. (1989). *Categorization and Naming in Children: Problems of Induction* Cambridge, MA: MIT Press.

Matsuzawa, T. (2003). The Ai project: Historical and ecological contexts. *Animal Cognition*, **6**, 199–211.

McCarrell, N. S. & Callanan, M. A. (1995). Form–function correspondences in children's inference. *Child Development*, **66**, 532–546.

Mintz, T. H. & Gleitman, L. R. (2002). Adjectives really do modify nouns: The incremental and restricted nature of early adjective acquisition. *Cognition*, **84**, 267–293.

Murphy, G. L. (2000). Explanatory concepts. In R. A. Wilson & F. C. Keil (Eds.), *Explanation and Cognition*, pp. 361–392, Cambridge, MA: MIT Press.

Murphy, G. L. (2002). *The Big Book of Concepts* Cambridge, MA: MIT Press.

Murphy, G. L. & Medin, D. L. (1985). The role of theories in conceptual coherence. *Psychological Review*, **92**, 289–316.

Naigles, L. (1990). Children use syntax to learn verb meanings. *Journal of Child Language*, 117, 357–374.

Namy, L. L. & Waxman, S. R. (1998). Words and gestures: Infants' interpretations of different forms of symbolic reference. *Child Development*, **69**, 295–308.

Namy, L. L. & Waxman, S. R. (2000). Naming and exclaiming: Infants' sensitivity to naming contexts. *Journal of Cognition and Development*, **1**, 405–428.

Namy, L. L. & Waxman, S. R. (2002). Patterns of spontaneous production of novel words and gestures within an experimental setting in children ages 1.6 and 2.2. *Journal of Child Language*, **29**, 911–921.

Pinker, S. & Bloom, P. (1990). Natural language and natural selection. *Behavioral and Brain Sciences*, **13**, 707–784.

Poulin-Dubois, D., Graham, S. A., & Sippola, L. (1995). Early lexical development: The contribution of parental labeling and infants' categorization abilities. *Journal of Child Language*, **22**, 325–343.

Povinelli, D. J. (2000). *Folk Physics for Apes: The Chimpanzee's Theory of How the World Works* Oxford: Oxford University Press.

Preissler, M. A. & Bloom, P. (2007). Two-year olds understand the duality of pictures. *Psychological Science*, **18**, 1–2.

Preissler, M. A. & Carey, S. (2004). Do both pictures and words function as symbols for 18- and 24-month-old children? *Journal of Cognition and Development*, **5**, 185–212.

Quine, W. V. O. (1960). *Word and Object: An Inquiry into the Linguistic Mechanisms of Objective Reference* New York: Wiley.

Rakison, D. H. & Lupyan, G. (2008). Developing object concepts in infancy: An associative learning perspective. *Monographs of SRCD*, **73**(1), 1–110.

Rehder, B. (2003). Categorization as causal reasoning. *Cognitive Science*, **27**, 709–748.

Reynaert, C. C. & Gelman, S. A. (2007). The influence of language form and conventional wording on judgments of illness. *Journal of Psycholinguistic Research*, **36**, 273–295.

Rossman, I. L. & Goss, A. E. (1951). The acquired distinctiveness of cues: The role of discriminative verbal responses in facilitating the acquisition of discriminative motor responses. *Journal of Experimental Psychology*, **42**, 173–182.

Sabbagh, M. A. & Baldwin, D. A. (2001). Learning words from knowledgeable versus ignorant speakers: Links between preschoolers' theory of mind and semantic development. *Child Development*, **72**, 1054–1070.

Samuelson, L. K. & Smith, L. B. (1999). Early noun vocabularies: Do ontology, category structure, and syntax correspond? *Cognition*, **73**, 1–33.

Saussure, F. de. (1966). *Course in General Linguistics*. C. Bally, A. Sechehaye, & A. Riedlinger (Eds.), W. Baskin (translator), New York: McGraw-Hill.

Savage-Rumbaugh, E. S. (1993). *Language Comprehension in Ape and Child* Chicago, IL: University of Chicago Press.

Saylor, M. M. & Baldwin, D. A. (2004). Discussing those not present: Comprehension of references to absent caregivers. *Journal of Child Language*, **31**, 537–560.

Seidenberg, M. S. & Petitto, L. A. (1979). Signing behavior in apes: A critical review. *Cognition*, **7**, 177–215.

Sloutsky, V. M. (2003). The role of similarity in the development of categorization. *Trends in Cognitive Sciences*, **7**, 246–251.

Sloutsky, V. M. & Fisher, A. V. (2004). Induction and categorization in young children: A similarity-based model. *Journal of Experimental Psychology: General*, **133**, 166–188.

Sloutsky, V. M., & Fisher, A. V. (2005). Similarity, induction, naming, and categorization (SINC): Generalization or verbal inductive reasoning? Response to Heit and Hayes. *Journal of Experimental Psychology: General*, **134**, 606–611.

Sloutsky, V. M. & Lo, Y.-F. (1999). How much does a shared name make things similar? Part 1: Linguistic labels and the development of similarity judgment. *Developmental Psychology*, **35**, 1478–1492.

Sloutsky, V. M., Kloos, H., & Fisher, A. V. (2007). When looks are everything: Appearance similarity versus kind information in early induction. *Psychological Science*, **18**, 179–185.

Smith, E. E. & Medin, D. L. (1981). *Categories and Concepts* Cambridge, MA: Harvard University Press.

Smith, L. B. (2000). Learning how to learn words: an associative crane. In R. M. Golinkoff, K. Hirsh-Pasek, L. Bloom, et al. (Eds.), *Becoming a Word Learner: A Debate on Lexical Acquisition*, pp. 51–80, New York: Oxford University Press.

Smith, L. B. & Heise, D. (1992). Perceptual similarity and conceptual structure. In B. Burns (Ed.), *Percepts, Concepts, and Categories*, pp. 233–272, New York: Elsevier Science Publishers.

Smith, L. B., Jones, S. S., & Landau, B. (1996). Naming in young children: A dumb attentional mechanism? *Cognition*, **60**, 143–171.

Smith, L. B., Jones, S. S., Yoshida, H., & Colunga, E. (2003). Whose DAM account? Attentional learning explains. *Cognition*, **87**, 209–213.

Tager-Flusberg, H. (2000). Understanding the language and communicative impairments in autism. In L. M. Glidden (Ed.), *International Review of Research on Mental Retardation*, Vol. 20, pp. 185–205, San Diego, CA: Academic Press.

Tarc, M. & Gelman, S. A. (in press). Determining that a label is kind-referring: Factors that influence children's and adults' novel word extensions. *Journal of Child Language*.

Terrace, H. S. (1979). *Nim* New York: Knopf.

Van de Walle, G., Carey, S., & Prevor, M. (2000). The use of kind distinctions for object individuation: Evidence from manual search. *Journal of Cognition and Development*, **1**, 249–280.

Vygotsky, L. S. (1962). *Thought and Language* Cambridge: MIT Press.

Walton, G. M. & Banaji, M. R. (2004). Being what you say: The effect of essentialist linguistic labels on preferences. *Social Cognition*, **22**, 193–213.

Ware, E. A. & Booth, A. E. (2007, April). Form follows function: The role of function information in the development of the shape bias. Poster Presented at the Biennial Meeting of the Society for Research in Child Development, Boston, MA.

Waxman, S. R. (1990). Linguistic biases and the establishment of conceptual hierarchies: Evidence from preschool children. *Cognitive Development*, **5**, 123–150.

Waxman, S. R. & Booth, A. E. (2003). The origins and evolution of links between word learning and conceptual organization: New evidence from 11-month-olds. *Developmental Science*, **6**, 130–137.

Waxman, S. R. & Braun, I. E. (2005). Consistent (but not variable) names as invitations to form object categories: New evidence from 12-month-old infants. *Cognition*, **95**, B59–B68.

Waxman, S. R. & Lidz, J. L. (2006). Early word learning. In W. Damon & R. M. Lerner (Series Eds.), and D. Kuhn & R. Siegler (Eds.), *Handbook of Child Psychology*, Vol. 2, 6th edn., pp. 299–335, Hoboken, NJ: Wiley.

Waxman, S. R. & Markow, D. B. (1995). Words as invitations to form categories: Evidence from 12-month-old infants. *Cognitive Psychology*, **29**, 257–302.

Waxman, S. R. & Markow, D. B. (1998). Object properties and object kind: 21-month-old infants' extension of novel adjectives. *Child Development*, **69**, 1313–1329.

Waxman, S. R. & Shumer, D. (2008). Naming and the Inductive Strength of Racial and Gender Categories: Evidence from Preschool-Aged Children. Unpublished manuscript, Northwestern University.

Waxman, S. R., Lynch, E. B., Casey, K. L., & Baer, L. (1997). Setters and samoyeds: The emergence of subordinate level categories as a basis for inductive inference. *Developmental Psychology*, **33**, 1074–1090.

Waxman, S. R., Lidz, J. L., Braun, I. E., & Lavin, T. (2009). Twenty-four month old infants' interpretations of novel verbs and nouns in dynamic scenes. *Cognitive Psychology*, **59**(1), 67–95.

Welder, A. N. & Graham, S. A. (2001). The influence of shape similarity and shared labels on infants' inductive inferences about nonobvious object properties. *Child Development*, **72**, 1653–1673.

Wellman, H. M. & Gelman, S. A. (1998). Knowledge acquisition in foundational domains. W. Damon and R. M. Lerner (Series Eds.), and D. Kuhn and R. Siegler (Ed.), *Handbook of child psychology: Vol. 2. Cognition, Language, and Perception*, 5th edn., pp. 523–573, New York: Wiley.

Wilcox, T. & Baillargeon, R. (1998). Object individuation in infancy: The use of featural information in reasoning about occlusion events. *Cognitive Psychology*, **37**, 97–155.

Woodward, A. L. & Hoyne, K. L. (1999). Infants' learning about words and sounds in relation to objects. *Child Development*, **70**, 65–77.

Woodward, A. L. & Markman, E. M. (1998). Early word learning. In W. Damon & R. M. Lerner (Series Eds.), and D. Kuhn & R. Siegler (Eds.), *Handbook of Child Psychology, Volume 2: Cognition, Perception, and Language*, pp. 371–420, New York: Wiley.

Xu, F. (1999). Object individuation and object identity in infancy: The role of spatiotemporal information, object property information, and language. *Acta Psychologica*, **102**, 113–136.

Xu, F. (2002). The role of language in acquiring object kind concepts in infancy. *Cognition*, **85**, 223–250.

Xu, F. & Carey, S. (1996). Infants' metaphysics: The case of numerical identity. *Cognitive Psychology*, **30**, 111–153.

Xu, F., Cote, M., & Baker, A. (2005). Labeling guides object individuation in 12-month-old infants. *Psychological Science*, **16**, 372–377.

Yamauchi, T. (2005). Labeling bias and categorical induction: Generative aspects of category information. *Journal of Experimental Psychology: Learning, Memory and Cognition*, **31**, 538–553.

Younger, B. A. (2003). Parsing objects into categories: Infants' perception and use of correlated attributes. In D. H. Rakison & L. M. Oakes (Eds.), *Early Category and Concept Development: Making Sense of the Blooming, Buzzing Confusion*, pp. 77–102, New York: Oxford University Press.

Chapter 7

Concepts and culture

Norbert Ross and Michael Tidwell

Editors' Preview

Chapter 7, 'Concepts and Culture', embraces an anthropological approach to concepts and highlights how they are learned and transmitted while situated or embedded within a context of social and cultural processes. Cultural concepts are described as mental representations that are relatively stable in a population. They are formed through mental activities that are relevant to an individual's life and, as such, reflect the goals, emotions, and social and physical investment of that individual. By studying concepts under diverse cultural conditions, one can hope to gain an understanding of the extent to which the principles of categorization are invariant across cultures and how much concepts can vary as a consequence of living in unique individual cultures.

Chapter 7 contrasts anthropological and psychological approaches to the study of concepts through an examination of how the acquisition of expertise influences conceptual structure. While psychological studies of expertise have emphasized how experts differ from novices in terms of the amount of knowledge they have about a domain, anthropological studies of expertise have stressed how experts may differ from novices (and other experts) in term of the kinds of knowledge they have about a domain. For example, in a novice–expert comparison, while University of Michigan undergraduates and Guatemalan farmers displayed similarity in classifying plants and animals, they reasoned about them differently. These data suggest that while the two groups' categories picked out similar referents, the underlying representations were based on different kinds of information. In another example relying on an expert–expert comparison, landscapers and botanists were shown to categorize trees differently. While botanists sorted trees based on scientific taxonomy, landscapers used goal-related knowledge as a basis for classification. This finding implies that different occupational groups have different sets of goals related to the same objects and as a consequence may classify them differently.

An additional study contrasted the fish-categorization behaviour of two expert 'fishing' populations in the northern Midwest of the United States: Euro-Americans and Menominee Indians. While the Euro-American categorizations were based on a recreational under-standing of fish (i.e. fishing as sport), the Menominee categorizations were based on the fish's habitat (i.e. the ecological relations of one fish to another in the food chain). As both groups were experts, they were considered to have the same knowledge base about fish; what differed was the information that was accessed. This study provides support for the idea that there are cultural differences in categoriza-tion and conceptualization that reflect differences in how objects within a domain are interacted with, which in turn reflect differences in goals and worldviews.

Chapter 7 also considers when, during development, cultural differences in conceptual systems may begin to arise and yield differ-ent kinds of expertise, and how cultural information is transmitted between generations. Although knowledge is clearly 'passed down' through the formal instruction that occurs via schooling, there is also an important role for informal conversation as it grows out of basic social interaction. Such conversation provides the input for encultura-tion. Chapter 7 further makes plain that in order to understand the 'uptake' of concepts by new generations, one must consider the preexisting concepts possessed by those generations when acquiring new knowledge. In this regard, children's belief in essentialism (i.e. the idea that objects within a category are united by an unchang-ing core) may generate internal resistance to acquiring the concept of evolution, where variation among individuals is a foundational notion.

Overall, Chapter 7 makes the case that while there will be similari-ties in categorization behaviour across different cultures, there will also be differences in knowledge across cultures that are related to goals and expertise. These differences bring about differences in con-ceptual representations, how accessible they are, and how we reason with them.

In this chapter we make two main points. First, concepts and categories are fundamental to understanding culture and cultural change. Second, understanding cognition as an *embodied* or *situated process* (as occurring within the context of sociocultural processes) is necessary to improve our understanding of the role of concepts and categories in human cognition. Being embedded and developed in specific cultural context, we argue, is what makes human concepts unique. We begin, therefore, by examining the definitions of culture, categories, and concepts.

Defining culture, categories, and concepts

In our view, culture comprises concepts (mental representations) as well as public representations like material productions, speech, and other aspects of behaviour (see Ross, 2004; Sperber, 1996). What we refer to as culture or cultural concepts are those representations that are relatively stable and distributed widely in a population (Atran et al., 2005; Ross, 2004). When we talk about cultural change, we are talking about conceptual change (within and across individuals) as well as about changes in the distribution of specific concepts across individuals. If we explore culture as the relatively wide and stable distribution of mental representations, then studying concepts, concept formation, and conceptual change becomes a centrepiece of our anthropological research. Questions about how concepts are formed and how they are transmitted across individuals (perhaps being restructured in the process of information transmission) are essential to understanding culture as the outcome of cognitive and social factors (Sperber, 1996).

Insofar as the formation and transmission of concepts depends on the flux of information, it is important to widen our analysis of *information* to include unintentional information inputs, including those that are constantly provided by the physical and social environments. Adopting this perspective has important consequences for the cognitive sciences, in that it forces us to perceive cognitive processes as *situated manifestations*; that is, as (1) mental activities relevant to an individual's actual life, which (2) take place within a specific social and physical context. These conditions are quite distinct from the situation we often encounter and create in the psychology laboratory, where we not only purposefully abstract away from social and physical conditions, but we also apply artificial conditions by using stimuli that are often irrelevant to our participants (see Atran et al., 1999; Ross, 2004; also Chapter 2 of this book). To be concrete, expertise acquired in the lab might take anywhere from 10 min to several days to acquire and is usually not related to any kind of special interest, commitment, or values. This contrasts with the kind of expertise anthropologists usually describe, where becoming an expert might take years and decades of engagement with a subject and as a consequence produces or requires an emotional investment, creating a different outlook on things at the same time.

There are several possible ways that we can conceive of 'cultural differences' in categorization and concepts. *Expertise* seems to be a good way of capturing at least some of these differences. For example, farmers of the tropical rainforest are more likely to be experts in the domain of folkbiology than the average US citizen. However, expertise is not a one-dimensional process of incremental knowledge. Instead incremental knowledge might be biased by *kinds of expertise* (e.g. as related to specific goals) directly affecting categorization, concepts, and framework theories. In this context, framework theories are seen as theory theories, themselves consisting of ideas, biases, and theories that are grounded within a domain. In fact, categories, concepts, and framework theories seem to be three inseparable parts of the same notion. Following Barsalou's argument of goal-driven categorization (1991), we might assume that both different goals as well as framework theories, which themselves might be responsible for different goals, might produce different *kinds of expertise*. This account describes expertise as a multidimensional phenomenon rather than only the time-trained aspect of certain (as mentioned often meaningless) activities (see Medin et al., 2007).

When looking at culture and cultural processes from this perspective, it is clear that the individual cognitive processes explored by the cognitive sciences and the larger-scale cultural processes studied by anthropologists are inseparable. In a sense, culture becomes the emergent product of cognitive processes, themselves embedded in a specific social environment. But let us take a closer look at concepts.

Close et al. (Chapter 3, this book), point out that concepts can include rules for category membership. However, given that the primary function of categories is to organize the world in meaningful ways by providing additional, implied information, concepts must also include the rules of induction based on those categories. In this view, some categories – such as 'mammal', for example – might be seen as concepts. A similar point is made by Machery (2005), who argues that the notion of 'concept' actually describes three different things, all associated with the same signifier (e.g. dog): *exemplars, prototypes,* and *theories.* Exemplars are specific sensory experiences that instantiate a concept. According to Barsalou and his colleagues, these modality-specific experiences are necessary for concept formation (Barsalou et al., 2003), yet they are not sufficient. Prototypes consist of rules for category membership or statistical information about category members. Without something like a prototype, it would be impossible for disparate experiences to be recognized as instances of a concept. Finally, theories are the rules of induction by which a new instance inherits properties of the concept. Following this line of reasoning, differing concepts describe differing categories, and changes in concepts lead to changes in categories. Thus, maybe the easiest way to conceive of categories is to think of them as groupings of items based on specific rules laid out by category specific concepts. These category specific concepts themselves are subject to change. For example, Dupre has shown that historically our categorization of whales shifted, not in response to more knowledge about whales, but rather because of changing concepts of what it means to be a fish (Dupre, 1999). Part of the shift in categorization of whales is, of course, an increase in knowledge with respect to whales specifically, but also fish in general. As such, we discuss the role of differences in expertise in understanding cultural differences in concepts and categorization.

The relevance of *levels* and *kinds* of expertise in modifying conceptual structure

The role of expertise in cognitive processes has long been discussed, yet most of the time the discussion has been limited to considerations of *amounts of expertise* usually acquired during training sessions in the laboratory. To be sure, such research has provided us with important insights (see Palmeri et al., 2004). However, by definition it must ignore important aspects of real-life expertise, including emotional commitment as well as goal structures related to wider frameworks, and hence we need to look beyond the psychological experiment to compare our laboratory studies with real-life situations. Separating *levels* and *kinds of expertise* is actually much harder than initially assumed. Boster and Johnson (1989) examined knowledge and sorting pattern (categorization) among expert and novice fisherman. They noted that while morphological information about fish (provided on stimuli cards as pictures) is available to novices and experts alike, access to more specific information related to functional and utilitarian aspects requires expertise. In this account, experts should differ from novices (within their cultural setting) not only in the amount of information they possess, but also with respect to the *kind of information*. Similar arguments have been made about cognitive development (see, e.g. Chi et al., 1981; Chi & Koeske, 1983; or Gobbo & Chi, 1986).

Boster and Johnson (1989) found just that: novices relied more on morphology when sorting fish than did experts (post hoc justifications revealed the same pattern). As a consequence, the authors argue, shifts in expertise do not resemble a shift from an incoherent to a more coherent model, but represent a shift from a readily available default model to a newly acquired model, based on different goals and respective information. These data are interesting on two accounts. First, they posit the existence of a default system of categorization (at least for the domain of folkbiology) and second, they point towards the acquisition of expertise as a process of modifying conceptual structures to attune to different kinds of information and goals, resulting in new categorization schemes. Note that this first claim does not make any specific commitment to the causes of such a natural default categorization system. In other words, the fact that Itzá Maya slash and burn farmers in the tropical rainforest of Guatemala categorize their local mammals in ways similar to how Michigan students categorize mammals of their own environment (Lopez et al., 1997) might stem from the fact that individuals in both groups build on universal categorization principles that interact with the structure provided by the phylogenetic history of living kinds. In fact, Lopez et al. were specifically interested in exploring the role of different principles of category-based induction, namely similarity, typicality, and diversity (see Osherson et al., 1990). The *similarity* principle of induction describes the fact that two mammals seen as similar (closer related in terms of their taxonomic distance) are more likely to share a previously unknown (and invisible) characteristic than two mammals that are taxonomically more distant (mice and rats are more likely to share an unknown property than mice and elephants). The *typicality* principle describes the fact that more-typical members of a category are more likely to have features common to all the category members than less-typical ones (sparrow are more likely to share properties with all birds than penguins). Finally, the *diversity* principle describes the fact that knowing two different category members share a property, we are more likely to project this property to all category members than when two similar category members share a property (a projection from mice and whales to all mammals is stronger than a projection from mice and rats to all mammals). It is clear that the three principles are all different uses of category-based similarity.

Using these principles, Lopez et al. draw several important conclusions. First, despite cultural and expertise differences, members of the two groups basically share a common taxonomy for local mammals. Second, beyond some overall agreement, systematic group differences in categorization emerged. Third, these differences in categorization lead to predictable differences in reasoning strategies. Fourth and finally, while both Michigan students as well as Itzá Maya farmers apply similarity- and typicality-based reasoning when reasoning about mammals, only the Michigan students seem to apply the diversity principle in this specific context.

An alternative account is that Michigan students and Itzá Maya attend to different features for categorization purposes, yet these features are interrelated, converging to a common categorization scheme for the members of the two groups. The second point is of much interest for our discussion of culture and concepts as it hints at something we already alluded to above, namely, that the acquisition of expertise entails a change of conceptual structures. This has been shown in laboratory studies (Palmeri et al., 2004) and can of course be related to the work by Barsalou on goal-directed categories (1991), as well as one account of the causes of cognitive change in children (e.g. Chi et al., 1981; Chi & Koeske, 1983).

Building on these findings, Medin and colleagues studied three different groups of Euro-American tree experts including landscapers, park-maintenance workers, and taxonomists (Medin et al., 1997). Interestingly, landscapers, but not park workers, developed goal-related categories, while taxonomists basically categorized trees along scientific taxonomy (1997). These findings have been explained by the fact that landscapers approach trees from a perspective of limited goals, while park workers approach trees with a multitude of goals, being probably best captured by a multipurpose categorization scheme (Medin et al., 2002). These results provide clear evidence that *kinds of expertise* have clear implications for categorization and, via category-based induction (Osherson et al., 1990), for reasoning strategies.

So far, the studies with a wide range of participants from different cultural settings suggests certain universal tendencies both in the categorization of natural kinds and in the principles employed in category-based induction. Notably, researchers have found that human categorizations of plants and animals are fairly consistent and generally correspond to scientific taxonomies (see Atran, 1990; Berlin, 1992). Investigators generally report correlations of around 0.6 between different folk taxonomies as well as between folk taxonomies and scientific taxonomies (see e.g. Bailenson et al., 2002; Lopez et al., 1997; Medin et al., 2006). Similarly, category-based induction has been shown to be a domain-general way of using category membership for reasoning (see Chapter 3). In fact, one way of testing the psychological reality of categories has been to see whether they are used for reasoning strategies (Ross, 2004). So to sum up, across populations we find strong agreement in categorization and reasoning with respect to natural kinds. Does this mean that concepts are also shared across these populations? From the previous discussion the reader might have already guessed that we do not think so. Hence, we now turn our attention to findings of cross-cultural differences. Before doing so, we need one more clarification. Of course our argument is that agreement of categories is only superficial if the concepts of these categories are different across groups, precisely because concepts form an integral part of categories. We started out with an emphasis on expertise differences in categorization and reasoning. However, we argued that the acquisition of expertise entails a change of conceptual structures. Many cultural differences might be better described as differences in expertise. For example, Itzá Maya living off, and in, the rainforest of Guatemala clearly have more expertise with their natural environment than University of Michigan students.

As such the cultural comparison is akin to the study of professional fishermen and novices reported by Boster and Johnson (1989). However, while we argue that activity–related-expertise differences clearly form a part of cultural differences, as we shall see in the next section, this is not the end of the story.

The interaction of expertise and culture

Aside from the overall agreement in categorization across cultures, the data so far indicate systematic variations between the ways expert and novices as well as different kinds of experts order the natural world. We mentioned above that overall significant correlations exist between folk taxonomies as well as between folk and scientific taxonomies. However, another way of interpreting these correlations is that their predictive value is fairly low.

The differences are more interesting, in many respects, not as a conclusion, but as a focus of investigation. That is, once we encounter differences in categorization either between different kinds of experts (such as Medin et al., 1997) or between experts of different cultures (Medin et al., 2007), the challenge becomes understanding how differences between groups correspond with those differences in categorization and induction. The interviewed Itzá Maya differ in almost every aspect from the Michigan students: physical environment, age, education, expertise with the natural world, etc. Which one, then, is responsible for the differences encountered? It is tempting to analyse the data with a multiple regression analysis, with 'culture' becoming an independent variable usually shorthanded as 'ethnicity'. Such an account not only ignores decades of anthropological theories of culture, but comes with further implications that one might want to consider. First, treating culture as an independent variable either explains culture away (it becomes insignificant in our analyses if we get enough other variables) or mystifies culture as a black box that stands in for an explanation when other variables fail to explain the phenomena (see Medin et al., 2002). In other words, without a specific theory of culture, simply naming these differences 'cultural' does not really add anything to our understanding of either 'culture' and 'cultural processes' or of concepts, categorization, and reasoning. How then should we think of culture and how should we study it?

Results from studies on expertise and goal orientation might provide us with some leverage. Clearly, these studies show that expertise is not a one-dimensional process of 'knowing more'. Instead, the acquisition of expertise comes with a change in focus (driven by different goals in the widest sense) leading to different kinds of expertise. These different kinds of expertise might cause different ways of categorizing natural kinds.

Building on this idea, Medin et al. (2002, 2006, 2007) conducted a study comparing Menominee Native American and Euro-American nonprofessional fish experts in Wisconsin with respect to their categories and concepts of local freshwater fish[1]. All the participants were fish experts (described as such by the fellow community members).

---

[1] Parallel studies were conducted among Menominee and Euro-American hunters (Medin et al., 2007; Ross et al., 2007).

They were all male (as only men were mentioned as experts – even when we asked women) and all had over 15 years of fishing experience. Note that this research design tried to hold constant: (1) the level of expertise (years and kind of fishing); (2) the physical environment (both groups live immediately adjacent to one another); (3) factors such as age, education, income; as well as (4) the actual stimuli, local fish well known to all the study participants. Individuals had similar amounts of de facto knowledge (where to find fish, what specific fish eat, etc.). The most obvious differences between the groups were that Euro-Americans focus on fishing as a sport or competition, whereas the Menominee show a much higher interest in fishing for food. Menominee generally eat both musky and bass (although these are not their preferred fish), which is the primary species of sport fishing among Euro-Americans, who practise catch-and-release fishing. As far as goals and values form part of concepts, this indicates that members of the two groups differ substantially in their concepts of fish.

The differences in their concepts of fish were further explored with a categorization task as well as two experiments geared at understanding some conceptual dimensions, namely ideas about fish–fish interactions. With respect to the categorization task (card sorting of fish species; 'put the fish together that go together by nature'), Medin et al. (2006, 2007) report cross-group agreement in how individuals categorized the locally existing fish. However, this agreement was also paired with significant cross-group differences. Specifically, Euro-Americans categorized fish based on morphology (including size) as well as desirability. Euro-Americans named certain categories as 'sportfish', 'panfish'[2], and 'garbage fish' making their specific goal orientation very salient. Menominee also used morphology and desirability to sort fish species; however, a third dimension was necessary to best represent their categorization of fish. This dimension correlated significantly with ecological relations of fishes (mainly habitat, food chains, etc.). Given the pattern of residual agreement it is clear that the Euro-American model in this study represents a subset of the more-complex Menominee model.

Exploring these differences further, Medin et al. looked at how members of both groups think about interactions between species of fish (see below for a similar task with respect to tropical plants and animals among Maya farmers). In this task, individuals were asked to describe fish–fish interactions in a series of trials consisting of individual pairs of fish. Two versions of the task were applied. In the first round (speeded version), participants were asked to report on the relations of several hundred fish pairs in roughly 90 min. In the second round (un-speeded version), we focused only on the items for which we encountered group differences during trial 1. Here, participants answered approximately 40 questions in more or less the same amount of time.

The results provide important insights for both anthropology and the cognitive sciences. In the 'speeded condition', general agreement was found to be paired with systematic group differences. Euro-Americans described fish interactions to be mostly of the type 'big eats small' with respect to adult fish sizes (i.e. musky eats bass). Menominee reported these relations too, yet added or qualified some of them by

---

[2] Panfish refers, of course, to the frying pan.

including fish across the life cycle (a big bass can eat a young/small musky) and by considering actual questions of habitat (musky and brook trouts do not have any relations because they both live in different habitats). They also included types of helping, such as providing nesting opportunities, generally not mentioned by Euro-Americans. In general, Menominee described not only more, but also more complex interactions and in fact the relations described by Euro-American fish experts only related to pairs of fish that actually do not share a common habitat. Medin et al. designed a further task to explore whether these mistakes were based on a lack of knowledge (which of course would question the assumption of equal levels of expertise) but found that this was not the case. When describing shared habitats, Euro-Americans were just as accurate as Menominee. In fact, they did not assign shared habitats for some of the fish for which they had reported existing interactions in the above-described task! This indicates that in the speeded interaction task, Euro-American participants did not activate all the propositional knowledge available to them. More interesting still are the results of the un-speeded version of the task. When provided with more time, Euro-American responses looked just like the responses of Menominee. For Menominee, no differences were found between the two tasks.

This latter finding might come as a surprise to many anthropologists. The 'cultural' differences encountered only emerged when participants answered under time pressure. As a consequence, the differences are not caused by differences in base knowledge but by differences in access to existing knowledge. The kind of differences emerging from the task also linked these differences clearly to differences described in categorization as well as to the broader cultural models and goals individuals bring to the practice of fishing (Medin et al., 2006, 2007).

To sum up this study then, Menominee and Euro-American fish experts living in Wisconsin differ with respect to their goals and respective values towards fishing and, as a result, their concepts and categorizations of fish are different. While members of the two groups share the same level of base knowledge, access to certain aspects of that knowledge seems to be different and related to the difference in categorization of fish as well as the overarching goal structure and framework theories brought to fishing. These findings clearly demonstrate the linkage between: (1) categories and concepts; (2) kinds of expertise and categories; and (3) kinds of expertise, the social environment, and concepts.

Three questions emerge from this analysis:

1. Do we see similar differences for nonexperts?
2. At what age do these differences arise?
3. And maybe the most pressing question, what causes these differences?

The first question cannot be answered, as there are literally no fish novices in the Menominee community (i.e. as compared to Michigan undergraduate students!). Everyone fishes or has fished at least some times. Nevertheless, studies with lesser experts in both communities indicate similar group differences in categorization (Medin et al., 2002)[3]. In response to the second question, Ross et al. (2003) conducted

---

[3] The interaction task was not administered to nonexperts.

research with children in the two communities (as well as among children in Boston). Although this research pursued a somewhat different goal, it is clear from the data that Menominee children, as young as 6 years old, show a propensity to think about plants and animals in ecological terms, an attribute not seen in either rural or urban Euro-American children.

Finally, let us turn to the potential causes of these differences. From the above description it should be clear that Medin et al. ascribe the causes for these differences to different worldviews, or what they call *habits of the mind*, biases to look at the world in specific ways. For Menominee (also reported for other Native American groups) we find that people tend to see the environment as an interaction of humans, animals, plants, and natural kinds, where everything has a role to play and hence everything is interrelated and important (see Ross et al., 2007). On the other hand, for Euro-Americans, the environment seems to be in large part the background for important fish and game. Given that these differences are based on different underlying world-views, we do not expect these differences to carry over to completely different domains (e.g. such as concerning professional life). Rather, these differences should be domain specific (e.g. limited to the domain of living kinds).

Pilot studies indicate that when talking to their children about the environment Menominee parents are more likely to connect different species presented on the pages of a picture book (the *bear* climbs up the *tree* to eat the *honey* of the *bee*), than Euro-American parents, who tend to only point out the different species to their children (this is a *bear*, this is a *tree*, etc.). Clearly, more research is needed to elucidate fully the relationship between discursive practices in a community to both worldview and child-rearing practices. Nevertheless, at this point, the evidence suggests that different general ideas about the social and physical environment lead Menominee and Euro-American fish experts to develop different kinds of expertise, expressed by different categories, conceptual webs, values, and finally behaviours.

In terms of expertise, these studies should make one point clear. We can no longer think of expertise as a dimension of less to more knowledge, but rather as different kinds of expertise, closely linked to goal structures and worldviews. If kinds of expertise are related to goal structures and general worldviews, then we should expect conceptual knowledge to correlate with values and behaviours. This question was taken up by another research project (Atran et al., 2002). Again, the card-sorting procedure ('put the things together that go together by nature') as well as the above interaction task were used to elicit and compare categorization and conceptual knowledge across different cultural groups. The three groups were Itzá Maya farmers of Guatemala, immigrant Q'eqchi' Maya, and Ladinos (a term used for the Spanish-speaking nonindigenous population of Guatemala), all living adjacent to each other in the tropical rainforest of northern Guatemala. The stimuli were local animals and plants of the tropical rainforest.

The researchers found that the three groups not only differed in specific interaction models (which animal helps/hurts a plant and vice versa), but also in larger models (do animals actually help/hurt plants?), and that these differences were related to actual values of and behaviours towards specific plants. Itzá Maya, for example, reported to protect/help specific plants, which the plant–animal interaction model described as most beneficial to animals (through an index of positive relations). Further botanical explorations actually showed that reported behaviour coincided with actual behaviour, for example, Itzá Maya indeed protected the plants, which they reported to protect. Tree counts in agricultural plots of Itzá Maya showed a correlation between the frequency of a plant species encountered and the importance of that plant to animals. Nothing similar was found for the other two groups. For the Itzá Maya, these trees were also *spiritually protected* by the *Arux*, forest spirits that can help but also punish individuals according to their behaviour. In a sense then, this model is institutionalized via religious beliefs (Atran et al., 2002).

In summary, the research presented so far has shown that differences of *kinds of expertise*, related to goals and values might be one good way to think about cultural differences in conceptual systems. We suggested that such differences are present from early on in childhood and one way to think about their emergence is that they are the outcome of socially constructed frameworks that build on foundational theories (see Rogoff, 1990, 2003; Wellman & Gelman, 1992) creating the *habits of the mind*, as described by Medin et al. (2006, 2007) and Ross et al. (2007). In this account, a high level of plasticity is ascribed to the mind, a fact that seems to be supported by the neurosciences (Linden, 2007). Of course, this account would be much more convincing if we could actually show that these structures directly guide knowledge transmission, which, consequently, would provide some interesting space for theorizing about cultural change. We believe that relevant data now exist and turn our attention to these two points in the next section.

Knowledge transmission, conceptual change, and cultural change

In the study among Itzá Maya, Q'eqchi' Maya migrants, and Ladinos (described above), Atran et al. were not only interested in whether (and how) different cultural models are linked to behaviour and values, but also (1) whether and how cross-generational and cross-cultural learning takes place, and (2) what form it might take. While we do not wish to argue against the important role of observation and instruction for cultural learning, we would like to caution the reader not to overextend the importance of such processes. For example, it does not seem plausible to argue that animal–plant interactions within the tropical rainforest are learned literally by observation or instruction. There are simply too many species around. How then do individuals acquire their knowledge about such interactions?

To start answering this question the researchers interviewed young Itzá Maya (approximately 30 years old) on the same plant–animal-interaction task they administered to older Itzá Maya (approximately 50–65 years old). Members of both generations have considerable differences in experience in the forest, with expertise being positively correlated with age. Exploring similarities and differences in the plant–animal-interaction models of old and young Itzá Maya, it became apparent that young Itzá Maya generated new knowledge (probably while interviewed) based on the application of category-based induction). In other words, once they believed that a specific animal had a certain kind of relation to a specific plant, they extended this relation both to similar animals and similar plants. This led to some predictable mistakes in which young Itzá Maya overextended knowledge along category lines when this was in fact inappropriate. As a result, their emerging models differed systematically from their elders' models (Atran, 2002). In these cases, the categories appeared to provide the framework for the acquisition/generation of knowledge in ways that are not only highly predictable (if one knows the underlying categories and concepts), but also stable across individuals (because similar categories and concepts provide for similar inferences).

This finding goes back to the already mentioned fact that concepts and categories must include rules/theories of induction, rules that allow for inference making when knowledge is sketchy or entirely missing. What forms can such framework or rules of inductions take? We already mentioned the category structure itself as providing such a framework. Other possible frameworks might be general epistemological frameworks such as *everything has a role to play* (Ross et al., 2007) or *animals cannot help plants/animals cannot hurt plants*. We might think of these frameworks as general biases or assumptions about the elements under consideration.

Another example from the comparative study in Guatemala (described above) might illustrate this point further. In addition to comparing ecological models of the rainforest across cultural groups, Atran et al. were also interested in exploring the potential transmission of knowledge across groups. Two main points became evident: first, Spanish-speaking Ladinos systematically acquired knowledge from Itzá Maya. Knowledge acquisition worked along the lines of social and expertise networks connecting Itzá Maya experts of the forest with their Ladino counterparts, who themselves are connected with their nonexpert (or rather less-expert) fellow Ladinos (Atran et al., 2002). Second, this knowledge transfer only includes *how plants relate to animals*, but not *how animals relate to plants*. More specifically, the existing framework of the Ladinos allowed for the acquisition of knowledge related to (1) plants helping animals (food, shelter, etc.) as well as (2) animals hurting plants (playing with the fruits and destroying them, etc.). However, they rejected (and as a result did not acquire) knowledge about some animals helping specific plants (seed dispersal, weeding out other plants, etc.). The notion of animals can actually help plants seemed to have been incompatible with their general framework of thinking about plants and animals and as a result this general framework constrained respective knowledge acquisition.

Again, this underscores the previous observation that knowledge acquisition does not take the form of copying presented information but includes the active generation of knowledge by the learner (through inference making). This *active generation of knowledge by the learner* explains not only the amount of new knowledge learned as well as the relative stability of knowledge transmission, but also helps us understand the role of framework theories in this process. The fact that Ladinos did not learn or *did not make the relevant inferences* that animals help plants, seems to be exactly *because* their already established framework theories did not allow for such inferences. As a result, this whole part of the Itzá Maya model has been lost in the transmission process. To be sure, in this context learning does not – or very rarely – take the form of formal or even conscious instruction. While Ladinos at times directly approached Itzá Maya about specific plants and animals (mostly with respect to usage), most of the learning took place in informal talks. This finding has of course huge implications for the acquisition of conceptual knowledge as well as for conceptual change. And we urge for much more research along these lines of inquiry. From the above discussion, it should be evident that these frameworks are themselves an emergent property of human social interaction and as such constitute a unique human aspect of categorization and concepts. They are part of the input condition within the context of *enculturation* (a child's upbringing within a specific culture), such as when Menominee parents tell stories about the local flora and fauna (compared to Euro-Americas). Of course, as products of social interactions such frameworks are not static, but change over time. For example, local plant knowledge in England has considerably changed over the last centuries with individuals knowing fewer plants and on less-specific levels (see Wolff et al., 1999). One can easily imagine, how such a decrease in knowledge might lead to changing structures in stories told, affecting the overall framework within which new knowledge is acquired and integrated into existing structures. As a result, these frameworks provide some stability, yet undergo some changes while transmitted, depending on other input conditions.

This change in interpretative frameworks has been in part the focus of the lead author's research among the Lacandon Maya of Chiapas, Mexico. In this research, Ross (2001, 2002) describes the intergenerational differences of ecological knowledge administering the same plant–animal-interaction task described above and used with Itzá Maya and Spanish-speaking Ladinos of Guatemala. Given the history of the community (recent forced transition to a settled community) as well as observed generational changes (religious change, generation-specific settlement pattern, change in values of life, etc.), Ross hypothesized that these changes would be paralleled by similar changes in conceptual knowledge, because members of the two generations grew up in two very different environments. Older Lacandon Maya grew up living in individual households close to their agricultural fields in the midst of the rainforest, moving their houses along with the movement of their agricultural fields (a practice called swidden agriculture). Much of their life was focused on the relation with the rainforest. This, however, had dramatically changed for younger Lacandon Maya. For sure, they still knew a lot about the forest, yet they showed very different relations and attitudes towards agriculture, hunting, and the forest itself (see Ross, 2001). The two groups differed with respect to (1) values and goals, and (2) level of expertise as related to the rainforest.

Overall, older members of the community were much less likely to report animals as hurting plants, despite the fact that members of both groups would describe animals eating or playing with unripe fruits, destroying thereby the seeds of the plant. While members of both groups made the same observation, or at least shared the same knowledge in these cases, the evaluation of these events differed. Older members of the community generally rejected the notion of any animal hurting a plant (note again the role of inference!). The ultimate reasoning behind rejecting such inferences was the framework theory that *animals only did what they were created to do and hence no hurting could be involved in their actions* (Ross, 2001, 2002). The same argument applied, in fact, to human behaviour as well. As long as humans behave in accordance with the Lacandon Maya traditions (e.g. in the way they were created by the gods), they do not and in fact cannot harm a plant. In this setting, then, cutting down a tree to get to honey is not hurting the plant species. In contrast, cutting down the tree to create a cattle pasture or to simply sell the wood does hurt the species.

These examples illustrate how framework theories/concepts influence the rules of inferences and hence how conceptual knowledge guides the acquisition/generation of new knowledge (within and across populations). However, conceptual knowledge and rules of inferences themselves are the products of cognitive and social factors and hence differ across social groups and change across times.

Our ideas on conceptual change and the acquisition of new knowledge through processes of inference-making echo research conducted in the educational sciences (defined in a wide sense). While few psychologists would consider these studies as relevant to thinking about 'culture', this seems to be largely due to a limited theory of culture. As we pointed out at the beginning of the chapter, culture, comprises widely shared and relatively stable models or representations of the world, as well as the public representations produced in accordance with those models. We presented a view in which conceptual structures (including rules of inferences) constitute the input condition for knowledge acquisition/learning. Similarly, Strike and Posner (1992) argue that in order to understand conceptual change in educational settings, it is critical to understand the student's *conceptual ecology*, the collection of concepts and relations among them that is implicated in understanding experience (including class lessons) and generating knowledge from lessons. It is important to keep in mind, that the very same conceptions (and misconceptions) that are the target of instruction provide the framework to integrate new information. In other words, the very concepts that pedagogues wish to change are actively used by students to interpret lessons.

An excellent example of this is provided by Vosniadou and Brewer (1992), who describe how students' conceptions of gravity (that things fall down, down being an absolute direction) made it difficult for them to conceive of earth as a sphere (since people on the opposite side ought to fall off). A similar situation may be occurring during the teaching of biological evolution (cf. Mayr, 1982). In this case, it is observed that humans tend to conceive of species of organisms in essentialist terms (see Gelman & Wellman, 1991; Wellman & Gelman, 1992). Stated briefly, humans assume by default that living things belong to natural categories by virtue of shared essence (foundational theory), which is passed from parent to offspring, generates obvious traits that are seen as indicative of the kind, and maintains identity through time. Such concepts colour everyday perception of living things and aid dramatically in generating new knowledge that goes beyond first-hand experience (category-based induction). Thus, for example, by assuming that squirrels share an underlying essence, one may infer a great deal more, particularly that something true of one squirrel is true of all of them. This tendency seems to lead to misconceptions of evolution as described in research on evolution education (e.g. Evans, 2000; Poling & Evans, 2002; Samarapungavan & Wiers, 1997). Of course this kind of 'typological thinking' (Mayr, 1982) undermines perception of variation in traits within a species, creating a great disadvantage for learning about species variation and evolution.

Before proceeding further, let us step back for a second and sum up. There are several ways we can think of 'cultural differences' with respect to concepts and categories. Expertise seems to be a good way of capturing at least some important aspects of these differences. We distinguished both *levels of expertise* as well as *kinds of expertise*. The research presented so far illustrates not only how both can affect categorization, concepts, and framework theories, but also how these three are inseparable. Of course, expertise must be explored within individual domains and with respect to the pathways through which different levels and kinds of expertise emerge within and across different populations. It is here that the social and the cognitive need to come together improve in a parallel fashion, our understanding of both cultural and cognitive processes. Our understanding of cultural processes is improved by grounding them in specific cognitive and social factors. In turn, our understanding of cognitive processes (concepts, categories, and framework theories) is improved by understanding them within the social context in which they emerge. It is not by accident that our arguments can be extended to educational psychology. In this vein, conceptions of education as imparting knowledge to students are incomplete insofar as they do not include the kinds of conceptual changes or transformations in thinking that science educators desire. In other words, such cross-cultural studies of conceptual change may be thought of as models or garden experiments for understanding similar issues in our schools. In both cases, we need to understand the outcome of learning as the result of both social and cognitive processes, including preexisting models and conceptual structures.

Conclusion

Our account has been as much about categories and concepts as it has been about differences in expertise and about culture. This is not by accident, as we have argued that the processes of categorization and concept formation are deeply embedded in social processes and 'culture' in the common sense of the world. Building on research in the cognitive sciences that showed both *expertise* and *specific goal structures* to influence categorization and concept formation, we propose both factors as candidates to start understanding what is often termed 'cultural differences'. Based on recent research, we propose that expertise must not be seen as a one-dimensional phenomenon, that is, *levels of expertise*, but must be understood in terms of *kinds of expertise* as well. The latter dimension appears to be closely related to different goal structures, leading individuals to focus on different aspects when acquiring new knowledge. Given this intimate relationship between expertise, categorization, and concepts it is clear that parts of our research need to be dedicated to the question of what it means to be and become an expert in a domain within a specific social setting. This is necessarily very different from our laboratory studies; hence the need to combine cognitive research with ethnographic work.

We proposed potential ways of how to do so. However, we did so by bringing together data from different projects, each carried out with somewhat different goals in mind. We do not know of one single project that combined the different levels of analyses that we think are needed for a full understanding of the issues at hand.

Such a project would include and start out with detailed ethnographic research that would among other things answer the following questions:

◆ How do people think about the domain at hand?

◆ What are some of the broader frameworks people apply when thinking about the domain?

◆ How does one become an expert in this domain and what does it mean to be an expert?

If the study were cross-cultural in nature, then of course one would apply the same ethnographic framework in both contexts. In this case, we might then start out by comparing categories and concepts across experts and nonexperts of the two groups. Ideally, the experimental tasks would include testing of hypotheses generated based on the ethnographic study. If differences are encountered, we could then go on and query them along the above lines (what is the content as well as the nature of these differences); yet we certainly would want to see how these differences emerge in developmental studies. Once we can pinpoint the developmental course of conceptual learning in our domain, we can then query again the environmental aspects for cues that might trigger these differences (education, parental input, etc.). In this phase again, we would use both ethnographic and experimental methods.

What have we just described? We described the best of two – as of yet unfortunately separated – worlds, where anthropology and the cognitive sciences are actually one and the same and treated as mutually informing one another.

In this account, culture ceases to be a mystical unit that evades any clear understanding. Instead, it becomes an emergent phenomenon that can be studied and understood. Human cognition at the same time ceases to be an abstract process taking place in people's heads and in isolation of the social world. By carefully exploring the interaction of the social and the cognitive, we will be in a better position to appreciate the uniquely human aspects of our cognition, for example, the fact that human concepts are situated and produced by cognitive mechanisms working deeply embedded into the social world. It is this intricate connection between the social and the cognitive that produces uniquely human aspects of cognition. Compared to other species, humans not only take environmental input to produce knowledge, but create the input conditions through which new information is acquired and integrated into existing frameworks. Different ecological niches might lead to different conceptual categories in different species. This very likely also applies to humans. However, only humans seem to be capable of creating the cognitive frames through which new information is acquired, independent of external input conditions.

Acknowledgements

The writing of this chapter was supported by NSF grants 0726107 to Norbert Ross and 0527707 to Norbert Ross and Tom Palmeri.

References

Atran, S. (1990). *Cognitive Foundations of Natural History: Towards an Anthropology of Science* New York: Cambridge University Press.

Atran, S., Medin, D., Ross, N., et al. (1999). Folkecology and commons management in the Maya Lowlands. *Proceedings of the National Academy of Sciences of the United States of America,* **96,** 7598–7603.

Atran, S., Medin, D., Ross, N., et al. (2002). Folkecology, cultural epidemiology, and the spirit of the commons: A garden experiment in the Maya lowlands, 1991–2001. *Current Anthropology,* **43**(3), 421–450.

Atran, S., Medin, D., & Ross, N. (2005). The cultural mind: environmental decision making and cultural modeling within and across populations. *Psychological Review,* **112**(4), 744–776.

Bailenson, J. M., Shum, M. S., Atran, S., Medin, D., & Coley, J. D. (2002). A bird's eye view: Triangulating biological categorization and reasoning within and across cultures and expertise levels. *Cognition,* **84**(1), 1–53.

Barsalou, L. W. (1991). Deriving categories to achieve goals. In G. H. Bower (Ed.), *The Psychology of Learning and Motivation,* pp. 1–64, New York: Academic Press.

Barsalou, L. W., Simmons, W. K., Barbey, A. K., & Wilson, C. D. (2003). Grounding conceptual knowledge in modality-specific systems. *Trend in Cognitive Sciences,* **7**(2), 84–91.

Berlin, B. (1992). *Ethnobiological Classification: Principles of Categorization of Plants and Animals in Traditional Societies* Princeton, NJ: Princeton University Press.

Boster, J. S. (1987). Agreement between biological classification systems is not dependent on cultural transmission. *American Anthropologist,* **89,** 914–920.

Boster, J. S. & Johnson, J. C. (1989). Form or function: A comparison of expert and novice judgments of similarity among fish. *American Anthropologist,* **91**(4), 866–889.

Boster, J. S., Berlin, B., & O'Neill, J. (1986). The correspondence of Jivaroan to scientific ornithology. *American Anthropologist,* **88**(3), 569–583.

Carey, S. (2000). Science as conceptual change. *Journal of Applied Developmental Psychology,* **21**(1), 13–19.

Chi, M. T. H., Feltovitch, P. J., & Glasr, R. (1981). Categorization and representation of physics problems by experts and novices. *Cognitive Science,* 5, 121–152.

Chi, M. T. H., & Koeske, R. D. (1983). Network representation of a child's dinosaur knowledge. *Developmental Psychology,* **19,** 29–39.

diSessa, A. A. & Sherin, B. L. (1998). What changes in conceptual change. *International Journal of Science Education,* **20**(10), 1155–1191.

Dupre, J. (1999). Are whales fish? In D. Medin & S. Atran (Eds.), *Folkbiology,* pp. 461–476, Cambridge: MIT Press.

Evans, E. M. (2000). The emergence of beliefs about the origins of species in school-age children. *Merrill-Palmer Quarterly,* **46**(2), 221–254.

Gelman, S. & Wellman, H. (1991). Insides and essences: Early understandings of the nonobvious. *Cognition,* **38,** 213–244.

Gobbo, C. & Chi, M. (1986). How knowledge is structured and used by experts and novice children. *Cognitive Development,* **1**(3), 221–237.

Linden, D. (2007). *The Accidental Mind* Cambridge: Harvard University Press.

Lopez, A., Atran, S., Coley, J. D., Medin, D., & Smith, E. (1997). The tree of life: Universals of folkbiological taxonomies and inductions. *Cognitive Psychology,* **32,** 251–295.

Machery, E. (2005). Concepts are not a natural kind. *Philosophy of Science,* **72,** 444–467.

Mayr, E. (1982). *The Growth of Biological Thought: Diversity, Evolution, and Inheritance* Cambridge: Belknap Press.

Medin, D., Lynch, D., Coley, J. D., & Atran, S. (1997). Categorization and reasoning among tree experts: Do all roads lead to Rome? *Cognitive Psychology*, **32**, 49–96.

Medin, D., Ross, N., Atran, S., Burnett, R. C., & Blok, S. V. (2002). Categorization and reasoning in relation to culture and expertise. *Psychology of Learning and Motivation*, **41**, 1–41.

Medin, D., Ross, N., Atran, S., et al. (2006). Folkbiology of freshwater fish. *Cognition*, **99**(3), 237–273.

Medin, D., Ross, N., Cox, D., & Atran, S. (2007). Why folkbiology matters: Resource conflict despite shared goals and knowledge. *Human Ecology*, **35**(3), 315–329.

Osherson, D., Smith, E., Wilkie, O., Lopez, A., & Shafir, E. (1990). Category-based induction. *Psychological Review*, **97**, 85–200.

Palmeri, T. J., Wong, A. C.-N., & Gauthier, I. (2004). Computational approaches to the development of perceptual expertise. *Trends in Cognitive Sciences*, **8**(8), 378–386.

Poling, D. & Evans, E. M. (2002). Why do birds of a feather flock together? Developmental change in the use of multiple explanations: Intention, teleology and essentialism. *British Journal of Developmental Psychology*, **20**, 89–112.

Rogoff, B. (1990). *Apprenticeship in Thinking* New York: Oxford University Press.

Rogoff, B. (2003). *The Cultural Nature of Human Development* New York: Oxford University Press.

Ross, N. (2001). *Bilder vom Regenwald, Mentale Modelle, Kulturwandel und Umweltverhalten bei den Lakandonen in Mexiko (Images of the rainforest: Mental models, cultural change and environmental behavior among the Lacandon Maya of Chiapas)* Munster: LIT Verlag.

Ross, N. (2004). *Culture & Cognition: Implications for Theory and Method* Thousand Oaks, CA: Sage Publications.

Ross, N., Medin, D., Coley, J. D., & Atran, S. (2003). Cultural and experiential differences in the development of folkbiological induction. *Cognitive Development*, **18**, 25–47.

Ross, N., Medin, D., & Cox, D. (2007). Epistemological models and culture conflict: Menominee and Euro-American hunters in Wisconsin. *Ethos*, **35**(4), 478–515.

Samarapungavan, A. & Wiers, R. (1997). Children's thoughts on the origin of species: A study of explanatory coherence. *Cognitive Science*, **21**(2), 147–177.

Sperber, D. (1996). *Explaining Culture: A Naturalistic Approach* Cambridge: Blackwell Publisher, Inc.

Strike, K. A. & Posner, G. J. (1992). A revisionist theory of conceptual change. In R. A. Duschl (Ed.), *Philosophy of Science, Cognitive Psychology, and Educational Theory and Practice*, pp. 147–176, Albany, NY: SUNY Press.

Vosniadou, S. & Brewer, W. F. (1992). Mental models of the Earth: A study of conceptual change in childhood. *Cognitive Psychology*, **24**, 535–585.

Wellman, H. & Gelman, S. (1992). Cognitive development: foundational theories of core domains. *Annual Review of Psychology*, **43**, 337–375.

Wolff, P, Medin, D. & Pankratz, C (1999). Evolution and devolution of folkbiological knowledge. *Cognition*, **73**, 177–204.

Part 2

Concept learning across species

Chapter 8

Category learning and concept learning in birds

Olga F. Lazareva and Edward A. Wasserman

Editors' Preview

Chapter 8, 'Category learning and concept learning in birds', reviews evidence on the abilities of pigeons to learn a variety of categories. The categories that have been investigated include those based on perceptual similarity, association, and more abstract relations among stimuli. Given that pigeons are not verbal and cannot demonstrate their categorization skill through differential naming behaviour, researchers have in many instances relied on a methodology in which pigeons are taught category discrimination by learning to peck at one key for one class of stimuli and peck at another key for another class of stimuli. Concept formation is in evidence if pigeons generalize their key pecking behaviour to novel instances of the classes.

Use of the training plus generalization paradigm has revealed that pigeons readily learn perceptual concepts, including presence versus absence concepts that are based on whether the stimuli presented contain or do not contain instances of trees, fish, people, or conspecifics. Likewise, pigeons form concepts of mutually exclusive classes at an intermediate or basic level of generality, cats versus dogs, for example. This categorical responding also extends to contexts where more than two classes are contrasted. In one instance, pigeons were able to respond differentially to instances from 16 different object categories.

Sceptics of animal cognition may argue that the pigeons were trained via reinforcement to make the various category distinctions among object classes. However, it is the case that the pigeons, even without training, seem to experience the perceptual coherence of the object classes. That is, they display a greater likelihood of confusing instances from within a category than between categories. In addition, pigeons find it easier to learn perceptually coherent categories (e.g. cats vs. flowers vs. cars vs. chairs) than arbitrary categories consisting of members from different basic-level categories. Moreover, pigeons can acquire fine-grained, subordinate-level concepts that in humans are associated with the attainment of perceptual expertise (e.g. king-fishers vs. other types of birds).

Although pigeons are sensitive to the perceptual cohesiveness of categories, they can learn broad, superordinate-level categories where the stimuli within a category, while coherent, can vary widely from one another (e.g. mammals, animals, living things). They can also form categories that are based more on association than perception. Furthermore, pigeons can acquire concepts based on abstract relations detected among stimuli. For example, when trained to perform differential pecking responses to stimuli varying in size, pigeons behave as if they have extracted a 'smaller than' rule. Similarly, when presented with arrays of objects in which the objects are all the same or all different from one another, pigeons respond as if they have abstracted 'same' versus 'different' concepts.

Chapter 8 points out that many of the studies of pigeon categorization provide demonstrations or existence proofs that pigeons can form one or another concept. Given that there are morphological differences between avian and mammalian perceptual systems, one may wonder whether the categorization behaviours of pigeons are governed by the same mechanisms that underlie the categorization behaviours of mammals. More comparative research is therefore needed to probe how the concepts are being acquired by various species. A step in this direction involves investigating how the same variables affect categorization performance across species. Notably, concept formation in pigeons does seem to be facilitated with increases in the number of training stimuli, a finding that has been reported in other participant populations including humans.

Most psychologists would readily agree that 'concepts and categories serve as building blocks for human thought and behavior' (Medin, 1989, p. 1469). Humans group objects together because they look alike (e.g. cars or trees), because they perform the same function (e.g. tools or musical instruments), or because they entail the same relationship (e.g. above or inside). Consequently, some researchers have proposed a classification scheme that divides concepts into three broad classes: *perceptual concepts* based on physical similarities among their members; *nonsimilarity-based concepts* based on common functions or associations among their members; and *abstract concepts* based on relations between or among stimuli instead of physical properties (Lazareva & Wasserman, 2008; Zentall et al., 2002).

But, what is categorization? And, what behaviour must we observe in nonhuman animals in order to conclude that categorization has occurred? For the purposes of this chapter, we define categorization as an organism's ability to respond equivalently to members of the same class, to respond differently to members of different class, and to transfer those report responses to novel, discriminably different members of these classes (Keller & Schoenfeld, 1950; Wasserman et al., 1988). So, when a child says 'cat' if she sees any cat and when the child says 'dog' if she sees any dog, we say that the child has displayed the ability to categorize cats and dogs. Likewise, when a pigeon selects the left key if the displayed photograph contains a car and the right key if the displayed photograph contains a chair, then even though the pigeon may never have seen these particular images before, we say that it can categorize cars and chairs.

It is important to distinguish categorization from discrimination. We speak of categorization when the organism discriminates among *classes* of multiple stimuli rather than among individual *instances* of each class. So, if a pigeon has been trained to make one response to a single photograph of a car and to make a second response to a single photograph of a chair, then we say that the pigeon discriminates the car from the chair. But, if a pigeon has been trained to make one response to multiple exemplars of cars and to make a second response to multiple exemplars of chairs, then we say that the pigeon categorizes the cars and chairs. In essence, categorization entails a small subset of discrimination problems in which multiple stimuli are associated with a common response.

Perceptual concepts can be related to human basic-level (e.g. cat or chair) and subordinate-level (e.g. Persian cat or armchair) categorization. Basic-level categorization is based on high perceptual similarity among members of the same category and low perceptual similarity among members of different categories, rendering this level of categorization most preferred by humans (Rosch & Mervis, 1975; Rosch et al., 1976). Subordinate-level categorization differentiates subgroups within basic-level categories and, consequently, entails high within- and between-category similarity. With some exceptions (e.g. Tanaka & Taylor, 1991), subordinate-level categorization is less preferred by humans than basic-level categorization.

Perceptual concepts

Studies of perceptual concepts in animals typically involve discrimination of photographs from human-language basic-level categories using a variety of behavioural techniques. In their pioneering study, Herrnstein and Loveland (1964) trained pigeons to perform a *person/no-person* discrimination using a go/no-go procedure in which one class of pictures (*person*) was associated with reinforcement and another class of pictures (*no-person*) was associated with experimental extinction (Table 8.1). That is, pigeons were required to peck if a photograph contained a person and to refrain from pecking if the photograph did not contain a person. Pigeons learned the task and transferred the discrimination to novel photographs, although Herrnstein and Loveland did not explicitly demonstrate that the novel photographs were discriminably different from those used in training. Many reports have since demonstrated that birds can acquire this *presence/absence* discrimination using photographs or pictures of trees, fish, people, or conspecifics, and to transfer this discrimination to novel images (Aust & Huber, 2001, 2002; Ghosh et al., 2004; Matsukawa et al. 2004). Most of these studies used a single category (e.g. *person*) together with its complementary category

Table 8.1 Studies of basic-level categorization in pigeons

Training type	Category	References
Go/no-go	Fish	Herrnstein & de Villiers, 1980
Go/no-go	Trees	Herrnstein et al., 1976
Go/no-go	Humans	Aust & Huber, 2001, 2002; Matsukawa et al., 2004
Go/no-go	Cats, dogs	Ghosh et al., 2004
Forced-alternative choice task	Cars, chairs, humans, flowers	Bhatt et al., 1988; Lazareva et al., 2004, 2006; Wasserman et al., 1988
Forced-alternative choice task	Cars, babies, bottles, keys, cakes, ducks, planes, pens, crackers, trees, phones, flowers, dogs, fish, shoes, hats	Wasserman et al., 2007

(e.g. *nonperson*). A few studies have used the go/no-go procedure with noncomplementary categories such as *dog versus cat* (e.g. Ghosh et al., 2004; Roberts & Mazmanian, 1988): for example, a pigeon would be required to respond if the photograph contained a dog and to refrain from pecking if the photograph contained a cat. Still, this categorization learning is restricted to only two categories.

Some authors have suggested that 'only primates may sort the world, i.e. divide it into its indeterminately many classes' (Premack, 1976, p. 215), whereas all other species can only learn *presence/absence* categories. Wasserman and colleagues (Bhatt et al., 1988; Wasserman et al., 1988) addressed this possible limitation by using a multiple-alternative forced-choice procedure which provided the opportunity of training animals to classify multiple noncomplementary categories. For example, Bhatt et al. (1988) trained pigeons to classify photographs of cats, flowers, cars, and chairs by pecking at four distinctively different choice keys. Pigeons readily learned the task and reliably transferred their discrimination to novel images that were shown to be discriminably different from the training images (Bhatt et al., 1988; Lazareva et al., 2004, 2006; Wasserman et al., 1988).

After more than four decades of research on basic-level categorization in animals, it is clear that pigeons can discriminate among many basic-level categories, including multiple noncomplementary categories. Although some early reports suggested that pigeons may be unable to categorize human-made stimuli, such as cars or bottles (Herrnstein, 1985), later studies have found that pigeons can easily associate multiple images of cars, chairs, cats, and flowers with four different responses (Bhatt et al., 1988; Lazareva et al., 2004). Moreover, ongoing research in our laboratory suggests that pigeons' categorization is not limited to only four classes of stimuli: birds can learn to discriminate 16 noncomplementary categories, such as ducks, bottles, trees, hats, and so on (Wasserman et al., 2007).

Still, to what extent is this ability comparable to basic-level categorization in people? Do animals view the members of these categories as being perceptually coherent or more similar to one another than to members of other categories *before* any categorization training, as do people?

Perceptual coherence of basic-level categories

Although some human-language categories may not be based on perceptual similarity, extensive evidence suggests that our most common approach to categorizing the world is to use multiple clusters of objects that are perceptually similar to each other, such as trees, bottles, or airplanes (see Chapter 14 of this book, for a review). This possibility was clearly and emphatically championed by Quine (1969):

> If then I say that there is an innate standard of similarity, I am making a condensed statement that can be interpreted, and truly interpreted, in behavioral terms. Moreover, in this behavioral sense it can be said equally of other animals that they have an innate standard of similarity too. It is part of our birthright. And, interestingly enough, it is characteristically animal in its lack of intellectual status (p. 11).

Do nonhuman animals actually partition the outside world into perceptually coherent clusters of objects? Do they perceive cars to be more similar to other cars than they are to flowers and flowers to be more similar to other flowers than they are to cars? The common approaches to studying basic-level categories in nonhuman animals that were described in Part 1 involved explicit training to discriminate one class of stimuli from another. Thus, the mere ability to learn such discrimination does not tell us whether the animals perceived the members of one class to be more similar to each other than to the members of the other class *before* such training was undertaken. Fortunately, several reports have explored the perception of similarity among members of basic-level categories using more innovative experimental methods.

In one experiment, rhesus monkeys were trained to perform a same–different discrimination (Sands et al., 1982); the animals had to perform one response if two successively shown pictures were identical and to perform a different response if the two pictures were not identical. Therefore, this procedure did not involve explicit categorization training. The set of pictures included six different exemplars of human faces, monkey faces, trees, flowers, and fruits. To explore the perception of similarity among these categories, the researchers analysed the pattern of confusion errors produced by the monkeys. If the monkeys perceived members of the same category (e.g. fruit) to be more similar to each other, then they should have been more likely to erroneously respond 'same' when a picture of an apple was followed by a picture of an orange than when the picture of the apple was followed by a picture from another category (e.g. an oak). Figure 8.1 shows two-dimensional maps derived from these confusion errors for two monkeys. With few exceptions, both monkeys perceived members of the same category to be more similar to each other than to members of

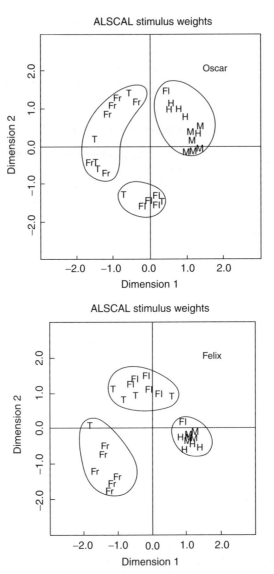

Fig. 8.1 Two-dimensional scaling map for two monkeys, Oscar (top) and Felix (bottom). Letters represent different types of the pictures: H – human faces, M – monkey faces, T – trees, Fr – fruits, Fl – flowers.

Reprinted from Sands, S. F., Lincoln, C. E., & Wright, A. A. (1982). Pictorial similarity judgments and the organization of visual memory in the rhesus monkey. *Journal of Experimental Psychology: General*, **111**, 369–389 with permission from Elsevier.

other categories, as indicated by placement of the pictures belonging to one category in the same region of multidimensional space. Together, these studies suggest that visual perception in primates is influenced by the categorical structure of the world, just as it is in human visual perception.

What about birds? Morphologically, the mammalian visual system is strikingly different from the avian visual system, which consists mainly of nuclear structures and lacks the distinctive layered organization of the mammalian neocortex. Yet, despite these dramatic disparities, avian and mammalian visual systems have similar basic neural organization (see Jarvis et al., 2005; Shimizu & Bowers, 1999, for reviews). Moreover, many reports suggest considerable similarities in visual processing at a behavioural level. Odd-item search and texture segregation provide particularly good examples. When trained to detect a single odd item among uniform distractors, pigeons' search time and accuracy reflect the similarity of the target and the distractors: if the target is highly discriminable from the distractors, then pigeons' detection time does not increase with an increase in the number of the distractors (Blough, 1989). Pigeons trained to discriminate the odd region in a texture display do so more accurately when the visual elements come from the same dimension (e.g. colour) than when visual elements are represented by a conjunction of features (e.g. colour and shape). Pigeons were able to detect texture differences within 100 ms, implying that texture discrimination and perceptual grouping are early processes in pigeon vision, just as they are in human vision (Cook et al., 1996, 1997). Taking all of this evidence together, we might expect that pigeons will be sensitive to the perceptual cohesiveness of basic-level categories, just as are humans and primates.

Wasserman et al. (1988) were the first to experimentally address this possibility. In one experiment, they randomly divided 20 photographs, of cats, flowers, cars, and chairs, into two subcategories each containing 10 photographs. Each subcategory was associated with a distinctive response key, so that the pigeons were required to make one response in the presence of the first subcategory and a different response in the presence of the second subcategory. For example, a pigeon might be shown a picture of a flower along with four choice-response keys. Two out of four response keys were associated with the two subcategories of flowers and the other two response keys were associated with the two subcategories of cars. The variable of interest was the error rate associated with each of the *incorrect* (i.e. nonreinforced) response keys. If the pigeons perceived flowers to be no more similar to each others than to cars, then we would expect to observe a random distribution of errors among the three incorrect responses (incorrect flower subcategory and two subcategories of cars). However, if the pigeons viewed the categories as being perceptually coherent, then we would expect to see more confusion errors to the response key associated with the incorrect subcategory of flowers.

Indeed, pigeons made significantly more categorical errors (56%) than expected by chance (33%). In other words, when the pigeons saw a photograph of a flower belonging to one subcategory, they were much more likely to select the incorrect key associated with flowers from the other subcategory than the two keys associated with cars.

Therefore, pigeons behaved as if members of the same human-language basic-level category were less discriminable than members of different basic-level categories.

In a subsequent experiment, Wasserman et al. (1988) further examined this matter by comparing the speed of learning a true categorization task and a pseudocategorization task. Pigeons trained to perform the true categorization task had to associate four human-language basic-level categories with four distinctive response keys. Pigeons trained to perform the pseudocategorization task had to sort the same stimuli into four arbitrary groupings, each of which contained the same number of members of all four basic-level categories. Again, if all of the stimuli were equally discriminable, then both groups ought to have learned their respective tasks at the same speed. Instead, the pseudo-category group was much slower to learn than the true category group (Figure 8.2); after 40 days of training, the pseudocategory group averaged just over 40% correct, whereas the category group averaged almost 80% correct. This result again suggests that pigeons perceive members of the same basic-level category as being more similar to each other than to members of different basic-level categories.

Later, Astley and Wasserman (1992) developed a new experimental procedure for examining the perception of categorical similarity by pigeons. The birds were presented with 12 exemplars drawn from a single basic-level category that were reinforced during training as well as with 12 different exemplars drawn from four basic-level categories that were not reinforced during training. For example, a pigeon might be shown 12 photographs of cars followed by reinforcement plus 12 different photographs

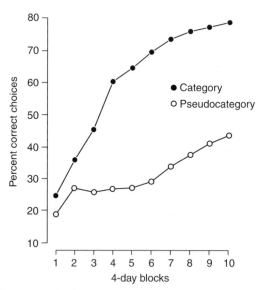

Fig. 8.2 Mean percentage of correct responses for category and pseudocategory groups.

From Wasserman, E. A., Kiedinger, R. E. & Bhatt, R. S. (1988). Conceptual behavior in pigeons: Categories, subcategories, and pseudocategories. *Journal of Experimental Psychology: Animal Behavior Processes*, **14**, 235–246.

of cars, 12 photographs of chairs, 12 photographs of people, and 12 photographs of flowers, all followed by nonreinforcement. If all 48 nonreinforced stimuli appeared equally similar to the 12 reinforced stimuli, then the response rate to all of the categories of nonreinforced stimuli should have fallen at the same rate. To establish an initial high and uniform rate of response, pigeons were first presented with all of the stimuli that were to appear during discrimination training reinforced with a probability of 0.25.

Figure 8.3 shows the results from experiment 2 of Astley and Wasserman (1992) calculated as a proportion of change from the baseline rate of response. It is evident that nonreinforced stimuli drawn from the same category as the reinforced stimuli were more resistant to extinction than were nonreinforced stimuli drawn from different categories. These results again suggest that pigeons perceive human-language basic-level categories as perceptually coherent clusters of objects.

Subordinate categories as an example of perceptual concepts

Subordinate categories are nested within basic-level categories: for example, the category *tree* includes maples, oaks, and pines. Subordinate categories have high within-category similarity. But, unlike basic-level categories, they also have high between-category similarity; after all, most trees look quite similar to each other. Consequently, categorization at the basic level is preferred to categorization at the subordinate level (Rosch & Mervis, 1975). Nevertheless, the less-privileged status of subordinate categories can be moderated by expertise: dog experts and bird experts

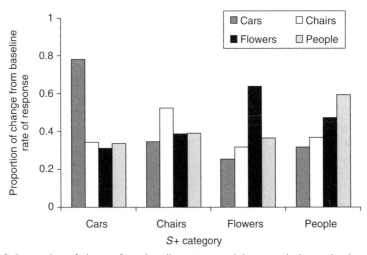

Fig. 8.3 Proportion of change from baseline rate to training rate during extinction training.

Compiled from Astley, S. L. & Wasserman, E. A. (1992). Categorical discrimination and generalization in pigeons: All negative stimuli are not created equal. *Journal of Experimental Psychology: Animal Behavior Processes*, **18**, 193–207.

identify objects at the subordinate level just as fast as at the basic level within their domain of expertise (Johnson & Mervis 1997; Tanaka & Taylor, 1991).

Can animals learn to categorize at the subordinate level? Although categorization at the subordinate level has received far less attention than categorization at the basic or superordinate levels, Roberts and Mazmanian (1988) successfully trained pigeons to categorize at the subordinate level (*kingfisher/non-kingfisher*). Curiously, pigeons in this study readily learned and transferred the subordinate-level *kingfisher/non-kingfisher* discrimination, but they were unable to master the basic-level *bird/non-bird* discrimination (Roberts & Mazmanian, 1988). However, other reports suggest that pigeons can successfully master the *bird/mammal* discrimination (Cook et al., 1990). Future research systematically examining the preferred level of categorization across different species is needed to disclose potential disparities and similarities in subordinate-level categorization in animals and humans.

Nonsimilarity-based concepts

Nonsimilarity-based concepts (e.g. tools or furniture) include perceptually diverse stimuli that are grouped on the basis of common function or common association. A chair, a lamp, a rug, and a table do not look alike, but they are all items of furniture. What permits this aggregation of perceptually dissimilar stimuli into a single category? One possibility is related to *learned or acquired equivalence*: the stimuli associated with a common response or a common outcome will be grouped together, despite their perceptual heterogeneity (Keller & Schoenfeld, 1950; Schusterman et al., 2000; Sidman, 2000; Wasserman et al., 1992; Zentall, 2000). Can nonhuman animals also construct categories based on their functional, rather than perceptual, properties?

In the representative experiment depicted in Figure 8.4 (Wasserman et al., 1992), pigeons were trained to peck one button when photographs of two basic-level categories (e.g. flowers and chairs) were presented and to peck a second button when photographs of other two basic-level categories (e.g. cars and people) were presented. Then, with the first two buttons unavailable, the pigeons were trained to peck a third button to photographs of flowers and to peck a fourth button to photographs of people – a procedure called reassignment training (Lea, 1984). No photographs of cars or chairs were shown during reassignment training. Finally, the researchers showed the pigeons photographs of cars and chairs with only the third and fourth buttons available. If, during original training, the pigeons grouped the two basic-level categories associated with a common response into a higher-order category, then they should have been able to select the response associated with the complementary basic-level category during reassignment training.

In the testing phase, the pigeons did predominately peck the button that had been associated with the complementary basic-level category during reassignment training, thus documenting functional stimulus equivalence. Later research in our laboratory has revealed that pigeons can form functional equivalence classes via associations with a common delay, a common probability, and a common quantity of reinforcement (Astley et al., 2001; Astley & Wasserman, 1999; see also Frank & Wasserman, 2005). For example, when cars and flowers were associated with a 15-s delay to reinforcement,

Original training   **Reassignment training**

Category 1

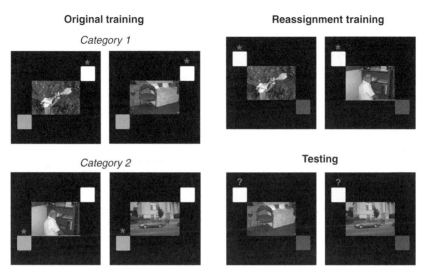

Category 2   **Testing**

Fig. 8.4 Schematic depiction of the training and testing procedures used in Wasserman et al. (1992). First, pigeons were trained to associate two basic-level categories with one response and two other basic-level categories with a different response (*original training*), creating two higher-level, superordinate categories. Later, one of the basic-level categories from each superordinate category was associated with a different response (*reassignment training*). Finally, the withheld basic-level categories were presented with the novel choice responses (*testing*). If the birds were forming superordinate-level categories during original training, then they should be able to select the correct response associated with the other class of stimuli during reassignment training. Asterisks indicate the correct response.

or were reinforced on one out of ten trials, or were reinforced by five pellets, pigeons grouped these two basic-level categories together into a functional equivalence class. In sum, these results show that pigeons group together perceptually dissimilar stimuli when they are associated with a common response or a common outcome, much as people group together socks, shirts, and hats as items called 'clothing'. Moreover, when some members of these classes are associated with a novel response during reassignment training, pigeons are able to extend this response to all other exemplars of the functional equivalence class. In a similar manner, when we learn that 'apparel' is a synonym of 'clothing', we instantly conclude that socks, shirts, and hats are all members of this new class, without being explicitly told so.

The examples above used perceptually diverse stimuli to create a model of superordinate-level categories. Starting with Herrnstein's studies, many studies have also demonstrated that pigeons can learn to respond differentially to superordinate human-language categories, such as bodies of water, man-made objects, or food (Table 8.2). However, most published studies have explored animals' categorization at different levels in different experiments and usually with different visual stimuli. Yet, flexible classification of objects and events at different levels is thought to be one of the

Table 8.2 Studies of categorization at the superordinate level in pigeons

Category	References
Bodies of water	Herrnstein et al., 1976
Mammals, birds, or animals	Roberts & Mazmanian, 1988
Man-made vs. natural, or living vs. nonliving	Cook et al., 1990; Lazareva et al., 2004, 2006; Lubow, 1974; Roberts & Mazmanian, 1988
Food	Awazu & Fujita, 2006

most important and perhaps the unique feature of human categorization (Markman, 1989): humans can refer to the same object as a Toyota, a car, or a vehicle, depending on context. Recently, work in our laboratory has explored whether pigeons can flexibly classify the same photographs at the basic level or at the superordinate level depending on task demands (Lazareva et al., 2004).

Our experiment used four basic-level categories (cars, chairs, flowers, and humans) that were arranged into two superordinate-level categories (artificial: cars and chairs, natural: flowers and humans). During training, the same photograph randomly required basic-level discrimination if four choice keys were presented and superordinate-level discrimination if two other choice keys were presented (Figure 8.5). Our pigeons readily mastered both discriminations, attesting to their ability to flexibly categorize the photos; as well, our pigeons demonstrated reliable transfer to novel exemplars at both basic and superordinate levels. Flexible categorization therefore appears not to be a uniquely human ability.

Abstract concepts

Many theorists have drawn a distinction between 'natural' concepts, such as *tree* or *furniture*, and 'abstract' or 'relational' concepts, such as *above/below* or *same/different*

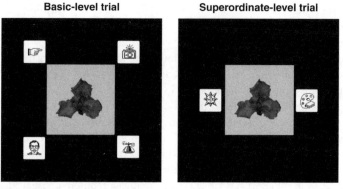

Fig. 8.5 Schematic layout of a basic-level trial and a superordinate-level trial used in Lazareva et al. (2004).

(Cook & Wasserman, 2006; Herrnstein, 1990; Lea, 1984; Mackintosh, 2000; Pearce, 1994; Premack, 1983; Thompson, 1995; Wasserman, 1995; Wright et al., 2003). Members of natural concepts are grouped either by perceptual, associative, or functional similarity, whereas abstract concepts are believed to go beyond the specific features of the stimuli. Instead, abstract concepts are based on *relations* between or among those stimuli.

Relational concepts using transposition

Can birds respond to the relations between or among stimuli rather than to the absolute properties of the stimuli? Perhaps the most famous attempt to experimentally examine this possibility comes from the case of transposition, first explored by Köhler (1918/1938). Suppose that an organism is given a simultaneous discrimination task in which the positive discriminative stimulus (S+) is a 2-cm diameter circle and the negative discriminative stimulus (S-) is a 3-cm diameter circle. When the organism masters the visual discrimination, has it learned that only the 2-cm circle signals food or has it learned the concept *smaller*? Köhler suggested that the answer to this question can be found by considering how the organism ought to respond to new pairs of stimuli. If the former S+ is presented along with the even *smaller* 1-cm diameter circle, then having learned to respond to the relation between the circles, the organism may actually choose the untrained stimulus over the former S+. In his pioneering studies, Köhler (1929, 1938) found that chicken did indeed respond in this relational manner – a result which led him to propose that stimuli are not only judged in absolute terms, but also relative to one another.

However, later research has shown that the choice of the untrained stimulus over the former S+ does not necessarily guarantee control by the relation between stimuli. Kenneth W. Spence (1937) famously demonstrated that 'relational' responding in the transposition paradigm can be explained as the result of the interaction of learned tendencies to make responses to S+ and to withhold responses to S–. If both training stimuli are located along the same dimension, then the algebraic summation of those learned tendencies leads to two *peak shifts*: the peak of maximal associative strength shifts away from the former S– and the peak of minimal associative strength shifts away from the former S+. In other words, the organism may prefer the 1-cm circle because the associative strength of this stimulus is actually higher than associative strength of the formerly reinforced 2-cm circle. So, according to Spence's generalization theory, the preference for the novel stimulus over the former S+ found by Köhler was no more relational than was the tendency to approach S+ and the tendency to avoid S– after standard discrimination training. Spence's stimulus generalization theory yielded several important predictions that have been confirmed in different species, including humans, and in different situations (e.g. Cheng, 1999; Cheng & Spetch, 2002; Ehrenfreund, 1952; Honig, 1962; reviewed by Purtle 1973; Reese, 1968; Riley, 1968).

Several reports, however, have challenged generalization theory as the sole account of an organism's behaviour in transposition tasks. Marsh (1967) trained pigeons to discriminate four stimuli of different wavelengths. One group of 12 pigeons was trained with S1+ versus S2– and S3+ versus S4–; a second group of 12 pigeons was trained with S1+ versus S2– and S3– versus S4+. The numbers here represent ordinal placement of the stimuli along the wavelength continuum. Within each group, half of the pigeons were given successive discrimination training, so that the birds could not directly compare two training stimuli. The other half of the pigeons were given simultaneous discrimination training; they were able to directly compare the wavelengths of the training stimuli. In the test, all of the pigeons were given the choice of S2 versus S3. Marsh found that pigeons trained with the same relation in both pairs of the simultaneous discrimination (S1+ vs. S2– and S3+ vs. S4–) selected the previously nonreinforced S2 over the previously reinforced S3 an average of 76% of the time, whereas all of the other pigeons responded in accord with the absolute reinforcement histories of the discriminative stimuli. Marsh claimed that it is impossible to find excitatory and inhibitory gradients that can account for both discrimination mastery and choice of a previously nonreinforced stimulus (S2–) over the previously reinforced stimulus (S3+).

In our own recent studies (Lazareva et al., 2005, 2008), we further explored transposition behaviour by exposing pigeons to multiple training pairs. In one such test (Lazareva et al., 2008), we trained pigeons to discriminate circles of different sizes indicated by the different numerals in Figure 8.6. Pigeons in one-pair training had to discriminate S1+ versus S2–; pigeons in two-pair training had to discriminate S1+ versus S2– and S2+ versus S3; and, pigeons in three-pair training had to discriminate S1+ versus S2–, S2+ versus S3–, and S3+ versus S4–. The critical testing pairs are S4 versus S5 and S5 versus S6. As relationally correct stimuli S4 (in pair S4 vs. S5) and S5 (in pair S5 vs. S6) gradually come closer to the stimulus that was not reinforced during training, we expect transposition to be lower after three-pair training than after one-pair training. As right panel of Figure 8.6 shows, after one-pair training, the post-discrimination generalization gradients predicted chance responding to both testing pairs. With more training pairs, however, the gradients predicted a *decrease* in transposition from one-pair training to two-pair training to three-pair training. Figure 8.7 shows the results of our experiment. We found a steady *increase* in relational responding from one-pair to two-pair to three-pair training, instead of the decrease predicted by post-discrimination generalization gradients.

It is well known that increasing the number of exemplars leads to better acquisition of a concept in many species of animals, including pigeons (Cook, 2002; Katz et al., 2002; Wright et al., 1988; Wright, 1997). Similarly, pigeons may need to encounter multiple instances of a rule in order to exhibit strong relational responding. Unfortunately, we do not yet know whether the same is true for other animal species.

Concept of identity

The concept of identity or sameness (and the counterparts' nonidentity and difference) is perhaps the most extensively studied concept in nonhuman animals. The most frequently used experimental procedures are matching-to-sample and same–different discrimination. In the standard matching-to-sample task, an animal first views a single stimulus, or *sample*, and performs several observing responses to it (e.g. pecking the sample). After that, the animal is shown two *comparison stimuli* and is required to select the comparison that matches the sample (identity matching) or that

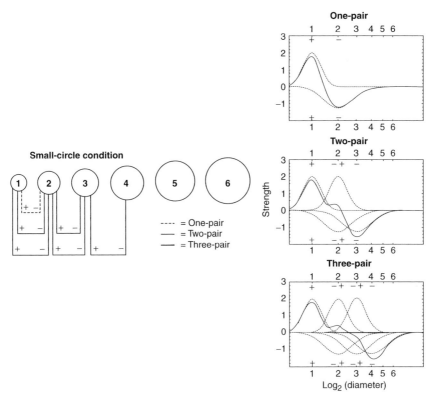

Fig. 8.6 Schematic representation of the experimental design, together with post-discrimination gradients (smooth lines) obtained by summation of the excitatory and inhibitory gradients (dashed lines), for the small-circle condition, smaller plus discrimination task, used in Lazareva et al. (2008).

does not match the sample (oddity matching). The simultaneous same–different discrimination task requires the choice of one arbitrary response if the two presented stimuli are identical and a second arbitrary response if the two stimuli are nonidentical.

To demonstrate the identity concept, animals need to be able to successfully transfer their discriminative behaviour to novel stimuli. The most stringent test of *full concept learning* requires the animal to discriminate the novel stimuli as accurately as the training stimuli. In many cases, animals discriminate novel stimuli less accurately than the training stimuli, signifying the stimulus-dependent nature of the acquired behaviour, even when discriminative performance is reliably above chance; this is sometimes termed *partial concept learning*.

Do birds demonstrate partial or full learning of the concept of identity? Many studies listed in Table 8.3 show that they indeed can. Interestingly, the number of stimuli used during training appears to be an important parameter affecting identity concept learning. When the number of stimuli used during training is small, birds often memorize associations between individual stimuli resulting in poor transfer to

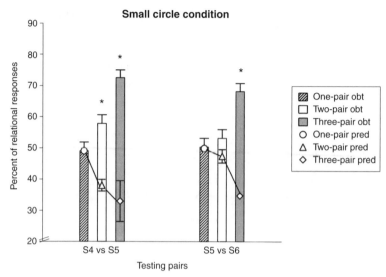

Fig. 8.7 Mean percent of transposition responses obtained after one-pair, two-pair, and three-pair training and predicted by the best-fitting post-discrimination stimulus generalization gradients based on Shepard's (1987) stimulus-generalization function.

novel exemplars. When the number of training stimuli is increased, a procedure that makes memorizing individual stimulus associations a more difficult and costly strategy, transfer to novel exemplars improves dramatically. This effect has been replicated across different species (crows: Smirnova et al. 2000; pigeons: Bodily et al., 2008; primates: Wright et al., 2003) and different experimental procedures (Bodily et al., 2008), suggesting that the improvement in concept learning with an

Table 8.3 Studies of same–different concept learning in birds

Species	Experimental procedure	Degree of concept learning	References
Pigeons	Matching-to-sample	Partial to full, depending on training procedure	Bodily et al., 2008; Wright, 1997; Wright & Delius, 1994; Wright et al., 1988
Pigeons	Same–different	Partial	Blaisdell & Cook, 2005; Cook et al., 2003; Wasserman et al., 1995; Young et al., 1997; Young & Wasserman, 1997
Hooded crows	Matching-to-sample	Full	Smirnova et al., 2000
Jays and jackdaws	Matching-to-sample	Partial	Wilson et al., 1985

increase in the number of exemplars instantiating the concept may be a general cognitive trait.

Other reports suggest that seemingly minor changes in experimental procedure may lead to the deployment of dramatically different strategies for task mastery. Gibson et al. (2006) trained pigeons to perform a simultaneous same–different discrimination. In the *16S* versus *16D* condition (Figure 8.8), the birds had to select one choice key if all 16 items in the display were the same and to select the other choice key if all 16 items in the display were different. In the *16S versus 15S:1D* condition, *different* displays contained 15 identical items and 1 odd item. In other words, in the 16S versus 16D condition, pigeons could potentially perform the discrimination by comparing any two items in the display, but in the 16S versus 15S:1D condition, they had to locate the single odd item in order to learn the task.

After the pigeons learnt the task, they were trained to concurrently perform the already learned 16S versus 16D discrimination plus the newly introduced 16S versus 15S:1D discrimination. If all of the birds were using the same strategy in both tasks, then they should begin to make many more errors on *same* trials in the 16S versus 16D task, as the 16S displays are quite similar to the 15S:1D displays. On the contrary, the birds should make many fewer errors on *different* trials, as the 16D displays should appear even more different than the 16S display when the 15S:1D displays are introduced. Yet, none of these changes were observed. Acquisition of the 16S versus 15S:1D task did not come at the expense of 16S versus 16D task performance, suggesting that

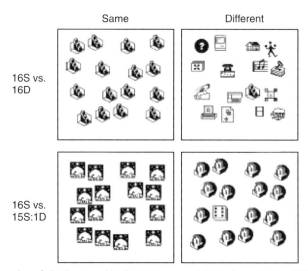

Fig. 8.8 Examples of displays used in the 16S versus 16D task and in the 16S versus 15S:1D task.

Modified from Gibson, B. M., Wasserman, E. A., & Cook, R. G. (2006). Not all same–different discriminations are created equal: Evidence contrary to a unidimensional account of same–different learning. *Learning and Motivation, **37**,* 189–208, with permission from Elsevier.

the pigeons may have used two different strategies to solve these two different tasks. Other evidence also points to the conclusion that these two tasks are qualitatively different (reviewed by Cook & Wasserman, 2006; Wasserman et al., 2004). More research is clearly necessary to elucidate the factors affecting the acquisition of the identity concept and the mechanisms underlying conceptual behaviour in different experimental procedures.

Conclusion

Why do we need categories or concepts? Sorting different objects that are nevertheless similar to each other in some important aspects into the same group, or category, gives us the opportunity to make inferences about those stimuli and to apply those inferences when we encounter new members of this category. The impressive development of human conceptual abilities often leads theorists to conclude that our abilities to categorize and to conceptualize are not only superior that of other animals, but that they are unique to our species. Yet, other species have undoubtedly had to overcome environmental problems that required the deployment of an assortment of cognitive processes. After all, it is clearly beneficial for a pigeon to recognize different species of hawks as predators or to recognize different trees as potential nest locations. As stated by Charles Darwin, 'the senses and intuitions, the various emotions and faculties, such as . . . memory, attention, . . . reason, etc., of which man boasts, may be found in an incipient, or even sometimes in a well-developed condition, in the lower animals' (Darwin, 1896, p. 126).

The research reviewed in this chapter strongly suggests that, if asked in the appropriate way, then birds too can provide convincing evidence of their conceptual abilities that bears sometimes striking similarities to human conceptual abilities. Birds form concepts based on perceptual similarity among their members, classifying objects into basic-level categories and subordinate-level categories. They appear to sense the perceptual structure of their environment, viewing members of basic-level categories (such as humans or trees) as being more similar to one another than to members of other categories. They can sort objects into nonsimilarity-based, superordinate categories, flexibly switching from basic-level categorization to superordinate-level categorization. Even the ability to form abstract concepts based on the relation between or among stimuli is not exclusively human.

However, we are still far from understanding to what extent the mechanisms underlying human conceptual behaviour are similar to those in nonhuman animals. Most of the research up to this point has focused on whether a particular species is able to form a specific concept. Although such studies are an important first step in our understanding of categorization and conceptualization in animals, they do not tell us *how* the species attains concept mastery. As Stewart Hulse (2006) aptly notes, we need 'less and less research on existence proof, that is, whether or not a given species has the same cognitive capacity as we, or some other species, do' (p. 674), and more and more research on how these cognitive capacities operate.

References

Astley, S. L. & Wasserman, E. A. (1992). Categorical discrimination and generalization in pigeons: All negative stimuli are not created equal. *Journal of Experimental Psychology: Animal Behavior Processes*, **18**(2), 193–207.

Astley, S. L. & Wasserman, E. A. (1999). Superordinate category formation in pigeons: Association with a common delay or probability of food reinforcement makes perceptually dissimilar stimuli functionally equivalent. *Journal of Experimental Psychology: Animal Behavior Processes*, **25**(4), 415–432.

Astley, S. L., Peissig, J. J., & Wasserman, E. A. (2001). Superordinate categorization via learned stimulus equivalence: Quantity of reinforcement, hedonic value, and the nature of the mediator. *Journal of Experimental Psychology: Animal Behavior Processes*, **27**(3), 252–268.

Aust, U. & Huber, L. (2001). The role of item- and category-specific information in the discrimination of people versus nonpeople images by pigeons. *Animal Learning and Behavior*, **29**(2), 107–119.

Aust, U. & Huber, L. (2002). Target-defining features in a 'people-present/people-absent' discrimination task by pigeons. *Animal Learning and Behavior*, **30**(2), 165–176.

Awazu, S. & Fujita, K. (2006). Transfer from 'edible' categorization training to feeding behavior in pigeons (Columba livia). *Japanese Psychological Research*, **48**(1), 27–33.

Bhatt, R. S., Wasserman, E. A., Reynolds, W. F., & Knauss, K. S. (1988). Conceptual behavior in pigeons: Categorization of both familiar and novel examples from four classes of natural and artifical stimuli. *Journal of Experimental Psychology: Animal Behavior Processes*, **14**(3), 219–234.

Blaisdell, A. P. & Cook, R. G. (2005). Two-item same-different concept learning in pigeons. *Learning and Behavior*, **33**(1), 67–77.

Blough, D. (1989). Odd-item search in pigeons: Display size and transfer effects. *Journal of Experimental Psychology: Animal Behavior Processes*, **15**(1), 14–22.

Bodily, K. D., Katz, J. S., & Wright, A. A. (2008). Matching-to-sample abstract-concept learning by pigeons. *Journal of Experimental Psychology: Animal Behavior Processes*, **34**(1), 178–184.

Cheng, K. (1999). Spatial generalization in honeybees confirms Shepard's law. *Behavioural Processes*, **44**(3), 309–316.

Cheng, K. & Spetch, M. L. (2002). Spatial generalization and peak shift in humans. *Learning and Motivation*, **33**, 358–389.

Cook, R. G. (2002). The structure of pigeon multiple-class same-different learning. *Journal of Experimental Analysis of Behavior*, **78**(3), 345–364.

Cook, R. G. & Wasserman, E. A. (2006). Relational discrimination learning in pigeons. In E. A. Wasserman & T. R. Zentall (Eds.), *Comparative Cognition: Experimental Explorations of Animal Intelligence*, pp. 307–324, Oxford: Oxford University Press.

Cook, R. G., Wright, A. A., & Kendrick, D. F. (1990), Visual categorization by pigeons. In M. L. Commons & R. J. Herrnstein (Eds), *Behavioral Approaches to Pattern Recognition and Concept Formation*, pp. 187–214, Hillsdale, NJ: Lawrence Erlbaum Associates.

Cook, R. G., Cavoto, K. K., & Cavoto, B. R. (1996). Mechanisms of multidimensional grouping, fusion, and search in avian texture discrimination. *Animal Learning and Behavior*, **24**(2), 150–167.

Cook, R. G., Cavoto, B. R., Katz, J. S., & Cavoto, K. K. (1997). Pigeon perception and discrimination of rapidly changing texture stimuli. *Journal of Experimental Psychology: Animal Behavior Processes*, **23**(4), 390–400.

Cook, B. R., Kelly, D. M., & Katz, J. S. (2003). Successive two-item same-different discrimination and concept learning by pigeons. *Behavioural Processes*, **62**(1–3), 125–144.

Darwin, C. (1896). *The descent of man, and selection in relation to sex* New York: D. Appleton and Company.

Ehrenfreund, D. (1952). A study of the transposition gradient. *Journal of Experimental Psychology*, **43**(2), 81–87.

Frank, A. & Wasserman, E. A. (2005). Response rate is not an effective mediator of learned stimulus equivalence in pigeons. *Learning and Behavior*, **33**(3), 287–295.

Ghosh, N., Lea, S. E. G., & Noury, M. (2004). Transfer to intermediate forms following concept discrimination by pigeons: Chimeras and morphs. *Journal of Experimental Analysis of Behavior*, **82**(2), 125–141.

Gibson, B. M., Wasserman, E. A., & Cook, R. G. (2006). Not all same–different discriminations are created equal: Evidence contrary to a unidimensional account of same–different learning. *Learning and Motivation*, **37**(3), 189–208.

Herrnstein, R. J. (1985). Riddles of natural categorization. *Philosophical Transactions of the Royal Society of London.Series B, Biological Sciences*, **308**(1135), 129–143.

Herrnstein, R. J. (1990). Levels of stimulus control: A functional approach. *Cognition*, **37**, 133–166.

Herrnstein, R. J. & de Villiers, P. A. (1980). Fish as natural category for people and pigeons. In G. H. Bower (Ed.), *The Psychology of Learning and Motivation: Advances in Research and Theory*, Vol. 14, pp. 59–95, New York: Academic Press.

Herrnstein, R. J. & Loveland, D. H. (1964). Complex visual concept in the pigeon. *Science*, **146**(3643), 549–551.

Herrnstein, R. J., Loveland, D. H., & Cable, C. (1976). Natural concepts in pigeons. *Journal of Experimental Psychology: Animal Behavior Processes*, **2**(4), 285–302.

Honig, W. K. (1962). Prediction of preference, transposition, transposition–reversal from the generalization gradient. *Journal of Experimental Psychology*, **64**(3), 239–248.

Hulse, S. H. (2006). Postscript: An essay on the study of cognition in animals. In E. A. Wasserman & T. R. Zentall (Eds.), *Comparative Cognition: Experimental Explorations of Animal Intelligence*, pp. 668–678, New York: Oxford University Press.

Jarvis, E. D., Guentuerkuen, O., Bruce, L., et al. (2005). Avian brains and a new understanding of vertebrate brain evolution. *Nature Reviews Neuroscience*, **6**, 151–159.

Johnson, K. E. & Mervis, C. B. (1997). Effects of varying levels of expertise on the basic level of categorization. *Journal of Experimental Psychology: General*, **126**(3), 248–277.

Katz, J. S., Wright, A. A., & Bachevalier, J. (2002). Mechanisms of same/different abstract-concept learning by rhesus monkeys (*Macaca mulatta*). *Journal of Experimental Psychology: Animal Behavior Processes*, **28**(4), 358–368.

Keller, F. S. & Schoenfeld, W. N. (1950). *Principles of Psychology: A Systematic Text in the Science of Behavior* New York: Appleton-Century-Crofts, Inc.

Köhler, W. (1929). *Gestalt Psychology* New York: H. Liveright.

Köhler, W. (1938). Simple structural functions in the chimpanzee and in the chicken. In W. D. Ellis (Ed.), *A Source Book of Gestalt Psychology*, pp. 217–227, London: Routledge & Kegan Paul. (Original work published 1918.)

Lazareva, O. F. & Wasserman, E. A. (2008). Categories and concepts in animals. In R. Menzel (Ed.), *Learning Theory and Behavior. Vol. 1 of Learning and Memory: A Comprehensive Reference (edited by J. Byrne)*, pp. 197–226, Oxford: Elsevier.

Lazareva, O. F., Freiburger, K. L., & Wasserman, E. A. (2004). Pigeons concurrently categorize photographs at both basic and superordinate levels. *Psychonomic Bulletin and Review*, **11**(6), 1111–1117.

Lazareva, O. F., Wasserman, E. A., & Young, M. E. (2005). Transposition in pigeons: Reassessing Spence (1937) with multiple discrimination training. *Learning and Behavior*, **33**(1), 22–46.

Lazareva, O. F., Freiburger, K. L., & Wasserman, E. A. (2006). Effects of stimulus manipulations on visual categorization in pigeons. *Behavioural Processes*, **72**, 224–233.

Lazareva, O. F., Miner, M., Wasserman, E. A., & Young, M. E. (2008). Multiple-pair training enhances transposition in pigeons. *Learning and Behavior*, **36**(3), 174–187.

Lea, S. E. G. (1984). In what sense do pigeons learn concepts? In H. L. Roitblat, T. G. Bever, & H. S. Terrace (Eds.), *Animal Cognition*, pp. 263–277, Hillsdale, NJ: Erlbaum.

Lubow, R. E. (1974). High-order concept formation in the pigeon. *Journal of Experimental Analysis of Behavior*, **21**(3), 475–483.

Mackintosh, N. J. (2000). Abstraction and discrimination. In C. Heyes & L. Huber (Eds.), *The Evolution of Cognition*, pp. 123–142, Cambridge, MA: MIT Press.

Markman, E. M. (1989). *Categorization and Naming in Children*: *Problems of Induction* Cambridge, MA: MIT Press.

Marsh, G. (1967). Relational learning in the pigeon. *Journal of Comparative and Physiological Psychology*, **64**(3), 519–521.

Matsukawa, A., Inoue, S., & Jitsumori, M. (2004). Pigeon's recognition of cartoons: Effect of fragmentation, scrambling, and deletion of elements. *Behavioural Processes*, **65**, 23–34.

Medin, D. L. (1989). Concepts and conceptual structure. *American Psychologist*, **44**, 1469–1481.

Pearce, J. M. (1994). Discrimination and categorization. In N. J. Mackintosh (Ed.), *Animal learning and Cognition. Handbook of Perception and Cognition Series*, 2nd edn., pp. 109–134, New York, London: Academic Press.

Premack, D. (1976). *Intelligence in Ape and Man* Hillsdale, NJ: John Wiley & Sons.

Premack, D. (1983). Animal cognition. *Annual Reviews in Psychology*, **34**, 351–362.

Purtle, R. B. (1973). Peak shift: A review. *Psychological Bulletin*, **80**(5), 408–421.

Quine, W. V. (1969). Natural kinds. In N.Rescher (Ed.), *Essays in honor of Carl G. Hempel*, pp. 5–23, Dordrecht, Holland: D. Reidel.

Reese, H. W. (1968). *The Perception of Stimulus Relation: Discrimination Learning and Transposition* New York, London: Academic Press.

Riley, D. A. (1968). *Discrimination Learning* Boston, MA: Allyn and Bacon, Inc.

Roberts, W. A. & Mazmanian, D. S. (1988). Concept learning at different levels of abstraction by pigeons, monkeys, and people. *Journal of Experimental Psychology: Animal Behavior Processes*, **14**(3), 247–260.

Rosch, E. & Mervis, C. B. (1975). Family resemblances: Studies in the internal structure of categories. *Cognitive Psychology*, **7**(4), 573–605.

Rosch, E., Mervis, K. B., Gray, W. D., Johnson, D. M., & Boyes-Braem, P. (1976). Basic objects in natural categories. *Cognitive Psychology*, **8**, 382–439.

Sands, S. F., Lincoln, C. E., & Wright, A. A. (1982). Pictorial similarity judgments and the organization of visual memory in the rhesus monkey. *Journal of Experimental Psychology: General*, **111**(4), 369–389.

Schusterman, R. J., Reichmuth, C. J., & Kastak, D. (2000). How animals classify friends and foes. *Current Directions in Psychological Science*, **9**(1) 1–6.

Shimizu, T. & Bowers, A. N. (1999). Visual circuits of the avian telencephalon: Evolutionary implications. *Behavioural Brain Research*, **98**, 183–191.

Sidman, M. (2000). Equivalence relations and the reinforcement contingency. *Journal of Experimental Analysis of Behavior*, **74**(1) 127–146.

Smirnova, A. A., Lazareva, O. F., & Zorina, Z. A. (2000). Use of number by crows: Investigation by matching and oddity learning. *Journal of Experimental Analysis of Behavior*, **73**(2) 163–176.

Spence, K.W. (1937). The differential response in animals to stimuli varying within a single dimension. *Psychological Bulletin*, **44**(5), 430–444.

Tanaka, J. W. & Taylor, M. (1991). Object categories and expertise: Is the basic level in the eye of the beholder? *Cognitive Psychology*, **23**(3), 457–482.

Thompson, R. K. R. (1995). Natural and relational concepts in animals. In H. L. Roitblatt & J.-A. Meyer (Eds.), *Comparative Approaches to Cognitive Science*, pp. 176–224, Cambridge, MA: MIT Press.

Wasserman, E. A. (1995). The conceptual abilities in pigeons. *American Scientist*, **83**, 246–255.

Wasserman, E. A., Kiedinger, R. E., & Bhatt, R. S. (1988). Conceptual behavior in pigeons: Categories, subcategories, and pseudocategories. *Journal of Experimental Psychology: Animal Behavior Processes*, **14**(3), 235–246.

Wasserman, E. A., DeVolder, C. L., & Coppage, D. J. (1992). Nonsimilarity-based conceptualization in pigeons via secondary or mediated generalization. *Psychological Science*, **3**(6), 374–378.

Wasserman, E. A., Hugart, J. A., & Kirkpatrick-Steger, K. (1995). Pigeons show same-different conceptualization after training with complex visual stimuli. *Journal of Experimental Psychology: Animal Behavior Processes*, **21**(3), 248–252.

Wasserman, E. A., Young, M. E., & Cook, R. G. (2004). Variability discrimination in humans and animals. *American Psychologist*, **59**(9), 879–880.

Wilson, P. N., Mackintosh, N. J., & Boakes, R. (1985). Transfer of relational rules in matching and oddity learning by pigeons and corvids. *Quarterly Journal of Experimental Psychology*, **37B**, 313–332.

Wright, A. A. (1997). Concept learning and learning strategies. *Psychological Science*, **8**(2), 119–123.

Wright, A. A. & Delius, J. D. (1994). Scratch and match: Pigeons learn matching and oddity with gravel stimuli. *Journal of Experimental Psychology: Animal Behavior Processes*, **20**(1), 108–112.

Wright, A. A., Cook, R. G., Rivera, J. U., Sands, S. F., & Delius, J. D. (1988). Concept learning by pigeon: Matching-to-sample with trial-unique video picture stimuli. *Animal Learning and Behavior*, **16**(4), 236–444.

Wright, A. A., Rivera, J. U., Katz, J. S., & Bachevalier, J. (2003). Abstract-concept learning and list-memory processing by capuchin and rhesus monkeys. *Journal of Experimental Psychology: Animal Behavior Processes*, **29**(3), 184–198.

Young, M. E. & Wasserman, E. A. (1997). Entropy detected by pigeons: Response to mixed visual displays after same-different discrimination training. *Journal of Experimental Psychology: Animal Behavior Processes*, **23**(2) 157–170.

Young, M. E., Wasserman, E. A., & Dalrymple, R. M. (1997). Memory-based same-different conceptualization by pigeons. *Psychonomic Bulletin and Review*, **4**(4), 552–558.

Zentall, T. R. (2000). Symbolic representation by pigeons. *Current Directions in Psychological Science*, **9**(4), 118–123.

Zentall, T. R., Galizio, M., & Critchfield, T. S. (2002). Categorization, concept learning, and behavioral analysis: An introduction. *Journal of Experimental Analysis of Behavior*, **78**, 237–248.

Chapter 9

Concept learning in nonprimate mammals: In search of evidence

Stephen E. G. Lea

Editors' Preview

Chapter 9, 'Concept learning in nonprimate mammals: In search of evidence', helps to fill the gap between the chapters on conceptual behaviour in birds (Chapter 8) and primates (Chapters 10 and 11) by examining conceptual behaviour in a wide variety of nonprimate mammals including cows, coyotes, dogs, dolphins, elephants, hamsters, horses, meerkats, rats, seals, sheep, and squirrels. The phrase in the title 'in search of evidence' introduces a major theme of the chapter, namely, that only a small amount of research on nonprimate mammals has made connection with the literature on the cognitive psychology of concepts. It is not completely clear why this state of affairs exists, although the fact that birds and primates are vision dominated means that they can easily be presented with the many visual stimulus sets that have been used to study categorization in humans. By contrast, many nonprimate mammals rely more on olfaction and audition, senses for which there has been less empirical focus on concept formation in humans.

The evidence that does exist has generally involved tests of conceptually-based discrimination where the animals are trained to perform one common response when exemplars of one category are presented and to perform a different common response when instances of another category are presented. The discrimination is construed to be 'conceptually based' because there are variations in the individual instances of the concepts (e.g. different appearances, poses, views, lighting conditions), and in the best studies, the animals must demonstrate generalization of response to new instances of the categories not presented during training.

It is also the case that many of the conceptually-based discriminations that have been investigated in nonprimate mammals have important social and ecological significance. These discriminations have included tests of whether animals can respond differentially to same species (i.e. conspecifics) versus other species, kin versus nonkin, self versus other, male versus female, predator versus prey, and one individual versus another individual from the same or a different species. However, there is also a more limited base of evidence examining nonprimate mammal discrimination of nonsocial perceptual categories and more abstract categories including geometric forms (i.e. triangles vs. circles that vary in size), number as it varies across modality of presentation, phonetic categories of human speech sounds (e.g. ba vs. pa), and same versus different (the type of general concept tested in monkeys, see Chapter 10).

The fact that nonprimate mammals are less vision dominated underscores the importance of categorization as it occurs via audition and olfaction. It is through scent that many animals carry out crucial cognitive functions with survival implications such as identification of place, detection of predators, tracking of prey, and distinguishing food from nonfood, in addition to performing the social parsings described above (own vs. other species, etc.). Likewise, it is through animals' recognition of the sound of (1) distress calls that mothers can track their offspring (and vice versa), and (2) alarm calls that conspecifics can alert each other to the presence of threats.

The evidence on the conceptually-based discriminations tested in nonprimate mammals has generally been positive, thereby providing support for the idea that the concepts are continuous with those of birds and primates. Whether the concepts are also continuous with those of humans is of course the major question posed by the volume as a whole. As noted in this chapter, it is important to consider in response to this question, not just whether the concepts can be demonstrated, but also whether training (and how much of it) is necessary to elicit the conceptual behaviour.

Introduction

As we seek to trace the phylogenetic emergence of human conceptual abilities, it is logical to devote a chapter to the evidence for conceptual learning in nonprimate mammals. It is well established that some human conceptual abilities are shared with some of our fellow primates, as subsequent chapters in this book will discuss (Chapters 10 and 11). But to what extent are those abilities unique to primates? We know that they are shared to some extent with birds (see Chapter 8), but is that because of convergent evolution in the two groups of warm-blooded vertebrates, or should we be looking for its origins in our common reptilian ancestors? That would be a tricky task, bearing in mind that the mammal and bird lineages probably diverged about 200 million years ago and our common ancestors have long since disappeared.

Examining the evidence for conceptual abilities in nonprimate mammals should throw light on these questions. Unfortunately, the available evidence is largely indirect. Whereas there is a significant amount of work on concepts in at least some primate species, and a substantial and fairly orderly literature exists on concept learning in birds (though largely restricted to a handful of species and to pigeons in particular), only a little research has been done using similar methods in nonprimate mammals. Although some early papers on the mechanisms of discrimination learning in rats used ideas like 'hypotheses' to account for such learning (e.g. Krechevsky, 1932), and this strongly suggests conceptual ability, only a handful of experiments with nonprimate mammals have used what has become the hallmark test of conceptual learning in animals (see Chapter 8) – showing that the animal can learn to make a common response to multiple discriminable stimuli within one category, and a different common response to multiple discriminable stimuli within a different category.

On the other hand, the natural lives of many species involve discriminations that seem likely to have a conceptual basis. Several of these kinds of discrimination have been investigated in more detail in nonprimate mammals than in other taxa. Moreover, some kinds of learning that either occur spontaneously or are induced by training in domestic animals may have a conceptual basis, and most domestic animal species are nonprimate mammals.

'Nonprimate mammals' might seem a rather odd grouping. The exclusion of the primates makes it paraphyletic; why should such a group have anything in common that is distinct from other taxa, cognitively or indeed in any other way? However as a grouping it may make better sense psychologically than it does cladistically. Many primates have excellent vision, and this seems to be their dominant sense. Humans are included in this group, and this fact has a methodological implication – it is easy for us to design stimuli for use with our fellow-primates, and our intuitions about how those stimuli will look and what will be salient about them are likely to be well founded. Birds too are a visually dominated group. The basis of their vision is very different from ours, and our intuitions about the appearance and salience of stimuli to them are likely to be less accurate than they are for nonhuman primates. Nonetheless, the significance of vision for both primates and birds is a sufficient explanation for the concentration of research into concept learning on those groups. It is a reasonable guess that many nonprimate mammals' conceptual abilities are more likely to be shown in the auditory or olfactory domains than the visual. Certainly in the psychology laboratory, ever since the heroic efforts of Lashley (1938) to explore complex visual pattern learning in the albino rat (a mammal with very poor vision indeed), the conventional wisdom has been that this kind of research is better done with pigeons or other birds, if it is not going to be done with primates.

To some extent, this characterization of nonprimate mammals as nonvisual is a mistake. For example, the common belief that most mammals are colour-blind is quite wrong: although only primates (and not all primates) have trichromatic colour vision, most mammals do have dichromatic colour vision. The major exceptions are pinnipeds and cetaceans, though individual species within other taxa may be mono-chromats if they have a rigidly nocturnal lifestyle (e.g. some species of flying squirrel; Carvalho et al., 2006). Similarly, the claim that mammals rely less on vision because they tend to be nocturnal is obviously wrong; although there are more nocturnal mammals than nocturnal birds, for example, there are many species of mammals that are more active during the day than by night – not least, nearly all the common domestic species. And even a species such as the domestic cat, which is specialized for crepuscular hunting, clearly makes substantial use of vision.

However, it remains probable that nonprimate mammals' most elaborate cognitions are about stimuli that are at least in part olfactory or auditory rather than visual. In looking for evidence of concept use or concept discrimination in this group, therefore, we cannot afford to ignore senses other than vision.

Most of the data we consider in this chapter involve discriminations that are important in the social life of the species concerned – typically discriminations between members and nonmembers of the species, between kin and nonkin, or between particular individuals. Because of the ecological importance of such discriminations, much of the experimental literature on concept discrimination has used stimuli related to them; in addition, our inferences of concept discrimination from natural behaviour will inevitably involve them. At least at the visual level, such discriminations almost inevitably meet the definition of concept discrimination: the individual stimuli in the positive and negative sets will necessarily vary from trial to trial in an experiment or from exposure to exposure in the natural life of the animal. In a species or kin discrimination, different individual con- and allospecifics, or individual kin and nonkin, will differ in appearance; and in an individual discrimination, the target individuals will be seen in different postures, different lights, and so forth. However, this variation is not so surely guaranteed where auditory or olfactory cues are concerned: for example, it is possible that all members of a species could secrete a single chemical substance that would give them all the same odour that was discriminably different from the odour of any other species. Humans' olfactory limitations mean that experimenters are less likely to spot such simple bases for discrimination in the olfactory than in the visual domain.

Social partners are not the only ecologically important stimuli that may require category-level discrimination. Both prey and predators are likely to be encountered in diverse forms, all of which require a common response. Places (whether highly local such as a nest site, or on a larger scale such as the target of an annual migration) are also likely to be perceived in diverse ways depending on circumstances. However, little research has so far been devoted to studying the discrimination of such stimuli.

Explicit studies of (mainly visual) concepts in nonprimate mammals

First, we look at the limited number of studies that have investigated visual concept discrimination or concept use in nonhuman mammals in the same way as has been done so extensively with birds and primates. We begin with perceptual concepts, in which the exemplars all bear a perceptual similarity to one another, and then consider data on more abstract concepts, where the similarities are at a formal or logical level. In some of the experiments, olfactory or auditory cues were available in addition to visual cues.

Fields (1932, 1935, 1936) carried out a series of experiments which explicitly tested rats' ability to discriminate between perceptual classes. Although his stimuli were simple geometrical forms (triangles and circles), he varied the properties of both stimuli in several different ways, and showed that rats could maintain the discrimination; he therefore claimed that rats possessed the concept of triangularity. Unlike most recent experiments with pigeons or primates, Fields used simultaneous rather than successive discrimination. In a successive discrimination, a single stimulus is presented, and the animal has to choose whether to approach it or not. In a simultaneous discrimination, a positive and a negative stimulus are presented together, and the animal has to choose which one to approach. This may well have made the task easier. An especially interesting result comes from Fields (1936): in this experiment, he tested both rats and racoons. The racoons were slower to acquire the original discrimination (a result Fields attributed to the apparatus being less suitable for them) but performed better at generalizing it to new types of triangle, suggesting that even though circumstances made the original task hard for them, they were more likely to treat it at a conceptual level.

Range et al. (2008) trained dogs in a pictorial own/other species discrimination using procedures very like those that have been used with birds and primates. The dogs were required to respond to a touchscreen, and to discriminate between pictures that contained an image of a dog and pictures that did not. They used relatively large sets of positive and negative images (40 of each) in training. Like Fields (1932, 1935, 1936), they used a simultaneous discrimination procedure. One of the few pigeon experiments to have used simultaneous discrimination was an early study by Siegel and Honig (1970) of pigeons' discrimination between pictures that did or did not include an image of a human being; Range et al.'s dogs learned slightly faster than Siegel and Honig's pigeons, reaching a criterion of consistent 80% correct performance in 720–2040 trials, whereas Siegel and Honig's pigeons were still below 75% correct after 1480 trials. However Siegel and Honig used a rather larger set of stimuli (280 each of positive and negative), and the discrimination did not involve images of conspecifics. Following training, Range et al.'s dogs showed successful transfer to new images of dogs, even if they were superimposed on familiar (negative) landscape images, suggesting that they paid selective attention to the features of the dogs.

A number of experiments have tested discriminations using live animals as the objects to be discriminated in food-rewarded tasks. Using this technique Coulon et al. (2007) demonstrated an own/other species discrimination in domestic cattle. They also used a food-rewarded simultaneous discrimination task with photographic images as stimuli, but in a maze rather than with a touchscreen. Their stimulus sets were rather smaller than those used by Range et al. (2008) with dogs (10 exemplars in each), and they did not test for transfer to new exemplars. However, they did carry out a reversal test and showed that the same heifers could also learn to choose the noncow stimulus, so there was no dramatic own-species advantage.

A more demanding task is to discriminate between individuals. As noted above, under natural conditions, at least in the visual domain, even discriminating a single individual requires a concept-level discrimination, since the individual will be seen in many different poses, from many different viewpoints, and in many different lighting conditions. Hagen and Broom (2003) demonstrated that cattle are capable of discriminating between live individual members of their own species in a food-rewarded task. Using live individuals as the stimuli to be discriminated at the visual level guarantees that the stimuli seen by the subjects would vary from trial to trial. However they were not able to determine what sensory modality was supporting the discrimination, so it is possible that some simple olfactory or auditory cues were available. Similar results were obtained by McLeman et al. (2005) using young female pigs, again in a food-rewarded discrimination task; Souza et al. (2006) confirmed their conclusions in a habituation-based design which reduced the amount of handling and disturbance of the subject animals.

Discriminating individual conspecifics might be aided by instinctual cues, so discriminating individuals of another species is a purer test of animals' discrimination-learning abilities. Davis et al. (1998) showed, using a food-rewarded discrimination task, that sheep can discriminate accurately between individual human handlers, though they did not investigate what sensory modalities or cues were being used. Taylor and Davis (1998) obtained similar results with cows. Munksgaard et al. (1997) also showed discrimination between individual humans in cattle, though instead of using food reward they examined whether the cows distinguished between a rough and a gentle handler. Koba and Tanida (2001) investigated the basis for pigs' discrimination between individual humans; in an extensive series of experiments they showed that pigs could discriminate between individual humans and that multiple modalities and cues seemed to be involved in the discrimination, with no one cue necessary to the task. Rybarczyk et al. (2001) used a similar approach with cows, and found that although multiple cues were used (especially body height and face), none of them produced good discrimination on their own, suggesting that information integration was required. However, under some conditions, the basis for discrimination may be simpler: Rybarczyk et al. (2003) found that calves could discriminate between handlers based on the colour of their clothing alone.

The most extensive research relevant to visual concepts in nonprimate mammals is the work of Kendrick and his colleagues on the recognition of faces by sheep. While these experiments have been carried out in the service of investigations of the brain physiology underlying face recognition (e.g. Kendrick & Baldwin, 1987), they have provided a solid base of evidence that sheep can make the sort of perceptual category discrimination that has been extensively investigated in birds and primates. Using a Y-maze simultaneous discrimination test, Kendrick et al. (1995, 1996) showed that sheep quickly learned to discriminate between images of the faces of familiar sheep of their own breed and faces of other breeds or species. There is both behavioural and physiological evidence that sheep-face discriminations are mediated specifically by the right temporal cortex in sheep, as human-face discriminations are in humans (Broad et al., 2000; Peirce et al., 2000). Interestingly, Kendrick et al. (1996) showed that learning to discriminate between individual faces was fast (the majority of animals reached an 80% correct criterion in under 40 trials), and faster than learning to discriminate between two abstract shapes; learning to discriminate lamb faces was also slow. Peirce et al. (2001) showed that although sheep can learn to discriminate human as well as sheep faces, the left hemifield advantage that suggests right-cortex specialization is much less with these stimuli.

As demonstrations of concept discrimination, some of these experiments are weak, since there was little variation in the positive and negative stimuli, only a few exemplars of each category being used. The experiments typically did not include the usual test with novel instances of the categories to check whether the category discrimination was being performed by simple exemplar learning. Indeed, it seems likely that the sheep were learning by absolute discrimination, since they were able to remember the classification of 50 different sheep faces as positive or negative with undiminished accuracy for up to 600 days (Kendrick et al., 2001). However, given that the discriminations were learned so readily, that they were learned more readily than other discriminations, that they were severely disrupted by manipulations like inversion of the stimuli, and that they seem to be supported by distinct brain structures, it seems certain that the discriminations Kendrick et al. (1995, 1996) observed were based on a natural ability to discriminate sheep faces, which as Kendrick et al. (2001) point out is an essential social skill given the social structure of sheep. Ferreira et al. (2004) have demonstrated that sheep can generalize a discrimination between photographs of conspecific faces to new orientations and new ages at the time when the picture was taken, giving strong support to the idea that learning is occurring at a categorical level. The evidence for preferential learning of adult sheep faces and for anatomical specialization underlying such learning do make it open to question whether sheep have a general capacity for concept discrimination of the kind that has been demonstrated in birds.

A special case of individual discrimination is recognizing oneself. There has been much controversy about animals' capacity to respond to mirror or similar images in a way that suggests that the subject knows that the image is of itself. Typically, experiments on this topic involve the 'mark test' introduced for use with primates by Gallup (1970). Most of the discussion has focused around the theoretical importance of such experiments for the question of whether animals have a theory of mind, and this is not our primary concern here. However the perceptual ability to distinguish oneself from other individuals, if it can be demonstrated, would be good evidence for individual discrimination. Claims of self-recognition have been made for a handful of species of nonprimate mammals, though such claims are controversial. Plotnik et al. (2006) reported that elephants behaved like chimpanzees in Gallup's mark test, but Povinelli (1989) had earlier failed to find any such evidence and the difference of results remains unexplained. Marten and Psarakos (1995) claimed that dolphins possessed a self concept, on the basis of their differential behaviour towards live video images of themselves as compared with images of other dolphins. This claim was greeted with much scepticism, but Reiss and Marino (2001) also showed more typical evidence of self-recognition using mark tests with reflective surfaces. It does appear that human children show self-recognition at a later age with video tests rather than mirror tests (Suddendorf et al., 2007), so the video methodology used by Marten and Psarakos may have been a severe test of the dolphins' abilities. Delfour and Marten (2001) showed positive responses to marks in a mirror test in at least one other species of delphinid, the killer whale, and possibly also in a false killer whale; interestingly, they could not find comparable evidence in a sea lion. Bekoff (2001) has also argued that dogs possess a self-concept, but on the basis of an entirely different kind of evidence: he showed that they are capable of distinguishing their own urine from that of others.

A handful of experiments have used nonsocial stimuli that varied between trials in a way that requires category-level discrimination. Hanggi (1999) trained horses to discriminate an open from a filled circle, and then added additional pairs of stimuli (squares, triangles, and so on) and found that after one or two pairs, transfer was effectively immediate, suggesting that a concept of openness rather than individual item associations had been learned. In tests, the relative size of the stimuli was varied to control for the possibility that the discrimination was based on total light area. In research that has not yet been published in full, Harley et al. (2007) reported that bottlenose dolphins that could be trained in a matching to sample task in which the stimuli were either objects or photographs of them, and would match pictures to objects or vice versa without difficulty.

Additional evidence for concept-level discrimination comes from experiments on cross-modal transfer with bottlenose dolphins. Although the stimuli used in such experiments are relatively simple and invariant, if an animal can recognize a stimulus by echolocation having learned to respond to it visually, it seems clear that the subject must have some kind of higher-order representation of the object, which it would be reasonable to refer to as a concept. Harley et al. (1996) demonstrated that matching to sample performance in dolphins was improved when both visual and echolocation modes were available, and furthermore that the subjects could correctly choose a match using vision when the sample had been perceived only by echolocation, and vice versa. The objects used in the cross-modal tests were all already familiar to the dolphins, but in a further test of cross-modal matching, Herman et al. (1998) showed that dolphins perform well in the same task with unfamiliar objects as well. Furthermore Pack and Herman (1995) found that dolphins could match echolocated objects to visual images presented on a video screen. Pack et al. (2002) used this cross-modal matching procedure to show that echolocating dolphins were using global rather than local features of objects to make the match.

All the experiments described so far have involved perceptual concepts (although the self-recognition experiments may also involve a much more abstract concept, that of the self). At a more abstract level, the concept that has been most studied is that of sameness – or, conversely, difference. There has been much debate as to whether accurate performance in a matching-to-sample task implies that an animal is able to use concepts of 'sameness' or 'difference'. It is now generally accepted that we can only draw that inference if performance is maintained above chance levels when totally new sample and comparison stimuli are introduced, or if different stimuli are used on every trial. Concept-based matching-to-sample performance has been claimed for a number of species of nonprimate mammals, including a monotreme, the short-beaked echidna (Burke & Russell, 2007), though this experiment has not yet been formally published. In a series of experiments on visual discrimination, Nakagawa (1993, 2002, 2003) has claimed that rats transfer a matching or nonmatching task to new stimuli, and Bailey and Thomas (1998) support this for the nonmatching (or oddity) case in an olfactory discrimination. Mauck and Dehnhardt (2005) demonstrated excellent transfer of matching to new stimuli in a common (harbour) seal. Kowalska (1997) reported successful training of auditory matching to sample in dogs with stimuli that were different on every trial, but noted that performance declined with extended training, suggesting that the performance may have been at the limits of the animals' cognitive abilities. A related way of investigating concepts of sameness and difference is to train animals to respond differentially to small sets of stimuli that are either all the same or include some different elements; using this technique, Mercado et al. (2000) showed that bottlenose dolphins could generalize the discrimination to new objects.

Other abstract concepts that can be considered include symmetry (which may or may not depend on a concept of sameness), time, and number. Most of the recent comparative literature on such concepts has focused either on birds or on primates. Nonetheless, there have been a number of demonstrations of discrimination on the basis of number by nonprimate mammals, including rats (in which there have been several studies using different methods, e.g. Church & Meck, 1984; Davis & Bradford, 1986; Capaldi & Miller, 1988), a raccoon (Davis, 1984), and a bottlenose dolphin (Kilian et al., 2003). Number discriminations can obviously be important in a social context, for example in determining the strength of a rival group, and McComb et al. (1994) have claimed that lionesses can discriminate numbers for this purpose. The clearest evidence that an abstract concept is involved here comes from claims (e.g. Church & Meck, 1984; Meck, 1987) that rats can transfer a number discrimination across perceptual modalities; Meck & Church (1982) make the same claim for time discriminations.

Natural visual concepts

In addition to these more formal experimental tests, there is evidence for visual concept-level discrimination occurring within the natural life of nonprimate mammals. Most examples concern individual, kin, or species recognition. Given the variability of the views that a subject animal will receive of any other individual, reliable visual individual recognition almost inevitably requires concept-level discrimination. However, given the importance of olfaction and audition, experimental procedures are usually required to tease apart the contribution of vision to natural discriminations.

An example is the work of Ligout and Porter (2004) on the discrimination of individual age-mates by domestic lambs. The authors first showed that vision was not necessary for individual recognition, but then tested the lambs with life-size projected images of a familiar penmate, their own (familiar) twin, or an unfamiliar unrelated lamb. The lambs showed more response to their twin than to the other two images, but did not differentiate between those, suggesting that only a rather coarse discrimination was possible. Porter et al. (1997) also showed that vision played some role in lambs' recognition of their twins: the presence of a twin reduces bleating in lambs isolated from their mothers, and Porter et al. found that lambs bleated less if they could see their twin through bars than if the barrier between them was opaque. Porter and Bouissou (1999) showed that lambs behaved differently towards an image of a sheep than towards a scrambled version of the same image, suggesting that they were responding to the intact image as a conspecific in some sense.

Another context in which concept-level discrimination may be required is in the recognition of locations: varying viewpoints and climatic conditions mean that the stimulus presented by a location will vary greatly from time to time. This case has been little investigated in nonprimate mammals, though Mauck and Dehnhardt (2007) used a matching-to-sample task to show that common seals encode landscape information in terms of numerous mutually redundant cues rather than a few key features, a good basis for concept-level discrimination.

In summary, the available literature on explicit tests of concept discrimination, or on natural visual concept discriminations, in nonprimate mammals is clearly limited. The experimental literature has involved a fairly arbitrary selection of species, and there has been little systematic investigation of questions of interest within the psychology of concepts. Some of the most numerous and species-rich groups of mammals, such as rodents and bats, have been investigated little or not at all. Nonetheless, there is nothing in the literature we have reported so far to suggest that concept-discrimination abilities in nonprimate mammals are either better or worse than would be expected from the much more thorough investigations that have been made of birds and primates. Perhaps, however, that is because the research has largely involved visual stimuli. Perhaps a different pattern will emerge when we examine evidence from the senses that have been little investigated in birds or primates, olfaction and audition.

Is there evidence for olfactory concept discrimination?

Mammals of many groups rely on olfaction for many purposes: identifying places, detecting predators, detecting and tracking prey, and determining the condition of food items. However the great majority of the literature relevant to possible olfactory concept discrimination concerns the use of olfaction to discriminate between other animals, either to place them into categories (own/other species, member/nonmember of a social group, neighbour/stranger, kin/nonkin, male/female, suitable/unsuitable mates) or to identify them as individuals. Individual recognition in turn has many functions: animals may need to identify their parents or offspring, their mates, members of their social group who are dominant or subordinate to them or reliable or unreliable sources of information, or a territorial neighbour who is or is not in his usual location.

Olfactory recognition depends on the object animal making or leaving a chemical trace in the environment. Such traces may arise as an inevitable result of normal physiological processes, of breathing, sweating, urinating, and defecating. However, many mammals have specific glands that secrete and exude chemical substances that are used as signals. In some cases, these glands are located so that they add the chemical signal to a normal body product such as sweat or faeces; in others, the animal has specific behaviours, at least partly instinctive, that place the signals into the environment. Cats, for example, instinctively rub their faces and flanks on each other and on objects within their environment, and in so doing they transfer secretions from sebaceous glands in their skin (see Bradshaw & Cameron-Beaumont, 2000; Feldman, 1994). Where the chemical mark is introduced into normal body products, excretory behaviour may be modified so that the signal is placed strategically, as, for example, in urine marking by dogs (e.g. Bekoff, 1979; Pal, 2003).

Evidence for the deposit of scent marks and for their use by other individuals is widespread among the nonprimate mammals. However, it is much less clear what exact signals are being detected, and evidence of how they are processed cognitively is correspondingly thin (Johnston, 2003; Thom & Hurst, 2004). In a few cases, chemical analysis of the signals involved has been possible. For example, in domestic mice, it appears that individual recognition is mediated through genetically-based differences in the major urinary proteins (Cheetham et al., 2007); surprisingly, odours associated with the much discussed major histocompatibility complex (MHC) are neither necessary nor sufficient for individual recognition in mice (Hurst et al., 2005).

Even in these relatively well-explored cases, research has rarely gone beyond demonstrating the behavioural or discriminatory impact of one or more substances. So there is little to show whether or not animals are able to treat a wide range of discriminably different scents as all being a signal of the presence of a single individual, or a single type of individual. In most cases, the data could be explained by a single 'trigger' substance whose presence or absence gives unequivocal evidence for the presence or absence of a particular individual or its membership in a particular social group, an idea which in the study of olfaction and pheromones is usually referred to as a 'labelled-line' theory. However most authors (e.g. Laurent, 2002) find this implausible, noting that natural odourants usually consist of mixtures of numerous substances, whose relative concentrations vary greatly from occasion to occasion – exactly the conditions where category-level discrimination is likely to be required. Unfortunately for our present purposes, most of this discussion has gone on in connection with olfaction in insects – including some experimental work that would otherwise be ideal for demonstrating conceptual processing (e.g. Wright & Smith, 2004).

Conditions requiring concept-level olfactory discrimination undoubtedly occur in the natural lives of nonprimate mammals. It is common for mammals to have multiple sources of scent (e.g. meadow voles have at least three, and hamsters at least five: Ferkin & Johnston, 1995; Johnston & Peng, 2008). The scent trace of an individual may involve stimuli that vary from time to time, and may change as an individual matures (as Mateo, 2006, has demonstrated for Belding's ground squirrels), creating a need for conceptual processing of scents. What we mostly lack is evidence that such processing actually occurs. However, a few papers have claimed to produce such evidence. Golden hamsters have multiple sources of scent, at least five of which have potential for use in individual recognition. Johnston and Jernigan (1994) showed that habituation by male hamsters to one of the characteristic odours of a given female only generalized to another scent from the same female if the male had had direct contact with the female, and Johnston and Peng (2008) extended this result to five different odours. The authors therefore argued that if and only if the male had experienced the female, the different odours were all remembered as attributes of that individual female, which as Johnston and Peng remark, 'might also be described as having a concept of individuals' (p. 128).

Because of the ecological importance of olfactory recognition, and because the diverse circumstances in which each scent is recognized (and, in the case of kin, species or other group recognition, the diverse individuals to whom a single response is made) make a prima facie case for category-level discrimination, it is worth discussing the main mechanisms of olfactory recognition and giving some further examples of its use, even in the absence of stronger evidence that it does take place at the categorical level.

Logically, the first step in investigating olfactory discrimination is to establish that there are differences that could in principle be used for such discrimination. In some cases, this is as far as research has yet progressed; for example, in Bechstein's bat, Safi and Kerth (2003) demonstrated chemically that interaural gland secretions differed between individuals, but it has not yet been established whether the bats are sensitive to these differences. More often, however, behavioural discrimination is obvious but its chemical basis cannot be established. Animals frequently leave multiple chemical traces, some of which are more important in individual recognition than others; for example Swaisgood et al. (1999) showed that giant pandas responded differentially to individuals' anogenital gland secretions, but could not prove that there was any discrimination of individuals' urine.

There are many mechanisms by which animals could in principle acquire olfactory discriminations between individuals or groups (Mateo, 2004). Recognition of species, sex or sexual condition, dominance status, and some other categories could well occur on an instinctual basis, using information carried genetically. It might be thought that kin or social group recognition must involve some element of learning. However, especially for kin recognition, there is always the possibility of 'self-referent phenotype matching': the individual may recognize that the scent (or indeed the calls or visual appearance) of another individual is in some way like its own. Phenotype matching in the more general sense, of responding to the learned similarities in the scents of familiar related individuals, has been strongly urged as a suitable mechanism for supporting discrimination between kin and nonkin, especially in cases where such discrimination extends to paternal kin and there is no paternal care; and there is a good deal of evidence that it occurs (Mateo, 2003), as we shall discuss shortly. It has often been linked to research into the MHC genes, which are known to be highly variable and to code for the synthesis of proteins that are important in the immune system. However, evidence in favour of specifically self-referent phenotype matching, which need not require any learning, is scarce. Among nonprimate mammals, the most strongly argued case is for golden hamsters (Mateo & Johnston, 2000), though this case has been contested (Hare et al., 2003).

If the referent is not the self, then phenotype matching must involve learning, and arguably it involves abstraction of information from multiple stimuli in the way we would normally recognize as concept discrimination. If an animal learns the scents of its close kin through experience, then newly encountered individuals can be classified as kin or not on the basis of their similarity to the scents of known kin – which must themselves be variable. Mateo (2003) reviews a large number of studies of rodents, and in around half of the species that have been studied, the evidence supports this kind of phenotype matching as a mechanism of kin recognition. She then reports a series of experiments on Belding's ground squirrels using the habituation/dishabituation technique to show that the squirrels do indeed treat unfamiliar kin as similar to familiar kin, with the degree of similarity varying with the degree of relatedness. Since she also shows that individual Belding's ground squirrels have at least two distinct sources of scent, this too looks like an example of concept learning. Busquet and Baudoin (2005) obtained similar results in mound-building mice. Learned phenotype matching is of course not confined to rodents: for example, Moore (2007) has argued that the demonstration of inbreeding avoidance in African elephants by Archie et al. (2007) also constitutes strong evidence for phenotype matching.

The alternative to phenotype matching is usually termed kin recognition by 'familiarity' – in other words, by simply learning the characteristics of individuals (and possibly abstracting the common characteristics of groups). Unlike phenotype matching, this does not require the individual to first know (or learn) about a core group, either itself or its closest kin. There are many examples of such learning and only a few can be given here. Gheusi et al. (1997) used an instrumental discrimination task to show that rats could discriminate between individual conspecifics, and that this discrimination was maintained when only the object rats' odours were presented. Using a habituation/dishabituation technique, Vache et al. (2001) showed that American red squirrels discriminated the odours of unfamiliar conspecifics from those of familiar territorial neighbours. Similar results have been found by Rosell and Bjorkoyli (2002) in beavers, and by Zenuto and Fanjul (2002) in tucotucos. Phenotype matching and familiarity mechanisms are not mutually exclusive: for example, Kruczek (2007) showed that both are involved in kin discrimination in bank voles, depending on the stage of life of the subject.

A number of experiments have explored what scent source is involved in such discriminations, and how it is processed. Palphramand and White (2007) showed that faecal odour was sufficient for familiar/unfamiliar discrimination in badgers, and as noted above, Swaisgood et al. (1999) found that giant pandas could discriminate faeces from different individuals on the basis of the secretions introduced into them by the anogenital gland. Tang-Martinez et al. (1993) showed that female golden hamsters could distinguish individual differences in the odours of flank gland secretions, urine, faeces, and soiled bedding from males, and were more likely to mate successfully with familiar males. Ramm et al. (2008) showed that wild female house mice were only attracted to the urinary odours of males whom they had previously encountered, implying that individual recognition based on familiarity rather than a labelled-line pheromonic response was involved in the attraction. In some conditions, however, familiarity would not be a sufficient basis for the discriminations that animals demonstrate; for example, degus nest communally, and Jesseau et al. (2008) showed that nursing mothers can discriminate the odour of their own offspring from those of a nestmate's offspring, even if the offspring have been separated from them. After weaning, however, recognition is based entirely on familiarity.

Beyond the level of the individual, O'Riain and Jarvis (1997) showed that naked mole rats could discriminate the odours for members of their own colony from the odours of strangers, even when genetic relatedness was high, and in a preference test they chose to go towards their own colony odour. Using a dishabituation technique, Todrank and Heth (1996) showed that mole rats could also distinguish the odours of their own species from those of other, closely related species.

A case where there has been much discussion of the role of olfaction, as against other senses, is in the recognition of newborn young by their mothers in ungulates (hoofed mammals). Because ungulate newborns are typically highly precocial and mobile, this is a situation where rapid learning is required, especially under domestic conditions where large numbers of mother–offspring pairs are kept together. Romeyer et al. (1994) showed that nanny goats with experimentally damaged olfactory systems bonded effectively with their kids in the first hour after birth, but unlike intact goats they were unable to discriminate them from other kids 3 h later. This implies that in the normal case, there is rapid olfactory learning shortly afterbirth; however, olfaction is not the only sense involved in this recognition system since mothers can also discriminate differences in their kids' bleats (Terrazas et al., 2003). Maletinska et al. (2002) used cross-fostering to show that sows recognized day-old piglets on the basis of their individual odours, regardless of genetic similarity.

As well as recognizing individuals of their own species, some nonprimate mammals can learn to recognize individuals or groups of other species. Most of the cases that have been studied involve recognition of humans. For example, Bates et al. (2007) showed that African elephants living in the Amboseli can distinguish the odour of young Maasai men from that of young Kamba men. Both ethnic groups live in the Amboseli, but whereas the Maasai are required to spear elephants as part of a rite of passage, Kamba men are not. The elephants show fear responses only to the odour of the Maasai.

The most substantial literature is on the recognition of individual humans by dogs, because of the importance of this system for forensic purposes. In a realistic tracking situation, Kalmus (1955) showed that such discrimination was possible up to the level of family members. Monozygotic twins' scents could be discriminated in a simultaneous test, when both scents were available, but not in successive tests. The ability to discriminate humans on the basis of genetic similarity is not confined to dogs: Ables et al. (2007) obtained a similar result from rats.

Kalmus's (1955) basic findings on dogs' abilities have been replicated and extended since; for example Harvey et al. (2006) showed that bloodhounds' confusion between twins depended only on their genetic relationship, not on whether they were living together, though Hepper (1988) found that environmental factors did have some effect on discrimination – dogs could discriminate the scents of adult but not infant human twins. In an identification line-up situation, Schoon (1996) confirmed that dogs could identify people from smell samples with fair but not 100% accuracy, though performance varied substantially depending on the way the test was conducted. From the conceptual point of view, however, the key issue is whether dogs can recognize different odour sources as coming from the same individual human. Brisbin and Austad (1991) found that dogs who could recognize the scent of their handlers' hands did not transfer this recognition to the scent of their armpits, and therefore argued that the discrimination could not have a conceptual basis. However Sommerville et al. (1993) disputed this conclusion, pointing out that in Kalmus's (1955) tests and in others that they had conducted, scent samples were taken from the individual humans' armpits. Since the dogs then tracked where people had walked, they must have been transferring between armpit and foot odour. Settle et al. (1994) explicitly tested dogs with cloth samples that were obtained from four different parts of the target humans' bodies, and found clear evidence of generalization. Their design was not perfect, since the odour donors had to handle all four cloths, and furthermore the four samples from each donor were stored together for a time, allowing cross-contamination. Nonetheless, the balance of the evidence suggests that, as in the conspecific recognition of hamsters studied by Johnston and Jernigan (1994) and Johnston and Peng (2008), dogs can recognize different sources of scent (which no doubt have different chemical compositions) as coming from the same human.

In addition to discriminating the scent of an individual human, dogs can be trained to track classes of object. These tasks seem likely to involve category-level discrimination, since presumably different objects of the same class will have somewhat different odours. Examples include the use of dogs to find either living or dead people (interestingly, dogs are more accurate if they are trained on only one of these classes: Lit & Crawford, 2006), or to find animals of a particular species, or their traces, in ecological research (e.g. Cablk & Heaton, 2006; Smith et al., 2003). Less persuasive as evidence of concept-level discrimination, at least in the present state of the evidence, are the uses of dogs to identify medical conditions (e.g. melanoma: Pickel et al., 2004), since in these cases a relatively invariant chemical signature is a distinct possibility.

Is there evidence of auditory concept discrimination?

The evidence for auditory concepts in nonprimate mammals follows a pattern that will by now be familiar. There is a small literature that has tested category-level discrimination more or less explicitly, and then a substantial literature on ecologically important discriminations, mainly between individuals.

The literature on artificial auditory concepts, where the content of the stimuli is well controlled and we can be confident that category-level discrimination is required, is mainly concerned with the discrimination of human speech sounds by other species. The purpose of this research has usually been to test claims that humans are specifically adapted to make particular discriminations that are important in speech; if other species can make the same discriminations with equal relative ease, that argument falls. A series of experiments of this sort have been carried out, with variations of the speech sounds used as stimuli within the range recognized by human language users as representing the same phoneme. Successful training of such discriminations has been reported in cats (Dewson, 1964; Hienz et al., 1996) and chinchillas (Burdick & Miller, 1975; Kuhl & Miller, 1978), and is now being investigated systematically in rats (Erikkson & Villa, 2006; Pons, 2006; Reed et al., 2003; Toro & Trobalon, 2005; Toro et al., 2005). Similar results have been obtained with birds (e.g. Kluender, et al., 1998, using starlings) and primates (e.g. Dewson et al., 1969, using rhesus monkeys), though these are not the subject of the present chapter. Whether or not these experiments really do shake the conclusion that speech sounds are special for humans is open to dispute, since in at least some cases the discrimination is not learned nearly as fast as it is in human infants. But they certainly do demonstrate that nonprimate mammals can learn concept-level auditory discriminations.

As regards natural discriminations, the focus has been strongly on individual or group discrimination on the basis of calls. As in olfactory identification, some studies are simply concerned to show that there is enough information in the calls to enable individual (and, in some cases, also kin) recognition. Examples include McCowan & Hooper's (2002) analysis of chirp calls in Belding's ground squirrels; Scherrer and Wilkinson's (1993) analysis of evening bat calls and Mora et al.'s (2005) analysis of Cuban evening bat calls; Pfalzer and Kusch's (2003) analysis of the social calls of 16 species of European bat; Vannoni and McElligott's (2007) analysis of the groan vocalizations of fallow deer; Soltis et al.'s (2005) analysis of the rumble calls of African elephants; and Mitchell et al.'s (2006) analysis of the barks and howls of coyotes.

However, there are many studies that have demonstrated that animals do in fact respond differently to calls from different individuals and groups. In some cases, the calls concerned are made for other purposes than individual recognition. For example, little brown bats can discriminate gender of the caller (Kazial & Masters, 2004) and the individual caller (Kazial et al., 2008) on the basis of the echolocation calls they make for hunting purposes. African elephants seem to be able to distinguish the alarm calls of familiar and unfamiliar groups when they are transmitted seismically (O'Connell-Rodwell et al., 2007).

In other cases, individual recognition is a major function of the call. An important example occurs in precocial, group-living animals, where the offspring are capable of moving away from the mother among other juveniles. It is common in such species for infants or mothers, or both, to make characteristic vocalizations if they become separated from each other: these are referred to as isolation calls. In a number of such species it has been demonstrated that mothers can recognize and respond to their own offspring's isolation calls among a group (e.g. guinea pigs, Kober et al., 2007; noctule bats, Knornschild et al., 2007; greater spear-nose bats, Bohn et al., 2007; pigs, Illman et al., 2002; goats, Terrazas et al., 2003; Weddell seals, Collins et al., 2006; harp seals and common seals, Perry & Renouf, 1988). Perry and Renouf's data on seals are particularly relevant to our present concerns, because they showed that mothers could recognize their pups' calls despite the acoustical differences introduced by their being transmitted through either air or water.

However, not all mothers in social, precocial species show successful individual recognition: for example, Lingle et al. (2007) suggest that, at least in the hectic conditions of a predator attack, offspring calls alone would not be sufficient for white-tailed deer mothers to establish the identity of their fawns, though they would enable discrimination from the fawns of mule deer, which live in the same areas as white-tailed deer. Cows also show poor recognition of their own calves' calls, at least when they are separated from them in the first day of life (Marchant-Forde et al., 2002).

In precocial species, not only do mothers need to be able to recognize their own offspring, offspring need to be able to identify their own mothers. In fact, Marchant-Forde et al. (2002) showed that calves were better at discriminating their mothers by voice than cows were at discriminating their calves. In fur seals, both mothers and pups contribute to recognition, but they use different kinds of cues to do it (Charrier et al., 2003). Ewes and lambs, however, use the same types of cue to recognize each other (Searby & Jouventin, 2003).

In many social species, cohesion is important in groups other than the mother–offspring dyad, and acoustical recognition can be important in such groups. For example, twin lambs can recognize each other by voice (Ligout et al., 2004). Where animals can discriminate between larger groups by acoustical signals, there is a good case that concept-level discrimination must be involved, since it is unlikely that groups could each have distinct trigger features in their variants of the contact call, and it is equally unlikely that all members of the group will make the call in exactly the same way. Examples of this kind of discrimination include the discrimination of screech calls by greater spear-nosed bats: Boughman and Wilkinson (1998) demonstrated that female bats from different caves had discriminably different screech calls and that they did in fact react differently to the calls of bats from their own and other caves.

Another situation where individual recognition might be advantageous is alarm calling: if some individuals are more reliable at detecting predators, and less likely to give false alarms than others, conspecifics might gain by responding more to reliable callers (Cheney & Seyfarth, 1988). Although this is an attractive theoretical possibility, evidence that it occurs widely among nonprimate mammals is weak. Hare and Atkins (2001) argue that it can be seen in Richardson's ground squirrels, but Schibler and Manser (2007) showed that although there is enough information in meerkat alarm calls for individuals to be recognized with considerable accuracy, there was no evidence that other meerkats responded differentially to alarm calls from different individuals.

The isolation calls of precocial offspring and their mothers have individual recognition as one of their main functions, but they also serve to indicate distress and to help mothers and offspring locate each other. A substantial literature has developed around the suggestion that cetaceans have calls, or call components, that have no other function but to indicate individual identity; these are usually called signature whistles because they occur at the end of whistled vocalizations, though the more neutral term coda is sometimes used and is in some ways preferable, especially since the identifying function of the whistles is still disputed. Evidence for signature whistles was first produced by Caldwell and Caldwell (1965), and a series of studies by Tyack, Sayigh, and their colleagues (e.g. Janik & Slater, 1998; Sayigh et al., 1990, 1999; Tyack, 1986) has investigated their properties. A number of other cetaceans have been reported to use a similar system (e.g. narwhals, Shapiro, 2006; orcas, Nousek et al., 2006; Weiss et al., 2006; humpback whales, Cerchio & Dahlheim, 2001; sperm whales, Rendell & Whitehead, 2004, though in this case the coda is claimed to provide a group rather than an individual signature). However, the field was thrown into dispute by McCowan and Reiss (2001), who used the same methods as in the original report by Caldwell and Caldwell, and found that the isolation calls of dolphins were stereotyped and not individually distinctive. This analysis has in turn been disputed, notably by Sayigh et al. (2007).

Harley (2008) reviewed the dispute, and recognized that there is genuine uncertainty about how whistles should be categorized, and corresponding uncertainty about their interpretation. Nonetheless, she concluded that the balance of the evidence does favour the signature-whistle hypothesis. However, she also noted that to date research on dolphins' own recognition of the differences between signature whistles has lagged behind research seeking to demonstrate that individual differences exist and to explore how they are acquired developmentally. She therefore tested a dolphin's capacity to distinguish between the whistles of six individuals, and found excellent discrimination. Such discrimination tests are of the greatest concern in the present chapter, although a fully persuasive argument for the identification function of signature whistles would more or less demand the conclusion that they can be discriminated.

Acoustic signals with the sole purpose of advertising individual identity have been suggested in other groups of nonprimate mammals. For example, Randall (1994) suggested that foot-drumming in the kangaroo rat might serve this purpose, and an extensive literature has developed around this behaviour. Furthermore, as with olfaction, some animals may be able to discriminate individual humans on the basis of auditory cues: there is some evidence for this in dogs, for example (Coutellier, 2006).

Conclusions

Our starting point in this chapter was that, compared with the situation for birds and primates, relatively little research has been carried out to examine category discrimination in nonprimate mammals. In particular, there is no body of experimentation that parallels the intensive exploration of visual concepts in (especially) pigeons that has taken place over the past 50 years.

However, there are a few experiments that are reasonably parallel to those that have been carried out with birds and primates, and these do give comparable results. Furthermore, extensive literatures on olfactory and auditory discrimination provide further evidence that concept discrimination is possible, and in the case of these sensory modalities, the evidence is probably better for nonprimate mammals than it is for primates or birds. On the basis of the evidence that we have reviewed here, there can be no reasonable doubt that highly complex stimuli in the visual, olfactory, and auditory domains can all be reliably discriminated by mammals from a range of groups. The evidence that such discrimination is at the conceptual level (i.e. that discriminably different stimuli are all assigned the same response) rather than involving a simple trigger feature or labelled line is less conclusive: in some cases it is simply absent, in others it is indirect or inferential. However, in at least some cases, variation in the stimuli has been demonstrated directly, and the data give no reason to doubt that category discrimination is fully possible in these groups.

The sampling of the nonprimate mammals across these experiments is inevitably nonsystematic. There has been a focus on a few species because of their practical or economic importance (e.g. dogs and farm animals), or because they are thought of as having high intelligence (e.g. cetaceans and elephants, and to a lesser extent dogs and horses), or because they occupy ecological niches with unusual cognitive demands (e.g. bats and cetaceans). Nonetheless, the evidence we have reviewed has involved mammals from almost all the major orders. Given the popularity of rabbits as laboratory animals, it is surprising and perhaps significant that no relevant data have been reported from lagomorphs. It is less surprising that none have been reported from the marsupials, or from the orders Erinaceomorpha and Soricomorpha (the mammals formerly classified as Insectivora), because there has been relatively little cognitive study of these animals and many of the insectivores would be very difficult to work with under laboratory conditions.

As we seek a broad understanding of the development of human concepts, a study of category learning in nonprimate mammals seems at first sight to be no more than a gap-filling exercise – a necessary check that there is no discontinuity between the well-studied birds and primates, but not something that is likely to contribute new insights.

However the present review leads to at least two conclusions that would not be evident from the literature on more popular taxa.

First, category discrimination is as important in other sensory modalities as it is in vision. It follows that an undue focus on the visual modality is likely to underestimate the conceptual abilities of any species; this may be particularly relevant for humans, where recent decades have seen a great deal of speculation, and some data, on the role of olfaction in social perception. A further consequence is that many categories may be functionally defined in terms of more than one sensory modality — if it is going to be a duck, it not only has to walk like a duck, it has to quack like a duck too. This is an issue that is largely unexplored, and not just in nonprimate mammals: it has hardly been taken up in any taxon, even in humans.

Second, category discriminations are vital in the social life of animals. For lack of direct experimental data, we had to look for evidence of category-level cognition in the discriminations that animals have to make in order to carry on their daily life. Such evidence was plentifully available. The use of concepts is not an arcane or abstract cognitive ability, unrelated to the natural life of animals, as some fields of human cognition (e.g. reading or formal mathematics) might be thought to be. Concepts are valuable tools in enabling a rapid but flexible response to a complex perceptual world.

References

Ables, E. M., Kay, L. M., & Mateo, J. M. (2007). Rats assess degree of relatedness from human odors. *Physiology & Behavior*, **90**, 726–732.

Archie, E. A., Hollister-Smith, J. A., Poole, J. H., et al. (2007). Behavioural inbreeding avoidance in wild African elephants. *Molecular Ecology*, **16**, 4138–4148.

Bailey, A. M. & Thomas, R. K. (1998). An investigation of oddity concept learning by rats. *Psychological Record*, **48**, 333–344.

Bates, L. A., Sayialel, K. N., Njiraini, N. W., Moss, C. J., Poole, J. H., & Byrne, R. W. (2007). Elephants classify human ethnic groups by odor and garment color. *Current Biology*, **17**, 1938–1942.

Bekoff, M. (1979). Scent marking by free-ranging domestic dogs. *Biology of Behavior*, **4**, 123–139.

Bekoff, M. (2001). Observations of scent-marking and discriminating self from others by a domestic dog (*Canis familiaris*): Tales of displaced yellow snow. *Behavioural Processes*, **55**, 75–79.

Bohn, K. M., Wilkinson, G. S., & Moss, C. F. (2007). Discrimination of infant isolation calls by female greater spear-nosed bats, *Phyllostomus hastatus. Animal Behaviour*, **73**, 423–432.

Boughman, J. W. & Wilkinson, G. S. (1998). Greater spear-nosed bats discriminate group mates by vocalizations. *Animal Behaviour*, **55**, 1717–1732.

Bradshaw, J. & Cameron-Beaumont, C. (2000). The signalling repertoire of the domestic cat and its undomesticated relatives. In D. C. Turner & P. Bateson (Eds.), *The Domestic Cat: The Biology of Its Behaviour*, 2nd edn., pp. 67–94, Cambridge: Cambridge University Press.

Brisbin, I. L. & Austad, S. N. (1991). Testing the individual odor theory of canine olfaction. *Animal Behaviour*, **42**, 63–69.

Broad, K. D., Mimmack, M. L., & Kendrick, K. M. (2000). Is right hemisphere specialization for face discrimination specific to humans? *European Journal of Neuroscience*, **12**, 731–741.

Burdick, C. K. & Miller, J. D. (1975). Speech perception by the chinchilla. *Journal of the Acoustical Society of America*, **58**, 415–427.

Burke, D. & Russell, F. (2007). Conditional same-different categorisation in the short-beaked echidna. Conference on Comparative Cognition, Melbourne, FL, March.

Busquet, N. & Baudoin, C. (2005). Odour similarities as a basis for discriminating degrees of kinship in rodents: evidence from *Mus spicilegus*. *Animal Behaviour*, **70**, 997–1002.

Cablk, M. E. & Heaton, J. S. (2006). Accuracy and reliability of dogs in surveying for desert tortoise (*Gopherus agassizii*). *Ecological Applications*, **16**, 1926–1935.

Caldwell, M. C. & Caldwell, D. K. (1965). Individualized whistle contours in bottlenosed dolphins (*Tursiops truncatus*). *Nature*, **207**, 434–435.

Capaldi, E. J. & Miller, D. J. (1988). Counting in rats: Its functional significance and the independent cognitive processes that constitute it. *Journal of Experimental Psychology: Animal Behavior Processes*, **14**, 3–17.

Carvalho, L. D., Cowing, J. A., Wilkie, S. E., Bowmaker, J. K., & Hunt, D. M. (2006). Shortwave visual sensitivity in tree and flying squirrels reflects changes in lifestyle. *Current Biology*, **16**, R81–R83.

Cerchio, S. & Dahlheim, M. (2001). Variation in feeding vocalizations of humpback whales *Megaptera novaeangliae* from southeast Alaska. *Bioacoustics*, **11**, 277–295.

Charrier, I., Mathevon, N., & Jouventin, P. (2003). Vocal signature recognition of mothers by fur seal pups. *Animal Behaviour*, **65**, 543–550.

Cheetham, S. A., Thom, M. D., Jury, F., Ollier, W. E. R., Beynon, R. J., & Hurst, J. L. (2007). The genetic basis of individual recognition signals in the mouse. *Current Biology*, **17**, 1771–1777.

Cheney, D. L. & Seyfarth, R. M. (1988). Assessment of meaning and the detection of unreliable signals by vervet monkeys. *Animal Behaviour*, **36**, 477–486.

Church, R. M. & Meck, W. H. (1984). The numerical attribute of stimuli. In H. L. Roitblat, T. G. Bever, & H. S. Terrace (Eds.), *Animal Cognition*, pp. 445–464, Hillsdale, NJ: Erlbaum.

Collins, K. T., Terhune, J. M., Rogers, T. L., Wheatley, K. E., & Harcourt, R. G. (2006). Vocal individuality of in-air Weddell seal (*Leptonychotes weddellii*) pup 'primary' calls. *Marine Mammal Science*, **22**, 933–951.

Coulon, M., Deputte, B. L., Heyman, Y., Delatouche, L., & Richard, C. (2007). Visual discrimination by heifers (*Bos taurus*) of their own species. *Journal of Comparative Psychology*, **121**, 198–204.

Coutellier, L. (2006). Are dogs able to recognize their handler's voice? A preliminary study. *Anthrozoös*, **19**, 278–284.

Davis, H. (1984). Discrimination of the number three by a racoon (*Procyon lotor*). *Animal Learning and Behavior*, **12**, 409–413.

Davis, H. & Bradford, S. A. (1986). Counting behavior by rats in a simulated natural environment. *Ethology*, **73**, 265–280.

Davis, H., Norris, C., & Taylor, A. (1998). Whether ewe know me or not: The discrimination of individual humans by sheep. *Behavioural Processes*, **43**, 27–32.

Delfour, F. & Marten, K. (2001). Mirror image processing in three marine mammal species: Killer whales (*Orcinus orca*), false killer whales (*Pseudorca crassidens*) and California sea lions (*Zalophus californianus*). *Behavioural Processes*, **53**, 181–190.

Dewson, J. H. (1964). Speech sound discrimination by cats. *Science*, **144**, 555–556.

Dewson, J. H., Pribram, K. H., & Lynch, J. C. (1969). Effects of ablations of temporal cortex upon speech sound discrimination in monkey. *Experimental Neurology*, **24**, 579–591.

Eriksson, J. L. & Villa, A. E. P. (2006). Learning of auditory equivalence classes for vowels by rats. *Behavioural Processes*, **73**, 348–359.

Feldman, H. N. (1994). Methods of scent marking in the domestic cat. *Canadian Journal of Zoology*, **72**, 1093–1099.

Ferkin, M. H. & Johnston, R. E. (1995). Meadow voles, *Microtus pennsylvanicus*, use multiple sources of scent for sex recognition. *Animal Behaviour*, **49**, 37–44.

Ferreira, G., Keller, M., Saint-Dizier, H., Perrin, G., & Levy, F. (2004). Transfer between views of conspecific faces at different ages or in different orientations by sheep. *Behavioural Processes*, **67**, 491–499.

Fields, P. E. (1932). Studies in concept formation. I. The development of the concept of triangularity by the white rat. *Comparative Psychology Monographs*, **9**, 1–70.

Fields, P. E. (1935). Studies in concept formation: II. A new multiple stimulus jumping apparatus for visual figure discrimination. *Journal of Comparative Psychology*, **20**, 183–203.

Fields, P. E. (1936). Studies in concept formation: III. A note on the retention of visual figure discriminations. *Journal of Comparative Psychology*, **21**, 131–136.

Gallup, G. G. (1970). Chimpanzees: Self-recognition. *Science*, **167**, 86–87.

Gheusi, G., Goodall, G., & Dantzer, R. (1997). Individually distinctive odours represent individual conspecifics in rats. *Animal Behaviour*, **53**, 935–944.

Hagen, K. & Broom, D. M. (2003). Cattle discriminate between individual familiar herd members in a learning experiment. *Applied Animal Behaviour Science*, **82**, 13–28.

Hanggi, E. B. (1999). Categorization learning in horses (*Equus caballus*). *Journal of Comparative Psychology*, **113**, 243–252.

Hare, J. F. & Atkins, B. A. (2001). The squirrel that cried wolf: reliability detection by juvenile Richardson's ground squirrels (*Spermophilus richardsonii*). *Behavioral Ecology and Sociobiology*, 51, 108–12.

Hare, J. F., Sealy, S. G., Underwood, T. J., Ellison, K. S., & Stewart, R. L. M. (2003). Evidence of self-referent phenotype matching revisited: Airing out the armpit effect. *Animal Cognition*, **6**, 65–68.

Harley, H. E. (2008). Whistle discrimination and categorization by the Atlantic bottlenose dolphin (*Tursiops truncatus*): A review of the signature whistle framework and a perceptual test. *Behavioural Processes*, **77**, 243–268.

Harley, H. E., Roitblat, H. L., & Nachtigall, P. E. (1996). Object representation in the bottlenose dolphin (*Tursiops truncatus*): Integration of visual and echoic information. *Journal of Experimental Psychology: Animal Behavior Processes*, **22**, 164–174.

Harvey, L. M., Harvey, S. J., Hom, M., Perna, A., & Salib, J. (2006). The use of bloodhounds in determining the impact of genetics and the environment on the expression of human odortype. *Journal of Forensic Sciences*, **51**, 1109–1114.

Harley, H. E., Fellner, W., & Odell, K. (2007). Object–photo/photo–object matching by the bottlenose dolphin. Conference on Comparative Cognition, Melbourne, FL: March.

Hepper, P. G. (1988). The discrimination of human odour by the dog. *Perception*, **17**, 549–554.

Herman, L. M., Pack, A. A., & Hoffmann-Kuhnt, M. (1998). Seeing through sound: Dolphins (*Tursiops truncatus*) perceive the spatial structure of objects through echolocation. *Journal of Comparative Psychology*, **112**, 292–305.

Hienz, R. D., Aleszczyk, C. M., & May, B. J. (1996). Vowel discrimination in cats: Acquisition effects of stimulus level, and performance in noise. *Journal of the Acoustical Society of America*, **99**, 3656–3668.

Hurst, J. L., Thom, M. D., Nevison, C. M., Humphries, R. E., & Beynon, R. J. (2005). MHC odours are not required or sufficient for recognition of individual scent owners. *Proceedings of the Royal Society of London Series B: Biological Sciences*, 272, 715–724.

Illmann, G., Schrader, L., Spinka, M., & Sustr, P. (2002). Acoustical mother–offspring recognition in pigs (*Sus scrofa domestica*). *Behaviour*, 139, 487–505.

Janik, V. M. & Slater, P. J. B. (1998). Context-specific use suggests that bottlenose dolphin signature whistles are cohesion calls. *Animal Behaviour*, 56, 829–838.

Jesseau, S. A., Holmes, W. G., & Lee, T. M. (2008). Mother–offspring recognition in communally nesting degus, *Octodon degus*. *Animal Behaviour*, 75, 573–582.

Johnston, R. E. (2003). Chemical communication in rodents: From pheromones to individual recognition. *Journal of Mammalogy*, 84, 1141–1162.

Johnston, R. E. & Jernigan, P. (1994). Golden hamsters recognize individuals, not just individual scents. *Animal Behaviour*, 48, 129–136.

Johnston, R. E. & Peng, A. (2008). Memory for individuals: Hamsters (*Mesocricetus auratus*) require contact to develop multicomponent representations (concepts) of others. *Journal of Comparative Psychology*, 122, 121–131.

Kalmus, H. (1955). The discrimination by the nose of the dog of individual human odours and in particular the odours of twins. *British Journal of Animal Behavior*, 3, 1–25.

Kazial, K. A. & Masters, W. M. (2004). Female big brown bats, *Eptesicus fuscus*, recognize sex from a caller's echolocation signals. *Animal Behaviour*, 67, 855–863.

Kazial, K. A., Kenny, T. L., & Burnett, S. C. (2008). Little brown bats (*Myotis lucifugus*) recognize individual identity of conspecifics using sonar calls. *Ethology*, 114, 469–478.

Kendrick, K. M. & Baldwin, B. A. (1987). Cells in temporal cortex of conscious sheep can respond preferentially to the sight of faces. *Science*, 236, 448–450.

Kendrick, K. M., Atkins, K., Hinton, M. R., Broad, K. D., Fabre-Nys, C., & Keverne, B. (1995). Facial and vocal discrimination in sheep. *Animal Behaviour*, 49, 1665–1676.

Kendrick, K. M., Atkins, K., Hinton, M. R., Heavens, P., & Keverne, B. (1996). Are faces special for sheep? Evidence from facial and object discrimination learning tests showing effects of inversion and social familiarity. *Behavioural Processes*, 38, 19–35.

Kendrick, K. M., Da Costa, A. P., Leigh, A. E., Hinton, M. R., & Peirce, J. W. (2001). Sheep don't forget a face. *Nature*, 414, 165–166.

Kilian, A., Yaman, S., Von Fersen, L., & Günturkün, O. (2003). A bottlenose dolphin discriminates visual stimuli differing in numerosity. *Learning & Behavior*, 31, 133–42.

Kluender, K. R., Lotto, A. J., Holt, L. L., & Bloedel, S. L. (1998). Role of experience for language-specific functional mappings of vowel sounds. *Journal of the Acoustical Society of America*, 104, 3568–3582.

Knornschild, M., Von Helversen, O., & Mayer, F. (2007). Twin siblings sound alike: Isolation call variation in the noctule bat, *Nyctalus noctula*. *Animal Behaviour*, 74, 1055–1063.

Koba, Y. & Tanida, H. (2001). How do miniature pigs discriminate between people? Discrimination between people wearing coveralls of the same colour. *Applied Animal Behaviour Science*, 73, 45–58.

Kober, M., Trillmich, F., & Naguib, M. (2007). Vocal mother–pup communication in guinea pigs: Effects of call familiarity and female reproductive state. *Animal Behaviour*, 73, 917–925.

Kowalska, D. M. (1997). The method of training dogs in auditory recognition memory tasks with trial-unique stimuli. *Acta Neurobiologiae Experimentalis*, 57, 345–352.

Krechevsky, I. (1932). Hypotheses in rats. *Psychological Review*, **39**, 516–532.

Kruczek, M. (2007). Recognition of kin in bank voles (*Clethrionomys glareolus*). *Physiology & Behavior*, **90**, 483–489.

Kuhl, P. K. & Miller, J. D. (1978). Speech perception by chinchilla: Identification functions for synthetic VOT stimuli. *Journal of the Acoustical Society of America*, **63**, 905–917.

Lashley, K. S. (1938). The mechanism of vision: XV. Preliminary studies of the rat's capacity for detailed vision. *Journal of General Psychology*, **18**, 123–193.

Laurent, G. (2002). Olfactory network dynamics and the coding of multidimensional signals. *Nature Reviews Neuroscience*, **3**, 884–895.

Ligout, S. & Porter, R. H. (2004). Effect of maternal presence on the development of social relationships among lambs. *Applied Animal Behaviour Science*, **88**, 47–59.

Ligout, S., Sebe, F., & Porter, R. H. (2004). Vocal discrimination of kin and non-kin agemates among lambs. *Behaviour*, **141**, 355–369.

Lingle, S., Rendall, D., & Pellis, S. M. (2007). Altruism and recognition in the antipredator defence of deer: 1. Species and individual variation in fawn distress calls. *Animal Behaviour*, **73**, 897–905.

Lit, L. & Crawford, C. A. (2006). Effects of training paradigms on search dog performance. *Applied Animal Behaviour Science*, **98**, 277–292.

Maletinska, J., Spinka, M., Vichova, J., & Stehulova, I. (2002). Individual recognition of piglets by sows in the early post-partum period. *Behaviour*, **139**, 975–991.

Marchant-Forde, J. N., Marchant-Forde, R. N., & Weary, D. M. (2002). Responses of dairy cows and calves to each other's vocalisations after early separation. *Applied Animal Behaviour Science*, **78**, 19–28.

Marten, K. & Psarakos, S. (1995). Using self-view television to distinguish between self-examination and social behavior in the bottlenose dolphin (*Tursiops truncatus*). *Consciousness and Cognition*, **4**, 205–225.

Mateo, J. M. (2003). Kin recognition in ground squirrels and other rodents. *Journal of Mammalogy*, **84**, 1163–1181.

Mateo, J. M. (2004). Recognition systems and biological organization: The perception component of social recognition. *Annales Zoologici Fennici*, **41**, 729–745.

Mateo, J. M. (2006). Development of individually distinct recognition cues. *Developmental Psychobiology*, **48**, 508–519.

Mateo, J. M. & Johnston, R. E. (2000). Kin recognition and the 'armpit effect': Evidence of self-referent phenotype matching. *Proceedings of the Royal Society of London Series B: Biological Sciences*, **267**, 695–700.

Mauck, B. & Dehnhardt, G. (2005). Identity concept formation during visual multiple-choice matching in a harbor seal (*Phoca vitulina*). *Learning & Behavior*, **33**, 428–436.

Mauck, B. & Dehnhardt, G. (2007). Spatial multiple-choice matching in a harbour seal (*Phoca vitulina*): differential encoding of landscape versus local feature information? *Animal Cognition*, **10**, 397–405.

McCowan, B. & Hooper, S. L. (2002). Individual acoustic variation in Belding's ground squirrel alarm chirps in the High Sierra Nevada. *Journal of the Acoustical Society of America*, **111**, 1157–1160.

McCowan, B. & Reiss, D. (2001). The fallacy of 'signature whistles' in bottlenose dolphins: A comparative perspective of 'signature information' in animal vocalizations. *Animal Behaviour*, **62**, 1151–1162.

McLeman, M. A., Mendl, M., Jones, R. B., White, R., & Wathes, C. M. (2005). Discrimination of conspecifics by juvenile domestic pigs, *Sus scrofa*. *Animal Behaviour*, 70, 451–461.

Meck, W. H. (1997). Application of a mode-control model of temporal integration to counting and timing behaviour. In C. M. Bradshaw & E. Szabadi (Eds.), *Time and Behaviour: Psychological and Neurobiological Analyses*, pp. 133–184, New York: Elsevier.

Meck, W. H. & Church, R. M. (1982). Abstraction of temporal attributes. *Journal of Experimental Psychology: Animal Behavior Processes*, 8, 226–243.

Mercado, E., Killebrew, D. A., Pack, A. A., Macha, I. V. B., & Herman, L. M. (2000). Generalization of 'same–different' classification abilities in bottlenosed dolphins. *Behavioural Processes*, 50, 79–94.

Mitchell, B. R., Makagon, M. M., Jaeger, M. M., & Barrett, R. H. (2006). Information content of coyote barks and howls. *Bioacoustics*, 15, 289–314.

Moore, J. (2007). Phenotype matching and inbreeding avoidance in African elephants. *Molecular Ecology*, 16, 4421–4423.

Mora, E. C., Rodriguez, A., Macias, S., Quinonez, I., & Mellado, M. M. (2005). The echolocation behaviour of *Nycticeius cubanus* (Chiroptera: Vespertilionidae): Inter- and intra-individual plasticity in vocal signatures. *Bioacoustics*, 15, 175–193.

Munksgaard, L., De Passille, A. M., Rushen, J., Thodberg, K., & Jensen, M. B. (1997). Discrimination of people by dairy cows based on handling. *Journal of Dairy Science*, 80, 1106–1112.

Nakagawa, E. (1993). Relational rule learning in the rat. *Psychobiology*, 21, 293–298.

Nakagawa, E. (2002). Shift learning in matching-to-sample discriminations in rats as a function of overtraining. *Psychological Record*, 52, 107–26.

Nakagawa, E. (2003). Shift learning in same-different conditional discriminations in rats. *Psychological Record*, 53, 487–506.

Nousek, A. E., Slater, P. J. B., Wang, C., & Miller, P. J. O. (2006). The influence of social affiliation on individual vocal signatures of northern resident killer whales (*Orcinus orca*). *Biology Letters*, 2, 481–484.

O'Connell-Rodwell, C. E., Wood, J. D., Kinzley, C., Rodwell, T. C., & Poole, J. H. (2007). Wild African elephants (*Loxodonta africana*) discriminate between familiar and unfamiliar conspecific seismic alarm calls. *Journal of the Acoustical Society of America*, 122, 823–830.

O'Riain, M. J. & Jarvis, J. U. M. (1997). Colony member recognition and xenophobia in the naked mole-rat. *Animal Behaviour*, 53, 487–498.

Pack, A. A. & Herman, L. M. (1995). Sensory integration in the bottlenosed dolphin: Immediate recognition of complex shapes across the senses of echolocation and vision. *Journal of the Acoustical Society of America*, 98, 722–733.

Pack, A. A., Herman, L. M., Hoffmann-Kuhnt, M., & Branstetter, B. K. (2002). The object behind the echo: Dolphins (*Tursiops truncatus*) perceive object shape globally through echolocation. *Behavioural Processes*, 58, 1–26.

Palphramand, K. L. & White, P. C. L. (2007). Badgers, *Meles meles*, discriminate between neighbour, alien and self scent. *Animal Behaviour*, 74, 429–436.

Pal, S. K. (2003). Urine marking by free-ranging dogs (*Canis familiaris*) in relation to sex, season, place and posture. *Applied Animal Behaviour Science*, 80, 45–49.

Peirce, J. W., Leigh, A. E., & Kendrick, K. M. (2000). Configurational coding, familiarity and the right hemisphere advantage for face recognition in sheep. *Neuropsychologia*, 38, 475–483.

Peirce, J. W., Leigh, A. E., da Costa, A. P. C., & Kendrick, K. M. (2001). Human face recognition in sheep: Lack of configurational coding and right hemisphere advantage. *Behavioural Processes*, **55**, 13–26.

Perry, E. A. & Renouf, D. (1988). Further studies of the role of harbor seal (*Phoca vitulina*) pup vocalizations in preventing separation of mother pup pairs. *Canadian Journal of Zoology*, **66**, 934–938.

Pfalzer, G. & Kusch, J. (2003). Structure and variability of bat social calls: Implications for specificity and individual recognition. *Journal of Zoology*, **261**, 21–33.

Pickel, D., Manucy, G. P., Walker, D. B., Hall, S. B., & Walker, J. C. (2004). Evidence for canine olfactory detection of melanoma. *Applied Animal Behaviour Science*, **89**, 107–116.

Plotnik, J. M., DeWaal, F. B. M., & Reiss, D. (2006). Self-recognition in an Asian elephant. *Proceedings of the National Academy of Sciences of the United States of America*, **103**, 17053–17057.

Pons, F. (2006). The effects of distributional learning on rats' sensitivity to phonetic information. *Journal of Experimental Psychology: Animal Behavior Processes*, **32**, 97–101.

Porter, R. H. & Bouissou, M. F. (1999). Discriminative responsiveness by lambs to visual images of conspecifics. *Behavioural Processes*, **48**, 101–110.

Porter, R. H., Nowak, R., Orgeur, P., Levy, F., & Schaal, B. (1997). Twin/non-twin discrimination by lambs: An investigation of salient stimulus characteristics. *Behaviour*, **134**, 463–475.

Povinelli, D. J. (1989). Failure to find self-recognition in Asian elephants (*Elephas maximus*) in contrast to their use of mirror cues to discover hidden food. *Journal of Comparative Psychology*, **103**, 122–131.

Ramm, S. A., Cheetham, S. A., & Hurst, J. L. (2008). Encoding choosiness: Female attraction requires prior physical contact with individual male scents in mice. *Proceedings of the Royal Society B: Biological Sciences*, **275**, 1727–1735.

Randall, J. A. (1994). Discrimination of footdrumming signatures by kangaroo rats, *Dipodomys spectabilis*. *Animal Behaviour*, **47**, 45–54.

Range, F., Aust, U., Steurer, M., & Huber, L. (2008). Visual categorization of natural stimuli by domestic dogs. *Animal Cognition*, **11**, 339–347.

Reed, P., Howell, P., Sackin, S., Pizzimenti, L., & Rosen, S. (2003). Speech perception in rats: Use of duration and rise time cues in labeling of affricate/fricative sounds. *Journal of the Experimental Analysis of Behavior*, **80**, 205–215.

Reiss, D. & Marino, L. (2001). Mirror self-recognition in the bottlenose dolphin: A case of cognitive convergence. *Proceedings of the National Academy of Sciences of the United States of America*, **98**, 5937–5942.

Rendell, L. & Whitehead, H. (2004). Do sperm whales share coda vocalizations? Insights into coda usage from acoustic size measurement. *Animal Behaviour*, **67**, 865–874.

Romeyer, A., Poindron, P., & Orgeur, P. (1994). Olfaction mediates the establishment of selective bonding in goats. *Physiology & Behavior*, **56**, 693–700.

Rosell, F. & Bjorkoyli, T. (2002). A test of the dear enemy phenomenon in the Eurasian beaver. *Animal Behaviour*, **63**, 1073–1078.

Rybarczyk, P., Koba, Y., Rushen, J., Tanida, H., & Passillé, A. M. de (2001). Can cows discriminate people by their faces? *Applied Animal Behaviour Science*, **74**, 175–189.

Rybarczyk, P., Rushen, J., & de Passillé, A. M. (2003). Recognition of people by dairy calves using colour of clothing. *Applied Animal Behaviour Science*, **81**, 307–319.

Safi, K. & Kerth, G. (2003). Secretions of the interaural gland contain information about individuality and colony membership in the Bechstein's bat. *Animal Behaviour*, **65**, 363–369.

Sayigh, L. S., Tyack, P. L., Wells, R. S., & Scott, M. D. (1990). Signature whistles of free-ranging bottlenose dolphins *Tursiops truncatus*: Stability and mother-offspring comparisons. *Behavioral Ecology & Sociobiology*, **26**, 247–260.

Sayigh, L. S., Tyack, P. L., Wells, R. S., Solow, A. R., Scott, M. D., & Irvine, A. B. (1999). Individual recognition in wild bottlenose dolphins: A field test using playback experiments. *Animal Behaviour*, **57**, 41–50.

Sayigh, L. S., Esch, H. C., Wells, R. S., & Janik, V. M. (2007). Facts about signature whistles of bottlenose dolphins, *Tursiops truncatus*. *Animal Behaviour*, **74**, 1631–1642.

Scherrer, J. A. & Wilkinson, G. S. (1993). Evening bat isolation calls provide evidence for heritable signatures. *Animal Behaviour*, **46**, 847–860.

Schibler, F. & Manser, M. B. (2007). The irrelevance of individual discrimination in meerkat alarm calls. *Animal Behaviour*, **74**, 1259–1268.

Schoon, G. A. A. (1996). Scent identification lineups by dogs (*Canis familiaris*): Experimental design and forensic application. *Applied Animal Behaviour Science*, **49**, 257–267.

Searby, A. & Jouventin, P. (2003). Mother-lamb acoustic recognition in sheep: A frequency coding. *Proceedings of the Royal Society of London Series B: Biological Sciences*, **270**, 1765–1771.

Settle, R. H., Sommerville, B. A., McCormick, J., & Broom, D. M. (1994). Human scent matching using specially trained dogs. *Animal Behaviour*, **48**, 1443–1448.

Shapiro, A. D. (2006). Preliminary evidence for signature vocalizations among free-ranging narwhals (*Monodon monoceros*). *Journal of the Acoustical Society of America*, **120**, 1695–1705.

Siegel, R. K. & Honig, W. K. (1970). Pigeon concept formation: Successive and simultaneous acquisition. *Journal of the Experimental Analysis of Behavior*, **13**, 385–390.

Smith, D. A., Ralls, K., Hurt, A., et al. (2003). Detection and accuracy rates of dogs trained to find scats of San Joaquin kit foxes (*Vulpes macrotis mutica*). *Animal Conservation*, **6**, 339–346.

Soltis, J., Leong, K., & Savage, A. (2005). African elephant vocal communication II: Rumble variation reflects the individual identity and emotional state of callers. *Animal Behaviour*, **70**, 589–599.

Sommerville, B. A., Settle, R. H., Darling, F. M. C., & Broom, D. M. (1993). The use of trained dogs to discriminate human scent. *Animal Behaviour*, **46**, 189–190.

Souza, A. S., Jansen, J., Tempelman, R. J., Mendl, M., & Zanella, A. J. (2006). A novel method for testing social recognition in young pigs and the modulating effects of relocation. *Applied Animal Behaviour Science*, **99**, 77–87.

Suddendorf, T., Simcock, G., & Nielsen, M. (2007). Visual self-recognition in mirrors and live videos: Evidence for a developmental asynchrony. *Cognitive Development*, **22**, 185–196.

Swaisgood, R. R., Lindburg, D. G., & Zhou, X. P. (1999). Giant pandas discriminate individual differences in conspecific scent. *Animal Behaviour*, **57**, 1045–1053.

Tang-Martinez, Z., Mueller, L. L., & Taylor, G. T. (1993). Individual odours and mating success in the golden hamster, *Mesocricetus auratus*. *Animal Behaviour*, **45**, 1141–1151.

Taylor, A. A. & Davis, H. (1998). Individual humans as discriminative stimuli for cattle (*Bos taurus*). *Applied Animal Behaviour Science*, **58**, 13–21.

Terrazas, A., Serafin, N., Hernandez, H., Nowak, R., & Poindron, P. (2003). Early recognition of newborn goat kids by their mother: II. Auditory recognition and evidence of an individual acoustic signature in the neonate. *Developmental Psychobiology*, **43**, 311–320.

Thom, M. D. & Hurst, J. L. (2004). Individual recognition by scent. *Annales Zoologici Fennici*, **41**, 765–787.

Todrank, J. & Heth, G. (1996). Individual odours in two chromosomal species of blind, subterranean mole rat (*Spalax ehrenbergi*): Conspecific and cross-species discrimination. *Ethology*, **102**, 806–811.

Toro, J. M. & Trobalon, J. B. (2005). Statistical computations over a speech stream in a rodent. *Perception & Psychophysics*, **67**, 867–875.

Toro, J. M., Trobalon, J. B., & Sebastián-Gallés, N. (2005). Effects of backward speech and speaker variability in language discrimination by rats. *Journal of Experimental Psychology: Animal Behavior Processes*, **31**, 95–100.

Tyack, P. (1986). Whistle repertoires of two bottlenosed dolphins, *Tursiops truncatus*: Mimicry of signature whistles? *Behavioral Ecology & Sociobiology*, **18**, 251–257.

Vache, M., Ferron, J., & Gouat, P. (2001). The ability of red squirrels (*Tamiasciurus hudsonicus*) to discriminate conspecific olfactory signatures. *Canadian Journal of Zoology*, **79**, 1296–1300.

Vannoni, E. & McElligott, A. G. (2007). Individual acoustic variation in fallow deer (*Dama dama*) common and harsh groans: A source-filter theory perspective. *Ethology*, **113**, 223–234.

Weiss, B. M., Ladich, F., Spong, P., & Symonds, H. (2006). Vocal behavior of resident killer whale matrilines with newborn calves: The role of family signatures. *Journal of the Acoustical Society of America*, **119**, 627–635.

Wright, G. A. & Smith, B. H. (2004). Variation in complex olfactory stimuli and its influence on odour recognition. *Proceedings of the Royal Society of London Series B: Biological Sciences*, **271**, 147–152.

Zenuto, R. R. & Fanjul, M. S. (2002). Olfactory discrimination of individual scents in the subterranean rodent *Ctenomys talarum* (tuco-tuco). *Ethology*, **108**, 629–641.

Chapter 10

Concepts in monkeys

Michèle Fabre-Thorpe

Editors' Preview

Chapter 10, 'Concepts in monkeys', continues the comparative review of concepts in animals other than human beings. In this instance, the focus is on primates (monkeys), but there is also additional coverage of the concept-formation abilities of pigeons.

One point of organization for the chapter concerns the kinds and levels of concepts that can be formed by animals. Concepts span a continuum from those based on rote memorization to those based on abstract relations. For example, at one end of the scale, monkeys (baboons) were trained to perform one response for one set of pictures and another response for another set of pictures with an estimate of the total number of pictures presented approximating 5000. While this type of task can be solved via association between the individual pictures and one or the other response, the findings speak to the large memory capacity of animals, which in turn provides evidence that is consistent with the exemplar view of concepts described in several of the earlier chapters.

In addition to forming categories based on sheer repetition of a large number of individual instances, animals (including pigeons and monkeys) have been shown to form more open-ended categories based on perceptual similarity. The open-ended nature of the categories refers to the fact that responses learned to trained instances will generalize to novel instances of the categories. Thus, for example, monkeys have been shown to form open-ended categorical distinctions contrasting photographs containing people versus those not containing people. Monkeys have also been shown to form such concepts for conspecifics (e.g. rhesus monkeys form a category representation for rhesus monkeys that excludes Japanese macaques), birds exclusive of nonbird animals, and subordinate-level categories of birds (e.g. kingfishers exclusive of other types of birds). The concepts are not limited to people or animals, but can further be formed for trees, as well as artefact categories (e.g. 3s vs. Bs with exemplars from each category presented in multiple typefaces).

At the other end of the range, monkeys have been shown to form more abstract concepts based on same–different relations abstracted from the instances presented. For example, monkeys learn to discriminate between large arrays in which all of the items are the same versus those in which all or some of the items are unique. Importantly, the learned response to the same versus different arrays generalizes to novel arrays, indicating that it could not have been based on perceptual similarity. The abstract nature of the concepts that can be represented by monkeys is further documented by the fact that they can have an amodal nature (i.e. the categorical distinction between human and monkey faces can for monkeys be based on both sight and sound).

Chapter 10 also reviews evidence relating to characteristics of the concept formation processes in animals versus humans. For example, in studies investigating monkey and human adults' ability to divide pictures into classes with and without a person and with and without food, both monkeys and humans are able to respond quite rapidly (with monkeys showing even faster responses perhaps because of their smaller brains). In addition, both monkey and human performance are affected similarly when the stimulus sets are manipulated through changes to the colour and contrast of the pictures. For both monkeys and humans, removing colour cues and greatly reducing contrast does not adversely affect performance, suggesting that processing mechanisms responding to coarse visual information perform the categorization. This should perhaps not be viewed as surprising given the additional evidence reviewed in the chapter indicating that much of what we believe to be true about the neural circuitry underlying (at least visual) concepts in humans is based on studies using physiological recording techniques with monkeys. Also of note is that when the categorization task required a response at a greater level of specificity (birds among nonbirds), both monkey and human performance was slowed, suggesting a real-time progression in categorical processing from broad (animals) to narrow (birds) that may correspond with the trend observed in infant development from broad to narrow category representations that is described in Chapter 12.

Abstract concepts are the building blocks of higher cognitive capacities. However, because animals lack language to tell us what they think, they have long been denied any abstraction abilities. For both Descartes and Locke, the distinction between humans and animals lay in the specific capacity for abstraction derived by humans from their language ability. For Descartes, animals had no thoughts – they were unthinking machines that lacked even conscious perception. For Locke, animals could not generate abstract ideas because they could not use words or any other general signs. Thus, human abilities are usually described with words such as 'abstraction', 'conceptualization', 'thought', etc. whereas animals do little more than react to their environment, discriminate, associate, or learn by heart. Indeed, billions of years of selection have been so successful that the animal world overflows with examples of 'intelligent behaviour' that just involve stereotyped stimulus responses. There is little doubt that language can help shape categories and concepts, and allow mental representations of ideas, events, objects, or features independent of their real concrete existence. Are humans therefore unique?

Charles Darwin (1871) was the first to apply his theory of evolutionary continuity not only to physical characteristics, but also to minds, when he proposed 'the necessary acquirement of each mental power and capacity by gradation'. According to this view, mammalian and human mental abilities would essentially be of the same nature, although having attained different degrees of sophistication. To support such phylogenetic continuity, it is necessary to show that closely related species such as monkeys and humans share basic processes. Higher-level 'processing units' may have been progressively built on such first 'blocks' to reach the sophistication of human mental faculties.

With the title of the first pioneering study in the field: 'Complex visual concept in the pigeon', Herrnstein and Loveland (1964) dropped the first bombshell. Their study opened a large field aimed at exploring animal minds with progressively more and more refined behavioural methods. A second bombshell was dropped when humans discovered that their genetic code was more than 98% similar to that of a chimpanzee. Would this mean that we are just quantitatively different or would the 2% of human-specific genes allow us to be qualitatively different?

In this chapter, some very recent studies are reviewed that have reported conceptual behaviour in monkeys that are far more abstract than could have been expected just 10 years ago. Indeed, in the last 10 or even 5 years, research on internal representations and reasoning in animals has blossomed. This explosion of new data is due, first, to a wide range of newly available techniques for imaging cerebral activity (positron emission tomography [PET], functional magnetic resonance imaging [fMRI]). Initially developed for humans, fMRI has now been adapted by a small number of dedicated research teams to the study of monkey behaviour. This has allowed gigantic advances in the knowledge of cerebral functional homologies, enlightening both the similarities and dissimilarities between animals and humans performing similar cognitive tasks. However, there is still a long way to go from the activation of brain structures to the neuronal coding that supports the representation of percepts and concepts. There again, techniques that had only been used in animals – such as intracranial single-unit recording – have been, in very specific medical cases, developed in humans and have offered the possibility of comparing the neuronal response in both species. Finally, the creativity of some developmental cognitive researchers interested in the thinking abilities of human infants who lack language has led to the development of new protocols that can also be applied to monkeys.

The concept of mental representation has been central to the study of animal cognition (Gallistel, 1970; Vauclair, 1992). To interact adequately with the surrounding world, animals have to use memorized experience to mentally assess what to expect from objects and to manipulate mental representations.

In the present chapter, data supporting conceptual abilities of monkeys at different levels of abstraction, up to language abilities and even metacognition, are reported. Also, briefly addressed is the cerebral basis of such faculties of abstraction when comparative data are available in humans.

From visual to conceptual categorization

Categorization is an economical way to deal with the dense flow of information continuously processed by our brains. Attributing a previously unseen object to a given category is useful because all the memorized knowledge about this category can be applied to the new object. Imagine, for example, that an animal is facing a predator or a prey. It is easy to see the biological advantage for animals able to categorize a new 'object' appearing in its surrounding world as belonging to one of these two categories. Attributing an object to a given category implies the extraction of some invariant features. It means that among its many visual features, some have to be ignored as irrelevant for its categorization, whereas others have to be extracted because of their pertinence for classification. This is a very important characteristic of brain functioning. The ability to select what is important allows a large simplification of the world's complexity and is the basis for generalization. The fantasy story about '*Funes, el memorioso*' by Argentinian writer Jorge Luis Borges illustrates how unusable the internal world would be without abstraction. As Borges writes, 'to think is to forget a difference, to generalize, to abstract. In the overly replete world of Funes there were nothing but details, almost contiguous details'.

In 1990, Hernstein proposed a hierarchical organization of category levels. At the lowest level of abstraction, stand categorization by rote, which relies on memorization, and the open-ended categories based on perceptual similarity. Monkeys have repeatedly been shown to display the ability to form such categories.

In a recent study, the large long-term memory capacity of monkeys has clearly been demonstrated in Old World monkeys (Fagot & Cook, 2006). Baboons were trained to learn and retain the association of a picture with one of two possible responses. An increasing number of picture–response associations were progressively introduced over the 3 years of the study. At that time, 3500–5000 associations had been memorized and the authors estimated that the baboons could have retained thousands more with continued testing. Although humans have not been tested in exactly the same task, various studies have given theoretical estimates that all converge towards an enormous memory capacity (see Dudai, 1997, for a review). From their study, Fagot and Cook hypothesized that 'a progressive evolutionary growth in long term memory capacity may have served the development of increasingly complex cognitive functioning over time'. Their study also reported long-term memory capacities in pigeons. The comparison between pigeons and baboons revealed functional similarities suggesting that millions of years of divergent evolution 'may have mainly changed memory capacities but have had little impact on basic memory processes'.

Memory capacity is certainly one of the key factors, but our brain has to select the pertinent information to store. It has to choose the right balance between the necessary details for identification and useful abstraction for categorization.

Beyond categorization by rote, there is now enough evidence to say that monkeys can build open-ended categories. At such a level of categorization, objects belong to the same class because they are 'perceptually similar' (see Chapter 8, this book). Indeed, in the pioneering study by Herrnstein and Loveland (1964) pigeons were shown to accurately classify pictures on the basis of whether or not they contained a human being. Moreover, pigeons were shown to be able to transfer their categorization ability to photographs that they had never seen before. Thus, they went further than rote categorization and showed generalization. The existence of such a 'person' concept has also been reported for monkeys (D'Amato & Van Sant, 1988) and numerous studies have demonstrated monkeys' ability to form open-ended categories. Although, such pictures can be varied because of different view angles, partial or occluded views, or target scale that could include close-ups and far views, perceptual similarity could still be used to build such categories. One particularly significant open-ended category concerns members of one's own species, a biologically crucial faculty. Squirrel monkeys have been reported to form and use the concept of 'squirrel monkey' (Phillips, 1996), and the same has been reported for both baboons (Martin-Malivel & Fagot, 2001) and rhesus monkeys (Yoshikubo, 1985). Rhesus monkeys were shown to be quite strict with such classification, differentiating rhesus monkeys from Japanese macaques. Apart from conspecifics, monkeys can build natural open-ended categories such as 'trees' when tree exemplars are presented among other objects (Vogels, 1999a), 'kingfishers' among other birds or 'birds' among other animals (Roberts & Mazmanian, 1988). Moreover, they can also learn artefactual categories such as letters or numbers (Schrier et al., 1984; Vauclair & Fagot, 1996). Although baboons can perfectly discriminate between 'B' or '3' items when presented in different typefaces, they also can form a 'B' or a '3' category regardless of the font (Vauclair & Fagot, 1996).

For Hernstein (1990), the next level of abstraction after categories by rote and open-ended categories is one that goes beyond perceptual similarity. It involves 'conceptual categorization' because many disparate exemplars have to be grouped together. Twenty years ago a very interesting study compared perceptual categorization performance in squirrel monkeys and humans at three different levels of abstraction (Roberts & Mazmanian, 1988). At the most concrete level, similarity between exemplars was very high and subjects were required to categorize 'kingfisher', a very colourful bird, when presented among other birds. At an intermediate level, they were presented with animals and they had to form a 'bird' category. There again (although similarity between exemplars is not as high) birds share a large number of specific visual features. Finally, at the most abstract level, subjects had to form an 'animal' category among nonanimal distractors. For this third category level, they need to go well beyond physical similarities as it would be next to impossible to group on the basis of similarity, a swarm of swallows in the sky and a snake in the grass. The mental representation needed to span the huge variety of known animals is presumably highly abstract. Thus generalization should be more difficult, and monkey performance was expected to decrease with increasing conceptual abstraction. Interestingly, the results showed that both monkeys and humans performed best at the most abstract level, namely, at the superordinate level. On the other hand, monkeys had difficulties in forming a separate category for birds among animals (basic level) whereas humans performed at their best. Inversely, the worst human performance was found at the subordinate level – kingfisher among birds, where exemplars were most similar whereas monkeys performed also at their best. Whatever the level of categorization, both humans and monkeys could transfer their acquired abilities to previously unseen photographs. However, for the most abstract 'animal' category, the correct transfer rate for squirrel monkeys was not very high and was clearly dependant upon the training-set size.

Whereas the conclusion could be that monkeys exhibited difficulties in the transfer phase at the most abstract level, the observed difference between monkeys and humans might also be related to some specific aspects of the experimental protocol used by Roberts and Mazmanian (1988). First, the monkeys had to choose the target picture from a pair of simultaneously presented pictures. In this scenario, they can compare the two images for as long as they want and are encouraged to rely on discrimination abilities. Second, after being trained with a fixed set of photographs, they were tested in the transfer phase on a completely new set of image pairs. In my opinion, using such a transfer set induces two main biases. In their training phase, monkeys are encouraged to use a strategy based on the memorization of stimulus–response associations rather than to develop a strategy relying on the emergence of a real concept; and we know that monkeys are very good at memorizing stimulus–response associations (Fagot & Cook, 2006). Moreover, in the transfer phase, the exclusive use of new photographs tends to amplify any drop of performance. Indeed, an initial minor accuracy decrease during the testing session with new photographs will induce a decrease in reward rate and will alter the monkey's motivation and attention, resulting in further performance errors. Finally, another bias comes from the enormous difference between humans and monkeys in terms of training-set size. The concept of 'animals' is a human concept. Human subjects have 'processed' thousands of different exemplars since their birth and have become highly expert.

This stimulating study by Roberts and Mazmanian used a comparative approach between three animal species to determine the degree of abstraction of their categorical representations, but the performance levels reported for monkeys could have been underestimated, especially as they used a New World monkey. To further assess monkeys' abilities at building an 'animal' concept, we tried and designed a protocol that would prevent some of the above biases. We were also keen to compare monkeys and humans when both had to produce very fast responses. The rationale was that the sophisticated strategies that might be specific to humans must have evolved in addition to more basic mechanisms, and might therefore be time consuming. By imposing a severe time constraint on humans, we could force them to rely on more basic mechanisms that they might share with their monkey cousins.

Fast visual 'conceptual' categorization in monkeys and humans

The ability of rhesus macaques (an Old World monkey) to develop abstract concepts such as not only 'animals' but also 'food objects' was investigated and compared to human performance in a protocol of fast visual categorization first introduced in 1996 (Thorpe et al., 1996). For better comparison, monkeys and humans were tested using identical set-ups, following exactly the same protocol and using the same varied sets of natural images.

In our task, subjects are presented with one image at a time in a random sequence and must only respond to targets ('go' trials). They have to withhold their response on nontargets ('no-go' response). This is another important difference when compared with Roberts and Mazmanian's task, in which monkeys were always faced with a pair of stimuli and rewarded for choosing the target category. In our task, they cannot compare two images and decide which one contains most feature targets. To succeed, they have to reach a decision on the basis of their internal representation of what an 'animal' or a 'food object' is. Moreover, the task prevents monkeys from forming an object category based on the association with reward, because all correct decisions are rewarded (whether 'go' or 'no-go'). However, the main point concerns the assessment of the macaque's performance on previously unseen photographs. In order to encourage the monkey not to use a strategy based on memorization of stimulus–response associations, but rather to try and solve the problem by forming a 'concept', new photographs were added every day throughout training and testing sessions and mixed with familiar ones. New stimuli were thus embedded in a sequence of familiar stimuli, the reward rate was fairly stable and so was the animal's state of attention and motivation whenever a novel image was presented for the first time. This is of major importance: to really tackle generalization abilities without learning interference, transfer performance was specifically assessed on the monkey's response to the very first presentation of a previously unseen photograph. If ten new photographs were included each day, only ten trials were analysed, even though monkeys happily performed over 1000 trials a day.

Our aim was to apply extreme temporal constraints in task performance so that the subjects (both macaques and humans) had to rely on fast decisions and on early rapid processing of visual information. Stimuli were flashed for only 30 ms and the manual response (let go of a button and touch a tactile screen) had to be made in less than 1 s from stimulus onset. There is little doubt that with longer stimulus presentations, humans could have used additional time-consuming verification strategies to perform the task 100% correctly. With 30 ms of stimulus presentation, subjects had no time for eye movements and could not visually explore the photographs. Targets and distractors were very varied. Animal targets included fish, birds, mammals, reptiles, and even some insects presented in their natural environments. Distractors included landscapes, trees, flowers, buildings, vehicles, and all kinds of man-made objects.

Despite these constraints, monkeys scored around 90% correct with images they had never seen before (Delorme et al., 2000; Fabre-Thorpe et al., 1998). This performance should be compared with the rate of 94% correct for humans, a robust score similar to the performance reported in the original study (Thorpe et al., 1996). The most surprising finding was the speed at which monkeys could perform the tasks; they were much faster than humans, with a median reaction time in the range of 250–300 ms whereas human median reaction times were usually in the range 370–450 ms (Figure 10.1).

A post hoc analysis of monkey performance according to human rate of success showed that errors were concentrated on the same photographs. Stimuli that induced

Go responses (%)

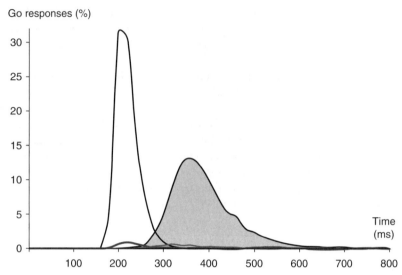

Fig. 10.1 Reaction-time distributions for 'go' responses. Top two curves for correct go responses towards targets and bottom two curves for incorrect go-responses towards nontargets. Reaction times of human (shaded curves) are much longer than those of monkeys (empty curves).

high, intermediate, and poor performance for humans induced similar success rates for monkeys. The same correlation holds for reaction times, as long or short response latencies were associated with similar sets of target images in humans and monkeys. This result suggests that the 'animals' and 'food objects' concepts built by monkeys in our task had considerable overlap with the human concepts. It also suggests that they both based their decisions on the processing of similar visual cues.

Among all the features contained in a natural photograph, colour might be an important cue to categorize an object as 'food' or 'animal'. In fact, D'Amato and Van Sant (1988) considered colour a key feature in monkey decision-making. Removing colour was shown to impair performance of both humans and monkeys (Roberts & Mazmanian, 1988) when 'kingfishers', very colourful birds, had to be categorized among other birds. But in these studies, subjects were not under high temporal constraints to reach a decision. In our rapid-categorization task, colour was not found to be a crucial feature. When humans and monkeys performed the task with a sequence that mixed randomly coloured photographs and grey-scale ones, removing colour information had only a very marginal effect on either accuracy or response speed. In fact, the effect was mainly seen in the human subjects that tended to produce slow responses, as if the use of colour needed additional processing time (Yao & Einhauser, 2008). Again, the set of photographs that induced errors in monkeys and in humans overlapped substantially for both coloured and grey-level images (Delorme et al., 2000).

Of course, reaching similar levels of performance does not necessarily imply that the underlying processes are similar and that similar cues are being used to reach a decision.

The faster speed at which monkeys performed the task relative to humans might indeed suggest that monkeys solve the task by using simple computations of low-level cues rather than an abstract concept. Rather than exploring a set of possible low-level cues, we investigated how performance would be affected in humans and monkeys when the task could easily be solved by the use of low-level cues. If performance in the fast-categorization task relied on an abstract concept, then subjects should be able to significantly shorten their reaction times when they only have to process low-level cues. On the other hand, if performance was already based on low-level cues, then reaction times should be stable. To tackle this question, the very same protocol was used, except that the target was a single well-known image presented in 50% of the trials among 50% of varied nontarget images. This unique target image had been well learned by the subjects. Analysis of the very few false alarms revealed that both humans and monkeys relied on low-level cues available in the image such as the scene spatial layout, the location, and orientation of foreground objects, and even patches of colour. The results showed that both humans (Delorme et al., 2004) and monkeys (Macé et al., 2005a) were able to speed up their responses, shifting the whole reaction-time distribution towards shorter latencies even for the very first responses.

Both monkeys and humans were able to respond faster in the 'one target task', when using low-level cues. Thus, the faster speed exhibited by monkeys relative to humans in the categorization task cannot be interpreted by the use of two different strategies; monkeys' responses being based on low-level cues whereas human reponses were based on conceptual processes. This does not mean that low-level cues do not play a crucial role in categorization, and indeed processing of low-level cues could coexist with conceptual processes in both species.

The fast speed of monkeys in the categorization task could also reflect their overtraining in the task. They were performing 5 days a week for as long as they wanted and one could wonder whether a monkey that had categorized the same photographs many times could process them faster. This hypothesis was investigated by comparing performance on new and familiar images. Whereas response accuracy and global speed were slightly improved for both monkeys and humans (Fabre-Thorpe et al., 2001), the latency of their fastest responses could not be shortened. This 'minimal response latency' reflects the minimal input–output-processing time in the categorical task. It stands at around 180 ms in monkeys and 250 ms in humans, regardless of whether the stimuli are new or familiar. The fact that overtraining cannot speed up the fast responses produced by monkeys and humans when categorizing previously unseen photographs suggest that for these very fast responses, all the computing steps are necessary and none can be bypassed.

In fact, humans and monkeys are so fast in this animal-categorization task that it raises the question of the kind of object representation that can be attained in such a short processing time. Further investigations showed that this representation must indeed be very rudimentary. Both humans and monkeys were tested with achromatic images in which original contrasts were reduced by a factor of 2, 4, 8, 10, 16, or 32. The performance was surprisingly robust (Figure 10.2) as chance level was only observed when the original contrast was divided by 32, that is, when photographs only contained 3% of the original contrast. Interestingly, monkeys (Macé, 2006; Macé et al., in press)

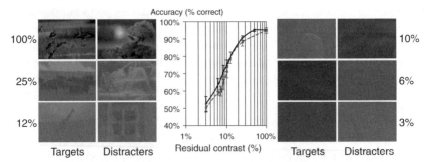

Fig. 10.2 Categorization accuracy is robust to reduction of contrast. Around 94% correct with the original black and white image (100% contrast) accuracy was still around 70% with only 10% residual contrast for both humans (dotted line) and monkeys (bold line). Chance level (50%) was attained for both humans and monkeys when only 3% of the initial contrast was preserved.

and humans (Macé et al. 2005c) showed a very similar performance decrease with decreasing contrasts, and with initial contrast divided by a factor of 10, they could both still score around 70% correct. The implications of such robustness to low-level contrasts have to be drawn from functional differences between the two different main-streams of visual information originating in the primate retina: the parvocellular and the magnocellular pathways. Schematically, at very low contrasts, the slow parvocellular visual system is not activated; performance has to rely on the contrast-sensitive magnocellular pathway. But the fast magnocellular pathway only processes low-spatial-frequency information and does not convey any colour information. The object representations built from such visual information must be very rudimentary and necessarily achromatic, a conclusion which is in agreement with the very limited role played by colours in the categorization task reported earlier in this chapter.

Whereas such rudimentary representation might be sufficient to decide whether an animal is present in the image, it might not be explicit enough to decide which animal it is. Indeed, when contrast was very low, humans often reported that they were not very confident in their response and that they would not be able to tell which animal was present. They report the same impression, still performing well over chance, when photographs were processed with very low acuity because they were flashed in far peripheral vision (Thorpe et al., 2001), or when a mask presented 10–20ms after the image interrupted the incoming image-information flow (Bacon-Mace et al., 2005). In such extreme conditions, the well-adapted behavioural responses observed could be triggered from abstract mental representations that might not even be consciously accessible.

The coarse object representations used by humans and monkeys in the rapid-animal-categorization task may need to be refined through additional processing to access which kind of animal was presented. Thus if monkeys and humans are required to categorize a given animal category (such as 'birds' among nonbirds), additional processing time might be reflected by an increase in response latency. This is indeed what was found in a recent experiment that compared 'bird' categorization with 'animal' categorization.

Mean latency was increased by 40–70 ms in humans and by 30 ms in monkeys. This shift towards longer reaction times was even seen on the latency of the earliest responses that was increased by about 40–50 ms in humans (Macé et al., 2009) and by 20 ms in monkeys (Macé et al., 2005b). Incidentally, this coarse–to–fine processing of visual stimuli is at odds with the commonly accepted view that basic categories are accessed first. Our result shows that in a purely visual task, the superordinate category (animals) can be accessed before a basic-level category (birds).

Taken as a whole, this series of experiments using a rapid-categorization task with briefly flashed stimuli and strong temporal constraints showed first that monkeys and humans reach very similar accuracy performance in the main animal/nonanimal-categorization task. Moreover, it showed that performance – in terms of accuracy and response speed – was also similarly affected by modifications to the categorization task requirements and stimulus manipulations in which performance was assessed both in monkeys and humans. These results suggest that monkeys and humans rely – at least partly – on common visual cues processed through similar mechanisms to reach decisions.

This is not to say that monkeys use the same 'animal' concept as humans. The first bias in any study of animal concepts comes from the fact that the experimental investigator is always a human being, designing an experiment with his own human concepts to try and address animal concepts. In our experiments the 'animal' concept built by monkeys through learning shows a considerable overlap with the human 'animal' concept and needs similar information processing to be activated by a previously unseen picture.

This conclusion is at odds with the fact that monkeys are much faster than humans in performing the task. So far, we have excluded an explanation based on the exclusive use of low-level cues and on the effect of overtraining. The speed difference might be explained, at least partially, by a speed/accuracy trade-off. Irrespective of the task at hand, it might be that monkeys tend to produce fast responses, whereas humans tend to favour accuracy over speed. This is certainly true in our task, in which monkeys are reliably less accurate than humans by about 5%. But this explanation can only partially account for the difference in speed between monkeys and humans, as human accuracy drops dramatically when subjects are required to speed up their responses. The most likely explanation takes into consideration the length of the path along which the information travels from the retina to the hand (Figure 10.3). Within the brain, travelling from one cortical area to another is time consuming because of the surprisingly low conduction velocity of the axons involved. Thus, between processing steps, a considerable amount of time is lost in just transferring information. As monkeys have much smaller brains than humans, travelling along the ventral visual pathway would simply be faster because of the shorter distances involved. In fact, monkey visuo-motor reaction times have been reported to be shorter than human ones for a variety of tasks. Express saccades, for example, are seen at 70 ms in monkeys and 100 ms in humans; vergence reflex or tracking are observed at latencies of 55–60 ms in monkeys and 80 ms in humans. And in general, monkey reaction times are typically about 2/3 of those seen in humans, a result in accordance with the faster responses of monkeys in our categorization task (Figure 10.1). Thus the faster speed of monkeys relatively to

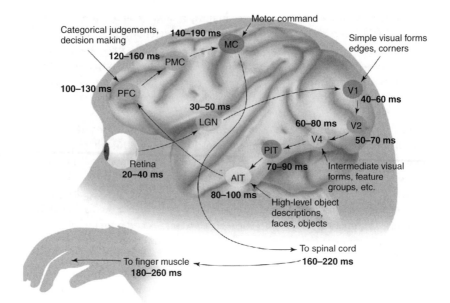

Fig. 10.3 Schematic progression of visual inputs along the ventral visual pathway in monkeys. At each processing step, the latency of recorded neuronal responses is indicated by two values: the shortest latency and the usual latency. A feedforward processing of information account for the monkeys' finger lift reaction time at 180–200 ms as shown in Figure 10.1.

Reproduced with permission from Thorpe, S. J. & Fabre-Thorpe, M. (2001). Neuroscience. Seeking categories in the brain. *Science*, **291**, 260–263.

humans in our rapid-categorization task would not reflect a difference in terms of elementary/sophisticated strategy but simply an artefact of their smaller brains.

In this example, the 'conceptual representation' of animals or food objects is purely visual. It deserves the word of conceptual because the subjects have to generalize to new exemplars of the learned category. Such new stimuli often have very little similarity with the ones they have already learned. Moreover, although they need training, monkeys can learn to modify the rule they apply for picture categorization. They can alternate between the animal-categorization task in which all objects in the nontarget pictures belong to nonanimal categories and a bird-categorization in which nontargets include other animal species. They can also alternate between two superordinate categories ('animal' and 'food'). In both cases, they have to consider as nontargets, some or even all the pictures that were previously rewarded when processed as targets and have to accordingly modify their motor behaviour (go vs. no-go responses).

But a category of objects is not only defined by its abstract visual representation. Birds have specific visual shapes, but you could also determine their shape through touch. Touch will add more information about the external texture of parts of their bodies. A 'bird' concept should be activated through various source of information through touch but also through audition and olfaction, because birds produce specific sounds, specific odours, etc. As such, an abstract concept cannot be unimodal; it has to be accessible through different modalities.

From visual to multimodal concepts

In order to be useful for cognitive operations from perception to action or even to thought, the conceptual representation of the surrounding world should be accessible through different sensory modalities. The demonstration of cross-modal object representations is thus very important. Apes and young human infants show cross-modal matching between touch and vision (Bryant et al., 1972; Davenport & Rogers, 1970; Davenport et al., 1973). Newborn babies have also been shown to extract shape within the tactile modality and transfer it to a visual representation. In a recent study, Streri and Gentaz (2004) used the natural behaviour of newborn human babies, who spend more time exploring a new situation or a new object than a familiar one. After a phase of haptic habituation to a given shape, during which an object, a prism, for example, was inserted into the newborn's hand until s/he dropped it repeatedly, they observed that when visually presented with the prism and a new object such as a cylinder, newborns would explore the new object for longer. This result suggests that this ability does not need any perceptual learning and might rely on innate faculties.

The ability of monkeys to perform cross-modal matching has long been debated but has been now demonstrated in different monkey species. The first convincing evidence was reported by Cowey and Weiskrantz (1975), who motivated rhesus monkeys to perform cross-modal matching from touch to vision by using edible versus inedible shapes. Cross-modal perception in monkeys has also been shown between auditory and visual information. Using matches between vocalizations of conspecifics and photographs or videos of faces producing such vocalizations, auditory–visual integration has been shown in both capuchin monkeys (Evans et al., 2005) and Japanese macaques (Adachi et al., 2006). Squirrel monkeys are also capable of auditory–visual cross-modal perception for their primary human caretakers (Adachi & Fujita, 2007).

Of particular interest is the study by Martin-Malivel and Fagot (2001) based on conceptual priming. Humans and baboons were tested in a go/no-go categorization task, in which they had to decide whether a 3-s vocalization was produced by a human or a baboon. This vocalization was preceded by a 120-ms visual prime in which they were shown a natural image containing either human(s) or baboon(s). If subjects could achieve multimodal conceptual categorization, the expected results would be a reduced latency of the response in congruent situations when image-prime and target-sound were conceptually related. This is indeed what happened for humans and for one of the two baboons. The visual prime was effective both when the colour photograph was shown in black and white or reduced to the subject's cutouts demonstrating that the effect was not related to either colour or contextual features but was really based on the subject (baboon or human) presented in the photograph. Cross-modal integration can thus occur across a class of objects and shows that categorization in monkeys cannot rely only on perceptual attributes of the stimuli. Like humans, it appears that baboons are able to form multimodal abstract concepts of object categories.

Mental representations in monkeys are not pure images of particular sensory inputs. They can be accessed through different sensory modalities, and can be mentally manipulated to produce pertinent behavioural responses.

Abstract relations: the same/different concept

Returning to Herrnstein's category hierarchy (Herrnstein, 1990), the ability to form concepts is followed by the ability to learn abstract relations between and among concepts.

Same/different judgements can vary enormously in abstraction. Match and nonmatch to sample tasks have been widely used in monkeys. First presented with a sample object, for example, an apple, the monkey is subsequently shown a pair of objects, one of them being the apple. If performing a match-to-sample task, the monkey must choose the apple. The same/different concept is just applied at a perceptual level. Match(or nonmatch)-to-sample tasks have also been used to study the memory trace of the sample object by introducing delays between the sample and the test stimuli. This sort of same/different response presumably relies on basic perceptual similarities between objects, but could also be based on the relative familiarity or novelty of an object. But monkeys can go further by matching appropriate cues to same/different relations between stimuli. They can either choose the appropriate – same or different – cue in the presence of the corresponding relational pair of stimuli, or choose the appropriate relational pair in the presence of a cue. Somehow, they are able to 'label' the relation between the two objects (Flemming et al., 2007). To succeed in labelling a pair of object as same or different is not easy for monkeys. In Flemming et al. (2007), monkeys first had to extract the same/different concept from large arrays of stimuli that were all identical or all different. Thus, monkeys would rely on stimulus entropy for concept acquisition; once learned, they would then be able to apply the concept to a two-item display. To explain what entropy is, it might be better to just say that entropy is equal to 0 with displays that contain all identical items (whatever the number of items) but with a multiple-item display, the entropy value increases both with the number of items and with their heterogeneity. Alternatively, monkeys have shown to be able to learn the same/different concept with pairs of objects, but in that case they need a large training set to succeed. Performance in a transfer phase was similar to baseline performance for capuchin and rhesus monkeys trained with a set of 128 pairs, although most rhesus monkeys performed very well after training with 64 pairs (Katz et al., 2002; Wright et al., 2003).

If monkeys are able to label the relation between two stimuli, are they able to use this relation as the pertinent cue to apply for responding to the next pair of stimuli? In other words, are monkeys able to succeed in a relation–between-relations paradigm (Thompson & Oden, 2000)? In that case, monkeys have to choose the match stimulus because its overall design is identical to the sample stimulus. Baboons have been shown to build such abstract concepts (Fagot et al., 2001). In the study, stimuli were square displays containing 16 little items that could be either all different or all identical. Shown an 'all-identical-items' display as the sample, they were subsequently presented with both kinds of displays and had to choose the 'all-identical-items' new display (Figure 10.4). They could not rely on perceptual similarity, because the items contained in the sample and the test stimuli were always different. They had to choose the right answer on the basis of the relationship between the items contained in the stimuli. In such a task, baboons and humans both rely on entropy. With 16 item displays, entropy ranges from 0 (all identical items) to 4 (all different items). Stimulus entropy was manipulated either by decreasing the number of included items from 16 to two, or by keeping the items to 16 but using different proportions of same and different items in any one stimulus. Baboons needed more items than humans to extract the same/different relationship from the sample display and humans exhibited a much stricter use of the 'same' relation than baboons. Thus, whereas humans and baboons both rely on entropy, human strategy might include additional processes linked to language, as the word 'same' is much more restrictive than the word 'different'. Nevertheless, this experiment clearly shows that baboons can discriminate the 'relation between relations'. The performance of a relational match to sample task needs transfer of a concept to a new situation; analogical thinking might not be so far out of reach of monkeys.

Finally, monkeys have also been shown to make judgements of conceptual identity. This is a very abstract concept that is not even possible for 3-year-old children. Baboons first learn to categorize objects into food and nonfood categories, and to master a

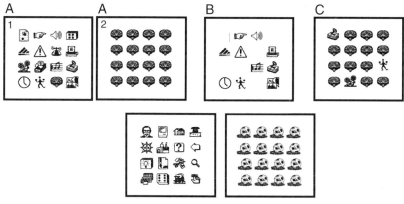

Stimulus Test

Fig. 10.4 An example of the 16 item stimuli used in Fagot et al. (2001). A sample is first displayed (A1, A2, B, or C), then the stimulus test is displayed and monkeys have to choose according to the relation-between-items in the sample. If an 'all different items' (A1) sample was shown choose the 'all different items' display in test. If an 'all identical items' (A2) sample was shown, choose the 'all identical items' display in test. Variantes in their experiment included the decrease of items in the sample display (B) and samples in which the ratio of same vs. different items was varied (in C 13S/3D).

From Fagot J., Wasserman E. A. and Young M. E., (2001). Discriminating the relation between relations: the role of entropy in abstract conceptualization by baboons (*Papio papio*) and humans (*Homo sapiens*). *Journal of Experimental Psychology: Animal Behavior Processes*, **27**, 316–328, APA publisher, adapted with permission.

perceptual matching in which they had to judge whether two objects were perceptually the same (an apple is the same as an apple, but is different than a hammer). In the final experiment, the authors showed that baboons could learn to apply the 'same/different' concept to two different objects belonging to the functional categories that they had learned. Such conceptual matching allowed them to respond that an apple and a banana were 'same objects' because they both belonged to the food category (Bovet & Vauclair, 2001). Although children at 3 years of age can categorize both apple and banana in the food category, they cannot infer the conceptual matching rule from just watching examples being sorted by someone else. They needed verbal explanation to work out the rule and perform the conceptual identity task (Bovet et al., 2005).

Baboons can learn conceptual categories, an ability that was long thought to be limited to apes and humans. They display analogical abilities that are out of reach of young children. Such abilities have long been denied to species lacking language. Although words might help us acquire new categories and shape the mental representation of items that have no perceptual features (see Chapter 6, this book), they are not always crucial for mental manipulations between and among concepts.

Neuronal basis of visual concepts

Humans and macaques have evolved separately for about 30 million years, and although some microscopic differences have recently been reported between apes' and humans' cortical organization, for example, concerning the primary visual cortex (Preuss & Coleman, 2002), their visual systems are largely analogous. Moreover, the anatomy and physiology of the macaque visual system is very well documented; so it makes a very good model to try and relate mental representations, mental manipulations, and neuronal mechanisms. Invasive techniques such as the recording of neuronal responses have thus often been used in monkeys with the obvious assumption that the results can be extrapolated to humans. But, as pointed out in the introduction, such invasive techniques are now used, albeit rarely, in humans. Even if such reports are very limited, they are priceless in appreciating the similarities and dissimilarities of neuronal responses in both species.

The information captured by the retina is transmitted to the primary visual cortex (V1) through the lateral geniculate nucleus. From V1, the visual information can be processed along two distinct, dorsal and ventral, cortical pathways. Object recognition and visual categorization mainly involve the ventral pathway (Figure 10.3). Beside this duality, a second dichotomy exists between the magnocellular and parvocellular pathways that originate from different cells in the retina and convey different kinds of information as described earlier in this chapter. Whereas the dorsal pathway is essentially magnocellular, the ventral pathway uses both magno- and parvocellular information. When progressing along the different steps of the ventral pathway, neurons show progressively longer response latencies and more complex visual responses. In the final step, in the anterior inferotemporal cortex (AIT), neuronal responses are linked to very complex visual stimuli such as faces or other very specific objects (Bruce et al., 1981; Logothetis et al., 1995; Perrett et al., 1982). Such cells are often more or less 'view-dependant', responding only to an object seen from a limited range of viewing angles (Logothetis & Sheinberg, 1996). However in a small proportion of neurons, the response can be totally 'view-invariant', in the sense that the neurons can be activated by all angles of view of an object (Booth & Rolls, 1998). This kind of response has been jokingly referred to as 'grandmother cells' and rejected at least in part because it would mean that the loss of such neurons would induce very specific deficits in object recognition. But in fact 'view-invariant' neurons respond to more than one object; so, the specific object identity can presumably be inferred only from the firing of a population of neurons. Recently, single-unit recording in humans reported highly invariant visual responses in the human median temporal lobe (Quiroga et al., 2005). One of the most impressive cells reported by these authors is a 'Halle Berry' cell that responded to all kinds of pictures of Halle Berry, even when her face was masked when costumed as 'Catwoman'. Furthermore, it responded to drawings and caricatures of the actress, and very impressively it responded to her written name! A 'Halle Berry' concept in a single cell? This is the schematic idea that the authors specifically do not want to defend (Quiroga et al., 2008), but somehow, between grandmother cells and models based on large distributed coding stands, the possibility arises of a 'sparse-invariant' coding, in which such a concept could emerge from the specificities of a restricted population of cells.

Neurons in monkeys' AIT have been reported to respond to a large variety of exemplars of a given category such as trees or fish (Vogels, 1999b), but clear category-related responses have not been reported (Op de Beeck et al., 2001). Cells can respond to many exemplars of a given category, but they do not respond to all of them, and they also respond to objects that do not belong to the category. On the other hand, the specificity of AIT cells for selected stimulus features can be shaped by the pertinence of such features to the task at hand. In a task requiring categorization of face drawings on the basis of eye separation and eye height, Sigala and Logothetis (2002) showed that AIT cells responded differentially to different eye separation and height while ignoring the variation affecting features that were nonpertinent for task resolution. This ability to ignore irrelevant variations while focusing on the pertinent dimension is a critical feature for abstraction.

In humans, neurons with a remarkable degree of category-specific firing have been reported in regions that receive inputs from AIT cortex. An example of such a neuron is described in the entorhinal cortex that responded selectively to pictures of all kinds of animals (Kreiman et al., 2000).

All the above results might suggest that the neuronal substrate for visual categorization may be located in the temporal cortex, but one important feature is missing. These very selective responses do not appear to be linked in any way with the behavioural outcome. In a study conducted by Sheinberg and Logothetis (2001), monkeys were trained to press a lever on the left or the right in response to two different sets of objects. Next, monkeys had to explore a natural scene in search of one such object hidden in the photograph to appropriately press the lever. Inferotemporal cells showed highly selective visual responses for such objects, but none was found that responded to all the objects requiring either a left or right response. Inferotemporal neurons might code for very sophisticated visual characteristics, but they do not seem interested in making a link with the appropriate behavioural outcome (Gold & Shadlen, 2001; Thorpe & Fabre-Thorpe, 2001).

The specification of the category boundaries relevant to motor responses could be done in another brain area, namely the prefrontal cortex (PFC). In that area, neuronal responses are much less sensitive to exemplar prototypicality. Instead, they appear to be interested in discriminating exemplars on the basis of the response they induce. In a very elegant study (Freedman et al., 2002), monkeys were trained to categorize cats and dogs. But the test stimuli used were obtained by morphing dogs' and cats' shapes in different proportions. Monkeys were very accurate even when stimuli mixed the two shapes in a 60:40% proportion. The interesting result was that many PFC neurons did code for cats and dogs regardless of how cat-like or dog-like the stimulus was. Moreover, neuronal activity really did reflect the visual categories pertinent for motor output. When visual stimuli were assigned to new categories, there was a re-shaping of the category boundaries that modified the responses of the neurons appropriately.

In the visual modality, PFC neurons are in constant interaction with AIT neurons (Figure 10.3). Thus, one possibility is that whereas AIT would encode visual features and stimulus prototypicality, PFC would set category boundaries in relation to the current behavioural requirements. PFC could influence the sensitivity of AIT neurons to enhance representation and discrimination of the stimulus features pertinent to solving a particular task.

The role of PFC in setting category borders is not limited to the visual system. PFC neurons have also been shown to spontaneously code for other biologically meaningful categories such as monkeys' vocalizations. In the absence of any training, neurons in the ventral PFC of rhesus monkeys discriminate between species-specific vocalizations associated with food versus nonfood events; a discrimination that has been shown to be independent of the acoustic properties of the vocalizations (Cohen et al., 2005).

One step further . . . language?

The repertoire of species-specific vocalizations in primates is rich. Monkeys communicate using complex sounds for finding food, emotions, particular relationships, and detection of predators. In vervet monkeys, alarm calls are specific to the predator that has been spotted: a loud bark for leopards, a short, double-syllable cough for eagles, and a 'chutter' sound for snakes. The response of other monkeys is appropriate as they respectively run to the trees, seek shelter, or stand up and look in the grass (Seyfarth et al., 1980). During infancy, monkeys learn to produce the appropriate calls for particular predators and the appropriate behavioural response upon hearing the calls (Seyfarth & Cheney, 1986). These signals are plastic, since monkeys can acquire new alarm calls to signal new predators (Gil-da-Costa et al., 2003). After being trained to use a tool to get food, Japanese macaques spontaneously produced differentiated coo-calls to ask experimenters for either food or tools (Hihara et al., 2003). Such communication signals reflect conceptual abilities that can be seen as perceptual multimodal representations associated with appropriate actions.

In the last 10 years, many studies performed with humans have shown that knowledge about particular categories is distributed across the modality-specific systems that process their properties (Barsalou, 2005). For example, when viewing or just naming a tool, the brain networks activated in humans include visual, premotor, and 'spatial' areas, as if linking mental representations of the specific visual features and attributes of tools with the appropriate hand and finger movements necessary for using them (Chao & Martin, 2000). Using the brain-imaging techniques now available in animals, scientists have started the investigation of the cerebral network involved in the conceptual system of monkeys. Gil-da-Costa et al. (2004) used PET to monitor the cerebral activity of rhesus monkeys while hearing coos, screams, and nonbiological sounds such as musical instruments or environmental sounds. Coos are associated with friendly behaviours and food approach, while screams are submissive vocalizations after an attack by a dominant. They are acoustically different. All biological and nonbiological sounds activated auditory brain areas, but conspecific vocalizations activated areas from the visual ventral stream including the temporal cortex (AIT), and brain regions associated with the perception of biological movements. With screams, moreover, enhanced activation was also found in areas associated with the encoding of affective situations.

The cerebral 'conceptual' network activated by coos and screams in monkeys is a very crucial result because of its striking similarities to the human cerebral network that is activated in similar emotional circumstances, for example, when meaningful words conveying emotional states are read to human subjects (Kensinger & Corkin, 2004). Macaques might activate multimodal representations strongly associated through repetitive experience with coos and screams. They might generate mental visual images of a conspecific producing the vocalization. Such representations could include monkey faces, expressions, or even threatening actions, together with emotional responses, especially with screams that have a strong negative emotional value.

Indeed, rhesus monkeys showed cross-modal visuo-auditory integration for vocal expressions (Ghazanfar & Logothetis, 2003). Coos are produced with a small mouth opening, whereas screams are associated with a large mouth opening. Tested with the preferential-looking paradigm used with prelinguistic human infants, rhesus monkeys stared longer at the video (from a choice of two videos) that matched the vocalization. Monkeys can also match the number of voices they hear to the number of faces they expect to see (Jordan et al., 2005). Thus, monkeys and humans might have a common neural substrate for conceptual representations that was already present in their common ancestors about 30 millions years ago, a system that might be important for the evolution of language in humans (Jordan et al., 2005).

Brain-imaging techniques are an extraordinary tool for comparing neuronal substrates in humans and monkeys, in the same or similar situations. But only very recently has the technique been sufficiently well adapted to allow studies in behaving monkeys. This research area is particularly active in trying to find homologies between humans and monkeys, or to determine the areas that show substantial modifications specific to humans. In the domain of language, very recent imaging studies have been trying to delineate cortical areas in monkeys that could be considered as homologous to human cortical regions specifically involved in language. For example, monkey homologues for human's Broca and Wernicke areas respectively involved in speech production and comprehension have been reported (Gil-da-Costa et al., 2006). Monkeys have also been reported to have a brain 'voice region' (Petkov et al., 2008). In humans, the voice region is specifically activated by human voices and vocalizations

(Belin et al., 2000). It is also sensitive to acoustic features that are specific to different human voices and might thus be involved in the recognition of individual voices (Belin & Zatorre, 2003). Even the left cerebral hemispheric dominance for language functions in humans may have some roots in monkeys. The left lateralization of language could have evolved from the left lateralization of a communication system using gestures, since baboons have been reported to use their right hand for species-specific communicative gestures (Meguerditchian & Vauclair, 2006).

These results show just how active this field of research is and how quickly it evolves. Establishing the details of homologies between monkeys, apes, and humans is invaluable for the evolutionary scientist. We need to delineate the basic neuronal systems present in all primates and the additional mechanisms specific to humans that have evolved to allow the sophistication of our conceptual systems and language functions.

Language is often thought of and presented as involving a single unified faculty. A distinction between language in a broad sense and a narrow sense has been proposed (Hauser et al., 2002). In a broad sense, language would involve interactions of a language system with nonlinguistic systems, whereas in a narrow sense, it would refer to all the processes that distinguish human language from communication in other species. As Hurford has argued, language 'should not be considered as a 'single monolithic behavior' (Hurford, 2006). Language evolved out of nonlanguage. The comparative study of animals and humans might be a very fruitful approach to the understanding of human language.

Even further?

Arguably, a unique aspect of human concepts is an awareness of them. Studies published in the last 5 years have shown a degree of self-awareness in monkeys that was not really expected.

For example, humans typically know whether they know an answer or not; if they do not know they will seek for hints. This metacognitive ability to judge one's knowledge is often considered to be exclusively human. However, very recently, rhesus macaques have convincingly been shown to make retrospective confidence judgements and to ask for hints when lacking knowledge (Kornell et al., 2007). Monkeys were rewarded by tokens that accumulated in a bank for correctly responding in a perceptual task. When reaching 12 tokens, they got a reward and three tokens were removed from the bank. After responding in their perceptual task, monkeys were offered a choice between a 'high-confidence' icon and a 'low-confidence' icon. Choosing the high-confidence icon was risky as the monkey earned three tokens with a correct response but lost three tokens with an erroneous response. Choosing the low-confidence icon always led to one token reward. Monkeys were shown to choose more frequently the low-confidence icon after an erroneous response. Thus, they knew how confident they were in their response. A crucial point is that they immediately transferred this confidence judgement to a memory task. Finally, when tested in a task that could only be solved by trial and error, they were shown to look for hints to solve the problem and to decrease hint seeking in correlation with accuracy increase. This sort of behaviour is very similar to that seen in humans under similar circumstances. This series of experiments shows that monkeys are capable of metacognitive monitoring. They can evaluate the accuracy of their response and control their knowledge – two components of human metacognition.

The conclusions on conceptual representations in monkeys are far from consensual. But it is clear that monkeys share conceptual abilities with humans and appear to rely, at least partly, on similar processes. As shown throughout this chapter, this area of research has developed very quickly in the last 5 years. The failure of animals on some cognitive tasks has sometimes been shown to result from poorly adapted experimental paradigms rather than cognitive inabilities. Cognitive scientists have progressed enormously in testing animal faculties by adapting behavioural tasks primarily developed for prelinguistic infants. New cognitive abilities have been demonstrated in monkeys that resulted in new requirements being imposed for demonstrating conceptual abilities. An even better understanding requires an interdisciplinary approach involving the integration of knowledge resulting from a variety of methodologies and different levels of integration (organisms, brain circuits, brain structures, single cells, genes). The advent of brain studies using fMRI helps enormously to better understand brain homologies in humans and monkeys (Sereno & Tootell, 2005). We can now compare the cerebral network activated in monkeys, apes, and humans when solving the same task to determine 'where' in the brain abstract concepts might be encoded. Similarities and dissimilarities in cerebral activation can guide the electrophysiologists attempting to understand 'how' neuronal responses reflect the encoding of such abstract concepts. Homologous cerebral areas activated in all species are good candidate areas in which to look for neuronal computations common to all primates. In contrast, additional activation in other brain regions might indicate species-specific neuronal processes acquired by monkeys and humans since their evolutionary paths have separated. The understanding of what is common and what is species-specific in the neuronal encoding underlying cognitive abilities is a crucial key in understanding the evolution of cognition, and in this case the evolution of concepts.

References

Adachi, I. & Fujita, K. (2007) Cross-modal representation of human caretakers in squirrel monkeys. *Behavioral Processes*, **74**, 27–32.

Adachi, I., Kuwahata, H., Fujita, K., Tomonaga, M., & Matsuzawa, T. (2006). Japanese macaques form a cross-modal representation of their own species in their first year of life. *Primates*, **47**, 350–354.

Bacon-Mace, N., Mace, M. J., Fabre-Thorpe, M., & Thorpe, S. J. (2005). The time course of visual processing: Backward masking and natural scene categorisation. *Vision Research*, **45**, 1459–1469.

Barsalou, L. W. (2005). Continuity of the conceptual system across species. *Trends in Cognitive Sciences*, **9**, 309–311.

Belin, P. & Zatorre, R. J. (2003). Adaptation to speaker's voice in right anterior temporal lobe. *Neuroreport*, **14**, 2105–2109.

Belin, P., Zatorre, R. J., Lafaille, P., Ahad, P., & Pike, B. (2000). Voice-selective areas in human auditory cortex. *Nature*, **403**, 309–312.

Booth, M. C. A. & Rolls, E. T. (1998). View-invariant representations of familiar objects by neurons in the inferior temporal visual cortex. *Cerebral Cortex*, **8**, 510–523.

Bovet D. & Vauclair J. (2001). Judgment of conceptual identity in monkeys. *Psychonomic Bulletin and Review*, **8**, 470–475.

Bovet D., Vauclair J., & Blaye A. (2005). Categorization and abstraction abilities in 3-year-old children: a comparison with monkey data. *Animal Cognition*, **8**, 53–59.

Bruce, C., Desimone, R., & Gross, C. G. (1981). Visual properties of neurons in a polysensory area in superior temporal sulcus of the macaque. *Journal of Neurophysiology*, **46**, 369–384.

Bryant, P. E., Jones, P., Claxton, V., & Perkins, G. M. (1972). Recognition of shapes across modalities by infants. *Nature*, **240**, 303–304.

Chao, L. L. & Martin, A. (2000). Representation of manipulable man-made objects in the dorsal stream. *Neuroimage*, **12**, 478–484.

Cohen, Y. E., Hauser, M. D., & Russ, B. E. (2005). Spontaneous processing of abstract categorical information in the ventrolateral prefrontal cortex. *Biology Letters*, **2**, 261–265.

Cowey, A. & Weiskrantz, L. (1975). Demonstration of cross-modal matching in rhesus monkeys, *Macaca mulatta*. *Neuropsychologia*, **13**, 117–120.

D'Amato, M. R. & Van Sant, P. (1988). The person concept in monkeys (*Cebus apella*). *Journal of Experimental Psychology: Animal Behavior Processes*, **14**, 43–55.

Darwin, C. (1871). *The Descent of Man, and Selection in Relation to Sex* London: Murray.

Davenport, R. K. & Rogers, C. M. (1970). Intermodal equivalence of stimuli in apes. *Science*, **168**, 279–280.

Davenport, R. K., Rogers, C. M., & Russell, I. S. (1973). Cross modal perception in apes. *Neuropsychologia*, **11**, 21–28.

Delorme, A., Richard, G., & Fabre-Thorpe, M. (2000). Ultra-rapid categorisation of natural scenes does not rely on colour cues: A study in monkeys and humans. *Vision Research*, **40**, 2187–2200.

Delorme, A., Rousselet, G. A., Mace, M. J., & Fabre-Thorpe, M. (2004). Interaction of top-down and bottom-up processing in the fast visual analysis of natural scenes. *Brain Research. Cognitive Brain Research*, **19**, 103–113.

Dudai, Y. (1997). How big is human memory, or on being just useful enough. *Learning and Memory*, **3**, 341–365.

Evans, T. A., Howell, S., & Westergaard, G. C. (2005). Auditory–visual cross-modal perception of communicative stimuli in tufted capuchin monkeys (*Cebus apella*). *Journal of Experimental Psychology: Animal Behavior Processes*, **31**, 399–406.

Fabre-Thorpe, M., Delorme, A., Marlot, C., & Thorpe, S. J. (2001). A limit to the speed of processing in ultra-rapid visual categorization of novel natural scenes. *Journal of Cognitive Neurosciences*, **13**, 171–180.

Fabre-Thorpe, M., Richard, G., & Thorpe, S. J. (1998). Rapid categorization of natural images by rhesus monkeys. *Neuroreport*, **9**, 303–308.

Fagot, J. & Cook, R. G. (2006). Evidence for large long-term memory capacities in baboons and pigeons and its implications for learning and the evolution of cognition. *Proceedings from the National Academy of Sciences, USA*, **103**, 17564–17567.

Fagot, J., Wasserman, E. A., & Young, M. E. (2001). Discriminating the relation between relations: the role of entropy in abstract conceptualization by baboons (*Papio papio*) and humans (Homo sapiens). *Journal of Experimental Psychology: Animal Behavior Processes*, **27**, 316–328.

Flemming, T. M., Beran, M. J., & Washburn, D. A. (2007). Disconnect in concept learning by rhesus monkeys (*Macaca mulatta*): Judgment of relations and relations-between-relations. *Journal of Experimental Psychology: Animal Behavior Processes*, **33**, 55–63.

Freedman, D. J., Riesenhuber, M., Poggio, T., & Miller, E. K. (2002). Visual categorization and the primate prefrontal cortex: neurophysiology and behavior. *Journal of Neurophysiology*, **88**, 929–941.

Gallistel, C. R. (1970). *The Organisation of Learning* Cambridge, MA: MIT Press.

Ghazanfar, A. A. & Logothetis, N. K. (2003). Neuroperception: Facial expressions linked to monkey calls. *Nature*, **423**, 937–938.

Gil-da-Costa, R., Braun, A., Lopes, M., et al. (2004). Toward an evolutionary perspective on conceptual representation: Species-specific calls activate visual and affective processing systems in the macaque. *Proceedings from the National Academy of Sciences, USA*, **101**, 17516–17521.

Gil-da-Costa, R., Martin, A., Lopes, M. A., Munoz, M., Fritz, J. B., & Braun, A. R. (2006). Species-specific calls activate homologs of Broca's and Wernicke's areas in the macaque. *Nature Neuroscience*, **9**, 1064–1070.

Gil-da-Costa R., Palleroni A., Hauser M. D., Touchton J., & Kelley J. P. (2003). Rapid acquisition of an alarm response by a neotropical primate to a newly introduced avian predator. *Proceedings, Biological Sciences*, **270**, 605–610.

Gold, J. I. & Shadlen, M. N. (2001). Neural computations that underlie decisions about sensory stimuli. *Trends in Cognitive Sciences*, **5**, 10–16.

Hauser, M. D., Chomsky, N., & Fitch, W. T. (2002). The faculty of language: What is it, who has it, and how did it evolve? *Science*, **298**, 1569–1579.

Herrnstein, R. J. (1990). Levels of stimulus control: a functional approach. *Cognition,* **37**, 133–166.

Herrnstein, R. J. & Loveland, D. H. (1964). Complex visual concept in the pigeon. *Science*, **146**, 549–551.

Hihara, S., Yamada, H., Iriki, A., & Okanoya, K. (2003). Spontaneous vocal differentiation of coo-calls for tools and food in Japanese monkeys. *Neuroscience Research*, **45**, 383–389.

Hurford, J. R. (2006). Recent developments in the evolution of language. *Cognitive Systems*, 7, 23–32.

Jordan, K. E., Brannon, E. M., Logothetis, N. K., & Ghazanfar, A. A. (2005). Monkeys match the number of voices they hear to the number of faces they see. *Current Biology*, **15**, 1034–1038.

Katz, J. S., Wright, A. A., & Bachevalier, J. (2002). Mechanisms of same/different abstract-concept learning by rhesus monkeys (*Macaca mulatta*). *Journal of Experimental Psychology: Animal Behavior Processes*, **28**, 358–368.

Kensinger, E. A. & Corkin, S. (2004). Two routes to emotional memory: Distinct neural processes for valence and arousal. *Proceedings from the National Academy of Sciences, USA*, **101**, 3310–3315.

Kornell, N., Son, L. K., & Terrace, H. S. (2007). Transfer of metacognitive skills and hint seeking in monkeys. *Psychological Science*, **18**, 64–71.

Kreiman, G., Koch, C., & Fried, I. (2000). Category-specific visual responses of single neurons in the human medial temporal lobe. *Nature Neuroscience*, **3**, 946–953.

Logothetis, N. K. & Sheinberg, D. L. (1996). Visual object recognition. *Annual Review of Neurosciences*, **19**, 577–621.

Logothetis, N. K., Pauls, J., & Poggio, T. (1995). Shape representation in the inferior temporal cortex of monkeys. *Current Biology*, 5, 552–563.

Macé, M. J-M. (2006). Représentations visuelles précoces dans la catégorisation rapide de scènes naturelles chez l'homme et le singe. Thèse de l' Université Paul Sabatier Toulouse. Available at http://tel.ccsd.cnrs.fr/tel-00077594, p.238. (Accessed July 2009).

Macé, M. J-M., Richard, G., Delorme, A., & Fabre-Thorpe, M. (2005a). Rapid categorization of natural scenes in monkeys: Target predictability and processing speed. *Neuroreport*, 16, 349–354.

Macé, M. J-M., Richard, G., Thorpe S., & Fabre-Thorpe, M. (2005b). Category-level hierarchy: What comes first in vision? *Acta Neurobiologica Experimentalis*, 63 (suppl.) 24.

Macé, M. J-M., Thorpe, S. J., & Fabre-Thorpe, M. (2005c). Rapid categorization of achromatic natural scenes: how robust at very low contrasts? *European Journal of Neurosciences*, 21, 2007–2018.

Macé M. J-M., Joubert, O. R., Nespoulous, J-L., & Fabre-Thorpe, M. (2009). Time-course of visual categorizations: You spot the animal faster than the bird. *PLoS ONE*, 4(6), e5927.

Macé M. J-M., Delorme, A. Richard, G., & Fabre-Thorpe, M. (in press). Spotting animals in natural scenes: efficiency of humans and monkeys at very low contrasts. *Animal Cognition*.

Martin-Malivel, J. & Fagot, J. (2001). Cross-modal integration and conceptual categorization in baboons. *Behavioral Brain Research*, 122, 209–213.

Meguerditchian, A. & Vauclair, J. (2006). Baboons communicate with their right hand. *Behavioral Brain Research*, 171, 170–174.

Op de Beeck, H., Wagemans, J., & Vogels, R. (2001). Inferotemporal neurons represent low-dimensional configurations of parameterized shapes. *Nature Neuroscience*, 4, 1244–1252.

Perrett, D. I., Rolls, E. T., & Caan, W. (1982). Visual neurones responsive to faces in the monkey temporal cortex. *Experimental Brain Research*, 47, 329–342.

Petkov, C. I., Kayser, C., Steudel, T., Whittingstall, K., Augath, M., & Logothetis, N. K. (2008). A voice region in the monkey brain. *Nature Neuroscience*, 11, 367–374.

Phillips, K. A. (1996). Natural conceptual behavior in squirrel monkeys (*saimiri sciureus*): An experimental investigation. *Primates*, 37, 327–332.

Preuss, T. M. & Coleman, G. Q. (2002). Human-specific organization of primary visual cortex: alternating compartments of dense Cat-301 and calbindin immunoreactivity in layer 4A. *Cerebral Cortex*, 12, 671–691.

Quiroga, R. Q., Reddy, L., Kreiman, G., Koch, C., & Fried, I. (2005). Invariant visual representation by single neurons in the human brain. *Nature*, 435, 1102–1107.

Quiroga, R. Q., Kreiman, G., Koch, C., & Fried, I. (2008). Sparse but not 'grandmother-cell' coding in the medial temporal lobe. *Trends in Cognitive Sciences*, 12, 87–91.

Roberts, W. A. & Mazmanian, D. S. (1988). Concept learning at different levels of abstraction by pigeons, monkeys, and people. *Journal of Experimental Psychology: Animal Behavior Processes*, 14, 247–260.

Schrier, A. M., Angarella, R., & Povar, M. L. (1984). Studies of concept formation by stumptailed monkeys: concepts humans, monkeys, and letter A. *Journal of Experimental Psychology: Animal Behavior Processes*, 10, 564–584.

Sereno, M. I. & Tootell, R. B. (2005). From monkeys to humans: what do we now know about brain homologies? *Current Opinions in Neurobiology*, 15, 135–144.

Seyfarth R. M. & Cheney D. L. (1986) Vocal development in vervet monkeys. *Animal Behaviour*, 34, 1640–1658.

Seyfarth, R. M., Cheney, D. L., & Marler, P. (1980). Monkey responses to three different alarm calls: Evidence of predator classification and semantic communication. *Science*, 210, 801–803.

Sheinberg, D. L. & Logothetis, N. K. (2001). Noticing familiar objects in real world scenes: the role of temporal cortical neurons in natural vision. *Journal of Neurosciences*, 21, 1340–1350.

Sigala, N. & Logothetis, N. K. (2002). Visual categorization shapes feature selectivity in the primate temporal cortex. *Nature*, 415, 318–320.

Streri, A. & Gentaz, E. (2004). Cross-modal recognition of shape from hand to eyes and handedness in human newborns. *Neuropsychologia*, 42, 1365–1369.

Thompson, R. K., & Oden, D. L. (2000). Categorical perception and conceptual judgments by nonhuman primates: The paleological monkey and the analogical ape. *Cognitive Science*, 24, 363–396.

Thorpe, S. J. & Fabre-Thorpe, M. (2001). Neuroscience. Seeking categories in the brain. *Science*, 291, 260–263.

Thorpe, S.J., Fize, D., & Marlot, C. (1996). Speed of processing in the human visual system. *Nature*, 381, 520–522.

Thorpe, S. J., Gegenfurtner, K. R., Fabre-Thorpe, M., & Bulthoff, H. H. (2001). Detection of animals in natural images using far peripheral vision. *European Journal of Neurosciences*, 14, 869–876.

Vauclair, J. (1992). *L'intelligence de l'animal* Paris: Seuil.

Vauclair, J. & Fagot, J. (1996). Categorization of alphanumeric characters by baboons (*Papio papio*): Within and between class stimulus discrimination. *Current Psychology and Cognition*, 15, 449–462.

Vogels, R. (1999a). Categorization of complex visual images by rhesus monkeys. Part 1: Behavioural study. *European Journal of Neurosciences*, 11, 1223–1238.

Vogels, R. (1999b). Categorization of complex visual images by rhesus monkeys. Part 2: Single-cell study. *European Journal of Neurosciences*, 11, 1239–1255.

Wright, A. A., Rivera, J. J., Katz, J.S., & Bachevalier, J. (2003). Abstract-concept learning and list-memory processing by capuchin and rhesus monkeys. *Journal of Experimental Psychology: Animal Behavior Processes*, 29, 184–198.

Yao, A. Y. & Einhauser, W. (2008) Color aids late but not early stages of rapid natural scene recognition. *J Vis*, 8: 1211–1213.

Yoshikubo, S. (1985). Species discrimination and concept formation by rhesus monkeys (*macaca mulatta*). *Primates*, 26, 258–299.

Chapter 11

Cognitive development in chimpanzees: A trade-off between memory and abstraction?

Tetsuro Matsuzawa

Editors' Preview

Chapter 11, 'Cognitive development in chimpanzees: A trade-off between memory and abstraction?', presents a complex picture of similarities and differences between developing chimpanzees and humans and their emerging cognitive abilities. Even though humans are nearly 99% chimpanzee in terms of shared DNA, and both species undergo extensive postnatal development, it is also the case that humans develop a brain that is three times the size of the chimpanzee brain. While both human and chimp infants receive extensive parenting, many human infants are reared by an extended network of caregivers (inclusive of parents, grandparents, and child-care workers), whereas chimp infants are reared exclusively by their mothers.

Although motor development is rapid in both human and chimp infants, human infants have an advantage in terms of remaining stable when in a supine posture, thereby freeing hands for object manipulation, which in turn may contribute to humans' greater sophistication at tool usage. Still, developing chimps do learn to use tools, even to the point where they are coordinating up to three objects (e.g. stones) to operate on a fourth object (e.g. removing food from a nut). Notably, while tool-use behaviours are learnt in chimps, there is no explicit instruction; the learning occurs on the basis of imitating an observed model.

Attempts have been made to teach chimps language, but with limited success. Vocabularies attained have been modest in size and slow in acquisition rate when compared to humans. In addition, chimpanzees have not shown evidence of grammatical rule use or speech sound production. Nevertheless, the few studies that have examined how language affects cognition in chimps have shown similarities with how language affects cognition in humans, thereby linking with the themes of Chapter 6. For example, chimps with different amounts of language-training experience sort colours into category-like clusters (resembling those of human colour categories), but greater language experience seems to produce more stable classification performance. This finding is consistent with the idea that language can help to secure the boundaries on the cognitive structures that are provided by perception. In addition, there seems to be overlap in the perceptual categories formed by human and chimp infants, with both groups demonstrating the ability to form broad, global category distinctions (e.g. mammals vs. vehicles).

Chimpanzees have also demonstrated that they possess some of the conceptual machinery for representing number, thereby providing a foretaste of the information to be presented in Chapter 13. For example, chimps can learn the ordinal properties of numbers (i.e. representing the numerical order of things in a set) as well as their cardinality (i.e. the number of things in a set). Chimps further possess an extraordinary capacity for remembering numerals, comprehending many numerals in a single glance, surpassing even the performance of adult humans.

Chapter 11 offers speculation that the strong, near-photographic memory of chimps for number may be one manifestation of a more general characteristic of a representational system that provides extraordinarily detailed records of visual scenes. Such a system may be viewed as adaptive in a cognitive niche in which rapid, categorical decisions need to be made about objects encountered (e.g. ripe vs. unripe food, friend vs. foe). By contrast, the human cognitive niche emphasizes linguistic description of events that capture an abstract gist which can be communicated to others. In this sense, chimps may be likened to humans with autism who display weak central coherence (i.e. an eye for detail, but without the corresponding big-picture idea).

Recent advances in the study of the human and chimpanzee genome (The Chimpanzee Sequencing and Analysis Consortium, 2005) have revealed that chimpanzees are the closest evolutionary living relatives of humans. The difference in the DNA between the two is only about 1.23%. In other words, humans are 98.77% chimpanzee. This genetic difference is comparable to that between horses and zebras, estimated to be about 1.5% (Walner et al., 2003). You may think that zebras are horses that have black and white stripes. If so, you should then also think that chimpanzees are humans that have long black hair on their bodies.

The chimpanzee is classified as a member of order primates, family *Hominidae*, genus *Pan*, while humans are members of the order primates, family *Hominidae*, genus *Homo*. Chimpanzees belong to the family of hominoid, both in the biological classification and also in conventions such as Convention on International Trade in Endangered Species (CITES). It must also be noted that humans are one of 350 or so primate species. Thus, the comparison of the human primate with other primate species may be the best way to understand human nature and to answer questions such as 'What is uniquely human?' or 'Where did we come from?'.

Humans have a large brain (about three times as large as that of chimpanzees). However, the postnatal growth of the brain is roughly the same in humans and chimpanzees. The neonatal brain of the two species triples in size before reaching adult size (3.26 times in humans and 3.20 times in chimpanzees). This suggests that chimpanzees may experience similar cognitive developmental changes as humans. Chimpanzees learn through experience during postnatal development, as do humans. The cognitive world of the infant chimpanzee (see Figure 11.1) is markedly different from that of juveniles, adolescents, and adults, which is why we need to study not only chimpanzee cognition, but also the developmental changes of cognitive abilities (Matsuzawa, 2007; Matsuzawa et al., 2006).

The stable supine posture hypothesis: an evolutionary basis of language and tool use

A long socialization process is not uniquely human, but is a unique characteristic of hominoids (i.e. humans and apes). Fieldwork has helped to shed light on the life history of chimpanzees (Emery-Thompson et al., 2007). The life span of wild chimpanzees is about 50 years. Weaning is also earlier in humans in comparison to chimpanzees and other great apes. Chimpanzee infants suckle until they are at least 4–5 years old. The average inter-birth interval is 5–6 years in chimpanzees, longer than in humans. In other words, during the first 5–6 years, the infant monopolizes the mother. There are no siblings separated by only 2 or 3 years; yet, this is a popular age gap in human societies. The chimpanzee mother–infant relationship is characterized by the rearing of a single offspring at any one time by the mother only – a situation

Fig. 11.1 Chimpanzee mother and a 2-month-old baby.
Photo by Tomomi Ochiai.

resembling the case of the single mother. On the contrary, the human mother–infant relationship is characterized by the rearing of multiple children simultaneously, with the assistance of multiple caretakers. Children are looked after not only by the mother but also the father, grandparents, aunts, and helpers, and in many cases aided even by a wide network of community support. Humans are a prosocial and collaborative breeding species.

Humans rear multiple children at one time. Thus mothers cannot hold the immature infant all the time. The physical separation of mother and infant immediately after birth is a unique feature of humans. Human infants can be stable in a supine posture, while great ape infants cannot. The human infant has a relatively high level of fat content, with about 20% of body weight consisting of fat. This may be partly due to adaptation to the cold temperature at ground level in the savannah, in a new niche of hominids such as *Australopithcus* and *Homo* spp. In contrast, the chimpanzee infant has very little fat content: only 4% of their body weight is comprised of fat. For at least the first 3 months of their lives, chimpanzee infants are never separated from the mother. In contrast, human infants are physically separated from their mother from the very first day. Clinging-embracing is the characteristics of primate (especially simian) mother–infant relationship in general (reported in Matsuzawa, 2007). However, human mothers do not always carry their infants, but must sometimes put the baby down. Human neonates (less than 2 weeks of age) have several innate responses, such as clinging (Moro's reflex), grasping, rooting, and sucking. However, human infants cannot actually cling to the mother by him/herself, in contrast to chimpanzee neonates.

In sum, humans are characterized by putting the babies on the back immediately after birth. The mother–infant relationship in humans is somewhat unique in terms of collaborative breeding, physical separation, stable supine posture, and early weaning compared to other hominoids. These characteristics may lead to the uniquely human way of communication and tool use.

Many people still believe that bipedal upright posture and bipedal locomotion are uniquely human, and the ultimate cause for human cognitive evolution. According to this explanation, when quadripedal creatures stood up, their hands were free to manipulate objects. However, human infants do not start to stand up bipedally until around 1 year old, but clearly there is cognitive development before this age. Early cognitive development is of course important. In recent publications, we have proposed the hypothesis of stable supine posture as the important cause of human evolution (Matsuzawa, 2007; Takeshita, 2009).

Chimpanzee infants, as well as orangutan infants, cannot assume a stable supine posture when they are laid on their back. They slowly lift up one arm and the contralateral leg, then a few seconds later, they switch both arms and legs and lift those on the opposite side. The alternation in limb movement suggests that this is not a stable posture for them – ape infants need to cling to the mother. The stable supine posture leads to a great deal of face-to-face communication, including looking into each other's eyes, smiling, waving, and vocal exchange. Chimpanzee infants never cry at night: they have no need to do so as they are constantly embraced by the mother. Human infants, on the other hand, are often physically separated from the mother during both day and night, and receive a lot of allomothering behaviour from family members. The importance of the supine posture in terms of tool use is not well recognized. When supine, an individual's hands are free from clinging. Although bipedalism starts at around 1 year of age, it is the stable supine posture beginning right after birth that frees the infant's hands and facilitates a much earlier onset of object manipulation in a uniquely human fashion.

Cognitive development in chimpanzees in the wild

The study of chimpanzees helps us understand the evolutionary foundations of human nature. Each chimpanzee community in the wild has its own unique set of cultural traditions (McGrew, 1992; Whiten et al., 1999). Chimpanzees seem to pass on knowledge and skills from one generation to the next. Our studies have focused on tool use and cultural behaviour in the chimpanzees of Bossou, Guinea, West Africa (Biro et al., 2003).

The chimpanzees at Bossou are known to use a pair of stones as hammer and anvil to crack open the hard shells of oil-palm nuts to obtain the edible kernel (Figure 11.2). In addition to stone-tool use, the Bossou chimpanzees' repertoire of tool manufacture and use includes a variety of unique examples such as pestle-pounding, algae-scooping, hyrax-toying, the use of folding leaves for drinking, the use of leaves as cushions, and so on (Matsuzawa, 1999). These tool-use behaviours are limited to the Bossou community. Ant-dipping is known in several communities across Africa. However, if you look carefully at the target ant species, the material of the tool, the length of the tool, and the technique of using the tool, there are features unique to each community (Humle & Matsuzawa, 2002).

Thanks to the ongoing efforts of many colleagues, we have continued to illustrate the unique aspects of the material and social culture of the Bossou chimpanzees. In addition to traditional ways of carrying out fieldwork, we have also established a

Fig. 11.2 Bossou chimpanzee use stone tools to crack open oil-palm nuts to get the edible kernel inside the hard shell.

Photo by Etsuko Nogami.

unique way of studying chimpanzee cognition in the wild. We refer to this approach as 'field experiments' for tool use (Matsuzawa, 1994). We created an open-air 'laboratory' for analysing many aspects of stone-tool use in close detail. In the core part of the chimpanzees' ranging area, we set up a laboratory site by laying out stones and nuts. We then simply waited for chimpanzees to pass by and use the objects provided. Here, stone-tool use could be directly observed and videotaped. This experimental set-up allows us to analyse the details of chimpanzee tool use.

Let us focus on the concepts that appear through object manipulation. Field experiments show that tool use can be classified into several levels by focusing on how the objects are related to each other (Matsuzawa, 1996). At around 2 years of age, wild chimpanzees start to acquire 'level-1 tool use' – relating one object to another – such as ant-fishing, algae-scooping, and use of leaves for drinking water. Almost all of chimpanzee tool use in the wild can be classified into this level-1 tool.

At around 4 years of age, chimpanzees start to show 'level-2 tool use' – relating three objects in a hierarchical fashion – such as using two mobile stone tools for cracking nuts. For example, in stone-tool use, they place a nut on the anvil stone, and then hit it with a hammer stone to crack the hard shell and get the edible kernel within. Thus, there are two nodes to relate the objects in a hierarchical way.

At around 6 years of age, they develop 'level-3 tool use' – relating four objects in a hierarchical order – such as the use of a wedge stone to stabilize the anvil stone, where the nut is placed, and then hitting the nut with a hammer stone. There is no clear evidence that the chimpanzees can reach level-4 tool use or even more. There seems to be a limit on how many objects they are able to combine in a hierarchical order.

In contrast, humans can develop hierarchical combinatorial manipulations to infinite levels. Humans also use meta-tools, that is, tools for making or using another tool. There must be a meta–meta-tool to utilize the meta-tool, and so on. Human technology is characterized by the self-embedding and recursive structure of tool use (Greenfield, 1991; Hayashi, 2007; Matsuzawa, 1991, 1996). The tree-structure analysis of the action grammar of manipulating objects may tell us the similarity of cognitive behaviour between humans and chimpanzees (Matsuzawa, 1996; Hayashi, 2007).

It takes time to learn the tool-use repertoire unique to each chimp community. There is a uniquely chimpanzee way of social learning that we have called 'education by master–apprenticeship' (Matsuzawa et al., 2001). Education by master–apprenticeship is characterized by: (1) prolonged exposure based on the mother–infant bond; (2) no teaching (no formal instruction, and no positive/negative feedback from the mother); (3) intrinsic motivation of the young to copy his/her mother's behaviour; and (4) high tolerance of the mother towards her infant.

In sum, there is no active teaching in chimpanzees. They do not show the moulding or prompting found in human teaching. The mothers and the adult members simply show the right model while the apprentice has the strong intrinsic motivation to copy the model. It is also important to know that there is very little evidence of social referencing in chimpanzees (Ueno & Matsuzawa, 2005). In contrast, much of human learning occurs in the context of a triadic interaction of mother–infant–object. Rich social referencing is uniquely human. Chimpanzee learning is characterized by the dyadic interaction of the infant and the target objects, without the referential model, even though they carefully watch other chimpanzees' behaviour.

From the study of ape language to comparative cognitive science

Wolfgang Köhler (1925) and Ladygina-Kohts (1935, 2002) carried out pioneering work in comparing the development of chimpanzee infants with that of human infants. Other early attempts also focused on human-rearing chimpanzees in a home setting, and teaching spoken language to chimpanzees (Hayes, 1951; Hayes & Hayes, 1952; Kellogg & Kellogg, 1933).

In parallel to the rise of fieldwork in Africa in the 1960s (Goodall, 1986; Nishida, 1990), there was a corresponding attempt to understand the chimpanzee mind in the laboratory. These were called 'ape-language studies': researchers tried to teach American sign language (ASL) or corresponding visual symbols to home-reared chimpanzees (Fouts & Mills, 1998, Gardner & Gardner, 1969; Premack, 1971; Savage-Rumbaugh et al., 1993; Terrace, 1979), gorillas (Patterson, 1978), and to an orangutan (Miles, 1990). The ape-language paradigm was later extended to the parrots, dolphins, dogs, etc.

At present, almost three decades later, we can summarize the results of ape-language studies from the 1960s to the 1980s as follows: it is clear that chimpanzees and other great apes can master language-like skills to some extent. However, there are clear constraints on their ability to demonstrate the semantics, syntax, phonetics, and pragmatics central to human language.

Regarding semantics, chimpanzees can learn the use of symbols, such as ASL, plastic signs, letters, or Arabic numerals to represent each object, colour, number, and so on. However, their ability is limited in several ways. The number of signs or 'words' learned is several hundred at most and never exceeds 1000. The acquisition rate of words does not increase but reaches a plateau in the apes, while it increases exponentially in humans.

Regarding syntax, chimpanzees show very little evidence of learning grammatical rules. The apes seldom used multiple signs in communicative contexts except the simple repetition of the same signs within their repertoire. The mean length of 'utterances' (MLU) is less than two and even in the case of multiple sign use, there is no clear evidence of syntactical rule use. This kind of grammatical constraints of symbol use is paralleled by the constraints found in object use (Matsuzawa, 1996). For example, chimpanzees seldom use the subassembly strategy when combining multiple objects (Greenfield, 1991; Hayashi, 2007).

Regarding phonetics, no research has succeeded in making apes use their vocal tract to produce various sounds, although humans and chimpanzees share the common developmental process of laryngeal descent (Nishimura et al., 2005).

Regarding pragmatics, the language-like skills mastered by apes has faced criticism by Terrace and others. The apes often showed imitation of the human signers and showed replication of same signs (Terrace, 1979).

The year 1978 was an important moment for changing the paradigms and the trends used for studying the chimpanzee mind. One crucial event was the landmark paper published by Premack and Woodruff (1978), entitled 'Do chimpanzees have a theory of mind?'. They coined the term 'theory of mind'; that is, the ability to understand the other's mind. Since then, there have been many publications on the social aspects of chimpanzee mind (Byrne & Whiten, 1988; Call & Carpenter, 2001; Hare et al., 2000; Povinelli & Eddy, 1996; Tomasello, 1998; de Waal, 1982). The theory-of-mind issues also entered into the studies on human cognitive development (Baron-Cohen et al., 1985; Wimmer & Perner, 1983).

Another key moment in 1978 was the creation of a research paradigm called comparative cognitive science (CCS). We started the long-running project known as the Ai project in 1978. CCS is the combined study of psychophysics and ape-language, using computer-controlled apparatus. The original form of CCS aimed to compare the perception, memory, and cognition of humans and closely related species, such as chimpanzees, using the same method, the same apparatus, and the same procedure.

Psychophysics is the classic psychological discipline of measuring human sensation, perception, memory, and cognition in general. Psychophysics tried to find the relationship between psychological events and the physical events. The research methods have been refined in the past 100 years. Psychophysics has established many laws such as Weber-Fechner's law and Steven's power law. There are many established methods to measure the relationship between the presented stimuli and the corresponding internal psychological states. Thus, psychophysics can be extended to study the issues related to concept formation.

CCS applied psychophysical methods to understand the chimpanzee mind. A series of studies began with the chimpanzee Ai when she first touched a keyboard on April 15th, 1978. Ai was the first chimpanzee who learned to discriminate the 26 letters of the alphabet. The letters were then used to quantitatively compare her visual acuity with that of humans, to assess her perception of shapes, and to investigate the other-races effect in chimpanzees (Matsuzawa, 1990).

Ai also mastered visual symbols such as Kanji (Japanese–Chinese characters) for the abstract concept of colour. Then, colour naming and classification could be directly compared with that of humans, using identical materials and testing methods (Matsuzawa, 1985a). In humans, there is a universal aspect of colour classification regardless of the cultural background. It seems that this kind of universality, so-called basic colour terms, should be extended to the chimpanzee too. Ai had intensive experience of using colour names (Sousa & Matsuzawa, 2004, see Figure 11.3). In a recent study, we compared a language-trained chimpanzee (Ai) and a naïve chimpanzee (Pendesa) in a colour-classification task (Matsuno et al., 2004; 2006). We tested these chimpanzees on the classification of 124 colours on the cathode ray tube (CRT) monitor. The two subjects exhibited a similar tendency of classifying the colours into some clusters. However, there was a clear difference between the two: Ai produced consistent colour classification significantly more often (65% of the test colours) than did Pendesa (45%). Thus, intensive experience in colour naming may refine categorical colour recognition in chimpanzees.

Ai is also the first chimpanzee who mastered the use of Arabic numerals to represent numbers (Matsuzawa, 1985b). She learned both cardinal and ordinal aspects of the

Fig. 11.3 Chimpanzee Ai is performing the symbolic matching to sample of colour. She can choose the corresponding colour name written in Kanji (Japanese–Chinese characters) when a colour is presented on a monitor.

Photo by Tetsuro Matsuzawa.

number system: she used numerals to label the number of real-life items such as 'five red toothbrushes' shown in a display window. She also mastered how to touch Arabic numerals in ascending order, even including the numeral '0' (Biro & Matsuzawa, 1999, 2001). Her numerical knowledge was further used for testing her short-term memory (Kawai & Matsuzawa, 2000). In the CCS approach, studies did not focus on teaching human language to the apes. There is little concern about the communication between humans and chimpanzees through language-like skills. Instead, CCS focused on testing the perceptual and cognitive skills of humans and nonhuman animals using the same apparatus, following the same procedure (Fujita & Matsuzawa, 1990; Hayashi & Matsuzawa, 2003; Matsuzawa, 2001, 2003; Tomonaga & Matsuzawa, 2002; Tomonaga et al. 1993).

Chimpanzee cognitive development as shown by participation observation

Numerous studies have examined chimpanzee cognition in captivity with regard to such capacities as tool use, insightful problem solving, and rudimentary forms of collaboration. However, very little literature has paid attention to developmental changes in chimpanzee cognition. To address this deficit, a research paradigm was developed to study cognitive development (Matsuzawa et al., 2006) known as 'participation observation'. In this study, we followed the course of three infants born in the year 2000. These chimpanzee infants were raised by their biological mothers. The researchers observed the behaviour of the chimpanzee mother–infant pairs and tested them through participation in their everyday life. Thanks to the long-term relationship between the mother and the human researchers, we were able to test the cognition of infant chimpanzees with the assistance of the mother chimpanzees (Figure 11.4). The three mother–infant pairs are members of a community of 14 chimpanzees consisting of three generations living in an enriched environment. This is important, because we

Fig. 11.4 Participation observation, a unique way to test the cognitive development of infant chimpanzees with the assistance of the chimpanzee mothers. A tester is opening his mouth to elicit neonatal imitation in the infant chimpanzee. A tiny video camera recorded the facial expression of the infant.

Photo by Nancy Enslin.

need to provide social contexts equivalent to ones in the wild to understand cognitive development.

Chimpanzee infants preferred a straight gaze to an averted gaze (Myowa-Yamakoshi et al., 2003), and could utilize gaze cues (Okamoto et al., 2002). Mutual gaze is also marked between mothers and infants (Bard et al., 2005). In parallel to their gaze preference, chimpanzees also developed a preference for their mother's face (Myowa-Yamakoshi et al., 2005). In the first month of life, the chimpanzee infants did not show any special preference for his/her own mother's face. However, they developed a significant preference to their mother's face when they were 1–2 months old. This preference later disappeared.

Infant chimpanzees start to move away from their mothers for brief periods at around 3–4 months old. They start exploring the outer world and interacting with other members of the community at this point. Chimpanzee infants first show object–object manipulation, the precursor of tool use, at the age of 10 months (Hayashi & Matsuzawa, 2003). The first tool use, using a probing tool to get honey through a small hole, was recorded at slightly earlier than 2 years old in the three infants studied (Hirata & Celli, 2003). Participation observation revealed that the developmental change in object manipulation and tool use correspond to that observed in their natural habitat (Biro et al., 2003; Inoue & Matsuzawa, 1997).

We also explored the rudimentary form of concept formation or categorization in infant chimpanzees using object manipulation and looking time (Murai, 2006; Murai et al., 2006). Human infants display complex categorization abilities (Mareschal & Quinn, 2001). We utilized the object-categorization test based on the familiarization–novelty preference. In sum, humans (10–24 months) and chimpanzees (10–23 months) showed a similar ability to form categorical representation in terms of the familiarization–novelty task, although the chimpanzees' performance was closer to that of younger infants (10–17 months). This kind of similarity based on the perceptual concept is also found in spontaneous object-sorting behaviour (Spinozzi, 1993; Spinozzi et al., 1998).

In sum, chimpanzees showed similar cognitive development to humans, especially in the first 10 months of life (Tomonaga et al., 2004). However, the developmental process must be different from that of humans in some key respects. The following section focuses on a unique feature of chimpanzee cognition in comparison to humans.

Working memory of numerals in chimpanzees

The chimpanzee mind has been extensively studied and the general assumption is that it is inferior to that of humans (Premack, 2007). However, Inoue and Matsuzawa (2007) showed for the first time that young chimpanzees have an extraordinary working-memory capability for numerical recollection. It was better than that of human adults tested on the same apparatus following the same procedure. The subjects of the study were six chimpanzees, three mother–offspring pairs.

In 2004, when the three young chimpanzees reached the age of 4 years, the mother–offspring pairs started to learn the sequence of Arabic numerals from 1 to 9, using a touch-screen monitor connected to a computer. In the numerical sequence task, each trial was unique; the nine numerals appeared in different locations on the screen. Accurate performance with 1-2-3-4-5-6-7-8-9 spontaneously transferred to nonadjacent sequences such as 2-3-5-8-9. All naïve chimpanzees successfully learned this numerical-sequence task.

A memory task called the 'masking task' was introduced around the time when the young chimps reached 5 years old. In this task, after touching the first numeral, all other numerals were replaced by white squares. The subject had to remember which numeral appeared in which location, and then touch them in the correct ascending order. All five naïve chimpanzees mastered the masking task just like Ai (Kawai & Matsuzawa, 2000). It must be noted that the chance level of this task is extremely low: $p = 1/24$ for 4 numerals, $1/120$ for 5 numerals, ... $1/362\,880$ for 9 numerals, etc.

In general, the performance of the three young chimpanzees was better than that of the three mothers. Ayumu, the son of Ai, was the best performer among the three subjects (Figure 11.5). Response times in human adults were slower than in the three young chimpanzees.

Next, we invented a new test called the 'limited-hold memory task'. This is a novel way of comparing the working memory of chimpanzee and human subjects in exactly the same way. In this task, after touching the initial white circle, the numerals appeared only for a certain limited duration, and were then automatically replaced by white squares. We tested both chimpanzees and humans on three different hold-duration conditions: 650, 430, and 210 ms. The duration of 650 ms was equivalent to the average initial latency of the five-numeral masking task described above. The shortest duration, 210 ms, is close to the frequency of occurrence of human saccadic eye movement. This condition does not leave subjects enough time to explore the screen by eye movement. The limited-hold memory task provided a means of performing an objective

Fig. 11.5 Chimpanzee Ayumu performing the memory task of Arabic numerals.
Photo by Tetsuro Matsuzawa.

comparison between the two species under exactly identical conditions. We compared Ai (the best mother performer), Ayumu (the best young performer), and humans subjects ($n = 9$, all were university students) on this task.

Figure 11.6 shows the results of the comparison between the two chimpanzees and human subjects in the limited-hold memory task. The number of numerals was limited to five items. For example, the numerals 2, 3, 5, 8, 9 might appear very briefly on the screen and then be replaced by white squares. Subjects had to touch the squares in the correct ascending order indicated by the original numerals.

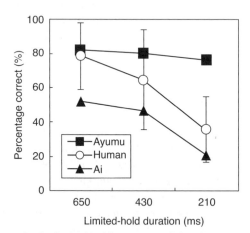

Fig. 11.6 Performance in the limited-hold memory task by Ai, Ayumu, and human subjects ($n = 9$, the bars represented the SD). X-axis shows the three different limited-hold durations tested; percentage of trials correctly completed under each condition is shown on the Y-axis. Each session consists of 50 trials. Each chimpanzee received 10 sessions and each of nine humans received a single test session. Post hoc tests revealed that Ayumu's performance did not change as a function of hold duration, whereas Ai and the human subject's performance decreased with shorter duration lengths.

See the details in Inoue, S. & Matsuzawa, T. (2007). Working memory of numerals in chimpanzees. *Current Biology*, **17**, R1004–R1005.

In human subjects, the percentage of correct trials decreased as a function of hold duration: the shorter the duration became, the worse the accuracy was. Ai's performance was below that of the human subjects' average, but stayed within the range of human variation and showed the same tendency of decrement. However, from the very first session, Ayumu's performance remained at almost the same level irrespective of hold duration, and showed no decrement. These data clearly show that chimpanzees can memorize, at a glance, Arabic numerals scattered on the touch-screen monitor and that Ayumu outperformed all of the human subjects both in speed and accuracy. Video clips of the task can be found at http://www.pri.kyoto-u.ac.jp/ai/.

The results may be reminiscent of the phenomenon known as 'eidetic imagery' found by a German psychologist, Jaensch (1930). Eidetic imagery has been defined as the memory capability to retain an accurate, detailed image of a complex scene or pattern. It is known to be present in some human children, and then the ability declines with age.

Ayumu was not the only one to show this extraordinary ability. The other two young chimpanzees also showed the same remarkable memory capability. Young chimpanzees have a working-memory capability for numerical recollection which is better than that of human adults.

The trade-off between memory and abstraction

Why do chimpanzees have better immediate memory than humans? One plausible explanation is as follows. The data can be interpreted according to an evolutionary trade-off hypothesis. The common ancestor of humans and chimpanzees may have possessed an extraordinary memory capability, much like that exhibited by Ayumu. At a certain point in evolution, because of limitations on brain capacity, the human brain may have acquired new functions in parallel with losing others – such as acquiring language while losing the visuo-spatial temporal storage ability shown in the present task.

Previous studies have revealed that there are some other cognitive tasks in which chimpanzee performance exceeds human performance. Chimpanzees are good at identifying pictures of faces presented upside down, while this is very difficult for humans (Tomonaga et al., 1993). Chimpanzees are also good at voice–face matching-to-sample tasks, in which a chimpanzee's voice is presented as a sample and then the subject has to choose the photo of the vocalizer among the alternatives. This is also a very difficult task for human subjects (Izumi & Kojima, 2004; Martinez & Matsuzawa, 2009). In sum, chimpanzees are good at tasks that seem to have ecological validity for them.

It is important for wild chimpanzees to recognize things at a glance. Suppose that a chimpanzee arrives at a huge fig tree. Where are the ripe red fruits? Where are the dominant males? It is essential to get this kind of information at a glance in order to choose the right place for gathering figs. Another example: suppose the chimpanzees encounter the neighbouring community when they are patrolling the boundary of their territory. It is important to know how many opponent chimpanzees are hidden in the bush, and how many allied chimpanzees are on his side.

In contrast, humans may have developed a different kind of cognitive capability, focusing on conceptualization, or establishing abstract concepts. Suppose you watched a creature quickly pass in front of you. You may realize that its body was covered with brown hair, it had a white spot on the forehead, and a black part on the right front leg. This may be one (useful) way of seeing things in the world. However, there might also be a different way to view things in the world. Based on the complete features you just saw, you may sum up the information to label the creature as a 'horse'. This kind of representation may work because it can save memorizing the details and also generalize the experience to similar encounters in the future.

In the movie 'Rain Man', Dustin Hoffman played an autistic person who can immediately recognize the number of matches scattered on the floor. It is amazing to witness this kind of extraordinary ability. However, it is not clear what the advantage of having this kind of memory in our daily life is. It is probably better to have a representation of the scene that neglects the details, but to have the capability of communicating about that scene with other members of the community. Communication must have been more important than immediate memory in the social life of early hominids. Humans are creatures who can learn from the experiences of the others.

The trade-off theory makes sense not only in phylogeny but also in ontogeny. In humans, youngsters can be better than adults on certain memory tasks. For example, for chimpanzee-like memory tasks such as remembering cards upside-down, human children can be better than human adults. In the course of cognitive development, human children may acquire linguistic skills while losing their chimpanzee-like photographic memory. This may be due to the time lag of myelination of neuronal axons in each part of the brain. It is known that the association cortex that is responsible for complex representation and linguistic skills develops more slowly than the other primary areas. Further study on the mind–brain relationship will illuminate this kind of trade-off across phylogeny and ontogeny.

Acknowledgements

The present study was financially supported by grants from MEXT (#16002001, 20002001), as well as by the following grants: JSPS Global COE program for biodiversity (A06), JSPS International training program HOPE. I would like to thank my colleagues, students, caretakers, veterinarians, administration staff, and chimpanzees at the Primate Research Institute of Kyoto University. Special thanks are due to Masaki Tomonaga, Masayuki Tanaka, and Misato Hayashi. I am also very grateful to Michiko Sakai, Sumiharu Nagumo, Sana Inoue, Tomoko Takashima, and Suzuka Hori for their help with the laboratory study. Without their efforts, I could not continue our study of chimpanzees in KUPRI. I also acknowledge the help by our field assistants in Bossou, Seringbara, and Yeale in West Africa. Thanks are also due to the government of the Republic of Guinea, especially the DNRST (Direction Nationale de la Recherche Scientifique et Technologique) and IREB (Institut de Recherche Environmentale de Bossou), and the government of Côte d'Ivoire.

References

Bard, K., Myowa-Yamakoshi, M., Tomonaga, M., Tanaka, M., Costall, A., & Matsuzawa, T. (2005). Group differences in the mutual gaze of chimpanzees (*Pan troglodytes*). *Developmental Psychology*, **41**, 616–624.

Baron-Cohen S., Leslie A. M., & Frith U. (1985). Does the autistic child have a 'theory of mind'? *Cognition*, **21**, 37–46.

Biro, D., Inoue-Nakamura, N., Tonooka, R., Yamakoshi, G., Sousa, C., & Matsuzawa, T. (2003). Cultural innovation and transmission of tool use in wild chimpanzees: Evidence from field experiments. *Animal Cognition*, **6**, 213–223.

Biro, D. & Matsuzawa, T. (1999), Numerical ordering in a chimpanzee (*Pan troglodytes*): Planning, executing, monitoring. *Journal of Comparative Psychology*, **113**, 178–185.

Biro, D. & Matsuzawa, T. (2001). Use of numerical symbols by the chimpanzee (*Pan troglodytes*): Cardinals, ordinals, and the introduction of zero. *Animal Cognition*, **4**, 193–199.

Byrne, R. & Whiten, A. (Eds) (1988). *Machiavellian Intelligence: Social Expertise and the Evolution of Intellect in Monkeys, Apes, and Humans* New York: Oxford University Press.

Call, J. & Carpenter, M. (2001). Do apes and children know what they have seen? *Animal Cognition*, **4**, 207–220.

Emery-Thompson, M., Jones, J.H., Pusey, A.E., et al. (2007). Aging and fertility patterns in wild chimpanzees provide insights into the evolution of menopause. *Current Biology*, **17**, 1–7.

Fouts, R. & Mills, S. T. (1998). *Next of Kin: My Conversations with Chimpanzees* New York: Harper Paperbacks.

Fujita, K. & Matsuzawa, T. (1990). Delayed figure reconstruction by a chimpanzee (*Pan troglodytes*) and humans (*Homo sapiens*). *Journal of Comparative Psychology*, **104**, 345–351.

Gardner, R. A. & Gardner, B. T. (1969). Teaching sign language to a chimpanzee. *Science*, **165**, 664–672.

Goodall, J. (1986). *The Chimpanzees of Gombe: Patterns of Behavior* Cambridge, MA: Harvard University Press.

Greenfield, P. (1991). Language, tools, and brain: The ontogeny and phylogeny of hierarchically organized sequential behavior. *Behavioral and Brain Sciences*, **14**, 531–595.

Hare, B., Call, J., Agnetta, B. & Tomasello, M. (2000). Chimpanzees know what conspecifics do and do not see. *Animal Behavior*, **59**, 771–785.

Hayashi, M. (2007). A new notation system of object manipulation in the nesting-cup task for chimpanzees and humans. *Cortex*, **43**, 308–318.

Hayashi, M. & Matsuzawa, T. (2003). Cognitive development in object manipulation by infant chimpanzees. *Animal Cognition*, **6**, 225–233.

Hayes, C. (1951). *The Ape in Our House* New York: Harper.

Hayes, K. J. & Hayes, C. (1952). Imitation in a home-raised chimpanzee. *Journal of Comparative Psychology*, **45**, 450–459.

Hirata, S. & Celli, M. (2003). Role of mothers in the acquisition of tool-use behaviours by captive infant chimpanzees. *Animal Cognition*, **6**, 235–244.

Humle, T. & Matsuzawa, T. (2002). Ant-dipping among the chimpanzees of Bossou, Guinea, and some comparisons with other sites. *American Journal of Primatology*, **58**(3), 133–148.

Inoue, S. & Matsuzawa, T. (2007). Working memory of numerals in chimpanzees. *Current Biology*, **17**, R1004–R1005.

Inoue-Nakamura, N. & Matsuzawa, T. (1997). Development of stone tool-use by wild chimpanzees (*Pan troglodytes*). *Journal of Comparative Psychology*, **111**(2), 159–173.

Izumi, A. & Kojima, S. (2004). Matching vocalizations to vocalizing faces in a chimpanzee (*Pan troglodytes*). *Animal Cognition*, **7**, 179–184.

Jaensch, E. R. (1930). *Eidetic Imagery and Typological Methods of Investigation*, 2nd edn., (trans. Oscar Oeser) New York: Harcourt, Brace and Co.

Kawai, N. & Matsuzawa, T. (2000). Numerical memory span in a chimpanzee. *Nature*, **403**, 39–40.

Kellogg, W. N. & Kellogg, L. A. (1933). *The Ape and the Child: A Comparative Study of the Environmental Influence Upon Early Behavior* New York: Hafner Publishing Company.

Köhler, W. (1925). *The Mentality of Apes* New York: Harcourt, Brace.

Ladygina-Kohts, N.N. (2002). *Infant Chimpanzee and Human Child: A Classic 1935 Comparative Study of Ape Emotions and Intelligence* New York: Oxford University Press.

Mareschal, D. & Quinn, P.C. (2001). Categorization in infancy. *Trends in Cognitive Science*, **5**, 443–450.

Martinez, L. & Matsuzawa, T. (2009). Effect of species-specificity in auditory-visual intermodal matching in a chimpanzee *(Pan troglodytes)* and humans. *Behavioural Processes*, **82**, 160–163.

Matsuno, T., Kawai, N., & Matsuzawa, T. (2004). Color classification by chimpanzees (*Pan troglodytes*) in a matching-to-sample task. *Behavioural Brain Research*, **148**, 157–165.

Matsuno, T., Kawai, N., & Matsuzawa, T. (2006). Color recognition in chimpanzees (*Pan troglodytes*). In T. Matsuzawa, M. Tomonaga, & M. Tanaka (Eds.), *Cognitive Development in Chimpanzees*, pp. 317–329, Tokyo: Springer.

Matsuzawa, T. (1985a). Color naming and classification in a chimpanzee (*Pan troglodytes*). *Journal of Human Evolution*, **14**, 283–291.

Matsuzawa, T. (1985b). Use of numbers by a chimpanzee. *Nature*, **315**, 57–59.

Matsuzawa, T. (1990). Form perception and visual acuity in a chimpanzee. *Folia Primatologica*, **55**, 24–32.

Matsuzawa, T. (1991). Nesting cups and meta-tool in chimpanzees. *Behavioral and Brain Sciences*, **14**(4), 570–571.

Matsuzawa, T. (1994). Field experiments on use of stone tools by chimpanzees in the wild. In R. Wrangham, W. C., McGrew, F. B. M. de Waal, & P.G. Heltne (Eds.), *Chimpanzee Cultures*, pp. 351–370, Cambridge, MA: Harvard University. Press.

Matsuzawa, T. (1996). Chimpanzee intelligence in nature and in captivity: Isomorphism of symbol use and tool use. In W. McGrew, L.F. Marchant, & T. Nishida (Eds.), *Great Ape Societies*, pp. 196–209, Cambridge: Cambridge University Press.

Matsuzawa, T. (1999). Communication and tool use in chimpanzee: Cultural and social contexts. In M. Hauser & M. Konishi (Eds.), *The Design of Animal Communication*, pp. 645–671, Cambridge, MA: MIT Press, 645–671.

Matsuzawa, T. (Ed.) (2001). *Primate Origins of Human Cognition and Behavior* Tokyo, Japan: Springer-Verlag.

Matsuzawa, T. (2003). The Ai project: Historical and ecological contexts. *Animal Cognition*, **6**, 199–211.

Matsuzawa, T. (2007). Comparative cognitive development. *Develpmental Science*, **10**, 97–103.

Matsuzawa, T., Biro, D., Humle, T., Inoue-Nakamura, N., Tonooka, R., & Yamakoshi, G. (2001). Emergence of culture in wild chimpanzees: Education by master-apprenticeship. In T. Matsuzawa (Ed.), *Primate Origins of Human Cognition and Behavior*, pp. 557–574, Tokyo, Japan: Springer.

Matsuzawa, T., Tomonaga, M., & Tanaka, M. (2006). *Cognitive Development in Chimpanzees* Tokyo: Springer.

McGrew, W. C. (1992). *Chimpanzee Material Culture: Implications for Human Evolution* Cambridge: Cambridge University Press.

Meltzoff, A. N. & Moore, M. K. (1977). Imitation of facial and manual gestures by human neonates. *Science*, **198**, 75–78.

Miles, L. (1990). The cognitive foundations for reference in a signing orangutan. In S.T. Parker & K.R. Gibson (Eds.), *'Language' and Intelligence in Monkeys and Apes*, pp. 511–539, Cambridge: Cambridge University Press.

Mizuno, Y., Takeshita, H., & Matsuzawa, T. (2006). Behavior of infant chimpanzees during the night in the first four months of life: Smiling and suckling in relation to behavioral state. *Infancy*, **9**, 215–234.

Murai, C. (2006). Early spontaneous categorization in primate infants – chimpanzees, humans, and Japanese macaques – with the familiarization-novelty preference task. In T. Matsuzawa, M. Tomonaga, & M. Tanaka (Eds.), *Cognitive Development in Chimpanzees*, pp. 279–304, Tokyo: Springer.

Murai, C., Kosugi, D., Tomonaga, M., Tanaka, M., Matsuzawa, T., & Itakura, S. (2005). Can chimpanzee infants (*Pan troglodytes*) form categorical representations in the same manner as human infants (*Homo sapiens*)? *Developmental Science*, **8**, 240–254.

Myowa-Yamakoshi, M., Tomonaga, M., Tanaka, M., & Matsuzawa, T. (2003). Preference for human direct gaze in infant chimpanzees (*Pan troglodytes*). *Cognition*, **89**, 113–124.

Myowa-Yamakoshi, M., Tomonaga, M., Tanaka, M., & Matsuzawa, T. (2004). Imitation in neonatal chimpanzees (*Pan troglodytes*). *Developmental Science*, **7**(4), 437–442.

Myowa-Yamakoshi, M., Yamaguchi, M., Tomonaga, M., Tanaka, M., & Matsuzawa, T. (2005). Development of face recognition in infant chimpanzees (*Pan troglodytes*). *Cognitive Development*, **20**, 49–63.

Nishida, T. (1990). *The Chimpanzees of the Mahale Mountains* Tokyo: University of Tokyo Press.

Okamoto, S., Tomonaga, M., Ishii, K., Kawai, N., Tanaka, M., & Matsuzawa, T. (2002). An infant chimpanzee (*Pan troglodytes*) follows human gaze. *Animal Cognition*, **5**, 107–114.

Patterson, F. G. (1978). The gestures of a gorilla: Language acquisition in another pongid. *Brain and Language*, **5**, 72–97.

Povinelli, D. J. & Eddy, T. J. (1996). What young chimpanzees know about seeing. *Monographs of the Society for Research on Child Development*, **61**(247), 1–189.

Premack, D. (1971). Language in chimpanzees? *Science*, **172**, 808–822.

Premack, D. (2007). Human and animal cognition: Continuity and discontinuity. *Proceedings of the National Academy of Sciences of the USA*, **104**, 13861–13867.

Premack, D. & Woodruff, G. (1978). Does the chimpanzee have a theory of mind? *Behavioral and Brian Sciences*, **1**, 515–526.

Ross, C. (2002). Park or ride? Evolution of infant carrying in primates. *International Journal of Primatology*, **22**, 749–771.

Rumbaugh, D., Gill, T. V., & von Glasersfeld, E. (1973). Reading and sentence completion by a chimpanzee. *Science*, **182**, 731–733.

Savage-Rumbaugh, S., Murphy, J., Sevcik, R. A., Brakke, K. E., Williams, S. L., & Rumbaugh, D. (1993). Language comprehension in ape and child. *Monographs of the Society for Research in Child Development*, (Ser 233) **58**, 1–252.

Sousa, C. & Matsuzawa, T. (2001). The use of tokens as rewards and tools by chimpanzees (*Pan troglodytes*). *Animal Cognition*, **4**, 213–221.

Spinozzi, G. (1993). Development of spontaneous classificatory behavior in chimpanzees (*Pan troglodytes*). *Journal of Comparative Psychology*, **107**, 193–200.

Spinozzi, G., Natale, F., Langer, J., & Schlesinger, M. (1998). Developing classification in action: II. Young chimpanzees (*Pan troglodytes*). *Human Evolution*, **13**, 125–139.

Takeshita, H., Myowa-Yamakoshi, M., & Hirata, S. (2009). The supine position of postnatal human infants: Implications for the development of cognitive intelligence. *Interaction Studies*, **10**, 252–269.

Terrace, H. (1979). *Nim* New York: Knopf.

The Chimpanzee Sequencing and Analysis Consortium. (2005). Initial sequence of the chimpanzee genome and comparison with human genome. *Nature*, **437**, 69–87.

Tomasello, M. (1998). Emulation learning and cultural learning. *Behavioral and Brain Sciences*, **21**, 703–704.

Tomonaga, M., Itakura, S., & Matsuzawa, T. (1993). Superiority of conspecific faces and reduced inversion effect in face perception by a chimpanzee. *Folia Primatologica*, **61**, 110–114.

Tomonaga, M. & Matsuzawa, T. (2002). Enumeration of briefly presented items by the chimpanzee (*Pan troglodytes*) and humans (*Homo sapiens*). *Animal Learning and Behavior*, **30**, 143–157.

Tomonaga, M., Tanaka, M., Matsuzawa, T., et al. (2004). Development of social cognition in infant chimpanzees (*Pan troglodytes*): Face recognition, smiling, gaze, and the lack of triadic interactions. *Japanese Psychological Research*, **46**(3), 227–235.

Ueno, A. & Matsuzawa, T. (2005). Response to novel food in infant chimpanzees: Do infants refer to mothers before ingesting food on their own? *Behavioral Processes*, **68**, 85–90.

de Waal, F. (1982). *Chimpanzee Politics: Power and Sex Among Apes* London: Jonathan Cape.

Walner, B., Brem, G., Muellwer, M., & Achman, R. (2003). Fixed nucleotide differences on the Y chromosome indicate clear divergence between *Equus prizewlskii* and *Equus caballus*. *Animal Genetics*, **34**, 453–456.

Whiten, A., Goodall, J., McGrew, W. et al. (1999). Cultures in chimpanzees. *Nature*, **399**, 682–685.

Wimmer, H. & Perner, J. (1983). Beliefs about beliefs: Representation and constraining function of wrong beliefs in young children's understanding of deception. *Cognition*, **13**, 103–128.

Chapter 12

Categorization and concept formation in human infants

Barbara A. Younger

Editors' Preview

Chapter 12, 'Categorization and concept formation in human infants', reviews the literature on the categorization abilities of human infants. Given that one cannot verbally query infants about their classification skills, investigators have made use of looking-time or manual-exploration procedures that rely on an inherent preference for novelty. Infants are presented with multiple instances from a common category (in the form of two-dimensional [2D] images or small three-dimensional [3D] toy replicas) and then with a novel instance from the familiar category and a novel instance from a novel category. Categorization is inferred if infants generalize responsiveness to novel instance from the familiar category and display differential responsiveness to the novel instance from the novel category.

Investigations following this logic have provided evidence support-ing the idea that infants have core cognitive processes at their dis-posal (see also Chapter 13) which allow them to form representations for at least one of the major types of categories discussed in the volume as a whole, namely, similarity-based categories. One core categorization process is that of prototype abstraction. For example, infants presented with exemplars from a category and subsequently with a preference test pairing the novel prototype from the familiar-ized category with a previously seen exemplar from the familiarized category will display a paradoxical novelty preference for the previ-ously seen exemplar (indicating that the novel prototype was actually recognized as more familiar). A second core categorization process possessed by infants is the ability to process correlations among attributes. For instance, infants presented with two groups of sche-matic animals marked by different bundles of correlated attributes (e.g. those with feathers and ears vs. those with fur and antlers) will generalize to novel exemplars that preserve the attribute correlations, but respond differentially to novel exemplars that break the attribute correlations (e.g. instances with feathers and antlers).

Looking-time procedures (as well as object-manipulation procedures that assess whether infants touch objects from the same category in succession or engage in actions appropriate to the objects) have also produced evidence suggesting that infant category representations start out as broadly inclusive and become more exclusive with development. Thus, infants may start out with representations at a superordinate or global level (e.g. animals or prototypic mammals), with representations at an intermediate or basic level (e.g. cats, horses) and subordinate level (e.g. Siamese cats) emerging subsequently. There is also some evidence to suggest that once the different levels of representation become available, a certain primacy may accrue to the intermediate level.

Chapter 12 further reviews some of the issues that are lively sources of debate among theorists and investigators of infant categorization. For example, there is the question of whether the experimental procedures used with infants are revealing category representations that are formed online during the course of an experiment or are alternatively tapping into category representations that existed prior to the start of the procedure. There is also the related question of whether infants are forming their category representations based on bottom-up perceptual processing of the surface attributes of the stimuli or whether the representations are based more on a top-down conceptual understanding of the 'kind of thing' presented. A further associated issue is how the beginning category representations of infants give rise to the more mature conceptual representations of children and adults. Two empirical phenomena that may bear on these debates include the existence of performance asymmetries (i.e infants prefer category *B* after familiarization with category *A*, but do not prefer category *A* after familiarization with category *B*) and whether experiences occurring initially for infants at home may influence their subsequent performance in laboratory-based categorization tasks.

The ability to recognize perceptually distinct entities as the same kinds of things and to treat them as such is fundamental to intelligent behaviour. Research examining categorization in human infants now spans over three decades. In the preverbal infant, 'treating different entities as the same kinds of things' traditionally has been operationalized through patterns of looking behaviour – categorization is inferred when infants generalize habituated levels of looking to a novel instance of a familiarized category and/or increase their looking to a novel exemplar from a different category.

Much of the evidence regarding categorization in infants thus derives from visual-familiarization/preference-type procedures. In a typical study, infants are shown multiple exemplars of a single experimenter-defined category over a series of discrete trials (e.g. 12 cat images might be presented over six trials). Infants then are presented (using a paired-comparison test format or over successive trials) with novel instance(s) of the familiarized category (e.g. a different cat) as well as novel exemplar(s) from a different category (e.g. a dog or bird). Longer looking at item(s) from the contrast category is regarded as evidence of categorization. In older infants, nonverbal categorization may be operationalized differently, for example, through sequences of touches to varied items within a category, relative to items that cross a category boundary. Several variants of both looking time and object-manipulation procedures have been used in the infant-categorization literature. Details of these procedures are provided as needed in this selective review of the literature.

Adult-categorization researchers (Chapter 3 and Chapter 14, this book) make distinctions between rule-based and similarity-based categories. This review follows the empirical emphasis in the human infant literature in its focus on similarity-based categories. The use of the terms category, category (or categorical) representation, and concept also reflect common usage in the infancy literature, and deviate somewhat from that defined at the outset of this book. In keeping with Murphy (Chapter 2), the term category generally is used here to refer to sets of objects or entities in the world (and to sets of exemplars presented to infants in studies of categorization). Infants' mental representations of those sets of objects generally are referred to as category (or categorical) representations. This is intended as a theoretically neutral term that could refer to representations that are primarily perceptual in nature, as well as representations that begin to reflect conceptual understanding (equivalent to concept; Chapter 2). In this chapter, the term concept (when applied to infants) is used in a theory-specific fashion to refer to mental representations that are specifically conceptual in nature (Mandler, 2004).

The chapter begins with a discussion of core processes yielding structured category representations in infancy. It then turns to the content of infants' category representations, with an emphasis of the level of inclusiveness of infants' object categories. Next comes an issue that is perhaps unique to the human infant literature, arising to some degree from the methods used to assess categorization in young infants. Are the category representations revealed in studies of categorization represented a priori in the mind of the infant (and brought to bear on the task at hand), or are category representations formed or 'trained' in the context of the task? Much of the evidence presented in the chapter suggests that infant's early category representations are perceptually grounded (thus, easily supported by associative similarity-based learning). The chapter concludes by addressing the relationship between the infant's early similarity-based representations and more mature concepts.

Structured category representations

In this section, the focus is on core categorization processes supporting two key structural features of infants' category representations: typicality gradients and correlated attributes. Several years ago, Rosch (1978; Mervis & Rosch, 1981) argued persuasively for a graded notion of everyday concepts. A category like bird, for example, was said to consist of elements that have unequal status: a robin is more central to, or prototypical of, its category than is an ostrich or a penguin. Rosch also highlighted the correlational structure of natural object categories. Creatures with feathers, for example, are very likely to have wings and beaks; those with fur tend instead to have legs and mouths. In the following review, the focus is on evidence that even the youngest of human category learners exhibit typicality gradients in their categorical representations, followed by evidence that infants represent correlations among attributes and form correlation-based categories.

Graded category representations

Based on studies using artificial categories, it has been argued that infants under a year of age are able to generate an internal, graded representation based on experience with varied instances of category. Throughout much of the first year, infants (much like adults) demonstrate prototype effects in their categorization of novel stimuli (Bomba & Siqueland, 1983; Quinn, 1987; Strauss, 1979; Younger, 1990; Younger & Gotlieb, 1988). Presented with varied exemplars of a category (i.e. distortions of prototypical dot patterns; faces or animals having discrete values along some set of continuous dimensions), infants routinely recognize the previously unseen prototype over a member of a novel category. Under most conditions of category exposure, infants also recognize the prototype (or prototypical exemplars) over nonprototypical category members, including the specific items presented to the infant during category familiarization. This pattern obtains under varied conditions of category familiarization, including extended familiarization time with a small set of exemplars (Sherman, 1985; Younger, 1990; for an exception, see Quinn, 1987). In the Sherman and Younger studies, individual items were presented repeatedly until infants demonstrated a novelty preference for the next item in the familiarization sequence. Despite being 'forced' to attend to differences among the individual items during category familiarization, infants treated the previously unseen prototype as more familiar than the nonprototypical exemplars they had just seen.

Focusing on natural object categories, Quinn (2002) proposed that the nature of infants' category representations might vary as a function of prior experience with category members. Specifically, a demonstrated asymmetry in very young infants' categorization of humans versus nonhuman animals (Quinn & Eimas, 1998) was said to reflect differing representations: a broad, exemplar-based representation of humans (reflecting the beginnings of an 'expert' representation) and a narrower, summary-level representation or prototype for generic object categories (including species of non-human animals). Support for the proposal came from a study in which 3–4-month-old infants were familiarized either with pictures of 12 humans or 12 cats. Following familiarization, infants were given two paired-preference tests. In one, a novel human was paired with a novel cat (as a test of categorization). In the other, a novel member of the familiarized category was paired with an exemplar taken from the familiarization set (as test of exemplar memory). Infants familiarized with cats demonstrated standard prototype effects: they looked longer to the human than to a novel cat (a typical novel category preference), but they did not distinguish new and old exemplars of the familiarized category. Infants familiarized with humans showed a very different pattern of looking at test. They did not prefer a novel cat to a novel human. They did, however, exhibit exemplar memory, looking longer to a novel human than to one that had been included in the familiarization set. Either as a function of exposure to large numbers of humans (outside the experimental context) or as a function of extended interactions with a small number of humans, infants' representation of humans presumably had expanded beyond prototypes to form a cognitive reference region in representational space (Quinn, 2002).

Sensitivity to correlated attributes

As noted above, correlated attributes figured prominently in Rosch's intuitions about the structure of natural object categories as well as the psychological 'privilege' of basic-level categories (Mervis & Rosch, 1981; Rosch, 1978). By Rosch's view, an organism able to detect and represent clusters of correlated attributes is capable of categorization. Correlational learning also figures prominently in recent computational approaches to concept development (e.g. Mareschal & French, 2000; Rakison & Lupyan, 2008; Rogers & McClelland, 2005).

Infants under a year of age have been shown to be sensitive to correlations among attributes (Younger, 1990; Younger & Cohen, 1983, 1986; Younger & Fearing, 1998). The properties involved in the initial studies were static appearance features. Typically, sets of whimsical animals were shown to infants in the familiarization phase of a habituation task. In each study, the set of familiarization stimuli featured pairs (or trios) of correlated attributes. For example, creatures with feathered tails had ears; those with furry tails had antlers (Younger, 1990). Following familiarization, infants demonstrated their encoding of the feature relation by generalizing habituated levels of looking to a novel stimulus that maintained the experienced pattern of correlation (e.g. another creature with a feathered tail and ears) and by increasing their looking to a stimulus that violated the pattern of correlation (a creature with a feathered tail and antlers).

Infants have also been shown to spontaneously parse exemplars into correlation-based categories having graded representations (Younger, 1985). The stimuli in this case were cartoon animals that assumed one of five discrete values along each of the four continuous dimensions. There were two stimulus conditions: in one, values on one dimension could combine with the full range of values on other dimensions (broad familiarization condition); in the other, values on one dimension were predictive of values on other dimensions (narrow familiarization condition). Thus, in the broad condition, animals with short legs had either short or long necks, thick or thin tails, etc. In the narrow condition, animals with the shorter legs always had the longer necks and thicker tails (and vice versa). The critical question was how infants would respond (in a visual paired-comparison test trial) to a stimulus that contained values that represented the average along each of the four dimensions. As predicted, infants in the broad condition regarded the average stimulus to be familiar, suggesting that they had formed a single category represented by an average prototype (Strauss, 1979). In contrast, infants in the narrow condition treated the average stimulus as the more novel one (relative to a stimulus comprised of more extreme values on each dimension). In this case, the nonaverage stimulus was representative of one of the two correlation-based categories. The average stimulus belonged to neither category (essentially, it fell at the boundary between the two categories). Infants in the narrow condition thus appeared to have spontaneously parsed exemplars into two separate categories.

With increased age – presumably as a function of increasingly sophisticated information-processing abilities – infants become attentive to and encode a broader range of properties and property relations (Oakes & Madole, 2003; Rakison & Lupyan, 2008). Findings from Rakison and Poulin-Dubois (2002) serve to illustrate the point. The investigators presented infants between the ages of 10–18 months with video displays depicting geometric (bug-like) figures traversing the display screen. A range of properties (static and dynamic) and property relations were evident in the displays. Although 10-month-old infants were attentive to static appearance features of the depicted objects (body types), they appeared not to have processed differences in moving parts or in the motion trajectories as objects travelled across the display screen. By 14 months, infants clearly had encoded relations between the local movements of body parts and the motion trajectory of the object as a whole (i.e. whether the whole object followed a rectilinear or curvilinear path as it traversed the display screen). It was not until 18 months, however, that infants demonstrated their attentiveness to the full range of property relations (i.e. part–trajectory, object–trajectory, part–object, and part–object–trajectory relations).

Correlation-based learning appears to become increasingly constrained as well, presumably in a top-down fashion as infants gain experience with statistical regularities in the world (Rakison, 2005, 2006; Rakison & Lupyan, 2008). To illustrate, Madole and Cohen (1995) reported that in 14-month-olds, the encoding of part–form correlations in novel objects was largely unconstrained: infants demonstrated their sensitivity to the correlation whether the form of a particular part predicted the function of the same part or the function of a different part. In contrast, 18-month-olds were attentive to the correlation only when the form of the part predicted the function of the same part. The speculation was that the older infants were attentive to a type of relation that makes sense given their experience with objects in the real world.

Using computational modelling, Rakison and Lupyan (2008) obtained evidence of a comparable trajectory as networks gained experience with correlations between specific features (of objects) and the object's role in causal events. As the networks gained experience, they progressed from showing no sensitivity to the correlation, to learning all relations (including those inconsistent with the training set), to learning only relations that were consistent with the original training set. Apparently, as networks (and presumably infants) build representations linking specific parts with specific causal roles, those representations begin to constrain future learning and generalization.

The discussion thus far has centred on core categorization processes in infancy. We have seen that even quite young infants are able to generate a summary representation that is graded in structure. As infants gain experience within a domain (e.g. human faces), they may progress towards broader, exemplar-based representations. We have seen as well that infants are able to form correlation-based categories. As their information-processing abilities improve, they gain access not only to static appearance features but also to dynamic features relating to function and to motion characteristics of objects. Correlation-based learning also appears to become increasingly constrained over time as emerging representations begin to constrain future learning and generalization. In the next section, the focus is shifted to the content of infants' early category representations.

Level of exclusivity of category representations

The level of exclusivity of children's first categories or concepts has been a focal issue in the study of categorization. Do infants first form category representations that are relatively narrow in scope (e.g. dog, chair), or are their first categories broader and more inclusive (animal, vehicle)? Arguing on several grounds that the basic level is more fundamental psychologically than categories at either a more superordinate or subordinate level, Rosch (1978; Rosch et al., 1976) set the stage for current debate in the infancy literature. Structurally, categories at the basic level were said to stand out as categories because they contain bundles of correlated attributes that tend not to overlap with other categories at the same level. The basic level also was said to be the level first named and understood by children (Anglin, 1977; Mervis & Crisafi, 1982).

In contrast to the basic-first assumption, Mandler (2004) has argued forcefully that infants' first concepts are at a broader, global level of differentiation (the term 'global' rather than 'superordinate' is used to emphasize that basic-level category representations are not nested within infants' broad concepts). Evidence offered in support of the global-first hypothesis initially came from studies using a sequential touching technique (Mandler & Bauer, 1988; Mandler et al., 1991). The task is one in which infants (generally between the ages of 12–24 months) handle objects rather than look at pictures. In the standard version of the task, infants are presented with arrays of eight objects – four exemplars from each of two classes. In a test of global categorization, the object arrays might include four scale-model animals (e.g. fish, bird, cat, frog) and four model vehicles (e.g. car, plane, boat, bus). In a test of basic categorization, the array might include four kinds of fish and four kinds of dogs (or four cars and four trucks). Typically, infants are given 2 min to explore the set of objects in any way they wish. The assumption is that infants will systematically touch objects in a way that indicates their awareness (or discovery) of a categorical contrast. Thus, the order of touches to particular objects is recorded. The inference that a child's behaviour in the task is category-driven is supported when sequences of touches to items from the same category (i.e. within-category 'runs') exceed sequence lengths expected by chance. The proportion of infants who categorize may then be used to determine whether infants of a particular age recognize a particular categorical contrast. The general finding has been that infants (as a group) attend to global category contrasts at a younger age than basic contrasts within a domain (Mandler et al., 1991).

The global-first hypothesis received additional support from patterns of inference assessed through the generalized imitation task (Mandler & McDonough, 1996, 1998). Upon recognizing that an instance (A) manifests property X, inductive inference entails first noticing similarities between (A) and a second instance (B) and then inferring that (B) must also share property X. In the generalized imitation task, infants (between the ages of 14 months and 24 months) interact with scale models like those used in the sequential touching task. In a baseline phase of testing, the infant is given two choice objects (e.g. cat and bus) and a prop (toy cup) to assess spontaneous enactments of the target property. In a subsequent modelling phase, the experimenter demonstrates the target property for the infant, using a modelling exemplar and prop (e.g. the toy cup is tipped to the face of a dog to model 'drinking'). Then, in the test phase of the procedure, the infant is once again given the pair of choice objects and the prop to assess generalized imitation. Infants' attempts to enact the target property are recorded along with their choice of object(s) for imitation. For example, if infants infer that a cat will drink, they should more often select the cat to imitate 'giving a drink'. Using this task, infants have been shown to extend properties broadly within domains, but generally not across domain boundaries (Mandler & McDonough, 1996, 1998; for an exception, see Rakison, 2003). Thus, toy animals (cat, bird, fish) are given drinks more frequently than are toy vehicles. Studies using the generalized imitation task also have yielded evidence that property extension narrows as children approach 2 years of age (Mandler & McDonough, 2000). Although younger infants are as likely to feed a bone to a bird as to a dog, for example, 2-year-olds tend to restrict their response to the member of the appropriate basic category.

In Mandler's (2004) view, these findings reflect the meanings objects have for infants. Mandler makes a clear distinction between percepts and concepts – between perceptual categorization (e.g. seeing the difference between dogs and cats) and conceptualization (i.e. having a conceptual understanding of the differences between them). She argues that the two processes often do not work in tandem for the infant and that different testing procedures used with infants emphasize one process over the other. Looking tasks in her view tend to emphasize perceptual categorization whereas object-manipulation tasks emphasize conceptual understanding. Thus, an infant might in one context (including visual-familiarization tasks) identify an object as a dog based on perceptual likeness to other dogs. In another context, the infant might choose to group the dog with other animals based on conceptual likeness. Although Mandler leaves open the possibility that basic categories may be special for the infant with regard to perceptual categorization (and the identification function of categories), she maintains that the basic level does not reflect a special level of conceptualization for the infant.

Mandler's (2004) claims regarding separate perceptual and conceptual categorization systems have been challenged on numerous grounds, as has the notion that picture-looking and object-manipulation tasks tap into different categorization systems (for in-depth discussion, the reader is referred to Rakison & Oakes, 2003; see also Quinn, 2004; Rakison & Lupyan, 2008). In fact, there is some evidence to suggest that pictures (as a form of symbolic artefact) are more readily linked to category knowledge than are model objects (Gelman et al., 2005). Over much of the child's first 2 years of life, model competence (defined as the child's understanding of the correspondence between model objects and their real-world counterparts) also appears to lag behind pictorial competence (DeLoache, et al., 2003; Younger & Johnson, 2006). Thus, caution may be warranted in drawing general conclusions about the child's emerging conceptual system based solely on evidence from the object-manipulation tasks.

Evidence favouring a global-to-basic (or broad-to-narrow) developmental progression has been obtained as well, however, in studies using visual-preference procedures with infants under a year of age. It has been known for some time that infants as young as 3–4 months of age are able to form either broad or narrow categorical representations, depending at least in part on the range of exemplars shown to infants during category familiarization. For example, presented with perceptually diverse images of mammals, infants form a category representation that includes novel mammals but excludes items of furniture (Behl Chadha, 1996). In contrast, presented with images of domestic cats only, 3–4-month-old infants form a narrow representation that includes novel cats but excludes other mammals (e.g. elephants, rabbits, dogs; Eimas & Quinn, 1994). This flexibility to categorize either at a broad or narrow level was not observed in infants under 3 months of age (Quinn & Johnson, 2000). Although 2-month-olds were shown to form a categorical representation for mammals that excluded items of furniture, they did not form a narrower representation for cats that excludes other mammals.

This global-to-basic sequence of category emergence had been predicted based on connectionist simulations (Quinn & Johnson, 1997, 2000; see also Rogers & McClelland, 2005). Inputs to the autoassociative networks were entirely perceptually based (they were derived from surface measurements of the mammal and furniture exemplars shown to infants). The observed pattern of progressive differentiation (i.e. the emergence of animal–furniture clusters first, followed by particular types of animals or items of furniture) likely reflected a confluence of properties shared by exemplars within domains as well as the salience or accessibility of large property differences (in relation to the initial state of network or to the young category learner). The authors speculate that, with increased experience, a basic-level superiority might replace the initial global superiority as representational resources become increasingly devoted to the basic level (Quinn & Johnson, 1997).

Younger and Fearing (1999, 2000) reported findings that may reflect an emerging basic-level superiority over the course of the child's first year of life. Rather than presenting infants with varied exemplars of a single category during the familiarization phase of a visual preference task, Younger and Fearing familiarized infants with varied exemplars of two categories (e.g. cat images on some trials, horse images on others). The question was whether infants would form a single-category representation inclusive of the range of exemplars presented during familiarization, or whether they would form two narrower representations (consistent with basic-like categories). In keeping with the broad-to-narrow pattern highlighted above, the answer depended on the specific categories presented. Although 7-month-olds responded to cats and cars as separate categories, there was no evidence to suggest that they did so for cats and horses (or cats and birds). Ten-month-olds, in contrast, did appear to have spontaneously parsed exemplars into the narrower categories, as indicated by novel-category preferences for close taxonomic relatives of each of the presented categories. Thus, in the sense that infants could have formed either a broad, inclusive categorical representation or two narrower representations, findings from the Younger and Fearing (1999, 2000; see also Younger, 1985) studies suggest a primacy for basic-level representations towards the end the child's first year (a time at which infants are beginning to comprehend, if not produce, words for basic categories).

Infants also exhibit (within the second year of life) the flexibility to categorize simultaneously at the global and basic level (Mareschal & Tan, 2007). In the standard eight-object version of the sequential touching task, infants are tested at one level or the other on a given trial (e.g. they are given four animals and four vehicles, or four fish and four cows). To allow for sequential touching to occur in a given trial at the global level of differentiation (animal–vehicle) and/or at the basic level within a domain, Mareschal and Tan (2007) modified the sequential touching task to include sets of 12 objects (e.g. three fish, three cows; three planes, three trucks). Individual infants exhibited different patterns of behaviour. In the sense that more infants categorized at the basic level only than at the global level only, there was some indication here as well of a primacy for the basic level (at age 18 months). In the sense that some infants exhibited evidence of categorization at both levels within a single trial, there was evidence as well of infants' flexibility to attend to categories at different levels of abstraction.

In summary, we have seen that the pattern of responding to broad contrasts at a younger age than narrower ones is evident in different task contexts across different age ranges. In visual-familiarization tasks, infants under a year of age form broad category representations at a younger age than narrower ones (Quinn & Johnson, 2000; Younger & Fearing, 2000). The same pattern has been reported between infants 1 and 2 years of age in studies utilizing object-manipulation techniques (Mandler & McDonough, 1996, 2000; Mandler et al., 1991). Other findings, however, indicate that 18-month-olds have the flexibility to categorize model objects simultaneously at both levels of abstraction (Mareschal & Tan, 2007).

Such findings have generated considerable debate in the infancy literature over the perceptual versus conceptual bases for early categorization (and the need to posit separate perceptual and conceptual categorization systems). It is often assumed that, in the context of visual-familiarization tasks, category representations are formed online as category exemplars are presented to the infant. As only perceptual information is presented, it may be assumed that the category representation is entirely perceptually based. In studies using object-manipulation tasks (sequential touching, generalized imitation), it is often assumed that the infant comes to the task with a category or conceptual representation (derived elsewhere) that guides behaviour in the task (Mandler, 2004). In the next section, evidence that bears more directly on these assumptions is examined.

Influence of prior representations

In this section, evidence is examined to determine that category or conceptual representations exist a priori in the mind of the infant and are brought to bear on performance in laboratory tasks, as well as the alternative that infants' category representations are, to a large extent, formed in the immediate context of the task at hand. To date, relatively few studies have directly addressed the issue. We do know that infants can rapidly form representations for new categories as exemplified through studies utilizing artificially constructed categories (Younger, 1985; Younger & Gotlieb, 1988), as well as novel categories drawn from 'natural kind' domains (e.g. black-and-white animals;

Ribar et al., 2004). We also know that infants sometimes discover alternative bases for categorization in the immediate context of the task at hand (Ellis & Oakes, 2006; Horst et al., 2009). However, when infants are presented with contrasts drawn from real-world categories (e.g. animal–vehicle, cat–horse, car–truck), it is often unclear whether (or the degree to which) prior representations influence infants' behaviour in the task. In this section, the focus is on two lines of evidence regarding the influence of prior representations on categorization in infants.

Asymmetries in early categorization

One particularly fruitful approach to the question has involved detailed examination of asymmetries in early categorization (Quinn, 2002). It is standard practice in studies of infant categorization to counterbalance the set of items shown to infants during category familiarization. If infants are to be tested with a contrast between categories A and B, half of the infants are familiarized with exemplars of A, half with exemplars of B. In most cases, there is no effect of familiarized category. Infants in both familiarization groups look longer at members of the novel category at test.

There have, however, been isolated reports of asymmetries in early categorization (e.g. Leinbach & Fagot, 1993; Quinn & Eimas, 1998; Quinn et al., 1993). Infants familiarized with members of category A, for example, may form a categorical representation for A that excludes members of category B. In contrast, infants familiarized with members of category B may include exemplars of A in their categorical representation of B. As detailed in the discussion that follows, the bases for particular asymmetries are revealing with regard to the influence of prior representations. In some cases, the evidence indicates that prior representations form the basis for the asymmetry. In other cases, the asymmetry emerges online, supported by infants' sensitivity to statistical properties of the perceptual input.

As discussed previously in this chapter (in the section on prototypes), an asymmetry demonstrated in young infants' categorization of humans and nonhuman animals is thought to reflect infants' prior experience with and representation of humans (Quinn, 2002). An asymmetry has been reported as well in infants' categorization of male and female faces (Leinbach & Fagot, 1993). In this case, the asymmetry appears to be supported by a preference for looking at female over male faces (Quinn et al., 2002). Evidence is accumulating that this response preference is supported by representations that are tuned through infants' prior experience with faces. First, it appears that the female face preference emerges over the early months of life: Although 3-month-old infants generally respond preferentially to female faces over male faces, newborn infants do not (Quinn et al., 2008). Second, the female-face preference appears to be specific to the race of the infant. Caucasian infants displayed a preference for female over male faces when the faces were Caucasian, but not when the faces were Asian (Quinn et al., 2008). Finally, there is some evidence to suggest that the direction of preference reflects the gender of the infant's primary caretaker (Quinn, 2002). Although the sample of infants was small, Quinn reported that infants reared by a male primary caretaker prefer male to female faces.

Moreover, examination of asymmetries in categorization provide compelling evidence of a largely bottom-up process operating in the early months of life when infants are presented with members of generic object categories. Presented with cat or dog images in a visual-categorization task, young infants have been shown to exclude dogs from their category representation for cat, but to include cats in their representation for dog (Quinn et al., 1993). Importantly, the dog–cat asymmetry was shown not to reflect an a priori response preference favouring cat images over dog images. Rather, the evidence is strong that the asymmetry is supported by asymmetrical inclusion relationships for several surface features (e.g. head length, ear separation) of the cat and dog images (Mareschal et al., 2000). In effect, the authors argued based on their examination of property distributions that half of the cats used in the study could be categorized as dogs, though very few dogs could be categorized as cats. In a follow-up study the authors further demonstrated, both through computational modelling and behavioural testing with infants, that the asymmetry could be eliminated or reversed through manipulation of the stimulus images (French et al., 2004).

Following the logic that the cat–dog asymmetry in early categorization reflects a largely bottom-up process, Furrer and Younger (2005) argued that the decline or disappearance of the asymmetry likely reflects the emergence of top-down influences (i.e. prior representations) on categorization. Using cat and dog images shown previously to support an asymmetry both in 3–4-month-old infants' categorization and in computational modelling (Mareschal et al., 2000; Quinn et al., 1993), Furrer and Younger (2005) documented a shift from the asymmetric pattern evident in 4-month-olds (as well as 7–9-month-olds; Mareschal et al., 2004) to a fully symmetric pattern in 10-month-olds. Whether they were shown images of cats or dogs during category familiarization, 10-month-old infants formed category representations that included novel members of the familiarized category, but excluded members of the contrast category. The symmetric pattern was evident in 10-month-olds under varied familiarization conditions, including in-task exposure to very few category exemplars, leading to the suggestion that 10-month-olds' behaviour in the laboratory task was influenced by prior category representations. The plausibility of this argument rested in part on label-comprehension norms showing that 50% of infants between 10 and 11 months of age comprehend the words 'dog' and 'kitty' (Fenson et al., 1994). The argument is further strengthened by recent experimental evidence showing that the labels 10-month-old infants hear can override the formation of correlation-based perceptual categories (Plunkett et al., 2008).

Experiential history of the child

A second approach to the question of the impact of prior representations on categorization is to focus on the experiential history of the individual category learner (Furrer & Younger, 2008; Kovack-Lesh et al., 2008; Quinn, 2002). As discussed in the previous section of this chapter, inferences assessed through the generalized imitation task have been offered in support of the view that infants and toddlers conceptualize objects at a global level of differentiation (Mandler, 2004). An infant's tendency to select a cat over a bus to 'give a drink' presumably is guided by a relatively stable conceptual representation akin to animal (or animate). Having been shown that one animal drinks, the infant infers that another animal (the cat) will drink as well. Likewise, infants will select a bird as readily as another dog to 'give a bone' because both the bird and dog fall within the infants' undifferentiated concept of animal.

Other investigators have argued for a more dynamic view of infants' performance in tasks assessing early categorization. Rather than reflecting a stable conceptual representation, infants' responses in the generalized imitation task are thought to emerge flexibly as a function of a variety of influences (Furrer & Younger, 2008; Rakison & Hahn, 2004). Focusing specifically on the short-term experiential history of the individual child, Furrer and Younger (2008) conducted an experimental training study. Prior to their participation in the generalized imitation task, 15-month-old infants were shown picture books designed to convey specific category–property relations (e.g. monkeys eat bananas, frogs eat bugs). Eight properties were used in the study, two aligned with each of four basic animal categories. Individual infants were trained on one property per category. Basic category labels were not provided, though verbal references were made to the target properties (e.g. 'Look! This one eats bugs' was offered in reference to photos depicting frogs and bugs). A brief delay followed training, and then infants were tested on two of the trained properties as well as two untrained properties (counterbalanced to ensure that specific properties aligned with each of the four categories served equally often as trained and untrained properties).

Prior exposure to particular category–property relations was shown to impact infants' behaviour in the generalized imitation task. In the absence of prior experience with a particular category–property relation, infants did tend to generalize broadly within the domain as reported by Mandler and McDonough (2000). Thus, despite having seen the experimenter model the target property using a single exemplar of the target category (e.g. pretending to feed a bug to one frog), infants extended the untrained properties broadly (i.e. they selected a novel monkey as often as a novel frog for their imitation).

Infants' performance for properties that had been included in their training set differed markedly. Having been exposed beforehand (in the training session) to evidence consistent with that presented in the modelling phase of the task, infants were much more likely to constrain their responses to members of the modelling category. These findings generally support the view that categorization occurs flexibly, at least within domains. The ease with which infants learned to link novel properties to particular basic-level kinds also draws into question the claim that behaviour in the task is guided by a broad, undifferentiated concept of animal.

Origin of concepts in infancy

The predominant focus in the infant-categorization literature has been on similarity-based categorization processes. From a very young age (likely from birth), infants exhibit core categorization processes that allow for organized and efficient storage and retrieval of category information. These core processes include prototype-formation abilities. Although infants are not able to provide us with judgements of 'best examples' of a category, their category representations do appear to reflect typicality gradients as reflected in their attention to prototypical versus nonprototypical category members (Strauss, 1979; Younger, 1990). As infants gain experience within a particular domain (e.g. humans), areas of representational space initially characterized by narrow prototype structures may expand to accommodate more detailed, exemplar-based representations (Quinn, 2002).

Infants also exhibit sensitivity to the clusters of correlated attributes that form the basis for many object categories (Younger, 1985; Younger & Cohen, 1986). More generally, we can characterize infants as excellent statistical learners. Within the realm of object categorization, the evidence reviewed indicated that the asymmetry in young infants' categorization of cat and dog images reflects, in part, asymmetric inclusion relations evident within the perceptual input (French et al., 2004; Mareschal et al., 2000). To elaborate somewhat, Mareschal and colleagues appeal to general associative learning mechanisms in combination with asymmetric properties of the perceptual input in their account of the cat–dog asymmetry. Associative learning mechanisms have also been shown to support the formation of simple correlation-based categories (Mareschal & French, 2000). Evidence of statistical learning in infants (and adults) is perhaps most evident in work that is outside the scope of this chapter, in the field of language acquisition (Gomez & Gerken, 2000; Maye et al., 2002; Saffran et al., 1996). It is important to note – in relation to the aims of this book – that the statistical learning mechanisms demonstrated in studies of speech perception with infants have been shown to operate both across modalities (Kirkham et al., 2002) and across species (Hauser et al., 2001). Statistical learning in general thus appears to be supported at least in part by general-purpose learning mechanisms.

Much of the evidence presented in this chapter suggests that infants' early categories are perceptually grounded and thus, easily supported by associative similarity-based learning. But what is the relation between these early similarity-based categories, and later concepts? For Mandler (2004), there is a fundamental difference. Infants' earliest category representations are grounded in the surface appearance of things: 3-month-old infants categorize cats as equivalent because they share appearance features with one another. Concepts, however, are stripped away from appearances and are based on a more abstract notion of kind (or meaning). The early concept of animal (or animate), for example, is derived through a process of perceptual meaning analysis that involves a re-description of dynamic perceptual information into a simpler, conceptual format. Animals (of all sorts) are understood, for example, as self-propelled entities that can serve as agents in causal events.

Many of us who study categorization in infants do not hold to the assumption that there is a principled distinction between perceptual and conceptual concepts (Madole & Oakes, 1999; Quinn et al., 2000). Although the specifics vary, alternative accounts of early concept development generally involve some kind of continuous process of representational enrichment grounded in a perceptual system that allows for the extraction of regularities in both static and dynamic properties of objects (e.g. Quinn & Eimas, 2000; Rakison & Lupyan, 2008). Much of the evidence reviewed in this chapter is consistent with this viewpoint (though the available evidence is often limited by the methods we employ in our laboratory studies). Consider again infants' categorization of cats and dogs. Presented with static images in the laboratory, young infants have been shown to form category representations that directly mirror the statistical properties of the input (i.e. the asymmetric inclusion relations of surface features of cats and dogs; French et al., 2004; Mareschal et al., 2000). Before the end of the child's first year, infants' category representations are no longer tied so closely to the input. In fact, very little input was required in the lab to support a categorical distinction in 10-month-olds between cat and dog (Furrer & Younger, 2005). At this point, we do not have a clear understanding of what happens in between, though it stands to reason that the richness of the experience infants are likely to have with members of these categories (encompassing not only static appearances but also the sounds they make, the behaviours they exhibit, the ways they move) are likely to be reflected in the concepts the child has formed by the end of the first year. In fact, there is now some evidence to suggest that for even quite young infants, experience with pets in the home can impact infants' categorization of cat and dog images in a laboratory task (Kovack-Lesh et al., 2008).

Perhaps the most detailed account to date of how a concept akin to 'animal', for example, can be grounded in perception is the one recently offered by Rakison and Lupyan (2008). The authors demonstrate the viability of a largely bottom-up approach to account for the child's growing recognition of the animate–inanimate distinction. They begin with the observation that categories of animate and inanimate entities in the world are sufficiently rich in structure to allow an associative learning mechanism to extract the relevant regularities from the input: animate and inanimate entities, for example, differ in the number of motion-related surface features. To get the system off the ground, the authors propose that the infant comes into the world with low-level perceptual biases that increase the salience of particular aspects of the perceptual array. As discussed previously in the chapter, attention to dynamic properties of objects increases in the child's second year of life, primarily as a function of developmental advances in information-processing abilities (memory capacity, speed of processing). Over time, new constraints on learning emerge as a product of prior learning (see Chapter 16, this book, for a related discussion regarding emerging constraints on word learning). By 18–24 months of age, associative mechanisms give rise to representations that reflect correlations among static and dynamic properties typical of animate and inanimate entities in the world. Through these representations, infants come to identify things in the world that are likely to exhibit self-propelled motion (Rakison, 2006), or things that are likely to serve as agents in causal events (Rakison, 2005).

What is uniquely human about concepts? From the perspective offered here, at least within the timeframe of the child's first 2 years, probably nothing. Early concepts are built from the bottom up, through associative processes that allow for the gradual and continuous elaboration of early, perceptually based category representations. Over time, infants' category representations may exhibit greater exclusivity and more top-down influence as prior experience and learning is brought to bear on subsequent attempts to organize and make sense of the world.

References

Anglin, J. M. (1977). *Word, Object and Conceptual Development* New York: W. W. Norton & Co.

Behl-Chadha, G. (1996). Basic-level and superordinate-like categorical representations in early infancy. *Cognition, 60*, 105–141.

Bomba, P. C. & Siqueland, E. R. (1983). The nature and structure of infant form categories. *Journal of Experimental Child Psychology*, **35**, 294–328.

DeLoache, J. S., Pierroutsakos, S. L., & Uttal, D. H. (2003). The origins of pictorial competence. *Current Directions in Psychological Science*, **12**, 114–118.

Eimas, P. D. & Quinn, P. C. (1994). Studies on the formation of perceptually based basic-level categories in young infants. *Child Development*, **65**, 903–917.

Ellis, A. E. & Oakes, L. M. (2006). Infants' flexibly use different dimensions to categorize objects. *Developmental Psychology*, **42**, 1000–1011.

Fenson, L., Dale, P. S., Reznick, J. S., Bates, E., Thal, D. J., & Pethink, S. J. (1994). Variability in early communicative development. *Monographs of the Society for Research in Child Development*, **59**(5), 1–189.

French, R. M., Mareschal, D., Mermillod, M., & Quinn, P. C. (2004). The role of bottom-up processing in perceptual categorization by 3-and 4-month-old infants: simulations and data. *Journal of Experimental Psychology: General*, **133**, 382–397.

Furrer, S. D. & Younger, B. A. (2005). Beyond the distributional input? A developmental investigation of asymmetry in infants' categorization of cats and dogs. *Developmental Science*, **8**(6), 544–550.

Furrer, S. D. & Younger, B. A. (2008). The impact of specific prior experiences on infants' extension of animal properties. *Developmental Science*, **11**(5), 712–721.

Gelman, S. A., Chesnick, R. J., & Waxman, S. R. (2005). Mother–child conversations about pictures and objects: Referring to categories and individuals. *Child Development*, **76**, 1129–1143.

Gomez, R. L. & Gerken, L. (2000). Infant artificial language learning and language acquisition. *Trends in Cognitive Sciences*, **4**, 178–186.

Horst, J. S., Ellis, A. E., Samuelson, L. K., et al. (2009). Toddlers can adaptively change how they categorize: Same objects, same session, two different categorical distinctions. *Developmental Science*, **12**(1), 96–105.

Kirkham, N., Slemmer, L., & Johnson, S. P. (2002). Visual statistical learning in infancy: Evidence for a domain general learning mechanism. *Cognition*, **83**, B35–B42.

Kovack-Lesh, K. A., Horst, J. H., & Oakes, L. M. (2008). The cat is out of the bag: The joint influence of previous experience and looking behavior on infant categorization. *Infancy*, **13**(4), 285–307.

Leinbach, M. D. & Fagot, B. I. (1993). Categorical habituation to male and female faces: Gender schematic processing in infancy. *Infant Behavior & Development*, **16**, 317–332.

Madole, K. L. & Cohen, L. B. (1995). The role of object parts in infants' attention to form–function correlations. *Developmental Psychology*, **31**, 637–648.

Madole, K. L. & Oakes, L. M. (1999). Making sense of infant categorization: Stable processes and changing representations. *Developmental Review*, **19**, 263–296.

Mandler, J. M. (2004). *The Foundations of Mind* New York: Oxford University Press.

Mandler, J. M. & Bauer, P. J. (1988). The cradle of categorization: Is the basic level basic? *Cognitive Development*, **3**, 247–264.

Mandler, J. M. & McDonough, L. (1996). Drinking and driving don't mix: Inductive generalization in infancy. *Cognition*, **59**, 307–335.

Mandler, J. M. & McDonough, L. (1998). Studies in inductive inference in infancy. *Cognitive Psychology*, **37**, 60–96.

Mandler, J. M. & McDonough, L. (2000). Advancing downward to the basic level. *Journal of Cognition and Development,* 1, 379–403.

Mandler, J. M., Bauer, P. J., & McDonough, L. (1991). Separating the sheep from the goats: Differentiating global categories. *Cognitive Psychology,* 23, 263–298.

Mareschal, D. & French, R. (2000). Mechanisms of categorization in infancy. *Infancy,* 1, 59–76.

Mareschal, D. & Tan, S. H. (2007). Flexible and context-dependent categorization by eighteen-month-olds. *Child Development,* 78, 19–37.

Mareschal, D., French, R. M., & Quinn, P. C. (2000). A connectionist account of asymmetric category learning in early infancy. *Developmental Psychology,* 36, 635–645.

Mareschal, D., Powell, D., & Volein, A. (2004). Basic-level category discrimination by 7-and 9-month-olds in an object examination task. *Journal of Experimental Child Psychology,* 86, 87–107.

Maye, J., Werker, J., & Gerken, L. (2002). Infant sensitivity to distributional information can affect phonetic discrimination. *Cognition,* 82, B101–B111.

Mervis, C. B. & Crisafi, M. A. (1982). Order of acquisition of subordinate, basic, and superordinate categories. *Child Development,* 53, 258–266.

Mervis, C. B. & Rosch, E. (1981). Categorization of natural objects. *Annual Review of Psychology,* 32, 89–115.

Oakes, L. M. & Madole, K. L. (2003). Principles of developmental change in infants' category formation. In D. H. Rakison & L. M. Oakes (Eds.), *Early Concept and Category Development: Making Sense of the Blooming, Buzzing Confusion,* pp. 132–158, New York: Oxford University Press.

Plunkett, K., Hu, J., & Cohen, L. B. (2008). Labels can override perceptual categories in early infancy. *Cognition,* 106, 665–681.

Quinn, P. C. (1987). The categorical representation of visual pattern information by young infants. *Cognition,* 27(2), 145–179.

Quinn, P.C. (2002). Beyond prototypes: asymmetries in infant categorization and what they teach us about the mechanisms guiding early knowledge acquisition. *Advances in Child Development and Behavior,* 29, 161–193.

Quinn, P. C. (2004). Multiple sources of information and their integration, not dissociation, as an organizing framework for understanding infant concept formation. *Developmental Science,* 7, 511–513.

Quinn, P. C. & Eimas, P. D. (1998). Evidence for a global categorical representation for humans by young infants. *Journal of Experimental Child Psychology,* 69, 151–174.

Quinn, P. C. & Eimas, P. D. (2000). The emergence of category representations during infancy: Are separate perceptual and conceptual processes required? *Journal of Cognition and Development,* 1, 55–61.

Quinn, P. C. & Johnson, M. H. (1997). The emergence of perceptual category representations in young infants: A connectionist analysis. *Journal of Experimental Child Psychology,* 66, 236–263.

Quinn, P. C. & Johnson, M. H. (2000). Global-before-basic object categorization in connectionist networks and 2-month-old infants. *Infancy,* 1(1), 31–46.

Quinn, P. C., Eimas, P. D., & Rosenkrantz, S. L. (1993). Evidence for representations of perceptually similar natural categories by 3-month-old and 4-month-old infants. *Perception,* 22, 463–475.

Quinn, P. C., Johnson, M. H., Mareschal, D., Rakison, D., & Younger, B. A. (2000). Response to Mandler and Smith: A dual process framework for understanding early categorization? *Infancy,* 1(1), 111–122.

Quinn, P. C., Yahr, J., Kuhn, A., Slater, A. M., & Pascalis, O. (2002). Representation of the gender of human faces by infants: A preference for female. *Perception,* 31, 1109–1121.

Quinn, P. C., Uttley, L., Lee, K., Gibson, A., Smith, M., Slater, A. M., & Pascalis, O. (2008). Infant preference for female faces occurs for same- but not other-race faces. *Journal of Neuropsychology,* 2, 15–26.

Rakison, D. H. (2003). Parts, categorization, and the animate-inanimate distinction in infancy. In D. H. Rakison & Oakes, L. M. (Eds.), *Early Concept and Category Development: Making Sense of the Blooming Buzzing Confusion* New York: Oxford University Press.

Rakison, D. H. (2005). A secret agent? How infants learn about the identity of objects in a causal scene. *Journal of Experimental Child Psychology,* 91, 271–296.

Rakison, D. H. (2006). Make the first move: How infants learn the identity of self-propelled objects. *Developmental Psychology,* 42, 900–912.

Rakison, D. H. & Hahn, E. (2004). The mechanisms of early categorization and induction: Smart or dumb infants? In R. Kail (Ed.), *Advances in Child Development and Behavior.* Vol 32, New York: Academic Press.

Rakison, D. H. & Lupyan, G. (2008). Developing object concepts in infancy: An associative learning perspective. *Monographs of Society for Research in Child Development,* 73(1), 1–110.

Rakison, D. H. & Oakes, L. M. (2003). *Early Concept and Category Development: Making Sense of the Blooming Buzzing Confusion* New York: Oxford University Press.

Rakison, D. H. & Poulin-Dubois, D. (2002). You go this way and I'll go that way: Developmental changes in infants' detection of correlations among static and dynamic features in motion events. *Child Development,* 73, 682–699.

Ribar, R. J., Oakes, L. M., & Spalding, T. L. (2004). Infants can rapidly form new categorical representations. *Psychonomic Bulletin & Review,* 11, 536–541.

Rogers, T. T. & McClelland, J. L. (2005). A parallel distributed processing approach to semantic cognition: Applications to conceptual development. In L. Gershkoff-Stowe & D. Rakison (Eds.), *Building Object Categories in Developmental Time,* pp. 335–387, Mahwah, NJ: LEA.

Rosch, E. H. (1978). Principles of categorization. In E. Rosch & B. Lloyd (Eds.), *Cognition and Categorization,* pp. 27–48, Hillsdale, NJ: Erlbaum Associates.

Rosch, E., Mervis, C. B., Gray,W., Johnson, M., & Boyes-Braem, P. (1976). Basic objects in natural categories. *Cognitive Psychology,* 8, 382–439.

Saffran, J. R., Aslin, R. N., & Newport, E. L. (1996). Statistical learning by 8-month-old infants. *Science,* 274, 1926–1928.

Sherman, T. (1985). Categorization skills in infants. *Child Development,* 56, 1561–1573.

Strauss, M. S. (1979). Abstraction of prototypical information by adults and 10-month-old infants. *Journal of Experimental Psychology: Human Learning and Memory,* 5, 618–635.

Younger, B. A. (1985). The segregation of items into categories by 10-month-old infants. *Child Development,* 56, 1574–1583.

Younger, B. A. (1990). Infant categorization: Memory for category-level and specific item information. *Journal of Experimental Child Psychology,* 50, 131–155.

Younger, B. A. & Cohen, L. B. (1983). Infant perception of correlations among attributes. *Child Development, 54*, 858–867.

Younger, B. A. & Cohen, L. B. (1986). Developmental change in infants' perception of correlations among attributes. *Child Development, 57*, 803–815.

Younger, B. & Fearing, D. (1998). Detecting correlations among form attributes: An object-examining test with infants. *Infant Behavior and Development, 21*, 289–297.

Younger, B. A. & Fearing, D. (1999). Parsing items into separate categories: Developmental change in infant categorization. *Child Development, 70*, 291–303.

Younger, B. A. & Fearing, D. (2000). A global to basic trend in early categorization: Evidence from a dual-category habituation task. *Infancy, 1*, 47–58.

Younger, B. A. & Gotlieb, S. (1988). Development of categorization skills: Changes in the nature or structure of infant form categories? *Developmental Psychology, 24*, 611–619.

Younger, B. A. & Johnson, K. E. (2006). Infants' developing appreciation of similarities between model objects and their real world referents. *Child Development, 77*, 1680–1697.

The making of an abstract concept: Natural number

Susan Carey

Editors' Preview

Chapter 13, 'The making of an abstract concept: Natural number', provides an account of how number concepts are acquired. Crucial to the account are: (1) core cognitive systems that enable representation of abstract numerical concepts; (2) qualitative change from the representations produced by the core cognitive systems to the more mature verbal concepts of numerical lists possessed by older children and adults; and (3) a learning mechanism which underlies that qualitative change and which allows a cognitive 'placeholder' structure to be created initially without numerical content, but which eventually allows that content to be 'bootstrapped' onto the placeholder structure.

One of the core cognitive systems allows for analogue representation in which number is represented by physical magnitude or quantity. This system is believed to have a long evolutionary history and behavioral evidence of it can be found in both nonhuman animals and human infants. The critical signature of such behavioural evidence is that numerical discriminations follow Weber's law (i.e. the two numbers being contrasted must exceed a certain ratio in order for them to be discriminated). Thus, for example, 7-month-old infants discriminate between arrays consisting of 8 versus 16 dots, but do not discriminate between contrasting arrays of 8 versus 12 dots. Notably, this signature exists for a range of stimulus classes including numbers of sounds and events (i.e. jump sequences), suggesting that the representations mediating the behavioural responses have an abstract nature.

A second core cognitive system (also believed to be present in nonhuman animals and human infants) allows for parallel individuation of small sets up to three in number. This system arises from the operation of working memory, which is believed to generate an object file for each individual item presented up to three. The evidence for such a system is provided by a behavioural signature (different from the Weber ratio marker of the analogue magnitude system) in which successful performance is observed for numerical operations within small sets up to three, but where performance breaks down for numerical operations involving comparison of a small set (three or less) with some larger set (four or more). For instance, 10- to 12-month-old infants will succeed in tasks involving comparisons between two versus three items, but fail in tasks comparing one versus four items.

Chapter 13 maintains that there is discontinuity between the numerical representations provided by the analogue magnitude and parallel individuation systems and the systems that underlie verbal list representation of positive integers (i.e. natural numbers, 1, 2, 3, 4, 5. . .). The analogue magnitude system even in its most mature form fails at ratios smaller than 8/9 and the parallel individuation system is limited to three items. Neither system can explain, then, an older child or adult's knowledge that 19 is exactly one more than 18.

The qualitative change that takes place in the changeover between numerical representations mediated solely by the core systems and representations that allow for verbal counting of successive positive integers occurs over a lengthy developmental period between 2–4 years of age. During this time, children transition from being 'subset knowers' in which 'one' is first distinguished from 'more than one', and then 'one' and 'two' are distinguished from each other and from 'more than two'. This progression continues up to 'one' versus 'two' versus 'three' versus 'four' versus 'more than four' at which point children make the move to being 'cardinal principle knowers', where they understand that the last word reached in a count represents the cardinal value in a set. The learning processes that underlie the shift include learning a list of meaningless lexical items (i.e. the count list) and attaching numerical content to each item.

A theory of human conceptual development must provide an empirically supported description of our innate representational resources. We must discover what features of the world evolution have endowed us with the capacity to encode. Even the most radical empiricists, and the most radical constructivists with propensities towards the leanest initial state, agree with nativists on this point. Learning is a computational process, and all computations require representations as input. At issue between empiricists and nativists is how *rich*, how *abstract*, the initial representational resources are. Classical empiricists such as Locke, and many modern empiricists as well, hypothesize that the initial representational resources are exhausted by sensory primitives – those features of the world detected by sense organs at the surface of the body. Piaget's innate sensorimotor schemata are similarly lean. Classical nativists, such as Descartes, and their modern descendants, such as Fodor, Chomsky, and Spelke, suggest that our innate endowment supports much richer and more abstract representations – such as *object, agent, number, depth, noun phrase,* and in a *reductio ad absurdum, carburator* (Fodor, 1975).

A theory of conceptual development must also provide an account of how later-developing conceptual resources differ from those that are part of the initial endowment. Are there discontinuities in conceptual development, and if so, what kinds? In what ways do later developing representational resources transcend their input? If discontinuities in development exist, they pose the ultimate challenge to theories of conceptual development: what learning mechanisms underlie the creation of representational resources more powerful than their input?

The above questions frame the controversies discussed in this book. With respect to developmental primitives, the question is whether nonhuman animals and preverbal infants represent abstract concepts, and if so, which ones? With respect to developmental discontinuity, the question is whether the conceptual repertoire changes in qualitative ways (e.g. from containing no abstract concepts of some specified type to containing many) either over evolutionary or ontogenetic time, and if so, the question is what kinds of mechanisms underlie those changes.

Here, I argue for three points: First, like many in this book (e.g. Chapters 6, 10 and 15), I deny that nonhuman animals or human infants lack the capacity to represent abstract concepts. In particular, I argue that the initial state includes several systems of core cognition with long evolutionary histories. Core cognition includes abstract concepts with conceptual content. Second, nonetheless, there are discontinuities in conceptual development at two different levels of generality. At a general level, most of human concepts differ from those embedded in core cognition in many ways, and at a specific level, core cognition does not have the resources to represent most specific abstract concepts. Third, I characterize one class of learning mechanism that underlies the discontinuities of interest – Quinian bootstrapping. With this analysis in hand, I speculate on some aspects of conceptual representations unique to humans.

Here, I illustrate these points with a single case study of the making of the human capacity to represent natural number (*natural* number is what mathematicians call the positive integers). See Carey (2009) for other case studies of core cognition: representations of objects and agents. My book also presents several other case studies of specific conceptual discontinuities, both within individual cognitive development and within the history of science: the acquisition of concepts of rational number, matter, weight, density, heat, temperature, gravity, and the mathematics of field theories.

The concept of natural number

Representations of number play a huge role in human mental life, as they are central to mathematics and science, as well as to modern commerce. Accounting for the origins of human numerical abilities seems to pose a formidable challenge. Number is a quintessential abstract entity. Piaget believed that numerical representations are built from logical capacities (the capacity for linear order and the capacity to represent sets), logical capacities that were not themselves constructed until the early elementary school years. Accordingly, he believed that children could not represent natural

number until then, and indeed, offered his famous work on number conservation as evidence for his view (Piaget, 1952).

An alternative to Piaget's position makes natural number representations themselves innate. The remark of the great constructivist mathematician Leopold Kronecker, 'The integers were created by God; all else is man-made' (cited in Weyl, 1949, p 33), can be taken to expresses a view of the *cognitive foundations* of arithmetical thought. If we replace *God* with *evolution*, the position would be that evolution provided us with an innate capacity to create symbols that express the cardinal values of sets of individuals. Let me be clear about this alternative. Obviously we have the *capacity* to construct (by adulthood) representations of natural number – this is obvious because what is actual is possible. The nativist position is that there is an innate computational machinery that operates on representations of sets of individuals that creates mental symbols for positive integers, and that such symbols have some computational role to play in infancy. Indeed, many modern cognitive scientists, most notably Rochel Gelman and Randy Gallistel, have argued for the continuity of integer representations throughout development (Gallistel & Gelman, 1992; Gelman & Gallistel, 1978).

Continuing to interpret Kronecker psychologically, he would be saying that all the rest of mathematics, including the rest of the number concepts (rational, negative, 0, real, imaginary, etc.), was culturally constructed by human beings, and may require conceptual change to be mastered by individuals.

The rest of this chapter argues that the facts support a third position. Continuity theorists are right: there are innate symbols with numerical content. But discontinuity theorists are also right: mature mathematical concepts are very unlike those in core cognition, which even lacks the capacity to form symbols with the content *natural number*. Finally, cognitive science is up to the challenge of characterizing the bootstrapping process that underlies this discontinuity.

Core cognition

The core cognition hypothesis is just that: an empirically falsifiable hypothesis that human infants are endowed with systems of representations with several distinctive properties: (1) the representations in core cognition are the output of innate, modular, input analysers; (2) the representations in core cognition are continuous throughout the life span; (3) systems of human core cognition have a long evolutionary history, and are often observed in other animals; (4) the format of representation of symbols in core cognition is most likely pictorial; and (5) the symbols that are the output of core cognition are conceptual in two distinct senses – they have a rich central conceptual role, interacting inferentially with the output of other systems of core cognition and with central conceptual representations such as causal ones, and they have abstract content that patently transcends the vocabulary of sensory and perceptual primitives.

Point 5 is worth dwelling on, for it is central to the concerns of this book. In several respects, the representations within core cognition are like paradigm perceptual representations, such as representations of depth (e.g. 1–4, above). Perceptual representations (representations that reflect constancies), like conceptual representations, also go beyond sensory representations, in that they represent the distal world. However, (point 5), the representations in core cognition are richer even than paradigmatic perceptual representations, in the ways specified above. There is core cognition of objects and their causal interactions, agents, and their goals, and of number, and representations in these domains interact centrally. These representations are abstract in that they encode entities of many different types (e.g. goals are attributed not only to people, but also to geometric figures interacting with each other in certain ways; numerical representations are computed over sets of objects, sounds, and events), and are conceptual in their rich central conceptual role, and the role they play in the acquisition of fully conceptual representations.

We must also recognize the ways that core cognition is perception like (properties 1–4), for it is these properties that underlie the general-level discontinuities between core cognition and humans' later-developing conceptual representations. Although conceptual in some respects, the representations in core cognition are utterly unlike later-developing conceptual representations. Take almost any linguistically encoded concepts you like: *wolf, virtue, cancer, oxygen, London*, and, I shall argue, *seven*. The format of these representations is not pictorial, they are not the output of innate input analyzers, they do not have a deep evolutionary history, and they are part of conceptual systems that are not continuous during development. That is, there are no innate representations with these contents. Furthermore, historically, conceptual changes within intuitive and explicit theories were necessary for the construction of some of them in the first place (e.g. *cancer, oxygen*). Thus, at a general level of description, core cognition is discontinuous with later developing explicit cognition, as these two types of representations have very different properties. Specific discontinuities at the level of repertoires of individual concepts will be illustrated with the concept *seven*, as I will show that the representations of core cognition cannot express it.

I now illustrate the nature of and evidence for core cognition, taking two systems of core cognition with numerical content as my examples.

Core system 1: analogue magnitude representations of number

Human adults, human infants, and nonhuman animals deploy a system of analogue magnitude representations of number. Number is represented by a physical magnitude that is roughly proportional to the number of individuals in the set being enumerated. Figure 13.1 depicts an external analogue magnitude representational system in which lengths represent number. A psychophysical signature of analogue magnitude representations is that discriminability of any two magnitudes is a function of their ratio. That is, discriminability is in accordance with Weber's law. Examining the external analogues in Figure 13.1, it is easy to see that 1 and 2 should be more discriminable than 7 and 8 (what is called the magnitude effect). Here are 1 and 2: ——, and here are 7 and 8: ——————— ————————. Similarly, it should be easier to discriminate 1 from 3 than 2 from 3 (what is called the distance effect). Here are 1 and 3: — ———, and here are 2 and 3: —— ———. Indeed, studies of numerical discrimination robustly reveal both magnitude and distance effects, which follow from Weber's law (Dehaene, 1997; Gallistel, 1990).

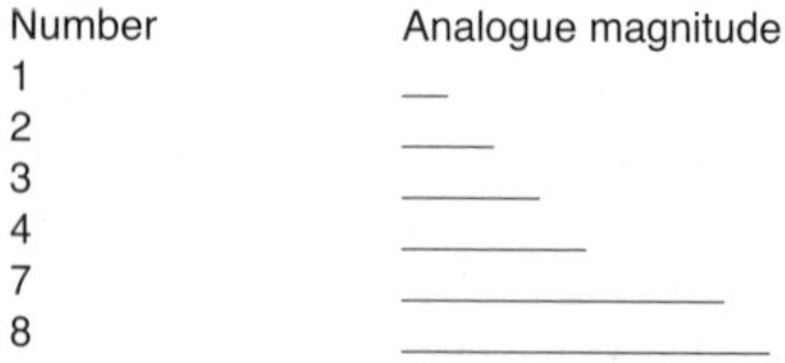

Number	Analogue magnitude representation
1	—
2	——
3	———
4	————
7	———————
8	————————

Fig. 13.1 External analogue magnitude representation of number in which number is represented by line length.

Dehaene (1997) and Gallistel (1990) review the evidence for the long evolutionary history of analogue magnitude number representations. Animals as disparate as pigeons, rats, and nonhuman primates represent number, using the representational system sketched above. Space precludes a full treatment of this gorgeous literature, so I will sketch only one series of studies. Elizabeth Brannon and Herb Terrace demonstrated that rhesus macaques are sensitive to number and represent sets differing in cardinal value as numerically ordered. These researchers began with Terrace's previous demonstrations that rhesus macaques can learn to order arbitrary sets of simultaneously presented stimuli. Presented with an array of four objects randomly distributed on a touch screen on each trial, for example, a red circle, a brown table, a black cat, and a blue flower, the monkeys can learn to touch the stimuli in a specified order. Thus, Terrace's earlier work suggests that the capacity to represent serial order is itself part of our evolutionary endowment and does not await the end of Piaget's stage of 'preoperational' thought for its emergence (Swartz et al., 1991; Terrace et al., 2003). Brannon and Terrace established that rhesus' number representations are intrinsically ordered (Brannon & Terrace, 1998). I will illustrate with data from two monkeys, Rosencrantz and Macduff. They were first taught to do the ordered list task, with arbitrary lists such as: first circle, then table, then cat, then flower. Of course, whenever they were shown four new stimuli, they could have no idea what order they were supposed to touch them in, so there was an extended period of trial and error before they learnt the order. After Rosencrantz and Macduff became good at that trial-and-error discovery process, Brannon and Terrace started giving them lists such as those in Figure 13.2. As can be seen, each list consisted of four pictures, containing respectively, sets with 1, 2, 3, and 4 items. In each list, the order the monkeys were supposed to press was 1, 2, 3, and 4. Across all the lists, all continuous variables confounded with number were controlled for. At the beginning, the monkeys treated each list the same as any arbitrary list, requiring extensive trial and error to learn the order called for on that list. But over the course of learning 35 such lists, Rosencrantz and Macduff got faster and faster. This could be because they were becoming ever more efficient at the trial-and-error strategies for learning whatever arbitrary list the experimenter had in mind, or it could be because they had learned a numerical rule.

To decide between these two possibilities, Brannon and Terrace gave Rosencrantz and Macduff 150 trials in which they saw new lists only once, thus preventing any trial-and-error learning. They did as well as on these lists as on those at the end of the 35 training-sets series, where they had seen each list 60 times. They had learnt a

Equal size

Clip art mixed

Equal surface area

Random size and shape

Random size

Random size, shape, and colour

Clip art

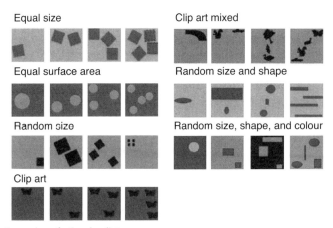

Fig. 13.2 Examples of stimulus lists.

Reprinted from Brannon, E. M. & Terrace, H. S. (1998). Ordering of the numerosities 1 to 9 by monkeys. *Science*, **282**, 746–749, with permission from Elsevier.

numerical rule. But which one? 'Press 1 object, then 2 objects, then 3 objects, and then 4 objects?' Or 'press in order of increasing numerical magnitude?'. To find out, Brannon and Terrace then presented the monkeys with novel trials involving sets of 4, 6, 7, 8, and 9 items. Now the task was simply to order two stimuli: for example, 2 versus 4, 3 versus 6, or 5 versus 9. Some included numbers within the trained lists and some were entirely novel pairs. Each pair was shown only once. Again, both monkeys transferred the rule to the novel lists including numbers outside of the training set. Apparently, they had learned the rule, 'touch in order of increasing numerical magnitude'.

Analogue magnitude representations of number underlie performance on this task. Clear evidence for distance effects was observed – accuracy was a function of the numerical distance between the stimuli (e.g. the monkeys' ability to order 6 and 9 was more accurate than their ability to order 7 and 8). Recent data from Brannon's laboratory confirm these generalizations. Monkeys were trained to touch two arrays in numerical order; all training pairs were taken from sets of 1–9 elements and over all pairs, other variables were controlled as in the Brannon and Terrace studies. After training, sets of 10, 15, 20, and 30 were added. Again, monkeys continued to succeed at the task upon first encountering these larger sets, and performance accorded with Weber's law (Cantlon & Brannon, 2005).

These data support the existence of an evolutionarily ancient representational system in which number is encoded by an analogue magnitude proportional to the number of objects in the set. These representations support computations of numerical equivalence and numerical order. There is also evidence that animals can add analogue magnitudes (e.g. Flombaum et al., 2005). In sum, that these analogue magnitude representations are *number* representations is shown by the fact that they track number rather than other dimensions of the sets attended to, and by the fact that numerically relevant computations are defined over them.

In the past 5 years, four different laboratories have provided unequivocal evidence that preverbal infants form analogue magnitude representations of number (Brannon, 2002; Brannon et al., 2004; Lipon & Spelke, 2003, 2004; McCrink & Wynn, 2004a; Wood & Spelke, 2005; Xu & Spelke, 2000; Xu et al., 2005). The first paper in this flurry of studies is by Fei Xu and Elizabeth Spelke, who solved the problem of how to control for other possible bases of judgement (cumulative surface area, element size, density) in a large number-habituation paradigm. Xu and Spelke habituated 6-month-old infants to displays containing 8 dots or to displays containing 16 dots (Figure 13.3). Possible confounds between number and other variables were controlled either by equating the two series of stimuli on those variables, or by making the test displays equidistant from the habituation displays on them. Habituated to 8-dot displays, 7-month-old infants recovered interest when shown the novel 16-dot displays, while generalizing habituation to the novel 8-dot displays. Those habituated to 16-dot displays showed the reverse pattern. Subsequent studies duplicated this design (and the positive result) with 16-dot versus 32-dot comparisons and with 4-dot versus 8-dot comparisons. Thus, the infants showed a sensitivity to cardinal values of sets outside

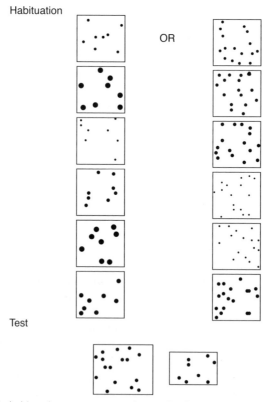

Fig. 13.3 Sample habituation sequences and test stimuli.

Reprinted from Xu, F. & Spelke, E. S. (2000). Large number discrimination in 6-month-old infants. *Cognition*, **74**, B1–B11, with permission from Elsevier.

the range of object-tracking mechanisms (see below), when potential confounds were strictly controlled for.

That analogue magnitude representations support these discriminations is shown by the fact that success is a function of the ratio of the set sizes. In all of the above studies, in which infants succeeded with a 2:1 ratio, they failed in comparisons that involved a 3:2 ratio (i.e. they failed to discriminate 8-dot from 12-dot arrays, 16-dot from 24-dot arrays, and 4-dot from 6-dot arrays). Morevoer, these researchers have found that sensitivity improves by 9 months of age. Infants of this age succeed at 3:2 comparisons across a wide variety of absolute set sizes, but fail at 4:3 comparisons.

These baby experiments involve dot arrays. Animals create analogue magnitude representations of number of sounds, number of bar presses, and number of key pecks, as well as of sets of visually presented individuals (Dehaene, 1997; Gallistel, 1990). Infants also represent the cardinal values of sets of individuals that are not visually specified. Jennifer Lipton and Elizabeth Spelke showed that 6-month-old infants discriminate 8 from 16 tones, and also 4 from 8 tones, when continuous variables are controlled in a manner analogous to the Xu and Spelke studies, and they fail to discriminate 8-tone from 12-tone sequences, or 4-tone from 6-tone sequences. Not only do 6-month-old infants create analogue magnitude representations of number in a sequence of tones, their sensitivity to numerical differences is in the same ratio as for arrays of dots (between 2:1, where they succeed, and 3:2, where they fail); also, paralleling the results with dot arrays, by 9 months, infants succeed at this latter ratio, distinguishing 8-tone sequences from 12-tone sequences and distinguishing 4-tone sequences from 6-tone sequences. Succeeding at 3:2 ratios, irrespective of set size, infants this age fail at 5:4 ratios, failing to distinguish 5-tone sequences from 4-tone sequences and also 10-tone from 8-tone sequences. Thus, at each age, sensitivity is a function of the ratios of the number of elements in the sets to be compared, with older infants showing greater sensitivity (3:2 at 9 months; and 2:1 at 6 months; Lipton & Spelke, 2003, 2004).

Furthermore, infants also represent the number of jumps in a sequence of jumps with the same sensitivity. Justin Wood and Elizabeth Spelke showed that 6-month-olds distinguish 4-jump sequences from 8-jump sequences, but not from 6-jump sequences, whereas 9-month-olds succeed at 4-jump versus 6-jump comparisons (Wood & Spelke, 2005). Thus, analogue magnitude representations are abstract in the sense of representing the cardinal values of sets of very different types of individuals.

In all of the above studies, we can be confident it is the number that infants are responding to, because every other variable is equated either across the habituation stimuli or across the test stimuli. In these studies, the child's attention is drawn when there is a *different number* of dots, jumps, or tones in a test set from the number in each of the habituation sets, and discrimination follows Weber's law. Thus, the child is using the analogue magnitude system to compute numerical equivalence. Of course, if the analogue magnitude representations underlying performance in these habituation studies are truly numerical representations, number-relevant computations other than establishing numerical equivalence should be defined over them, and indeed this is so.

Elizabeth Brannon showed that 11-month-old infants represent numerical order using analogue magnitude representations of sets. Infants were habituated to 3-array sequences, always increasing in number by a ratio of 2:1 (e.g. 2, 4, 8; 4, 8, 16; 1, 2, 4). Continuous variables were controlled as in the Xu and Spelke studies. After habituation, infants were shown a novel increasing sequence (3, 6, 12) or a decreasing sequence (12, 6, 3). They generalized habituation to the former and dishabituated to the latter. Another group of infants were habituated to decreasing sequences; they generalized habituation to the test sequence that decreased in numerical value and dishabituated to the one that increased (Brannon, 2002).

Finally, Koleen McCrink and Karen Wynn showed that 9-month-olds can manipulate sets of objects in the analogue magnitude range to support addition and subtraction (McCrink & Wynn, 2004a). Shown 5 objects move behind a screen, followed by another 5, infants look longer if the screen is removed revealing a set of 5 than if a set of 10 is revealed. Conversely, if the first set was 10 and 5 objects were seen to leave, infants looked longer if upon the screen's removal, 10 were revealed. These objects were each constantly expanding and contracting, and so, it was possible to control for summed continuous variables as a basis of response. In sum, analogue magnitude representations of number are available at least by 7 months of age. Preverbal infants represent the approximate cardinal value of sets, and compute numerical equivalence, numerical order, addition, subtraction, and ratios (McCrink & Wynn, 2004b) over these representations. Given the ancient evolutionary history of analogue magnitude number representations, it is very likely they are the output of innate perceptual analysers. Indeed, a variety of models of the exact nature of these input analysers have been proposed, from Church and Meck's (1984) serial accumulator model, to various models that operate in parallel on an attended set of individuals to abstract a summary representation of number (e.g. Dehaene & Changeux, 1993).

Analogue magnitude number representations display all of the properties of a system of core cognition. Number representations are conceptual in the sense of their content going beyond spatiotemporal and sensory vocabulary (their content is *cardinal value*), as well as in the sense of being abstract; they are computed over sets of individuals of many different types. The domain-specific perceptual analysers that encode number, as well as the arithmetic computations defined over the resulting representations, are evolutionarily ancient, most likely innate, and operate throughout the life span (see Butterworth, 1999; Dehaene, 1997). Their format is analogue (hence their name), and thus pictorial, in the sense that a representation of 3 dots is a part of a representation of 4 dots, just as a set of 4 dots has a set of 3 dots as part of it.

In sum, the evidence points to a system of representation in which number is encoded in the brain by some symbol that is itself a linear or logarithmic function of number. If this is right, we can say more about what is represented *explicitly* and what *implicitly* by this system. Explicit, in the sense I mean it here, is not the same as public. Rather, the explicit aspect of a system of representations is the meaning expressed by the symbols themselves.

The word 'seven', the Roman numeral symbol 'VII', and the Arabic numeral '7' are both public and explicit symbols. A representational theory of mind is committed to the existence of *mental* symbols, and a theory of them must specify their format, their content (what they represent), and the computations they support. Some of their content is determined by their conceptual role. That is, the meaning of the whole system goes beyond the meaning of the symbols themselves. In the case of the analogue magnitude system, the symbols themselves are the explicit representations. They are the output of the input analysers and are available to central processors for a wide variety of computations. But much of the numerical content of this system of representation is implicit. There is no explicit representation of the axioms of arithmetic, no representation that one–one correspondence guarantees numerical equivalence. These principles are implicit in the operation of the input analysers and in the computations defined over analogue magnitudes, but they need not be available for the child to base any decisions on. This case illustrates that once one has a well-confirmed model of some representational system, one can examine that model to establish exactly what is represented and how. Analogue magnitudes are explicit, but approximate, symbols of cardinal values of sets. Other numerical content is embodied in operations that compute over these symbols; that latter knowledge is not symbolized and thus is not input to further computations.

A second core system with numerical content: parallel individuation of small sets

Science moves rapidly, and the infant studies reviewed above came relatively late in the history of studies designed to show that infants are sensitive to number. The first studies, some 20 years earlier than Xu and Spelke's studies on analogue magnitude representations, concerned *small* sets – discriminations among sets of 1, 2, and 3 objects. These include many 2 versus 3 habituation studies and Wynn's 1 + 1 = 2 or 1 violation of expectancy studies (Antell & Keating, 1983; Starkey & Cooper, 1980; Wynn, 1992b). Although some have suggested that analogue magnitude number representations underlie success in these experiments (e.g. Dehaene, 1997), the evidence conclusively implicates a very different representational system (Feigenson & Carey, 2003; Feigenson et al., 2002a; Scholl & Leslie, 1999; Simon, 1997; Uller et al., 1999). In this alternative representational system, number is only implicitly encoded; there are no symbols for number at all, not even analogue magnitude ones. Instead, the representations include a symbol for each individual in an attended set. Thus, a set containing one apple might be represented: 'O' (an iconic object file) or 'apple' (a symbol for an individual of the kind apple) and a set containing two apples might be represented 'O O' or 'apple apple', and so forth. These representations consist of one symbol (file) for each individual, and when the content of a symbol is a spatiotemporally determined object, it is an object file (Kahnemann et al., 1992). Infants also create working-memory models of small sets of other types of individuals, such as sound bursts or events, and so I shall call the system of representation 'parallel individuation' and the explicit symbols within it 'individual files'. When those individual files are object files, I sometimes refer to them as such.

There are many reasons to favour individual file representations over analogue magnitude representations as underlying performance in most of the infant small-number studies (see Carey, 2009, for a more thorough review). First, and most important, success on many spontaneous number-representation tasks involving small sets do not show the Weber-fraction signature of analogue magnitude representations; rather, they show the set-size signature of individual file representations. This, is, small sets (sets of 1, 2, or 3) can be represented, and sets outside of that limit cannot, even when the sets to be contrasted are related by the same ratio as those large sets which the infant easily discriminates.

The set-size signature of object-file representations is motivated by evidence that even for adults there are sharp limits on the number of object files that can be simultaneously attended to and held in working memory. If object-file representations underlie infants' performance in some tasks meant to reflect number representations, then infants should succeed only when the sets being encoded consist of small numbers of objects. Success at discriminating 1 versus 2, and 2 versus 3, in the face of failure with 3 versus 4 or 4 versus 5 is not enough to confirm that object-file representations underlie success, for Weber-fraction differences could equally well explain such a pattern of performance. That is, ratios of 3:4 or 4:5 might exceed the sensitivity of the analogue magnitude system at that age. Rather, what is needed is success at 1 versus 2 and perhaps 2 versus 3 in the face of failure at 3 versus 6 – failure at the higher numbers when the Weber fraction is the same or even more favourable than that within the range of small numbers at which success has been obtained. This is the set-size signature of individual file representations.

This set-size signature of object-file representations is precisely what is found in some infant habituation studies – success at discriminating 2 versus 3 objects in the face of failure at discriminating 4 versus 6 objects (Starkey & Cooper, 1980). Similarly, two other paradigms provide vivid illustrations of the set-size signature of object-file representations. In one of them, an infant watches as each of two opaque containers, previously shown to be empty, is baited with a different number of graham crackers. For example, the experimenter might put two graham crackers in one container and three in the other. After placement, the parent allows the infant to crawl toward the containers. The dependant measure is which container the baby chooses. The data reflect the set-size signature of parallel individuation. Apparently, three is limit on parallel individuation in babies. Ten- to 12-month-old infants succeed at 1 versus 2, 2 versus 3; and 1 versus 3, and fail at 3 versus 4, 2 versus 4, and even 1 versus 4 (Feigenson & Carey, 2005; Feigenson et al., 2002a). One:four is a more favourable ratio than 2:3, but infants fail at 1 versus 4 comparisons and succeed at 2 versus 3. Note also that 5 crackers are involved in each choice, so the total length of time of placements is equated over these two comparisons. This is a striking result. Infants could succeed at 1 versus 4 comparisons on many different bases: putting 4 crackers into a bucket takes much longer, draws more attention to that bucket, and so on, yet infants are at chance. Although infants could solve this problem in many different ways, apparently they are attending to each cracker, creating a model of what's in the container that contains one object-file for each cracker. As soon as one of the sets exceeds the limits on parallel individuation, performance falls apart. This finding provides very strong evidence that parallel individuation underlies success on this task.

Convergent data from a second paradigm involving small sets of objects demonstrate the set-size signature of parallel individuation. The task requires infants to search inside a box into which they can reach but not see. When 12–14-month-old infants have seen 1, 2, or 3 objects placed into a box, they search for exactly 1, 2, or 3, respectively. But when they have seen 4 objects placed in the box, they are satisfied when they have retrieved only 2 or even only 1. That is, as in the cracker-choice experiments, infants distinguish 2 from 3 (see 3 hidden, retrieve 2, expect another in there), but fail to distinguish 4 from 1 (see 4 hidden, retrieve 1, do not search further for any more in there; Feigenson & Carey, 2003, 2005). Performance falls apart when the set to be represented exceeds the limit on parallel individuation of objects, not when the ratio of objects exceeds some limit. Again, 4:1 is a more favourable ratio than 3:2, yet infants search for additional objects having seen 3 placed into the box and having retrieved only 2, but fail to search for additional objects having seen 4 placed into the box and having retrieved only 1. This set-size signature of object-file representations rules out the possibility that analogue magnitude representations of number underlie the baby's actions on this task.

That infants' performance shows the set-size signature of parallel individuation rather than the constant Weber-ratio signature of analogue magnitudes shows that analogue magnitude representations do not subserve performance on the small-number tasks described above. Readers confronting these data for the first time always ask 'why not?'. Why do infants not draw on analogue magnitude representation of 4 balls to distinguish arrays of 4 from arrays of 2 or 1 in the box-search task, and why do infants not draw on analogue magnitude representations of 6, 3, 4, 2, or 1 crackers to choose consistently when presented with 6 versus 3 crackers, 4 versus 2, or 4 versus 1 choices in the cracker-choice tasks? I do not know for sure; apparently, something about these experimental paradigms encourages infants' attention to specific individuals, such that these arrays are being represented in short-term memory models that consist of one symbol for each individual in the small set being represented. These experiments do not in any way undercut the evidence provided above that in some circumstances, infants deploy analogue magnitude representations. But for some reason, they do not deploy them in these studies. Rather, in these studies, infants display a consistent pattern of responses that implicate quite a different system of representation, the symbols which represent the individuals in the set, not the number of them (except implicitly, for there is one symbol for each individual).

If parallel individuation models do not include symbols for number, why am I discussing them in a chapter on the origin of number concepts? Two recent studies show that infants carry out computations on these models that are numerical. They compute one–one correspondence between representations of small sets held in short-term memory, determining numerical equivalence and numerical order. Lisa Feigenson and I showed that it is *number* of objects represented in the box that guides search in the task in which infants reach into a box into which they cannot see to retrieve hidden objects. We carried out a version of this study in which infants saw 2 small objects, for example, cars, placed into the box, one at a time. We then gave them the box, and they reached in and retrieved a car – either one of the cars they had seen, or a car that was twice the surface area and 4 times the volume but was otherwise identical to the cars they saw hidden. Infants showed by their subsequent search that they expected exactly one more in either case. They were oblivious to the cumulative continuous variables; their reaches were guided by how many objects they represented in the box (Feigenson & Carey, 2003). They must have been computing one–one correspondence between the individuals in their model of what was represented in the box and their representations of what they had so far retrieved from the box.

Feigenson also showed that infants are sensitive to number in a simple habituation task, as long as the individuals in the set are distinct from one another (Feigenson, 2005,) unlike in experiments involving homogeneous stimuli, where infants compute total surface area or total contour length over their models of the individuals held in working memory. When habituated to arrays as in Figure 13.4, infants dishabituated to the array with a novel number and generalized their habituation to the array that matched in total surface area. Apparently, homogeneity in properties of individuals facilitates computations of cumulative continuous variables from representations of small sets of individuals, and heterogeneity of properties focuses attention on representations of distinct individuals. An important feature of this study is that it requires an abstract representation of the sets of objects (sets of 1 or sets of 2). During habituation, two different sets of heterogeneous objects were presented. Thus a working-memory model of two objects must be abstracted from these habituation arrays, which then must be compared to a model of the outcome array, which in turn contained very different objects from those in each of the habituation arrays, on the basis of one–one correspondence. The important conclusion is that one–one correspondence computations that establish numerical equivalence and numerical order *can* be carried out over object-file representations held in parallel in working-memory models, in spite of the fact that in many experiments they are not (Feigenson et al., 2002b; Mix et al., 2002).

Space precludes summarizing the evidence for parallel individuation of individuals that are not object files; under some circumstances, representations of small sets of jumps or of sounds also display the set-size signature of parallel individuation, as well

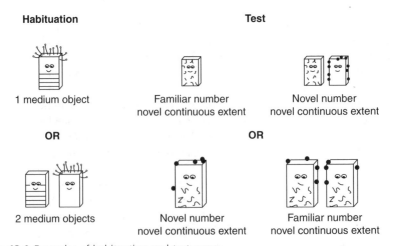

Fig. 13.4 Examples of habituation and test arrays.

Reprinted from Feigenson, L. (2005). A double dissociation in infants' representation of object arrays. *Cognition*, **95**, B37–B48, with permission from Elsevier.

as all of the other signatures of parallel individuation not reviewed here (see Carey, 2009, for a review).

Although some describe what I am calling the system of parallel individuation as a 'small-number system', that is a misnomer. The purpose of parallel individuation is to create working-memory models of small sets of individuals, in order to represent spatial, causal, and intentional relations among them. Unlike analogue magnitude number representations, the parallel individuation system is not a dedicated number representation system. Far from it. The symbols in the parallel individuation system explicitly represent individuals. Figure 13.5 depicts two different individual file representations of two boxes. In neither of these alternative models is there a symbol that has the content *two*; rather, the symbols in working memory represent the boxes. The whole model {obj obj} represents two boxes, of course, but only implicitly. Furthermore, as I have mentioned, the quantitative calculations over parallel individuation models in working memory often privilege continuous variables (such as total event energy, total contour length, total surface area) over numerical equivalence. Still, parallel individuation models are shot through with numerical content, even though that numerical content is merely implicit in the computations that pick out and index small sets to represent, that govern the opening of new individual files, that update working-memory models of sets as individuals are added or subtracted, and that compare sets on numerical criteria. The creation of a new individual file requires principles of individuation and numerical identity; models must keep track of whether this object or jump, seen now, is the same *one* as that object seen before, or this sound just heard, is the same *one* as that just heard previously. The decision the system makes dictates

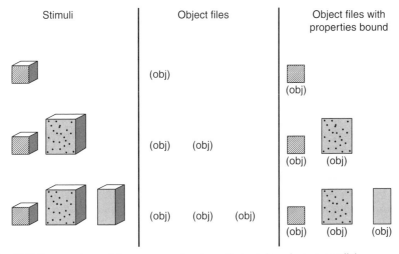

Fig. 13.5 Two versions of the memory structures that might subserve parallel individuation of small sets of objects. In one, each object is represented by an object file that abstracts away from specific features (OBJ). In the other, each object is represented by an object file on which shape, colour, texture, and spatial extent features have been bound.

whether an additional individual file is established, and this guarantees that a model of a set of three boxes will contain three box symbols. Computations of numerical identity are (as their name says) numerical computations. The opening of a new individual file in the presence of other active files also provides an implicit representation of the process of adding one to an array of individuals. Finally, working-memory models of two sets of individuals can be simultaneously maintained, and when individual file models are compared on the basis of one–one correspondence, the computations over these symbols establish numerical equivalence and numerical order.

Finally, I remind you that parallel individuation of sets of individuals displays all of the properties of core cognition. The capacity is evolutionarily ancient (shared with nonhuman primates; see Hauser and Carey, 2003; Hauser et al., 2000), evident in very young infants, and thus most likely part of our innate endowment. It is continuous throughout the lifespan. For example, the set-size signature of the number of individuals stored in working memory is seen in adults in studies of multiple object tracking and change detection (Carey, 2009; Luck & Vogel, 1997; Trick & Pylyshyn, 2004, describes many other signatures of parallel individuation that are continuous through the life span). Very likely, the format of representation of the individuals held in working memory is pictorial (see Carey, 2009, Chapter 4). And it is conceptual in the senses that other systems of core cognition are. That is, the individuals represented have content that goes beyond the vocabulary of sensory primitives, the representations abstract across many different sensory modalities, and the representations interact centrally with other representations. Note, the fact that we can see objects does not mean that representations of objects are perceptual representations. We can see nuclear reactors also, but we would not be tempted to think that *nuclear reactor* is a perceptual representation. Throughout recent intellectual history, how humans create representations with the content *object* has been one of the theoretical arenas in which the empiricist/rationalist debate has played out. See Piaget (1954) and Quine (1960), for why object representations go beyond perception, and Carey (2009), for evidence for core cognition of objects. Furthermore, parallel individuation abstracts across many different modalities, and the quantificational computations carried out over representations of sets of individuals held in working memory are abstract, encompassing individuals that are not objects.

Conceptual discontinuity: specific level of description

As mentioned above, conceptual discontinuity is possible at two different levels of description. At the general level, later-developing conceptual representations may have properties utterly unlike the properties of core cognition. At the specific level, later-developing representations may have the capacity to express particular concepts that were not expressible in the earlier representational systems. The transition between core cognition of number and the first public, linguistically encoded, system of number representation (the numeral list, as deployed in counting) involves discontinuity at both levels of description. I begin by discussing discontinuity at the specific level.

In cases of conceptual discontinuity, no antecedent system of representation can express the concepts of a later-developing one. To establish discontinuity, then, one must characterize two empirically supported successive systems of representation (conceptual systems 1 and 2; CS1 and CS2), and demonstrate why CS2 had more expressive power than CS1. I consider each core cognition system as CS1. For illustrative purposes, I will take CS2 to be the verbal numeral list representation of the positive integers, characterized by Gelman and Gallistel's (1978) counting principles. This system of representation is typically mastered by age 3½ or 4 by children growing up in a numerate culture. It expresses a finite subset of the natural numbers. The principles that underlie it are recognized to be extendable to arbitrarily large numbers by children a few years older (Hartnett & Gelman, 1998), at which point children have constructed a representation of natural number.

Analogue magnitude representations of number lack the expressive power of any system of representation of the natural numbers, including numeral list representations, in three crucial respects. First, they have an upper limit; they represent the cardinal values of sets that can actually be apprehended, and so they lack the capacity to represent discrete infinity. Second, because analogue magnitude representations are inexact and discriminable only to a given Weber ratio, they fail to capture small numerical differences between large sets of objects. The distinction between 18 and 19, 11 and 12, 124 and 127, and so on, cannot be captured reliably by the analogue magnitude representations of human adults, because as a matter of contingent fact, the Weber ratio for sensitivity to numerical differences is 8:9 (at best). Relatedly, they are not built around, nor can they express, the successor function, the operation of adding one to a given integer in order to generate the next integer. Rather, they positively obscure the successor function. They contain no representation for exactly one. Moreover, since numerical values are compared by computing a ratio, the difference between one and two is experienced as different from that between two and three, which is again experienced as different from that between three and four. Of course, the difference between nine and ten, is not experienced at all, since nine and ten, like any higher successive numerical values, cannot be discriminated.

In sum, analogue magnitude representations are not powerful enough to represent the natural numbers and their key property of discrete infinity. They do not provide exact representations of numbers and they obscure the successor function, which is constitutive of natural number.

The parallel individuation does not remotely have the capacity to represent natural number. Unlike the analogue magnitude number representation system, the parallel individuation system is not dedicated to number representations. Number is only implicitly represented, in that computations of one–one correspondence are made over symbols for individuals represented in parallel in models of arrays of objects and events. The system of parallel individuation, like that of analogue magnitude number representations, contains machinery for indexing and tracking sets of individuals, but it contains no symbols for cardinal values. The only symbols in such models represent the individuals themselves. In addition, the system of parallel individuation has an upper bound at very low set sizes indeed – three for infants. With this system of representation, infants cannot even represent 4 (even implicitly), let alone 7 or 32 or 1 345 698.

In sum, neither of the CS1 has the capacity to represent natural number, whereas CS2 (the numeral list representation of number) does. CS2 is discontinuous with either CS1.

Conceptual discontinuity: general level of description

The differences between the numeral list representation of number and the core cognition systems also illustrate the general-level discontinuities between core cognition and later-developing linguistically encoded systems of representation. The format of representation of the later-developing systems is not pictorial or analogue (three is represented 'three' or '3', not '——' or 'O O O'). There are no innately specified input analysers that output representations like 'three' (as seen above). Numeral list representations are not evolutionarily ancient, nor are they cross-culturally universal (Gordon, 2004; Hurford, 1987; Pica et al., 2004). Finally, they do not remain constant throughout development; the concept of number as natural number captured in the count routine undergoes conceptual change in the course of mathematical development, becoming more abstract and divorced from representations of cardinal values of particular sets, and expanded to include negative number, rational number, and the like.

Thus, cognitive science faces two challenges: accounting for how systems of representation with properties so utterly different from those of core cognition arise (accounting for discontinuities at the general level of description) and accounting for how particular concepts not expressible in the systems of representation that are input to learning can be acquired (accounting for discontinuities at the specific level of description).

Empirical evidence for conceptual discontinuity

Hypothesized conceptual discontinuities make two crucial predictions. First, CS2 should be very difficult to learn; because CS2 is very different in type from CS1 (general-level discontinuity) and has more expressive power than CS1 (specific-level discontinuity). Second, learners should make systematic, far-reaching errors, as they initially assimilate the evidence for CS2 to representational systems very different from it. Both of these predictions are confirmed in the case of children's mastering the numeral list representation of natural number.

Children learn to count during the ages of 2–4 years, and learning to count is far from easy. Although young toddlers use a stably ordered list and count each object just once, honouring the stable order and one–one correspondence principles (two of the counting principles that guarantee that counting represents natural number), they do so for almost a year and a half before they figure out the cardinality principle (that the last number reached in a count represents the cardinal value of the set) – that is, before they figure out how counting represents number (Fuson, 1988; Le Corre et al., 2006; Wynn, 1990, 1992a). Indeed, initially, they have assigned no numerical meaning to any of the numerals in the count list. They cannot even hand a person 'one penny' (from several) if asked, or indicate which of two sets (a set of one and a set of several) has 'one'. I will use Wynn's work to illustrate the evidence for these claims. Wynn (1990, 1992a) showed that, from very early in the process of learning to count, children know what 'one' means. They can give you one penny from a pile of pennies if asked to, and they correctly distinguish a card with one fish from a card with any other number of fish if asked to indicate the card with 'one fish'. But they have not assigned a cardinal meaning to any other numeral on their count list. The striking phenomenon (and you can definitely try this at home if you have a handy 2-year-old) is that if you ask for 'two pennies' or 'four pennies', they merely grab a handful, with no relations to the number requested (they do not give more for when asked for four than for two). Notice that this shows that they know that the other words in the count sequence contrast with 'one'. They always grab a random number of objects greater than one when asked to hand over 'two, three, four. . .' objects, and they also successfully point to a card with three fish when it is contrasted with a card with one, even though their choices are random when three is contrasted with two. Such children are called 'one'-knowers, for they know the meaning only of the verbal numeral 'one'. They have no idea which particular cardinality any of their other number words refers to. Moreover, consistent with the claims that preverbal representations of number are quite different from counting, and that learning the meaning of the count list is very difficult, children remain 'one'-knowers for 6–8 months before they figure out what 'two' means. Upon becoming 'two'-knowers, they can construct sets of two when asked for 'two', and tell which of two cards has 'two fish' when given a contrast between a set of two fish and any other set. But they still respond randomly on 'three'. They are 'two'-knowers for several months, and then become 'three'-knowers. Le Corre and Carey (2007) showed that all children who have worked out how counting represents number, have previously assigned 'four' a numerical meaning. Thus, children labouriously work out numerical meanings for the numerals 'one' through 'four' over a year and a half before they figure out how to use counting to implement the successor function. Call the children who have not yet figured out the cardinality principle (the last numeral reached in a count represents the cardinal value of the set) 'subset'-knowers, for they have assigned cardinal meanings to only a subset of the numerals in the count list.

The ways in which CS2 transcends core cognition makes sense of why it takes children a year and a half or 2 years to figure out how counting represents number. Not only does the discontinuity hypothesis require that constructing CS2 should be difficult, but it also predicts that behavioural measures will reflect a qualitative change in representational capacity as CS2 is constructed. We should see within-child consistency on a whole variety of tasks that reflect CS2 – and indeed we do. There is evidence from a wide variety of measures for a qualitative shift between subset-knowers, on the one hand, and cardinal-principle knowers, on the other. There is also evidence for consistency within knower-level. A 'one'-knower reveals knowledge only of the numeral 'one' on every task that probes for such knowledge? Ditto for 'two'-, 'three'- and 'four'-knowers.

Le Corre et al. (2006, 2007) provide a thorough documentation of these claims; here, I give just a few examples of the striking within-child consistency on several measures that suggests a qualitative shift in understanding how counting represents number upon becoming a cardinal principle knower. In Karen Wynn's (1990, 1992a) original studies, subset-knowers almost never counted to produce sets, either within their knower-level range or outside it (asked to give five apples, they merely grabbed a handful), whereas cardinal principle knowers almost always counted out large sets.

Moreover, when simply asked to count a set of objects, children in both groups could do so with few errors, but then after counting, if asked 'How many was that'? the cardinal principle knowers almost always merely repeated the last word of their previous count, whereas subset-knowers rarely did so. Rather, subset-knowers recount, or provide a numeral that does not match the last word of their count. This suggests that subset-knowers do not realize that the last word reached in a count represents the cardinal value of the set. Later studies confirmed these findings and extended them. Even cardinal principle knowers sometimes make mistakes when creating sets of a requested number. Children are asked to count and check their answers. When the count reveals an incorrect set size, cardinal principle knowers virtually always correct appropriately. Subset-knowers, in contrast, leave the set unchanged or correct in the wrong direction (e.g. add more objects when the count revealed that there were already too many) on more than 70% of the trials (Le Corre et al., 2006; Wynn, 1990, 1992a).

Within knower level, being a 'one'-knower according to Wynn's 'give-a-number' task predicts which pairs of sets children will succeed on when asked 'which is n' (i.e. any contrast between a set of one and a set with any other number; no other contrast). Ditto for 'two'-, 'three'-, and 'four'- knowers. Similarly, knower level on Wynn's task predicts which set sizes children can successfully estimate (without counting) when simply shown a set of entities and asked how many it contains (Le Corre & Carey, 2007; Le Corre et al., 2006). A 'two'-knower says 'one' for sets of 1 and 'two' for sets of 2 and uses higher numerals randomly for sets from 3 to 10.

In sum, two kinds of analyses support the claim that the representational system that is the verbal count list is discontinuous with antecedent representations. Most importantly, I have offered empirically supported characterizations of two such antecedent systems of representations with numerical content, and shown how they lack the expressive power of the count list. Second, I have offered evidence that the count list representation of number is, as predicted, very difficult to learn, and is systematically misinterpreted during the learning process.

The explanatory challenge: Quinian bootstrapping

I turn now to the explanatory challenge – what learning processes can create representational resources with more expressive power than, or qualitatively different from, their input; that is, what learning processes underlie discontinuity at both the specific and general levels. With respect to the general level, I appeal to the old favourite – the uniquely human capacity to create external symbols. Like many writers in this book (see especially Chapter 6), I assume that the human capacity for language distinguishes us from nonhuman animals, and that language plays an essential role in conceptual development. I assume (but will not argue the point here) that the capacity for human language – the capacity to form lexical, syntactic, and morphological representations – has innate support, as do the logical capacities needed to express meanings and the inferential relations among propositions. It is these capacities that partially underlie discontinuity at the general level. Indeed, I will help myself to many of these capacities in accounting for the capacity to represent natural number.

But what I want to emphasize here is that these powerful capacities do not by themselves explain discontinuity at the specific level. The human capacity for language and logic does not, by itself, account for the origin of concepts like *32, infinity, gene, cancer,* and *democracy*. It is not normal language acquisition that accounts for the making of the concept of 'seven', even though external symbols are essential to the process.

This explanatory challenge of accounting for specific conceptual innovations has been extensively discussed by historians and philosophers of science, and many appeal to what are called 'bootstrapping' processes as an explanation for how representational resources that transcend their input can be created. The very word bootstrapping is a metaphor, meant to capture the deep difficulty of the problem. After all, it is impossible to pull oneself up by one's bootstraps. Neurath's metaphor of building a boat while already in the middle of the ocean also captures the difficulty of the problem – that while not grounded one must build a structure that will float and support you. Not grounded in this case means that the planks one is building the boat with are not interpreted concepts one already represents. In other metaphors, the learner's concepts are partially grounded, as in Quine's ladder metaphor. Here, one builds a ladder grounded in one conceptual system until one has a platform that is self-sustaining, and then one kicks the ladder out from under. In a final Quinian metaphor, one is scrambling up a chimney supporting oneself by pressing against the sides one is building as one goes along. Quine again captures that the new conceptual system that supports you is being built as you go along. This metaphor stresses, as does Neurath's boat, that the structure one builds consists of relations among the concepts one will eventually attain – it is that structure of interrelations among the to-be-attained concepts (the sides of the evolving chimney, the boat itself, the platform from which the ladder can be kicked away) that serves the crucial bootstrapping role. See Quine (1960, 1969, 1974) for his own elaboration of Quinian bootstrapping.

Although such metaphors are evocative – of both the problem to be solved and the solution – Quine never describes in detail how this learning process operates. These metaphors are hardly satisfying to a cognitive scientist trying to understand bootstrapping mechanisms. As I illustrate here, I believe it is possible to flesh out the metaphors with appeals to processes that are well understood at a computational level.

Quinian bootstrapping processes require explicit symbols, such as those in written and spoken language or mathematical notational systems. The aspect of the bootstrapping metaphor that consists of building a structure while not grounded is applied as the learner initially learning the relations of a system of symbols to one another, directly, rather than by mapping each symbol onto preexisting concepts (Block, 1986). The symbols so represented thus serve as placeholders, at most only partially interpreted with respect to antecedent concepts. This is one essential component of Quinian bootstrapping. The second essential component is the process through which the placeholders become interpreted. As historian and philosopher of science, Nancy Nersessian (1992) argues, these are modelling processes. Often, but not always, processes of analogical mapping are involved. Other modelling processes, such as abduction, thought experimentation, limiting-case analyses, and induction, all have roles in Quinian bootstrapping. Two properties of these modelling processes are important. First, they are not deductive. There are no guarantees in bootstrapping. The structures that are tentatively posited either work, in the sense of continuing to capture the observed data that constrain them, or they do not. Second, they are all problem-solving mechanisms that play a role in thought more generally. They are bootstrapping mechanisms only when harnessed in the service of creating a representational resource with more power than those that are their input.

Bootstrapping the numeral list representation of natural number

The output of the learning process we seek to understand is the numeral list representation of natural number – an ordered list of numerals such that the first one on the list represents 1 and for any word on the list that represents the cardinal value n, the next word on the list represents $n + 1$. The successor function is the heart of numeral list representations of integers. The numeral list representation of number is characterized by Gelman and Gallistel's counting principles (the list is stably ordered; individuals in a given count are put in one–one correspondence with number words, and the cardinal value of the set is the ordinal position of the word in the count list).

The problem of how the child builds a numeral list representation decomposes into the related subproblems of learning the ordered list itself ('one, two, three, four, five, six. . .'), learning the meaning of each symbol on the list (e.g. 'three' means three and 'seven' means seven), and learning how the list itself represents number, such that the child can infer the meaning of a newly mastered numeral symbol (e.g. 'eleven') from its position in the numeral list.

As mentioned above, the child first learns 'one, two, three, four, five. . .' as a list of meaningless lexical items. There is no doubt that children have the capacity to learn meaningless ordered lists of words – they learn sequences such as 'eeny, meeny, miny, mo', the alphabet, the days of the week, and so on. Indeed, nonhuman primates have this capacity, and so it is likely part of innate computational machinery (e.g. Terrace et al., 2003). This step in the learning process – learning an arbitrary ordered list ('one, two, three, four, five, six. . .') is a paradigmatic example of one aspect of Quinian bootstrapping: the meanings of the counting words are exhausted, initially, by their interrelations, their relative order in the list, and their place in the numerically meaningless count routine. At this point in the process, the verbal numerals are placeholders with respect to the numerical meaning they will come to have.

Children do not learn the numerical meaning of 'one' in the context of counting. 'One' is much more frequent in speech to the child's input as a quantifier than embedded in the count routine (Sarnecka et al., 2007). 'Can you give me one'? 'Would you like that one'? 'I'd like one cupcake'. As Paul Bloom and Karen Wynn (1997) argued, from the outset of numeral production, children correctly use them in the syntactic positions of quantifiers. The semantics of quantifiers helps children recognize the numerical meaning of 'one'. Three sources of evidence support Bloom and Wynn's conjecture. First of all, the partial meanings children in the subset-knower stage assign to numerals they have not yet assigned a cardinal meaning to implicate hypothesis testing over the space of quantifier meanings. For example, for 'one'-knowers, 'two, three, four', and so on each mean essentially 'plural'. Second, learners of Japanese and Mandarin, classifier languages with no singular–plural distinction, learn to count as early as do learners of English, and have equivalent number word input, but do not become 'one'-knowers until several months later than do English-speakers (Le Corre et al., 2003; Sarnecka et al., 2007). Relatively sparse number marking in syntax slows down assigning partial meanings to the placeholder symbols in the count list. Finally, Palestinian Arabic has a dual marker system and also distinguishes plural morphology and collective morphology. In a study of children's learning number marking in Palestinian Arabic, Ravid and Hayek (2003) found that 3-year-olds often used the numeral translated 'two' instead of the dual when referring to sets of two objects, whereas older children were unlikely to do this. This finding is consistent with the suggestion that 'two' is initially a dual marker (see also Clark and Nikatina, in press).

Before we can understand how children work out the meaning of the count list, we must establish what 'one', 'two', 'three', and 'four' mean for a 'four'-knower, for it is only after being 'four'-knowers that children figure out the cardinal principle. What is the format of the mental representations that underlie the numerical meanings subset-knowers have created for numerals? If 'two' is a dual marker for 'two'-knowers, what representations give numerical meaning to dual markers? What is the process through which a given set is assigned one numeral rather than another?

Le Corre and I proposed a system of representations that could underlie the meanings of numerals for subset-knowers that draw on the resources both of natural language quantification and parallel individuation, and thus we dubbed it 'enriched parallel individuation' (Le Corre & Carey, 2007; see Mix et al., 2002).

The parallel individuation system that is part of core cognition creates working-memory models of sets. The symbols in these models represent particular individuals – *this box, that box*. However, as detailed above, even when drawing on parallel individuation alone, infants have the capacity to represent two models and compare them on the basis of one–one correspondence. For representations of this format to subserve the meanings of the singular determiner or the numeral 'one' for subset-knowers, the child may create a long-term memory model of a set of one individual and map it to the linguistic expression 'a' or 'one'. Similarly, a long-term memory model of a set of two individuals could be created and mapped to the linguistic expression for a dual marker or 'two', and so on for 'three' and 'four'. These models could contain abstract symbols for individuals ($\{i\}$, $\{j\ k\}$, $\{m\ n\ o\}$, $\{w\ x\ y\ z\}$) or they could simply be long-term memory models of particular sets of individuals ($\{Mommy\}$, $\{Daddy\ Johnnie\}$...). What makes these models represent 'one' 'two', and so forth is their computational role. They are deployed in assigning numerals to sets as follows: the child makes a working-memory model of a particular set he or she wants to quantify {e.g. cookie cookie}. He/she then searches the models in long-term memory to find that which can be put in one–one correspondence with this working-memory model, retrieving the quantifier that has been mapped to that model.

All of the computational resources required for enriched parallel individuation are known to be available to prelinguistic infants (see above, and Carey, 2009, for full evidence for this claim). Prelinguistic infants create working-memory models of at least two separate sets and compare these on the basis of one–one correspondence. They also treat sets as objects, quantifying over them as required by natural language quantifiers. Still, it is important to stress that the long-term memory models that support the meanings of singular, dual, and triple markers, as well as the child's first numerals, are not themselves part of core cognition. These must be created in the course of language learning, and for English-learning children, this process unfolds for a period of over a year. This why Le Corre and I designate the hypothesized system of representation 'enriched parallel individuation'.

The two important planks of the bootstrapping process are constructed in parallel, largely independent of each other. The child learns the explicit numeral list and the count routine as a numerically meaningless game. The child also creates numerical meanings for some numerals – in this case 'one' through 'four'. These meanings are supplied by enriched parallel individuation.

The stage is set for the completion of the bootstrapping processes. Children use the placeholder structure to model sets of individuals in the world. They must note the identity of the words 'one, two', 'three', and 'four which now have numerical meaning, and the first words in the otherwise meaningless counting list. Moreover, in the course of counting, children discover that when an attended set would be quantified with the dual marker 'two', the count goes 'one, two', and when an attended set would be quantified with the trial marker 'three', the count goes 'one, two, three'. The child is thus in the position to notice that for these words at least, the last word reached in a count refers to the cardinal value of the whole set (as captured by enriched parallel individuation).

At this point, the stage is set for the crucial induction. The child must notice an analogy between next in the numeral list and next in the series of mental models ($\{i\}$, $\{j\ k\}$, $\{m\ n\ o\}$, $\{w\ x\ y\ z\}$) related by adding an individual. Remember, core cognition supports the comparison of two sets simultaneously held in memory on the basis of one–one correspondence, so the child has the capacity to represent this latter basis of ordering sets. This analogy licenses the crucial induction: if 'x' is followed by 'y' in the counting sequence, adding an individual to a set with cardinal value x results in a set with cardinal value y. This generalization does not yet embody the arithmetic successor function, but one additional step is all that is needed. Since the child has already mapped single individuals onto 'one', adding a new individual is equivalent to adding one.

This proposal makes sense of the actual partial meanings children assign to number words as they try to fill in the placeholders. The semantics of quantifiers explain these facts. It makes sense of the fact that subset-knowers acquire the cardinal meanings of 'one' 'two' 'three', and 'four', and no other numeral, on the assumption that by age 3, the limits on parallel individuation have reached the adult level of 4 (see Oakes et al., 2006 for evidence that the adult level is evident even in infancy under some circumstances). Only sets of these sizes are representable by models of the sets of individuals held in parallel in working memory, thus to be matched via one–one correspondence to long-term memory models of sets of one, two, three, and four individuals.

We sought an answer to several questions. How do children assign numerical meanings to verbal numerals, and how do children learn how the list itself represents number? The bootstrapping proposal provides answers to both. The meanings of 'one' through 'four' are acquired just as quantifiers in natural languages are – as quantifiers for single individuals, pairs, triples, and quadruples. These words, as well as higher numerals, also get initial interpretations as part of a placeholder structure, the count list itself, in which meaning is exhausted by the fact that the list is ordered. The bootstrapping process explains how children learn how the list itself represents number, which in turn explains how they assign numerical meaning to numerals like 'five' and 'seven'. When children first become cardinal-principle knowers, the meaning of 'five' is exhausted by the child's mastery of counting. The counting principles ensure that the content of 'five' is one more than four, and the meaning of 'seven' is one more than six, which is one more than five, which is one more than four.

Conclusions

I have argued here that the numeral list representation of number is a representational resource with power that transcends any single representational system available to prelinguistic infants. When the child, at around age 3½, has mastered how the count sequence represents number, he or she can represent any exact cardinality expressed in their count list. Before that, he or she has only the quantificational resources of natural languages, parallel individuation representations that implicitly represent small numbers and analogue magnitude representations that provide approximate representations of the cardinal values of sets.

Additionally, I have taken on the challenge of specifying a learning mechanism that can underlie specific developmental discontinuities – Quinian bootstrapping. Quinian bootstrapping involves, but is not exhausted by, garden-variety learning processes: association, the mechanisms that support language learning, and so on. In addition, it involves noticing analogies and making inductive and abductive leaps. The specific bootstrapping proposal depends on the analogy between next on the numeral list and next state after additional individual has been added to a set.

In Quinian bootstrapping, an explicit structure is learned initially without the meaning it will eventually have, and at least some relations among the explicit symbols are learned directly in terms of each other. The list of numeral words and the counting routine are learned as numerically meaningless structures. Whereas order is essential to numerical representations, ordered relations in themselves are much more general and thus not uniquely numerical. The ordering of the number words exhausts their initial representational content within the counting routine and plays a role in the mappings and inductions through which counting comes to have numerical content.

Quinian bootstrapping depends upon integrating previously distinct representations. This is where the new representational power comes from. The concepts *set, individual, singular, plural, dual,* and *triple* are explicitly available to support the learning of quantifiers, but are only implicit or absent in parallel individuation and analogue magnitude representations. In analogue magnitude representations, numerical distinctions are explicitly symbolized that are unmarked in natural language quantifiers or parallel individuation (e.g. 35 vs. 40), and although analogue magnitude representations may play no role in the child's learning how counting represents number, they are integrated with counting some 6 months later (Le Corre & Carey, 2007). The representations that articulate the parallel individuation system contain computations that embody the successor function, whereas neither of the other systems does. The bootstrapping process (which depends on analogical mapping) creates an explicit representational system with all of these properties, a representational system that maps onto each of its sources and thus serves to integrate them.

Kronecker was wrong. Neither God nor evolution gave humans natural number. Natural number is a human construction. I have provided here one worked example of the creation of a new representational resource with more power than the representations upon which it is built. The lessons I wish to draw, however, are very general. Such creations occur repeatedly, both historically and within the individual child. Within mathematical representations, much has been written about the creation of 0, negative numbers, and rational numbers. Each of these developments transcends the power of the numeral list representation that is the focus of the present chapter, and each requires further episodes of Quinian bootstrapping (see Carey, 2009, for a discussion of the construction of rational number). Similarly, within the history of science, theory changes that involve conceptual change require the creation of new representational resources that allow thoughts that were previously unthinkable, and these theory changes also require Quinian bootstrapping (Carey, 2009).

Where does this leave us with respect to the questions that motivate this book? Many authors implicate language as one engine for the creation of abstract concepts, an engine that is uniquely human. Obviously, I agree with this speculation. But I offer a particular twist to it. Core cognition, shared with other animals, includes conceptual representations that are abstract in the sense of being amodal and in the sense of having meanings that cannot be stated in terms of a sensory vocabulary (e.g. *approximately seven, goal, cause.* . .). So language is not necessary for the creation of all abstract concepts. More importantly, the language faculty, on its own, does not account for the uniquely human conceptual repertoire, for all normal humans command one or more human language, and only some humans can think about rational numbers, global warming, or pancreatic cancer. Here, I have characterized one learning mechanism, Quinian bootstrapping, that crucially depends upon language (for the placeholder structures are typically formulated in language) but that draws on a variety of modelling techniques as well (analogy being the case in point in the present example). Modelling one conceptual domain in terms of the representations of the other is an abstraction technique; what remains is a structure that honours the constraints of each. Accounting for the evolutionary origins of Quinian bootstrapping processes is an open research question. Did the modelling techniques of Quinian bootstrapping evolve as part of the language faculty more generally, thus being available to support conceptual innovations, when harnessed, as in this present case study? Or did some other selection pressure support the construction of these powerful problem-solving devices? Would language trained animals, such as Matsuzawa's Ai or Pepperberg's Alex, be capable of Quinian bootstrapping? These questions are completely unexplored.

References

Antell, S. & Keating, D. P. (1983). Perception of numerical invariance in neonates. *Child Development*, **54**, 695–701.

Block, N. (1986). Advertisement for a semantics for psychology. In P. A. French (Ed.), *Midwest Studies in Philosophy*, pp. 615–678, Minneapolis, MN: University of Minnesota.

Bloom, P. & Wynn, K. (1997). Linguistic cues in the acquisition of number words. *Journal of Child Language*, **24**(3), 511–533.

Brannon, E. M. (2002). The development of ordinal numerical knowledge in infancy. *Cognition*, **83**, 223–240.

Brannon, E. M. & Terrace, H. S. (1998). Ordering of the numerosities 1 to 9 by monkeys. *Science*, **282**, 746–749.

Brannon, E. M., Abbott, S., & Lutz, D. J. (2004). Number bias for the discrimination of large visual sets in infancy. *Cognition*, **93**, B59–B68.

Butterworth, B. (1999). *What Counts: How Every Brain is Hardwired for Math* New York: Free Press.

Cantlon, J. & Brannon, E. M. (2005). The effect of hetereogeneity on numerical ordering in rhesus monkeys. *Infancy*, **9**(2), 173–189.

Carey, S. (2009). *The Origins of Concepts* New York: Oxford University Press.

Church, R. M. & Meck, W. H. (1984). The numerical attribute of stimuli. In H. L. Roitblatt, T. G. Bever, & H. S. Terrace (Eds.), *Animal cognition*, pp. 445–464, Hillsdale, NJ: Erlbaum.

Clark, E. V. & Nikatina, T. N. (in press). One vs. more than one: Antecedents to plurality in early language acquisition. *Linguistics.*

Dehaene, S. (1997). *The Number Sense* Oxford: Oxford University Press.

Dehaene, S. & Changeux, J-P. (1993). Development of elementary numerical abilities: A neuronal model. *Journal of Cognitive Neuroscience*, **5**, 390–407.

Feigenson, L. & Carey, S. (2003). Tracking individuals via object files: Evidence from infants' manual search. *Developmental Science*, **6**(5), 568–584.

Feigenson, L. & Carey, S. (2005). On the limits of infants' quantification of small object arrays. *Cognition*, **97**(3), 295–313.

Feigenson, L., Carey, S., & Hauser, M. D. (2002a). The representations underlying infants' choice of more: Object files versus analog magnitudes. *Psychological Science*, **13**, 150–156.

Feigenson, L., Carey, S., & Spelke, E. (2002b). Infants' discrimination of number vs. continuous extent. *Cognitive Psychology*, **44**, 33–66.

Flombaum, J. I., Junge, J. A., & Hauser, M. D. (2005). Rhesus monkeys (*Macaca mulatta*) spontaneously compute addition operations over large numbers. *Cognition*, **97**(3), 315–325.

Fodor, J. (1975). *The Language of Thought* Cambridge, MA: Harvard University Press.

Fuson, K. C. (1988). *Children's Counting and Concepts of Number* New York: Springer-Verlag.

Gallistel, C. R. (1990). *The Organization of Learning* Cambridge, MA: MIT Press.

Gallistel, C. R. & Gelman, R. (1992). Preverbal and verbal counting and computation. *Cognition*, **44**, 43–74.

Gelman, R. & Gallistel, C. R. (1978). *The Child's Understanding of Number* Cambridge, MA: Harvard University Press.

Gordon, P. (2004). Numerical Cognition Without Words: Evidence from Amazonia. *Science*, **306**(5695), 496–499.

Hartnett, P. & Gelman, R. (1998). Early understandings of numbers: Paths or barriers to the construction of new understandings? *Learning and Instruction*, **8**(4), 341–374.

Hauser, M. D. & Carey, S. (2003). Spontaneous representations of small numbers of objects by rhesus macaques: Examinations of content and format. *Cognitive Psychology*, **47**(4), 367–401.

Hauser, M. D., Carey, S., & Hauser, L. B. (2000). Spontaneous number representation in semi-free-ranging rhesus monkeys. *Proceedings of the Royal Society, London*, **267**, 829–833.

Hurford, J. (1987). *Language and Number: The Emergence of a Cognitive System* Oxford: Blackwell.

Kahneman, D., Treisman, A., & Gibbs, B. (1992). The reviewing of object files: Object-specific integration of information. *Cognitive Psychology*, **24**, 175–219.

Le Corre, M. & Carey, S. (2007). One, two, three, four, nothing more: How numerals are mapped onto core knowledge of number in the acquisition of the counting principles. *Cognition*, **105**, 395–438.

Le Corre, M., Li, P., & Jia, G. (2003, April). Effects of plural syntax on number word learning: A cross-linguistic study. Poster presented at the 70th Biennial Meeting of the Society for Research in Child Development. Tampa, FL.

Le Corre, M., Brannon, E. M., Van de Walle, G. A., & Carey, S. (2006). Re-visiting the competence/performance debate in the acquisition of the counting principles. *Cognitive Psychology*, **52**(2), 130–169.

Lipton, J. S. & Spelke, E. S. (2003). Origins of number sense: Large number discrimination in human infants. *Psychological Science*, **15**(5), 396–401.

Lipton, J. S. & Spelke, E. (2004). Discrimination of large and small numerosities by human infants. *Infancy*, **5**(3), 271–290.

Luck, S. J. & Vogel, E. K. (1997). The capacity of visual working memory for features and conjunctions. *Nature*, **390**, 279–281.

McCrink, K. & Wynn, K. (2004a). Large-number addition and subtraction by 9-month-old infants. *Psychological Science*, **15**(11), 776–781.

McCrink, K. & Wynn, K. (2004b). Ratio abstraction by 6-month-old infants. Paper presented at the International Conference on Infant Studies, Chicago, IL.

Mix, K., Levine, S. C., & Huttenlocher, J. (2002). *Quantitative Development in Infancy and Early Childhood* Oxford: Oxford University Press.

Nersessian, N. (1992). How do scientists think? Capturing the dynamics of conceptual change in science. In R. Giere (Ed.) *Cognitive Models of Science*, pp 3–44, Minneapolis, MN: University of Minnesota Press.

Oakes, L. M., Ross-Sheehy, S., & Luck, S. J. (2006). Rapid development of feature binding in visual short-term memory. *Psychological Science*, **17**, 781–787.

Piaget, J. (1952). *The Child's Conception of Number* (C. Gattegno & F. M. Hodgson, Trans.) London: Routledge & Kegan Paul.

Piaget, J. (1954). *The construction of reality in the child* New York: Basic Books.

Pica, P., Lemer, C., & Izard, V. (2004). Exact and approximate arithmetic in an Amazonian indigene group. *Science*, **306**(5695), 499–503.

Pylyshyn, Z. W. (2001). Visual indexes, preconceptual objects, and situated vision. *Cognition*, **80**(1–2), 127–158.

Quine, W. V. O. (1960). *Word and Object* Cambridge, MA: MIT Press.

Quine, W. V. O. (1969). *Ontological Relativity and Other Essays* New York: Columbia University Press.

Quine, W.V.O. (1974). *Roots of Reference* New York: Columbia University Press.

Ravid, D. & Hayek, L. (2003). Learning about different ways of expressing number in the development of Palestinian Arabic. *First Language*, **23**(1), 41–63.

Sarnecka, B. W., Kamenskaya, V.G., Ogura, T., Yamana, Y., & Yudovina, J. B. (2007). From grammatical number to exact numbers: Early meanings of 'one,' 'two,' and 'three,' in English, Russian, and Japanese. *Cognitive Psychology*, **55**(2), 136–168.

Scholl, B. J. & Leslie, A. M. (1999). Explaining the infant's object concept: Beyond the perception/cognition dichotomy. In E. Lepore & Z. Pylyshyn (Eds.), *What Is Cognitive Science?* pp. 26–73, Oxford: Blackwell.

Simon, T. J. (1997). Reconceptualizing the origins of number knowledge: A "non-numerical" account *Cognitive Development*, **12**, 349–372.

Starkey, P. & Cooper, R. (1980). Perception of numbers by human infants. *Science*, **210**, 1033–1035.

Swartz, K. B., Chen, S., & Terrace, H. (1991). Serial learning by rhesus monkeys: Acquisition and retention of multiple four-item lists. *Journal of Experimental Psychology: Animal Behavior Processes*, **17**(4), 396–410.

Terrace, H. S., Son, L. K., & Brannon, E. M. (2003). Serial expertise of rhesus macaques. *Psychological Science*, **14**(1), 66–73.

Trick, L. M. & Pylyshyn, Z. W. (1994). Why are small and large numbers enumerated differently? A limited capacity preattentive stage in vision. *Psychological Review*, **101**(1), 80–102.

Uller, C., Carey, S., Huntley-Fenner, G., & Klatt, L. (1999). What representations might underlie infant numerical knowledge. *Cognitive Development*, **14**, 1–36.

Weyl, H. (1949). *Philosophy of Mathematics and Natural Science* Princeton, NJ: Princeton University Press.

Wood, J. & Spelke, E. (2005). Infants' enumeration of actions: Numerical discrimination and its signature limits. *Developmental Science*, **8**(2), 173–181.

Wynn, K. (1990). Children's understanding of counting. *Cognition*, **36**, 155–193.

Wynn, K. (1992a). Children's acquisition of the number words and the counting system. *Cognitive Psychology*, **24**, 220–251.

Wynn, K. (1992b). Addition and subtraction by human infants. *Nature*, **358**, 749–750.

Xu, F. & Spelke, E. S. (2000). Large number discrimination in 6-month-old infants. *Cognition*, **74**, B1–B11.

Xu, F., Spelke, E., & Goddard, S. (2005). Number sense in human infants. *Developmental Science*, **8**(1), 88–101.

Chapter 14

Concepts in human adults

James A. Hampton

Editors' Preview

Chapter 14, 'Concepts in human adults', focuses on concept usage by human adults, and is organized around the idea that there are both continuities and discontinuities between the concepts possessed by human adults on the one hand, and the concepts represented by nonhuman animals and human infants on the other.

In continuity with the concepts of nonhuman animals and human infants, human adults represent individual folk concepts for everyday categories (e.g. dog, lunch, truck, chair) based on direct input from actual events. Day-to-day experiences with members from various categories allow adult humans to learn correlations of attributes and generalize to novel category instances based on similarity to abstracted prototypes and stored exemplars. This manner of learning and representing concepts based on experiential data should remind readers of the type of concept learning that was described in Chapters 3 and 4. It is also consistent with the concept-formation processes described for nonhuman animals and human infants in Chapters 8 to 12. It is in this respect that the concepts of human adults can be said to share an influential evolutionary and developmental past with nonhuman animals and human infants, respectively.

However, in discontinuity with the concepts of human infants and nonhuman animals, Chapter 14 also describes how the concepts of human adults are verbal concepts. We have words for 'dog', 'lunch', 'truck', and 'chair', and as was conveyed in Chapter 6, there is in human children (beginning at around 12 months) and adults, a strong interdependence between language and concepts. In this sense, language can be likened to an additional input system (one supplementing direct experience) that allows for the cultural transmission of information through means such as informal and formal instruction from more experienced tutors, the reading of books, and the watching of films. It is this additional mode of concept acquisition, which encompasses the scholarship received from proper schooling and higher education, that can bring human adults to more abstract ways of representing concepts, including understanding of their deeper ontologies.

The data reviewed in the chapter make the interesting point that although human adults seem to have both modes of concept construal (individual–folk and cultural–theoretical) available in their representational repertoires, it is the individual–folk mode that can often take precedence in tasks assessing adult concept usage. For example, in a study in which college students were told about a bird that had changed appearance to that of an insect through toxic contamination, a majority of participants judged that the creature's category membership had in fact changed from bird to insect. In addition, there is the phenomenon of the illusion of explanatory depth in which people often think they know how things work at a deep level when in fact they do not know. That is, in keeping with the notion of psychological essentialism, human adults may believe that concepts have definitions, but when pressed, learn that either they do not have the definitions, or that they do not have conscious access to those definitions. Finally, there is the occurrence of the inverse-conjunction fallacy. In this case, if reasoning followed purely logical rules, then people who believe that some property is true of all members of a class, such as sofas, should also believe that the same property is true of all members of a subset of that class such as uncomfortable handmade sofas. However, as Chapter 14 observes, people are more likely to believe the more general statement than the more specific one. The findings suggest that there are important ways in which the verbal concepts possessed by adult humans do not respect the constraints of logic. This observation implies that although years of schooling may facilitate adult humans' abilities to use abstract, formal powers of reasoning about concepts, there may be a more primitive, default mode of human adult concept representation (one held in common with nonhuman animals and human infants) that comes to the surface in a variety of tasks assessing concept usage.

Physics tells us that the world that we live in is 'really' composed of vast numbers of tiny waves/particles, defined and individuated by their mass, energy, charge, velocity, and position. That is all there is, the rest being empty space. In contrast, the world that we interact with in our everyday lives is composed of rooms with windows, people, and cats, and plates filled with milk and cornflakes. It is a world of individual objects and stuff, most of which can be effortlessly identified and labelled as being of a particular kind. Like an illustration in a child's reader, we could look around our environment and attach labels to all of the objects and kinds of things around us. We can also label events that occur across different time scales – breakfast, driving to the shops, going to college – as well as states, qualities, activities, and the rest. These labels represent the repertoire of verbal concepts that we have for interpreting and interacting with the world around us. As far as we know, language is not a necessary element for humans to possess this ability to conceptualize the world. Nonetheless, language is clearly integral to human conceptual knowledge, to the extent that one cannot study one without the other. Language also provides a huge boost to the cognitive capacities of the human species in relation to other primates (see Chapter 6 and other chapters in this book). This chapter focuses on these verbal concepts, and primarily on the nature of the concepts underlying kind terms such as 'cat', 'car', or 'breakfast'. For discussion of other kinds of conceptual knowledge see Chapter 2 of this book.

To situate the discussion in the light of earlier chapters, the conceptual repertoire of an average adult consists of a large amount of highly overlearned knowledge. Unlike the concepts acquired in the concept-learning experiments described in Chapters 3, 4, and 5 of this book, or indeed those in Chapters 8, 9, and 10 describing concept training with other species, an adult will have had daily exposure to numerous exemplars of familiar categories (breakfasts, cars, beds) for many years, even decades. We therefore need to keep an open mind about how such concepts will be represented. The models that best explain performance in concept-learning experiments may have only limited relevance to how adult verbal concepts are either learnt, represented, or utilized. It is probable that most of our more-advanced conceptual knowledge is acquired verbally without any direct experiential input. My knowledge of malaria, for example, is entirely based on verbal accounts of the disease's causes, symptoms, and transmission mechanism. Most people's concepts of a wide range of things is likely to be limited to what they have been told, what they have seen on TV, or what they have read in books. Humans have the ability to be told the answer without needing to work things out for themselves. Often, (although not always) that will be sufficient to generate an immediate change in behaviour. If I am told by a reliable source that a particular headache pill increases my risk of serious illness, I will at once stop taking it and look for an alternative. I do not need successive trials with corrective feedback in order to change my behaviour.[1]

The strong interdependence of language and concepts is central to understanding a vital distinction in discussing and exploring human adult concepts. The language faculty is a set of skills and knowledge contained in the head of a speaker, but a language is also an abstract cultural artefact with an independent existence of its own. The same is true of the concepts that constitute the meaning of the terms in any language. When we speak of a concept, such as 'cat', there are two very different ways in which we can understand the notion of concept. Taking a psychological stance, we consider the concept to be information stored in the brains of all people who can reasonably be said to understand what a cat is. Rey (1983) called this the 'conception' of a cat. We could imagine the research programme for studying this concept as follows: take a random

---

[1] On the other hand health messages about fatty foods or tobacco may have less immediate effect!

sample of competent adult speakers of English. Ask them if they know what a cat is, and if so to tell you all that they know about them. The set of information that is common to most of the respondents will correspond to the concept of cat as it is understood by this group – the folk concept of cat (see Chapter 7, this book). There is obviously room for individual variation in concepts studied this way. Some individuals may have eccentric views that disagree with beliefs commonly held by others. One might also differentiate the concept of 'cat' of pet owners from those of farmers, an urban versus a rural concept, and so forth. Medin et al. (1997) provided an excellent example of this type of research when they contrasted the concept of 'tree' as possessed by groups of taxonomists, landscape designers, and parks workers. Importantly, it is not possible for everyone to be *wrong* about what a cat is, if the concept is defined this way. Anything fitting the descriptive information in the right kind of way has to be a cat, and nothing else can be.

On the other hand, we could turn to a dictionary and an encyclopaedia in order to learn what the term 'cat' refers to. There we would learn another, overlapping, set of information including commonly known facts (about being mammals, hunters of mice, etc.) as well as less well-known facts – for example, about the evolution of the current race of domestic pets from desert cat ancestors in the Near East some 10 000 years ago. For this alternative notion of concept, it is at least conceivable that we could all be wrong about a concept. Scientific advance and careful systematic observation can redefine the categories of what 'really' exists, so that, for example, whales are no longer classified as fish. The question is then which of these two approaches gives us the 'real' concept of a cat?

The cultural transmission of conceptual information through the use of language, both spoken and written, plays a key role in enabling us to use our concepts for communication. It also generates a sociological dynamic by which certain concepts are owned by particular groups in society, who construct and maintain the meaning of terms, often with perfectly explicit goals. An example is the deliberate use of language in the struggle against prejudice in areas such as gender, disability, and mental health. It is therefore inaccurate to suppose that we learn our concepts simply through daily interaction with the world and by conversing informally with others. Consider that in most of the developed world, a human will spend a minimum of 10–12 years in full-time education, and those who intend to pursue an occupation that requires advanced levels of abstract thought will typically require 3–6 years more. Speaking as an educator, it would be nice to think that at least some of our conceptual repertoire as adults was the result of this process.[2]

A brief consideration of history confirms the central importance of cultural transmission of concepts. Even a concept as simple as that of negative number was poorly understood until the end of the eighteenth century (Boyer, 1968, p. 501) with some textbook writers in the mid-1700s still rejecting categorically the notion that two negative numbers could be multiplied together. The notion that zero is a number,

---

[2] Children's concepts too may be heavily influenced by the topics that they are studying in class, as Lloyde et al. (2003) discovered.

rather than the absence of a number, also took a surprisingly long time to evolve (Kaplan, 1999), just as did the physical notion that space could be empty (Aristotle had worked out that this was impossible, see Lafferty, 1993, p. 91). Concepts in mathematics and science exemplify culturally transmitted concepts (see Chapter 13, this book). Not only do school children around the world rapidly grasp concepts that eluded the most talented mathematicians of former times, but there is also an embarrassingly huge gulf between the conceptual grasp shown by the most able and the least able in the same society, depending on their ability and opportunity to benefit from education.

The discussion so far has been to set the scene for our review of human adult concepts. As students of the human species, we have two very different accounts to provide. One is to explain how the mind is able to develop, understand, and competently use abstract relational systems such as mathematics, logic, or scientific theories. Study of this question has been largely driven by theoretical and philosophical argument – what are the processes that drive scientific advance, and what sort of cognitive architecture would enable thinking of this kind to take place? There have also been fascinating studies of the processes of scientific reasoning and conceptual change in the lab (Dunbar, 1997). This type of culturally transmitted understanding is obviously something that sets human adults apart from both other species and from the pre-educated young of their own. A quite different issue to explain is how the mind operates in everyday life, away from the rigours of abstract cogitation. To preview the rest of the chapter, it will be argued that most of the evidence about this second issue is that we depend very heavily on a similarity-based, flexible, and a relatively vague set of conceptual terms, often with little awareness of the deeper ontological questions that concern philosophers. People are aware of their conceptual cultural heritage, and are, in the right circumstances, willing to accept that their understanding of a concept may be incorrect if it does not correspond to how the experts in society understand the term. But for the most part, they classify and label the world using inexact conceptual representations that they have picked up through being members of a community who share and fix the meanings through their daily usage of the conceptual terms. We shall then turn to the sometimes vexed question of how it is possible to think true thoughts that obey the laws of logic, given the inexactness of our concepts in everyday thought.

The research to be reviewed should also be seen in its social context. It is almost exclusively research conducted with highly educated and conceptually able samples of university students, whose minds have had many years of training in how to think. We should expect therefore that at least some of the results obtained may prove limited in generality (see, e.g. Atran & Medin, 2008; Proctor & Keil, 2006; Chapter 7, this book). Most importantly, in terms of context-independent, abstract, logical thought, we should be cautious about taking the results of these experiments as representative of the conceptual competence of the average human adult.

Concepts in practice

How do we represent a concept in our minds? How can we determine the content of any particular concept and individuate it from others that we might possess? Some of our concepts have explicit definitions that we could learn and use: a fever is the raising of body temperature above its normal range due to internal processes; a prime number is a number divisible without remainder only by itself and 1; or the crime of murder is the unlawful killing of a person with 'malice aforethought'. It is in fact a major part of the job of legislators to find usable verbal definitions and of the courts to decide how to apply them in different circumstances. However, most concepts in everyday use do not have definitions – a point now widely accepted (Fodor et al., 1980; Rosch & Mervis, 1975; Smith & Medin, 1981). Furthermore, even when the definition may be known, people's use of the term in everyday thought is likely to extend its application beyond its strict sense. Saturday night fever, or a game played at fever-pitch do not explicitly require a raised body temperature. Murder in a naïve juror's mind may correspond to a broader concept than the concept laid down in law – something more akin to the technical notion of homicide.

In the absence of definitions, it appears that we are forced to accept that the concepts found in the mind have more fluid, vague content. Four phenomena in particular led theorists to propose a prototype representation for concepts (Hampton, 1979, 1995, 2006; Rosch & Mervis, 1975). These are:

1. *Vagueness.* Concepts refer to categories of things, but the borders of the categories are often poorly delineated, with people both disagreeing and even being inconsistent about the class of things to which a concept refers (Hampton, 1998; McCloskey & Glucksberg, 1978).

2. *Typicality.* Within a semantic category like 'bird' or 'car' there are some items that people agree are highly typical or representative of the category, while other equally familiar items may be atypical. Nightingales and larks are typical birds, though rarely encountered, whereas turkeys and penguins are atypical (Rosch, 1975).

3. *Opaque definitions.* People find it hard to give an explicit account of why objects should fall in a particular category. As remarked above, few of our concepts have explicit definitions (Hampton, 1979; McNamara & Sternberg, 1978).

4. *Genericity.* Not being able to provide definitions does not mean that people do not know what is relevant to category membership. They will readily list aspects of a creature that are relevant to it being a bird, or aspects of a vehicle that make it a car. However these aspects are often only true of a majority of the category – they are generically but not universally true (Hampton, 2008).[3]

Early versions of prototype theory (Hampton, 1979; Rosch, 1975) proposed that concepts capture similarity clusters of the kind studied in category learning experiments (see Chapters 3 and 4, this book). Effectively, it was assumed that a prototype was

---

[3] An early treatise on logic made the distinction of metaphysically universal truths such as 'every human being is living' and morally universal truths such as St. Paul's rather un-Christian endorsement in Titus 1:12 of the view that 'Cretans are always liars, evil brutes, and gluttons', or Horace's equally pithy 'All singers have this fault: if asked to sing among their friends they are never so inclined; if unasked, they never stop'. The authors commented that for moral truths 'it is enough if things are usually this way', Arnauld & Nicole, 1662/1996, p. 114.

constituted by a set of inter-correlated features each of which was predictive of category membership. Both membership and typicality in a category were determined by the weighted sum of features possessed by a candidate item. Vagueness resulted from noise in the calculation of feature weights relative to some vaguely drawn criterion for membership. Typicality was simply a function of how many features an item possessed. Nightingales have more of the properties characteristic of most birds than do ostriches. The lack of explicit definitions and the ready production of generic properties were directly explained in terms of people representing the concept by a list of features each of which could be generally, but not necessarily, true of the concept. Note that the model still allows that *some* features may be necessarily or universally true of a concept. However such features *on their own* do not serve to define the concept sufficiently precisely. In Hampton (1995) it was also pointed out that by a judicious selection of feature weights, a well-defined concept may also be represented as a prototype, so the fact that humans were defined by Plato as featherless bipeds does not imply that 'human' may not be a prototype concept for Plato.[4]

Subsequent research has led to the rejection of this relatively simple notion of a prototype. One suggestion has been to supplement the notion by proposing that the set of features is not a simple list, but is structured into a knowledge schema or frame (Barsalou & Hale, 1993; Hampton, 2006). The schema represents additional information about the relations, causal and other, between the features. For example, a car has a motor, requires fuel, and is self-propelled. These three features are of course intimately related, and their relationship is part of our concept of 'car'. If the motor ran on clockwork and drove the windshield wipers only, the fuel was for heating the passenger compartment and the car was pulled along by sails it would be a highly atypical car, in spite of matching all three features.

However, such schemas may be quite patchy in terms of how much of the 'true' cultural concept of car is represented. As Keil and his colleagues have shown in their studies of the illusion of explanatory depth, people are often unaware of how little actual knowledge of causal links in complex artefacts they possess (Keil, 2003). People are probably quite good at conditional reasoning based on such schemas (if there is no fuel in the car it will not go anywhere), but are usually very bad at being able to say just how the presence of the fuel is actually translated into the forward motion of the car. Schemas can still be thought of as prototypes for two important reasons: 1) they provide abstract representations of the typical features of a class while losing details of individual members, and 2) they represent the typical centre of a class but are vague about the borderline. There is no precise specification of just how close the match to a schema needs to be in order for an individual or subclass to count as falling under that concept. Cars may be powered by electricity or have three wheels with the steering at the rear, but still be cars.

In Hampton (1998), I investigated the degree to which the probability of a borderline item being categorized in a given category was simply a function of its typicality

---

4 Rumour has it that when Diogenes brought a plucked chicken to Plato in his academy, the latter was forced to amend his definition to 'featherless biped *with broad nails*'.

for that category, as would be predicted by prototype theory. For most categories, the function was very regular – the higher the average rating of typicality for an item, the greater the proportion of people who would include it in the category. I also found however that for biological categories, categorization could deviate systematically from typicality. This deviation occurred where a creature was known to be of one kind but looked like another. The most obvious creatures of this kind were bats and penguins, whales, and dolphins. For example, a whale was rated to be quite typical of a fish, but was unlikely to be categorized as such. Dissociations of categorization and typicality in verbal concepts have been reported elsewhere. Rips (1989) presented a number of studies in which the two variables were dissociated. Typicality is usually judged on the basis of surface appearance. The notion of being a typical example seems to require that an item look right. On the other hand, categorization requires deeper hidden parts to be correct. Thus a bird that changes its appearance into an insect through toxic contamination was judged in Rips's study to be more typical of an insect, yet more likely to be a bird. Such results suggest that similarity to a category schema could be calculated in different ways depending on the task context (although Rips used his result to motivate the more radical claim that categorization is not based on similarity to a schema at all).

Hampton, Estes, and Simmons (2007) replicated Rips's metamorphosis study and found that there were in fact quite large individual differences amongst college students in how they responded. When asked simultaneously to judge both typicality and category membership for each scenario, as was done in Rips's study, a majority (17) judged that the creature was still of the same kind after the change, but a sizeable minority (12) made the reverse judgement. In a second experiment, where students in the relevant condition only judged category membership and not typicality, only eight judged that the creature's kind had not changed, whereas 19 now thought it had. A third experiment confirmed that most students had the intuition that in fact the creature was no longer a bird (as in Rips, 1989, the experiments all actually used multiple examples of the transformations and incorporated other conditions and controls). Hampton et al. argued that students were making this choice on the basis that the transformation, even though externally caused, was so great that it must have affected the inner workings of the creature to the point where it was now more of an insect than a bird.

The prototype theory has also been challenged by growing evidence for the role of exemplar knowledge in conceptual tasks (see Murphy, 2002, Chapter 4; Smits et al., 2002; Storms et al., 2000, 2001) which would suggest that the process of abstraction of conceptual prototypes is incomplete. For example, Smits et al. (2002) considered how people would decide whether to categorize a number of unfamiliar exotic edible plant products as fruits or vegetables. Classification was best modelled with an exemplar-based model that used similarity to individual known fruits and vegetables rather than similarity to an abstraction of each category to determine classification. Similarly Storms et al. (2000) found that typicality in categories is usually better captured by an exemplar model (summed distance in similarity space from stored exemplars) than by a prototype model (distance from a central average point of the category in similarity space).

A recent book by Rogers and McClelland (2004) provides a detailed model of how both prototype and exemplar effects could be generated through the same simple associative learning process. They adapted a model proposed by Rumelhart (1990) in which a PDP feedforward network is trained with facts such as (a robin *can* sing) or (a canary *is* yellow). The subject noun (robin) is activated in one input array, and the relation (*can*) in a second input array, and then connections are adjusted by gradual incremental learning in order to activate the correct element (sing) in an output array. The model shows a range of interesting effects, including learning broad category distinctions before narrower ones (e.g. animals vs. plants before birds vs. fish), and retaining broad categories over more specific ones when the network is damaged. Both of these effects correspond to well-known effects in the literature (Mandler & McDonough, 1993; Quinn & Johnson, 2000; Warrington, 1975). The model abstracts away from individual inputs by forming generalizations over similar inputs, so that its representation of a category resembles a prototype. However, it also retains enough within-category structure to be able to account for exemplar effects.

A particularly interesting feature of the model is that it provides a possible account of centrality effects. Sloman, Love, and Ahn (1998) described how the features of a concept differ in their centrality for the concept. Centrality can be defined and measured in different ways, but the basic notion is the degree to which the feature could be changed without otherwise affecting the rest of the concept. Washing machines are typically white, but they could be yellow without any need to revise any of their other features. They typically also contain a drum for the clothes, and it would not be easy to change this feature without at the same time making major adjustments to the rest of the concept schema. Centrality is therefore related to the number of causal dependencies that a feature enters into within the schema that represents the concept. Sloman and colleagues have shown that centrality of an attribute is correlated with a number of other behavioural measures such as the importance of the attribute for predicting category membership.

Simple prototype or exemplar models have no obvious way to derive feature centrality. The prototype model weights features by their covariation with category membership, but does not represent the covariation or dependency amongst features. The exemplar model simply situates exemplars in a similarity space and has no more to say about the features of a concept than that. Rogers and McClelland's model however retains information about the complex covariation of features within a domain, so that it can determine which features are more central in terms of the total pattern of correlation that they have with the other features. It captures what makes a concept coherent, without the need for a higher level of causal understanding to be superimposed on the representation.

Psychological essentialism and beliefs about concepts

As most humans live in social groups, and concepts are a fundamental part of communication with other people, we have seen how learning models that simply relate the mind's contents to its learning history are going to be inadequate. I have already made the important point that many of our concepts are not ours to use or change as we would wish but belong to our culture. I could choose to start including whales and other cetaceans in my category of fish, but I would then stand accused of using the word fish in a nonstandard way (but see Dupré, 1999). Note however, that the lay population has not accepted all of science's terms. Botanically speaking, many of the vegetables that we eat are fruits – a green bean forms from the ovary on the plant after the flower has been fertilized, and contains the seeds for the next generation, just as a plum or an orange does. Sometimes indeed even established sciences have terminological problems. Recently, the world press reported difficulties with the definition of the term 'planet' in astronomy. Originally a planet was a large body circling a sun, but the problem arose when it turned out that Pluto, the furthest recognized planet in our solar system, was smaller and had a less-circular orbit than two other objects that had not been awarded the status of planets. A concept that appeared to be clear and well understood turned out to be vague and arbitrary to an embarrassing degree. The world is not always as neat as we would wish it to be.

These problems aside, the average student participant in concept experiments, no doubt like other members of the adult population, is aware that there are experts who may know more about a concept than they do. Kalish (1995) posed the following kind of problem to his participants. Imagine that there is an animal in the zoo, and that George says it is a possum while John says it is not. Does one of them have to be right and the other wrong, or could it just be a matter of opinion? Kalish found a systematic tendency to say that one of the two must be right – most particularly for biological kinds. This tendency to assume that there is an externally determined correct answer to a question of categorization has been associated with the thesis of psychological essentialism (Medin & Ortony, 1989). The thesis holds that people believe that things are of a particular kind because of some hidden essence deep within them. We may not know what the essence actually is, in which case our representation of the concept may contain an empty placeholder. (Keil et al., 2008, have shown that both adults and children know about where expertise on different domains is to be found.)

Kalish's result was replicated in a study by Claire Simmons as part of her PhD thesis (Simmons & Hampton, 2006). She investigated three different manifestations of essentialist beliefs. In addition to the question of fact versus opinion, students were asked to judge whether a category had all-or-none membership, as opposed to admitting of partial membership, and whether or not they would defer to an expert's opinion if it differed from their own. Across a range of categories, there was evidence for stronger essentialist beliefs about biological categories than about artefacts. Willingness to defer to experts was however very limited (see also Braisby, 2001, 2004; Proctor & Keil, 2006). Interestingly, in common with the Hampton, Estes, and Simmons (2007) study, there were systematic individual differences. Thinking that membership should be all-or-none correlated positively across individuals with thinking that categorization was a matter of fact rather than opinion. Degree of deference, however, did not correlate with either of the other measures. There is also reason to suppose that deference may be more a question of social conformity than of essentialist beliefs. Braisby (2001) found that when asked about whether a genetically modified salmon would still be a salmon his respondents deferred not only to the opinions of biologists but also, to a lesser extent to the opinions of shoppers.

Concepts and causality

A recurring theme in the concepts literature since Murphy & Medin (1985) is that concepts are part of a broader causal-explanatory scheme with which we understand the world. As Rogers and McClelland (2004) point out, a simple learning model, such as might easily occur in other species, can learn about the centrality of different properties of a conceptual domain, without invoking notions of cause or explanation. However, we do frequently invoke conceptual information as explanations for events and properties that we observe in the world.

A set of studies conducted by Daniel Heussen for his PhD thesis (Heussen and Hampton, 2007; Heussen, 2009) explored the ways in which people explain the properties of a concept. Heussen asked student participants to explain things such as why axes are dangerous. An initial qualitative analysis revealed that they frequently appealed to another property as an explanation. They said, for example, that axes are dangerous because they are sharp. Heussen then obtained ratings of how satisfying such explanations were for a sample of paired properties in the frame 'concept X has property p because it has property q'. He predicted the variance in these ratings on the basis of different measures of the properties in question. Where applicable, these measures were taken in each direction (p to q and q to p). The measures were co-occurrence (Of all man-made things that are dangerous, what percentage is also sharp?), counterfactuals (If axes were not dangerous, would they still be sharp?), and the mutability of each individual property (How difficult is it to imagine axes that are not dangerous/axes that are not sharp?). He also showed another group of participants a diagram listing the most salient properties of the concept, and asked them to draw arrows to indicate when one property depended on another. A measure of centrality was then taken in terms of the number and strength of links involving each target property.

In a subsequent regression analysis, he found that the primary predictor of the plausibility of an explanation with a standardized regression weight, beta, of 0.48 was the dependence of p on q – that is, the degree to which being dangerous was judged to depend on being sharp in the network-dependency diagram. In addition, the two counterfactual measures predicted additional variance with betas of around 0.23 each – the questions of whether if axes were not dangerous, they would still be sharp, and if they were not sharp, they would still be dangerous. Interestingly neither of the co-occurrence measures, reflecting intuitions about the statistical correlation between the properties, predicted any variance in the plausibility of explanations.[5] Apparently, the fact that people consider most sharp things to be dangerous did not enter into people's thinking when deciding that it makes sense to say that axes are dangerous because they are sharp. (For a detailed model of causal understanding see Sloman, 2005.)

Concepts and truth

I have so far concentrated on the role of concepts in our everyday mental life – seeing the world as composed of types, and using that conceptual framework in order to

---

[5] Reliability of the different rating measures used as predictors was comparable.

learn about the world and explain it to ourselves and others. But concepts also serve another purpose. As described in my opening remarks, concepts are not just personal mental entities, but have a life of their own in a social community. An important function for a theory of concepts therefore is to explain how it is possible for thoughts to refer to the world so that we can assert or believe things that are true, and recognize that other things are false. Concepts are the building blocks of propositions, and many propositions can be given semantic value in terms of being true or false in our world. If I declare that there is a hippopotamus in the room, the truth of the statement will depend on their being a creature in the room and on that creature being a hippopotamus. Enabling words and sentences to refer to the world, that is, establishing reference is a major part of the role of concepts in our thought. There is a large literature in the philosophy of mind and language, and in semantics itself, on how words and sentences establish reference and the conditions under which propositions of different kinds are true or false. The interface of this literature with the psychology of concepts has led to some interesting debates on the nature of concepts (e.g. Fodor, 1998).

Much of the debate turns on the question of whether concepts are constituted by the type of thing in the world that they refer to (externalism) or by the type of content that is represented in the mind (internalism). For most philosophers (e.g. Rey, 1983) the concept of 'cat' is an abstract entity that refers to the class *Felis silvestris catus*. Most speakers of English will have the name of this concept in their vocabulary, and will represent it in some way, which may be more or less correct. This externalist view would allow that we may all be wrong about the content of a concept. It could turn out that water is not after all H_2O, in which case we would all change our represented concept to match what we now know to be the case (see Putnam, 1975, and Kripke, 1980, for famous papers on this topic). The externalist view subscribes to the distinction that I made at the start of the chapter between cultural concepts and individual concepts. In addition, they would say that for many concepts, and particularly those referring to natural kinds in the world, the cultural concept itself has to defer to the real class of things in external reality.

The advantage of specifying conceptual content in terms of external criteria should be obvious for the treatment of truth and falsehood. If concepts can be individuated with external criteria, the truth of propositions involving those concepts can be easily defined in terms of set-theoretic semantics. The statement 'all cats purr' will be true just in the case that the class of 'things that purr' is a superset of the class of 'cats'. If on the other hand, the notion of purring is something that depends on how an average-educated speaker of English understands the meaning of the term, it becomes problematic to separate out issues of truth from issues of meaning. Whether all cats purr or not will depend on how you understand what kind of creature may count as a cat, and on what kind of sound should count as a purr. Truth becomes relative to an individual's set of meanings, and can not be determined independent of individual contexts.

This relativity relates to another problem in philosophical logic, namely vagueness (Keefe & Smith, 1997). In deciding whether all cats purr, it is necessary to determine for every creature (1) whether or not it is a cat, and (2) whether or not it purrs. But many statements of this kind appear to rely on vague predicates. The classic examples relate to the so-called Sorites paradox. How does one determine the set of adult men for whom 'X is bald' is true? If we start with those with no hair at all, the predicate clearly applies. If we then consider someone with just a single hair, the statement is still clearly true. But if we then proceed by adding one hair at a time, we are on the uncomfortable horns of a dilemma. Either we must say that there is a particular number of hairs at which 'X is bald' switches abruptly from true to false, or we must allow that adding just one hair can never change the truth of the statement in this way. The first appears counterintuitive, since it would imply that one could have two individuals, one with just one hair less than the other, but we would call one bald and the other not bald. The second is even worse, since it implies that everyone is bald, or if one starts at the other end of the sequence, it implies that no one is bald.

One way to handle vagueness is to stipulate that it does not exist. Thus, Frege (1892/1980) declared that all meaningful propositions involving concepts had to be true or false, and any concept that admitted of partial truth was not a concept at all. Alternatively, it has been suggested that natural language statements should allow of varied degrees of truth (so called fuzzy truth, Zadeh, 1965). If baldness is a matter of degree, the truth of 'X is bald' can be mapped onto the number of hairs through a continuous function (Hampton, 2007). There are however unresolved problems with this solution (Kamp & Partee, 1995; Osherson & Smith, 1981, 1982, 1997), in particular because once fuzziness is allowed into truth values, other desirable properties of truth functions tend to be lost. For example, Harold may be 50% bald, but 'Harold is either bald or not bald' would appear to be necessarily true, while 'Harold is both bald and not bald' should be necessarily false. No completely satisfactory way to derive this intuition has been proposed.

A possible solution was proposed by Kamp and Partee (1995). Without going into the technical detail, they proposed that there may be three types of truth value – true, false, and undecided. Vague borderline cases would fall in the undecided category. To test this notion, I conducted some studies with my students Bayo Aina, Mathias Andersson, and Sejal Parmar to investigate whether people would actually recognize a category of undecided or borderline cases. The method we used was to ask one group of people to categorize borderline cases (e.g. Is a tomato a fruit?) using just a Yes/No answer, and a second group to categorize them but with three response choices: definitely yes, definitely no, and not definitely sure. Our intuition was that if there were cases that a person knew were problematic in some way, they would use this last category. Moreover, if asked to do the task again 2 weeks later, the same items would still be seen as problematic and would remain in the unsure category. In contrast, we predicted that those participants who were forced to choose between yes and no would tend to choose a response in an arbitrary way and so would be more likely to give a different response when asked again at a later date. In the event, across two studies we found that the level of instability in categorization responses was identical in the two groups. People were no more reliable at selecting the items for which they were 'definitely sure it's in the category' versus the rest than they were at just categorizing the items with yes or no. The conclusion is that vagueness does not just apply to a certain set of items. The boundaries of the vague region are themselves just as vague as the category boundary.

Within the psychological literature on truth and vagueness, there is plenty of evidence that people fail to appreciate the set-theoretic approach to truth based on externally defined sets. Informal testimony from logic teachers suggests that the average person's mind is unreceptive to logical theorems. Research into syllogistic reasoning confirms that people have a very hard time drawing inferences based on propositional form, and that most reasoning is performed through simulating situations in one's mind, in effect constructing mental models (Johnson-Laird & Byrne, 1996). The reader may like to try the following puzzle taken from Lewis Carroll (1958, p.119):

> No kitten, that loves fish, is unteachable.
> No kitten without a tail will play with a gorilla.
> Kittens with whiskers always love fish.
> No teachable kitten has green eyes.
> No kittens have tails unless they have whiskers.

The mind quickly fills with images of kittens, tails, whiskers, bowls of fish, and lonely gorillas seeking a playmate. Logical form is buried beneath the conceptual content and discovering it takes considerable effort.

Verbal concepts also display a lack of respect for the constraints of logic. An early demonstration, following Randall (1976), was a study in which I showed that conceptual categorization is not necessarily transitive (Hampton, 1982). People may agree that X is a type of Y, and Y is a type of Z, but balk at the conclusion that X is also a type of Z. For example, car-seats are a type of chair, and chairs are a type of furniture, but car-seats are not furniture. The effect is not just due to fuzziness or partial category membership, since chairs are very typical kinds of furniture, mentioned by just about everyone when asked to list examples of the category. Rather, the effect demonstrates that people judge truth of semantic statements like these on the basis of the overlap of conceptual content, rather than on the basis of the inclusion of one extensional class within another.

Similar evidence of failure to respect the logic of extensions was found in a series of studies I conducted on how people categorize items in complex categories formed using logical connectives (see Hampton, 1997). When people judged what belongs in categories such as 'sports which are games', or 'fruits or vegetables', or 'dwellings that are not buildings', they frequently made judgements that contradicted the apparent logical relations involved of set intersection, set union, and set complements. In Hampton (1987) I proposed a model for how the semantic content of two concepts could be integrated when forming a conjunctive concept such as sports which are games. As it combines generic, default, features of the two concept prototypes, and then subjects them to a coherence check, the model actually predicts that people will not respect logical constraints in their judgements in just the way that was found.

A similar effect is a phenomenon discovered by Shafir, Smith, & Osherson (1990) that I explored in a recent paper with Martin Jönsson (Jönsson & Hampton, 2006). People judged universally quantified sentences in which the subject noun was either unmodified or modified with an atypical adjective. Examples are:

1. All sofas have back-rests.

2. All uncomfortable handmade sofas have back-rests.

There was an apparently irresistible tendency to consider the first sentence more likely to be true than the second. The reader should check their own intuitions before reading on. The problem with this intuition is that, of course, if (1) is true, (2) must necessarily follow. (A separate group of students confirmed that all uncomfortable handmade sofas were in fact sofas.) Equally if (2) were false, (1) must necessarily also be false since (2) provides a counterexample. We tried different variants of the task, including placing the sentences side by side and asking students to select which was more likely to be true, and replacing the quantifier with the phrases 'Every single sofa...', 'All sofas always...' and '100% of sofas...'. None of these manipulations removed the tendency to rate the unmodified sentence as more likely to be true. In our final experiment, we adopted a format in which each pair of statements was printed one sentence above the other, and participants simply had to state whether each one was true or false. Filler sentences were included in which either (1) or (2) was clearly and legitimately more true. For example, it is quite correct to say that 'all trucks are noisy' is more likely to be true than 'all toy trucks are noisy', since toy trucks may not be a subset of trucks in its default sense. In this final experiment, we managed to reduce the incidence of the fallacy to a more respectable level, although the trend was still in the same direction. We termed the effect the inverse-conjunction fallacy, in recognition of its close relation to Tversky and Kahneman's (1983) more familiar conjunction fallacy, which is another example of people using conceptual similarity in a situation where extensional reasoning is called for.

In sum, all of these demonstrations suggest that people are committed to thinking conceptually in terms of internally constituted meanings rather than in terms of external classes. Psychological truth is not equivalent to logical or semantic truth, and they should not be confused.

Concepts as grounded in perception and action

Much of the preceding discussion of how people use their concepts is compatible with a theory of conceptual representation propounded by Barsalou (2003, 2008). Barsalou challenges the traditional assumption that conceptual information is represented in the mind by the use of amodal symbols. Instead, he suggests that concepts are never completely divorced from the experiential component of their instantiations. Encounters with cats will leave context-dependent traces of multi-modal experiences, including affective responses, vision, sound, and smell. These are used to construct a simulator – a brain mechanism that allows us to reconstruct and interrogate representations of cats under different conditions. If the simulator is unable to construct a cat that is not at the same time an animal, then the system can infer that all cats are animals. Space does not permit a review of the increasing evidence for this view, but much of the evidence comes from showing that the perceptual properties of a concept continue to influence the processing of the concept even when it is presented in abstract symbolic form (e.g. as written text). It should be clear that this approach would lend itself very readily to explaining the flexibility and vagueness of adult human concepts. It is also consistent with developmental accounts that take the perceptual experiences of infants as the starting point for the development of mature concepts (e.g. Quinn & Eimas, 2000).

Conclusions

In this chapter, we have been looking at the end result of the long and complex process of the making of human concepts. It is suggested that our evolutionary past is still very much a part of our conceptual system. There is plenty of evidence that our minds still make heavy use of associative systems for learning, with similarity-based generalization and a dependence on actually experienced objects and events, just as might be proposed for the concepts learnt by rats or pigeons. Having an adaptable and fuzzy system of knowledge is much better suited to handling our daily interaction with the world than a discrete symbolic system – as the advocates of fuzzy logic systems for artificial intelligence have demonstrated (Kosko, 1993).

However, this basic system for learning the prototype classes in the world around us is overlaid with the culturally transmitted accumulation of concepts enshrined in the language we speak, the books we read, the films we watch, and indeed the university courses we take. These concepts become elaborated through generations of scholarship and provide the solid foundations for knowledge and science. The term 'concept' has to cover the full gamut of representations from the concept of 'red' as a basic perceptual experience through to the concept of 'mass–energy' in Einsteinian physics. It is clear that, particularly through the evolution of language for social communication, and through cultural transmission of knowledge from one generation to the next, we have left other species far behind in our capacity to develop concepts beyond the simple prototypes we started with.

Research on adult human concepts has expanded greatly in the last three decades, and in addition to psychology there is also important and relevant work being done in linguistics, semantics, artificial intelligence, philosophy, and neuroscience. In fact, the topic is a prototype of the interdisciplinary interests of cognitive science. The applications of the research also spill over into a range of areas, including branding and marketing of consumer products and companies, social stereotyping, racism and prejudice, and public understanding of science. The challenge for the future is to encourage researchers to cross the disciplinary boundaries and to start to integrate the different theories and perspectives. We need to take our concept of 'concept' from its current prototype stage (fluid, vague, similarity-based, and polymorphous) into an explicit scientifically respectable concept, playing its role in a causal theory of mental representation and cognition.

References

Arnauld, A. & Nicole, P. (1662/1996). *Logic or the Art of Thinking* (Translated and edited by J. V. Buroker) Cambridge: Cambridge University Press.

Atran, S. & Medin, D. L. (2008). *The Native Mind and the Cultural Construction of Nature* Cambridge, MA: MIT Press.

Barsalou, L. W. (2003). Situated simulation in the human conceptual system. In H. E. Moss & J. A. Hampton (Eds.), *Conceptual Representation*, pp. 513–562, Hove: Psychology Press.

Barsalou, L. W. (2008). Grounded cognition. *Annual Review of Psychology*, 59, 617–645.

Barsalou, L. W. & Hale, C. R. (1993). Components of conceptual representation: from feature lists to recursive frames. In I. van Mechelen, J. A. Hampton, R. S. Michalski, & P. Theuns (Eds.),

Categories and Concepts: Theoretical Views and Inductive Data Analysis, pp. 97–144, London: Academic Press.

Boyer, C. (1968). *A History of Mathematics* New York: Wiley.

Braisby, N. R. (2001). Deference in categorisation: evidence for essentialism? In Moore, J. D. & Stenning, K. (Eds.), *Proceedings of the 23rd Annual Conference of the Cognitive Science Society*, pp. 122–127, Mahwah, NJ: Erlbaum.

Braisby, N. R. (2004). Deference and essentialism in the categorization of chemical kinds. In R. Alterman & D. Kirsch (Eds.), *Proceedings of the 25th Annual Conference of the Cognitive Science Society*, pp. 174–179, Mahwah, NJ: Erlbaum.

Carroll, L. (1958). *Symbolic Logic and the Game of Logic* New York: Dover Publications.

Dunbar, K. (1997). How scientists think: Online creativity and conceptual change in science. In T. B. Ward, S. M. Smith, & S. Vaid (Eds.), *Conceptual Structures and Processes: Emergence, Discovery and Change*, pp. 461–493, Washington, DC: APA Press.

Dupré, J. (1999). Are whales fish? In D. L. Medin & S. Atran (Eds.), *Folkbiology*, pp. 461–476, Cambridge, MA: MIT Press.

Fodor, J. A. (1998). *Concepts: Where Cognitive Science Went Wrong* Oxford: Oxford University Press.

Fodor, J. A., Garrett, M., Walker, E., & Parkes, C. (1980). Against definitions. *Cognition*, 8, 263–367.

Frege, G. (1892/1980). On sense and meaning. In P. Geach & M. Black (Eds.), *Translations from the Philosophical Writings of Gottlob Frege*, 3rd edn., Oxford: Basil Blackwell.

Hampton, J. A. (1979). Polymorphous concepts in semantic memory. *Journal of Verbal Learning and Verbal Behavior*, 18, 441–461.

Hampton, J. A. (1982). A demonstration of intransitivity in natural categories. *Cognition*, 12, 151–164.

Hampton, J. A. (1987). Inheritance of attributes in natural concept conjunctions. *Memory & Cognition*, 15, 55–71.

Hampton, J. A. (1995). Testing prototype theory of concepts. *Journal of Memory and Language*, 34, 686–708.

Hampton, J. A. (1997). Conceptual combination. In K. Lamberts & D. R. Shanks (Eds.), *Knowledge, Concepts and Categories*, pp. 135–162, Hove: Psychology Press.

Hampton, J. A. (1998). Similarity-based categorization and fuzziness of natural categories. *Cognition*, 65, 137–165.

Hampton, J. A. (2006). Concepts as prototypes. In B. H. Ross (Ed.), *The Psychology of Learning and Motivation: Advances in Research and Theory*, Vol. 46, pp. 79–113, Amsterdam: Elsevier.

Hampton, J. A. (2007). Typicality, graded membership and vagueness. *Cognitive Science*, 31, 355–383.

Hampton, J. A. (2009). Stability in concepts and evaluating the truth of generic statements. In F. J. Pelletier (Ed.), *Kinds, Things, and Stuff: Concepts of Generics and Mass Terms. New Directions in Cognitive Science*, Vol. 12, pp. 80–99, Oxford: Oxford University Press.

Hampton, J. A., Estes, Z., & Simmons, S. G. (2007). Metamorphosis: Essence, appearance and behavior in the categorization of natural kinds. *Memory & Cognition*, 35, 1785–1800.

Heussen, D. (2009). Property explanations: When one property explains another. PhD thesis, City University London.

Heussen, D. & Hampton, J. A. (2007). 'Emeralds are expensive because they are rare'; Plausibility of property explanations. In S. Vosniadou, D. Kayser, & A. Protopapas (Eds.),

Proceedings of Eurocogsci07, The European Cognitive Science Conference, pp. 101–106, Hove: Erlbaum.

Johnson-Laird, P. N. & Byrne, R. M. J. (1996). Mental models and syllogisms. *Behavioral and Brain Sciences*, **19**, 543–546.

Jönsson, M. L. & Hampton, J. A. (2006). The inverse conjunction fallacy. *Journal of Memory and Language*, **55**, 317–334.

Kalish, C. W. (1995). Essentialism and graded membership in animal and artifact categories. *Memory & Cognition*, **23**, 335–353.

Kamp, H. & Partee, B. (1995). Prototype theory and compositionality. *Cognition*, **57**, 129–191.

Kaplan, R. (1999). *The Nothing That Is; A Natural History of Zero* London: Penguin Books.

Keefe, R. & Smith, P. (1997). Theories of vagueness. In R. Keefe & P. Smith (Eds.), *Vagueness: A Reader*, pp. 1–57, Cambridge, MA: MIT Press.

Keil, F. C. (2003). Categorization, causation, and the limits of understanding. In H. E.Moss & J. A.Hampton (Eds.), *Conceptual Representation*, pp. 663–692, Hove: Psychology Press.

Keil, F. C., Stein, C., Webb, L., Billings, V. D., & Rozenblit, L. (2008). Discerning the division of cognitive labor: An emerging understanding of how knowledge is clustered in other minds. *Cognitive Science*, **32**(2), 259–300.

Kosko, B. (1993). *Fuzzy Thinking: The New Science of Fuzzy Logic* New York: Hyperion.

Kripke, S. (1980). *Naming and Necessity* Cambridge, MA: Harvard University Press.

Lafferty, J. M. (1993). History of vacuum science: A visual aids project. In P. A. Redhead (Ed.), *Vacuum Science and Technology; Pioneers of the 20th Century*, pp. 91–106, New York: Springer.

Lloyde, J., Braisby, N., & Brace, N (2003). Seeds of doubt: Are children taught to be essentialists? In F. Schmalhofer, R. M. Young & G. Katz (Eds), *Proceedings of EuroCogSci03*, pp. 211–216, Mahwah, NJ: Erlbaum.

Mandler, J. M. & McDonough, L. (1993). Concept formation in infancy. *Cognitive Development*, **8**, 291–318.

McCloskey, M. & Glucksberg, S. (1978). Natural categories: Well-defined or fuzzy sets? *Memory & Cognition*, **6**, 462–472.

McNamara, T. P. & Sternberg, R. J. (1983). Mental models of word meaning. *Journal of Verbal Learning and Verbal Behavior*, **22**, 449–474.

Medin. D. L., Lynch, E. B., & Coley, J. D. (1997). Categorization and reasoning among tree experts: Do all roads lead to Rome? *Cognitive Psychology*, **32**, 49–96.

Medin, D. L. & Ortony, A. (1989). Psychological essentialism. In S.Vosniadou & A. Ortony (Eds.), *Similarity and Analogical Reasoning*, pp. 179–195, Cambridge: Cambridge University Press.

Murphy, G. L. (2002). *The Big Book of Concepts* Cambridge, MA: MIT Press.

Murphy, G. L. & Medin, D. L. (1985). The role of theories in conceptual coherence. *Psychological Review*, **92**, 289–316.

Osherson, D. N. & Smith, E. E. (1981). On the adequacy of prototype theory as a theory of concepts. *Cognition*, **11**, 35–58.

Osherson, D. N. & Smith, E. E. (1982). Gradeness and conceptual conjunction. *Cognition*, **12**, 299–318.

Osherson, D. N. & Smith, E. E. (1997). On typicality and vagueness. *Cognition*, **64**, 189–206.

Proctor, C. & Keil, F. C. (2006). Differences in deference: Essences and insights. In R. Sun & N. Miyake (Eds), *Proceedings of the 28th Annual Conference of the Cognitive Science Society*, pp. 1974–1979, Mahwah, NJ: Lawrence Erlbaum.

Putnam, H. (1975). The meaning of 'meaning'. In H. Putnam (Ed.), *Mind, Language, and Reality: Philosophical Papers*, Vol. 2, pp. 215–271, Cambridge: Cambridge University Press.

Quinn, P. C. & Eimas, P. D. (2000). The emergence of category representations during infancy: Are separate perceptual and conceptual processes required? *Journal of Cognition and Development*, 1, 55–61.

Quinn, P. C. & Johnson, M. H. (2000). Global-before-basic object categorization in connectionist networks and 2-month-old infants. *Infancy*, 1, 31–46.

Randall, R. A. (1976). How tall is a taxonomic tree? Some evidence for dwarfism. *American Ethnologist*, 3, 543–553.

Rey, G. (1983). Concepts and stereotypes. *Cognition*, 15, 237–262.

Rips, L. J. (1989). Similarity, typicality and categorization. In S. Vosniadou & A. Ortony (Eds.), *Similarity and Analogical Reasoning*, pp. 21–59, Cambridge: Cambridge University Press.

Rosch, E. R. (1975). Cognitive representations of semantic categories. *Journal of Experimental Psychology: General*, 104, 192–232.

Rogers, T. T. & McClelland, J. L. (2004). *Semantic Cognition* Cambridge, MA: MIT Press.

Rosch, E. R. & Mervis, C. B. (1975). Family resemblances: Studies in the internal structure of categories. *Cognitive Psychology*, 7, 573–605.

Rumelhart, D. E. (1990). Brain style computation: Learning and generalization. In S. F. Zornetzer, J. L. Davis, & C. Lau (Eds.), *An Introduction to Neural and Electronic Networks*, pp. 405–420, San Diego, CA: Academic Press.

Shaffir, E., Smith, E. E., & Osherson, D. N. (1990). Typicality and reasoning fallacies. *Memory & Cognition*, 18, 229–239.

Simmons, C. L. & Hampton, J. A. (2006). Essentialist beliefs about basic and superordinate level categories. Poster Presented at the 47th Annual Meeting of the Psychonomic Society, Houston, TX, November.

Sloman, S. A. (2005). *Causal models: How People Think about the World and Its Alternatives* Oxford: Oxford University Press.

Sloman, S. A., Love, B. C., & Ahn, W. K. (1998). Feature centrality and conceptual coherence. *Cognitive Science*, 22, 189–228.

Smith, E. E. & Medin, D. L. (1981). *Categories and Concepts* Cambridge, MA: Harvard University Press.

Smits, T., Storms, G., Rosseel, Y., & De Boeck, P. (2002). Fruits and vegetables categorized: An application of the generalized context model. *Psychonomic Bulletin and Review*, 9, 836–844.

Storms, G., De Boeck, P., & Ruts, W. (2000). Prototype and exemplar based information in natural language categories. *Journal of Memory and Language*, 42, 51–73.

Storms, G., De Boeck, P., & Ruts, W. (2001). Categorization of unknown stimuli in well-known natural concepts: A case study. *Psychonomic Bulletin and Review*, 8, 377–384.

Tversky, A. & Kahneman, D. (1983). Extensional versus intuitive reasoning: The conjunction fallacy in probability judgment. *Psychological Review*, 90, 293–315.

Warrington, E. K. (1975). Selective impairment of semantic memory. *Quarterly Journal of Experimental Psychology*, 27, 635–657.

Zadeh, L. (1965). Fuzzy sets. *Information and Control*, 8, 338–353.

Part 3

The making of uniquely human concepts

Chapter 15

Darwin and development: Why ontogeny does not recapitulate phylogeny for human concepts

Frank C. Keil and George E. Newman

Editors' Preview

Chapter 15, 'Darwin and development: Why ontogeny does not recapitulate phylogeny for human concepts', critically examines the idea that concept development in children shows an 'ontogeny recapitulating phylogeny' pattern. In a book dedicated to understanding the similarities and differences of concepts in human infants and children, human adults, and nonhuman animal species from both developmental and evolutionary perspectives, a reasonable starting point from which to launch one's analysis would be to assume that a simple-to-complex progression of conceptual structure would be observed during both ontogenesis (development) and phylogenesis (evolution). This assumption would imply that nonhuman animal species and human infants and children would display evidence only for the simple forms of conceptual structure and only human adults would provide support for the more complex types of conceptual structure.

Chapter 15 reviews evidence for a number of different trends that have been reported for conceptual development, and finds that in each case, there is reason to question whether such development can be said to move along a straightforward progression from uncomplicated to more sophisticated. For example, it has been argued that one way conceptual development advances is from the more concrete to the more abstract. However, Chapter 15 cites counterexamples in which monkeys make abstract inferences about the causal properties of objects and in which young children reason abstractly about concepts (for instance, relying on the belief that objects have an underlying essence rather than adhering to physical appearance when determining category membership) and also seem to form concepts on a trajectory from more inclusive (more general) to less inclusive

(more specific). It has also been argued that concept development can be characterized as moving from category representations based on associations to those based on rules. Once more, though, Chapter 15 describes instances where young children can overlook associations and display knowledge of rules, and neuroimaging evidence that nonhuman animals possess the different kinds of brain circuits believed to represent both associations and rules in human adults. Finally, it has been contended that conceptual development moves from implicit, procedural representations to explicit, declarative representations. Yet, as observed in the chapter, this conclusion is confounded with the fact that human adults can talk whereas human infants and non-human animals cannot, and as clever procedures for assessing explicit knowledge in human infants and nonhuman animals have emerged, the implicit-to-explicit developmental shift has been called into question. The review of the data thus suggests that it is difficult to pin down simple-to-complex trends in conceptual development that are also observed across species.

Chapter 15 does consider two possible candidates for what might make concepts unique in humans. One is language, with its strong potential as a combinatorial mechanism that links together distinct domains such as objects and space, and concepts of different levels of specificity (e.g. object- and basic-level category). It is also the case that language may boost the range of concepts acquired by humans through communication of culturally accumulated forms of knowledge. This latter consideration leads to a second possibility for what may promote the uniqueness of human concepts, namely, the socially embedded nature of our interactions in a world populated by conspecifics. Chapter 15 notes that humans are capable of complex forms of social reasoning that are rooted in the perception of intentionality and the ability to make inferences about goal-directedness. These abilities connect to the world of concepts more generally by allowing humans to use the intentional actions of others to infer the causal structure of artefacts in ways that nonhuman animals do not.

Developmental biologists have for some time rejected the idea that ontogeny recapitulates phylogeny in terms of the development of the physical body. It is useful to briefly summarize this story and its neural analogue as a way of setting up the key issue of this chapter. To what extent can we understand the origins of human cognition by thinking of younger and younger children as simpler and simpler species on a phylogenetic scale? In the end, we suggest that such an approach is doomed to failure, but that it seems to implicitly, and sometimes even explicitly, recur in our field again and again. In its place, we suggest that human cognitive development does tell us a great deal about what makes human thinking qualitatively unique, but it does so in the same way that current evolutionary biologists explain how organisms are particularly well adapted to niches – that is, the way in which human concepts are specialized, rather than the product of a linear increase in complexity (see Penn et al., 2008, for a similar position).

The biology story

The idea that an organism's development progresses in a way that mirrors a continuum of species complexity has roots in classical antiquity (Gould, 1977). However, it is probably most strongly associated with Darwin's contemporary, Ernst Haeckel (1899). Haeckel was convinced (for almost mystical reasons) that the evolutionary history of species was directly causally linked to embryology – countless medical students have been misleadingly told that the human embryo 'recapitulates' the evolutionary history of organisms with the 'simplest' ones developing sooner. Dr. Spock helped further the myth by describing in detail how human babies go through a fish-like stage while in the womb (Spock, 1957).

This view can be discredited in many ways, ranging from distortion of the empirical facts to conceptual problems. For example, Haeckel's drawings are quite different from accurate renderings of the embryological stages of fishes, mammals, and the like. Human embryos at earlier stages of development do not really look identical to the embryos of other species. Moreover, the problem is conceptually muddled because it assumes a *scala natura,* or 'great chain of being', in which organisms can be neatly arranged along a single continuum of progress, in which every organism has a certain degree of primitiveness relative to another. Clearly, this is false because whereas human development happens along a single continuum, evolution is inherently not a single line of progression and is instead most aptly described in terms of a branching tree structure. One could see the development of a species as a single line going back to a single-celled organism, but one cannot see current species as ordered along a continuum since they long ago branched off from now-extinct common ancestors and acquired new specializations and complexities that may be unique on that branch. Thus, although the myth of a *scala natura* perseveres, especially in some creationist circles (for unclear reasons), it certainly has no traction among contemporary biologists.

The same theme has also been proposed with respect to brain development. John Hughlings Jackson, for example, proposed a theory of 'neurophylogenesis', in which the development of the brain recapitulates the evolution of the brain across species of increasing complexity (Jackson, 1884). Thus, the brain stem precedes midbrain structures, which in turn precede the cortex; and accordingly, the least-complex species are largely brain-stem creatures, followed by moderately complex midbrain creatures, followed by organisms with complex cortical structures. Jackson and others went further to tell the same story again in the cortex with sensory-projection areas maturing before cortical-association areas, which in turn matured earlier than the frontal and prefrontal cortical areas. However, this 'neuro' version of ontogeny recapitulating phylogeny runs into the same problems that occurred for whole-body embryology. A close examination of brains in early development does not mirror the brains of simpler species (Huttenlocher, 1990). Moreover, it is just as impossible to order brains along a neat, single chain of increasing complexity, as it is to order whole bodies. Nonetheless, it is still common today for 'lower-brain' structures to be discussed as those that we inherited from our more 'primitive' evolutionary ancestors.

As is often the case with myths, there are grains of truth that help perpetuate them. In this case, there are rough correlations that can support the general idea. For example, some of the design features of development may converge moderately with those of evolution (Gould, 1977). Thus, in development it might make sense that the first structures to appear are those that are most essential to the survival of an organism and those that directly support the functioning of other organisms. In addition, developing organisms, unlike artefacts, must remain functional (i.e. alive) at all points in their development – so, both in ontogenetic and phylogenetic development, there is the clear pressure to find workable solutions that meet the demands of the environment (Gilbert, 2006).

Consider how these ideas together, cause a rough correlation between phylogeny, evolutionary history, and development. One of the first challenges facing organisms that existed early in evolution related to energy collection and utilization. This was accomplished via chemical senses that caused an attraction towards nutrient-rich sources and mechanisms for releasing energy from organic molecules. Similarly, the first task facing the fertilized egg is to engage in energy recovery and use. As the embryo increases in complexity, it soon needs a circulatory system to bring nutrients to all locations and take the waste away. Hence, a beating heart emerges very early in development, around week 5, while functional eyes are not needed until much later. Finally, consider that development is also related to evolution by the idea that critical control points in development are ideal places for natural selection to operate – for example, by extending or minimizing the duration of a particular developmental period through changes in gene regulation. Thus, in places where adaptation occurred via leveraging off prior patterns of development, more complex organisms will often have some vestiges of those earlier developmental patterns.

In sum, while the notion of embryonic and neural recapitulation is flatly wrong for both factual and theoretical reasons, there are still a number of apparent similarities between ontogeny and phylogeny that result from common environmental pressures and common solutions to those demands. However, the story for biology is much more that just an interesting bit of history. It also helps to explain why similar biases may exist for theories of cognitive development. In the following sections, we outline a few key developmental transitions that are commonly assumed in human cognitive development and demonstrate how these ontogenetic distinctions fail to contribute to our understanding of cross-species differences.

Blurring the boundaries of developmental dichotomies

The study of human cognitive development is fundamentally about change – that is, we want to know how thinking at one point in development is different from thinking at another and how children progress from one level of competence to another in terms of mechanisms that mediate and cause change. This approach leads naturally to dichotomies wherein it is common to distinguish between two qualitatively different modes of thought. Moreover, relative to our discussion of ontogeny recapitulating phylogeny, such distinctions often share common assumptions: for example, the idea that one kind of thinking is 'simple', while the other kind is 'complex'; cognitive development moves in increasing complexity; and, other species have only the simple form of reasoning, while the complex form is often reserved for adult humans. In this section, we outline several of the distinctions that have been proposed over the years and explore the ways in which each of these distinctions may in fact be much more blurred than is commonly assumed. Moreover, where appropriate, we include evidence for the 'complex' form of reasoning in other species. Of course, we do not mean to argue that change does not occur in human cognitive development. Rather, our goal is merely to demonstrate why it may often be mistaken to confuse developmentally early modes of thought with the 'simple processing' of 'simple species'.

Concrete to abstract progressions

It is an old developmental story that concepts evolve from a concrete form in infants and young children to an abstract form in adults (e.g. Bruner, 1967; Inhelder & Piaget, 1958; Vygotsky, 1962; Werner, 1940). Such accounts often revolve around the representational formats of concepts, assuming either that concepts have a true internal structure that can be examined for developmental change, or that if an internal structure cannot be evinced, one can still make broad claims about the medium in which those concepts are expressed. If this idea is correct, it suggests a natural comparison across species, namely that concrete representations are widely shared across species, while abstract concepts are unique to human adults. However, this argument encounters three key problems. The first is that it is exceedingly difficult to get clarity on what is meant by 'abstract' and 'concrete' concepts in the first place. As Fodor has argued previously (Fodor, 1998), it may be difficult (if not impossible) to uncover the true internal structure for nearly all concepts. Thus, accounts of conceptual change that move from one type of representational format to another are difficult to sustain because of the challenges of precisely identifying *what* has changed at a level other than behaviour.

Second, in cases where this contrast has been made explicit, empirical findings actually argue against the idea that such a contrast exists in humans. For example, consider young children's beliefs about the underlying differences between categories. One might think that young children first differentiate between broad ontological domains such as animals and artefacts on the basis of concrete features. However, the empirical data suggest quite the opposite. Kindergartners, and in fact considerably younger preschoolers, seem to think that there are deep-seeded essential features that differentiate animals from artefacts. They know that there is 'something' that is inside living things that makes them look and behave differently from artefacts (e.g. Gelman, 2003). Yet, even when confronted with actual animal innards and actual car parts, kindergartners are frequently unable to say which ones go with which kind (Simons & Keil, 1995). Moreover, these abstract beliefs can change over time from one view to another. For example, young children, while still not knowing what insides look like, tend to think that animal essences are located in one focal point, deep in the centre of the animal, while older children and adults think of essences as evenly distributed throughout the entire body (Newman & Keil, 2008). Thus, children can apparently have a wide range of seemingly abstract beliefs about the underlying nature of different categories, while not knowing any of the particulars. This is not to say that sometimes concrete-to-abstract patterns cannot also be observed (e.g. infant spatial cognitions can be initially more influenced by distinctive perceptual features of individual objects before they use spatial relations that are more independent of object particulars, Cassasola, 2005; Quinn, 2007). In addition, even adults may, in some contexts, eschew essentialist assumptions in favour of more graded 'causal-homeostasis' models of how surfaces features are causally related (Hampton et al., 2007). The primary point is that there is no invariant progression in which abstract elements are built up out of earlier learned concrete ones.

Similarly, if one looks at the process of categorization, the earliest groupings are not necessarily the lowest ones in a hierarchical tree. By some accounts, young children might be expected to first categorize the world in terms of small local categories, such as dachshunds, then dogs, then mammals, and so on up the tree of expanding category size. Another view might argue that children will first enter the hierarchy of categories at the 'basic level' of categorization, where kinds 'bristle' with distinctive perceptual features that optimally contrast themselves from other kinds at the same level (Murphy, 2004; Rosch, 1975). Either way, the data actually seem to argue against this sort of concrete-to-abstract shift in categorization. In many cases, infants and toddlers initially apprehend categories at levels far above the basic level and will constrain their inferences about the future accordingly. For example, even infants seem to be sensitive to abstract categories such as vehicles and animals (Mandler, 2008; Mandler & McDonough, 1996; see also Chapter 12, this book), or even higher-level differences such as those between goal-directed agents and inanimate objects (e.g. Gergeley et al., 1995; Saxe et al., 2005). In some cases, broad categories may be first apprehended by young infants on the basis of simple perceptual attributes (Quinn & Johnson, 1997, 2000). When this occurs, the dichotomy between abstract and concrete starts to break down as well. A very broad category is normally considered more abstract than a local one; yet, a category constructed out of simple perceptual features seems to have concrete components as well.

Finally, the idea that other species are limited to only concrete representations is questionable as well. For example, free-ranging rhesus macaques appear to generate causal inferences about unfamiliar objects. They will, for example, respond differently to a physically possible outcome in which a knife appears to cut an apple in half, than to an impossible outcome in which the apple appears to be cut by a glass of water (Hauser & Spaulding, 2006). Indeed, such expectations minimally require an abstract notion of physical affordances and a vague sense of cause. Of course, all of this is not to say that human concepts are identical to the concepts of other species. Rather, we are suggesting that it is probably not the case that prelingual humans and other species are restricted to concrete representations alone, at least by most ways of specifying what concrete means.

Associative to rule based

A different type of contrast between concepts involves the idea that simpler, earlier concepts are more associative or 'similarity based', while developmentally older ones are more rule based. There are certainly many tasks that seem to show this kind of shift, and indeed it has figured prominently in the writings of such major theorists as Vygotsky, Werner, Piaget, and Bruner. It can take many forms, but usually refers to findings that younger children seem to focus on all salient features in categorization, while older children focus on a few critical features. Consider a case involving word meanings: if young children learn about exemplars that have many salient typical features, but lack a critical defining feature, they will judge those instances to be members of the category, while older children will not. Conversely, if young children are told of instances that lack salient typical features but do have all the critical defining ones, they may often judge that such instances are not members of a category, while older children will judge that they are good members (Keil, 1989; Keil & Batterman, 1984). For example, a young child might label a kind, gift-giving adult who *is not* related to their parent to be an uncle, while rejecting a young, obnoxious boy who is. Even adults, in the right contexts can be biased so as to favour characteristic features over essential ones for natural kinds (Hampton et al., 2007); but for well-defined terms such as 'uncle' or 'island', the characteristic-to-defining shift is a very robust pattern.

This shift might seem to be a perfect example of going from holistic to analytic representations or from associations to rules. But, in fact, it seems instead to represent one way in which people of all ages go from being a relative novice to being a relative expert. The shift occurs at very different ages depending on the domain involved (Diesendruck, 2004; Keil, 1989). Thus, children shift much earlier for instances of moral categories (lying, stealing) than they do for kinship categories (Keil, 1989). Moreover, even the youngest children are never completely driven by the most typical features. Thus, even preschoolers will not assume that uncles must wear baseball caps even if all known instances happen to have done so.

When one knows little in a domain, it usually pays to hedge bets and weigh as many features as possible in terms of their frequencies of occurrence and co-occurrence. But that very reasonable strategy does not represent a fundamental change in conceptual format or imply that children before a certain age are unable to have rule-based representations. Certainly, young children may have difficulty explicitly stating the rule (especially if they have not mastered much of their native language). Nonetheless, their behaviour alone demonstrates what seems to be knowledge of a wide variety of rules, for example, in the early mastery of grammatical relations or rules of social interaction. In fact, there are vigourous debates about whether the rule-based versus associative contrast is a dichotomy that has been falsely imposed on a continuum (Hampton, 2005; Pothos, 2005), or whether it represents an important key distinction between different forms of cognition (Ashby, 2005; Diesendruck, 2005; Marcus, 2001). Both sides of this debate, however, are no longer committed to the idea that there is a stage-like shift in development from initially conceiving of the world in terms of associations to conceiving of the world in terms of principles and rules. For our purposes, whether the dichotomy between rule-based and associative representations is real or illusory is not as central as the degree to which this contrast might apply to other species – that is, is it the case that rule-based reasoning is a uniquely human capacity?

The animal literature on rules versus associations is not as extensive, but as with earlier dichotomies, it is not easy to 'rule out' rule-based knowledge in a wide variety of other species. The idea that animals have both types of representations gains support from imaging studies suggesting two different brain systems for rule-based and similarity-based reasoning in human brains (Patalano et al., 2001), and the existence of roughly comparable structures in other species (see Chapters 5, 9, and 10, this book, in which recent advances in experimental methods show a wide range of conceptual abilities in primates and other mammals). It is true that various frontal circuits seem more developed in humans (Smith et al., 2004), but less-elaborated structures along the same lines may still allow simpler versions of rule-based categorization in other species. Indeed, even pigeons have been observed to undergo shifts in the course of category learning that are strongly suggestive of a shift from associative to more rule-based forms or representation (Cook & Smith, 2006).

Procedural to declarative and implicit to explicit

In various forms, it has long been speculated that children switch from procedural to declarative representations early in life (Karmiloff-Smith, 1992). The idea seems simple enough. Children initially seem to learn about objects and perhaps categories through reference to actions. A brush is the kind of thing that I do *this* with, and a chair is the kind of thing that I do *that* with, etc. Only later in development via a process of translation do those procedural representations become declarative. One version of that process is called representational redescription (Karmiloff-Smith, 1992), in which the child brings action-based representations into awareness and re-encodes them into declarative terms. Karmiloff-Smith also argues that later, they can still automate widely practised declarative actions, such as reading, and make them procedural once again.

It is tempting to embrace the idea of a procedural-to-declarative shift and then map it onto a comparative analysis of species. After all, if a species is simple enough, how could its learning be anything more than procedural? Does not declarative learning require a kind of metacognitive awareness that certainly would not be present in a moth or a bee? Two problems arise here that are similar to those we encountered earlier. Traditionally, the shift was often thought to occur sometime after language was acquired and those views largely followed from the ease with which declarative knowledge could be assessed through language. However, as researchers develop non-linguistic measures of declarative memory, it is actually beginning to look like such mechanisms may be present by at least 6 months of age (Bauer, 2004; Collie & Hayne, 1999). For example, in one task involving deferred imitation, young infants remember actions that they observe more than 24 h later, without having produced the actions themselves and often using different muscle groups from the actor. This achievement is argued to be a form of declarative memory (Bauer, 2004; Collie & Hayne, 1999; Jones & Herbert, 2006; Mandler, 2004). In addition, some studies suggest that very young children can verbally recall and describe actions that they learnt to do at an earlier age when they were preverbal (Bauer et al., 2002). It also seems to be the case that spatial terms are learned in the same order in which the concepts were learnt preverbally (Quinn, 2007). It seems much simpler to assume that these young children initially encoded the action in declarative terms and then accessed that knowledge verbally in the same format, rather than that they initially encoded it procedurally and then somehow transformed that encoding into a format that made it accessible to language at a later date. It is therefore, not obvious that even the youngest of humans are merely representing the world in terms of actions.

With nonhumans, there is not as much research examining if they are capable of declarative representations, but there are at least some arguments that they are. It has been argued, for example, that domestic hens will remember food choices in ways that are not procedural and action based but which seem to require a more declarative form of representation (Forkman, 2000). This may be because of basic functional/ anatomical structures in the hippocampus that cut across a wide range of species (Eichenbaum, 2004). Indeed, it has even been argued that the presence of declarative-like memories in fish implies that they can evaluate experiences, are capable of suffering, and are therefore capable of being treated cruelly (Chandroo et al., 2004). It is certainly far beyond the scope of this chapter to tackle questions about sentience in fish and the implications for their treatment by humans, but the mere presence of that issue in the literature suggests just how murky questions about declarative representations across species can be.

The same story seems to hold for the idea of developmental changes from implicit to explicit cognition. Instead of seeing the infant as essentially an implicit creature that only gains explicit knowledge as language becomes internalized, it is now more commonly believed that strands of both kinds of knowledge may be present from the earliest moments of infancy (Bauer, 2006, 2007; Rovee-Collier, 1997). As soon as one tries to operationalize notions of explicit cognition that are independent of language, it becomes very difficult to find a downward age limit before which humans completely lack such forms of cognition. To be sure, the robustness of such systems increases with age, but it is not clear when, if ever, they are completely absent. Moreover, when researchers turn to animals and use nonverbal assessment techniques, there are claims of episodic memory in animals as 'simple' as pigeons (Zentall et al., 2001) and of dissociations signalling an implicit/explicit contrast in a wide range of species (Cho et al., 2007).

In sum, although it is tempting to see the preverbal child as a different kind of mental creature who, in a language-free state, must represent the world in ways that are concrete, associative, procedural, tacit, and nonepisodic, these views seem to have been driven by the presence of language itself in older children. It is clearly easier to be sure of the presence of abstract, declarative thought in individuals that speak, but as soon as one attempts to disentangle these forms of thought from language and measure them in nonverbal ways, there is little evidence for developmental shifts. Without such independent accounts, claims of shifts amount to little more than stating the obvious fact that children before a certain age cannot speak or comprehend language. If the actual format of concepts is somehow related to these dichotomies, as many researchers have argued, then there is little evidence that concepts themselves undergo qualitative shifts in structure in the first few years of life. Infants' and young children's concepts may certainly differ from older children and adults, but not in ways that easily map onto these dichotomies. Moreover, it is difficult to be sure of the extent to which any of the more 'advanced' forms of representation are absent in other species as there are many instances suggesting systems strongly analogous to the purportedly more sophisticated reasoning found in humans.

The point here is not to abandon research trying to understand the nature of conceptual representations. It is, however, to suggest that unambiguous evidence for changes in conceptual structure over time is difficult to come by and that it is often more fruitful to look at what patterns of information organisms are able to exploit at different points in development and how they able to use that information to act. Ultimately, converging studies on the kinds of information used and how they are used may point strongly towards certain internal representational formats; but it in a great many cases, it may be more useful to first gather more detailed information on sensitivities to particular kinds of information in specific contexts and biases or constraints on how that information is tracked and used.

We have suggested so far that it is in fact quite difficult to nail down patterns of conceptual change that may be uniquely human. Moreover, many candidates, which loosely follow an 'ontogeny-recapitulating-phylogeny' theme, are not well supported. There are, however, two domains, language and social reasoning, in which human cognition does seem to be unique and which may provide a better way of asking if there are unique patterns to human conceptual change.

Is language the magic bullet?

The discussion so far has largely downplayed claims concerning qualitative changes in the representational formats of concepts. However, this is not meant to deny that concepts do change with development and that some human concepts are different from those found in other animals. One way to reconcile these points may simply lie in turning some of the dichotomies mentioned above into continua. Perhaps, adult concepts are less associative in nature than those in children and other animals. Perhaps, adults have richer and more elaborated episodic and declarative forms of knowledge. To some extent, this is certainly true, although it is rarely as simple as it seems. We have seen that the concrete/abstract distinction may not follow any easy developmental rule. Similarly, declarative knowledge can sometimes, with further experience, become procedural once again. Thus, even talking about these differences as differences in degree, rather than differences in kind, poses a strong challenge to the idea that these dichotomies reflect qualitatively different modes of thought.

The more important differences may not lie in the internal structures of concepts themselves but in the ways concepts are related to each other and to the social and physical world – that is, from an empirical perspective, perhaps it is more beneficial to consider the relationships between concepts, rather than their underlying nature. This perspective has the additional benefit of somewhat sidestepping controversies over whether there is any internal structure to concepts. If Fodor's (1998) worries about the decomposability of concepts are correct, then most of the contrasts considered earlier in this chapter are either misguided or have to be recast in ways that are really about the use and processing of concepts, rather than about their internal structure and the nature of representation.

Certainly, some proposals revolve around the idea that language provides a powerful transforming effect on cognition in general, and concepts in particular. For example, language has been argued to provide 'invitations to form categories' through the use of salient words (Waxman & Markow, 1995; see also Chapter 6, this book). Vygotsky argued that the internalization of language gave thought a more analytic and logical capacity and an ability to go beyond the here and now (Vygotsky, 1934/1962), and there are repeated accounts of language as a kind of cognitive prosthesis that enables one to keep more thoughts in mind at a time and to see more analytical relations between them. There certainly seems to be some truth to this claim. Quite simply, when we put ideas into words and sentences, we do seem to gain added power.

However, this may be an addition that is more akin to the support provided by writing things down on paper. We have all had explanations that we think we fully understand when they exist solely in thought, only to discover huge gaping holes when we actually try to articulate them in writing. The writing pad or computer screen provides a form of external support that greatly amplifies our ability to look for consistency and coherence in large chains of thought (cf. Clark, 2001). But it may well be that language does not transform unspoken thought any more than written language transforms spoken language. And, even the most ardent supporters of the effects of written language do not see it as changing the fundamental nature of thought in dramatic, qualitative ways (e.g. Olson, 1994; Olson & Torrance, 2001).

A second popular and longstanding theme has been the idea that language provides a form of cognitive glue that allows people to bring together distinct domains of thought, perhaps even modules. Several scholars have proposed that language enables a child to take relatively autonomous domains and bring them together in ways that can cause leaps forward in cognition, such as much more robust ways of tracking objects (e.g. Xu & Carey, 1996). Moeover, language may bring together processes that engage in different kinds of operations on number, and spatial navigation; and it may unite plants and animals into a common domain 'living things' (Carey, 2002; Caruthers, 2002, 2004; Gentner, 2003; Inagaki & Hatano, 2003; Mithen, 1996; Spelke, 2003; Spelke & Tviskin, 2001). Such accounts are naturally appealing if for no other reason than that they move from discrete processing to a more integrated view of cognition. If one maintains, as many infant researchers do, there are only a few core domains and/or modules of thought, then a device that can combine those core elements can unleash a vastly larger and more complex set of cognitive structures.

However, there are two issues that still need further elaboration in attempts to understand such accounts. First, it is important to specify in some detail how language allows two autonomous domains to be integrated. What work does it do to make the connections apparent? Second, if language is to play such a pivotal role in accomplishing conceptual integration, it is important to show that the integration cannot occur in the absence of language either in humans or in other species. Why, for example, can't similar integrations occur through various forms of imagery or spatial reasoning, or through prelinguistic thought, or even through another domain such as theory of mind (Atran, 2002; Hampton, 2002)? If language can be shown to have a unique facilitating effect, these arguments will be stronger. One promising example is an argument about how the quantifier structure of language 'bootstraps' the analogue number estimation system and the small discrete number system into a more sophisticated concept of discrete, symbolically represented numbers of indefinite size (Carey, 2004; Le Corre & Carey, 2007; Chapter 13, this book). Evidence for the importance of language to such a process comes from cultures that lack formal count systems. In these cultures, even adult speakers do not possess a fully developed concept of number that can conceptually distinguish between magnitudes larger than 4 or 5 (Gordon, 2004). At the same time, the bootstrapping process has been criticized as lacking in explanatory detail (Bloom & Keil, 2001; Gallistel, 2007; Rips et al., 2005).

It is important to note that there is, however, an alternative account in which all children, well before they learn language and probably from birth, are endowed with a 'language of thought', which is similar to spoken language in that it has propositional nature with quasi-logical principles of inference and entailment. This account assumes that spoken language is mapped onto the language of thought rather than emerging as an utterly new kind of mental structure (Fodor, 1975). By such an account, natural language in itself could not transform thought since it is not such a radical departure from the language of thought. There is still the possibility, however, that if a spoken language in some way reflects culturally accumulated and transmitted knowledge – for example, by guiding individuals to domains of expertise (Keil et al., 2008; Putnam, 1975) – it might have additional benefits that go beyond a preverbal language of thought. And, if language can amplify cognition by making salient culturally accumulated forms of knowledge, it makes sense to ask if the most dramatic aspects of conceptual development, as well as of animal/human differences, revolve around the ways in which concepts are linked to the knowledge of others. Consequently, in the following section, we turn to the nature of social knowledge and the role that social learning might play in concept formation and change.

Conceptual development and the social world

Apart from language, there are some other striking differences between humans and other animals that may have strong consequences for making human concepts different – consequences that are often revealed by the study of conceptual development in children. Many of these revolve around the perception of intentionality and inferences about other goal-directed beings. Humans are certainly not the only creatures that think differently about social beings, but they seem to have unique or greatly amplified skills in this respect, skills that in turn have consequences for concepts and conceptual change. As many scholars have noted, human infants are intensely tuned to social stimuli and seem to think about them differently from a very early age. They seem to be especially tuned to deciphering the goals of agents and using that information to make inferences about the meanings of situations. For example, infants will imitate the goals of an actor rather than the actions (Meltzoff, 1995), in some cases revealing such interpretations well before the first year of life (Woodward, 1998). Infants are also sensitive to the 'rationality' of actions, imitating an action when they assume there was an underlying goal that made it sensible (Gergeley & Csibra, 2003; Gergeley et al., 2002).

In general, by the time children start to learn language, they have shown a long-standing interest and skill in interpreting the goals of others and using those interpretations to guide their actions. But the most dramatic influence on concepts and conceptual change may occur in the years that follow. For example, young children rely heavily on intentions to infer word meanings, knowing that intentional actions are key indicators of likely categories of reference (Baldwin & Markman, 1996; Bloom, 2000). Similarly, they use intention to make inferences about procedural knowledge and the way in which to operate unfamiliar objects in their environment. Indeed, in some cases, the effects of social learning may be so powerful that they override rational decision making, as in the case of over-imitation: when reproducing the actions of a human trainer operating an unfamiliar device, chimpanzees will often drop out unnecessary actions to take the most efficient course of actions. However, in the same learning context, young children will reproduce all of the actions, even those that clearly seem quite unnecessary (Horner & Whiten, 2005). This phenomenon was originally thought to reflect a simple desire on the part of children to 'play the game', but later work demonstrated that children only over-imitate when they think an actor is intentionally engaging in the actions (Lyons et al., 2007). If the actor behaves unintentionally, children only reproduce the necessary actions. Even more importantly, when presented intentionally, children seem to internalize all of the actions as casually *necessary* and thereby infer that irrelevant parts of an object are actually causally important. At the same time, this seeming error that demonstrates the power of social learning may also be highly adaptive as it is an extremely useful way to learn about causal properties and relationships that are too complex to immediately figure out on one's own.

However, perhaps the most powerful influence of social learning lies in the way in which tracking intentionality allows children to benefit from the accumulated knowledge in the minds of others and the culture at large. Surely one of the most dramatic differences between human concepts and those in other animals involves the ease with which we rely on the expertise of others. An ability, that, for example, is obviously not limited to inferences about the state of the world based on the others' behaviour (as when a distress call or fleeing cues the existence of a predator), but rather incorporates highly nuanced appreciation about the ways in which knowledge itself is distributed among other people and society. For example, even kindergartners seem to be sensitive to the way in which knowledge and expertise cluster into domains that resemble academic disciplines (Keil et al., 2008). Of course, much of this knowledge could be transmitted via language, but critically much of it can also be gathered in other ways that do not seem to involve language or even direct instruction. A simple act of pointing, a gesture, a drawing, or the end-state of an action that was goal directed can clue a child into a property or relation of special importance. Critically, such learning seems to be almost immediately and effortlessly woven into a rich, overarching tapestry that unites information from these different sources and highlights the deep, underlying commonalities between them. This skill may be related to the unique nature of pedagogy in humans (Gergely & Csibra, 2006; Premack, 1984; Chapter 11, this book), but it may well go beyond any explicit goal to teach. Just the process of intentionally acting on an object may be vastly informative to a young child even when the actor is not intending to convey something to the observer (Warneken & Tomasello, 2006). By watching the intentional actions of others, children can learn a great deal about how the world works by simply assuming that intentional actions are directed towards causally important properties, parts, or junctions in events.

Also related to the idea of accumulating knowledge socially, is the process by which humans learn to defer. Children quickly learn to be comfortable with the idea that much of their knowledge is grounded in the minds of others as well as learning when and when not to rely on testimony offered by others (Harris & Koenig, 2006). For example, children believe that ferrets are different from weasels (even though they often cannot possibly tell them apart), because they believe that there are those who do know. From as early as preschool, children see themselves as part of a vast terrain of knowledge in which their concepts rely on important links to others, whose knowledge is richer than their own (Keil et al., 2008; Lutz & Keil, 2003). This last ability may also rely partly on the notion that most people intend to inform and not to deceive. Thus, at many levels of thought, children and even infants are quite sensitive to the way in which their own knowledge is immersed in a much more elaborate social network that is heavily dependent upon the ability to discern the goals and intentions of others. Moreover, this social sensitivity does seem in many ways uniquely human (Tomasello et al., 2005), though there is certainly always the possibility that this view may be revised, given the right kind of evidence.

Conclusion

In this last section we briefly return to the broader theme of the relationship between ontogeny and phylogeny. Roughly, we have outlined several cases in which an apparent conceptual division between different points in development or different species seems to blur and give way to a continuum of cognitive abilities. In many cases, it actually seems quite difficult to isolate discernable 'break-points' that may punctuate difference in the nature of reasoning across species or within human development (see, e.g. Chapters 10 and 11, this book).

If there is a distinctive aspect of human conceptual change, it may arise from the ways in which the acquisition of language and the embedding social context influence the endpoints of conceptual change – in other words, the way in which such mechanisms may boost the sophistication and saliency of existing conceptual structures. The potential influences of language have been heavily discussed and, while we acknowledge the possibility of such influences, we want to inject a note of caution in asking whether language is just one of many ways in which conceptual systems might be combined and amplified, as opposed to a mechanism by which qualitatively unique modes of thought are obtained.

Use of intentional behaviour, however, seems to be a powerful device for greatly expanding the power and range of concepts. We have suggested that humans are uniquely attuned to intentional behaviour as a cue to important information for grounding concepts and elaborating on them. The simple phenomenon of deference, which seems so critical to so many human concepts, may be largely absent in any other species. Even here, however, we do not see a dramatic qualitative transition as much as an important role of social context and intentionality from quite early in infancy. In sum, the ontogeny-recapitulates-phylogeny idea tends to bias one towards the view that infants start out largely as lower-order animals and then move beyond that state. We have suggested here that such a view may be deeply flawed because a great degree of analogous processing is observed between species and that whatever processing does appear to be unique to human concepts and human conceptual change may be part of the basic architecture that is present from the start.

Acknowledgement

Preparation of this paper and some of the research described therein was supported by NIH Grant R37-HD23922 to Frank Keil.

References

Asbhy G. & Casale, M. B. (2005). Empirical dissociations between rule-based and similarity-based categorization. *Behavioral and Brain Sciences*, **28**, 15–16.

Atran, S. (2002). In *Gods We Trust: The Evolutionary Landscape of Religion* New York: Oxford University Press.

Baldwin, D. & Markman, E. (1996). Infants' reliance on a social criterion for establishing word-object relations. *Child Development*, **67**, 3135–3153.

Bauer, P. J. (2004). Getting explicit memory off the ground: Steps toward construction of a neuro-developmental account of changes in the first two years of life, *Developmental Review*, **24**, 347–373.

Bauer, P. J. (2006). Constructing a past in infancy: a neuro-developmental account. *Trends in Cognitive Science*, **10**, 175–181.

Bauer, P. J. (2007). Recall in infancy: A neurodevelopmental account. *Current Directions in Psychological Science*, **16**, 142–146.

Bauer, P. J., Wenner, J. A., & Kroupina, M. (2002). Making the past present: Verbal reports of preverbal memories. *Journal of Cognition and Development*, **3**, 21–47.

Bloom, P. (2000). *How Children Learn the Meaning of Words* Cambridge, MA: MIT Press.

Bloom, P. & Keil, F. C. (2001). Thinking through language. *Mind and Language*, **16**, 351–367.

Bruner, J. S. (1967). On cognitive growth I & II. In J. Bruner, R. Olver, P. Greenfield, et al. (Eds.) *Studies in Cognitive Growth: A Collaboration at the Center of Cognitive Studies*, pp. 1–67, New York: John Wiley & Sons.

Carey, S. (2004). Bootstrapping and the origins of concepts. *Daedalus*, **133**, 59–68.

Carruthers, P. (2002). The cognitive functions of language: Modularity, language, and the flexibility of thought. *Behavioral and Brain Sciences*, **25**, 657–726.

Carruthers, P. (2004). Practical reasoning in a modular mind. *Mind and Language*, **19**, 259–278.

Casasola, M. (2005). When less is more: How infants learn to form an abstract categorical representation of support. *Child Development*, **76**, 279–290.

Chandroo, K. P., Duncan, I. J. H., & Moccia, R.D. (2004). Can fish suffer? Perspectives on sentience, pain, fear and stress. *Applied Animal Behaviour Science*, **86**, 225–250.

Cho, Y.H., Delcasso, S., Israel A., & Jeantet, Y. (2007). A long list visuo-spatial sequential learning in mice. *Behavioral Brain Research*, **179**, 152–158.

Clark, A. (2001). Reasons, robots and the extended mind. *Mind and Language*, **16**, 121–145.

Collie, R. & Hayne, H. (1999). Deferred imitation by 6- and 9-month-oldinfants: More evidence for declarative memory. *Developmental Psychobiology, 35,* 83–90.

Cook, R. G. & J. D. Smith. (2006). Stages of abstraction and exemplar memorization in pigeon category learning. *Psychological Science, 12,* 1059–1067.

Diesendruck, G. F. (2005). Commitment distinguishes between rules and similarity: A developmental perspective. *Brain and Behavioral Science, 28,* 21–22.

Eichenbaum, H. (2004). Hippocampus: cognitive processes and neural representations that underlie declarative memory. *Neuron,* **44,** 109–120.

Fodor, J. A. (1975). *The Language of Thought* Cambridge, MA: Harvard University Press.

Fodor, J.A. (1998). *Concepts: Where Cognitive Science Went Wrong* Oxford Cognitive Science Series, Oxford: Oxford University Press.

Forkman, B. (2000) Domestic hens have declarative representations. *Animal Cognition,* **3,** 135–137.

Gallistel, C. R. (2007). Commentary on Le Corre & Carey. *Cognition,* **105,** 439–445.

Gelman, S. A. (2003). *The essential child: Origins of essentialism in everyday thought.* New York, NY: Oxford University Press.

Gentner, D. (2003). Why we're so smart. In D. Gentner & S. Goldin-Meadow (Eds.), *Language in mind: Advances in the Study of Language and Thought,* pp.195–235, Cambridge, MA: MIT Press.

Gergely, G. & Csibra, G. (2003). Teleological reasoning in infancy: The naive theory of rational action. *Trends in Cognitive Sciences,* **7,** 287–292.

Gergely, G. & Csibra, G. (2006). Sylvia's recipe: The role of imitation, and pedagogy in the transmission of cultural knowledge. In N. J. Enfield & S. C. Levinson (Eds.), *Roots of Human Sociality: Culture, Cognition, and Interaction,* pp. 229–255, Oxford: Berg Press.

Gergely, G., Nadasdy, Z., Csibra, G., & Biro, S. (1995). Taking the intentional stance at 12 months of age. *Cognition,* **56,** 165–93.

Gergely, G., Bekkering, H., & Kiraly, I. (2002). Rational imitation in preverbal infants. *Nature,* **415,** 755.

Gilbert, S. F. (2006). *Developmental Biology,* 8th edn., Sunderland, MA: Sinauer Associates.

Gordon, P. (2004). Numerical cognition without words: Evidence from Amazonia. *Science,* **306,** 496–499.

Gould, S. J. (1977). *Ontogeny and Phylogeny* Cambridge, MA: Belknap Press.

Haeckel, E. (1899). *The Riddle of the Universe* (Translated J. McCabe) New York: Harper & Brothers Publishers.

Hampton, J. (2002). Language's role in enabling abstract, logical thought. *Behavioral and Brain Sciences,* **25,** 688.

Hampton, J. A. (2005). Rules and similarity – a false dichotomy. *Behavioral and Brain Sciences,* **28,** 26.

Hampton, J. A., Estes, Z., & Simmons, S. (2007). Metamorphosis: Essence, appearance and behavior in the categorization of natural kinds. *Memory & Cognition,* **35** (7), 1785–1800.

Harris, P. L. & Koenig, M. (2006). Trust in testimony: How children learn about science and religion. *Child Development,* **77,** 505–524.

Hauser, M. & Spaulding, B. (2006). Wild rhesus monkeys generate causal inferences about possible and impossible physical transformations in the absence of experience. *Proceedings of the National Academy of Sciences,* **103,** 7181–7185.

Horner, V. & Whiten, A. (2005). Causal knowledge and imitation/emulation switching in chimpanzees (*Pan troglodytes*) and children (*Homo sapiens*). *Animal Cognition,* **8,** 164–181.

Huttenlocher, P. R. (1990). Morphometric study of human cerebral cortex development. *Neuropsychologia*, **28**, 517–527.

Inhelder, B. & Piaget, J. (1958). *The Growth of Logical Thinking* New York: Basic Books.

Inagaki, K. & Hatano, G. (2003). Conceptual and linguistic factors in inductive projection: How do young children recognize commonalities between animals and plants? In Gentner, D. & S. Goldin-Meadow (Eds.), *Language in Mind: Advances in the Study of Language and Thought*, pp. 313–333, Cambridge, MA: MIT Press.

Jackson, J. H. (1994). Evolution and dissolution of the nervous system. Croonian Lectures delivered at the Royal College of Physicians, March 1884. *Lancet*, **1**: 739–744.

Jones, E. J. H. & Herbert, J. S. (2006). Exploring memory in infancy: Deferred imitation and the development of declarative memory. *Infant and Child Development*, **15**, 195–205.

Karmiloff-Smith, A. (1992). *Beyond Modularity* Cambridge, MA: MIT Press.

Karmiloff-Smith, A. (1999). Taking development seriously. *Human Development*, **42**, 325–327.

Keil, F. C. (1989). *Concepts, Kinds, and Cognitive Development* Cambridge, MA: MIT Press.

Keil, F. C. & Batterman, N. (1984). A characteristic-to-defining shift in the acquisition of word meaning. *Journal of Verbal Learning and Verbal Behavior*, **23**, 221–236.

Keil, F. C., Stein, C., Webb, L., Billings, V., & Rozenblit, L. (2008). Discerning the division of cognitive labor: An emerging understanding of how knowledge is clustered in other minds. *Cognitive Science*, **32**(2), 259–300.

Le Corre, M. & Carey, S. (2007). One, two, three, four, nothing more: An investigation of the conceptual sources of the verbal counting principles. *Cognition*, **105**, 395–438.

Lutz, D. R. & Keil, F. C. (2002). Early understanding of the division of cognitive labor. *Child Development*, **73**, 1073–1084.

Lyons, D.E., Young, A.G., & Keil, F. C. (2007). The hidden structure of overimitation. *Proceedings of the National Academy of Sciences*, **104**, 19751–19756.

Mandler, J. M. (2004). *The Foundations of Mind: Origins of Conceptual Thought* Oxford: Oxford University Press.

Mandler, J. M. (2008). On the birth and growth of concepts. *Philosophical Psychology*, **21**(2), pp. 207–203.

Mandler, J. M. & McDonough, L. (1996). Drinking and driving don't mix: Inductive generalization in infancy. *Cognition*, **59**, 307–335.

Marcus, G. F. (2001). *The Algebraic Mind: Integrating Connectionism and Cognitive Science* Cambridge, MA: MIT Press.

Meltzoff, A. N. (1995). Understanding the intentions of others: Re-enactment of intended acts by 18-month-old children. *Developmental Psychology*, **31**(5), 838–850.

Mithen, S. (1996) *The Prehistory of the Mind* London: Thames and Hudson.

Murphy, G. L. (2004). The Big Book of Concepts. Cambridge, MA: MIT Press

Newman, G. E. & Keil, F. C. (2008). Where's the essence? Developmental shifts in children's beliefs about internal features. *Child Development*, **79** (5), 1344–1356.

Olson, D. (1994). Demythologizing literacy. In D. R. Olson (Ed.), *The World on Paper: The Conceptual and Cognitive Implications of Writing and Reading*, pp. 1–19, Cambridge: Cambridge University Press.

Olson, D. R. & Torrance, N. (Ed.) (2001). *The Making of Literate Societies* Oxford: Blackwell Publishers.

Patalano, A. L., Smith, E. E., Jonides, J., & Koeppe, R. A. (2001). PET evidence for multiple strategies of categorization. *Cognitive, Affective, and Behavioral Neuroscience*, **1**, 360–370.

Penn, D. C., Holyoak, K. J., & Povinelli, D. J. (2008). Darwin's mistake: Explaining the discontinuity between human and nonhuman minds. *Brain and Behavioral Sciences*, **31**, 109–178.

Pothos, E. (2005). The rules versus similarity distinction. *Behavioral and Brain Sciences, 28*, 1–14.

Premack, (1984). Pedagogy and aesthetics as sources of culture. In M. Gazzaniga (Ed.), *Handbook of Cognitive Neuroscience*, pp. 15–35, New York: Plenum Press.

Putnam, H. (1975). The meaning of 'meaning'. In K. Gunderson (Ed.), *Language, Mind and Knowledge*, pp. 131–193, Minneapolis, MN: University of Minnesota Press.

Quinn, P. C. (2007). On the infant's prelinguistic conception of spatial relations: Three developmental trends and their implications for spatial language learning. In J. M. Plumert & J. P. Spencer (Eds.), *The Emerging Spatial Mind*, pp. 117–141, New York: Oxford University Press.

Quinn, P. C. & Johnson, M. H. (1997). The emergence of perceptual category representations in young infants: A connectionist analysis. *Journal of Experimental Child Psychology, 66*, 236–263.

Rips, L. J., Asmuth, J., & Bloomfield, A. (2006). Giving the boot to the bootstrap: How not to learn the natural numbers. *Cognition, 101*, B51–B60.

Rosch, E. (1975). Cognitive representations of semantic categories. *Journal of Experiment Psychology: General, 104*, 192–234.

Rovee-Collier, C. (1997). Dissociations in infant memory: Rethinking the development of implicit and explicit memory. *Psychological Review, 104*, 467–498.

Saxe, R., Tenenbaum, J. B., & Carey, S. (2005). Secret agents: Inferences about hidden causes by 10- and 12-month-old infants. *Psychological Science, 16*(12), 995–1001.

Simons, D. J. & Keil, F. C. (1995). An abstract to concrete shift in the development of biological thought: The inside story. *Cognition, 56*, 129–163.

Smith J.D., Minda J.P., & Washburn D. A. (2004). Category learning in Rhesus monkeys: A study of the Shepard, Hovland, and Jenkins tasks. *Journal of Experimental Psychology: General, 133*, 398–414.

Spelke, E. S. (2003). What makes us smart: Core knowledge and natural language. In D. Gentner & S. Goldin-Meadow (Eds.), *Language in Mind: Advances in the study of Language and Thought*, pp. 277–311, Cambridge, MA: MIT Press.

Spelke, E. S. & Tsivkin, S. (2001). Initial knowledge and conceptual change: Space and number. In M. Bowerman & S. C. Levinson (Eds.), *Language Acquisition and Conceptual Development*. Cambridge: Cambridge University Press.

Spock, B. (1957). *The Common Sense Book of Baby and Child Care* New York: Pocket Books.

Tomasello, M., Carpenter, M., Call, J., Behne, T., & Moll, H. (2005). Understanding and sharing intentions: The origins of cultural cognition. *Behavioral and Brain Sciences, 28*, 675–691.

Vygotsky, L. S. (1962). *Thought and Language* Cambridge, MA: MIT Press. (Original work published 1934.)

Waxman, S. R. & Markow, D. B. (1995). Words as invitations to form categories: Evidence from 12- to 13-month-old infants. *Cognitive Psychology, 29*, 257–302.

Warneken, F. & Tomasello, M. (2006). Altruistic helping in human infants and young chimpanzees. *Science*, 1301–1303.

Werner, H. (1940). *Comparative Psychology of Mental Development* New York: International Universities Press, Inc.

Woodward, A. (1998). Infants selectively encode the goal of an actor's reach. *Cognition, 69*, 1–34.

Xu, F. & Carey, S. (1996). Infants' metaphysics: the case of numerical identity. *Cognitive Psychology, 30*, 111–153.

Zentall, T. R., Clement, R. S., Bhatt, R. S., & Allen, J. (2001) Episodic-like memory in pigeons. *Psychonomic Bulletin and Review, 8*, 685–690.

Chapter 16

More than concepts: How multiple integrations make human intelligence

Linda B. Smith

Editors' Preview

Chapter 16, 'More than concepts: How multiple integrations make human intelligence', provides a departure from the other chapters in the book because it questions from the start whether the term concept is a necessary theoretical construct. It questions the traditional cognitive framework, that is, sense–think–act, for explaining behaviour. In the standard cognitive account, behaviour arises as a consequence of mental representations or concepts of experience. However, in the framework advocated in Chapter 16, mental representations are more the 'ghost in the machine', and are perhaps better regarded as byproducts of more primary systems such as perception, action, emotion, and social interaction, each of which is closely coupled to the others in its activity, and all of which are connected to the world in which they operate. In other words, in this more 'dynamic-systems' framework, concepts are an epiphenomenal product of the coordination of multiple sensory–motor systems that allow us to respond to the world in intelligent ways.

Development plays a crucial role in the dynamic-systems framework and Chapter 16 provides illustrative examples of how multimodal subsystems become coordinated during real-time change to create concepts. For instance, infants who wear sticky mittens and are provided with the opportunity to act on (i.e. reach for) objects while looking at them (before they develop mental exploration skills) subsequently show increased object exploration through both vision and oral manipulation (i.e. mouthing behaviours). The enhanced sensory–motor coordination provided by the sticky mittens manipulation may thus promote the formation of object concepts by infants. In addition, infants who are provided with the opportunity to explore transparent containers through both vision and touch display subsequent strong performance in object-permanence tasks involving transparent boxes and in visual cliff tasks that involve traversing across a transparent surface that offers support, but which is visually specified as a falling-off point. By the dynamic-systems account, the exploration of the containers allows infants to coordinate sight and touch experiences, which in turn enables the development of a concept of a solid surface of support. Note that the concept in this case displays a hallmark characteristic of human intelligence which is that it is transportable and can be generalized from one context to another (from object search to spatial locomotion).

Chapter 16 also considers the ways in which human intelligence may be unique, at least relative to different species of nonhuman animals. One candidate difference is that animal species do not always have the same type of coupling of various sensory and action systems. In the dynamic-systems account, such coupling is what allows the systems to learn from each other, thereby promoting the development of abstract concepts. For example, birds may have difficulty acquiring a generalizable concept of solid surface (that can be extended to transparent surfaces) because they cannot engage in the kind of eye–hand coordination that infants by 9 months of age are capable of. Another candidate difference is that of language. Hearkening back to the theme previously discussed in Chapters 6 and 13, words may equip humans with a more discrete, categorical, rule-like form of intelligence that provides a complement to a continuous, graded, more commonsense way of knowing the world. One final candidate (suggested also in Chapters 14 and 15) is the fact that our perceptions of and actions on the world are constrained and guided by the presence of conspecifics (who possess the same machinery for carrying out intelligent behaviour). Thus, according to Chapter 16, what may be uniquely human about concepts or intelligence (the latter being the preferred term in the chapter) are: (1) the overlapping operations of various perception–action systems (which in turn provide the redundant structure from which concepts are formed); (2) language; and (3) the socially embedded nature of our interaction with the world.

Understanding how and why human intelligence has the properties it does is certainly one of the most compelling questions in all of science. The phenomena in need of explanation are vast and varied, including behaviours of categorization, language and communication, imitation and learning from example, tool use, the invention of advanced symbol systems such as mathematics, as well as art and architecture. However, the topic of this book, 'concepts', is *not* a phenomenon in need of explanation. 'Concepts' are hypothetical constructs proposed by theorists to explain the sorts of phenomena listed above, and the jury is very much still out on whether such a theoretical construct is even needed (for differing views, see Beer, 2000; Brooks, 1991; Fodor, 1998; Keil, 1994; Smith & Katz, 1996) As venerable a figure as William James (1890) considered them misleading 'figments' and suggested psychologists abandon the construct altogether.

The construct of a 'concept' derives from the classic view in which mental life is divided into the discrete steps of 'sense–think–act'. Cognition, by definition, is about the 'think' part, the knowledge and processes that mediate perceiving and acting. Concepts, from this perspective provide the content for cognition and are amodal and propositional, consisting of relatively fixed and compositional representations. The work the concepts do as theoretical constructs, the argument for hypothesizing their existence in the first place, is that they provide stability and structure in the cognitive system. How can we recognize all varieties of dogs as 'dogs'? In this view, it is because all varieties of dogs activate the same fixed concept (e.g. Keil, 1994). How do we recognize the common structure of the solar system to an atom? In this view, it is because the componential and relational structure of the underlying concepts share significant similarities (Gentner, 1983). This approach has long dominated the study of human intelligence and without doubt has been the source of many significant insights. However, there are serious limitations to this approach, including explanations of the flexibility of human intelligence, its capacity to do the truly new (e.g. Smith & Katz, 1996), the unsolved problem of how anything like propositions emerge in the dynamic events of neural processing (Sporns, 2000), the problem of how new propositional representations (that are not new combinations of innate primitives) can emerge (see Barsalou, 1993; Fodor, 1999; Thelen & Smith 1994), and the disconnect between propositional representations and the real time and decidedly physical aspects of behaviour, learning, and development (e.g. Elman, 2004; O'Regan & Noe, 2001; Port & van Gelder, 1995; Smith & Gasser, 2005).

Accordingly, there are increasing discussions of an alternative view that does not segregate mental life into cognitive versus noncognitive processes and in which the construct of a 'concept' has a minimal role (or perhaps no role at all, see, Barsalou et al., 2003, 2007; Beer, 2000; Spencer & Schutte, 2004; Zwaan, 2004). This chapter considers human intelligence from this alternative 'more-than-concepts' point of view. There are several evolving forms of this newer approach (see Anderson, 2003; Wilson, 2002) but there are also common principles across these variants that are foundational to the ideas presented here:

1. *Knowledge has no existence separate from process*, but is instead embedded in, distributed across, and thus inseparable from real-time processes (e.g. Ballard et al., 1997; O'Regan & Noe, 2001; Samuelson & Smith, 2000; Spivey, 2006). From this perspective, there is no fixed and separate representation of anything, no concepts at all in the usual sense.

2. *Intelligence is made out of what have traditionally been viewed as noncognitive systems*, perception, action, emotion, and the coupling of these processes to the world and across individuals in social interactions (Hutchins, 1995; Rogoff, 2003; Tomasello et al., 1993). Rather than cognition being distinct from noncognitive processes, cognition *may simply be* the operation of this complex system as a whole.

3. *To understand intelligence is to know how to 'build' a behaving system that behaves intelligently.* One way to do this is to study how cognition develops from birth over time in biological systems. Another way is to pursue the evolutionary processes (and cross-species differences) that exploit developmental process. Alternatively, one could try to engineer intelligence by creating developing robots or by evolving artificial cognitive systems (Beer, 2000; Smith & Breazeal, 2007).

4. *Intelligence resides in a complex dynamic system that includes brain, body, and world* and can be understood only by understanding the continuous, real-time and closed-loop interactions of the brain through the body to the world and *back again.*

Given these starting principles, how does one explain the 'specialness' of human intelligence? Evolution provides an important clue. Many species do very smart things – navigate, calculate, detect, and smartly use subtle forms of regularities. But in many species, this intelligence is limited to specific tasks and contexts and is not transportable, nor inventive (Rozin, 1976). In contrast, the species we think of as having the most advanced forms of biological intelligence are advanced precisely because they are open systems, influenced by many sources of information, generalizing broadly and inventing new solutions. These same species also have long post-birth periods of immaturity. If this long period of immaturity is key to the inventive and open nature of human intelligence, then we need to understand just what is happening over that long period of development.

The theme of this chapter is that human intelligence emerges in the accrued effects of many different integrations of heterogeneous processes, each integration occurring as the consequence of *doing* some task. A complex system that must find solutions to many different overlapping tasks creates the specialness of human intelligence, an intelligence capable of inventing alphabets, writing poetry, building bridges, and jerry-rigging a broken door lock. The developmental processes that make human intelligence are bound to a structured world that includes conspecifics with a shared language, culture, and enduring artefacts and thus these contexts in which human development occurs are also important parts of the process. In brief, what is 'special' about human intelligence is precisely opposite of those accounts that propose specially evolved, innate, dedicated, and encapsulated systems.

Integration

In his book, *The Origins of Intelligence in Children*, Piaget (1952) described a pattern of infant activity that he called a secondary circular reaction. A rattle would be placed in a 4-month-old infant's hands. As the infant moved the rattle, it would both come into sight and also make a noise, arousing and agitating the infant, causing more body motions, and thus causing the rattle to move into and out of sight and to make more noise. Infants at this age have very little organized control over hand and eye. They cannot yet reach for a rattle and if given one, they do not necessarily shake it. But if the infant accidentally moves it, and sees and hears the consequences, the infant will become captured by the activity – moving and shaking, looking and listening – and incrementally through this repeated action gain control over the shaking of the rattle and, indeed, acquire the intention to shake to produce noise. This pattern of activity – an accidental action that leads to an interesting and arousing outcome and to the intention to re-experience of the outcome – is foundational to intelligence.

In his book, *Neural Darwinism*, Edelman (1987) also pointed to the coupling of heterogeneous sensory–motor systems in the creation of cognition. Edelman's theory, like that of Piaget, starts by recognizing the multimodal nature of the brain at birth; it is – from the start – a complex system made up of many heterogeneous subsystems with their own intrinsic dynamics; but these subsystems are also highly interactive and densely interconnected within themselves and also over longer pathways to other subsystems. Like Piaget, Edelman proposed that development occurs through the coupled interactions of these subsystems to each other and to the physical world as they are engaged in real-time tasks. In the context of a specific task, distinct processes are time-locked to each other *and* to the world, and this creates adaptive change in the internal operating characteristics of those subsystems and in their connections to each other.

To illustrate this, Reeke and Edelman (1984) built a simple computational device. The device's task was to learn to recognize all varieties of the letter A, from the mere experience of looking at As. Figure 16.1 provides a schematic illustration. The feature-analysis subsystem consists of line detectors excited by corresponding patterns of stimulation. The tracing subsystem gathers information about shape through 'eye-movements' as the letter is scanned. The developmental power arises because these activation patterns in these two subsystems are time-locked to each other and to the same physical world enabling straightforward Hebbian learning to create systematic and adaptive change.

That is, at the same time that the feature analyser is analysing features, the shape tracer is extracting a global description of shape. The outputs of these two heterogeneous processes, at every step in time, are mapped to each other. There are actually seven mappings being accomplished simultaneously in real time. One mapping, the feature analysis map, maps an input letter to a list of features. The second mapping, the tracing map, maps the input letter to the action sequences of scanning. The third map – from the tracing process to the physical world – selects moment by moment the input (the specific letter part) to both subsystems. The fourth and fifth maps are the recurrent activity within each subsystem: at any moment in time, the activity in the feature analysis subsystem, for example, depends not only on the current input but also on its just preceding state. The sixth and seventh maps are what Edelman calls re-entrant maps; they map the activities of the two subsystems to each other. Thus, two independent mappings of the stimulus to internal activity take qualitatively different glosses on the perceptual information and through their re-entrant connections, by being correlated in real time and by being coupled to the same physical world, they educate each other. Reeke and Edelman's simulation successfully taught itself to recognize all varieties of A, generalizing to novel fonts and handwriting, merely from actively looking at As.

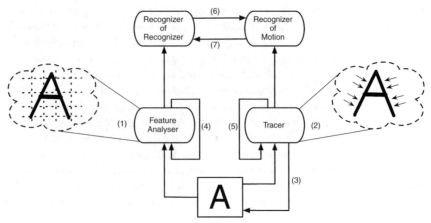

Fig. 16.1 A schematic of Reeke's and Edelman's (1984) network model of letter recognition. The letter A at the bottom of the figure depicts the two-dimensional input array. This input is connected to both a feature analysis system and a tracing system. The recurrent connection for each of these systems represents the system's dependence not only on input but on its own history. The feature analysis system is composed of feature detectors which track the local structure of the input array, like an oriented line segment. This system outputs to a more abstract detector which integrates information across the local detectors capturing the global structure of the input array. The tracing system scans the input array and detects the contour of objects. This system, like the feature analysis system, outputs to a higher-level network which captures shared characteristics of related input arrays. The two higher-level networks are connected to each other enabling the two subsystems (feature analysis and tracing) to work together to classify letters.

The idea that coupled perception and action drives perceptual development is well supported by classic work such as Held and Hein's (1963) demonstration of changes in the visual system of kittens who actively explored their world and the lack of change in the visual system of kittens who passively viewed the same visual events (see also, Gonzalez et al., 2005; Harman et al., 1999; Hein & Diamond, 1972; Landrigan & Forsyth, 1974). The newer idea – with growing supporting evidence in cognitive neuroscience (Barsalou et al., 2005; Martin & Chao, 2001; Pulvermüller et al., 1999, 2005) and in computational studies of brain systems and learning (Lungarella & Sporns, 2006; Lungarella et al., 2005; McIntosh et al., 2001; Tononi, 2004) is that this self-generated activity through the coordination of multiple sensory–motor systems also creates the higher-level cognition characteristic of human intelligence.

Multiple modalities

The human sensory motor (i.e. cognitive) system is far more complex than the model system shown in Figure 16.1. There are many more component subsystems and variable and complex patterns of connectivity among them. For example, many cortical brain regions associated with specific modalities are comprised of densely connected subregions that capture specific feature states within that single modality and there are also systems of connections among those feature areas. And, there are integrations across modalities (e.g. Martin & Chao, 2001; Pulvermüller et al., 2005; Rogers et al., 2007). Rapidly advancing work in systems neuroscience and in cognitive neuroscience increasingly document the pervasiveness of these cross-area integrations and indeed the greater interconnectivity of different sensory systems early in development (see Stiles, 2008). Overlapping, interacting, and redundant ways of knowing are a fundamental aspect of the human brain and may well be the source of abstract and transportable knowledge.

Multimodality may be key because of what Edelman (1987) calls *degeneracy*. Originally from the mathematical sense of the word, degeneracy in neural structure means that any single function can be carried out by more than one configuration of neural signals and that different neural clusters also participate in a number of different functions. As indicated in Figure 16.2, degeneracy is an intermediate level of complexity in a network between modularity and complete (or random) connections. A modular system is such that inputs in one module are unaffected by the activity in other modules, yielding highly stable but also highly limited patterns of activity. In a completely connected or random network, everything affects everything with the consequences of limited stability and considerable variability. In between is a degenerate network, with partially overlapping patterns of connectivity that include dense local connections and sparser longer pathways. The consequence is considerable complexity and many dynamically stable states (Sporns, 2002). The human brain is generally understood to be degenerate in this sense.

One consequence of degeneracy is that the whole can function even with the loss of one component. There are multiple routes to the same behavioural outcome. For example, because we encounter space through sight, sound, movement, touch, and even smell, we can know space even if we lack one modality. Being blind, for example, does not wipe out spatial concepts; instead, as studies of blind children show (Landau & Gleitman, 1985), comparable – and highly abstract – spatial concepts can be developed, presumably through the coordination of remaining redundant and overlapping subsystems.

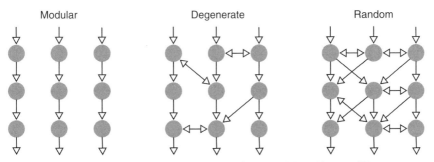

Fig. 16.2 A schematic illustration of three kinds of connectivity with very different properties with respect to stability and inventiveness: a modular system, a degenerate system, and a random and densely connected system.

The partial redundancies in functional connectivity also mean that different tasks can recruit different but overlapping consortiums of subsystems, a fact of considerable *developmental* importance. In one suggestive experiment, Needham et al. (2002) fit 2- to 5-month-old infants with Velcro-covered 'sticky mittens'. These mittens enabled the infants to grab objects merely by swiping at them, enabling them to precociously coordinate vision and reaching. Infants who were given 2 weeks of experiences with 'sticky' mittens subsequently showed more sophisticated object exploration even with the mittens off. They looked at objects more, made more visually coordinated swipes at objects than did control infants who had no exploratory experiences with 'sticky mittens'. Needham et al. found that the sticky-mitten task not only facilitated the development of reaching for objects but also visual–oral exploration. That is, infants who had experience with sticky mittens looked at objects more – even in nonreaching tasks – and also mouthed and orally explored objects in more advanced ways.

Figure 16.3 provides a schematic illustration of what may be the profound significance of these results. Two subsystems – reaching and looking – are coordinated in the sticky-mitten task and in so doing educate each other. But these components are also involved in other coordinations, in other tasks that recruit other coalitions of subsystems. Thus, extra experience in the coordination of reaching and looking with sticky mittens ends up not being just about looking and reaching but potentially about other developments, other coordinations, generating cascading developmental consequences in other tasks in which some of the same subsystems are involved.

Infants' learning about transparent surfaces presents another example of generalization from overlapping integrations, and perhaps also, evidence for an 'abstract idea' made through such integrations. Transparent surfaces are interesting precisely because they violate the usual hand–eye correlations in the world. In most cases, one can

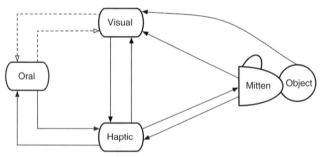

Fig. 16.3 A schematic illustration of affect of 'sticky' mittens on the visual, haptic, and oral systems. The use of 'sticky' mittens during manual exploration reorganizes the coordination of the visual and haptic systems. The oral system is greyed in the figure because it is not directly involved in the activity with the 'sticky' mittens. However, it is connected to the haptic system – infants often manually and orally explore objects – and through this connection is potentially influenced by the visual–haptic reorganization. The visual–haptic reorganization leads to the coupling of the visual and oral systems – depicted by empty arrows with dotted lines – which are not directly linked.

directly reach to a seen object by following the line of sight. In contrast to this usual case, transparent yet solid surfaces block direct line of sight-reaching paths. There can be no evolutionary programme for learning about transparency since transparent and solid surfaces are not common in nature but are artefacts, invented by people. And indeed, some species (birds) seem unable to resolve this problem of transparency (see Malakoff, 2004).

Babies (like birds) do not do well with this violation of usual expectations. The experimental demonstration of infants' difficulties is provided by Diamond (1990) who presented 9-month-old infants with toys hidden under boxes. The boxes were either opaque – hiding the toy – or transparent, enabling the infants to see the toy under the box. As illustrated in Figure 16.3, the boxes were open on the side, so that infants, by reaching to that side, could retrieve the object. Diamond found that infants were able to retrieve the toy from the opaque container, reaching around to the side opening. However, they frustratingly failed in the same task with a transparent container. The problem with the transparent container is that infants attempt to reach for the toy in the usual way (trying to put their hand through the transparent surface following the line of sight) and thus fail. They do not search for and find the opening.

But infants, unlike birds, are *not* stuck with what is a maladaptive approach in the modern artefact-filled world. Infants easily learn to solve this problem through their ordinary interactions with transparent containers. In a demonstration of this point, Titzer (1997, see also Smith & Gasser, 2005) conducted a microgenetic study in which 8-month-old infants were given either a set of opaque or transparent containers to play with at home. Parents were given no instructions other than to put these containers in the toy box, making them available to the infants during play. When the infants were 9 months old, they were tested in Diamond's task. The babies who had played at home with opaque containers failed to retrieve objects from transparent ones just as in the original Diamond study. However, infants who had played at home with the transparent containers sought out and rapidly found the openings and retrieved the object from the transparent boxes. Infants' at-home explorations of the transparent containers did *not* include the specific task of sideways retrieval of objects, although it seems likely that in their spontaneous play, objects were both put into and retrieved from the openings of the containers. Titzer proposed that during play – through the coordination of seeing and touching as they put objects in and out of the containers – infants learned to recognize the subtle visual cues that distinguish solid transparent surfaces from openings and had learned that surfaces with the visual properties of transparency are, in fact, solid and thus to reach around to the openings. In the framework of Figure 16.1, the haptic cues from touching the transparent surfaces educated vision, and vision educated reaching and touch, enabling infants when subsequently tested in Diamond's task to find the openings in transparent containers.

Critically, these coordinations of touch and sight had broader cascading consequences beyond retrieving objects from small transparent containers, cascading effects that some might want to summarize under the umbrella of a 'concept of solid and supporting surface'. The result was obtained in an additional transfer task, the visual cliff. The visual cliff was originally designed to study infant depth perception (Gibson & Walk, 1960; Walk & Gibson, 1961). It consists of a transparent but solid surface placed over a visual 'drop off'. In the classic version of the task, 8- and 9-month-old infants are placed on the 'safe' side of the surface. Infants this age typically avoid the visual drop, not moving onto the transparent surface that extends over the vertical drop.

Titzer tested the babies who had participated in their training study with transparent and opaque containers on the visual cliff and found that the infants who played with the transparent containers at home did not avoid the visual cliff. Instead, they happily crawled onto the transparent surface over the drop off, showing no apprehension whatsoever. The babies who had played with opaque containers, in contrast, avoided the 'edge' refusing – even when called by their parent – to approach the visually (but not tactually) apparent cliff. The infants, who had extensive play with transparent containers, were apparently both sensitive to the subtle visual cues that specify the solidity of a transparent surface and to the cues felt from their hands as they felt the surface and thus were confident of its support. Again, two subsystems – seeing and touching – are coordinated when playing with transparent containers, each system educating the other in the discovery of relevant regularities to that coupling. The changes in these component subsystems – the regularities found in one task will be transported to other tasks that also recruit these same subsystems (for another compelling example, see Bertenthal & Campos, 1990). In this way, the coordination of multimodal subsystems in specific tasks may create abstract and transportable ideas.

One might ask at this juncture: what do babies have that birds do not, that babies but not birds, so readily learn to distinguish transparent surfaces from openings in those surfaces? The correct answer is probably many, many different processes (and body parts). But in the case of transparency, one relevant difference may be the sensory–motor couplings and time-locked dynamic visual and haptic experiences that infants can generate with their hands as they manually and visually explore objects. Each sensory–motor system has its own processes and computational mechanisms. These unique takes on the world are a critical starting point to outcome and without doubt matter greatly. But what also matters is the *functional* coupling these heterogeneous processes *in multiple tasks*, such that the component systems change the internal workings of each other, finding higher-order regularities that transcend specific modalities and specific tasks (see Barsalou et al., 2003). What is unique in the human system relative to other species may not be so much any one bit of computational machinery but rather the higher-order integrative architecture, that is open to new and multiple solutions (see also Honey et al., 2007).

An open system

Human beings learn and do things that have never been done before. Even young children exhibit cognitive skills that were not imaginable generations ago, learning about transparency, pictures, and videos, about drag and click, how to program, and the rhythm and syntax of texting, as well as those older intellectual artefacts of reading and multiplication. There seems no limit to what we can potentially incorporate, make into everyday cognition, even into child's play. In this way, human cognition is decidedly not predetermined and not preset, but is rather open-ended. This open-endedness begins (but does not end) with our ability to discover goals, through our own activity.

The lesson from rattle-shaking and sticky mittens is this: goals are not prior to the task but are themselves emergent in the infant's engagement with the world. Prior to shaking the rattle, or catching a toy with the sticky mittens, infants can have no specific goal to shake to make noise, or to swat to snatch an object. Another example of goal discovery through action is 'infant conjugate reinforcement' (Argulo–Kinzler et al., 2002; Rovee-Collier & Hayne, 1987). Infants (as young as 3 months) are placed on their backs and their ankles are attached by a ribbon to a mobile which is suspended overhead. The mobile, which produces interesting sights and sounds, provides the infant with many time-locked patterns of correlations. More importantly, infants themselves discover these relations through their own movement patterns. The faster and harder infants kick, the more the mobile moves fuelling the infants' kicking. This is a highly engaging task for infants; they smile and laugh, and often become angry when the contingency is removed. This experimental procedure, like the world, provides complex, diverse, and never exactly repeating events but critically events perfectly time-locked with the infant's own actions. It is spontaneous nontask-related movement that starts the process off by creating the opportunity for the coordination of the infant's action with that of the mobile. It is this coordination which ultimately defines the task and thus becomes the goal.

Because the goals that drive intentional action (and learning) are not pregiven but are discovered by the individual through action, development itself is highly specific to the individual. Different children will follow different developmental paths that depend on the specific tasks they encounter and the intrinsic dynamics of their own system. One elegant demonstration of the individual nature of developmental trajectories is Thelen's et al. (1993) week-by-week study of the transition from not-reaching to reaching for visually presented objects. Thelen et al. studied four babies and found four different patterns of activity, and thus, four different patterns of development. The basic developmental pattern was: the presentation of an enticing toy is arousing and elicits all sorts of nonproductive actions, but different actions for different babies. These actions are first, quite literally, all over the place with no clear coherence in form or direction. But by acting, each baby in its own unique fashion, sooner or later makes contact with the toy – banging into or brushing against it or swiping it. These moments of contact select some movements, carving out patterns that are then repeated with increasing frequency. Over weeks, the cycle repeats – arousal by the sight of some toy, action, and occasional contact. Over cycles, increasingly stable, more efficient and more effective forms of reaching emerge.

As infants produce different movements – uncontrolled actions initiated by the arousing sight of the toy – they each discover initially different patterns and different developmental tasks to be solved. Some babies in the nonreaching period hardly lift their arms at all. Other babies flail and flap and are always moving. These different babies must solve different problems to grasp an object. The flailer needs to become less active lowering the hands to bring them to midline and create balance. The placid baby needs to be more active, to raise her hands and to lift them up.

What is remarkable in the developmental patterns observed by Thelen and collaborators is that each infant found a solution by following individual developmental pathways that eventually converged to highly similar outcomes. As action defines the task and as action – through the coordination of heterogeneous sensory systems – finds the solution, development is very much an individual and context-dependent matter, and not pre-defined prior to action itself. Given the constraints of the world, of human bodies, and of the heterogeneous and multimodal system out of which intelligence is made, different individuals will develop broadly similar systems (what one might summarize as 'universals') but at its core, development (like evolution) is opportunistic, individualistic, and local in its causes.

Doing with images

Actions create perceivable outcomes, some of which are stable and sit as new things in the world. For example, a child through a series of actions, stacks one thing onto the other, and then another, and then another, not only sees and feels the repetitive actions as they unfold but also in the end can also sit back, look at, and reflect on a tower of blocks that did not exist before. This link between actions and stable products in the world may be profoundly important to human intelligence and in particular, to the development of symbols. Alan Kay, one of the founding fathers of object-oriented programming and graphical-user interfaces (the idea behind the original MacIntosh drag-and-click we now all use) is a visionary computer scientist who gave a talk in 1987 with a cult-like following. The talk's title is 'Doing with images makes symbols'. (One can google the title of the talk to find hundreds of copies of it.) Inspired by Piaget (1952), Bruner (1956), and Vygotsky (1978), Kay proposed that abstract ideas (and symbolic thought) were built out of real-time sensory–motor interactions with images, that is, with the stable *perceivable consequences* of our own actions. This is like the idea of a closed loop in active vision in which every action creates perceivable consequences that also guide action at the next step. But the key idea here is that some perceivable consequences are special in being *image-like,* in that they are stable and enduring, a perceivable constant that is coupled to the messier context-specific and continuous dynamics of perception and action. These external stabilities – 'artefacts' that may be initially produced without plan or goal – are a profound force on human cognition.

The development of spatial classification provides an interesting phenomenon with which to consider these ideas. Between their first and third birthdays, children begin to use space to represent similarity, putting like things close together (Sugarman, 1983). Indeed, during this period, they become almost compulsive spatial sorters. Confronted with an array of four identical cars and four identical dolls, they physically group them – moving all the cars spatially close to each other and spatially apart from the groups of dolls even though there is no explicit task to do so. They are so reliable at doing this that many developmental psychologists use the task as a way to measure young children's knowledge of categories (e.g. Mandler et al., 1991; Nelson, 1973; Rakison & Butterworth, 1998). Their reasoning is that if a 2-year-old knows that two objects are the same kind of thing, she should spatially group them together. A perhaps just-as-interesting question is why the child spatially groups objects at all.

The developmental evidence suggests a progressive discovery of spatial classification. Nine- to 10-month-old infants when given sets of objects of like kinds do not systematically group them into categories. However, they do – more often than expected by chance – pick up like objects but not unlike objects, one in each hand, and bang them together (Forman, 1982). By 12 months of age these manipulations – like manipulations of like kinds – become more systematic and extended to all available like instances (Sugarman, 1983). For example, given four cars and four dolls, the child may systematically push each of the four cars. Around 18 months of age, children will not only manipulate objects from one category in sequence but also systematically manipulate in different ways objects from two different categories, for example, first pushing each of four cars, one after another and then touching each of four dolls in turn. Sometime after 24 months, the sorting seems more purposeful with all of one kind gathered to form one group and the other kind left unorganized. Later the systematic formation of two spatial groups emerges.

Sheya and Smith (Sheya, 2005; Sheya & Smith, 2008, in press) propose that this developmental pattern emerges though the child's own actions, actions that at first have no goal of creating a classification. Four behavioural tendencies are proposed to drive the process. The first is that infants reach to objects in which they are interested. The second is that infants have a tendency to repeat just-performed motor acts, and in particular to repeat reaches to nearby locations (e.g. Smith et al., 1999). The third is that perceptually similar objects are similarly enticing to infants. The fourth is that infants notice the outcomes of their own actions. These four tendencies can be understood in terms of a dynamic salience map, a map that determines where infants look to and reach next.

Imagine an array of eight toys, five of one kind and three of another as illustrated in Figure 16.4. Attention to and the touching of one toy alters the salience map, by

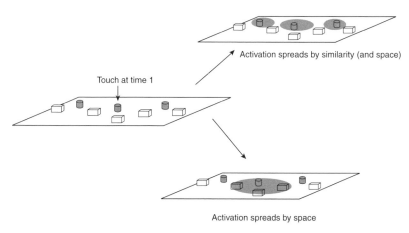

Activation spreads by similarity (and space)

Touch at time 1

Activation spreads by space

Salience (likelihood of next touch) at time 2

Fig. 16.4 An illustration of the two ways in which perceptual-motor activity at one moment in time may organize attention and behaviour at the next. A touch to one object may increase the salience of objects at locations near to that touch or a touch to one object may increase the salience of objects similar in their properties to the first object.

activating the spatial location of that toy. This activation can spread along two potential dimensions – physical space or a feature space according to the feature similarity of the objects. In their behavioural experiments, Sheya and Smith showed that activation in this salience space (as measured by the next toy touched) spreads mostly by space for younger infants (12-month-olds) but by feature similarity for older infants (18-month-olds). However, for all infants, both closeness and similarity interacted with *close* and *similar* things being more salient than close and dissimilar things.

These tendencies can create the sequential touching of like objects. As children are drawn to nearby and similar things, they are likely – through just these processes alone – to drop similar things near other, with the interactive effects of spatial proximity and physical similarity increasing the salience of reaching, again and again, to like and near things. A system whose activity is biased to both reach to similar locations and to reach to similar objects, will as consequence of reaching and dropping those things, end up with similar things near each other. It is here that Alan Kay's idea enters in. This unplanned consequence of similar things ending up near each other creates *an image*, a stable array of like things in proximity and apart from different things.

Namy et al., (1997) conducted a microgenetic study with the goal of encouraging the development of spatial classification in toddlers who did not yet spatially group like objects. The children's 'training' was a fun task of putting objects into a shape sorter. As illustrated in Figure 16.5, the shape sorter was a transparent container structured so that children could see the objects once they had been dropped inside. Children were given two different kinds of objects (e.g. blocks and bolls) that might be put into the container. The opening on the top of the shape container only allowed one type of object to fit inside the hole. Children at this age have strong perseverative tendencies to repeat the same action, and so they (quite happily) attempted to put all the objects into the container – the kind that fit and the kind that did not. But their actions led to only one kind actually being in the container together and thus in spatial proximity. Their actions thus produced a stable image of like things being near each other and apart from different things.

This experience turned these children in to spatial classifiers, advancing them several months in this developmental progression. In the transfer task, children were given sets of eight objects – four of one kind or four of another and no shaper sorter. Children who had previously sorted with the transparent shape sorter – that enabled the children to see the product of their activity – were much more likely to sort the objects

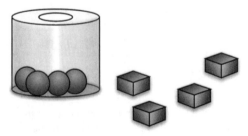

Fig. 16.5 Depicts the transparent sorter used in Namy et al. (1998). The sorter enabled young children to spatially segregate objects of different kinds.

into spatially organized groups than children in the control conditions. Namy et al. (1997) suggest that their experimental procedure intensified the experiences characteristic of children's every day activities. Children are attracted to objects that are physically similar, they tend to repeat similar acts and this leads to similar things often ending up close in space. As children play with things in their world, a world in which physically like things have similar propensities, like things will end up near each other. Moreover, as children interact with a world structured by adults with a similar psychology, they will encounter cups near cups on the shelves and socks all together in the sock drawer. In these ways, spatial proximity becomes *the* foundational metaphor for both informal ideas and formal mathematical theories about similarity.

Many (though not all) of the spatial classifications that children encounter and do in the world – the cups near the cups, the socks in the sock drawer – are man-made creations, artefacts. And they are everywhere, at least in our Western world. But it seems likely that if some child never saw a spatial classification of like-near-like that they would spontaneously produce it nonetheless. Spatial classification is an artefact that is likely to spontaneously emerge over and over again, even if unsupported by convention. This is because spatial classification is encouraged by the physical fact that like things have like propensities and the psychological fact of an attentional and action system governed by both nearness in space and similarity in features. Not all artefacts that shape human cognition are so easily or so readily re-invented by each of us. Instead, they are passed down (and incrementally adapted) across generations within a culture. In our culture, children grow up with several powerful systems of artefacts – tools, letters, books, stories, machines. In all human cultures, children grow up with language. These systems may literally make thought more computationally powerful (see Clark, 1998; 2003; Greenspan & Shanker, 2004; Premack, 2004; Vygotsky, 1978; Wertsch, 1985). Relevant examples that have been discussed by others include how the invention of zero made everyday arithmetic easy (Seife, 2000), how learning to read an alphabetic system changes how we perceive and process spoken sounds (e.g. Treiman & Kessler, 2007), how social interactions with tools potentiate the invention and use of tools (e.g. Call & Tomasello, 1994). The focus in the next section is how one shared symbol system – language – may empower intelligence.

Doing with symbols

Children grow in a sea of symbols that include spoken words, marks on paper, and gestures. These physical and thus perceivable symbols are a very special form of regularity with four characteristics potentially crucial to the 'specialness' of human cognition. First, symbol systems (including language and mathematics) are in-the-world regularities that are *shared* (e.g. Freyd, 1983; Hutchins & Hazelhurst, 1995). This shared aspect means that these systems are very stable, continually constrained by many local communicative acts. Second, symbol systems are *arbitrary*. For example, the form of the word *dog* gives us no hints about the kinds of thing to which it refers and there is nothing in the similarity of the forms of *dig* and *dog* that conveys a similarity in meaning. It is interesting to ask *why* language and other symbol systems are this way, and why invented symbol systems that often begin with strong iconicity between form and referent become increasingly noniconic. One might expect that a multimodal, grounded, sensorimotor sort of learning would favour a more iconic, pantomime-like language in which symbols were similar to referents. But symbol systems are decidedly not like this (see DeLoache, 2002). Third, the distinct physical tokens that comprise effective symbol systems are rapidly, automatically, and *categorically perceived*. For some such systems (e.g. spoken words) this may be because of evolved sensory systems. The shared and repeated use of symbols may also encourage them to take on easily perceived and produced forms (e.g. Christiansen & Kirby, 2003; Ohala, 1993). Finally, some symbol systems (e.g. orthographies, mathematics) are made easy to perceive through extensive training. In sum, effective symbol systems require that the symbols themselves not take too much cognitive processing so that they can be mere pointers to meaning. Finally, symbols *refer*. Symbols systems are not about themselves but are about their referents. These properties of symbols confer computational power through re-representation, by creating and enabling higher-order correlations, and by creating dynamically complex systems that can jump from one highly stable state to another.

Re-representation through replacement

The physical symbols that surround children – spoken words, letters, drawings – are dual entities: (1) physical things with their own properties and (2) entities which stand for other things. Operating on physical symbols as physical entities may empower cognition, simply as a consequence of replacing one entity (the referred to thing) with another (the physical symbol (see Son et al., 2008, for further discussion and evidence). This point can be illustrated by considering what we mean when we say that some thing is the 'same.' The problem with 'same' is that one can be talking about *any* kind of thing and *any* kind of similarity – how two books are alike, how whales are sort of the same as fish but not really, how two smells are alike, how the relative quality of two cars are the same, and so forth. Explaining this ability might actually require some underlying and innately given machinery that can compute sameness over anything (what some might call a concept, see Smith, 1993; Smith et al., 1997 for a discussion of this possible machinery).

The present concern, however, is how symbols as physical entities might leverage thought and cognitive development. A task invented by Premack (1976) to measure the transcendent and abstract nature of sameness judgements provides an interesting case. Understanding Premack's problem begins with a simpler problem, matching to sample. In matching-to-sample, the learner must find the two objects in a set of three that are the same, no matter what those two objects are. Various animal species can do this (see Cook & Wasserman, 2006). These judgements suggest an 'abstract concept of same', although such a conclusion from matching-to-sample tasks alone is highly controversial as success can also be explained in other more perceptual ways.

Premack's problem takes this matching-to-sample task a level higher. Table 16.1 shows the required responses. Given the joint presentation of the first two cards, the correct response is 'same'; given the joint presentation of the next two cards, the correct response is again 'same'; the next two cards when jointly presented require the

Table 16.1 Examples of the kinds of trials that make up Premack's problem

Presentation	Cards	Correct response
Card 1	X-X	
Card 2	Y-Y	
		Same
Card 1	X-Y	
Card 2	O-R	
		Same
Card 1	X-X	
Card 2	O-R	
		Different
Card 1	X-R	
Card 2	O-O	
		Different

response 'different' and the final two cards when jointly presented require the response different. The rule is that they are the 'same' when the *relation* in the two cards is the same. This is not easily learnt by children, nor most animals.

Chimpanzees can be taught to do this (see also, Oden, Thompson, & Premack, 1990). The method begins by first teaching them to label pairs of things that stood in an identity relation with one arbitrary physical token, such as a heart-token for same (e.g. ♥ → AA) and to label pairs of things that were different with another token (e.g. # → AB). Having learnt this, the chimpanzees can make second-order matches, judging AA to be related to BB. The informative idea is this Chimpanzees could potentially do this task, not by abstracting the relation of sameness across instances, but by knowing that AA→ ♥ and BB → ♥. Then they can simply respond to the sameness of ♥ and ♥. Notice that this second-order relation (the same relation between 'same' and 'same') can result from *direct computations over the labels*. By replacing AA with a heart-token and BB with a heart-token, these chimpanzees can reduce the problem to matching-to-sample. In this way, symbols can enable solutions to what might seem intractable problems, enabling manipulations of concrete entities (the symbols). Recent research on learning mathematical symbol systems such as algebra, suggest that even highly advanced forms of human intelligence might be tied to perceptual (and indeed motor) aspects of manipulating physical symbols as entities in the world (Landy & Goldstone, 2007).

Higher-order correlations

Symbols may not just replace their referents in computations but they may also enable the discovery of higher-order regularities (Colunga & Smith, 2005; Smith & Gasser, 2005). Young children's progressively more rapid learning of object names provides a case in point. Children's learning of such common names such as *chair, dog*, and *milk* begins by their learning the specific similarities that organize these specific categories. Considerable evidence suggests that this initial category-by-category learning *creates* higher-level knowledge that enables children to rapidly and correctly map a name to *the whole category* given just one single instance of that category (see Colunga & Smith, 2005, for review). Indeed, by the time children are 3 years of age, they generalize the names for novel artefacts by shape, names for novel animals by multiple similarities, and names for substances by material (Smith et al., 2002a).

Experimental and computational studies suggest four steps in children's learning. These are illustrated in Figure 16.6 (Smith et al., 2002b) which shows just one of the regularities that children learn – that artefact categories are organized by shape. Step 1 in the learning process is the mapping of names to objects – the name 'ball' to a particular ball and the name 'cup' to a particular cup, for example. This is done multiple times for each name as the child encounters multiple examples. And importantly, in the early lexicon, solid, rigidly shaped things are in categories typically well-organized by similarity in shape (Samuelson & Smith, 1999). This learning of individual names sets up step 2 – first-order generalizations about the structure of individual categories, that is, the knowledge that balls are round and cups are cup-shaped. The first-order generalization should enable the learner to recognize novel balls and cups.

Fig. 16.6 Steps in forming a higher-order generalizations: (1) learn specific word object associations; (2) make first-order generalizations for each of the specific categories; (3) make higher-order generalizations across the regularities discovered in those first-order generalizations; and (4) use these higher-order generalizations to rapidly learn new categories.

But the key to the rapid learning of *new* words is the formation of a higher-order generalization. As most of the solid and rigid things that children learn about are named by their shape, children may also learn the second-order generalization that names for artefacts (solid, rigid things) in general span categories of similar-shaped things. As illustrated in step 3 of the figure, this second-order generalization requires generalizations over specific names and specific category structures. Once such a higher-order generalization is formed, the child behaves as if it has an abstract and variablized rule: for any artefact, whatever its individual properties or individual shape, form a category by a shape. Step 4 illustrates the potential developmental consequence of this higher-order generalization – attention to the right property, shape – for learning new names for artefacts. The plausibility of this account has been demonstrated in experimental studies that effectively accelerate the vocabulary-acquisition function by teaching children the relevant correlations (Smith et al., 2002b) and in simulation studies with neural nets (Colunga, 2003). Although we describe the process here in step-by-step fashion to illustrate logic of what is learned, the system is actually and continuously making multiple mappings and this may be important to answering the question of just what enables a system to build higher-order, almost rule-like generalizations (see Colunga & Smith, 2005).

Critically, it may be symbols, or more correctly a learning process that makes generalizations over a *large* system of associations in which one class of associates are arbitrary and orthogonal to each other (that is having the properties of words) that makes these higher order generalizations possible. Words – in contrast to other kinds of associates of objects (e.g. the actions we perform on them, or their typical locations) are special because they are arbitrary and orthogonal. As Colunga (2003) has argued, arbitrary and nonoverlapping symbols will pull apart first-order categories in ways critical to forming the second-order generalizations (step 3) by connectionist networks. Indeed, her simulations indicate that networks that readily form second-order generalizations and yield accelerating rates of vocabulary acquisition do not do this if the labels, the words, are not orthogonal.

A second property of words that may also be critical to the formation of higher-order generalizations is that words present systems of correlations *among themselves* not just to things in the world. Yoshida and Smith (2005) demonstrated the potential importance of these word–word associations in a study that attempted to teach young children the higher-order generalizations that solid and artefact-like things are named by shape and that nonsolid substances are named by material. They attempted to teach this to Japanese-speaking children *at an age earlier* than when these children normally make this distinction (see Yoshida & Smith, 2003). They did this by intensively teaching children names for novel solid things in categories well-organized by shapes and names for novel nonsolid things in categories well organized by material, and they did this in two ways: without correlating linguistic cues or *with* correlating linguistic cues (roughly like count–mass determiners in English for which there are no counterparts in Japanese). The main result is that only children taught the correlations between the perceptual cues of solid → shape-based and nonsolid → material based *in the context of redundant linguistic cues that linguistically marked the novel nouns as being of two kinds* made the higher-order generalizations enabling generalizations of learning in transfer to the formation of novel lexical categories for novel solid and nonsolid things.

We know from corpus analyses and other forms of data-mining that there is considerable derivable latent structure in the co-occurrence probabilities and associations among words – that is the physical symbols – themselves. Importantly, word–word associations are *ungrounded* in the sense that associations and co-occurrence relations exist among symbols that can be considered in isolation from their referents and meaning. Considerable structure is derivable from the statistical regularites among the words themselves including phonological, semantic, and syntactic categories (Chater & Manning, 2006; Landauer & Dumais, 1997; Li et al., 2000; Mintz et al., 2002; Monaghan et al., 2005; Redington et al., 1998; Steyvers & Tenenbaum, 2005).

As illustrated in Figure 16.7, the human cognitive system has three kinds of very different but connected data sets out of which to build knowledge: (1) correlations among the multimodal sensory–motor processes time-locked to each other and the world in tasks; (2) statistical regularities – and the latent structure derivable from those regularities – that characterize the symbols themselves; and (3) then the regularities with which (some of) these symbols map to sensory–motor experiences.

Analogue and digital

Degenerate, integrative, and graded sensory–motor processes are inherently inventive and adaptive, not brittle. As many theorists have pointed out (e.g. Barsalou & Prinz, 1997; Clark, 2003; Pfeiffer & Scheier, 1999) these qualities of the human perception–action system lead to an intelligence that is very different from the standard digital computer, precisely because of the adaptive, graded, and blended nature of sensory–motor representations. Digital computers that route arbitrary symbol structures between memory structures and a central processor fail to capture the more subtle, complex, and graded regularities that comprise everyday intelligence. However, digital systems have some decided advantages. O'Reilly (2006) notes in a recent review in

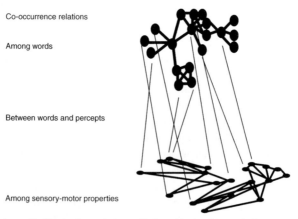

Co-occurrence relations

Among words

Between words and percepts

Among sensory-motor properties

Fig. 16.7 A schematic illustration of three distinct kinds of associative systems critical to human cognition: associations (co-occurrence regularities) among the symbols themselves; associations among perceivable properties of things in the world; and associations from symbols to perceivable properties in the world.

Science that digital systems have the advantage of being able to rapidly move from one highly stable solution to a very different but also stable one, without blending or passing through intermediate states (see also Clearfield et al., 2009; Hanania & Smith, in press; Munakata, 2001; Rougier et al., 2005).

One possibility is that language helps creates a digital-like function on top of the more graded and continuous and common sense way of knowing, giving human cognition two complementary ways of solving problems. One domain in which there is both evidence and theoretical models to support these ideas is the development of selective attention and attention shifting (Hanania & Smith, in press; Morton & Munakata, 2007; O'Reilly, 2006; Rougier et al., 2005). The key theoretical idea is that sufficient experience with words creates near-discrete and nondistributed activation patterns and these are necessary to bistable systems that exhibit 'rule-like' all-or-none gating of goals. Two different and independent simulations of these processes, each motivated by somewhat different concerns and data, came to the same conclusion (Rougier et al., 2005; Smith et al., 1997; see also Hanania & Smith, in press).

In the Rougier et al. simulations, the rapid shifting of attention in an all-or-none manner from one dimension to another required highly selective patterns of activation that corresponded to the input on one dimension independent of the other dimension. In these simulations, Rougier et al. (2005) specifically attempted to model the core properties thought to characterize the prefrontal cortex (PFC) and executive control: (1) recurrent and thus stabilizing patterns of activation; (2) an adaptive gating mechanism which maintains a rule so long as the outcome is predicted but that destabilizes the rule when the predictability of the outcome changes; and (3) modulation of processing in other areas, thus enabling the actively maintained rule to orchestrate and capture supporting processes in other systems (the so-called executive function of the PFC). The network was trained in three overlapping tasks: (1) labelling attributes on single dimensions (red, blue); (2) making judgements of sameness and difference on a single dimension (same colour, same shape); and (3) making comparisons on a single dimension (bigger, littler). Networks trained in all three of these tasks (but not just any one of them) developed highly abstract and orthogonal patterns of activation, not just to individual attributes (red, blue) but sameness along a single dimension independent of the particular attributes on that dimension (same colour, same shape). This result replicates a previous recurrent connectionist model by Smith et al. (1997) which also showed that highly abstract dimensional representations required training on both labelling (or selective responding to) attributes *and* same–different judgements on the dimension across a variety of different attributes and in the context of irrelevant variation on a different dimension. Both sets of simulations highlight two important contributions to the developmental processes that create the specialness of human cognition – overlapping tasks and language.

Doing with people

The highest forms of biological intelligence reside in a social world; development takes place among conspecifics with similar internal systems and similar external bodies. The importance of the social embeddedness of human cognition is well recognized in

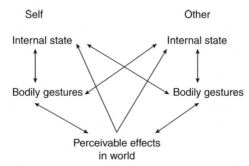

Fig. 16.8 The system of correlations added by being a social being in a social world. Coupled regularities between internal states, bodily gestures, and their perceivable effects in the world within and across individuals.

the literature (e.g. Markova & Legerstee, 2006; Rogoff, 2003; Striano & Reid, 2006). Perhaps less well recognized (but see, Smith, 2000a, 2000b; Yu et al., 2005) is how this social embeddedness is itself made manifest in sensory–motor coordinations (see Pereira et al., 2008; Smith & Breazeal, 2007).

Figure 16.8 illustrates the couplings between one's own internal states, one's outward bodily behaviours, the bodily behaviours of others, and their internal states. Crucially, the body and its behaviours are observable by others. But because observable behaviours are also linked to the actor's internal state, observable bodily behaviours also provide (albeit imperfect) information to others about those internal states. As one's bodily actions also influence the internal states of others, one's own actions are also (albeit indirectly) linked to the internal states of others. In brief, development occurs within a complex system of coupled behaviours, coupled bodies, and coupled cognitive systems.

These couplings generate a network of learnable correlations: between the appearance of the self and the appearance of others, between the behaviour of the self and the behaviour of others, between one's own bodily behaviours and one's internal states, between the external states of others and one own's internal states. In ways deeply analogous to the interactions of perception and action as illustrated in Figure 16.1, these correlations can yield transcendent higher-order regularities, in this case, about intentions and motivations (see Smith, 2000b; Smith & Breazeal, 2007). The dynamic socially embedded coupling of two intelligent systems – to each other through similar bodies and behaviours – is a potent agent of change and, is indeed, one component of developmental process that makes humans special.

What is special about human intelligence?

The task the contributors to this book were given by the editors was to specify what, if anything, is unique about human concepts and the role of evolution and development in this uniqueness. From the present perspective, this is an ill-formed question since 'concept' is an ill-defined theoretical construct that may or may not be needed in the end to explain human behaviour. This chapter began with the newer idea that intelligence does not reside in cognitive processes that are separate and distinct from the real-time sensory–motor processes which actively engage the world but that, instead, human intelligence can only be understood in terms of a complex system of brain, body, and world. A broad overview of what we know about the *making* of intelligent behaviour in human development from this perspective suggests the following:

- The open and inventive character of human cognition is made through a protracted period of immaturity in which children perceive and act in the world in the service of many different overlapping and discovered tasks.

- This developmental process (like evolution) is local, individualistic, and opportunistic and, therefore, highly creative.

- Many heterogeneous processes time-locked to each other and to the world change their internal dynamics (and thus the computations they can perform) as a consequence of these couplings.

- Many different tasks create different overlapping soft assemblies of these different component processes and cascading effects of learning from one task to others.

- Many different overlapping soft-assemblies NS integrations across many different tasks create abstract processes that transcend the specifics of specific modalities and the hear-and-now of specific tasks.

- Each action creates a new opportunity for perception and learning and some actions also create perceivable and stable images.

- A learning context with such self-created and also culturally provided images, artefacts, and symbols powers the cognitive system through re-representation, the creation of latent structure, and internal patterns of activation with multiple (discrete-like) stabilities.

- A learning context filled with mature conspecifics, with similar bodies and similar cognitive systems, enables systems of correlations across self and other, and ultimately creates predictions about the intentions and attentional states of others.

In brief, there is no simple answer to what makes human intelligence what it is, no one silver bullet, no one special thing, that makes human cognition. We are just kidding ourselves if we offer simple answers to these questions.

Finally, what are the roles of developmental process and evolution in all this? The bullet points above describe *developmental process*. It is complex, multilevelled, multicomponent, and in its entirety, it makes human intelligence what it is, and what it *can be*. Evolution selected this developmental process at all its levels of analysis from molecules to behaviour and including the multimodal sensory and motor systems (each with its own intrinsic dynamics and biases), the body's morphology, the possibilities for actions, the affiliative ties to conspecifics, and an integrative cognitive architecture that dynamically couples and uncouples components in functional tasks. In this complex system and in this developmental process, there will be many continuities with other organisms – no one magical difference anywhere – but the whole, and what it can create through its own activity, is uniquely human.

References

Angulo-Kinzler, R. M., Ulrich, B., & Thelen, E. (2002). Three-month-old infants can select specific leg motor solutions. *Motor Control*, **6**, 52–68.

Anderson, M. (2003). Embodied cognition: A field guide. *Artificial Intelligence*, **149**, 91–130.

Ballard, D., Hayhoe, M., Pook, P., & Rao, R. (1997). Deictic codes for the embodiment of cognition. *Behavioral and Brain Sciences*, **20**, 723–767.

Barsalou, L. W. (1993). Challenging assumptions about concepts. *Cognitive Development*, **8**(2), 169–180.

Barsalou, L. W. & Prinz, J. J. (1997). Mundane creativity in perceptual symbol systems. In T. B. Ward, S. M. Smith, & J. Vaid (Eds.), *Creative Thought: An Investigation of Conceptual Structures and Processes*, pp. 267–307, Washington, DC: American Psychological Association.

Barsalou, L. W., Pecher, D., Zeelenberg, R., Simmons, W. K., & Hamann, S. B. (2005). Multimodal simulation in conceptual processing. In W. Ahn, R. L. Goldstone, B. C. Love, A. Markman, & P. Wolff (Eds.), *Categorization Inside and Outside the Lab: Festschrift in Honor of Douglas L. Medin*, pp. 249–270, Washington, DC: American Psychological Association.

Barsalou, L. W., Simmons, W. K., Barbey, A. K., & Wilson, C. D. (2003). Grounding conceptual knowledge in modality-specific systems. *Trends in Cognitive Sciences*, 7, 84–91.

Barsalou, L., Breazeal, C., & Smith, L. B. (2007). Cognition as coordinated noncognition. *Cognitive Processing*, **8**, 79–91.

Beer, R. D. (2000). Dynamical approaches to cognitive science. *Trends in Cognitive Science*, **4**, 91–99.

Bertenthal, B. I. & Campos, J. J. (1990). A systems approach to the organizing effects of self-produced locomotion during infancy. In C. Rovee-Collier & L. P. Lipsitt (Eds.), *Advances in Infancy Research*, Vol. 6, pp. 1–60, Norwood, NJ: Ablex.

Brooks, R. A. (1991). 'Intelligence Without Representation'. *Artificial Intelligence Journal*, **47**, 139–159.

Bruner, J. S. (1996). *The Culture of Education* Cambridge, MA: Harvard University Press.

Bruner, J. S., Goodnow, J. J., & Austin, G. A. (1956). *A study of thinking* Oxford, England: John Wiley and Sons.

Call, J. & Tomasello, M. (1994). The social learning of tool use by orangutans (*Pongo pygmaeus*). *Human Evolution* 9, 297–313.

Chater, N. & Manning, C. D. (2006). Probabilistic models of language processing and acquisition. *Trends in Cognitive Sciences. Special Issue: Probabilistic Models of Cognition*, **10**(7), 335–344.

Christiansen, M. &. Kirby, S (2003). *Language Evolution* Oxford: Oxford University Press.

Clark, A. (1998). Magic words: How language augments human computation. In P. Carruthers & J. Boucher (Eds.), *Language and Thought: Interdisciplinary Themes*, pp. 162–183, Cambridge: Cambridge University Press.

Clark, A. (2003). *Natural-Born Cyborgs: Minds, Technologies and the Future of Human Intelligence*, New York: Oxford University Press.

Clearfield, M. W., Dineva, E., Smith, L. B., Diedrich, F. J., & Thelen, E. (2009). Cue salience and infant perseverative reaching: tests of the dynamic field theory. *Developmental Science*, **12**(1), 26–30.

Colunga, E. & Smith, L. B. (2005). From the lexicon to expectations about kinds: A role for associative learning. *Psychological Review*, **112**(2), 342–382.

Cook, R. G. & Wasserman, E. A. (2006). *Relational Discrimination Learning in Pigeons* New York: Oxford University Press.

DeLoache, J. (2002). The symbol-mindedness of young children. In W. W. Hartup & R. A. Weinberg (Eds.), *Child Psychology in Retrospect and Prospect: The Minnesota Symposia on Child Psychology*, Vol. 32, pp. 73–101, Mahwah, NJ: LEA Publishing.

Diamond, A. (1990). Developmental time course in human infants and infant monkeys and the neural bases of inhibitory control in reaching. In A. Diamond (Ed.) *The Development and Neural Bases of Higher Cognitive Functions*, pp. 637–676, New York: New York Academy of Sciences.

Edelman, G. (1987). *Neural Darwinism* New York: Basic Books.

Elman, J. L. (2004). An alternative view of the mental lexicon. *Trends in Cognitive Science*, **8**, 301–306.

Forman, G. (1982). A search for the origins of equivalence concepts through a microanalysis of block play. In G. Forman (Ed.), *Action and Thought: From Sensorimotor Schemes to Symbolic Operations*, pp. 97–135, New York: Academic Press.

Freyd, J. (1983). Shareability: The social psychology of epistemology. *Cognitive Science*, **7**(3), 191–210.

Gentner, D. (1983). Structure-mapping: A theoretical framework for analogy. *Cognitive Science*, **7**, 155–170.

Greenspan, S. I. & Shanker, S. G. (2004). *The First Idea: How Symbols, Language and Intelligence Evolved from Our Primate Ancestors to Modern Humans* New York: Da Capo Press.

Gibson, E. J. & Walk, R. D. (1960). The 'visual cliff'. *Scientific American*, **202**(4), 64–71.

González, J. C., Bach-y-Rita, P., & Haase, S. J. (2005). Perceptual recalibration in sensory substitution and perceptual modification. *Pragmatics & Cognition. Special Issue: Cognitive Technologies and the Pragmatics of Cognition*, **13**(3), 481–500.

Hanania, R. & Smith, L. B. (in press). Selective attention and attention switching: towards a unified developmental approach. *Developmental Science*, in press.

Harman, K. L., Humphrey, G. K., & Goodale, M. A. (1999). Active manual control of object views facilitates visual recognition. *Current Biology*, **9**(22), 1315–1318.

Hein, A. & Diamond, R. M. (1972). Locomotory space as a prerequisite for acquiring visually guided reaching in kittens. *Journal of Comparative and Physiological Psychology*, **81**(3), 394–398.

Held, R. & Hein, A. (1963). Movement-produced stimulation in the development of visually guided behavior. *Journal of Comparative and Physiological Psychology*, **56**(5), 872–876.

Honey, C. Kotter, R., Breakspear, M., & Sporns, O. (2007). Network structure of cerebral cortex shapes functional connectivity on multiple time scales. *Proceedings of the National Academy of Science*, **104**, 10240–10245.

Hutchins, E. (1995). *Cognition in the Wild* Cambridge, MA: MIT Press.

Hutchins, E. & Hazelhurst, B. (1995). *How to Invent a Lexicon: The Development of Shared Symbols in Interaction* London: UCL.

James, W. (1890). *The Principles of Psychology*, Vol. 1, New York: Holt.

Keil, F. C. (1994). The birth and nurturance of concepts by domains: The origins of concepts of living things. In L. A. Hirschfeld & S. A. Gelman (Eds.), *Mapping the Mind: Domain*

Specificity in Cognition and Culture, pp. 234–254, New York: Cambridge University Press.

Landau, B. & Gleitman, L. (1985). *Language and Experience* Cambridge, MA: Harvard University Press.

Landauer, T. K. & Dumais, S. T. (1997). A solution to Plato's problem: The latent semantic analysis theory of acquisition, induction, and representation of knowledge. *Psychological Review*, **104**(2), 211–240.

Landrigan, D. T. & Forsyth, G. A. (1974). Regulation and production of movement effects in exploration–recognition performance. *Journal of Experimental Psychology*, **103**(6), 1124–1130.

Landy, D. & Goldstone, R. L. (2007). Formal notations are diagrams: Evidence from a production task. *Memory & Cognition*, **35**, 2033–2040.

Li, P., Burgess, C., & Lund, K. (2000). The acquisition of word meaning through global lexical co-occurrences. In E. V. Clark (Ed.), *Proceedings of the 30th Annual Child Language Research Forum*, pp.167–178, Stanford, CA: Center for the Study of Language and Information.

Lungarella, M. & Sporns, O. (2006). Mapping information flow in sensorimotor networks. *PLoS Computational Biology*, **2**(10): e144–150.

Lungarella, M., Pegors, T., Bulwinkle, D., & Sporns, O. (2005). Methods for quantifying the informational structure of sensory and motor data. *Neuroinformatics*, **3**, 243–262.

Malakoff, D. (2004). Clear and present danger. *Audubon*, **106**(1), 65–68.

Mandler, J. M., Bauer, P. J., & McDonough, L. (1991). Separating the sheep from the goats: Differentiating global categories. *Cognitive Psychology*, **23**(2), 263–298.

Markova, G. & Legerstee, M. (2006). Contingency, imitation, and affect sharing: Foundations of infants' social awareness. *Developmental Psychology*, **42**(1), 132–141.

Martin, A. & Chao, L. L. (2001). Semantic memory and the brain: Structure and processes. *Current Opinion in Neurobiology Special Issue: Cognitive Neuroscience*, **11**(2), 194–201.

McIntosh, A. R., Fitzpatrick, S. M., & Friston, K. J. (2001). On the marriage of cognition and neuroscience. *Neuroimage*, **14**, 1231–1237.

Mintz, T. H., Newport, E. L., & Bever, T. G. (2002). The distributional structure of grammatical categories in speech to young children. *Cognitive Science*: A *Multidisciplinary Journal*, **26**(4), 393–424.

Monaghan, P., Christiansen, M. H., & Chater, N. (2007). The phonological–distributional coherence hypothesis: Cross-linguistic evidence in language acquisition. *Cognitive Psychology*, **55**(4), 259–305.

Morton, J. B. & Munakata, Y. (2002). Active versus latent representations: A neural network model of perseveration, dissociation, and decalage. *Developmental Psychobiology. Special Issue: Converging Method Approach to the Study of Developmental Science*, **40**(3), 255–265.

Munakata, Y. (2001). Graded representations in behavioral dissociations. *Trends in Cognitive Sciences*, **5**(7), 309–315.

Namy, L. L., Smith, L. B., & Gershkoff-Stowe, L. (1997). Young children discovery of spatial classification. *Cognitive Development*, **12**(2), 163–184.

Needham, A., Barrett, T., & Peterman, K. (2002). A pick me up for infants' exploratory skills: Early simulated experiences reaching for objects using 'sticky' mittens enhances young infants' object exploration skills. *Infant Behavior and Development*, **25**(3), 279–295.

Nelson, K. (1973). Some evidence for the cognitive primacy of categorization and its functional basis. *Merrill Palmer Quarterly*, **19**(1), 21–39.

Oden, D. L., Thompson, R. K., & Premack, D. (1990). Infant chimpanzees spontaneously perceive both concrete and abstract same/different relations. *Child Development*, **61**(3), 621–631.

Ohala, J. J. (1993). Sound change as nature's speech perception experiment. *Speech Communication*, **13**, 155–161.

O'Regan, J. K. & Noe, A. (2001). A sensorimotor account of vision and visual consciousness. *Behavioral and Brain Sciences*, **24**, 939–1031.

O'Reilly, R. C. (2006). Biologically based computational models of high-level cognition. *Science*, **314**(5796), 91–94.

Pereira, A., Smith, L. B., & Yu, C. (2008) Social coordination in toddler's word learning: Interacting systems of perception and action. *Connection Science*, **23**, 73–89.

Pfeifer, R. & Scheier, C. (1999). *Understanding Intelligence* Cambridge, MA: MIT Press.

Piaget, J. (1952). *The Origins of Intelligence in Children* Oxford: International Universities Press.

Port, R. & Van Gelder, T. (1995) *Mind as Motion* Cambridge, MA: MIT Press.

Premack, D. (1976). *Intelligence in Ape and Man* Oxford: Lawrence Erlbaum.

Premack, D. (2004). Is language the key to human intelligence? *Science*, **303**(5656), 318–320.

Pulvermüller, F. (1999). Words in the brain's language. *Behavioral and Brain Sciences*, **22**(2), 253–336.

Pulvermüller, F., Hauk, O., Nikulin, V. V., & llmoniemi, R. J. (2005). Functional links between motor and language systems. *European Journal of Neuroscience*, **21**(3), 793–797.

Rakison, D. H. & Butterworth, G. E. (1998). Infants' attention to object structure in early categorization. *Developmental Psychology*, **34**(6), 1310–1325.

Redington, M., Chater, N., & Finch, S. (1998). Distributional information: A powerful cue for acquiring syntactic categories. *Cognitive Science: A Multidisciplinary Journal*, **22**(4), 425–469.

Reeke, G. & Edelman, G. (1984). Selective networks and recognition automata. *Annals of the New York Academy of Sciences*, **426**, 181–201.

Rogers, T., Patterson, K., & Graham, K. (2007). Colour knowledge in semantic dementia: It is not all black and white. *Neuropsychologica*, **45**, 3285–3298.

Rogoff, B. (2003). *The Cultural Nature of Human Development* New York: Oxford University Press.

Rougier, N. P., Noelle, D. C., Braver, T. S., Cohen, J. D., & O'Reilly, R. C. (2005). Prefrontal cortex and flexible cognitive control: Rules without symbols. *Proceedings of the National Academy of Sciences of the United States of America*, **102**(20), 7338–7343.

Rovee-Collier, C. & Hayne, H. (1987). Reactivation of infant memory: Implications for cognitive development. In H. Reese (Ed.), *Advances in Child Development and Behavior*, Vol. 20, pp. 185–238, San Diego, CA: Academic Press, Inc.

Rozin, P. (1976). The evolution of intelligence and access to the cognitive unconscious. In J. M. Sprague & A. N. Epstein (Eds.), *Progress in Psychobiology and Physiological Psychology*, pp. 245–277, New York: Academic Press.

Samuelson, L. (2002). Statistical regularities in vocabulary guide language acquisition in connectionist models and 15–20-month olds. *Developmental Psychology*, **38**, 1011–1037.

Samuelson, L. K. & Smith, L. B. (1999). Early noun vocabularies: Do ontology, category structure and syntax correspond? *Cognition*, 73(1), 1–33.

Samuelson, L. & Smith, L. B. (2000). Grounding development in cognitive process. *Child Development*, 71, 98–106.

Seife, C. (2000). *Zero: The Biography of a Dangerous Idea* New York: Penguin.

Sheya, A. (2005, April). The origins of classification: Proximity, perseveration, and similarity. *Presented at the Biennial Meeting of the Society for Research on Child Development*, Atlanta, GA.

Sheya, A. & Smith, L. B. (in press). Changing priority maps in 12- to 18-month olds: An emerging role for object properties. *Psychonomic Bulletin & Review*.

Smith, L. B. (1993). The concept of same. *Advances in Child Development and Behavior*, 24, 216–253.

Smith, L. B. (2000a). How to learn words: An associative crane. In R. Golinkoff & K. Hirsh-Pasek (Eds.), *Breaking the Word Learning Barrier*, pp. 51–80, Oxford: Oxford University Press.

Smith, L. B. (2000b). Avoiding association when its behaviorism you really hate. In R. Golinkoff & K. Hirsh-Pasek (Eds.), *Breaking the Word Learning Barrier*, pp. 169–174, Oxford: Oxford University Press.

Smith, L. B. & Breazeal, C. (2007) The dynamic lift of developmental process. *Developmental Science*, 10, 61–68.

Smith, L. B. & Gasser, M. (2005). The development of embodied cognition: Six lessons from babies. *Artificial Life*, 11, 13–30.

Smith, L. B. & Katz, D. B. (1996) Activity-dependent processes in perceptual and cognitive development. In R Gelman & T. Au (Eds.), *Handbook of Perception and Cognition*, Vol. 13, pp. 413–445, San Francisco, CA: Academic Press.

Smith, L.B., Gasser, M., & Sandhofer, C. (1997). Learning to talk about the properties of objects: A network model of the development of dimensions. *The Psychology of Learning and Motivation*, 36, 220–256.

Smith, L. B., Thelen, E., Titzer, R., & McLin, D. (1999). Knowing in the context of acting: The task dynamics of the A-not-B error. *Psychological Review*, 106(2), 235–260.

Smith, L. B., Colunga, E., & Yoshida, H. (2002a). Making an ontology: Cross-linguistic evidence. In L.M. Oakes & D. H. Rakison (Eds), *Early Category and Concept Development: Making Sense of the Blooming Buzzing Confusion*, pp. 275–302, New York, NY: Cambridge University Press.

Smith, L. B., Jones, S. S., Landau, B., Gershkoff-Stowe, L., & Samuelson, S. (2002) Early noun learning provides on-the-job training for attention. *Psychological Science*, 13, 13–19.

Son, J. Y., Smith, L. B., & Goldstone, R. L. (2008). Simplicity and generalization: Short-cutting abstraction in children's object categorizations. *Cognition*, 108, 626–638.

Spencer, J. P. & Schutte, A. R. (2004). Unifying representations and responses: Perseverative biases arise from a single behavioral system. *Psychological Science*, 15, 187–193.

Spivey, M. (2006). *The Continuity of Mind* New York: Oxford University Press.

Sporns, O. (2002). Networks analysis, complexity, and brain function. *Complexity*, 8, 56–60.

Steyvers, M. & Tenenbaum, J. B. (2005). The large-scale structure of semantic networks: Statistical analyses and a model of semantic growth. *Cognitive Science*, 29(1), 41–78.

Stiles, J. (2008). *The Fundamentals of Brain Development* Cambridge, MA: Harvard University Press.

Striano, T. & Reid, V. M. (2006). Social cognition in the first year. *Trends in Cognitve Sciences*, **10**(10), 471–476.

Sugarman, S. (1983). *Children's Early Thought: Developments in Classification* New York: Cambridge University Press.

Thelen, E. & Smith. L. B. (1994). *A Dynamic Systems Approach to the Development of Cognition and Action* Cambridge, MA: MIT Press.

Thelen, E., Corbetta, D., Kamm, K., Spencer, J., Schneider, K., & Zernicke, R.F. (1993). The transition to reaching: Matching intention and intrinsic dynamics. *Child Development*, **64**, 1058–1098.

Titzer, R. C. (1997). Infants' understanding of transparency: A reinterpretation of studies using the object retrieval task and visual cliff. *Dissertation Abstracts International*, **58**, 1570–1586.

Tomasello, M. (1999). *The Cultural Origins of Human Cognition* Cambridge, MA: Harvard University Press.

Tomasello, M., Kruger, A., & Ratner, H. (1993). Cultural learning. *Behavioral and Brain Sciences*, **16**, 495–552.

Tononi, G. (2004). An information integration theory of consciousness. *BioMed Central Neuroscience*, **5**, 42.

Treiman, R. & Kessler, B. (2007). Learning to read. In M. G. Gaskell (Ed.), *Oxford Handbook of Psycholinguistics*, pp. 657–666, Oxford: Oxford University Press.

Vygotsky, L. (1978). *Mind in Society* Cambridge, MA: Harvard University Press.

Walk, R. D. & Gibson, E. J. (1961). A comparative and analytical study of visual depth perception. *Psychological Monographs*, **75**(15), 1–44.

Wertsch, J. V. (1985). *Culture, Communication and Cognition: Vygotskian Perspectives* NewYork: Cambridge University Press.

Wilson, M. (2002). Six Views of embodied cognition. *Psychonomic Bulletin & Review*, **9**(4), 625–636.

Yoshida, H. & Smith, L. B. (2005). Linguistic cues enhance the learning of perceptual cues. *Psychological Science*, **16**(2), 90–95.

Yoshida, H. & Smith, L. B. (2003). Shifting ontological boundaries: How Japanese- and English-speaking children generalize names for animals and artifacts. *Developmental Science*, **6**, 1–34.

Yu, C., Ballard, D.H., & Aslin, R.N. (2005). The role of embodied intention in early lexical acquisition. *Cognitive Science*, **29**(6), 961–1005.

Zwaan, R. A. (2004). The immersed experiencer: Toward an embodied theory of language comprehension. In B. H. Ross (Ed.), *The Psychology of Learning and Motivation: Advances in Research and Theory*, Vol. **44**, pp. 35–62, New York: Elsevier Science.

Chapter 17

The evolution of concepts: A timely look

Michael C. Corballis and Thomas Suddendorf

Editors' Preview

Chapter 17, 'The evolution of concepts: A timely look', provides a comparative/evolutionary view of what aspects of concepts are uniquely human. Referencing the work in Chapters 8 to 11 that reported on the conceptual abilities of pigeons, nonprimate mammals, monkeys, and chimps, respectively, Chapter 17 argues that the ability to form concepts is not uniquely human. Chapter 17 also cites evidence from (1) Rico, the dog who can select an unfamiliar object target from among familiar object distractors when provided with an unfamiliar label, and (2) Kanzi, the chimp who can use symbols on a keyboard to refer to objects and actions, to provide further support for the conclusion that concept formation abilities are not uniquely human.

What may be unique about human concepts, according to Chapter 17, stems from the structure of memory and a distinction that was first introduced in Chapter 5, where an explicit, declarative memory, the contents of which can be expressed in words (e.g. 'last night's dinner was roast chicken', 'Harrisburg is the capital of Pennsylvania'), was differentiated from an implicit, nondeclarative memory that is crucial for learning motor skills (e.g. tying one's shoes). The declarative memory can be further divided into a general semantic memory for remembering common facts about the world that transcend particular learning contexts (e.g. dogs have fur), and a more personal episodic memory that refers to specific occurrences in one's life (e.g. the events of last summer's beach vacation). Evidence that semantic and episodic memories can be dissociated comes from the findings that (1) individuals with semantic dementia have deficits in semantic memory, but have preserved episodic memory, and (2) individuals with amnesia do not remember past events, although they can retain semantic knowledge.

Chapter 17 makes the particular case that what is unique about human concepts is that humans have an episodic memory that allows not only for recollection of past events, but also planning for future events. In this sense, episodic memory allows humans to engage in mental time travel. Evidence supporting the notion that a common mechanism enables us to remember the past and anticipate the future comes from (1) the data of amnesiacs who are unable to both recall events that took place yesterday and predict what events will take place tomorrow, and (2) neuroimaging studies indicating that the same brain circuitry becomes activated when remembering past events and imagining future ones.

It is argued that mental time travel emerged evolutionarily during the Pleistocene period when *Homo sapiens* formed a cognitive niche to outsmart predatory animals, given the lack of strength and speed needed to fight off or escape from tigers and hyenas. Developmentally, there is evidence for mental time travel in children between 3 and 4 years of age, but not in preverbal infants. Comparatively, some species of birds display episodic-like memory for when and where they have stored food, and other species of birds demonstrate support for episodic-like memory by constructing food-gathering tools that can be used in the future. The memory of the animals is said to be episodic-like, rather than episodic, because the behaviours mediated by such a memory structure are not believed to be domain general and are not accompanied by phenomenal awareness, as is the case in humans.

Fodor (1968, 1975) has argued that virtually all of the concepts underlying words are innate. Pinker (2007, p. 90) refers to this as the theory that 'we are born with some 50,000 concepts', based on the number of words in the typical English speaker's vocabulary. The notion that our inventory of concepts is innate has proven highly controversial; Renaissance man was unlikely to have had the concept of *helicopter*, with the exception perhaps of Leonardo da Vinci, who designed such a contraption. Pinker (2007) argues instead that our concepts of reality are built from a smaller set of basic concepts of space, time, causality, and substance. But whether or not our concepts are innate, there can be no question that humans have at least the potential to develop vocabularies, and therefore concepts, of the order of tens of thousands. It is probably also a safe bet that no nonhuman species has a vocabulary even remotely approaching that number.

A large vocabulary is only part of the uniquely human capacity for language, or of conceptual thought. We can extend the number of messages we can convey by combining words into phrases and sentences, using grammatical rules. These rules are recursive, so that the potential number of messages we can convey is without limit. Just as Fodor proposed that our concepts are innate, so it has been argued that grammar depends on the innate and uniquely human endowment of *universal grammar* (Chomsky 1975).

However, studies of communities such as the Pirahã of Brazil suggest vocabularies much smaller than 50 000 and have called the notion of universal grammar into question (Everett, 2005; Tomasello, 2003a). Tomasello (2003b) suggests, in fact, that linguistic theories have been overly influenced by literacy and the 'unnaturalness' of written language, and comparative studies of languages, including those spoken by nonliterate populations, suggest that there are few if any grammatical constructions that are universally present in all languages. Rather, grammatical constructions may depend on what Locke and Bogin (2006), after Marler (1991), refer to as an 'instinct for inventiveness' that goes beyond language per se.

Although there are growing doubts as to whether human language, and its underlying concepts, depend on innate dispositions specific to language, there can be little doubt that humans are indeed distinct from other living creatures for sheer communicative and mental productivity. The open-ended nature of human language may be the result, not of mechanisms peculiar to language itself, but rather of more general prop- erties of the human mind. Humans may indeed be blessed with the capacity to form tens of thousands of concepts, and indeed to construct unlimited streams of thought in novel ways. Language may be primarily the messenger, allowing us to convey our thoughts and concepts to others, and to import those of others.

Although critical to language, the conceptual system is part of the broader memory system. In this chapter, we suggest that the special nature of human concepts depends on the way in which memory itself has evolved in our species. In particular, the evolution of memory has led to a unique understanding of time, and this in turn may have shaped the nature of language itself (Corballis & Suddendorf, 2007).

Memory systems

Memory is not a unitary system. First, and most fundamentally, a distinction is drawn between *declarative* and *nondeclarative* memory (sometimes known as implicit and explicit memory, respectively) (e.g. Squire, 2004). Nondeclarative memory refers to the stimulus-driven, unconscious memory systems that drive phenomena such as procedural skills and habits, priming, perceptual learning, and conditioning. Declarative memory is so named because we can report, or declare, these memories. Declarative memory is more flexible than nondeclarative memory in at least two ways. First, it provides an explicit detailed model of the world in which we live. We know precisely where we live, the neighbourhoods, the geographical areas in which we work, play, and travel. We have a huge array of facts at our disposal that enable us to make precise plans for the future, and meet different obligations and contingencies. Second, declarative memories can be voluntarily triggered top–down from the frontal lobes, rather than bottom–up through perception (Miyashita, 2004). They can therefore be brought into consciousness 'off-line' for flexible planning and decision making. We can contrast and compare different pieces of knowledge, and choose knowledge rele- vant to a particular activity, such as planning a career, or a vacation, or a dinner party.

Declarative memory can itself be divided into two categories: *Semantic* memory, which is memory for more or less enduring facts about the world, and *episodic* mem- ory, which is memory for specific events (Tulving, 1972). Roughly, semantic memory can be likened to a combined dictionary and encyclopaedia, and provides our basic concepts about the world, while episodic memory can be likened to a personal diary, and provides us with our sense of a personal past. Of course, part of our understanding of our personal past depends on semantic memory as well as on episodic memory, to make up what has been called *autobiographical* memory. The distinction between semantic and episodic memory has also been characterized as that between *knowing* and *remembering*, respectively (Tulving, 1985). For example, most of us know when we were born but do not remember the event, although we may possibly remember events of the first day at school. Episodic memory is perhaps the ultimate in flexibility, since it records the particularities of one's life, and enables projection of personal experience into the future (Suddendorf & Corballis, 2007).

Semantic and episodic memory are complementary, in that semantic memory codes for generalities remain more or less constant over time, whereas episodic memory codes for events occur at specific points in time. Nevertheless, there must be some interdependence between the two. Episodic memory must depend on the prior development of concepts in semantic memory and we argue that the recording of events in time would have created pressure to add to the number of concepts stored in semantic memory. Tulving (2001) also argues that the storage of episodic memories depends on semantic memories that are already in place, but are then related to the self in subjectively sensed time. This allows the actual experience of the event to be processed separately from the semantic system. In this view, episodic memories could not be stored in the absence of semantic memory, which is perhaps why our childhood episodic memories do not begin until the semantic system is firmly established, at around age 3–4 (e.g. Levine, 2004). Nevertheless, there is some evidence that episodic and semantic memories are more broadly dissociated. People with semantic dementia, a degenerative neurological disorder that afflicts some people in late adulthood, show severe decline in semantic memory, but their episodic memories remain remarkably and surprisingly intact (Hodges & Graham, 2001).

In most respects, though, it is episodic memory that is more fragile and incomplete. In cases of amnesia, it is typically episodic memories rather than semantic memories that are lost. In one dramatic case, for example, a patient with extensive damage to the frontal and temporal lobes was unable to recall any specific episode from his life, yet retained semantic knowledge (Tulving et al., 1988). Even without brain injury, people probably remember only a tiny fraction of actual past episodes (Loftus & Loftus, 1980), and events are often remembered inaccurately, even to the point that people will claim with some certainty to have remembered events that did not in fact happen (Loftus & Ketcham, 1994; Roediger & McDermott, 1995).

Given the unreliability of episodic memory, often a bane to courts of law, it seems clear that it did not evolve primarily to serve as a record of the past. Schacter (1996) suggests rather that its function is to build up a personal narrative, which may provide the basis for the concept of self, as well as a basis to ground future behavioural choices. The adaptive advantage of episodic memory may lie in what it offers for the future, rather than in how accurately it records the past (Schacter et al., 2007; Suddendorf & Busby, 2005). If semantic memory provides knowledge about relatively constant aspects of one's environment, episodic memory picks out singular events that can augment one's decisions about how to behave in similar circumstances in the future. Individual episodes provide a kind of vocabulary upon which to construct a self-narrative, and plan future episodes. By combining and recombining elements from past events as well as semantic knowledge one can imagine novel future scenarios, weigh their consequences, and act now to secure a future advantage. To maintain a complete record of the past, though, may be counterproductive, since this would occupy huge storage space, and involve needless repetition. As Anderson and Schooler (1991) note, forgetting itself can be adaptive, because it frees resources for future use and allows memory retrieval to continue quickly and efficiently.

Mental time travel

However incomplete, episodic memories are located in time, and so incorporate the time dimension into our mental lives. Episodic memory, then, can be regarded as part of a more general capacity for *mental time travel*, allowing us not only to mentally relive events in the past, but also to imagine the future in episodic detail (Suddendorf & Corballis, 1997, 2007). The capacity to envisage future episodes appears to emerge in children at around the same time as episodic memory itself, between the ages of 3 and 4 years (e.g. Atance & O'Neill, 2005; Busby & Suddendorf, 2005). Patients with amnesia are equally unable to answer simple questions about yesterday's events as to say what might happen tomorrow (Klein et al., 2002; Tulving, 1985). In a recent study, Hassabis et al. (2007) reported that patients with amnesia due to hippocampal damage were unable to use verbal cues to generate new imagined experiences. Amnesia for specific events, then, is at least in part a loss of the awareness of self in time.

The importance of mental time travel as a specific adaptation, enhancing the survival of the species, was anticipated by the British psychologist, Kenneth Craik (1943):

> If the organism carries a "small scale model" of external reality and of its own possible actions within its head, it is able to try out various alternatives, conclude which are the best of them, react to future situations before they arise, utilize the knowledge of past events in dealing with the present and future, and in every way to react in a much fuller, safer and more competent manner to the emergencies which face it (p. 61).

This is not to say, though, that this potential for foresight always manifests in prudent action. Unlike some innate future-directed adaptations in other animals (e.g. hoarding in squirrels), this human ability depends squarely on each individual attending to and computing a range of relevant information appropriately. Although there are common errors and biases in our recollections of the past and anticipations of the future (e.g. Gilbert, 2006), we routinely get it sufficiently right to benefit from our foresight. In fact, mental time travel and subsequent future-directed action is such an omnipresent human activity that it was long overlooked in academic psychology.

Another person to anticipate the current interest in foresight was the Swedish physiologist David Ingvar, a pioneer in the use of regional cerebral blood flow to measure brain activity, who concluded that activation in the prefrontal cortex was especially important in providing the internal connection between past and future (Ingvar, 1979). In a doubly premonitory passage, he wrote:

> On the basis of previous experiences, represented in memories, the brain—one's mind—is automatically busy with extrapolation of future events and, as it appears, constructing alternative hypothetical behavior patterns in order to be ready for what may happen (p. 21)

Using more refined techniques based on functional magnetic resonance imaging (fMRI), Addis et al. (2007) have shown that parts of the medial temporal lobe, as well as the prefrontal cortex, are activated when people are prompted to remember past events or to imagine future ones. They refer to the activated areas as a core network. But of course, people can usually distinguish past events from imagined future ones, and some studies have shown greater activation in several brain areas related to future than to past events (Okuda et al., 2003; Szpunar et al. 2007). Curiously, no brain area showed greater activation to past than to future events, perhaps indicating that imagining the future requires more intensive imaginative construction (Addis et al., 2007). This, perhaps, is akin to the finding that imagining is associated with greater activation in the visual cortex than perceiving (Kosslyn et al., 1993). Reliving the past may also involve active construction, sometimes to the detriment of veracity, and we suspect that people may occasionally confuse imagined future events with those that actually happened. The brain itself seems to hardly register the difference.

Uniquely human?

It has been proposed that episodic memory (Tulving, 1985), and more generally, mental time travel (Suddendorf & Corballis 1997, 2007), are uniquely human. This has posed a challenge to animal researchers to show that these capacities exist in nonhuman species. Since the testing of episodic memory and mental time travel in humans typically involves language, it has proven difficult to design comparable experiments to test nonlinguistic species. Nevertheless, there have been some concerted attempts to specify the defining properties of episodic memory, and then to test whether these properties hold in a nonhuman animal.

To date, the most industrious attempts have come from researchers working with birds that cache items of food, and are later able to recover the food from the stored locations. In particular, scrub jays can select food locations not only according to the type of food that is stored there, but also according to when it was stored. For example, they will recover recently cached worms in preference to nuts, since fresh worms are more palatable, but if the worms have been cached for too long they will retrieve nuts, because the worms will have decayed and become unpalatable (Clayton et al., 2003). (This cannot be attributed to a simple recency effect, since the worms and nuts were cached at the same time.) The mechanism underlying this behaviour has been dubbed 'what, where, when' (www)-memory (Suddendorf & Busby, 2003), because scrub jays apparently remember *what* has been cached, *where* it was cached, and *when* it was cached. In these respects, it seems to conform to the original criteria of episodic memory (Tulving, 1972).

Furthermore, if observed caching food, scrub jays will later re-cache it, presumably to avoid the observer stealing the food. They will only do this, however, if they have themselves stolen food in the past; that is, it takes a thief to know a thief (Emery & Clayton, 2004). The authors conclude from this and similar studies that scrub jays can not only remember past events, but can also anticipate the future by taking steps to ensure appropriate future food supply (Clayton et al., 2003; Correia et al., 2007).

This work is perhaps the most convincing evidence to date for something resembling mental time travel in a nonhuman species, but is it enough? Clark's nutcrackers seem to be among the most prolific, storing seeds in thousands of locations and recovering them with high (but not perfect) accuracy (e.g. Kamil & Balda, 1985). The question then is whether their ability to recover the cached food demonstrates knowing or remembering, in Tulving's (1985) distinction; in other words, do the birds actually remember the episode in which they cached the food, or do they simply have (semantic) knowledge of where it is? In one respect, at least, the data may not meet Tulving's (1985) more recent definition of episodic memory, which includes the phenomenological component. That is, recovery of an episodic memory involves *re-experiencing* the original episode. For this reason, Clayton and Dickinson (1998) have cautiously referred to www-memory in animals as 'episodic-like memory'. At the present time, at least, there seems no way to test subjectivity in nonhuman species, but there are other more tangible ways in which tests with scrub jays and other animals may fail to convincingly demonstrate episodic memory.

The ability of the scrub jays to retrieve nuts or worms depending on the time at which they were cached need not actually show that the birds remember when they cached the food. A simple internal clock mechanism might be sufficient to specify how long a memory has been established, creating a kind of 'use-by date' for retrieval, without any sense that the birds have a record of the act of caching itself. A recent study also suggests that rats can learn to retrieve food in a radial maze on the basis of *how long ago* it was stored, but not on *when* it was stored, suggesting that 'episodic-like memory in rats is qualitatively different from episodic memory in humans' (Roberts et al., 2008, p. 113). It is not yet established whether the scrub jays rely on when, or on how long ago. Moreover, caching in these birds is highly domain-specific, no doubt governed to a large extent by instinctive mechanisms, whereas declarative memory in humans is domain-general.

We think it unlikely that caching birds have anything resembling autobiographical memory in humans (see Suddendorf & Corballis, 2007, 2008, for further discussion). In fact, if one considers the birds' action in the broader context of their laboratory existence, it quickly becomes apparent that their foresight is nothing like that of a human. The trays the jays cache in are presented and removed by humans and the birds are always being fed. It is humans, not other birds, who steal their caches. In this context the caching of food and 'pilfering-avoidance' strategies, such as caching food out of sight of another jay in an adjacent cage, seem to somewhat lack in both foresight and insight.

Tool manufacture is sometimes taken as evidence for a sense of the future, especially when it is clear that a tool is manufactured on one occasion for later use. Again, birds seem to provide some of the most compelling evidence. For example, New Caledonian crows construct tools from pandanus leaves for the express purpose of extracting grubs from holes, and the design characteristics of these tools suggest a clear temporal distinction between construction and use (Hunt, 2000). There is little evidence that nonhuman primates make tools with any sense of future planning. Chimpanzees and other great apes may improvise objects for use as tools, such as using stones to crack open nuts, and they can be taught to use tools in specific ways, and even show culturally determined variation on how they use these tools (Whiten et al., 2005), but there is little evidence that they construct tools for some given future purpose, although they may be capable of a considerable degree of inventiveness (Whiten & Suddendorf, 2007). Oakley (1961) wrote of Sultan, the most resourceful of the chimpanzees observed by Köhler (1925), that he 'was capable of improvising tools in certain situations. Tool making occurred only in the presence of a visible reward, never without it. In the chimpanzee the mental range seems to be limited to present situations, with little conception of past or future' (p. 187). Perhaps this was too bleak a portrait, since a recent study by Mulcahy and Call (2006) suggests that one orangutan and one bonobo, at least, saved a tool for use 14 h later, which might suggest mental time travel, although it is not entirely clear that even here the animals were not responding simply on the basis of associations (Suddendorf, 2006). Further study is required to determine if our closest relatives have greater capacities for foresight than has been apparent so far.

The evidence on mental time travel in nonhuman species remains scant, but might be taken to indicate some domain-specific, rudimentary ability to refer to specific past experiences or to imagine future ones. Of course, if the same birds can be shown to provide evidence for mental time travel in both food caching and tool use, that would be a step towards domain generality, but still a long way from the broad range of contexts in which humans recover the past or imagine the future. Convergent evolution in more distantly related species may have produced various mechanisms designed to enhance future survival chances through cognitive capacities akin to mental time travel. Various curious future-directed capacities have been documented (e.g. natal homing of turtles), but most of them are largely based on domain-specific, innate mechanisms. The evidence for flexible foresight and episodic memory pales beside the undoubted ability of humans to re-experience their past lives or to imagine the future in detail (albeit incompletely). The manufacture of tools by humans is clearly governed by design characteristics that are oriented towards future use, and there is a clear temporal separation between manufacture and use. We have even manufactured tools that record time itself, or that are programmed to operate at given points in time – such as ovens that can be programmed in the morning to have your meal ready for you in the evening when you come home. Indeed, our human lives seem dominated by time, not in the instinctive way that migrating or hoarding animals respond to seasonal changes, but rather in the day-to-day sense of specific things that need to be done or plans that need to be made.

It remains something of an open question whether mental time travel in humans is different in degree or in kind from that in other species. Whichever is the case, we suspect that a major difference lies, not so much in the facts of remembering past events or imagining future ones, as in the flexible and combinatorial nature of our mental travels.

Time and the growth of concepts

The incorporation of time into our mental lives vastly increases the pressure to form concepts and representations. An animal living in the present can refer to objects or events as physical entities, and communication can be accomplished by drawing attention to those entities in the here and now. Of course, animals will sometimes use signals that draw attention to events that their conspecifics may not be able to see, such as when chimpanzees use pant hoot calls to signal the discovery of food (Goodall, 1986), or vervet monkeys use different signals that warn of different predators (Cheney & Seyfarth, 1990). The bonobo, Kanzi, is able to use visual symbols on a keyboard to refer to objects and actions; these symbols are again abstract in the sense that they were deliberately chosen by the human keepers so as not to resemble what they stand for (Savage-Rumbaugh et al., 1998). That is, one could have a mental representation for a particular object (a specific cat) experienced in the past so that it could be used in the present, but it need not be applicable to the class of objects (cats) in general.

In one especially revealing study, a border collie called Rico was able to respond accurately to spoken requests to fetch different objects from another room, and then to either place the designated object in a box or bring it to a particular person. If given an unfamiliar name of an object to fetch, he chose the object among the available selection that was novel. Four weeks later, he demonstrated that he still knew the name of this object, indicating what has been termed 'learning by exclusion' (Kaminsky et al., 2004). This ability to apply a label on a single trial is known as 'fast mapping', and has hitherto been thought to be restricted to humans. Furthermore, when asked to fetch items from one of two rooms, Rico typically returned directly to where the object was to be found, demonstrating knowledge of what was where (Kaminski et al., 2008). These findings show a clear ability to form concepts – although perhaps not necessarily at a broader taxonomic level – and understand verbal labels referring to them.

Nevertheless, the exploits of Kanzi and Rico can be explained in terms other than mental time travel. Rico's behaviour, for example, depends on semantic knowledge (learned associations) and short-term working memory, sufficient to bridge the time distance between receiving and carrying out the instruction. The human capacity to bring to mind events from the relatively distant past, or imagine events beyond the framework of working memory, means that the whole conceptual landscape is vastly increased. We need representations of people, places, objects, actions, covering experiences in space and time. Mental time travel also vastly extends the spatial canvas of our mental lives, since travelling through time generally implies travelling through space. We can remember events in different houses, streets, cafés, cities, countries – all at different times.

Memories are also structured. Semantic memory is hierarchically structured; we know, for example, that Paris is a city, the city of Paris is in France, France is in Europe, and so forth. Episodic memory, in contrast, is structured in combinatorial fashion. The uniqueness of an episode, like the uniqueness of a sentence, depends more on the specific combination of the familiar than on the insertion of the unfamiliar. We remember who did what to whom, where, when, and why, and what came of it. The combinatorial structure of episodic memory, we suggest, underlies the combinatorial structure of human language. This is not to say that we use language exclusively for recounting episodes; this article, for example, is an attempt to recount and construct semantic information, with no reference to actual episodes. Our suggestion is that language was shaped by the structure of episodes, and later exapted for more general communicative purposes.

Every episode is a potential sentence, or combinations of sentences. According to the eighteenth-century English philologist John Horne Tooke (1857), the earliest 'language' consisted only of nouns and verbs ('necessary words'), corresponding at the most fundamental level to objects and actions, the basic constituents of 'events'. Structural complexity would then be built from the combinations of objects and actions, experienced as events, and represented in language as nouns and verbs. Within language, at least, this complexity has been attributed to a process of 'grammaticalization' (Hopper & Traugott, 2003), driven by environmental pressure, although subject to biological constraints. However, Christiansen and Dale (2004) have suggested the structure of the brain did not adapt to accommodate language, as generally supposed, but rather that language adapted to biological constraints, and connectionist systems are increasingly successful in simulating the acquisition of language (e.g. Chang et al., 2006, Christiansen & Dale, 2004), without the necessity to postulate any preexisting, innately determined universal grammar, such as proposed by Chomsky (1975). The case against universal grammar is further developed by Christiansen and Chater (2008).

If this is so, then, the structure of language may depend partly on the structure of knowledge and episodic memory, and adaptations specific to language itself may depend, not on universal grammar, but rather on the medium of expression. Speech, for example, requires that events structured in four-dimensional space–time be transformed into a temporal sequence, a process known as 'linearization'. This may dictate conventions such as the ordering of subject, verb, and object, which are socially derived and maintained. Signed languages are differently and perhaps less constrained, since they allow expression in space–time, and expression can have more of a pantomime quality – although signed languages are nonetheless also highly conventionalized, largely in the interests of efficiency and practicality.

The incorporation of time into the mental apparatus has also added substantially to the number of concepts we possess. We understand concepts like *yesterday, last week*, and *9/11* to refer to the past, and *tomorrow, next year*, and *when the cows come home*, to refer to the future. But does this mean that humans are unique only in the sense of having more concepts than nonhuman animals? Is there anything unique about the nature and structure of these concepts? Actions and states are endowed with tense to indicate different points in time, as well as distinctions between conditional and unconditional, continuous and noncontinuous, and so on. Thus the words *eat, ate, eating*, and *eaten*, along with auxiliaries (e.g. *will eat, might have been eating*), refer to different concepts having to do with the intake of food. These examples also show that the expression of concepts may involve syntactic as well as morphological constructions. We have many different concepts to convey units of time, ranging from nanoseconds to aeons, as well as ways of locating points in time. Without the concept of time, it is doubtful whether we would have such concepts as past, present, future, birth, death, history, the Big Bang, heaven, or hell – perhaps, even global warming.

There is no evidence, to our knowledge, that nonhuman animals possess any of these concepts.

Different languages have different ways of representing time. Time is typically referred to in spatial terms, and English speakers talk about time as if it were horizontal, with the future stretched out in front and the past behind (*He looked to the future*, or *She looked back over her past life*).The Mandarin Chinese, though, tend to think of time as vertical, with earlier events seen as *up* and later events as *down*. Boroditsky (2001) reported evidence from priming experiments that these differences are language dependent, as suggested by the Whorfian hypothesis. Her findings, though, were not replicated by Chen (2007), who concluded that the Chinese speakers do not think about time differently from English speakers. A more striking difference between the two languages is that Chinese has no tenses, and the time of an event can be indicated by adverbs, such as *tomorrow*, and what are called aspectual markers, as in a sentence that might be roughly rendered as *He break his leg before* (Lin, 2005). This again might be taken as evidence against universal grammar, and more in keeping with the idea that different cultures may have simply invented different ways of weaving time into their language.

A more extreme example comes from the Pirahã, the Brazilian tribe referred to earlier, which has only a very restricted way of talking about relative time. This takes the form of two tense-like morphemes which indicate simply whether an event is in the present or not. Pirahã also includes a few words serving as temporal markers, such as *night*, *day*, *full moon*, and so on. The Pirahã are said to live largely in the present, with no creation myths, no art or drawing, no individual or collective memory for more than two generations past (Everett, 2005).

Pirahã language is highly simplified, at least in terms of syntax and semantics, in other ways. For example, it has no system for counting, no terms for colours, and no recursion, often considered the distinctive characteristic of human language (Hauser et al., 2002). Everett suggests that even these additional features derive fundamentally from their very limited sense of time, supporting the idea that the characteristics of language derive from mental time travel. He writes:

> . . . [the] apparently disjointed facts about the Pirahã language—gaps that are very surprising from just about any grammarian's perspective—ultimately derive from a single cultural constraint in Pirahã, namely, *the restriction of communication to the immediate experience of the interlocutors* (p. 622; Everett's italics).

Everett argues against the Whorfian view that Pirahã culture is dependent on language, suggesting instead that the language has adapted to the culture.

Language is the capacity most widely regarded as uniquely human (e.g. Chomsky 1975; Descartes, 1647/1985; Hauser et al., 2002; Pinker, 1994), and is also often held to play a special role in uniquely structuring human concepts (see Chapter 6, this book). Though some suggest that all that is unique about human cognition can be traced to language (e.g. Macphail, 1996), we have argued that the evolution of mental content must have preceded the evolution of means to communicate such content, or perhaps co-evolved with it (Suddendorf & Corballis, 1997, 2007). In particular, language shares a number of critical properties with mental time travel, and may derive to a significant extent from the need to communicate about events that occur in other places and at other times. As suggested by the Pirahã, language itself may vary depending on the extent to which time concepts are embedded in the culture.

Evolutionary considerations

Our closest relatives among living nonhuman animals are chimpanzees and bonobos (see Chapter 11, this book), who thus far have shown little evidence for mental time travel or for true syntactic language. Perhaps they have more competence than many other species, as suggested by 'ape-language' studies and emerging work on foresight, but the gap between their abilities and those of humans seems to be enormous. The major components of the human capacity for mental time travel, language, and a vast conceptual vocabulary therefore must have evolved since the hominin line split from the line leading to modern chimpanzees and bonobos. There is conflicting evidence as to the precise date of the split, with a recent suggestion that there was an initial separation some 7 million years ago, followed by a period of hybridization, then a second split sometime after 6.3 million years ago (Patterson et al., 2006).

Although the primary characteristic distinguishing the hominins from the quadrupedal great apes was their bipedalism, the more likely clue as to the cognitive advances that characterize our species has to do with the much later increase in brain size – on a priori grounds alone, these advances must have involved selection for increased storage and processing capacity. The human brain is some three times larger relative to body size than that of the great apes (Wood & Collard, 1999). When considering the absolute mass of brain tissue over that predicted for an average mammal of the same body size, humans have about 1.1 kg, or five times that of chimpanzees, in excess (Whiten & Suddendorf, 2007). The increase in brain size was relatively slow to emerge in the hominin lineage, and did not really begin until the emergence of the genus *Homo* some 2 million years ago.

The earliest members traditionally included in the genus were *Homo habilis* and *Homo rudolfensis*, still clumsily bipedal, but with brains slightly larger than those of the earlier hominins. Their brain capacities ranged from around 500 cc to about 750 cc, which is also significantly larger than that of the chimpanzee at around 393 cc and the larger-bodied gorilla at around 465 cc (Martin, 1992). It has been suggested, though, that these species had not really attained *Homo*-like characteristics, and should be classified still as Australopithecines (Wood & Collard, 1999). *Homo ergaster* emerged around 2 million years ago, and by 1.2 million years ago boasted a brain capacity as large as 1250 cc. Migrations out of Africa began around 1.8 million years ago, and the Asian counterpart to *ergaster*, known as *Homo erectus*, showed a similar increase. Thus in a space of about 750 000 years, brain size more than doubled.

Brain size appears to have reached a peak, not with *Homo sapiens*, dating from about 170 000 years ago, but with the Neanderthals, whose fossil remains have been found primarily in Western Europe, and as far east as Uzbekistan. Analysis of Neanderthal DNA suggests that the most recent common ancestor we share with the Neanderthals dates from about 700 000 years ago, and our ancestral populations split from about 370 000 years ago (Noonan et al., 2006), so the increase in brain size may have taken different trajectories. In some individual Neanderthals, brain capacity seems to have been as high as 1800 cc, with an average of around 1450 cc. Brain size in our own species, *Homo sapiens*, is a little lower, with a present-day average of about 1350 cc (Wood & Collard, 1999).

Another feature of the genus *Homo* is the prolongation of brain development. To conform to the general primate pattern, human babies should be born at around 18 months, not 9 months (Krogman, 1972), but as any mother will know this would be impossible, given the size of the birth canal. The brain of a newborn chimpanzee is about 60% of its adult weight, that of a newborn human only about 24%. This feature probably emerged in evolution with the increase in brain size, and there is evidence that it was present in *Homo erectus* by about 1.6 million years ago (Brown et al., 1985). Our prolonged childhood means that the human brain undergoes most of its growth while exposed to external influences, and is therefore more finely tuned to its environment.

Like the chimpanzee, the early hominins seem to have undergone two phases of development, known as infancy and juvenility, before reaching adulthood at around age 12 years. Beginning with *Homo habilis*, a third stage, known as childhood, appears to have been squeezed in between infancy and juvenility, and adulthood was delayed by about a year. Childhood and juvenility were progressively lengthened in *Homo erectus*, with the age of adulthood creeping up to around 15. In *Homo sapiens*, it has been suggested, another stage, known as adolescence, was inserted between juvenility and adulthood. According to this scenario, then, humans undergo four developmental stages: infancy from birth to age 2½, childhood from 2½ to about 7, juvenility from 7 to 10, and adolescence from 10 to about 17 (Locke & Bogin, 2006). It is during the period of childhood, unique to *Homo*, that both mental time travel and syntactic language emerge.[1]

These developments in the size and growth of the sudden increase in brain size probably had to do, at least in the first instance, with climate change. Other factors that are often suggested, such as a shift to a meat diet and the emergence of cooking (e.g. Wrangham et al., 1999), may be closely related to dealing with the fundamental challenges of climate change. The epoch prior to the arrival of the genus *Homo* was known as the Pliocene, beginning about 5.3 million years ago. Towards the end of the Pliocene, the earth became colder, and the ensuing Pleistocene gave rise to a series of crippling ice ages. The Pleistocene is formally dated from 1.81 million years ago to 11 500 years ago, although it has been argued that it should be dated from as early as 2.58 million years ago (Suc et al., 1997). The harsh conditions of the Pleistocene brought about the change from forest to the more open and exposed savanna in Africa and Asia, and may have at different times cut off various hominin populations from

---

[1] Younger infants may have some sense of the direction of time, but this need have no bearing on mental time travel. For example 8-month-old infants look longer at forward videotapes of events, such as pouring and spilling liquid, or the dropping of objects, than at 'unnatural' reversed videos of the same events (Friedman, 2002). It is not until the age of around 4, though, that children understand backward events to be anomalous, or 'magic' (Friedman, 2003), but even this need not mean that they can travel mentally in time in the sense of remembering previous episodes or imagining future ones.

one another. Our own species, *Homo sapiens*, arose from hominins who had remained in Africa, where cold episodes created extreme dryness, perhaps forcing our forebears to be more resourceful and cooperative to survive.

An especially dangerous feature of the savanna was the presence of large carnivorous animals, whose numbers peaked in the early Pleistocene. They included at least 12 species of saber-tooth cats and nine species of hyena (Foley, 1987). Our puny forebears had previously been able to seek cover from these dangerous predators in more forested areas, and perhaps by retreating into water, but such means of escape were relatively sparse on the savanna. Not only did the hominins have to avoid being hunted down by these professional killers, with their sharp teeth and claws, and immense speed and strength, but they also had to compete with them for food resources. Given their arboreal heritage, the hominins could not have competed physically with the aggressive cats of the savanna, nor escaped with the speed and agility of the antelope. Their survival must have depended in part on what might be termed the third way, which was to establish and occupy a so-called 'cognitive niche' (Tooby & DeVore, 1987). It was a question of survival of the smartest.

This third way involved enhanced memory, with the ability to record specific incidents, and to use this information to plan future activity that was at once safe and productive in terms of foraging for food. In short, episodic memory evolved to complement semantic memory to improve future-directed capacities. For example, hominins who based on past experience had the foresight to carry rocks when wandering through dangerous terrain, may have been able to fend off cats by hurling that ammunition in their defence. Cooperation would have been especially critical, not only because of safety in numbers, but also because individuals could be assigned to different roles directed to a common purpose. This culminated in the vast range of professions and occupations we see in the modern world. A structure of specialization would be superimposed on the hierarchical social structure typical of primate groups, leading to a diversity of concepts that differentiate individuals.

As our forebears gained control over the ecological challenges of the Pleistocene, they may have encountered a further threat – themselves. Paraphrasing Humphrey (1976), Alexander (1990) even suggested that 'the real challenge in the human environment throughout history that affected the evolution of the intellect was not climate, weather, food shortages, or parasites – or even predators. Rather, it was the necessity of dealing continually with our fellow humans in social circumstances that became ever more complex and unpredictable as the human line evolved' (p. 4). Future planning is probably as often concerned with overcoming human competitors as with cooperative enterprises. Paradoxically, mechanisms for group cohesion may have been enhanced by competition between groups. Our lives depend on a subtle calculus of sharing and greed – of left-wing socialism and right-wing individualism, if you like.

The emergence of *Homo* is also associated with the emergence of stone-tool industries. These have been dated from about 2.5 million years ago in Ethiopia (Semaw et al., 1997), and tentatively identified with *Homo rudolfensis*. However these early tools, known as the Oldowan industry, are relatively primitive and lacking in planned diversity. The more sophisticated Acheulian tool-making industry, with large bifacial tools and handaxes, dates from around 1.5 million years ago (Gowlett, 1992). Development actually then remained fairly static for over a million years, with an increase in diversity at around 300 000 years ago (Ambrose, 2001). A later, apparently dramatic expansion around 30 000–40 000 years ago that included objects such as projectiles, harpoons, awls, buttons, needles, and ornaments, has been described as a 'human revolution' (Mellars & Stringer, 1989), although it has also been argued that the development was continuous, if exponential, over the past 250 000–300 000 years (McBrearty & Brooks, 2000). Diversity has of course continued to accelerate, to the point that machines threaten to take over most human activity. Tool manufacture, too, may reflect challenges from our own species as well as from the physical environment; humans have proven as adept at killing each other as at killing other species.

The pressures of the Pleistocene on the cognitive niche our forebears began to occupy would have favoured brains capable of forming a large number of concepts. These would eventually have included differentiated roles played by individuals, increasingly diverse tools, conceptual understanding of different predators and prey, perhaps including plants and fruits, and various actions, states, and relations among these entities. This conceptual advance would have been semantic, but provided the vocabulary for, and was made increasingly necessary by, the prediction and planning of future events. A key advance in conceptualization across the domains just mentioned would have been the inclusion of a temporal dimension that allowed hominins to relate past and future occurrences of significant events. Understanding these links enables prediction and a new measure of planned control. Language may have co-evolved as a means of sharing episodes, thus vastly increasing each individual's episodic storehouse and planning capacity. Language adds to the storage requirement, of course, but this is presumably accomplished through association with existing concepts. Thus our conceptual knowledge of a helicopter includes, among many other attributes, its name. The telling of stories – extended episodes – is not necessarily concerned with faithful records of true events. We live in a wash of fiction, through novels, plays, movies, and soap operas. From an evolutionary perspective, what matters is not an accurate record of events in our personal lives so much as a portrayal of human activity in a realistic and revealing manner.

As exemplified by the bonobo, Kanzi, and the border collie, Rico, the formation of concepts and the capacity to label them is not unique to humans. Our uniqueness, we suggest, lies primarily in our ability to recreate specific episodes in the past, and to create potential episodes for the future. But both abilities depend in turn on vast storage capacity, both semantic and episodic. The creation of episodes applies not only to our personal futures, but is expressed in the vast outpourings of fictional stories, in the forms of literature, drama, films, and television. The sharing of episodes, whether fictional, planned, or remembered, also lead to uniquely human powers of expression, most obviously through language, but also through acting, mime, and even dance and music.

In summary, concepts are part of semantic memory, and are not confined to humans; there is ample evidence for concept formation in other primates, mammals, and even birds (e.g. Chapters 8, 9, 10, and 11 in this book). We argue, though, that the evolution of episodic memory and mental time travel created pressure to increase the conceptual vocabulary, and explains why humans possess a vastly more extensive and intricate semantic memory network than is apparent in any other species. Language co-evolved with mental time travel, and indeed shares many of its structural properties, to enable us to communicate both semantic and episodic information, and this would have created further pressure to increase the conceptual vocabulary, as well as create a lexical one. These adaptations, we suggest, were forced by conditions that prevailed during the Pleistocene, and can be tracked through the increase in brain size and more differentiated growth patterns, such as the insertion of childhood and adolescent phases, in the genus *Homo*.

References

Addis, D. R., Wong, A. T., & Schacter, D. L. (2007). Remembering the past and imagining the future: Common and distinct neural substrates during event construction. *Neuropsychologia*, **45**, 1363–1377.

Alexander, R. D. (1990). *How did Humans Evolve? Reflections on the Uniquely Unique Species* Ann Arbor, MI: Museum of Zoology, University of Michigan, Special Publication No. 1.

Ambrose, S. H. (2001). Paleolithic technology and human evolution. *Science,* **291**, 1748–1752.

Anderson, J. R. & Schooler, L. J. (1991). Reflections of the environment in memory. *Psychological Science,* **2**, 396–408.

Atance, C. M. & O'Neill, D. K. (2005). The emergence of episodic future thinking in humans. *Learning and Motivation,* **36**, 126–144.

Boroditsky, L. (2001). Does language shape thought? Mandarin and English speakers' conceptions of time. *Cognitive Psychology,* **43**, 1–22.

Brown, F., Harris, J., Leakey, R., & Walker, A. (1985). Early *Homo erectus* skeleton from west Lake Turkana, Kenya. *Nature,* **316**, 788–792.

Brunet, M., Guy, F., Pilbeam, D., et al. (2002). A new hominid from the Upper Miocene of Chad, Central Africa. *Nature,* **418**, 145–151.

Busby, J. & Suddendorf, T. (2005). Recalling yesterday and predicting tomorrow. *Cognitive Development,* **20**, 362–372.

Chang, F., Dell, G. S., & Bock, K. (2006). Becoming syntactic. *Psychological Review,* **113**, 234–272.

Chen, J-Y. (2007). Do Chinese and English speakers think about time differently? Failure of replicating Boroditsky (2001). *Cognition,* **104**, 427–436.

Cheney, D. L. & Seyfarth, R. S. (1990). *How Monkeys See the World* Chicago, IL: University of Chicago Press.

Chomsky, N. (1975). *Reflections on Language* New York: Pantheon.

Christiansen, M. H. & Chater, N. (2008). Language as shaped by the brain. *Behavioral and Brain Sciences*, **31**(5), 489–509.

Christiansen, M. H. & Dale, R. (2004). The role of learning and development in language evolution: A connectionist perspective. In D. K. Oller & U. Griebel (Eds.), *Evolution of Communication Systems*, pp. 91–109, Cambridge, MA: MIT Press.

Clayton, N. S. & Dickinson, A. (1998). Episodic-like memory during cache recovery by scrub jays. *Nature*, **395**, 272–278.

Clayton, N. S., Bussey, T. J., & Dickinson, A. (2003). Can animals recall the past and plan for the future? *Nature Reviews Neuroscience,* **4**, 685–691.

Corballis, M. C. & Suddendorf, T. (2007). Memory, time, and language. In C. Pasternak (Ed.), *What Makes us Human*, pp. 17–36, Oxford: Oneworld Publications.

Correia, S. P. C., Dickinson, A., & Clayton, N. S. (2007). Western scrub-jays anticipate future needs independently of their current motivational state. *Current Biology*, **17**, 856–861.

Craik, K. (1943). *The Nature of Explanation* Cambridge: Cambridge University Press.

Descartes, R. (1985). Discourse on method. In J. Cottingham, R. Stootfoff, & D. Murdock, D. (Eds. and Trans.), *The Philosophical Writings of Descartes* Cambridge: Cambridge University Press. (Orig. pub., 1647).

Emery, N. J. & Clayton, N. S. (2004). The mentality of crows: Convergent evolution of intelligence in corvids and apes. *Science*, **306**, 1903–1907.

Everett, D. L. (2005). Cultural constraints on grammar and cognition in Pirahã. *Current Anthropology*, **46**, 621–646.

Fodor, J. A. (1968). *Psychological Explanation: An Introduction to the Philosophy of Psychology* New York: Random House.

Fodor, J. A. (1975). *The Language of Thought* New York: Crowell.

Foley, R. (1987). *Another Unique Species: Patterns in Human Evolutionary Ecology* Harlow: Longman Scientific and Technical.

Friedman, W. J. (2002). Arrows of time in infancy: The representation of temporal–causal invariances. *Cognitive Psychology*, **44**, 252–296.

Friedman, W. J. (2003). Arrows of time in early childhood. *Child Development*, **74**, 155–167.

Gilbert, D. T. (2006). *Stumbling on Happiness* New York: Knopf.

Goodall, J. (1986). *The Chimpanzees of Gombe: Patterns of Behavior* Cambridge, MA: Harvard University Press.

Gowlett, J. A. J. (1992). Early human mental abilities. In S. Jones, R. Martin, & D. Pilbeam (Eds.), *The Cambridge Encyclopedia of Human Evolution*, pp. 341–345, Cambridge: Cambridge University Press.

Hassabis, D., Kumaran, D., Vann, S. D., & Maguire, E. A. (2007). Patients with hippocampal amnesia cannot imagine new experiences. *Proceedings of the National Academy of Sciences USA*, **104**, 1726–1733.

Hauser, M. D., Chomsky, N., & Fitch, W. T. (2002). The faculty of language: What is it, who has it, and how did it evolve? *Science*, **298**, 1569–1579.

Hodges, J. R. & Graham, K. S. (2001). Episodic memory: Insights from semantic dementia. *Philosophical Transactions of the Royal Society of London B: Biological Sciences,* **356**, 1423–1434.

Hopper, P. J. & Traugott, E. C. (2003). *Grammaticalization,* 2nd edn., Cambridge: Cambridge University Press.

Horne Tooke, J. (1857). *Epea Pteroenta or the Diversions of Purley* London: Tegg.

Humphrey, N. K. (1976). The social function of intellect. In P. P. G. Bateson & R. A. Hinde (Eds.), *Growing Points in Ethology*, pp. 303–318, New York: Cambridge University Press.

Hunt, G. R. (2000). Human-like, population-level specialization in the manufacture of pandanus tools by New Caledonian crows *Corvus moneduloides*. *Proceedings of the Royal Society of London B*, **267**, 403–413.

Ingvar, D. H. (1979). Hyperfrontal distribution of the cerebral grey matter flow in resting wakefulness: On the functional anatomy of the conscious state. *Neurological Scandinavica*, **60**, 12–25.

Kamil, A. C. & Balda, R. P. (1985). Cache recovery and spatial memory in Clark's nutcrackers (*Nucifraga columbiana*). *Journal of Experimental Psychology: Animal Behavior Processes*, 85, 95–111.

Kaminski, J., Call, J., & Fischer, J. (2004). Word learning in a domestic dog: Evidence for 'fast mapping'. *Science*, 304, 1682–1683.

Kaminski, J., Fischer, J., & Call, J. (2008). Prospective object search in dogs: Mixed evidence for knowledge of *what* and *where*. *Animal Cognition*, 11, 367–371.

Klein, S. B., Loftus, J., & Kihlstrom, J. F. (2002). Memory and temporal experience: The effects of episodic memory loss on an amnesiac patient's ability to remember the past and imagine the future. *Social Cognition*, 20, 353–379.

Köhler, W. (1925). *The Mentality of Apes* New York: Routledge and Kegan Paul. (Originally published in German in 1917).

Kosslyn, S. M., Alpert, N. M., Thompson, W. L. et al. (1993). Visual mental imagery activates topographically organized visual cortex: PET investigations. *Journal of Cognitive Neuroscience*, 5, 263–287.

Krogman, W. M. (1972). *Child Growth* Ann Arbor, MI: University of Michigan Press.

Levine, B. (2004). Autobiographical memory and the self in time: Brain lesion effects, functional neuroanatomy, and lifespan development. *Brain and Cognition*, 55, 54–68.

Lin, J-W. (2005). Time in a language without tense: The case of Chinese. *Journal of Semantics*, 23, 1–53.

Locke, J. L. & Bogin, B. (2006). Language and life history: A new perspective on the development and evolution of human language. *Behavioral and Brain Sciences*, 29, 259–325.

Loftus, E. F. & Loftus, G. R. (1980). On the permanence of stored information in the human-brain. *American Psychologist*, 35, 409–420.

Loftus, E. & Ketcham, K. (1994). *The Myth of Repressed Memory* New York: St. Martin's Press.

Macphail, E. M. (1996). Cognitive function in mammals: The evolutionary perspective. *Cognitive Brain Research*, 3, 279–290.

Marler, P. (1991). The instinct to learn. In S. Carey & B. Gelman (Eds.), *The Epigenesis of Mind: Essays on Biology and Cognition*, pp. 37–66, Hillsdale, NJ: Erlbaum.

Martin, R. (1992). Classification and evolutionary relationships. In S. Jones, R. Martin, & D. Pilbeam (Eds.), *The Cambridge Encyclopedia of Human Evolution*, pp. 17–23. Cambridge: Cambridge University Press.

McBrearty, S. & Brooks, A. S. (2000). The revolution that wasn't: A new interpretation of the origin of modern human behavior. *Journal of Human Evolution*, 39, 453–463.

Mellars, P. A. & Stringer, C. B. (Eds). (1989) *The Human Revolution: Behavioral and Biological Perspectives on the Origins of Modern Humans* Edinburgh: Edinburgh University Press.

Miyashita, Y. (2004). Cognitive memory: Cellular and network machineries and their top-down control. *Science*, 306, 435–440.

Mulcahy, N. J. & Call, J. (2006). Apes save tools for future use. *Science*, 312, 1038–1040.

Noonan, J. P., Coop, G., Kudaravalli, S., et al. (2006). Sequencing and analysis of Neanderthal genomic DNA. *Science*, 314, 1113–1121.

Oakley, K. P. (1961). On man's use of fire, with comments on tool-making and hunting. In S. L. Washburn (Ed.), *Social Life of Early Man*, pp. 176–193, Chicago, IL: Aldine.

Okuda, J., Fujii, T., Ohtake, H. et al. (2003). Thinking of the past and future: The roles of the frontal pole and the medial temporal lobes. *Neuroimage*, 19, 1369–1380.

Patterson, N., Richter, D. J., Gnerre, S., Lander, E. S., & Reich, D. (2006). Genetic evidence for complex speciation of humans and chimpanzees. *Nature*, **441**, 1103–1108.

Pinker, S. (1994). *The Language Instinct* New York: Morrow.

Pinker, S. (2007). *The Stuff of Thought* London: Penguin Books.

Roberts, W. A., Feeney, M. C., MacPherson, K., Petter, M., McMillan, N., & Musolino, E. (2008). Episodic-like memory in rats: Is it based on when or how long ago? *Science*, **320**, 113–115.

Roediger, H. L. & McDermott, K. B. (1995). Creating false memories – remembering words not presented in lists. *Journal of Experimental Psychology: Learning Memory and Cognition*, **21**, 803–814.

Savage-Rumbaugh, S., Shanker, S. G., & Taylor, T. J. (1998). *Apes, Language, and the Human Mind* New York: Oxford University Press.

Schacter, D. L. (1996). *Searching for Memory: The Brain, the Mind, and the Past* New York: Basic Books.

Schacter, D. L., Addis, D. R., & Buckner, R. L. (2007). Remembering the past to imagine the future: The prospective brain. *Nature Reviews Neuroscience*, **8**, 657–661.

Semaw, S. P., Renne, P., Harris, J. W., et al. (1997). 2.5-million-year-old stone tools from Gona, Ethiopia. *Nature*, **385**, 333–336.

Squire, L. R. (2004). Memory systems of the brain: A brief history and current perspective. *Neurobiology of Learning and Memory*, **82**, 171–177.

Suc, J-P., Bertini, A., Leroy, S. A. G., & Suballyova, D. (1997). Towards the lowering of the Pliocene/Pleistocene boundary to the Gauss–Matuyama reversal. *Quaternary International*, **40**, 37–42.

Suddendorf, T. (2006). Foresight and evolution of the human mind. *Science*, **312**, 1006–1007.

Suddendorf, T. & Busby, J. (2005). Making decisions with the future in mind: Developmental and comparative identification of mental time travel. *Learning and Motivation*, **36**, 110–125.

Suddendorf, T. & Busby, J. (2003). Mental time travel in animals? *Trends in Cognitive Sciences*, **7**, 391–396.

Suddendorf, T. & Corballis, M. C. (1997). Mental time travel and the evolution of the human mind. *Genetic, Social, and General Psychology Monographs*, **123**, 133–167.

Suddendorf, T. & Corballis, M. C. (2007). The evolution of foresight: What is mental time travel, and is it unique to humans? *Behavioral and Brain Sciences*, **30**, 299–351.

Suddendorf, T. & Corballis, M. C. (2008). New evidence for animal foresight? *Animal Behaviour*, **75**, e1–e3.

Szpunar, K. K., Watson, J. M., & McDermott, K. B. (2007). Neural substrates of envisioning the future. *Proceedings of the National Academy of Sciences, USA*, **104**, 642–647.

Tomasello, M. (2003a). *Constructing a Language: A Usage-based Theory of Language Acquisition* Cambridge: Cambridge University Press.

Tomasello, M. (2003b). Introduction: Some surprises for psychologists. In M. Tomasello (Ed.), *New Psychology of Language: Cognitive and Functional Approaches to Language Structure*, pp. 1–14, Mahwah, NJ: Lawrence Erlbaum.

Tooby, J. & DeVore, I. (1987). The reconstruction of hominid behavioural evolution through strategic modeling. In W. G. Kinzey (Ed.), *The Evolution of Human Behaviour: Primate Models*, pp. 183–237, New York: SUNY Press.

Tulving, E. (1972). Episodic and semantic memory. In E. Tulving & W. Donaldson (Ed.), *Organization of Memory*, pp. 381–430, New York: Academic Press.

Tulving, E. (1985). Memory and consciousness. *Canadian Psychology,* **26**, 1–12.

Tulving, E. (2001). Episodic memory and common sense: How far apart? *Philosophical Transactions of the Royal Society B: Biological Sciences*, **356**, 1505–1515.

Tulving, E., Schacter, D. L., McLachlan, D. R., & Moscovitch, M. (1988). Priming of semantic autobiographical knowledge: A case study of retrograde amnesia. *Brain and Cognition,* **8**, 3–20.

Whiten, A., Horner, V., & de Waal, F. B.M. (2005). Conformity to cultural norms of tool use in chimpanzees. *Nature,* **437**, 737–740.

Whiten, A. & Suddendorf, T. (2007). Great ape cognition and the evolutionary roots of human imagination. In I. Roth (Ed.), *Imaginative Minds*, pp. 31–60, Oxford: Oxford University Press.

Wood, B. & Collard, M. (1999). The human genus. *Science*, **284**, 65–71.

Wrangham, R.W., Jones, J. H, Laden, G., Pilbeam, D., & Conklin-Brittain, N. (1999). The raw and the stolen – Cooking and the ecology of human origins. *Current Anthropology*, **40**, 567–594.

Part 4
_____

Conclusions

Chapter 18

The making of human concepts: A final look

Denis Mareschal, Paul C. Quinn, and
Stephen E. G. Lea

If you know the terminology, but you don't know the
concepts, you're dangerous.
(*Jacob M. Appel, 2005, Arborophilia*)

A good compromise leaves everybody mad.
(*Calvin & Hobbes*)

Throughout this book we have sought to identify what it was that made human concepts unique (if unique they really are), and more specifically, what roles evolution and development may have played in the emergence of these unique concepts. We have asked whether it is possible to look back at the developing child and see the factors that shape the emergence of adult conceptual competence. Equally, is it possible to examine our biological cousins and ask what changes may have occurred over time to endow us with these distinctive abilities?

One immediate observation is that the popular myth that ontogeny simply recapitulates phylogeny is most certainly wrong (see Chapter 15). This simplistic view overlooks the nonlinear relationship that exists between different species. There is no single branch of evolutionary heritage along which we and other modern species have evolved: we are not descended from the monkeys and apes that currently exist, and it is at best an inference that the behaviour and cognition of current nonhuman primates reflects the behaviour and cognition of our common ancestors better than our own. Moreover, the cognitive skills that we have acquired (through learning or evolution) reflect the pressures and heritage that are unique to our own species, and there may be species of animals that are very far from our line of phylogenetic descent whose cognitions have been shaped by ecological pressures more similar to those our species has experienced than is the case for our near phylogenetic relatives. This is all the more clear when we recall that to specify the ecological niche of a species, we need to include the structure of the society in which it typically lives. So, if any aspect of our conceptual ability results from occupying the niche of a social, cursorial hunter, for example, one would be better off looking for parallels in dolphins or wolves than in the great apes. There is therefore no reason to expect phylogeny and ontogeny to bear any resemblance to one another.

A further bridge to cross on our journey is to ask first whether concepts exist in any meaningful way. In other words, does the construct of concept have any predictive value in helping us understand behaviour? Indeed, Smith (in Chapter 16) argues that the very notion of concept is a hangover from a misguided era in which cognition (and thought more generally) was believed to be somehow disembodied and disconnected from the physical world that we live in. According to the view that Smith is criticizing, concepts are abstract representations of the world that are somehow manipulated within an insulated inner mental world (e.g. Fodor, 1975). This approach immediately runs into the symbol-grounding problem (Harnad, 1990), or more generally, the problem of how to ground one's internal semantics (Fodor, 1998; Macnamara, 1982). In contrast, Smith and others (e.g. Barsalou, 2005, 2008; Clark, 1997) argue that we should do away with the notion of 'concept' and focus instead on the incredibly rich and powerful context-specific behaviours that humans demonstrate on a regular day-to-day basis. These are firmly grounded in sensory and motor experiences and do not need to appeal to some mystical process of semantic analysis. Such views draw on substantial evidence from research in ethology and neuroscience (See Clark, 1997; Mareschal et al., 2007).

This behaviourally oriented, sensorimotor view of intelligent behaviour is certainly consistent with the description of concepts prevalent in the animal cognition literature and implicit in many of the comparative chapters in this book, but it still remains a minority view within the human cognition literature. We will therefore take up the challenge of working with the notion of 'concept' as a useful construct in explaining behaviour, sidestep the question of how such representations are grounded in semantics, and return to our initial questions about the uniqueness and origins of human concepts.

We will, however, still need some kind of operational definition of concepts. To this end, we can turn to the chapters by Murphy and Hampton (Chapter 2 and Chapter 14) who each describe in some detail, the rich array of behaviours and possible representations that underlie human conceptual abilities. Let us agree, for the sake of argument, to simply adopt Murphy's operational definition that 'Categories are things in the world and concepts are the mental representations of those things'. To this we may add that they are mental representations that support action. Indeed, we are interested in concepts in so far as they guide behaviours in a meaningful and adaptively appropriate way.

At this stage, we make no commitment to the format of concepts, be they syntactically manipulable abstract symbols as argued by the 'language of thought hypothesis' (Fodor, 1975) or simply consistent patterns of neural activity induced by sensory and motor experiences (Ballard et al., 1997; Churchland & Sejnowski, 1994). The only way to compare competence across species in any meaningful way is through the careful observation of behaviours in natural and experimental situations. Theoretical considerations about the format of concepts do not (as far as we know) have any a priori reason for excluding any format from existing in one or another species or at any specific age across development. For example, the mechanistic debates concerning the role of rules versus associations in the learning of concepts discussed by Close et al. (Chapter 3)(and illustrated in the models presented by Love and Tomlinson (Chapter 4)) offer no in principle reasons for why one implementation rather than another could not be found within the cognitive systems of one species or another. Only empirically based arguments concerning the behavioural limitations of a particular species (e.g. their ability to generalize to novel stimuli) are used in attempts to restrict one format or another to distinct species.

The same can also be said of efforts to link unique representational formats to different ages. Furthermore, even more than doing so with different species, identifying different representational formats with different ages begs the question of how one format is transformed into the other. This question lies at the heart of modern cognitive-development research (e.g. Fodor, 1980; Karmiloff-Smith, 1992; Mareschal & Shultz, 1996; Piaget, 1980; Quartz & Sejnowski, 1997; Quinn & Eimas, 1997) with little empirical progress being made. So, for example, if infant cognition is linked to associative learning and the adult mind to rule-based cognition, this begs the question of how the associative mechanisms give rise to the rule-based mechanisms.

Are human concepts unique?

Throughout this book, and indeed throughout much of the comparative literature, there is ample evidence of a unique character to the way humans perform in concept-learning tasks, or tasks of a conceptual nature. With some very limited exceptions, humans are generally found to outperform all other species. This raises the very important question of why humans perform so well compared to the competition. One answer is to appeal to the uneven playing field with which we tend to assess other species. Indeed, much of the concept-learning world is interested in concepts that are of direct relevance in human adults. These are most often not ecologically relevant to other species, whose members will have spent most of their lives acquiring different conceptual structures, which may interfere with those being tested. For example, as Matsuzawa relates, chimps can be shown to have much better working memory than humans if tested in an ecologically relevant fashion (see also Chapter 10). In fact, the same has been said about tasks used to assess cognitive abilities in children. Simplifying tasks and making them more child relevant improves performance, suggesting that the conceptual abilities may be in place much earlier in development, if the test domain is relevant to the child (Donaldson, 1978).

Not only are the tasks selected because they are of relevance to humans, the modalities by which concepts are tested are largely biased towards the sensory modality most used by humans; namely, vision. As discussed by Lea (Chapter 9), the information provided by olfaction and audition may be important components of other mammals' conceptual representations. This emphasis on unisensory learning is also a consequence of the traditional scientific approach of separating phenomena into elementary causes, and is pervasive in the study of human concept learning. However, even humans live in a multisensory world, and providing multisensory information has been shown to improve learning retention and performance more generally in humans, let alone other species (Shams & Seitz, 2008).

Three things that do not make human concepts unique

Insofar as differences exist in the way humans (as compared to other species) behave in concept-learning tasks, we may legitimately ask what the origins of these differences could be. It may be that humans simply have better abilities to abstract information away from the immediate stimuli and therefore to generalize far more freely (e.g. the arguments presented by Carey in Chapter 13, with regards to numerical concepts). This ability is often related to the presence of language (see Chapter 6), which in its classic Chomskyan guise is characterized as an abstract and infinitely productive system (Chomsky, 1980). The link between language and abstract concepts has a long history, but with this view comes the chicken-and-egg problem of identifying which came first – that is, which ability is the more primitive one from which the other is built (e.g. Penn et al., 2008; Piatelli-Palmarini, 1980)?

The risk in appealing to language as the critical ingredient in the making of human concepts is that language and concepts may simply be re-descriptions of one another. If they are just two sides of the same cognitive coin, then one does not explain the origins of the other. So while language certainly plays an enormous role in allowing the conceptual system to flourish during development (and may presumably have played a similar evolutionary role), if the crucial difference is in the initial emergence of one or the other, then the tight coupling of language and concepts does not help us understand the origins of this symbiotic cognitive system. Indeed, Waxman and Gelman (Chapter 6) provide numerous examples of how language onset can facilitate concept acquisition, but say less about the initial bootstrapping of this process. We conclude, therefore, that it does not help us to declare that human concepts are unique simply because they are the product of language.

The richness of the social networks that we live and grow up in has also been proposed as a critical causal factor in determining the unique character of human concepts (Chapter 7, this book; Csibra & Gergely, 2006; Tomasello, 1999). We noted above that ecological niche (which includes a species' typical social structure) may be as big an influence on cognitive evolution as phylogeny. However, this overlooks the fact that there is a myriad of other species that exist within complex social networks. The eusocial insects (ants, bees, wasps, and termites) arguably outdo even humans in the size and complexity of the social groups they live in, but there are many species more closely related to us that live in large and intricate societies, including birds (penguins), nonprimate mammals (meerkats), non-ape primates (see Chapter 10), and especially the great apes (chimps; see Chapter 11). Complex social organization cannot therefore be the whole story. It may well play an important role (as we shall argue below), but it cannot be the sole critical feature as it is prevalent in so many other species.

A third approach is to appeal to differences in the underlying structure of the brain. Although there are undeniable differences between adult human brains and those of adult members of other species, there are also many important similarities (Finlay, 2008; Finlay et al., 2001). Humans are rarely if ever unique in any of the dimensions of brain structure usually associated with higher intelligence. For example, we have neither the largest brains, nor the largest cortices, nor the cortices with the most folds.

Indeed, many of the systems believed to underlie concept learning are, in fact, in place in other species (see Chapter 5) – hence the value of comparative studies in understanding the neurobiology of concept learning. So, finally, we do not believe that human concepts are unique because the human brain is unique, in any nontrivial sense. We do not expect neuroscientists to uncover a 'concepts centre' which humans possess and other species do not, or which differs in gross anatomy or physiology from the homologous structures in related species.

What is the role of development?

Humans are one of the species with the longest developmental periods; that is, a species in which the young take the longest to reach maturity (Joffe, 1997). This is usually put down to the increased size of the head (to accommodate the growing brain) combined with the mother's reduced pelvic breadth, in turn due to bipedalism. Thus, human infants are born both very immature and very plastic (Berger & Posner, 2001). The extensive period of development that occurs both within and outside the womb provides ample opportunity for the child to be slowly and gradually exposed to the physical and social worlds. It is this gradual and prolonged period of plasticity, argues Smith, that gives humans the unique flavour in their intelligent behaviour.

This period of extended development certainly allows for a gradual enrichment of experience, but it does come at a cost. It leaves the child more vulnerable for longer periods of time, in comparison with precocial species, whose young are able to function almost immediately after birth. Such rapid endowment of ability is perhaps necessary to ensure survival in the immediate, but limits the adaptability of the system.

So, where *do* human concepts come from?

Many factors contribute to the emergence of human conceptual abilities. Are these abilities unique? When considered separately, it appears not. All the factors (barring language, which as discussed above is of questionable explanatory value) exist in some shape or form in other species. What then is it that makes human conceptual abilities appear so different? The answer to this, we propose, is the confluence of all the factors. Not only is there an extended developmental period, but there is *also* a very rich social environment in which tutoring and scaffolding of the young play an essential role. Many species show complex social structures, but these are not associated with prolonged developmental periods. Those that have prolonged developmental periods often do not show the same degrees of social complexity and nurturing as do humans. In fact, those that are our closest cousins in terms of developmental periods and social structures (e.g. chimps, see Matsuzawa et al. 2006) are also those that have concepts most similar to ours.

To these factors is added the human ability not just to use tools, but crucially also to communicate with one another about the use of tools (Tomasello, 1999). This latter ability means that we can benefit from the experience of other members of our species, and through intergenerational transmission (Whiten, 2005; Whiten et al., 2007) we can benefit directly from past generations' experiences as well. There can then be a cumulative accrual of improved tools and improved tool use. Over many generations, this has resulted in the emergence of technologies such as writing, mathematics, and even language (indeed, Clark, 1997, argues that the invention of language is the ultimate in tool discovery) with profound cognitive implications. Such technologies greatly enhance our cognitive abilities by allowing us to use external supports to overcome our cognitive limitations (e.g. the use of pencil and paper to overcome memory limitations) or transform cognitive problems into formats that our brains are better suited to solve (e.g. the creation of maps where spatial information can be processed visually and in parallel). The importance of these external supports to amplify our cognitive abilities is so great that Clark (1997) suggests calling it 'wideware' in comparison to the terms 'software' or 'hardware' used in traditional computational and cognitive sciences.

This proposition is distinct from the suggestion that humans have some kind of unique social learning or tutoring instinct (Csibra & Gergely, 2006). We are not suggesting that any of the individual abilities are unique. Indeed, there are a handful of other species that directly tutor their young in some way or another, and a much greater number of species in which the young are receptive to the behavioural examples of their parents. Human uniqueness lies in the combination of the factors described above and the historical context in which we find ourselves now. In short, our current conceptual abilities have been shaped by the ecological and cultural histories of our species as well as by our own individual development.

Consider the concrete example of learning the concept of an electronic calculator used to solve numerical problems. Of course, some animals can be trained to recognize calculators and to behave as though they were using a calculator, by tapping on some keys in a particular order and in a specific context (see Candland's excellent [1993] book on feral children and clever animals). They will not however acquire the human concept of 'calculator' because it has no relevance to their ecology. They will not have received species-appropriate tutoring from conspecifics during development, so they will have formed a system of concepts in adulthood that is most probably incommensurate with calculators. The same could be said of humans trying to learn concepts that are central to say a bat's existence (Nagel, 1974). We doubt that this would be possible because such representations would have no embedding within our natural ecology. Indeed, in Chapter 17, Corballis and Suddendorf suggest that it was the need for *Homo sapiens* to communicate about events that occurred at times and places other than the present moment and context in order to outsmart faster and stronger predators that may have led to the formation of this particular cognitive niche.

Does this mean that no animals other than humans have a concept of a calculator? No, if we return to our pragmatic definition of concepts as mental representations, then even animals who fail to use or comprehend the calculator as we do will have a concept of calculator, just not the same as ours. This can also be said of young children. Before they have had extensive exposure to the culturally defined notions of number, mathematics, and even machines, they will not have a concept of calculator that is the same as the adult concept. This will come gradually with exposure, tutoring, and cultural embedding. It follows that many adults may not or may never be able to acquire the concept of calculator if it has no relevance to their everyday experiences and they have not had sufficient social tutoring throughout development. We may have a little more luck with animals tutored from birth, and indeed, there is some evidence that training animals on human-relevant concepts from birth provides some help (Chapter 11). But insofar as other animals will not benefit from the rich species-relevant input that human infants receive and which retrace many years of historical struggles in developing novel concepts, this will not suffice.

In sum, there is nothing unique about the distinct components that contribute to the making of human concepts, when these are considered individually. What is unique is their combined presence in a single species. Of particular note is the long developmental period that allows human infants to gradually acquire knowledge of the world and the rich social tapestry in which the child is embedded and that actively tutors the child to acquire species-relevant knowledge. Our current concepts are the outcome of tens of thousands of years of this process and reflect discoveries made at the societal level (such as language, writing, mathematics) each of which incrementally augments the conceptual abilities of successive generations of humans.

References

Ashby, F. G. & Lee, W. W. (1993). Perceptual variability as a fundamental axiom of perceptual science. *Advances in Psychology*, **99**, 369–399.

Ballard, D. H., Hayhoe, M. M., Pook, P. K., & Rao, R. P. N. (1997). Deictic codes for the embodiment of cognition. *Behavioral and Brain Sciences*, **20**, 723–767.

Barsalou, L. W. (2005). Continuity of the conceptual system across species. *Trends in Cognitive Sciences*, **9**, 309–311.

Barsalou, L. W. (2008). Grounded cognition. *Annual Review of Psychology*, **59**, 617–645.

Berger, A. & Posner, M. I. (2001). Ontogeny of brain and behaviour: A neuropsychological perspective. In A. F. Kalverboer & G. Gramsbergen (Eds.), *Handbook of Brain and Behaviour in Human Development*, pp. 11–32, Amsterdam: Kluwer Academic Publishers.

Candland, D. K. (1993). *Feral Children and Clever Animals: Reflections on Human Nature* Oxford: Oxford University Press.

Chomsky, N. (1980). *Rules and Representations* New York: Columbia University Press.

Churchland, P. & Sejnowski, T. J. (1994). *The Computational Brain* Cambridge, MA: MIT Press, Bradford Books.

Clark, A. (1997). *Being There* Cambridge, MA: MIT Press.

Csibra, G. & Gergely, G. (2006). Social learning and social cognition: The case for pedagogy. In Y. Munakata & M. H. Johnson (Eds.), *Processes of Change in Brain and Cognitive Development. Attention and Performance XXI*, pp. 249–274, Oxford: Oxford University Press.

Donaldson, M. (1978). *Children's Minds* London: Fontana Press.

Finlay B. L. (2008). Brain evolution: developmental constraints and relative developmental growth. In L. Squire, T. Albright, F. Bloom, F. Gage, & Spitzer, N. (Eds.), *New Encyclopedia of Neuroscience*, pp. 637–642, Amsterdam: Elsevier.

Finlay, B. L., Darlington, R. D., & Nicastro, N. (2001). Developmental structure of brain evolution. *Behavioral and Brain Sciences*, **23**, 263–308.

Fodor, J. A. (1975). *The Language of Thought* Cambridge, MA: Harvard University Press.

Fodor, J. A. (1980). Fixation of belief and concept acquisition. In Piatelli-Palmarini, M. (Ed.), *Language and Learning: The Debate between Chomsky and Piaget*, pp. 142–162, Cambridge, MA: Harvard University Press.

Fodor, J. A. (1998). *Concepts: Where Cognitive Science Went Wrong* Oxford: Oxford University Press.

Harnad, S. (1990). The symbol grounding problem. *Physica,* D **42**, 335–346.

Joffe, T. H. (1997). Social pressures have selected for an extended juvenile period in primates. *Journal of Human Evolution*, **32**, 593–605.

Karmiloff-Smith, A. (1992). *Beyond Modularity: A Developmental Perspective on Cognitive Science* Cambridge, MA: MIT Press.

Macnamara, J. L. (1982). *Names for Things* Cambridge, MA: MIT Press.

Mareschal, D., Johnson, M. H., Sirois, S., Spratling, M., Thomas, M., & Westermann, G. (2007). *Neuroconstuctivism Vol. 1: How the Brain Constructs Cognition* Oxford: Oxford University Press.

Mareschal, D. & Shultz, T. R. (1996). Generative connectionist architectures and constructivist cognitive development. *Cognitive Development*, **11**, 571–605.

Matsuzawa, T., Tomonaga, M., & Tanaka, M. (2006). *Cognitive Development in Chimpanzees* Tokyo: Springer.

Nagel, T. (1974). What is it like to be a bat? *Philosophical Review*, **83**, 435–450.

Penn, D. C., Holyoak, K. J., & Povinelli, D. J. (2008). Darwin's mistake: Explaining the discontinuity between human and non-human minds. *Behavioral and Brain Sciences*, **31**, 109–178.

Piaget, J. (1980). *Adaptation and Intelligence* Chicago: University of Chicago Press.

Piatelli-Palmarini, M. (1980). *Language and Learning: The Debate between Chomsky and Piaget* Cambridge, MA: Harvard University Press.

Quartz, S. R. & Sejnowski, T. J. (1997). The neural basis of cognitive development: A constructivist manifesto. *Behavioral and Brain Sciences*, **20**, 537–556.

Quinn, P. C. & Eimas, P. D. (1997). A reexamination of the perceptual-to-conceptual shift in mental representations. *Review of General Psychology*, **1**, 271–287.

Shams, L. & Seitz, A. R. (2008). Benefits of multisensory learning. *Trends in Cognitive Sciences*, **12**, 411–417.

Tomasello, M. (1999). *The Cultural Origins of Human Cognition* Cambridge, MA: Harvard University Press.

Whiten, A. (2005). The second inheritance system of chimpanzees and humans. *Nature*, **437**, 52–55.

Whiten, A., Spiteri, A., Horner, V., Bonnie, K. E., Lambeth, S. P., Schapiro, S. J., et al. (2007). Transmission of multiple traditions within and between chimpanzee groups. *Current Biology*, **17**, 1038–1043.

Index